THE OVERSEAS TARGETS

WAR REPORT

OF THE

OSS

Volume 2

THE OVERSEAS TARGETS

WAR REPORT

OF THE

OSS

(Office of Strategic Services)
Volume 2

with a new introduction
by

Kermit Roosevelt

Prepared by
History Project, Strategic Services Unit,
Office of the Assistant Secretary of War,
War Department, Washington, D.C.

WALKER AND COMPANY
New York
CARROLLTON PRESS, INC.
Washington, D.C.

This edition first published in the United States of America in 1976 by the Walker Publishing Company, Inc.

Published simultaneously in Canada by Fitzhenry & Whiteside, Limited, Toronto.

ISBN: 0-8027-0539-1

Library of Congress Catalog Card Number: 75-40760

Printed in the United States of America.

10 9 8 7 6 5 4 3 2 1

I feel that this War Report presents a well–rounded study of the first comprehensive organization for intelligence and unorthodox warfare in the history of the United States. I only regret that limitations of time prevented a fuller recording of OSS operations and experience.

The importance of OSS lies not only in its role in hastening military victory, but also in the development of the concept of unorthodox warfare which alone constitutes a major contribution.

Of even farther reaching importance are the lessons learned and the contributions made to the future of American defense and foreign policy.

The experience of OSS showed above all how essential it is for winning the war and keeping the peace to base national policy upon accurate and complete intelligence. Unorthodox warfare is now recognized as a vital part of our defense system.

WILLIAM J. DONOVAN

INTRODUCTION
to the 1976 edition

Kermit Roosevelt

This is the second volume of the War Report of the Office of Strategic Services (OSS), which covers the overseas operations. The first volume, which presented the history of the OSS predecessor organization, the Coordinator of Information (COI), and the headquarters history of OSS, was released in the spring of 1976.

In my introduction—written as the former Chief Historian of the War Report seeing this history for the first time in almost thirty years—I expressed a mixed reaction. The domestic material was necessarily concerned, in large part, with headquarters administration. But, especially when the story was dealing with overseas COI operations, there was a strong sense of "fascination and regret." The wartime lessons could have meant so much for the future, yet in recent years it has seemed that these lessons have been thrown away. In reading the second volume after thirty years, I find my feelings of regret are stronger than ever.

Once again, I regret the prohibition on use of American names involved in operations. There were few exceptions in volume one, and those were almost all non COI/OSS personnel, like State Department's Robert D. Murphy, who commanded North African operations leading up to the invasion. General Donovan himself was named, and there were a handful of others: Colonel William O. Eddy, USMCR, who was in charge, under Murphy, of the COI-OSS personnel in TORCH; David Bruce and Preston Goodfellow, in charge of SA/B, later SI, SA/G, and SO, respectively; and James P. Baxter III, head of R & A.* The entire history emphasizes the importance of individuals and small teams. The reader may contrast the size and relatively unspectacular contribution of the London office with the small team which made ANVIL (Europe) the "best briefed invasion in history," with the Swiss operation run by Allen Dulles with a staff of less than a dozen, and with TORCH itself, with only ten U.S. field personnel.

The emphasis in this introduction to Volume 2 will be upon the ETO section, largely because this was the first major, and very educational, experience of its kind in U.S. history.

Aside from small elements charged with particular, and generally technical, responsibilities, such as special funds or foreign groups within the U.S., OSS was organized into four principal working elements. Each was responsible for one of the major tasks assigned to the agency. Three of these have already been mentioned: SI, the intelligence function; SO, the conduct of sabotage, support to guerrillas, and general paramilitary opera-

---

*SA/B, Special Activities/Bruce; SI, Secret Intelligence; SA/G, Special Activities/Goodfellow; SO, Secret Operations; R & A, Research and Analysis

tions behind enemy lines; and R & A, the collation and interpretation of material—political, economic, geographic, and anything that might have a possible bearing on the conduct of the war—in whatever manner it was stored or available to the human mind. X-2 was responsible for counter-espionage and for ULTRA, information and operations derived from British penetration of the German Enigma machine cypher system which laid open the German military, naval, air, and secret intelligence communications to Allied reading. (There was little reference, even indirectly, to ULTRA in the War Report because of security considerations.) In the field, as one traveled further from Washington and overseas headquarters, the lines between the branches blurred, and personnel in one branch often became involved in the operations of others.

Early formulation of relationships in London was the key to the future. SO and X-2, for somewhat different reasons, accepted offers from Britain's SOE and MI 6(V)* of complete sharing of operations and techniques they developed over the years. In return, SOE and MI 6(V) demanded knowledge of SO and X-2 operations and a degree of coordination which often amounted to complete control. American acceptance was basically the result of Donovan's feeling that SO was a purely wartime activity which could afford, at least in its early stages, to surrender independence for rapid learning. X-2, which was not organized until March of 1943, had very little time to learn extremely complicated techniques and build up, without help, the massive files essential to operation.

SI, on the other hand, while beginning its London relations with SIS some ten months earlier, took longer to reach a solution on what those relations were to be. SIS claimed greater experience and broader coverage. This claim, well-founded as it was, gained the support of the U.S. members of COSSAC (Chief of Staff Supreme Allied Command) and SHAEF (Supreme Headquarters Allied Expeditionary Force). But General Donovan insisted that "freedom from the knowledge and control of any outside power was essential to long-range espionage." The issue came to a head in September of 1943, when the U.S. Theater Command, responsive to British objections, disapproved a Joint Chiefs of Staff directive authorizing OSS conduct of independent espionage in the European Theater of Operations. Donovan appealed the decision to the JCS which, on October 27th, gave OSS full, unqualified authority to conduct independent long-range espionage. This was an important move in making possible the independent development, after the war, of the Central Intelligence Agency (CIA).

North Africa, as the War Report correctly observes, was the proving ground for OSS. TORCH and ANVIL have already been mentioned. Later, working from North Africa into Italy and France, the techniques of recruitment and infiltration of indigenous agents across combat lines were developed. This volume gives more detail than did the first on the execution of TORCH, but is even more strict on the exclusion of COI/OSS names. Only Murphy is named. Of Colonel Eddy, it is simply noted that

*SOE, Special Operations Executive; MI 6(V), the Counter Espionage division of British Military Intelligence

COI dispatched "a chief agent" in the fall of 1941, and that he arrived in Tangier early in 1942. Murphy is described as responsible for the political negotiations with the French leadership, the COI head for directing the "secret aspects of intelligence, subversion and resistance." In effect, Allied clandestine operations before the landing in North Africa became a COI/OSS responsibility.

Once again I feel a sense of frustration because the War Report (page 13) says so little about "Strings," head of the most powerful religious brother-hood on northern Morocco, and "Tassels," a key tribal leader in the Rif. My recollection is that they were recruited by a professor of anthropology, Carleton S. Coon, who also was the developer of explosive horse and camel turds for anti-tank and anti-personnel use. (Somewhat similar devices were quite independently developed by Detachment 101 personnel in Burma.) The chief pilot of Port Lyautey was smuggled in a COI agent's car to Tangier and sent from there to Washington via Gibraltar. This is a tantalizing snippet of information, not sufficiently substantiated by word that his services with the landing fleet on D-Day were rewarded with the Silver Star and Navy Cross.

In retrospect—and this should have been evident at the time—it is clearly outrageous that individuals with knowledge of ULTRA (Allied reading of German codes and control of German agents) should have been allowed to expose themselves to possible capture. Donovan himself did this three times, in Sicily, Normandy, and Burma. In Sicily also, the SO chief, recently arrived from Washington and having extensive knowledge of OSS plans and organization, possibly including ULTRA, led a team sent by G-2 Seventh Army to penetrate Italian lines. Unfortunately they ran into a land mine which wounded the radio operator and an enlisted man. Even more un-fortunately, the explosion gave away their position to a German patrol. The team members ahead and behind the explosion escaped and regained the Allied Lines. But the SO chief remained with the two wounded men and was captured. Believing him mortally wounded, the Germans left the radio operator, who was later recovered by American units. The enlisted man managed to kill the German officer guarding him and also regained the U.S. lines. The SO chief was not heard from again, although several penetrations were attempted in order to recover him. Clearly there was no excuse for his being allowed to expose himself in enemy territory.

This kind of heroics in what was a new business, and by men essen-tially amateurs, may be understandable but is in no way excusable. It is simply not professional behavior. But, as pointed out a few pages later, prior to the Sicilian landing OSS had not participated in any major military campaign. "The OSS position in the Theater was inevitably that of a new agency about whose functions and relative position neither its own mem-bers, nor those to whom it was immediately responsible, were sure" (page 65). The early Italian operations appear generally enthusiastic, sometimes even inspired, but often so amateurish and ill-coordinated that foulups were not uncommon.

For example, the first strategic intelligence team was dispatched by Fifth Army Detachment on 12 October 1943 (see page 71). Its target was Rome.

The head of the team was "Coniglio"; other members included "Cervo" and "Corvo." They had considerable success in making valuable contacts in Rome but were unable to communicate by radio because it had been impossible to train the operator adequately before they left, and he was "unaccustomed to the SSTR-1." "Corvo" was therefore dispatched over-land to Naples, which he reached safely. In his absence it was discovered that an inadequate antenna had been used, and this was corrected. In the meantime "Pietro," a young American foreign correspondent who was Peter Tompkins, later killed in Viet Nam, had been specially recruited by General Donovan. He was ordered to contact radio VITTORIA, "Coniglio's" radio, and act as intelligence officer for the Fifth Army. Reaching Rome in late January 1944, he immediately conferred with "Coniglio." As long as they had VITTORIA and a second clandestine transmitter to handle the heavy flow of traffic, things were not too bad. But in March the security of the stations was "blown" and "Cervo" was captured. Although he knew virtually all the OSS agents in Rome, he endured five days of torture with-out revealing one detail. Then he was shot, along with 320 other Italians, in reprisal for the attack upon a German police truck on the streets in Rome. Both radio stations were gone, but the remainder of the agents were safe.

"The problems of hiding against the threat of further denunciations, reestablishing intelligence chains, and reopening contact with the base were further complicated by the overlapping jurisdictions of 'Coniglio' and 'Pietro'." Neither had been briefed about the other's mission or status. "Friction between agents in Rome, resulting from insufficient coordination and control by OSS operations officers, had prevented the evolution of a long-range intelligence organization from a tactical mission in support of a military operation. The initiative for action inside Rome was placed in the hands of agents themselves rather than retained by operations officers at the base."

What is somewhat extravagently described as the "largest OSS blunder of the war" was the unauthorized infiltration into Spain from Tunisia of Communists recruited through the "popular front" Union Democrita Espanol in Mexico and North Africa—BANANA (see pages 25-26). The infiltrators were captured by Spanish police having in their possession U.S. arms, SSTR-1 transmitters, code books for communications with Oujda, and, ac-cording to the Spanish, Communist code books as well. The commanding officer in Oujda was personally aware of the existence of other SI operations in Spain and had been warned that his recruits were unreliable. Nonetheless he had gone ahead, without checking with Washington headquarters for approval of the infiltration. He was released from OSS. In retrospect I think, however, that compared with the foul-ups in Northern Italy, for example, it is an exaggeration to call this the worst blunder of the war.

The major concentration of OSS effort—the War Report says during the European War, but I would now amend this to say during the whole war—was directed at France. The contrast between London, which concentrated upon SO, and Algiers, which concentrated upon SI, was most striking. London worked upon the SOE model; "SO recruiting, training, dispatching and servicing were handled in a military and largely impersonal fashion. . ." Officers and men were parachuted into France to organize and train resistance groups, handle air drops of supplies, direct sabotage, and—"incidentally"—transmit intelligence. From D–Day on, additional SO/SOE personnel were dispatched to serve as liaison and to coordinate resistance with the field armies. Eisenhower, Patton, and other generals, officially recognized "the remarkable resistance effort in causing diversions, covering undefended flanks, disrupting enemy communications, protecting vital installations and delaying and harrassing enemy troops in transit."

SI London carried out only one large–scale espionage operation, *Sussex*, done jointly with SIS, which placed just over fifty teams in areas not covered by the resistance.

Algiers, on the other hand, functioned principally "as an SI operations center and produced the outstanding direct intelligence record of the war. In contrast to agent processing at OSS/London, Algiers agents were recruited, trained, dispatched, and serviced on a personal basis, in an effort to make each man in the field feel that some one man at the home desk would do everything possible to support him." By D–Day the data locating enemy units and fortifications were so accurate and complete, as verified by the campaign itself, as to amaze the commanding general and his G–2 (see page 239).* After the landing, SI/Algiers, in addition to its superior record, had the only OSS radio station (DARTMOUTH) that was *"worked back"* by the enemy without our detection for almost eighteen months, close to one year in France and, after D–Day in South France, another six months in Germany. Four teams were sent in to the station during this period, and each was captured. Fortunately, the timing and whereabouts of the ANVIL landing were, in accord with regular procedure, not given to DARTMOUTH during this period.

This station had been opened by radio operator "Tommy," who established the first clandestine network organized by OSS for intelligence in metropolitan France. He had served operation TORCH in North Africa and also had set up the first mission in enemy–occupied Europe, in Corsica, three months after the African landing. Because of his extensive experience he was asked, during the first week of February 1943, to operate a clandestine station for the Deuxième Bureau in Marseille, reestablish radio contact for the British near Nice, form a new British sabotage post in the Alps, and create the beginnings of an OSS intelligence network and another clandestine station, MEXICO, in Toulon. In June he made his first parachutage to a Maquis reception group in the Vercors area. He helped reestablish an SOE station which had been lost to the enemy and activated a new station, BOSTON, to transmit to Algiers.

Months later, in October, MEXICO was captured and another Toulon station was either abandoned or caught. BOSTON was moved just in time to escape capture, but DARTMOUTH was lost very shortly afterward.

---

*Of this operation, General Eisenhower commented, "In no previous war, and in no other theater during this war, have resistance forces been so closely harnessed to the main military effort." 31 May 1945. page 222

A new operator working DARTMOUTH radio was detected in Algiers on 5 November; "Tommy" swore that the new man had been trained under his orders, but he was later shown to be mistaken.

DARTMOUTH was, as stated earlier, the only OSS station "doubled" successfully for such a long period, although such deception was frequently attempted by Axis and Allied C-E units. Two reasons were given for this: first, a two-fold violation of communications security—an operator recruited in the field without homebase briefing, and allowed to recruit other operators without the knowledge of the home base; second, the ingenuity of the Germans in making little use of the capture to seize other OSS agents of whom they knew, and allowing two key French underground personnel to pass through the station with important papers (see pages 173-77).

The story of the SO teams, and particularly the *Jedburghs* (see pages 199 ff.), operating from London with SOE, has been well told in the public press, notably by two *Jedburgh* members, the late Stewart Alsop and Thomas Braden in their book *Sub Rosa*. Of the 276 parachuted into France, Belgium, and Holland between June and September 1944, 83 were American, 90 British, and 103 French, forming three-man teams of two officers and one radio operator, all in Army uniforms and with no cover story. If captured they were to give name, rank, and serial number only and claim POW treatment under military law. Only two teams, HORACE and ALEXANDER, are described in the War Report.

The Operational Groups (OGs) have received less public coverage. They were dropped into France also between June and September 1944. They were mostly from Algiers but toward the end of the program four, two from Algiers and two "Norwegian" OGs, were diverted to France from London for lack of a Norwegian program. Since they were to operate either alone or with resistance groups in actions where large units were thought to be required, they generally consisted of fifteen men, including a radio operator and a medical technician. They were "the most military units in OSS. Their job was to carry out hit-and-run sabotage raids or to protect vital installations from destruction by the fleeing enemy. Always in U.S. Army uniform, they had to depend on the protection of resistance groups and their own ingenuity to avoid capture." (page 207)

The total SO-OG personnel working behind the lines in France during 1944 was 523; 85 were SO agents and radio operators, 83 Jedburghs, and 355 (composing 22 sections) were OGs. Their casualties were as follows: dead, 18, or 3.4% (5, or 6%, were Jedburghs); missing or captured, 17, or 3.3% (of which 10, or 11.8%, were SO); and wounded, 51, or 9.8% (of which 40, or 11.2%, were OGs). Thus total casualties were 86, close to 16.5% of the 523 personnel involved. (page 220)

There are no overall figures given for OSS casualties behind the lines, but the above would not be far from the average. Generally casualties were high in 1943, when the Allies were not so clearly winning the war and OSS had little experience. The figures lowered to close to zero as V. E. Day grew obviously near, but they are nonetheless higher than normal combat statistics for killed and wounded, and significantly lower for POWs.

Several "play-back" cases are described, of which the most interesting are DRAGOMAN, SKULL and WITCH (see pages 252-57). DRAGOMAN was a Spanish national living in Cherbourg and was the first American SCI case run on the continent. His reports gave a picture of American strength in Cherbourg that discouraged German attacks there. Post-war interrogation showed that the Germans considered DRAGOMAN one of their top stay-behind agents in France.

SKULL, member of a network originally run by Friedrich Kaulen, an Abwehr official in Le Havre, had moved south of Bordeaux when Le Havre was threatened by the Allied invasion. The Abwehr unit withdrew to Holland, but SKULL and five fellow agents remained in France and were captured between 26 August and 10 December 1944. SKULL was preserved for CE exploitation, and notionally put in touch with DRAGOMAN to explain the disappearance of his associates and his difficulty in communicating. In due course he became paymaster for all German agents in France. Subsequently Kaulen came to Bordeaux, which was still in German hands, and asked SKULL to meet him there. The prospect of capturing Kaulen alive was too good to be missed, in spite of the fact that it would have to mean the "death" of SKULL. In fact, the effort to capture Kaulen alive failed, but the instructions he was carrying for SKULL contained highly valuable information.

The third case, WITCH, after capture and several exchanges of information, was ordered by the Germans to the Metz-Thionville area just in time for the Battle of the Bulge. He and another controlled agent gave enough national coverage so that the Germans thought additional agents, who might have been able to work uncontrolled, unnecessary. SCI was able to report events and units just a few hours after their committment, when secrecy was no longer required but the information looked most valuable. WITCH was awarded the Iron Cross for outstanding work. Post-war interrogations revealed that German intelligence chiefs judged WITCH one of their very best stay-behind agents in France.

On the less satisfactory side, OSS Istanbul had its problems, due essentially to poor personnel (see pages 271-72). "Dogwood," who provided the channel through which Helmut Graf von Moltke, a leader in the anti-Hitler plot, tried unsuccessfully to contact pre-war American acquaintances at the end of 1943 and had most of his contacts arrested, due, in the opinion of OSS Headquarters, to insecure handling. There were two possibilities: one, that "Dogwood" was German-controlled; two, that he was arrogant and garrulous, believing that he had only to take a double-agent into his confidence to gain his support. His mission chief exercised no effective control and was himself famous in Istanbul for his talkativeness. In June 1944 he was replaced; the new chief fired "Dogwood" and his circle.

Finally, for the Europe, Africa, and Middle East section, there was Switzerland, the "happy hunting ground for the intelligence services of all the belligerent countries" (see page 273) during two world wars. The small staff there under Allen Dulles, later the director of the CIA, produced the "best OSS intelligence record of the war." Source "Wood," high in the German Foreign Office, brought diplomatic cables by the pound beginning in August 1943. In late 1944 travel problems led him to send rolls of film;

these included valuable information on Japan from the German Embassy in Tokyo (see pages 278-80). Hans Bernd Gisevius, one of the chief Abwehr representatives in Switzerland and later to become Allen Dulles's son-in-law, also established contact in early 1943. At one of his first meetings with Dulles, Gisevius produced copies of cables showing that the Germans had broken the Bern Legation code. This was gradually discarded by the Legation. Gisevius also disclosed bit by bit the plot to overthrow Hitler, which was given the code name "Breakers." He returned to Berlin in mid-July 1944, took part in the abortive putsch, but was lucky enough to escape when it failed, and finally with OSS help he reached Switzerland in January 1945.

OSS/Bern, on the basis of "Wood," Gisevius, and other evidence, believed that there was a "serious Allied over-estimate of the German will to resist." Bern believed that considerable success could have been achieved by following up the sudden allied military successes with "agent surrender missions to enemy commanding generals." Allen Dulles felt sure that, as the Normandy and south of France invasions progressed, there was a real opportunity to drive a wedge between the Hitler-SS group and the old line military forces. From Switzerland he sent full information on the plots against Hitler and on the defections among higher ranking Germans. However, he received no encouragement from Washington.

In the fall of 1944 he was urging a concentrated program to bring certain German generals on the west front to surrender. General Bradley and his G-2 expressed great interest in the project and supported it. However at the time of the Ardennes counter-offensive the project was dropped. By December 1944 the opportunity to bring about surrender on the west front had largely escaped the Allies. The Battle of the Bulge, with the attack spearheaded by SS Panzer divisions, made it clear that the Nazi party had seized final control. The OKW generals, who might earlier have been willing to surrender, had been removed and replaced by fanatical Nazis (see pages 321-322).

Another effort, directed at Hungary by the SI/Central Europe desk in Italy, was originally aimed at the Czech partisans, but two men were added to it to be escorted by partisans from the Czech territory south to the Hungarian frontier. One of them, "Moly," did succeed in reaching Budapest by train on 13 October. He arranged for an interview with Horsey through a personal friend. This took place on 14 October, at which time he delivered letters from AFHQ and from dissident Hungarian diplomats in Rome and elsewhere. Horsey was already in touch with the Russians and delivered his "Armistice Declaration" the day after his meeting with "Moly." Unfortunately, the declaration was followed by mass arrests by the Gestapo. A large diversion of German troops was made to maintain Axis control over Hungary (see page 322).

In North Italy the SUNRISE negotiations definitely led to surrender of Axis forces on 2 May 1945. German feelers had been reported as early as November of 1944 by an OSS team in Venice. They were followed by similar approaches to OSS Switzerland. On 25 February 1945 a Swiss intelligence officer informed Bern that an Italian industrialist was trying to establish contact with the Allies on behalf of SS General Karl Wolff. A meeting was arranged on 3 March. Eventually these negotiations did lead to the surrender of Axis forces on 2 May 1945. The culmination "underlined one of the unique contributions an undercover—and hence quasi-official—agency could make in the course of modern war" (see pages 323-325). Undercover personnel could handle preliminary dealings without risking embarrassment to the U.S. government. Meanwhile, OSS had the advantages of prompt access to top authorities in Washington and in the Mediterranean theater.

The Far East

The major stress in my new introduction to the War Report has been upon operations directed from London and Algiers because it was there that the important lessons for the post-war period were learned. The most important reason for this was that in the two Pacific theater commands—one under a series of admirals, the other under General Douglas MacArthur from beginning to end—OSS was severely limited in scope and activity. Thus it was forced to make its larger effort in the minor theaters on the Asiatic mainland, the China theater, and the India-Burma theater. This was as if in the European, African, and Middle Eastern area, OSS had been obliged to concentrate almost exclusively upon the Balkans and Norway. It resulted in a curious contrast. "No OSS unit in Europe equalled the tactical combat record of Detachment 101 in Northern Burma, just as no OSS group of any kind in the Far East could claim a direct contribution to [major invasions such as the landings in North Africa and France]. ... On the other hand, although numerous attempts at major subversion were made in Europe, none approached the thorough penetration of an entire nation such as was effected in Siam by OSS in Southeast Asia" (see page 358).

Here I am fascinated by a book, *Awakening from History*, published more than twenty years later in 1969 by my colleague on the War Record project, Edmond Taylor. Having both more space and greater freedom of expression than was available in the War Report, Taylor came up with a series of intriguing observations. One example describes General Joseph W. Stilwell, "simultaneously, and confusingly, supreme commander of the United States China-Burma-India Theater while serving as deputy to Admiral Mountbatten in the southern, British half of his command and to Generalissimo Chiang Kai-shek in the northern, Chinese half. A colorful, salty, testy old professional soldier who had abundantly earned his army nickname, Vinegar Joe, Stilwell labored with missionary zeal against foreign aggression and native corruption in the cause of his arrogant, suspicious, unteachable, Chinese overlord, while he voiced nothing but scorn and aversion for the pomps, the shams, and the greeds of British colonialism, symbolized in his eyes by his royal-blooded south-of-the-mountains British supreme commander."

Taylor had served in Algiers, where he had become involved with the French officers responsible for the assassination of General Giraud. Extricating himself, he returned to Washington where Donovan assigned him to the planning staff. Here he grew increasingly disillusioned. This disillusionment embraced Donovan as well as his job, and he accepted an offer from Major General Albert C. Wedemeyer to serve with him in the newly created South East Asia Command. Admiral Lord Louis Mountbatten was Theater Commander, based in New Delhi, and Wedemeyer his Deputy Chief of Staff. Colonel Richard P. Heppner, who died as a relatively young man some years ago, was the official OSS representative in Southeast Asia, on leave from Donovan's New York law firm. Taylor describes a meeting between Mountbatten, Donovan, Heppner, and himself in New Delhi on 28 November 1943. In civilian clothes—fastidiously neat Wall Street suits—Donovan looked like what he was, among other things: "a natural fighting man, a natural leader of men, a natural athlete who kept in permanent training. Dressed in his general's uniform he appeared incorrigibly civilian; the silvered, man-of-distinction's hair, the slightly florrid cheeks with the smooth, barber shop glow, the sleek, deceptively fleshy jowls suggested neither the dashing warrior nor the ruthless spymaster of his public image, but the moderately successful Republican politician and the prosperous able corporation lawyer that he actually was, the *bon vivant* he was not."

In the prejudiced view of soldiers or diplomats, Taylor notes, the general was suggestive of a bridge-club shark or even a shady stock promoter. His eyes were "too candid blue," his smiles too blandly courteous.

Following the late November meeting with Mountbatten came a talk with General Powell, Mountbatten's chief of staff. Donovan told him that if he (Powell) wanted something done for which he could not spare two or three thousand men, to just call on OSS, which would send twenty or thirty men to do the job. This was typical Donovan jocularity. When he spoke to his own officers later, he commented that he was a "prudent realist" and did know that in fact a minimum of fifty or sixty OSS men would be required to do the work of two or three thousand British, or for that matter American, soldiers.

On 9 December 1943 Donovan returned to New Delhi from China, where he had met with Captain (later Rear Admiral) M. E. Miles, USN, and General Tai Li, director of the Chinese security and counter-intelligence service. These two had earlier insisted, with full support from the U. S. Navy Department and the Chinese government, that Miles be designated head of OSS in China and that it be incorporated into a Sino-Navy-OSS operating group to be known as the Sino American Cooperative Organization (SACO). He told Mountbatten and Wedemeyer that he had removed Miles as the OSS representative and arranged that a triumvirate—Miles, Tai Li, and an OSS chief—would direct clandestine activities in China. He had given the Chinese six months to show results; otherwise he would withdraw all support material—e.g. tommy guns, wireless sets—he had been providing. (Many observers feared that these were intended for use against Chinese Communists rather than Japanese.)

Lord Louis was much amused by Donovan's spirited account of his dealings with Tai Li, whom legend had built into a "fabulously sinister figure, a blend of Himmler and the once-popular movie villain, the Insidious Dr. Fu Man Chu. To Donovan, Tai Li appeared a sentimentalist, if not a softie, a mediocre policeman with medieval ideas of intelligence work, but apart from that a rather likeable fellow."

"I said to him, (General Donovan speaking), General, I want you to know that I am going to send my men into China whether you like or not. I know that you can have them murdered one by one, but I want you to know that will not deter me." He then informed Mountbatten and Wedemeyer that he was sending Ed Taylor there immediately.

Actually Taylor never did get to China because he had been commissioned in the Navy specifically for service with Wedemeyer. He remained on Lord Louis' staff but was considered Donovan's agent and unofficial representative. His final comment on this episode is significant. Noting that the General's contribution through OSS to the Allied cause was far from negligible, he went on to observe that it was sometimes even more significant in establishing a pattern for "United States intervention in the revolutionary struggles of the post-war age. The Donovan influence on U.S. foreign military policy has continued to be felt ever since his death; for good and ill he left a lasting mark on the mind of the nation's power elite. However indirectly, many of our latter-day cold war successes, disasters, and entrapments can ultimately be traced back to him."*

Personally, I think it is slightly misleading for Taylor to say that the "Donovan influence" has been felt ever since. I agree that he did leave a "lasting mark," but I do not feel that most of those people who felt it, and in fact responded to it, would have identified it specifically with "Wild Bill" Donovan. The directors of the CIA were in themselves too individualistic and such strong characters—particularly "Beedle" Smith and Allen Dulles—for many to think back to their first predecessor.

By the spring of 1944 Donovan had effectively sprung OSS loose from Miles and formed a partnership with General Claire L. Chennault's Fourteenth Air Force. This was the Air and Ground Forces Resources and Technical Staff (AGERTS), which undertook SI, SO, MO, and R & A activities. It was made official on 26 August 1944 and was popularly referred to as "Agfighters." "The prestige in China of Chennault and the Fourteenth Air Force was so great that Tai Li was unable to oppose it . . . (and) in fact, was not formally notified . . . although he was fully aware of its status" (page 428). In the autumn of 1944 the U. S. CBI Theater was split into the India-Burma-Theater (IBT), which was subject to the U. S. South East Asia Command (SEAC) and the new China Theater. OSS/IBT, headquartered at Kandy in Ceylon, exercised control over all OSS elements south of the Hump and was responsible both to Admiral Mountbatten and the Commanding General USAF IBT. In China the new Theater Commander General Wedemeyer reorganized his theater in early 1945 and established OSS as an independent command responsible to him through the G-5. The struggle between Fourteenth Air Force and OSS was resolved and AGFRTS, its name changed to Air Ground Forces Technical and Resources Staff (AGFTRS), was assigned to the latter.

In Burma, meanwhile, Detachment 101 had established itself as the most effective tactical combat force in OSS after a shaky start. Supporting the first Allied offensive in Burma in March 1943, six Anglo-Burmese were landed in small British rubber dinghies on an uncharted beach which offered many rocks and heavy surf. Their radio equipment was swamped during the landing and nothing was ever heard from them again (Taylor, page 378).

*Edmond Taylor, *Awakening from History* (Boston: Gambit, 1969), pp. 341-351.

The reasons for failure were summarized by the Detachment commander: "Everybody in this theater knows who we are, what we are doing, and a lot of them actually know . . . what we are planning to do and when we will do it." This poor security was due, at least partly, to the fact that Detachment 101 did not have its own operational equipment. Its commander felt that it must use the techniques of the smuggler rather than the military, and should have, in addition to its own light planes and motor boats, at least one large vessel of the type used "for rum running during the days of prohibition." In December 1943 Donovan once again violated all security principles by flying in a small liaison plane to advanced Detachment 101 HQs behind the enemy lines. In retrospect, the reopening of the Burma Road appears to have had little impact on the China campaign, though it did of course contribute to the Thailand operation.

The Detachment's contributions to the campaign to reopen the Burma Road are summarized (see page 389) to include not only the collection and dissemination of all types of intelligence but, proudly, an analysis of casualties: Japanese, 4,350 killed and 53 captured; OSS, one American and 75 Kachins killed, 125 Kachins wounded. Including their own, the Detachment evacuated by light planes a total of 470 Americans, British, and native wounded troops. One amusing incident: when 101 personnel decided that a medal should be given to the Kachins, the Rear Echelon agreed but misunderstood the cabled request, which read "CMA medals"—CMA being the cable abbreviation for comma. Beautiful medals marked CMA were sent, which forward units distributed as that "rare American decoration, the Civilian Military Award." OSS Washington, somewhat shocked, ordered them recalled, but the field dismissed this as an impossible suggestion (see page 390).

The other major success in the Far East was the penetration of Siam. Ed Taylor believes that the reconciliation between General Stilwell and OSS was consummated when Stilwell approved "a rather bold scheme for parachuting a secret agent into Thailand in an attempt to subvert the Thai government from its nominal alliance with the Japanese." The British had already slipped in an agent of their own without official sanction. It was expected that they would shortly "surface" the operation and shut OSS off from any high level contacts in Bangkok. This, it was suggested to Stilwell, would isolate the leaders of Thai resistance from any liberalizing U.S. influence, making them little more than native mercenaries of British imperialism. Taylor himself firmly believed this argument, which proved irresistible to "Uncle Joe," as he refers to Stilwell, and from then on his "fear of OSS succumbing to the contagions of Western Colonialism in Asia gradually diminished."*

Thus two Thai agents, one closely related to the Regent, Luang Pradit, were dropped into northern Siam to contact the Regent and inform him of OSS interest in working with him. Though separated by a faulty drop, they finally reached Bangkok and were authorized to send word of his willingness to receive an OSS liaison officer. Since no one man could be

*Taylor, *Awakening from History*, pp. 352-53.

found with all the required capabilities, two were finally sent, one from SI, the other from SO. The latter was a young lawyer from Donovan's New York firm named Richard Greenlee, who died in 1970. The former was, I believe, the well-known Jim Thompson who developed a thriving trade in Thai silk after the war and vanished most mysteriously—probably victim to a native spear trap—from the hill trails around Bangkok in the mid 1950s.

When the Japanese surrender finally came, OSS operations in Siam had achieved conspicuous success. Although the guerrilla program had never come to fruition, intelligence of real importance was procured, many downed American aviators had been saved from Japanese capture, and, when hostilities ceased, it was learned that the Japanese, aware of Siamese "treachery," had redoubled their forces in the country, thus keeping a number of divisions from other fronts.

In the introduction to the 1976 edition of Volume 1, I commented on the parlous state of the CIA successor branch to OSS/X-2. Fear was expressed that since counterespionage had been secluded from other operational elements in CIA, the drastic dissolution of its senior staff in 1975 created a most dangerous vacuum. CE is clearly *the* vital element in a national intelligence program, and I expressed the hope that its reconstruction would receive the urgent attention required. I have, of course, no way of knowing whether this is being done.

The CE chief, whose "resignation" was requested in 1975, had ended the war with X-2 Italy. Later he developed a very close—possibly too close—relationship with the Israeli service. While X-2 in Europe, North Africa, and the Middle East had operated of necessity under the British wing during the war, in the Far East it was independent. This independence was made complete by 1946. When CIA struggled into existance in the post-war years, it did have that vital element as its very own. *Without* this, a "national" intelligence service would more truly be a "notional" intelligence service. *With* this, we have been able to establish close, highly valuable working relationships not only with the British services and (off again, on again) the French, but also with our defeated enemies, the Germans and the Japanese.

Now that we have the two volumes of the War Report of the OSS available, with the minor deletions and the major ommission, for security reasons at the time, of ULTRA, the American contribution to clandestine operations in World War Two may be fairly judged. I believe it can be considered a major contribution, far more important than might have been expected from a country so inexperienced in this kind of undertaking. Whether the impact of OSS upon later U.S. policy and operational capability can be credited primarily to Donovan, or, as seems more likely to be the case, and also more fair, to other principals in the earlier organization who continued on the high service in the CIA, is now a matter of largely academic interest. The point is that lessons were learned at the time, and that not all of these lessons were forgotten in later days. The OSS was America's first large scale and coherently directed organization of its kind. It opened new avenues for us as a country. We cannot afford to abandon those avenues, or to lose our way.

WAR DEPARTMENT
OFFICE OF THE ASSISTANT SECRETARY OF WAR
STRATEGIC SERVICES UNIT
25TH & E STREETS, N.W.
WASHINGTON 25, D.C.

5 September 1947.

SUBJECT: War Report, Office of Strategic Services.

TO: Director, SSU.

The project to prepare a War Report of the activities of the Office of Strategic Services was assigned to me by SSU Special Order 57. Following Admiral Leahy's memorandum of 26 July 1946, the staff for the History Project was assembled and work begun. Mr. Kermit Roosevelt was engaged as chief historian and directed the organization and preparation of the Report. After his departure on 1 May 1947 the final phases of editing and preparation were completed by the staff of the History Project.

The security classification of the Report is subject to determination by Joint Security Control. A glossary of certain terms and abbreviations used in the Report has been included in Volume I.

The bulk of the source material for the Report has been assembled in the files of the History Project and integrated into the OSS Archives, which, after 1 July 1947, were transferred to the jurisdiction of the Central Intelligence Group.

> (Signed) Serge Peter Karlow,
> (Typed)   SERGE PETER KARLOW,
>   Executive Officer for History Project.

TABLE OF CONTENTS
VOLUME 2

SECTION I
EUROPE, AFRICA, MIDDLE EAST

MAPS

Section I

EUROPE, AFRICA, MIDDLE EAST

INTRODUCTION

The previous volume has outlined the growth of COI/OSS in Washington and the development of the functions of its various branches. In this section, OSS activity in Europe, Africa, and the Middle East is related, not by branches, but according to each successive target area.

Eight parts cover: I, North Africa; II, the outlying neutral areas, Eire, Spain, Portugal, Africa, and the Middle East; III, the West Mediterranean Islands and Italy; IV, small nation resistance groups in the Balkans, Central Europe, and Scandinavia; V, France; VI, the indirect penetration of Germany from Stockholm, Istanbul, and Bern; VII, the final effort against Germany and Austria; and VIII, activities in liberated Europe up to the termination of OSS on 30 September 1945.

Subsequent parts of this Introduction outline relationships with the controlling theater commands, as well as the arrangements between OSS branches and the various corresponding British agencies who, for the most part, assisted OSS in acquiring the techniques of modern espionage and undercover warfare. Part II illustrates the importance in neutral territory of unfailing State Department support—difficult for the new agency to obtain.

For reasons given in the Preface to the War Report, none of the agency's personnel or representatives has been mentioned by name. This policy was followed in spite of the importance of individuals in the unorthodox activities of OSS. Secret intelligence, sabotage and subversion could not be run along standard military or bureaucratic lines. In the handling of agents the human element was primary, and it was discovered many times over that a few individuals who combined understanding of this factor with imagination in operations and objectivity in evaluating results could produce far better intelligence than could larger staffs which attempted to work on a more regular, more bureaucratic or more military basis.

Although external factors accounted for much, the notably disparate results of various competing OSS units attested the validity of the principle. Such a contrast was provided by the large but relatively unproductive SI/London staff compared with the small SI/Algiers unit which provided for Operation *ANVIL*, the best briefed invasion in history, as much information as the British and French services combined. A similar contrast appeared among OSS bases in neutral areas. Most of these offices employed some fifty American personnel, with the exception of OSS/Switzerland, which was limited to less than a dozen representatives but nevertheless acquired the outstanding U. S. indirect espionage record, including the exploitation of what the British Secret Intelligence Service termed the best intelligence source of the war. Similarly, the first large-scale COI/OSS operation, supporting *TORCH*, was carried out in the field by ten Americans, and the contrast extends even to small units attached to armies in the field.

For excellent examples of the various principal OSS activities in Europe, Africa, and the Middle East, the following sections should be noted:

Direct intelligence......Sections on South
 France
Indirect intelligence....Sections on OSS/Bern
Counter-espionage .....Section on X-2/France
"Black" propaganda....Sections on MO in North
 Italy and France
Building, supporting,...Sections on North
 and exploiting re-   France and on North
 sistance movements.   Italy
Tactical intelligence....Sections on Seventh
 for armies.   Army in South France
 and on the West Front

It should also be noted that full attention has been given to significant errors committed in the course of OSS operations, as in the sections on "Oujda Operations" and on "Istanbul". The lessons learned from them were as valuable as the experience gained on successful ventures.

2

ESTABLISHMENT OF LONDON BASE

Secret COI/OSS operations in North Africa, preparatory to the Allied landings there, preceded any similar activity out of London by a year and a half. However, the first base for COI/OSS operations in the areas of the European conflict was established in London in November 1941, and agreements concluded there with British intelligence agencies affected OSS activity in Europe, Africa, and the Middle East throughout the war. Operational and administrative relations, similar to those established in the European Theater, were subsequently matched in other theaters.

Preparations for a London base were made as early as August 1941 when General Donovan arranged for a COI office, which opened the following November. In June 1942 Secret Intelligence (SI), Special Operations (SO), and Research and Analysis (R&A) activities were already under way in London. By the Following December personnel had increased from 31 to more than 100, while activities were augmented by the addition of Field Photographic, Security, and Communications staffs. During 1943 and early 1944 the base crystallized into its final form. Morale Operations (MO) was activated in May; Counter-Espionage (X-2) in June; Services in September; Maritime Unit (MU) in December. In the spring of 1944 Documents (CD), Research and Development (R&D), and Medical Services were added. By that time the authorized personnel had increased to more than 2,000, and 14 branches were active.

Relations With British Agencies

The creation of COI had been warmly received by an Allied nation whose strategic military position was poor. British intelligence services offered training facilities in Canada and encouraged the establishment of a large base in London. In London COI/OSS would be well placed for operations into the Continent and simultaneously could follow British guidance in developing techniques, facilities, training and finally agent missions of its own.

SI, SO and later X-2 had been established as the three most secret large branches of OSS to correspond to the British Secret Intelligence Service (SIS), Special Operations Executive (SOE) and Military Intelligence 6 (Section V). SO and X-2 accepted the offers from their counterparts of complete entree into the operations and techniques the latter had developed during the preceding years. In return, SOE and MI-6 (V) each demanded knowledge of the developing operations of its corresponding OSS branch, and a degree of coordination of those operations, sometimes verging on control.

Donovan had early * made it clear that Special Operations would fill a role almost solely of a military nature, which would end with the cessation of hostilities. X-2 had been organized for counter-intelligence and counter-espionage as late as March 1943, and had an exceedingly short period in which to acquire the complicated techniques and the extensive files which it had taken foreign services decades to develop. SO and X-2, therefore, had little to lose and years to gain by the offer, and shortly moved their principal bases from Washington to London for close cooperation with SOE, MI-6 (V) and Allied services.

Secret Intelligence, on the other hand, was considered to be of long-range interest, a service which could adequately be provided, for U. S. purposes, only by independent U. S.

---

* See Washington section on Special Activities (COI), above.

representatives. SI never worked jointly with SIS and, as a partial result, encountered difficulties in mounting operations from London. But in the Mediterranean the Branch developed agent networks, particularly from bases under American control such as Algiers, which by 1944 far surpassed SIS coverage.

SO. The June 1942 agreement between SO and SOE was the first formal arrangement. SOE was the British organization responsible for aid to resistance, sabotage and similar subversive activities, and the need for defining its relations with SO was essential in order to minimize confusion and duplication.

After a series of joint discussions beginning in June 1942, a tentative agreement between SOE and OSS was approved by the JCS in August and confirmed by both agencies in September.* This agreement gave each organization certain geographic spheres of responsibility. All operations conducted by either organization would be under the control of the agency to which the area concerned was assigned.

SOE was designated the responsible agency for France, the Low Countries, Poland, Czechoslovakia, most of Norway, the Balkans, the Middle East and West Africa. Modifying clauses left the possibility of revision if Western Europe or West Africa ultimately became predominantly a U. S. Theater of Operations, and reserved to SO jurisdiction over North Africa, Finland and eventually Bulgaria, Rumania and the northern tip of Norway. According to a supplementary agreement of January 1943, SO renounced any independent operations or the establishment of an independent operational base for Western Europe. SO/London joined SOE in a joint operation for the support and direction of Western European resistance groups in occupied countries. The older, more experienced SOE provided SO with agent-training facilities and in-

struction. British special equipment, such as the S-phone communication device, was made available to U. S. agents.

SOE techniques in sabotage and parachutage were also freely given. SOE had made available to OSS the benefit of its know-how as early as November 1941. At that time a COI liaison officer was accepted by the British and given thorough indoctrination in the latest SOE methods of operation. The contribution of such British experience later proved invaluable when OSS put its own men into the field. SO in return gave funds, expert staff assistance, a packing station for preparing material for resistance groups, badly needed manpower, resistance supplies, three sub-chasers for Norwegian operations, squadrons of Liberators for air drop operations and a communication base more efficient than the two SOE stations.

SI. The SI/SIS relationship, which began in June 1942, took longer to iron out. Here, different, unrelated espionage networks were involved. The British again held that integration was essential in order to avoid wasted resources, prevent the accidental "blowing" of agents and assure maximum coverage of necessary targets. Moreover, SIS asserted that, since it was more experienced and had wider coverage already in existence, integration should be accomplished by placing SI activities under SIS control. American members of COSSAC and SHAEF, relying on the SIS reputation and wishing to maintain cordial U. S. relations, often supported SIS arguments.

The OSS position, however, was that freedom from the knowledge and control of any outside power was essential to long-range espionage. Over considerable British opposition, SI developed direct exchange of information with the various foreign intelligence services represented in London. Later, independent SI projects in France (VARLIN and *Proust*)* were mounted.

---

* SO War Diary Vol. 12, History Files, contains a copy.

---

* See "SI/North France," below.

However, these were small and the only large SI/London project, before the penetration of Germany in early 1945 was *Sussex*,* a joint SI/SIS operation.

Matters came to a head in September 1943 when the U. S. Theater Command sought British opinion before approving implementation of JCS Directive 406, which gave OSS authority to conduct espionage in the ETO. British objections resulted in the Theater Command's disapproval, and in October Donovan took the case to the JCS.

Regarding the British position, his appeal observed that the British proposal:

> . . . suggests "coordination" and "agreement," but as employed here the word "coordination" means "control" and "agreement" means "dependence."
> Physical circumstances permit the British to exercise complete control over United States intelligence. . . . The habit of control has grown up with them . . . through their relations with refugee Governments and refugee intelligence services. . . . We are not a refugee government.

In his conclusion Donovan summarized the OSS position as follows:

> Our basic comment is this: We think it proper that in strictly physical operations we should not only be coordinated but should accept the leadership of SOE. This we do. But the attempt of the British, by reason of their physical control of territory and of communication, to subordinate and control the American intelligence and counter-intelligence service is short-sighted and dangerous to the ultimate interest of both countries.**

As a result, JCS Directive 155/11/D *** of 27 October 1943 gave OSS full and unqualified authority to conduct Secret Intelligence. The Theater Command reversed its position accordingly and thenceforth the independence of OSS long-range espionage was assured. Although SI/London continued to encounter difficulties in running operations, SI independence soon produced results outdistancing SIS in other theaters.

* Ibid.

** Memorandum for the Secretary, the Joint U. S. Chiefs of Staff, from the Director, OSS, 18 October 1943, in Director's File 12,663, OSS Archives.

*** Washington Exhibit W-40.

5

. Furthermore, another U. S.
had already been accepted as
number of PWE and of MOI.
owever, as MO was absorbed
mework of the coordinating
Warfare Division of SHAEF,
with PWE increased. A num-
' radio, subversive leaflet and
igns were successfully run as
ns by equal partners.
tions. An unacceptable offer
inexperienced agency was the
al for joint communications.
ccepted, OSS would thus have
tire operations to the British,
er would undoubtedly have
e secrecy of theirs. In Janu-
roposal was rejected.

e Theater Framework

oo, as elsewhere, OSS encoun-
ems of fitting into the thea-
shifted from OSS/Washing-
ter commands. The new re-
d for a practical set-up which
ely as possible three sets of
(1) The Theater Commander
ed of service for his requests
r the organization and its ac-
; (2) JCS requirements for
o to be met and the Joint
e authority over OSS recog-
Washington had to be given
Considerations of security,
ture of OSS personnel re-
the need for unusual equip-
es increased the problem.
ndon was first established in
the office was placed under
ction for both cover and ad-
ooses. After OSS came into
e 1942, this arrangement
, and it remained in effect
SS overflowed its Embassy
own installations. Both
nant and Biddle were fav-
o the organization, and re-
oth except for a short pe-

riod in January 1942 when the Embassy attempted to supervise the flow of all cable
traffic. Throughout these early days American forces were few in number, the invasion
was far off, and OSS itself was small.

By the summer of 1942, however, ETOUSA
found the presence of such an independent
quasi-civilian agency, conducting highly
operational activities, incompatible with the
rigid organizational pattern that had rapidly enveloped the growing Theater. In
July the Theater Command, probably at SIS
insistence, demanded to be informed by OSS
whenever an agent was sent out. In August
JCS ordered that no OSS activities be undertaken without the Theater Commander's
consent.

Meanwhile OSS/London, too, was finding
its civilian status a growing handicap which
neither the Embassy connection nor over-all
responsibility to the Theater Command
could solve. Great numbers of personnel
were needed to implement new projects; supplies had to be drawn and billets obtained;
some mechanism to enable quick movement
of personnel was required. Difficulties were
enhanced rather than eased by the weak
nature of the first over-all directive from JCS
in December 1942 (155/4/D).* The terms
were vague and operational activities limited
to those in support of psychological warfare.

All these factors led OSS/London to seek
its incorporation into the Theater framework as a military unit. In late February
1943 the Strategic Services officer formally
requested militarization in a memo to the
Adjutant General-ETO. Further pressure
followed, and finally, on 4 June, OSS/Lon-
don was officially established by the Theater
as a military detachment, responsible to the
AC of S, G-2 ETOUSA. Henceforth all personnel and projects for OSS/ETO must have
prior Theater Command approval. This
arrangement was supplemented in October
by implementation of JCS 408, which defined
the organization's activities in ETO as well
as its responsibility to G-2 ETOUSA.

---

* Washington Exhibit W-33.

New jurisdictional complications arose early in 1944 with the activation of SHAEF. It was clear that the activities of OSS, which was now formally within the ETOUSA framework, were even more closely linked to the responsibilities of the new Supreme Headquarters.

As early as February 1944, OSS activities were informally transferred from ETOUSA to the SHAEF framework. Finally, in April the OSS position was officially redefined, with SHAEF assuming all operational control and ETOUSA acquiring control over routine administration. As finally worked out, the lines of authority were as follows: SI and X-2 were made responsible to G-2, SHAEF; SO and OG (jointly with the rest of the SFHQ organization) were put under control of G-3, SHAEF; MO was largely integrated into PWD/SHAEF, where its personnel were used for combat as well as for "black" propaganda; certain R&A representatives were similarly incorporated into the Civil Affairs Division and PWD/SHAEF; and all administrative phases of OSS were placed under authority of ETOUSA. The latter included such housekeeping activities as travel arrangements, personnel procurement and the requisitioning of equipment and supplies.

This represented the final crystallization of OSS within the Theater framework. OSS/London's only real outside responsibility was to SHAEF. JCS exercised no direct control, its authority arising only indirectly through its ultimate control over both the Theater itself and OSS as a whole. Similarly, OSS/Washington's legal control consisted chiefly in the right of veto, through its basic power always to withhold OSS personnel or participation if it disapproved of operations worked out between the Theater and OSS/ETO.

The advantages of OSS/London's status, as a military detachment responsible directly to the Theater Command, turned out as great as anticipated. ETOUSA's and in providing personnel to implement OSS/London's operational commitments was badly needed.

The main disadvantage stemmed from the Theater Command's occasional lack of understanding of, or sympathy with, OSS objectives. Most important in this respect was ETOUSA's policy throughout 1942-43 of favoring British secret intelligence at the expense of OSS participation in this field. The basis for the policy was greater British experience. The view, however, overlooked the compensating activities of an independent U. S. intelligence system which could provide fresh and different information, or which could supplement, confirm or refute intelligence from other sources and serve long-range U. S. strategic needs in a way that no other power could or would do. ETOUSA's omission to recognize these factors resulted not only in the American command's siding with the British against a U. S. unit, but also in ETOUSA's playing into the hands of SIS in the latter's efforts to curtail the development of an independent American secret intelligence service. It was only by the demonstrated effectiveness of OSS operations that OSS/SI finally found recognition.

The London arrangements and agreements were largely duplicated in other theaters in Europe, Africa and the Middle East. Thus, as in ETO, OSS bases and advance units worked for the theater commands and their subordinate units. OSS/Washington acted principally as a coordinating center. Services branches depended on the theater and local Army and Navy supply units. Vis-a-vis the British, SO established joint headquarters with SOE, and jointly directed OG activities. X-2 and MO collaborated closely with British services. SI and R&A remained independent, and their work as independent American organizations was of value not only to the United States but, in the exchange of information between equal Allied services, to the British as well.

Part I

NORTH AFRICA

North Africa was the testing ground for OSS. Initiated in January 1942, the first large-scale COI/OSS operation involved placing agents in an area where British services had been excluded, to gather intelligence, prepare sabotage units in the event of German invasion and prevail on military and other groups to support an Allied landing. Success was important, both in Washington for the future of the agency, and in the field as a demonstration to the theater commands (on whom OSS depended for facilities, transportation and other services) of its potentialities in support of the more orthodox forms of warfare. The operation was carried out by only ten Americans working under State Department cover in North Africa, and was commended in a letter of 23 December 1942 from General Marshall to Donovan.

Following the landings, OSS headquarters were established with AFHQ at Algiers, where it began operations both in North Africa and across the Mediterranean. General Clark requested an OSS detachment at Fifth Army Hq., Oujda, French Morocco, to help in counter-intelligence and on anti-Allied activities in adjacent Spanish territory. Although, in the course of operations, an OSS/Oujda officer failed to secure clearance from Washington and endangered all OSS activity in and out of Spain, he nevertheless performed such valuable service to Fifth Army that General Clark requested he take charge of a detachment to land at Salerno.

Meanwhile, during the Tunisian campaign, OSS and British SOE, which returned to Africa following the invasion, were attempting to work out the position and activities of their respective units with armies in combat. In this case, as subsequently in Sicily, their use on reconnaissance patrols constituted a waste of personnel trained for subversive activity. For over a month OSS assisted SOE in holding a sector of the front. It was not until later, in Italy and France, that the techniques of recruiting and infiltrating local agents through battle lines were developed.

A. OPERATION TORCH

The Vice-Consuls

In February 1941 an economic pact was concluded by the State Department with General Maxime Weygand, the Commander of Vichy French forces in North Africa. To supplement the agreement, twelve U. S. vice-consuls were added to U. S. representation in North Africa for the purpose of checking on the distribution of U. S. cotton, sugar, tea and petroleum to be allocated. They were to have access to ports to observe incoming American shipments and the distribution of goods when they arrived, and to check all outgoing ships carrying goods similar to those imported, in order to prevent their acquisition by the Axis.

The twelve control officers were selected by G-2 and ONI, in cooperation with State Department. . Ostensibly vice-consuls, they were briefed for intelligence activities. When military and naval undercover intelligence outside the Western Hemisphere was taken over by the new Coordinator of Information in the fall of 1941, COI dispatched a chief agent to set up a head office in the international port of Tangier. The agent arrived in early January 1942,

The subversive job in North Africa was divided between himself and Robert D. Murphy of State. While Murphy would handle the political negotiations with French leaders, COI would direct the secret aspects of intelligence, subversion and resistance. These involved, in addition to the actual collection of intelligence, disseminating propaganda designed to minimize French support of the Axis, obtaining the cooperation of French military groups and organizing units for sabotage and armed coup-de-main resistance to counteract the quasi-fascist organizations, S. O. L. and P. P. F.*

The British shelling of the French navy at Mers el Kebir and Dakar in July 1940 had closed French North Africa to open British activity. All British nationals were banned from the area and their diplomatic and intelligence representation evacuated to a perimeter position in the international city of Tangier overlooking the Straits of Gibraltar. Concomitant with this diplomatic break was the psychological severance that was to handicap seriously British relations with patriotic Frenchmen until the end of the war. The incident put the as yet non-belligerent Americans in a favorable position for subversive experimentation. They were able to assist the British Intelligence Services ** and borrow special equipment without having to rival these more experienced institutions. Intelligence in North Africa, preparatory to the landings, became a COI/-OSS responsibility.

* Service d'Ordre Legionnaire (a veterans organization) and Parti Populaire Francais.
** The U. S. State Department and COI/OSS considerably aided SIS when the latter's agent chains were jeopardized by its confinement to Tangier, e.g.: (1) Before Murphy's arrival, a regular U. S. vice-consul in Tunis helped an SIS agent, who had gone underground, to re-establish contact between his strong anti-Vichy group and SIS headquarters. A wireless transmitter was provided him by the U. S. Consul with which he maintained regular contact with SIS signals men on Malta, reporting enemy ship movements in Mediterranean waters from October 1941 to December 1942; (2) a U. S. vice-consul, in touch with the SIS/Tangier chief, agreed to pay British agents and collect, evaluate, and transmit their intelligence to Tangier; (3) a U. S. control consul in Casablanca serviced the British intelligence network in French Morocco, and from January 1942 until D-Day in November, handled 193 SIS requests covering agent contacts, transmissions of wireless sets and fuel, and the distribution of salaries and clothing.

11

Clandestine Radio Stations

Of the twelve vice-consuls, two each were operating in offices at Tunis, Oran and Algiers, and the remainder at Casablanca. The new COI chief immediately began the process of setting up a coordinated intelligence and special operations system, designed to meet the alternate possibilities of German or Allied invasion. Choosing six of the control officers and a regular State Department vice-consul of ten-years' standing, who had shown themselves most resourceful in organizing and working with agents, he appointed definite tasks of an intelligence and operational nature. He directed that all intelligence reports be channeled through Tangier for appropriate dissemination, instead of being dispatched direct to Washington from the various consulates.

An intrinsic part of Donovan's original plan for North Africa, as set forth in his memorandum to the President of 10 October 1941,* had been the establishment of rapid communications in such fashion that they could continue to operate in the event of a diplomatic break with the Vichy Government. COI's first and most pressing problem, therefore, was to establish—rapidly, in view of the continuing possibility of diplomatic rupture or military action by either the Germans or the Allies—a clandestine radio network for the ports where the control officers were operating.

Frenchmen with some knowledge of radio were recruited by the vice-consuls, sent secretly to Gibraltar to be drilled by the British, and returned to await the arrival of enough equipment to set up permanent field stations. The Casablanca office was the first to obtain both a wireless set and an operator with which to begin, in March 1942, a daily schedule to MIDWAY, the base station in Tangier. The location was a wine-press overlooking the airfield.

Agent sets of the small X-35 type and larger, together with transmitters, receivers

---

* Washington Exhibit W-21.

and parts, were consequently smuggled in from the British supplies in Gibraltar. By July wireless stations similar to the one in Casablanca (LINCOLN) had been clandestinely set up in Algiers (YANKEE), Tunis (PILGRIM) and Oran (FRANKLIN),* and were regularly contacting Tangier or Gibraltar.

The necessity for secrecy on extra-curricular activities led to a degree of misunderstanding on the part of the career members of the State Department, who frequently had cause to wonder about the movements of these food control officers. With the help of Murphy, and, later, the COI/OSS chief in the area, together with the precautions and stratagems of the men themselves, the invasion plan was never revealed to other U. S. representatives, even during the extremely active weeks directly preceding the Allied landing in November 1942.

Chains of Informants

Present in the main cities of North Africa, under the terms of the German treaty with a defeated France, were the Italian and German Armistice Commissions. These consisted of economists, military experts and agents gathering intelligence under cover of obtaining foodstuffs and minerals for the German war effort. The presence of these Axis officials helped to stiffen the Vichy-sponsored collaborationist government in North Africa and was a serious obstacle to the Americans in building up their own system.

Pearl Harbor and the official U. S. entry into the war in December 1941 brought about severe restrictions for Americans in North Africa and reprisals to Frenchmen seen associating with them. Americans were denied free access to docks, airfields and other

---

* The chief radio operator for the Division of Oran also worked the OSS station there. His position offered excellent concealment, for he was able to keep the radio set broken down in his office, assembling it only for transmission and reception.

strategic installations, while Gestapo agents in the German Armistice Commission, who had maintained a hands-off policy with regard to the Americans, now began to apply political and strong-arm pressure to oust them. Intelligence continued nevertheless to be supplied through well-placed sub-agents.

Even before the arrival of the American control officers, opposition to Axis rule in North Africa was being organized by Frenchmen themselves. These groups were especially active in Algiers and Tunis where they had established contacts with U. S. State Department representatives and with British SIS via radio to Tangier. Upon the advent of the vice-consuls, more and more Frenchmen, as well as Allied sympathizers of other nationalities who had escaped to North Africa, put themselves at the service of the Americans and their sub-agents. The head of a French youth movement, a police commissioner, officers in the French intelligence service (Deuxieme Bureau), an aviation workshops manager, a garage owner with widespread Moroccan contacts, a wealthy French industrialist, a host of French army officers, including many in high positions, Royalists, Communists, Jesuits, Arabs, Jews, de Gaullists and anti-de Gaullists worked with COI/OSS for the common purpose of helping to restore France as an independent power.

The threat of a German thrust through Spain to North Africa before, during and after the Allied landing was of constant concern to the planners of Operation TORCH. To help prepare for this contingency, two COI agents, trained in sabotage and other subversive techniques * and with first-hand knowledge of French and Spanish Morocco, arrived in April and May 1942 to work in and around Tangier.

Their task was to build within the heterogeneous native population of these Axis-infested areas pro-American intelligence and resistance groups. Since the menace to American security from this vulnerable flank was to continue until the Germans surrendered Tunisia on 8 May 1943, the groundwork laid by these men and the contacts made were to prove as important after the Allied landings as before.*

in the U. S. Legation at Tangier,** the new COI recruits set themselves up as dispensers of U. S. information, assisting with public relations disseminations and distributing other forms of printed propaganda. They made, almost immediately, key intelligence contacts among the main streams of Moroccan society. "Strings", the leader of the most powerful religious brotherhood in northern Morocco, and "Tassels", one of the most influential undercover tribal leaders in Er Rif,*** were put in touch with COI by one of its English-speaking Moslem agents, and financed by State Department and COI funds. Leaders of the diverse nationalist groups (elements of the Moroccan Nationalist Party), were also used, but to lesser advantage. The last were politically active intellectuals constantly under the surveillance of the French secret police, and therefore of little value for undercover work.

Members of the "Strings" group numbered tens of thousands of Moors from every walk of life, ready to obey unquestioningly the will of their divine leader. "Strings'" reports to COI came from caids and sheiks, holy men who penetrated areas forbidden by the French authorities to the general populace, and from farmers and shepherds who relayed pertinent items of intelligence in comparative anonymity.

---

* OSS activities in Morocco in the post-TORCH period are treated in the section on "Oujda Operations," below.

** Again, there was misunderstanding of their assignment by the U. S. Consul-General, and the men were put to work as code clerks until rescued by the OSS Chief.

*** The hilly coastal region transversing Central Spanish Morocco and extending into French Morocco.

---

* These men had received instruction in SOE schools in Canada.

13

The Riffs under "Tassels", on the other hand, were Berber adventurers, willing to carry out any job regardless of the danger involved, and highly adept at avoiding detection by Spanish or French police. These men knew how to handle arms and conduct guerrilla warfare in difficult terrain.*

COI handled both groups with caution, letting neither know of the other's cooperation. Secret meetings were held at regular intervals with "Tassels" and "Strings", or their leg-men, at frequently changed rendezvous. Here were reported at length detailed combat intelligence—Spanish battle order, troop movements, fortifications, etc.—and significant political events. Appropriate information was turned over by COI to G-2, ONI, the State Department and the British.

Individuals having natural occupational covers were also recruited as COI agents. A fisherman was able to report the exact locations of Spanish troops between Sidi Kassem and Cap Spartel, and turned in intelligence on Spanish AA guns overlooking the Straits and the movements of German submarines operating out of caves in the same vicinity. A sherif notified COI of secret fortifications in the Tetuan-Ceuta area. An Arab tribesman helped to explode the report of an enemy airport at Tammanrot.

Aside from the organizational phases of COI planning and intelligence in Morocco, the Tangier agents personally accomplished several on-the-spot services. Using State Department vehicles, they made frequent trips through the Spanish Zone to confirm specific items of reported intelligence or to make first-hand observations for the benefit of the Army and Navy. On one of these trips they checked on alleged Spanish airfields which were a matter of concern to G-2

---

* The Atlas Mountain tribes of Morocco were the greatest obstacle to French conquest of Morocco. "Marshal Petain required ten months and a force of 150,000 men and 30 batteries of 65 mm mountain guns to put down the Abd-el-Krim insurrection of 1925-26." From a Memo, Donovan to President, 9 January 1942. COI Exhibits, History Files.

and the British, and were able to report definitely that these consisted of nothing but a few anti-aircraft batteries. On another, they clocked the road from Tangier to Melilla and noted all possible targets for demolition or air attack. This road, extending along the coastal length of the Spanish Zone, was one which U. S. armies would have to use in the event of military operations in the area.

Two agents, secured by a COI representative at Casablanca,

supplied the Americans with decoded copies of all German Armistice Commission and Spanish Consulate cables passing through that office. An agent employed in the ticket office at the Casablanca airport reported Axis arrivals and departures, while the

contributed official figures on plane stocks and the plans of all airfields (including secondary ones) and their defenses, down to safety channels and recognition signals.

To supplement the detailed strategic reports on ports and other facilities already submitted to the Army, Navy and Air Force, OSS agents reported new defense measures or increased preparations in the ports, and followed the activities and methods of the Armistice Commissions. Movements of all ships and cargoes in and out of North African ports were noted. On the basis of this information, the RAF struck repeatedly at enemy planes and ships, to prevent vital supplies from going to the Germans.

By the time of U. S. entry into the war, the vice-consuls had established reliable chains of informants in each of the major North African ports and were transmitting intelligence of long-range and tactical value to Algiers and Washington via diplomatic pouch and cable. In the first category were many sketches and overlays of port installations (sent in answer to specific Army and Navy questionnaires) and information on the disposition of the French fleet, in particular on the presence of the 35,000 ton battleship

"Jean Bart" in Casablanca harbor. Examples of short-range intelligence were reports on shipments of crude rubber, iron ore and cobalt. These were, on different occasions, diminished in supply or denied exportation altogether as a result of the observations of native agents, translated into acts of sabotage or effective political pressure by the control consuls.

Sabotage Groups

To meet a possible German attack, the Riff and Moslem groups were directed by COI in laying definite plans for organized revolt, for the reception of Allied sea- and air-borne troops, the delivery of guns and the cutting off of roads and garrisons. A system of signals was laid on, arranging for Riffs to assemble and seize key positions. "Strings" was prepared to conceal the COI organizers should the Germans surprise them at Tangier, and to hide friendly Europeans for them. This planned uprising, involving some 80,000 natives, was part of a secret scheme

In Casablanca, the COI men divided their labors. While one narrowed his attention to the increasing demands of the new communications system, another concentrated on developing teams for special operational missions, such as the demolition of a bridge, the seizure and protection of a power house or signal station, or the detonation of mines. One group was given training in protecting rail installations and blocking the lines to prevent reinforcements of Axis troops from

the Arab centers of Fez, Meknes and Marrakech. Another group of twelve Frenchmen was recruited to lead ten-man strong-arm squads to kidnap the members of the German Armistice Commission on D-Day.*

Agents in the offices of Radio Maroc (Rabat) prepared to cut off the power and establish a secret studio from which to broadcast emergency signals without the knowledge of the Axis. The Chief of S. O. L. in Morocco was personally contacted by a COI agent, and won over to the U. S. viewpoint to the extent of dissolving his fascist organization altogether. Similar preparations were being made in the other ports where landings might be attempted. In Oran, combat groups ** totalled more than 2,500 men.

Since the Allied landing, first expected in May, was indefinitely postponed, the problem of maintaining the morale of the groups developed. Practice maneuvers were begun, but arms were difficult to obtain, and British SOE again offered invaluable assistance. It agreed to make available to the Americans supplies from its arsenal at Gibraltar, and a series of subterfuges was undertaken to get this equipment into North Africa. Sten guns, .45 pistols, ammunition, flares, explosives and other needed items were loaded in British diplomatic pouches in Gibraltar and shipped across on a Portuguese tugboat to the British Legation at Tangier. Here they were shifted to the U. S. Legation where they were reloaded into U. S. Navy or State Department pouches and smuggled through the Spanish Zone to Casablanca. Any Allied official might be asked to double as courier to deliver these items to the resistance groups in Algiers, Oran and Tunis. The vice-con-

* The need never arose, but fears of a flank attack through Spain continued as the American forces advanced eastward and Fifth Army requested OSS, following D-Day, to maintain contact with these organizations.

* This plot was stopped, along with a number of other OSS-planned maneuvers, when the French military group under directions from Algiers superseded civilians in the crucial hours before the invasion. See below.
** These groups were organized in cells. The men involved knew only their own leader, each leader knew no other but the ringleader, and the ringleader himself knew only the leaders of the various teams.

suls, travelling to Tangier for conferences, frequently acted in this capacity.

Hand grenades, a forbidden article in the British pouch, were obtained from a Riff leader who had access to a large supply left over from the Spanish Civil War. Grenades were smuggled over the Spanish Moroccan border on mule pack, disguised as contraband tea and sugar, to a COI agent who carted them to safety. These grenade-passing operations were conducted without detection, despite a large German reward offered for the name of the men responsible for their distribution.

Propaganda

In order to counteract derogatory and false reports about American military preparedness by the Axis-controlled Radio Maroc in Rabat, a COI vice-consul undertook, in January 1942, an extensive propaganda tour of Morocco, using a French interpreter popular among Moroccans.

A series of photographs of U. S. war materials being produced in factories, loaded on ships, etc., was shown to Frenchmen and natives in cities and outlying areas throughout French Morocco, including, in spite of the French Resident-General's warnings not to trespass, French military zones. French officers were impressed. Admiring Arab chieftains, notorious for their habit of playing the winning side, carried the reports via the grapevine to the German-controlled Arab center of Fez. Shortly afterwards COI agents were warned by the United States consul at Casablanca, as a result of pressure from the German Armistice Commission, to restrict their Arab contacts.

The hostile attitude displayed by Germans and collaborationists toward the Americans in North Africa became more pronounced with the rise to power of Laval in France in the spring of 1942. COI's program of influencing as many of the French and natives of North Africa as possible to favor the Allies was approached with greater caution, but nevertheless continued.

One outstanding performance was a free Arabic translation of President Roosevelt's Flag Day or "Four Freedoms" speech. The message was mailed all over the Spanish Zone (with some copies going accidentally to the French Zone) and broadcast several times over the Vichy-controlled Rabat radio station. It did more than anything else up to that time to assure the Moroccans of U. S. friendship and, at the same time, unfortunately convinced them that liberation from colonial status was near at hand. Other propaganda produced by the COI representatives included attacks on General Nogues (the Vichy Resident-General in Morocco) and complaints about black market conditions in Tangier.

Preparations for D-Day

Allied sympathizers in North Africa who were in danger, and persons capable of giving technical assistance to the invasion planners in Washington and London, were secretly exfiltrated with COI help. This was usually accomplished by shipping them at night aboard Portuguese schooners plying between Casablanca and Lisbon, or on British boats going from Tangier to Gibraltar. The chief pilot of Port Lyautey was thus secured, when a request was received from Washington for a guide who knew the harbor. He was cached in the baggage compartment of a COI agent's car going to Tangier, and sent to Washington via Gibraltar. The pilot's services with the incoming fleet on D-Day were recognized with a Silver Star and the Navy Cross.

During the summer of 1942, three COI vice-consuls who had helped organize intelligence and resistance at Casablanca, Oran and Algiers respectively, left to confer with military planners. They were personally to report to the invading Task Force on preparations for resistance in each of those ports and economic, geographic and political data obtained during their assignment to North Africa.

16

On 22 October 1942 General Mark Clark was secretly landed on the Cherchell beach (75 miles from Algiers) to meet with Ambassador Murphy and French military and naval leaders in a villa secured through an OSS/Oran agent. Here some of the final details of *TORCH* were revealed and plans coordinated. Cooperation of the French Army in North Africa was confirmed at this time, although, for security reasons, the Allied High Command did not divulge to any but the American undercover agents in North Africa the actual date and places of landing. In preparation for the secret arrival of General Giraud from Gibraltar on D-Day, French military commanders were appointed at each port to lead armed resistance in support of the Allied landing.

Rumors hinting at an Allied invasion at any number of possible points had been rife for some time. Both sides originated and encouraged these: the Axis in order to smoke out denials; the Allies for the purpose of misleading German opposition. COI agents spread the word that Americans would land at Dakar. Information later received by OSS agents working at Axis-controlled Radio Maroc and from an agent in the Spanish officers' mess at Tangier, revealed that the Axis governments did not suspect landings any place except Dakar, and that the Germans were, in fact, planning an invasion of their own at a somewhat later date than that chosen for *TORCH*. As a result of deliberately spread stories about Malta, the Germans were so convinced of a British decision to rush at all costs a food convoy to that starving island that they completely misinterpreted the move of 150 Allied ships through the Straits of Gibraltar on D-Day.

Final arrangements were made at each of the ports and beaches where Allied landings were to take place. Although the cooperation of French Army leaders was assured, the Allies expected the Navy to resist strongly. Persuasion of some, but not all, French naval battery commanders to withhold resistance was effected without revealing when the invasion would come. Strong-arm squads were appointed to guard all important public buildings and to make arrests if the order not to resist were ignored. Others were instructed to cut telegraph and telephone lines and to obstruct public utilities generally. Still others were to go just before H-Hour to detonate mines on roads and beaches which the Allies would have to use. Groups were assigned to beachheads and landing and parachute fields, with flares to signal in troops. Guides and interpreters were briefed with passwords to meet them and aid their ingress. An OSS/Oran representative, trained by the Army Signal Corps in the use of the secret "Rebecca" radio beacon device, led an armed group charged with the reception of paratroopers on the plain between La Senia and Tafaroui airports.

Headquarters at Tangier were shifted, five days before the invasion, to Gibraltar to coordinate all North Africa activity with AFHQ plans. OSS agents coded and decoded all secret messages between AFHQ and the North African stations, including, besides intelligence reports, all instructions from Eisenhower to Murphy and arrangements for the flight and reception of General Giraud. The signal to alert groups for action was to come to OSS communication operators as a BBC announcement: "Robert Arrive". General Giraud was scheduled, upon arrival at Algiers, to broadcast publicly the announcement of French entry into the war on the side of the Allies.

Cover for the heightened activity just before 8 November was provided by various means. One OSS man sent out invitations for a party to be given on a date shortly after that set for the landings. Another made arrangements for a trip to the country on the designated weekend. Since none of the French military or resistance groups knew exactly when the attack would occur, they could not reveal the plans by unnatural excitement or suspicious behavior. Many of the civilian resistance volunteers were actually absent from their posts at the time of the invasion, because they had not expected anything to happen so soon and had left for weekend vacations.

For varying reasons, including French defections and lack of American authorization to carry them out, several of the resistance and sabotage plans were not accomplished.* Many were. OSS furthermore brought intelligence to the landing forces throughout the operation. The large-scale deception plan was also effective. Some 107,000 Allied troops went ashore over a stretch of almost 2,000 miles of North African coast while seven squadrons of Sicily-based Luftwaffe fruitlessly circled the Mediterranean opposite Cap Bon, 300 miles to the east, to bomb a "Malta-bound" convoy.

U. S. troops were met on many beaches by friendly guides. On the previous night, an OSS/Oran agent had removed the caps from demolition charges in the tunnel connecting Mers el Kebir with Oran. The tunnel was vital to Allied movement and it was estimated that it would have required three months to rebuild.

In the absence of either a Spanish or German alarm, resistance to the Allies consisted

---

* The French Resident-General of Morocco was not arrested by a subordinate as planned. The French military leader in charge of resistance at Oran turned traitor at the last minute. (This development was reported by OSS radio station FRANKLIN, but the message appears to have been garbled.) American troops arrived in Algiers too late to relieve the resistance group which had seized control there, and Admiral Darlan waited three days to issue a "cease fire" order.

of a determined but short-lived opposition of a surprised French navy and scattered military troops. Allied Army, Navy and Air officers with the invasion fleet received until the last minute of H-Hour, and beyond, detailed information on what to expect (with the exception of the sudden defection of the Oran resistance leader) at every landing point. They had maps and diagrams of airport locations and measurements, and of port dimensions and facilities. They knew the disposition of the French fleet, the batteries actually being manned, and the number of planes on every airfield, with the amount of aviation gas available at each. They were aware of conditions of wind, weather and tide and they had the expert advice of guides who knew the harbors intimately. Before and after the landings, they were advised, by OSS representatives who accompanied them, on terrain, locations of French headquarters and of German Armistice Commission offices, and the officials on whom they could rely for assistance in the administration of civil affairs.

The techniques developed during *TORCH* for informing invasion commanders of last-minute conditions up to the moment of arrival represented a new kind of efficiency in warfare. The established value of OSS subsequently helped the new organization to gain support in both Washington and the theaters of military operations. OSS assistance to *TORCH* received special notice in a December 1942 letter from General Marshall to Donovan.*

---

* Washington Exhibit W-34.

B. TUNISIA

With the Armistice that was signed on 11 November 1942, control of French North Africa west of German-occupied Tunisia passed to AFHQ, and intelligence activities became the responsibility of the Counter-Intelligence Corps and G-2. OSS headquarters moved from Gibraltar to Algiers, where control was transferred from the State Department to Allied Force Headquarters (AFHQ).

Recognition of the OSS contribution to Operation *TORCH* and confidence in the ability of the new organization to attain strategic and tactical goals through irregular operations was given expression in General Clark's request, in early 1943, for an OSS contingent with the Fifth Army at Oujda * to further the work of counter-intelligence and sabotage built up for *TORCH* in Morocco.

Although operations into the Continent were uppermost in the minds of those making plans for the Algiers base, it was recognized that activity would have to be continued against German-occupied Tunisia on the east and a hostile Spanish Morocco on the west. Meanwhile, British SOE had reentered North Africa in force, with the *Brandon* and *Massingham* missions, the first for operations in Tunisia, the second for infiltration of agents into Europe.

OSS/Algiers improvised with what little personnel, transportation and supplies were available and cooperated with French and British services. Agents in Tangier and Casablanca, continuing intelligence channels and Moroccan contacts built up during *TORCH*, worked closely with Army counter-intelligence and G-2. An Algiers radio operator with *TORCH* experience began organizing a clandestine mission to Corsica,**

and, in order to learn the techniques of SO and guerrilla operations, OSS representatives accompanied the British SOE mission already active in Tunisia.

Brandon was the British SOE mission appointed to work with the British First Army and the American divisions attempting to oust the Germans from Tunisia. Agents were to infiltrate enemy lines for demolition and sabotage of enemy communications and transportation, and to gather tactical intelligence for G-3. With German troops concentrated around Tunis and Bizerte, the first, or northern, phase of *Brandon* consisted in the holding of the northern flank of the Allied line by SOE alone, against some 500 Italian troops. The second, or southern, phase began when German troops moved through the Kasserine Pass. So far as SOE and OSS were concerned, this phase involved front-line tactical intelligence.

Participation in this British operation constituted the first OSS experience in sabotage and combat intelligence teams in front areas and behind enemy lines. That the jobs actually done by the handful of OSS men who joined in the SOE Tunisian campaign were not typical of future activity was perhaps due as much to the exigencies of the battle situation as to the misunderstanding of their function by the British and American Army officers whom they served. Their activity was not that of an intelligence service, but consisted in effect of reconnaissance patrolling and in one case of holding a small sector of the front.

Five advance outposts were established by SOE for the northern phase of *Brandon*. Each was under the command of a British officer, with a few French junior officers, and manned by anti-fascist French and Spanish recruits from concentration camps, the Corps Franc d'Afrique and elsewhere. Few

---

* See next section.
** See "West Mediterranean Islands," below.

of these had military training; most were badly undernourished if not actually unfit for combat.

Radio communications were maintained between each of the bases, an advanced holding base, the main base at Guelma and with 5th Corps Hq. of the British First Army.

An OSS representative was dispatched to visit the outposts and acquaint himself with the way in which each performed intelligence and demolition work from its strategic position in no-man's land. As it worked out, he spent most of his time at the northernmost post, Cap Serrat, and was in charge of the group there during the absence of the British commander. This lighthouse post, located on the Mediterranean coast, was the best organized of the five, its British commander being the only one in *Brandon* with SOE training and experience.

During his assignment at Cap Serrat, the OSS observer performed three types of operational tasks—defensive, observational and offensive. Defensive operations included manning the lighthouse semaphore, the bridge over the Ziatine River and the beach. The OSS representative supervised the setting of booby traps, signal wires, rockets, etc., to warn of enemy approach. Observational activities consisted in scanning the surrounding countryside at the semaphore, in sending out patrols for information and in using Arab watchers and informers to advise of enemy movements. Offensive operations, owing to the small size of the garrison and the poor physical condition and morale of its men, were limited to several mining expeditions. These amounted to little, as the Italians were less active in the area than the German Messerschmitts, which regularly raided the few passable roads and made movement overland dangerous.

In addition to liaison duties, the OSS man was put in charge of work with the Arabs, involving interviews with hostages and prisoners for intelligence information. Allied relations with the Arabs were not of the best in Tunisia, mostly as a result of the open hostility that existed between Arabs and French. The Americans were associated with the latter, and not even the distribution of cotton, tea and sugar served to turn more than a very small percentage of the Tunisian Arabs to Allied assistance. A hostage system was employed:

We found that when we entered a distant village where loyalty was wavering, we could take the eldest son of the most important man and hold him in the lighthouse pending his father's arrival. The old man inevitably came, with gifts, demanding his son. He was sent back to get good information of enemy positions, and when he came the second time his son was released, if the information was satisfactory. . . . This use of hostages was our chief source of intelligence aside from the work of our own patrols.[*]

Only one demolition job is known to have been successfully carried out from Cap Serrat. Two Arabs who had supplied intelligence on Italian positions, supply dumps, etc., were trained by the OSS representative in railroad demolitions and sent to blow the Tindja-Ferryville railroad at Mateur. They infiltrated enemy lines on a mule, with explosives sewn in the pack-saddle. An OSS agent, who later visited the area, reported that the mission had been accomplished successfully.

Late in January 1943, seven OSS operatives came briefly to Guelma and trained forty released Spanish internees, at Mahouna, for the southern phase of *Brandon*. At least four of the OSS men were veterans of the Spanish Civil War, and although veteran leaders of guerrilla groups, they were given, prior to leaving America, the rating of Army sergeants. This low rating only served to weaken their position as special operatives and made it difficult to assign them to anything besides routine patrol and demolition tasks at the front.

All but one of the seven OSS men who instructed at Mahouna were assigned to the SOE unit at Sbeitla under a British major

* Report, *Brandon* Mission, pp. 98-99, History File 181.

responsible to G-3, II Corps at Tebessa. The remaining agent went to the *Brandon* holding area to coordinate G-2 and *Brandon* intelligence and later to help as liaison with an observation post on Hill 609. In an area where attack by superior German panzer divisions was imminent, the OSS men at Sbeitla were assigned by G-2 and G-3 officers to reconnaissance patrols. They were given orders to destroy tanks with Mills and Petard hand grenades. Two OSS men were wounded and had to be withdrawn as the result of such a mission. Two others were captured on patrol duty after one of them had been wounded by unsuspected enemy artillery. An OSS Marine officer and one of the sergeants were wounded by a mine while accompanying an advance reconnaissance unit looking for snipers; both were retired to hospitals in Algiers. Another OSS Marine observer volunteered to lead a combat patrol group and was wounded in the course of destroying a German machine-gun nest single-handed. With the OSS contingent thus depleted, it was recalled to Algiers on 22 March 1943.

That these men, many of them experts in the clandestine techniques of guerrilla warfare, should be used for infantry work had not been anticipated. Such use, though justifiable in an emergency, was inevitably wasteful of talented and trained men. However, despite the difficulties and disappointments encountered by *Brandon* personnel, the losses were less severe than they might have been. This problem—the degree of combat work to be undertaken by OSS—was later worked out in Italy and France.

C. OUJDA OPERATIONS

After the landings of 8 November 1942, the important job of protecting the western defenses of North Africa fell to the American occupation army.* Danger from within and without threatened the Allied supply line between Casablanca and the Tunisian battlefront: In Spanish Morocco and in Spain proper, Axis intelligence services trained agents for sabotage and espionage against Allied transport and communications; in Allied-occupied French Morocco and Algeria, pro-Vichy French officials and Falangist Spaniards openly menaced the security of Allied military and intelligence operations; in Tunisia, highly paid and heavily propagandized Arabs actively aided the German troops.

The army, thinly spread as it was, was further hampered by two conditions over which it had no control. Overt entrance into Spanish territory was prohibited by diplomatic and military agreement. Pro-Axis officials in French territories could not be ousted due to political considerations. Covert counter-intelligence and the arming of native groups were thus the Allies' sole defenses. This job was to be an OSS concern while it remained in North Africa, not only until the fall of Tunis, but through most of the war, as a result of the threat represented by Franco Spain.

The networks of agents in Spanish and French Morocco, developed for the *TORCH* operation, were put to immediate use. An OSS representative in Casablanca introduced to the local CIC officer his most valuable agent in Morocco, a former member of the French Services de Renseignements

(SR), who had built up an effective intelligence chain. Through his efficient handling of native sub-agents and access to friendly French organizations and officials, the agent was able to uncover a number of Axis spy rings in the border region and to effect the arrest, through French authorities, of Frenchmen illegally attempting to return to France through the Spanish Zone. In addition, this agent helped CIC establish intelligence contacts of its own in key Moroccan cities.

In Tangier, an SI representative set up a border patrol and increased the intelligence output of the "Strings" * chain. "Tassels' " ** Riffs, restless with inaction, and Moorish Nationalists, disappointed by U. S. failure to occupy the Spanish Zone, were kept carefully in hand by the Tangier agent, pending possible combat activity.

General Clark came to Morocco in December 1942 to begin training his Fifth Army for operations against the Continent. To meet the possibility of attack from Spain, the *BACKBONE* plan was prepared, to send American armored columns northward into Spanish Morocco in the event of a German advance. To tie in their organized Moslems and Riffs with *BACKBONE,* two OSS/Tangier men went to Oujda in February to confer with G-2, Fifth Army Headquarters. General Clark and G-2 officers were quick to see the advantages of using COI/OSS chains. Liaison, first established in Casablanca, was continued.

SO/SOE plans involving the "Strings-Tassels" subversive groups were laid on, with the Army agreeing to pay all operational expenses. Arms were withheld from the Tunisia battlefront for native use.

---

* At first under the jurisdiction of General Patton's Western Task Force, the area was transferred to Fifth Army under General Clark in December, upon the former's move to Tunisia for the Kasserine campaign.

---

* See "Operation *TORCH*," above.
** Ibid.

Aside from these precautions against the threat of actual military attack, General Clark's major concern was with political intelligence. This was necessitated by the extremely doubtful loyalties of persons in high position in the French territories, as well as the insecurity represented by Fascist persuasions among the French, Spanish and Arab populations. General Clark needed to know: (1) Military preparations by the Axis in Spain; (2) information about Axis intelligence services and sabotage schools; and (3) Vichy officials, "New Order" French, and Arabs undermining Allied security in North Africa.

Impressed with the assistance given CIC by OSS agents, General Clark arranged to have an OSS contingent attached to his G-2 branch. The OSS representatives were to maintain their undercover contacts in close collaboration with CIC, G-2, SOE and as many French organizations as possible. One OSS agent was to cover the Spanish Zone from Tangier, another remained at Oujda for liaison and work along the southern and eastern borders of Spanish Morocco. Two Frenchmen who had worked closely with OSS before and after *TORCH* were attached to the Oujda base as liaison officers. This was the first time that an OSS unit was attached to an American army at the specific request of its commander.

Through the French liaison agents, OSS established close relationships with the most important administrative officials in Oujda and elsewhere, including the local heads of the Police and of the French Deuxieme Bureau and key personnel in the Bureau des Affaires Indigenes. With their cooperation, French civil and military officials discovered by underground channels to be illegally working for the Axis, were removed from office. For example, the commander of the Fez garrison, an active Axis collaborator, was ousted.

German and Italian espionage schools at Tetuan in Spanish Morocco were penetrated. OSS-controlled agents were smuggled across the border to enlist in these schools on different occasions. A German-Swiss agent, obtained through the French Services, succeeded in entering the German service. He came back with German questionnaires on the American Army and on Casablanca harbor, and returned to Spanish Morocco a week later with answers deceptively filled in by Allied intelligence officers. The Italian school was penetrated by an Italian-born agent who was smuggled across the border with a radio. He was able to report to OSS/-Oujda 86 enemy saboteurs crossing the border to destroy railway lines and gasoline and ammunition dumps. Most of the 86 were caught.

A German spy ring which had been suspected of operating in the vicinity of Oran was uncovered. Several agents, sent from Oujda to try to discover enemy agents and methods, found that Riffian Arabs were carrying documents between the Spanish Consul at Oran and the German Consul at Melilla. This chain of agents and Arab couriers was revealed by buying out a member of the Spanish Consulate.

Once informed of such illegal crossings, OSS/Oujda passed on descriptions of the agents to the French Goums * deployed along the border. The Goum guards turned over all couriers and documents thus caught to French military authorities cooperating with the Allies. The Americans would have preferred to use Arabs, who were natives of the border region, for the seizure of Axis agents, since they were less apt to arouse the suspicions of the enemy. The French, however, with whom cooperation was essential for purposes of arrest, discouraged all American-Arab contacts and insisted on using their own troops. The border, as a result, remained porous in many places.

Clandestine contact with the Arabs was continued by OSS nevertheless, and, when large numbers of German escapees from Tunisia began streaming through, the French

* Goums are battalions of local, mostly Berber, militia, commanded by French officers.

did cooperate with the Oujda Detachment in establishing Arab networks and offering rewards to natives for the capture of Germans. Many of the Spanish and Arab shelterers of such prisoners were arrested by the French, when an OSS agent disguised himself as a German escapee and reported names and addresses of those who aided his egress toward the Spanish Zone.

The relative ease with which many of these penetrations were effected by Allied agents revealed weaknesses in an otherwise impressive Axis network. Neither this weakness nor the ejection of the Germans from Tunisia were enough, however, to make the area secure. It was common knowledge that, in violation of Franco's diplomatic assurances, Spain was giving every possible sub-rosa help to German and Italian subversive operations based on Spanish Morocco and directed against the security of the Allies in North Africa and the Fifth Army in particular.

In discussions between G-2, Fifth Army and OSS/Algiers in May 1943, it was decided to attempt more extensive over-the-border work to get highly important information directly from Spanish Morocco and Spain. During the summer of 1943 a clandestine route was established overland to the hub of Axis military and intelligence activity, Melilla, and agents infiltrated with radios into Malaga to obtain intelligence on the Spanish mainland.

To instruct Spaniards as intelligence agents for these new infiltrations, a training camp was established near Oujda by OSS, at the request of G-2, Fifth Army and with army equipment and funds. At this camp, on a mountain-top twenty miles from the nearest village, OSS veterans of the *Brandon* * mission trained 35 men recruited from the Spanish Republican underground. From the Oujda camp, the trainees were sent to the OSS base at Algiers to learn secret wireless communication at the newly-formed OSS radio school.

* See previous section.

The first agents were sent without radios to Melilla, to report via courier on developments at the espionage schools and military bases in the vicinity. Secret overland transportation for these infiltrations was arranged through a few Arab chieftains who volunteered their services and those of their relatives. OSS agents disguised as Arab natives were smuggled over the border and escorted through the Spanish Zone. Once established in key spots from which to observe German, Italian and Spanish activities first-hand, the agents sent back bi-weekly reports by couriers who were escorted in a like manner. Of the men who took advantage of this "underground railroad" none were lost; of those who attempted the trip alone, approximately fifty percent were captured.

Through this bi-weekly reporting system, from well-trained and strategically placed agents around Melilla, came intelligence of specific importance to the Fifth Army. A closer and more regular check than had before been possible was maintained on Spanish battle order, Spanish cooperation with the Axis, German personnel movements and German contacts with the Arabs.*

In July 1943, the first BANANA operation was launched from Oujda to obtain intelligence in Spain. Four trained Spanish agents and a Spanish operator were smuggled to Tangier via the Arab underground route and deposited at Malaga, Spain.

Radio communications started within seven days, and reports on Spanish defenses and other military information of interest to Fifth Army were received by OSS/Oujda. These messages were translated and turned over to G-2, with copies going to OSS/Algiers for AFHQ as well. Five more men entered Spain on 23 September and joined the first group.

* Similar activities were being carried out by the OSS station at Tangier. See "Africa," below.

Unfortunately, several errors were made in the BANANA operations:

(1) The agents were Communists, recruited through the "popular front" Union Democratica Espanol in Mexico and North Africa;

(2) They carried in neutral territory U. S. Army materiel, including grenades, submachine guns, ammunition and SSTR-1 radio sets, all with U. S. markings and serial numbers;

(3) The area was already covered, to the knowledge of the commanding officer of OSS/Oujda, by OSS/Spain, in fact by four American and better than fifty Spanish agents, who had turned in bi-weekly reports giving detailed plans of all fortifications of the south Spanish coast, plans of all airfields and complete order of battle information.

The agents were eventually captured by the Spanish police both in Malaga and Melilla. Communist code-books were reportedly discovered on them,* as well as the code-books for communication with Oujda. After suitable "processing" by the Spanish police, the men revealed the details of their American training in Oujda, the use of the SSTR-1's and like information, all of which was presumably passed on to German intelligence. They also gave away some of their leftist comrades, resulting in a widespread clean-up by the Falangist government with 261 arrests and 22 executions. A confidential brief was prepared by the Spanish police stating that the United States was backing the Communist movement in Spain. Since this was a neutral country with which the United States was maintaining friendly relations, it did not look well for American arms to be received by Communist elements there.

---

* Possibly these were planted by the Spanish police.

In this case the blame fell squarely on the commanding officer at Oujda, who was subsequently released. He had been warned that the recruits from the U. D. E. were unreliable and he was personally aware of the existence of SI in Spain. He never checked with OSS/Washington to obtain approval for the infiltration.

The U. S. Ambassador in Spain covered the OSS error, denying any U. S. implication in the operation.* However, BANANA nearly ended OSS activity in Spain and through Spain into southern France.** It was the largest OSS blunder of the war, and could only partly be excused by the youth of the U. S. espionage agency.

Despite the embarrassment to OSS in general, and to OSS/Spain and Ambassador Hayes in particular, OSS/Oujda had carried out General Clark's requests to his satisfaction. The weak supply line stretching east to the Tunisian battlefront had required active organization, intelligence and counter-intelligence to protect it from Axis activities in and around Spanish Morocco. Collaborators in the local French Government were ousted, German agents were caught in large numbers and military developments in Spanish Morocco and Spain were reported. The record in itself proved exceedingly useful in obtaining authorization for OSS activity in Italy.

On 9 September 1943 the OSS/Fifth Army Detachment left North Africa to accompany the landings at Salerno.*** Oujda was closed, and local OSS offices in Tangier, Oran, Casablanca and Tunis carried on the work of counter-intelligence until the end of the war.†

---

* U. S. guilt was never admitted to the Spanish Government.
** See "Spain and Portugal," below.
*** See "Fifth Army Detachment," below.
† See "Africa," below.

Part II

OUTLYING NEUTRAL TERRITORIES

During the early days of COI/OSS, agents were dispatched to Eire, Spain, Portugal, the African Continent and the Middle East. The initial purpose, of establishing stay-be-hind "sleeper" agents to prepare for the possibility of Axis invasion, gave way as Allied successes grew to secret intelligence, counter-intelligence and counter-smuggling.

In each of the areas, valuable experience in techniques normal to peacetime espionage was gained. The necessity for continuing State Department support became increasingly obvious. While secret operatives could best maintain their covers

(preferably permitting free time and travel), State Department offices provided the obvious headquarters for an open chief of U. S. intelligence in each area. State could also most safely offer communications, files and funds, where they could not be supervised by local cable, secret service and banking authorities.

The new U. S. espionage agency, however, often ran into State Department opposition, occasionally because of the mistakes of its own rapidly recruited, briefly trained and inexperienced representatives, and occasionally because some members of the State Department opposed U. S. secret intelligence in neutral territory. Lacking the firmest supporting directives from Washington, OSS had nearly always to depend on personal relationships with local Department representatives.

The operation in Eire, since fears of German invasion soon waned, was a small one and was taken over early in 1944 by X-2/-London. In Spain, Portugal and Africa, SI was initially active in collecting road maps, beach reports and local order of battle intelligence. Following Allied military successes, the large staffs in these countries turned to extensive counter-intelligence, counter-smuggling and general intelligence activity. In the Middle East, tightly controlled by British services, OSS principally gathered political and economic information on the conflicting activities of the major powers.

A. EIRE

A German invasion of Eire was feared to be imminent in 1940, and through 1941 and 1942 the threat remained serious. The Irish Government would allow no Allied forces in the country, necessitating the continued presence of a large Anglo-American contingent in North Ireland, prepared to enter Eire to repel the Germans before they could fully establish themselves on the southern coast. Local military support for the Germans was, furthermore, to be expected from the underground Irish Republican Army (I. R. A.), some of whose members were actively working for the Nazis.

On 23 December 1941 the first COI representative left for Dublin on a two-month "Special Temporary Mission to the Minister of Ireland."

He reported on the poor condition of Irish defenses and on the location of a Nazi spy center at Tralee. There he enlisted a local cattle inspector to communicate directly with the U. S. Military Attache in Dublin on local German activities.

In London, British intelligence services proved hesitant in turning over to the United States their intelligence on Ireland. It was hoped, however, that the Irish would be more willing to cooperate with Americans than they had with their British "big brothers". Accordingly, three OSS agents were dispatched.

One of these, the chief agent, worked from the U. S. Legation Two others went in under private cover, arriving in September 1942 and May 1943, respectively, but were shortly removed at the request of the U. S. Minister who stated that they made him "uneasy". The chief agent, "Hurst", meanwhile remained, despite the disapproval of the Minister, sending in reports on shipping to and from Eire, on Irish politics (the activities of the I. R. A. in particular), on German propaganda, on government attitudes and methods and on Irish radio direction-finding equipment. A quantity of counter-espionage material was also procured. Situation reports and censorship summaries received from the Washington base helped him in the analysis and collection of this information.

"Hurst's" major accomplishment was his official liaison with the Eire Government itself.

"Hurst's" main difficulties were with the American Minister. Although he submitted all intelligence to the Minister and took no step vis-a-vis the Irish without prior approval from him, personality difficulties

29

arose, and in November 1942 the Minister cabled the State Department recommending severance of connection with OSS because the Eire Government might resent the latter's activities.* This denial of Eire's clear cooperation was apparently ignored, other difficulties were ironed out and "Hurst" continued his work. His position as open, high-echelon OSS representative in neutral Eire

* An identical argument came from the U. S. Ambassador in Spain. See next section.

was fruitful. Although he built up nothing in the way of undercover agent networks, his liaison with the Irish secret police and foreign services produced substantial results in intelligence.

With D-Day in Normandy, Eire lost the significance of a potential military zone. "Hurst" turned over his official contacts to a London X-2 representative who made occasional trips to Dublin, and continuous OSS operation in Eire was concluded by July 1944.

B. SPAIN AND PORTUGAL

From America's entry into the war until the fall of Tunis in the spring of 1943, the possibility of a German occupation of Spain (with or without the consent of the Franco Government) represented a major strategic danger to the Allies. The danger was especially acute during the months immediately following the North African landings, when the extended supply lines across French North Africa to the Tunisian front offered an obvious and inviting target for an Axis striking force. That this danger was far from imaginary was adequately demonstrated by the discovery, after the liberation of France, of some 150 tons of German military maps of Spain, printed in 1941 and 1942, and stored since 1942 within a hundred miles of the Franco-Spanish border. Persistent rumors reached Washington of Hispano-German cooperation, extending considerably beyond accepted definitions of "non-belligerency", then the ostensible policy of the Spanish government.

The early intelligence assignments of OSS/Spain, largely shared by OSS/Portugal, were threefold: (1) The securing of all information, military, political and economic, about a possible Nazi coup or invasion; (2) the securing of intelligence regarding Spanish aid, economic and otherwise, to the Axis, to the end that such assistance might be exposed or blocked; and (3) the amassing of the sort of background material which would be vital to the Allies if the Iberian Peninsula became a battlefield (including the recruiting of agents who could be counted on in such an eventuality).

Consolidation of the Allied position in the Mediterranean meant that Spain gradually lost its military interest. The major attention of SI became centered on France, with X-2, aided by SI agents, concentrating on counter-espionage and counter-smuggling

activity, defecting many enemy agents and stopping secret transactions in such war materials as tungsten.

The task was made more difficult by the German control of Spain, although the venality of many Spanish officials rendered control something less than fully effective. Himmler's office had reorganized the Spanish police system in 1940. The head of the Spanish police was on the German pay roll, as were many of his subordinates. Numbers of Nazi police and intelligence personnel had been there since the beginning of the Spanish Civil War. Himmler's control combined with the high-level influence of the Abwehr,* covered every section of Spanish intelligence and counter-intelligence. Portugal, on the other hand, had the laxest of controls. Lisbon, as one of the important terminals of traffic to and from the United States, South America and Africa, was a nest of spies and informants at work for all the belligerents.

SI. In April 1942 the first two SI agents arrived in Lisbon and Madrid under State Department cover. As oil attaches they were to allocate half their time to observing the use of fuel supplied to Spain by the Allied governments, meanwhile giving the remainder to secret intelligence. By October 1944, twenty agents had been sent in under private cover

and fifty-two under State Department cover.

The centers of activity of these agents, many of whom had their own extensive networks of sub-agents and informers, are shown on the attached map. Diplomatic pouch and OSS courier constituted the chief method of intercommunication for the U. S.

---

* German foreign intelligence service.

31

agents. Occasionally the interconsular phones were used for coded messages, or the regular long-distance lines for American double-talk. From Madrid, intelligence was pouched to Washington, with priority information being transmitted from a secret radio station

     radio contact was maintained with OSS/Algiers (later Italy), OSS/Lisbon and OSS/France.

Communicating via these various lines were some forty chains, averaging twenty agents each. These were paralleled in Portugal by a network of over 250 agents and sub-agents.*

Under a broad general directive from the Joint Chiefs of Staff,** OSS in Spain and Portugal carried out its three major assignments. Irrefutable evidences of military cooperation between Spain and Germany were secured, including the use of Spanish military airfields by Axis planes, the supplying of German submarines, sabotage operations in Gibraltar harbor carried out by Italo-Spanish teams, the forced recruiting of Spanish technical personnel for service in Germany and the maintenance of the "Blue Division" on the Russian front after its official recall. Fully documented reports on all these subjects were forwarded to Washington, with digests cabled in OSS cipher through the Embassy.

On the subject of economic cooperation between Madrid and Berlin, OSS/Spain was able to report even more fully. Detailed and accurate copies of the bills of lading or manifests covering all merchandise shipped to France, whether by rail or sea, were received and transmitted weekly, including everything from orange juice, rice, wheat, barley

and olive oil (at a time when Spain was starving) to steel rails from Sagunto, quicksilver from Almaden and tungsten ore from Galicia. Equally complete intelligence was secured concerning the flagrant cooperation given the Germans in matters of espionage and counter-espionage by Spanish officials of all grades. OSS material in such fields was frequently used by the Ambassador in his reports, and the ONI gave a high rating to naval intelligence from Madrid.

It was, however, in the third of its three assignments that the record of OSS/Spain was particularly outstanding. A country almost as large as France, concerning which the available information of MID was both antiquated and extremely limited, was covered in eight months with remarkable thoroughness. In preparation for possible military operations in Spain, detailed road reports were prepared, with photographs of the more important bridges, grades and curves; these were rated by MID as the best road reports submitted on Spain and covered virtually every military or strategic highway in eastern and southern Spain. Complete descriptions, with plans and in many cases photographs, of all major Spanish airfields were sent in, and permanent watchers at most of these airfields, who reported weekly on all traffic and other activities, were made part of the OSS organization. A separate and detailed report (in many cases with samples of sand, in most cases with photographs, and in all cases with maps) was prepared for every possible landing beach on the Spanish coast. Over 1,000 maps of France and the Iberian Peninsula taxed the facilities of the diplomatic pouch. About eighty percent of these were to the scale of 1:50,000; many were originals prepared by agents, while others were maps not known by MID to be in existence. Among them were revised plans of important cities and towns, aerial photographs, hydrographic maps, sketches and a few highly secret military fortification plans. Finally, charts of possible bombing targets were prepared and

---

* The majority of the agents under private cover were compelled to travel by the nature of their ostensible activities, and had no fixed base. There were more or less fixed agents in or around Malaga (2 to 3), Teneriffe (Canaries), Seville (2 to 3), Palma (Mallorca), Lisbon (a staff), Madrid (a staff), Horta (Azores), Bilbao, Barcelona (3 to 5), Valencia, San Sebastian, Vigo and Coruna (2).

** JCS 170, Washington Exhibit W-38.

checked, including a partly documented report on gasoline and oil supplies.

After the North African landings, hundreds and eventually thousands of patriotic Frenchmen found means of crossing clandestinely into Spain, in the hope of joining the Allied forces in North Africa. Many of these were persons of great potential usefulness to the Allied cause—high ranking officers, SR personnel with recent intelligence of German activities, technical specialists or badly-needed fighter pilots. OSS/Spain, in order to facilitate their clandestine departure for African ports, set up safe houses in Barcelona and Madrid, and purchased three small sailing vessels, which ostensibly carried cargo between Barcelona and Cadiz or Huelva. Some twenty selected Frenchmen went aboard each ship and were transferred to British patrol boats off Gibraltar.

The ships were in poor condition when purchased, and frequently breakdowns interfered with their schedule. The crews, unquestionably loyal, had no notion of security and there is reason to believe that the Spanish Police was aware of the existence of this service within two months of its inception. It nevertheless permitted the evacuation to North Africa of the most seriously compromised Spanish agent of OSS (who had stolen the plans of the fortifications on the Balearic Islands), and later of his equally endangered wife and daughter. The two "directors" of the "shipping company" were eventually arrested and imprisoned. So far as is known, they gave no damaging information to the Spanish Police or the Falange.

In Madrid and Lisbon, close relations with the representatives of various Allied and enemy governments produced useful intelligence. Liaison with the Hungarian Minister provided coverage of Hungarian political developments. The diplomatic courier offered communication to Hungary itself. The Polish Exile Government representation offered reports from its returning agents, dropped by plane from London into Poland to make their way back across France and over the Pyrenees. Friendship with the Rumanian Charge d'Affaires in Lisbon brought a prediction a month ahead of time of the overthrow of the pro-German Antonescu regime, which was within a week of the exact date. Members of both the Swiss and Swedish Legations were helpful, particularly in passing on counter-espionage material. Often, in response to OSS requests, they would go directly to German representatives to obtain desired information.

Continued SI work in Spain was, however, hampered by State Department representation there. Agents under private cover were producing most of the intelligence. The first OSS Chief of Mission to arrive in Madrid was recalled to Washington * at the request of the Ambassador.

Members of the Madrid Embassy objected to OSS activities in general, feeling that they themselves were competent to cover developments in Spain. OSS salaries and allowances, often incorrectly understood, caused considerable envy, as did consular ranks of OSS officers (granted by the Department of State), especially when the OSS officials showed lack of training in consular practice. OSS supplies (which were used for bartering), OSS cars and OSS entertainment (of potentially useful persons) all contributed to the general irritation of Embassy personnel. The latter made little effort to conceal from Spanish officials the real activities of OSS representatives. As early as December 1942 an agent leaving Washington was told, "Good luck, you'll probably have more trouble keeping under cover from Americans than from the Gestapo." **

The Ambassador considered espionage against a "friendly" country to be "un-American". He stated that OSS activities were jeopardizing his efforts to maintain close bonds between Spain and the United States (although other nations, enemy and Allied,

---

* He later went to Portugal where he worked under State Department cover.
** Field Report of returning agent, 24 January 1945, History File 303.

with whom Spain was friendly, depended on large intelligence services). Several OSS sub-agents and two Americans were arrested between June and September 1943, the latter two for black market financial transactions in the purchase of European currencies for OSS operations.* This was felt by the Ambassador to be proof that OSS activities endangered relations with Franco. OSS argued, on the other hand, that Spain no longer represented a military threat, and that a certain percentage of embarrassments in espionage must be expected.

The Ambassador requested the complete withdrawal of OSS from the whole Iberian Peninsula; and, although this request was not granted, he was able, in November 1943, to gain certain concessions, principally that SI/Spain "will cover only such intelligence as may be requested or agreed to by the Ambassador and the Military and Naval Attaches, or be required by the Joint Chiefs of Staff with the concurrence of the State Department." **

The Ambassador also insisted on censoring all incoming and outgoing OSS messages. His job, as he saw it, was to maintain normal relations with the Franco government (even after the military threat had passed), and he wished to see that no other U. S. activities got out of line from that policy; that, above all, no "embarrassments" arise from the activities of any of the members of his official family. He insisted on "abstention from contracts and arrangements that might adversely affect the Chancery and our Consulates", and accordingly ruled that the Embassy must approve all agents hired (within the categories settled in the terms of the agreement) and all contracts and operational plans.

His actions, in effect, made him an accomplice to OSS undercover activity and put him in just that "embarrassing" position which he wished to avoid.

In addition, the Ambassador, through his censors, the Counselor and First Secretary of Embassy, prohibited any reports on Spain itself or tending to discredit the Spanish Government.

The Spanish Desk/SI in Washington made further efforts to locate private covers for agents, but could find few more than those already in use. Trade with Spain had been cut to a minimum, with the result that there was little excuse for a U. S. citizen to come to the country on business. Nearly all American residents had, furthermore, been evacuated at the outbreak of the war in 1939. OSS activity was continued, mainly by those free agents under private rather than State cover.

In October 1944 a branch of the AQUITAINE * mission was established with headquarters at Toulouse, under OSS/Paris direction, to infiltrate agents over the Pyrenees. Under cover of de-briefing old agent chains, one of the organizers of the pre-liberation chains into France contacted these agents and sent them back to Spain. Through Spaniards operating across the border, a check was kept on Spanish battle order in the area. Acquaintances in Basque circles produced a steady flow of information on the extent of Spanish aid to the beleaguered German garrisons along the French west coast. Considerable political intelligence was also gathered on Spanish Republican activities in the area. Interviews were conducted with officials of the refugee government. Through certain other contacts, intelligence was obtained on the secreting of German economic assets in Spain.

In Portugal and Spain tungsten smuggling was successfully traced and stopped. Contraband traffic had begun after the Allied governments exacted agreements from the Portuguese and Spanish governments to curtail sales to the Germans of this vital

---

* See "Oujda Operations," above, and Washington section on Special Funds.

** Memo on "Understanding between Embassy and OSS in Spain", 3 November 1943; copy in Director's Files, OSS.

---

* See section on "Liberated France" under Part VIII, below.

metal. The extensive OSS organization in northern Portugal and Spain had for some time been keeping accurate check on all shipments out of the Peninsula, and had been able to prevent smuggling of tin and other minerals. In the case of tungsten, the arrest of a large ring of smugglers in Portugal, involving Army officers and customs officials, was accomplished. In Spain, OSS intelligence made it possible for a British submarine to sink a German ship loading at a secret port near Bilboa. This action blocked the only sea outlet used for Axis tungsten smuggling.

X-2. X-2 representation arrived in Lisbon in November 1943. During the negotiations of the same month, Ambassador Hayes had agreed to the establishment of X-2 offices in Spain. In the following year these were set up in Madrid, Barcelona, Bilbao and San Sebastian, all under State cover.

During the first year of X-2 operation, the Branch was principally dependent on SI for contacts and personality data. Both SI and the British provided the material with which X-2 built up its basic files. SI contacts with various Spanish and enemy officials were turned over to X-2, as were many of the "tailing gangs" and other watchers.

The new X-2 stations served to coordinate counter-intelligence activities of the Embassy and other U. S. representatives in Spain and Portugal with the central registry in London, and to vet U. S. employees and visa applicants. Hampered by ambassadorial restriction, X-2 still performed successfully the penetration of German organizations in southwest France, the surveillance of enemy agent traffic between France and Spain, and the identification and eventual deportation of German undercover personnel and French collaborators who had fled to Spain in some numbers.

German reorganization of the Spanish Police apparently produced corruption and corruptibility on a large scale. The Spanish control officer at one of the most important points of entry into Spain from France re-ported, for a price, the comings and goings of important German agents and their missions. Inasmuch as these agents carried letters of identification to him, his coverage was thorough.

The Barcelona station kept a close surveillance of enemy agent traffic over the Pyrenees and controlled a number of double-agents who worked between Spain and France. None of this activity involved more than the usual local counter-espionage aims of (1) obtaining information about enemy personalities in Spain, and (2) rigging traps for enemy agents in France. The work of these double-agents supported the exploitation of enemy agent chains by the SCI (Special Counter-Intelligence) units in southwest France,* and provided useful information on the kind of data that the Germans were seeking on France. A network of advantageously placed informants, originall/ set up by SI, covered arrivals and departures not only at frontier points, but also at airports and at all hotels in the main cities.

By the time of the German collapse in May 1945, most of the German undercover agents in Spain had been identified, while their courier and other chains into northern Europe had been penetrated and placed under surveillance. The gaps in Allied data were filled in by defecting Germans who came in growing numbers to the American consulates. The liquidation of those services was furthered by a joint

list of German intelligence and subversion officers and agents, passed to the Spanish Foreign Office with a request for their deportation to Germany and France.

By VE-Day, X-2 files (largely based on British and SI reports) identified nearly 3,000 enemy agents, some 600 suspects, and more than 400 officials of enemy undercover services. Of those agents and officials, 45 were under X-2 control. A number of well-placed members of the Spanish Police and of the Servicio de Informacion Militar had

---

* See section on "X-2/France," below.

early been converted to a cooperative attitude by SI, and more were won over by X-2. These and other sources helped to uncover forty-six commercial firms in Spain being used by the enemy as cover for espionage purposes. Interrogations of enemy officials and agents, after the collapse of Germany, indicated that the control of the northern border, maintained in cooperation with SCI of southern France, was highly successful.

X-2 files in Lisbon contained identifications of 1,900 enemy agents, 200 enemy officials and 350 suspect agents. Of these, seven were defected and twenty controlled. Through representations to the Portuguese Government, 75 more were confined and 50 expelled.

One of the more interesting cases was a double-agent originally hired by SI/Portugal. This was Jean Charles Alexandre, alias Alendorf (real name probably Gessman or Gasman), reputed to be one of the most successful international intelligence wholesalers in Europe.

An Austrian, Alexandre had worked in Austria for the French Deuxieme Bureau as a double-agent in the German Abwehr. After the Anschluss the Germans learned this fact, but nevertheless used him later in Portugal. In 1939 he was sent to Portugal by the French and remained there after the fall of France, allying himself with the British and with the Czechoslovak Intelligence Service, which the British were controlling for operations into France. His official position was that of second-in-command of the Czech station. During this time the whole of the Czech network was blown to the Germans. Fritz Cramer, head of the counter-espionage department of the Abwehr in Lisbon, later stated that Alexandre was responsible for this betrayal.

The British, however, had learned this and quickly eased him out of service. Little more could be done about him at this point except to issue a general warning to Allied circles, since the British did not wish to burn the source of their information, and since

Alexandre had close connections with the Chief of the Secret Police. He parried all sorts of attractive offers for excursions to Allied territory—where he could have been interrogated and broken.

Nevertheless, Alexandre was almost immediately taken on by SI and set up by them as an important agent. He made adroit use of his new sponsorship to enhance his value to the Germans and to counter the effect of the British brush-off. He worked for SI from 1942 until mid-1943, introducing a group of agents who were used by SI. Others insinuated themselves on the SI pay roll by proffering their services under Alexandre's tutelage, without revealing that they were working for him.

The X-2 officer in Lisbon was able to put the full weight of the evidence against Alexandre, largely based on British reports, before SI and to convince them of his dangerous character. An investigation of all SI agents in Portugal was instigated, and, although no proof was found that Alexandre had actually sold his new information to the Germans, a purge of his agents was achieved. The man himself was safe in Portugal, but he was driven temporarily into semi-retirement.*

On the other hand, X-2 operated dozens of successful double-agents against the Germans. The Spanish border control officer has already been cited. The covert defection in the spring of 1945 of Fritz Cramer, Chief of Abwehr III (Counter-Espionage Department) in Lisbon, was especially rewarding. Cramer was in possession of all information on German personnel and operations in Portugal, and informed on German intelligence matters in Germany and elsewhere. His defection led the way to a promising X-2/FBI exploitation of a Japanese case. The Counselor of the Japanese Legation in Lisbon asked Cramer at this time to put him in touch with some of Cramer's agents in America who could serve as radio channels

---

* Later he was discovered in an Allied intelligence agency working under another name.

for certain Japanese agents to be set up in the United States. The FBI was interested, and arrangements were being worked out for the operation when the collapse of Japan intervened.

After VE-Day

Following the liberation of France, OSS chains through the Pyrenees were terminated. Meanwhile the Germans began to set up their own networks; X-2 in Barcelona succeeded shortly in penetrating this new organization and in locating the agents for apprehension by French authorities.

After the collapse of Germany, all the premises that had been occupied by agencies of that government were placed under the control of the U. S., British and French diplomatic missions. German passport and citizenship records revealed that naturalization in Spain had been used as a device by local Germans to avoid repatriation, and that these arrangements had been facilitated by Spanish officials. These and other sources indicated a post-war organization in Spain. The leaders were to be chosen from Germans who had escaped repatriation, the sub-agents from members of the Falange and the Blue Division. The organization counted on a slackening in Allied countermeasures as a result of conflicting political

and econ
able in tl
deposit i
X-2 acc
German
Madrid,

To tra
rope int
OSS co
personn
In Port
to give
safe de
ered by
obtaine
reques
count.
sion ir
tion.

Sinc
restric
Spain
count
assign
1945,
over-
rema

• T
to un
count
rope.
Part

C. AFRICA

During the first year of United States participation in World War II, Axis invasion of the whole African Continent was considered a distinct possibility. At bases in West Africa, German forces would threaten the lightly-defended Brazilian coast. Prior to the North African landings, the U. S. Army had planned, but did not execute, a small operation to invade the Cape Verde Islands. A British naval attempt to seize the port of Dakar had failed.

In the event that Africa became a battleground, every kind of military, naval, economic, political and psychological intelligence would be needed. State Department coverage was small; consulates were few and far between. In Angola, for instance, there had been no consular representation since 1925.

One agent had been dispatched by COI in February 1942. In April, an Africa Desk was organized in Washington, and its first agent left for Africa in that month. By the end of the war, posts had been established in Tangier, the Canary Islands, the Cape Verde Islands, French West Africa, Portuguese Guinea, Liberia, French Equatorial Africa, British East Africa, the Belgian Congo, Angola, the Union of South Africa, Mozambique, Ethiopia and French Somaliland. Finally, when the 2677th Regiment OSS (Prov.), Algiers moved to Italy, its posts at Casablanca, Morocco, Oran, Algeria and Tunis were transferred to the Africa Desk/SI and a similar post was set up at Algiers.

Certain special characteristics of the African Continent made the job of penetration and securing intelligence peculiarly difficult:

(a) Suitable agents who had had any previous residence or experience in Africa were scarce;

(b) The severity of the climate, and the resultant effect upon their health, made many of those who might otherwise have served unavailable;

(c) The problems of communication and transportation were so difficult of solution that preoccupation with them considerably hampered agent operations;

(d) The total number of white inhabitants on the entire Continent was so small (only 600,000 excluding French North Africa and the Union of South Africa), that it was next to impossible to infiltrate agents under effective cover. Every new arrival was suspect from the start.

Various covers were tried, with varying degrees of success.

Most of the agents were successful, although some were hampered by unsympathetic State Department officials. while others were poor recruits. SI/Africa first pursued the policy of selecting agents from persons who had already resided in the target areas. The policy was eventually abandoned when experience showed that such individuals were scarce and often not those most suited for intelligence work. Many agents thus chosen involved themselves too much in their previous activities; for example, one anthropologist spent his six-month tour of duty acquiring apes, caring for them when they fell ill and eventually catching their disease himself.

Nevertheless, these were only a small percentage of the total agents infiltrated in the following African countries, colonies and islands:

Tunisia (French)	3 men
Algeria (French)	7 men
Tangier (International)	7 men
Spanish Morocco	1 man
French Morocco	16 men
Canary Islands (Spanish)	1 man
Cape Verde Islands (Portuguese)	2 men
French West Africa	4 men
Portuguese Guinea	1 man
Liberia	7 men
French Equatorial Africa	1 man
British West Africa	18 men
Belgian Congo	4 men
Angola (Portuguese)	8 men
The Union of South Africa	5 men
Mozambique (Portuguese)	5 men
Ethiopia	2 men
French Somaliland	1 man*

* Egypt and the Sudan were covered by OSS/-Cairo.

Since the lack of transcontinental communication obviated the possibility of establishing a main base in Africa itself from which the work throughout the Continent could be supervised, Washington directed all agents. Casablanca served as an advance base for stations and agents in North Africa only. Accra served as an advance base for agents in West Africa only, and was the one overt mission set up south of the Sahara. All other installations there were covert or semi-covert.

It was possible to a certain extent to cooperate with British intelligence and certain elements of French intelligence.

An agreement between British SOE and OSS/SO prohibited U. S. undercover operations in British territory, but in return the British agreed to supply information from their own sources.

From the British services came basic topographic intelligence on the surrounding territory, French battle order in West Africa, regular reports on pro-Axis activities and on the political and economic developments in French West Africa. Notable contributions were the British files on Angola and the Cape Verde Islands. They included biographical data on government personalities together with data on airfields, terrain, military installations, resources, trade and shipping and Axis activity. Liaison with the U. S. Theater authorities in Africa, and in particular with G-2, provided supplies and pouch and wire service.

Most of the agents placed in Africa during the first year of operation were intended as defensive stay-behind agents, whose mission was to undertake sabotage and intelligence activities in the event that Axis forces should occupy Africa. An SO team of five was dispatched in August 1942 to Nigeria, with the mission of cooperating with SOE in setting up intelligence chains in the area and preparing for defensive action should it become necessary.*

The turning point came with the Allied landings in November 1942, when most of Africa became a field for counter-intelligence. An agreement between the X-2 and SI Branches in July 1943 provided for the joint briefing of agents dispatched by the Africa Desk/SI and for the joint use of intelligence transmitted. In late 1943, a plan was formulated to turn over the SI operations in North Africa to the SI Desk/Washington, but, with the exception of the Tangier station, this plan was not put into effect until October 1944.

* This team was transferred to SI in December 1942 and then recalled.

After the landings in 1942, a greater need was felt for Allied coverage of East and South Africa, in order to aid the discovery of Axis submarine refuelling, Axis diamond smuggling and Axis shipping intelligence. In particular this last enemy activity was causing high losses on the sea lanes outside Gibraltar, off the Cape of Good Hope and in the waters about Madagascar.

The success of all missions depended largely upon the degree of cooperation from State Department representatives. Unfortunately, most of the Foreign Service officers had not been properly briefed, and whether or not they contributed to or hampered the activities of OSS agents depended upon each individual's understanding of the situation and the extent to which Foreign Service and OSS representatives got along personally. In Tangier, for example, the Legation as a whole, and its various members personally, abetted OSS activities insofar as it was able and, in general, this was true in all of North Africa. South of the Sahara, where the war seemed more distant, difficulties were encountered. In Liberia, in French West Africa and in the Belgian Congo, the tendency seemed to be to regard OSS representatives as interlopers. Difficulties were also encountered with the British Ministry of Economic Warfare.

There follow accounts of the more important and typical operations carried out by OSS in Africa.

Liberia. In the summer of 1942, by agreement with its Government, American troops arrived in Liberia to protect it from Axis attack. Four OSS agents were sent out

Although all German nationals had been forced to leave the country by the time these agents were in place, nevertheless Axis agents were still active, especially in the Cape Palmas area. Bases in the Ivory Coast (French) were reported by agent "West,"
"West" further obtained, early in 1943, information showing that a   priest, Father   was collecting Allied military and naval information for the Axis and forwarding it by native runners to another priest who was reliably reported to be the most active Vichy-German agent in the Tabou area of the Ivory Coast. The evidence was so conclusive that both Colonel Kirchoff and General P. L. Sadler, successive Commanding Officers of the U. S. forces, requested Father   extradition. But when General Sadler outlined the case to the American Minister to Liberia, the latter refused to take any action.

General Sadler then ordered "West" to secure additional evidence. By this time the priests had, through the American Legation, become aware that they were under suspicion, and set a trap to discover who was reporting on their activities. When "West" was caught opening a letter
to Father   the Charge d'Affaires of the Holy See accused him of opening diplomatic mail, and he was obliged to leave Liberia, since the American Minister did not come to his defense.

French West Africa. In June 1943 Admiral Glassford was sent out to Dakar as the President's personal representative in French West Africa. He was accompanied by two OSS officers, who soon established close liaison with the Deuxieme Bureau to receive regular reports covering political, economic, military, naval and subversive activities from French sources along the west and northwest African coast.

Their work was hampered by the U. S. Consul-General, who opposed all OSS activity. The agents found it almost impossible to insure any security for their papers or privacy for their operations. The Consul-General persuaded the Admiral (a) that all military and naval intelligence should be left to the Military and Naval Observers attached to the Consulate, and (b) that no attempt should be made to cooperate with the French if the United States wished to establish undercover networks. As a result, the two agents were forbidden to conduct undercover work, although they had already set up successful operations in conjunction with the Deuxieme Bureau.

By the end of July 1943 both officers were ordered by the Admiral to duties unconnected with OSS. The Consul-General then reversed his stand with regard to the French and persuaded the Admiral to give them access to, and physical possession of, highly secret OSS radio installations and equipment there.* This was strenuously objected to by the OSS officers. The Admiral was forced to withdraw his offer of the equipment to the French, but in August OSS had to recall its two representatives.

Investigation of Diamond Smuggling. Germany's supply of industrial diamonds came, throughout the war, almost entirely from South and Central Africa by illegal channels. The U. S. Foreign Economic Administration became interested in attempting to block this clandestine supply line, and in the summer of 1943 the FEA representative in Angola asked OSS/Accra to assist in the investigation of the traffic. OSS and FEA investigations were successful, but action against enemy agents engaged in diamond smuggling was blocked by the action of both the British Ministry of Economic Warfare and by the U. S. Consul-General in the Congo.

Offers by both FEA and OSS representatives to cooperate with British MEW were rebuffed. On 9 October the OSS office was informed that London had no interest in the problem. A further inspection of the diamond fields in Angola by FEA, and in the Congo by OSS, brought a sudden reversal in the British attitude. Before the end of the same month, British investigators had been sent to the diamond fields. In November 1943, MEW issued a study showing that German stocks of industrial diamonds were down to an eight-month supply and that smuggling was the only possible source

---

* These were part of the Africa-101 Project, described in Washington sections on CD and Communications.

of replenishment. The British then approached the Americans, and agreements were concluded between OSS and SOE, and between FEA and MEW, to pursue the diamond investigation jointly.

Despite continuing MEW opposition, OSS agents established: (1) That, through contracts and ownership of purchasing and distributing channels, the DeBeers Syndicate controlled ninety-five percent of the world diamond market; (2) that three out of five members of the Diamond Committee of MEW represented the DeBeers interests; and (3) that for all practical purposes the Diamond Control Committee of MEW was controlled by the Syndicate. A report from the Chief of OSS/Accra stated:

We have now come to the conclusion (a) that our assistance was requested in this program primarily so that the Diamond Trading Corporation might discover how much we actually knew of the ramifications of the DeBeers world monopoly, and (b) that the OSS/Accra recommendations for a Security Committee were sabotaged, not by the British Government, but by the representatives of the Diamond Trading Corporation, Ltd. London, through their domination of the Diamond Committee of MEW.*

Further OSS/SOE investigation uncovered enemy smuggling channels through the Gold Coast, Mozambique, Angola, Cairo, the Belgian Congo and the Union of South Africa. Operators were named. A crisis arose when OSS agent "Teton" traced a smuggling chain to the Chief of Police at Leopoldville, capital of the Belgian Congo. "Teton," had established excellent contacts during an official tour of the Congo to register all American males of draft age. Available information indicated that the major source of leakage to Germany was the Forminiere mines in the Congo, and through his various contacts "Teton" discovered evidence that a full year's supply of diamonds had reached Germany from Forminiere through Red Cross parcels. He also uncovered an important

---

* "Report on Field Conditions," 7 September 1944, History File 140d.

42

secondary channel through Bulawayo in Southern Rhodesia.

In April 1943, SOE apprised OSS/Accra that MEW, London required more complete evidence before it could take official action against the enemy smuggling traffic, and OSS directed "Teton" to attempt the purchase of diamonds through illicit channels. "Teton" chose a pro-Allied Belgian to make the purchases for him and supplied him the funds. The Belgian was shortly thereafter arrested by the Belgian police, and a subsequent raid on "Teton's" house showed that "Teton" had in fact traced the smuggling to the Police Chief himself. Charges that "Teton" was engaged in "questionable activities" were then carried to the Governor General of the Congo, who referred them to the U. S. Consul-General. The latter knew of "Teton's" activities but merely asked the Governor General whether he considered him persona non grata. The Governor had only to nod an affirmative, and the OSS agent was forced to leave.

An OSS/SOE conference in Accra in February 1944 recommended the establishment of an advisory commission on diamond security, which met with a counter-proposal from MEW to conduct a survey of security measures employed in the Congo mines, by two experts, one a diamond mining engineer, the other a diamond security expert, both to be named by Sir Ernest Oppenheimer, Chairman of DeBeers. Thus the responsibility for security would have been turned over entirely to the industry, except that this plan also was dropped and eventually SOE worked out a program, which, though well planned, was unable to cope with the Syndicate's control of the industry and its dealings with the enemy.

Angola. In Angola complete information on the Benguela railroad, the only transcontinental line in Africa, was obtained, and plans were laid to blow the three most important bridges, should Marshal Rommel take North Africa. Observation of the coast line uncovered one spot where Nazi subma-

rines were being supplied from the shore, and, on representations from British SOE, with which OSS cooperated closely, the Governor General agreed to remove suspect individuals and close the area to all foreigners.

South Africa. In the Union of South Africa one OSS agent, cooperating with an OWI representative, uncovered evidence of pro-Axis activities on the part of the Ossewa Brandwag. This widespread local Fascist organization was strong enough to prevent Marshal Smuts from taking serious repressive action. By the fall of 1943, however, U. S. and British espionage services had accumulated sufficient evidence so that the British Foreign Office might approach General Smuts in London and thereby enable him to take action against the Ossewa Brandwag. It was learned later that the report, submitted by the OSS agent, on an interview with the Ossewa Brandwag leader, had played an important part in the South African cabinet decision to adopt a firm policy against that organization.

Mozambique. The most outstanding counter-espionage operation undertaken by representatives of SI/Africa took place in the Portuguese colony of Mozambique, and was carried out by OSS agent "Ebert."

Leopold Wertz, German vice-consul in Lourenco Marques, assisted by Campini, the Italian Consul General, and Manna, Director of the Stefani News Agency, operated a large espionage and sabotage ring in Mozambique and South Africa, gathering, in particular, shipping information, and actively spreading Nazi propaganda. "Ebert" arrived in December 1942 and, within a year, had acquired fairly complete data on the espionage chain. He sent to Washington a chart of the German and Italian intelligence organizations in Portuguese East Africa with backgrounds, photographs and descriptions of approximately 100 individuals conducting espionage activities for the Axis. Through wireless, couriers and the use of advertisements in Union newspapers, these agents were transmitting shipping news from Angola and South Africa to Lourenco Marques, whence it was sent directly to Berlin over the Marconi Radio Station, for relay to submarines.

"Ebert" worked jointly with British SIS and SOE on a plan to break up the entire ring. Operations were occasionally hampered by the rivalry between the two British organizations, but they were nearly blown by various indignant cables sent to the State Department by the Consul-General, who did not sympathize with the irregular activities of the American and British intelligence agencies. Nevertheless, action was taken against the Axis agents, and the first to be removed from effective operation was the number three man.

A renegade Greek journalist employed by the Germans was removed to Kenya in August, and in October, through pressure on the Portuguese authorities, a Union national, in charge of shipping intelligence for the Germans, was deported to the same place.

Several Italians were induced to break with the Mussolini Government and form the nucleus of a local Free Italy Movement which was directed by OSS agent "Ebert." Members of the Free Italy Movement demonstrated before the Italian Consulate and the Stefani News Agency in Lourenco Marques, threw a bomb into the former, propagandized their fellow nationals and gave information to OSS on the Italian intelligence system.

"Ebert" took over actual control of the U.S./British operations in 1944, when the SIS chief was recalled to London, and he then directed his activities principally toward the ousting of German agents

through legal means. A member of the German espionage organization, "Dram," joined him and helped to tap telephones, steal papers and persuade other Germans to break with the German Consulate. Sufficient evidence was obtained against the Germans so that Vice-Consul Wertz and four of his assistants were forced to leave Mozambique, and the German Consulate was closed by the Portuguese authorities.

In addition to his work against the German and Italian espionage chains, "Ebert" was able to send in reports on Portuguese battle order in Mozambique, with descriptions of every major airfield and sketches drawn to scale from aerial photographs, plus a considerable amount of economic and political intelligence.

The North African Stations. The first SI/Africa agent in North Africa was sent to Tangier to take over from the chief of the OSS unit of Operation *TORCH*. Representatives at this station continued the activity already initiated against official and unofficial Axis agents operating in the International and Spanish Zones of Morocco. They were able to identify all of the German, Italian and Japanese agents in the two Zones and, eventually, to submit such evidence against them as to require the Spanish High Commissioner to demand the withdrawal of their consular representatives and order the arrest of local collaborators.

Through their network of some fifty informants, they were able to report on German submarine activity near the Straits of Gibraltar. This intelligence, passed on to the American Naval Command at Casablanca, resulted in at least two sinkings. They uncovered to the Spanish High Commissioner a clandestine shipping, observation and submarine directing station operated in the town of Ceuta by German and

Spanish nationals, and personally participated in the official capture of the radio equipment, codes and personnel. Their counter-intelligence activity resulted in the expulsion by diplomatic means of a total of thirty-eight enemy agents.

The other stations in North Africa (Casablanca, Oran, Algiers and Tunis), originally established by the Control Vice-Consuls of Operation *TORCH,* were transferred in October 1944 to the Africa Desk. Their staffs were somewhat augmented by further SI personnel and by one representative from X-2. These stations continued the work of reporting on enemy agents and W/T installations, on enemy submarine, sabotage and subversion efforts, on the interrogation of captured enemy agents and of refugees and prisoners.

———————

SI/Africa continued counter-espionage in close cooperation with the British services throughout the war. Although the task was principally of an X-2 nature, it was carried out, with X-2 approval, by the SI agents and Desk originally established to penetrate Africa in anticipation of possible Axis military successes. Despite unusual climate, transportation and cover difficulties, OSS penetrated British, French, Italian, Portuguese, Spanish and independent countries on the Continent. Although there were some failures, many of them attributable to lack of cooperation from Allied agencies, several Axis spy rings were broken up, notably those based in Tangier and Lourenco Marques.

The greatly reduced budget of July 1945 caused the withdrawal of OSS agents from a majority of the outposts in Africa.

metal. The extensive OSS organization in northern Portugal and Spain had for some time been keeping accurate check on all shipments out of the Peninsula, and had been able to prevent smuggling of tin and other minerals. In the case of tungsten, the arrest of a large ring of smugglers in Portugal, involving Army officers and customs officials, was accomplished. In Spain, OSS intelligence made it possible for a British submarine to sink a German ship loading at a secret port near Bilboa. This action blocked the only sea outlet used for Axis tungsten smuggling.

X-2. X-2 representation arrived in Lisbon in November 1943. During the negotiations of the same month, Ambassador Hayes had agreed to the establishment of X-2 offices in Spain. In the following year these were set up in Madrid, Barcelona, Bilbao and San Sebastian, all under State cover.

During the first year of X-2 operation, the Branch was principally dependent on SI for contacts and personality data. Both SI and the British provided the material with which X-2 built up its basic files. SI contacts with various Spanish and enemy officials were turned over to X-2, as were many of the "tailing gangs" and other watchers.

The new X-2 stations served to coordinate counter-intelligence activities of the Embassy and other U. S. representatives in Spain and Portugal with the central registry in London, and to vet U. S. employees and visa applicants. Hampered by ambassadorial restriction, X-2 still performed successfully the penetration of German organizations in southwest France, the surveillance of enemy agent traffic between France and Spain, and the identification and eventual deportation of German undercover personnel and French collaborators who had fled to Spain in some numbers.

German reorganization of the Spanish Police apparently produced corruption and corruptibility on a large scale. The Spanish control officer at one of the most important points of entry into Spain from France reported, for a price, the comings and goings of important German agents and their missions. Inasmuch as these agents carried letters of identification to him, his coverage was thorough.

The Barcelona station kept a close surveillance of enemy agent traffic over the Pyrenees and controlled a number of double-agents who worked between Spain and France. None of this activity involved more than the usual local counter-espionage aims of (1) obtaining information about enemy personalities in Spain, and (2) rigging traps for enemy agents in France. The work of these double-agents supported the exploitation of enemy agent chains by the SCI (Special Counter-Intelligence) units in southwest France,* and provided useful information on the kind of data that the Germans were seeking on France. A network of advantageously placed informants, originally set up by SI, covered arrivals and departures not only at frontier points, but also at airports and at all hotels in the main cities.

By the time of the German collapse in May 1945, most of the German undercover agents in Spain had been identified, while their courier and other chains into northern Europe had been penetrated and placed under surveillance. The gaps in Allied data were filled in by defecting Germans who came in growing numbers to the American consulates. The liquidation of those services was furthered by a joint list of German intelligence and subversion officers and agents, passed to the Spanish Foreign Office with a request for their deportation to Germany and France.

By VE-Day, X-2 files (largely based on British and SI reports) identified nearly 3,000 enemy agents, some 600 suspects, and more than 400 officials of enemy undercover services. Of those agents and officials, 45 were under X-2 control. A number of well-placed members of the Spanish Police and of the Servicio de Informacion Militar had

* See section on "X-2/France," below.

35

early been converted to a cooperative attitude by SI, and more were won over by X-2. These and other sources helped to uncover forty-six commercial firms in Spain being used by the enemy as cover for espionage purposes. Interrogations of enemy officials and agents, after the collapse of Germany, indicated that the control of the northern border, maintained in cooperation with SCI of southern France, was highly successful.

X-2 files in Lisbon contained identifications of 1,900 enemy agents, 200 enemy officials and 350 suspect agents. Of these, seven were defected and twenty controlled. Through representations to the Portuguese Government, 75 more were confined and 50 expelled.

One of the more interesting cases was a double-agent originally hired by SI/Portugal. This was Jean Charles Alexandre, alias Alendorf (real name probably Gessman or Gasman), reputed to be one of the most successful international intelligence wholesalers in Europe.

An Austrian, Alexandre had worked in Austria for the French Deuxieme Bureau as a double-agent in the German Abwehr. After the Anschluss the Germans learned this fact, but nevertheless used him later in Portugal. In 1939 he was sent to Portugal by the French and remained there after the fall of France, allying himself with the British and with the Czechoslovak Intelligence Service, which the British were controlling for operations into France. His official position was that of second-in-command of the Czech station. During this time the whole of the Czech network was blown to the Germans. Fritz Cramer, head of the counterespionage department of the Abwehr in Lisbon, later stated that Alexandre was responsible for this betrayal.

The British, however, had learned this and quickly eased him out of service. Little more could be done about him at this point except to issue a general warning to Allied circles, since the British did not wish to burn the source of their information, and since

Alexandre had close connections with the Chief of the Secret Police. He parried all sorts of attractive offers for excursions to Allied territory—where he could have been interrogated and broken.

Nevertheless, Alexandre was almost immediately taken on by SI and set up by them as an important agent. He made adroit use of his new sponsorship to enhance his value to the Germans and to counter the effect of the British brush-off. He worked for SI from 1942 until mid-1943, introducing a group of agents who were used by SI. Others insinuated themselves on the SI pay roll by proffering their services under Alexandre's tutelage, without revealing that they were working for him.

The X-2 officer in Lisbon was able to put the full weight of the evidence against Alexandre, largely based on British reports, before SI and to convince them of his dangerous character. An investigation of all SI agents in Portugal was instigated, and, although no proof was found that Alexandre had actually sold his new information to the Germans, a purge of his agents was achieved. The man himself was safe in Portugal, but he was driven temporarily into semi-retirement.*

On the other hand, X-2 operated dozens of successful double-agents against the Germans. The Spanish border control officer has already been cited. The covert defection in the spring of 1945 of Fritz Cramer, Chief of Abwehr III (Counter-Espionage Department) in Lisbon, was especially rewarding. Cramer was in possession of all information on German personnel and operations in Portugal, and informed on German intelligence matters in Germany and elsewhere. His defection led the way to a promising X-2/FBI exploitation of a Japanese case. The Counselor of the Japanese Legation in Lisbon asked Cramer at this time to put him in touch with some of Cramer's agents in America who could serve as radio channels

* Later he was discovered in an Allied intelligence agency working under another name.

for certain Japanese agents to be set up in the United States. The FBI was interested, and arrangements were being worked out for the operation when the collapse of Japan intervened.

After VE-Day

Following the liberation of France, OSS chains through the Pyrenees were terminated. Meanwhile the Germans began to set up their own networks; X-2 in Barcelona succeeded shortly in penetrating this new organization and in locating the agents for apprehension by French authorities.

After the collapse of Germany, all the premises that had been occupied by agencies of that government were placed under the control of the U. S., British and French diplomatic missions. German passport and citizenship records revealed that naturalization in Spain had been used as a device by local Germans to avoid repatriation, and that these arrangements had been facilitated by Spanish officials. These and other sources indicated a post-war organization in Spain. The leaders were to be chosen from Germans who had escaped repatriation, the sub-agents from members of the Falange and the Blue Division. The organization counted on a slackening in Allied counter-measures as a result of conflicting political

and economic interests. Funds were available in the form of money and valuables on deposit in Spain. In the summer of 1945, X-2 accomplished the penetration of both German and Japanese espionage rings in Madrid, although no action could be taken.

To trace the flight of Axis funds from Europe into and through Spain and Portugal, OSS collaborated with State Department personnel in "Safe Haven" * investigations. In Portugal, a secret arrangement was made to give OSS access to information on enemy safe deposit boxes in all but four banks (covered by the British); a list of all boxes was obtained, together with specific information requested on any individual or business account. Contacts of the AQUITAINE mission in Toulouse gave additional information.

Since November 1943, by ambassadorial restriction, OSS had been limited, inside Spain itself, to counter-espionage and counter-smuggling. It had carried out these assignments successfully. In September 1945, SI/Spain was withdrawn, according to over-all State Department policy, and X-2 remained.

---

* The State Department "Safe Haven" program, to uncover the movement of assets out of enemy countries, was assisted by OSS throughout Europe. See subsequent sections; in particular, Part VIII, "The Liberation of Europe."

37

cate situation. Furthermore, another U. S. agency, OWI, had already been accepted as the opposite number of PWE and of MOI. Gradually, however, as MO was absorbed into the framework of the coordinating Psychological Warfare Division of SHAEF, collaboration with PWE increased. A number of "black" radio, subversive leaflet and rumor campaigns were successfully run as joint operations by equal partners.

Communications. An unacceptable offer to the new and inexperienced agency was the British proposal for joint communications. Had it been accepted, OSS would thus have revealed its entire operations to the British, while the latter would undoubtedly have maintained the secrecy of theirs. In January 1943 the proposal was rejected.

Fitting Into the Theater Framework

In London, too, as elsewhere, OSS encountered the problems of fitting into the theaters as control shifted from OSS/Washington to the theater commands. The new relationship called for a practical set-up which met as adequately as possible three sets of requirements: (1) The Theater Commander had to be assured of service for his requests and control over the organization and its activities in ETO; (2) JCS requirements for service had also to be met and the Joint Chiefs' ultimate authority over OSS recognized; (3) OSS/Washington had to be given proper service. Considerations of security, the peculiar nature of OSS personnel requirements, and the need for unusual equipment and facilities increased the problem.

When COI/London was first established in November 1941, the office was placed under Embassy jurisdiction for both cover and administrative purposes. After OSS came into existence in June 1942, this arrangement was carried over, and it remained in effect even though OSS overflowed its Embassy lodgings into its own installations. Both Ambassadors Winant and Biddle were favorably disposed to the organization, and relations were smooth except for a short period in January 1942 when the Embassy attempted to supervise the flow of all cable traffic. Throughout these early days American forces were few in number, the invasion was far off, and OSS itself was small.

By the summer of 1942, however, ETOUSA found the presence of such an independent quasi-civilian agency, conducting highly operational activities, incompatible with the rigid organizational pattern that had rapidly enveloped the growing Theater. In July the Theater Command, probably at SIS insistence, demanded to be informed by OSS whenever an agent was sent out. In August JCS ordered that no OSS activities be undertaken without the Theater Commander's consent.

Meanwhile OSS/London, too, was finding its civilian status a growing handicap which neither the Embassy connection nor over-all responsibility to the Theater Command could solve. Great numbers of personnel were needed to implement new projects; supplies had to be drawn and billets obtained; some mechanism to enable quick movement of personnel was required. Difficulties were enhanced rather than eased by the weak nature of the first over-all directive from JCS in December 1942 (155/4/D).* The terms were vague and operational activities limited to those in support of psychological warfare.

All these factors led OSS/London to seek its incorporation into the Theater framework as a military unit. In late February 1943 the Strategic Services officer formally requested militarization in a memo to the Adjutant General-ETO. Further pressure followed, and finally, on 4 June, OSS/London was officially established by the Theater as a military detachment, responsible to the AC of S, G-2 ETOUSA. Henceforth all personnel and projects for OSS/ETO must have prior Theater Command approval. This arrangement was supplemented in October by implementation of JCS 408, which defined the organization's activities in ETO as well as its responsibility to G-2 ETOUSA.

* Washington Exhibit W-33.

However, these were small and the only large SI/London project, before the penetration of Germany in early 1945 was *Sussex*,* a joint SI/SIS operation.

Matters came to a head in September 1943 when the U. S. Theater Command sought British opinion before approving implementation of JCS Directive 406, which gave OSS authority to conduct espionage in the ETO. British objections resulted in the Theater Command's disapproval, and in October Donovan took the case to the JCS.

Regarding the British position, his appeal observed that the British proposal:

... suggests "coordination" and "agreement," but as employed here the word "coordination" means "control" and "agreement" means "dependence."

Physical circumstances permit the British to exercise complete control over United States intelligence. . . . The habit of control has grown up with them . . . through their relations with refugee Governments and refugee intelligence services. . . . We are not a refugee government.

In his conclusion Donovan summarized the OSS position as follows:

Our basic comment is this: We think it proper that in strictly physical operations we should not only be coordinated but should accept the leadership of SOE. This we do. But the attempt of the British, by reason of their physical control of territory and of communication, to subordinate and control the American intelligence and counter-intelligence service is short-sighted and dangerous to the ultimate interest of both countries.**

As a result, JCS Directive 155/11/D *** of 27 October 1943 gave OSS full and unqualified authority to conduct Secret Intelligence. The Theater Command reversed its position accordingly and thenceforth the independence of OSS long-range espionage was assured. Although SI/London continued to encounter difficulties in running operations, SI independence soon produced results outdistancing SIS in other theaters.

* Ibid.
** Memorandum for the Secretary, the Joint U. S. Chiefs of Staff, from the Director, OSS, 18 October 1943, in Director's File 12,663, OSS Archives.
*** Washington Exhibit W-40.

X-2. Meanwhile, the development of X-2 required establishment of another set of relationships. In January 1943, British counter-espionage authorities decided that separate dealings on this subject with the U. S. Army, Navy and Air Force were unsatisfactory and requested liaison with OSS, as the single U. S. agency for all contacts. Accordingly, a CE Section of SI was established to work closely with British services, and thereafter shared British intelligence, contacts and sources. This CE Section evolved into the X-2 Branch in June 1943.

In contrast to the situation with respect to secret intelligence, the benefits OSS derived from operating under British control on CE matters far outweighed the disadvantages of collaboration. Here was a field in which OSS would have otherwise been unable to participate effectively at all. The British provided files, sources for information, operating techniques, trained assistance and facilities which proved indispensable. It would have taken OSS perhaps decades to gain by itself the experience reached in only two years of British tutelage, and to build up the extensive files it was able to copy from British sources.*

R&A. R&A's relations with the British never involved the issue of integration, probably because the British felt that the field of research, as opposed to espionage and aid to resistance, had little bearing on their long-range position in Europe.

MO. MO made unsuccessful efforts to begin joint operations with the Psychological Warfare Executive (PWE) in the summer of 1943. Since PWE controlled all propaganda dissemination facilities in the Theater, close collaboration seemed MO's only chance for effective contribution. However, in view of the recent clarification of its position with respect to other British agencies (Ministry of Information and SOE), PWE feared to introduce a new element into an already deli-

* For a full discussion of the special considerations surrounding the inception of X-2 see vol. 1, pp. 188 et seq.

D. MIDDLE EAST

OSS was organized in the Middle East, as in Eire, Spain and Africa, during the defense period against German advance. In the spring of 1942, Axis armies in North Africa and Southeastern Europe threatened a gigantic pincer movement around the Eastern Mediterranean. Preparations had to be made against possible German success.

Two COI representatives arrived in Cairo in April 1942 with the following general directive:

(1) To gather geographical-military, naval and economic intelligence in preparation for invasion;

(2) To conduct counter-intelligence;

(3) To collect political and economic information not available to official State Department sources; and

(4) To organize a stay-behind agent network, for future operation behind the advancing Axis lines.

A base was established at Cairo to direct SI, counter-intelligence and R&A activities in Syria, Lebanon, Palestine, Transjordan, Iraq, Saudi Arabia, Iran, Afghanistan and Turkey.*

Exchange of information was early arranged with the British Inter-Service Liaison Department, and this SIS sub-section made unusual concessions. On the understanding that OSS would forward them to Washington for U. S. officials only, ISLD agreed to turn over all its intelligence reports from the Middle East and southeastern Europe.**

Networks of agents were built up in the various Middle Eastern countries.

An arrangement for Foreign Economic Administration cover was attempted. However, the difficulties of conducting secret activities within such an open organization prevented success, at least within the brief time limit: agents could not take FEA jobs without revealing their OSS connections to large numbers of FEA personnel; FEA representatives were generally unaware of the necessary secrecy; FEA pay rolls were insecure; too much agent time would have to be devoted purely to FEA work, and a solution was never successfully worked out.

Business cover involved difficulties. If a job were accepted without informing the company of the purpose, the agent might be recalled or transferred, as was one agent operating in Iraq. Conversely, an X-2 agent in Egypt, who was known to his cover company, feared that the company books would reveal his activity to the auditing firm. Shortly after this agent's arrival, the auditors (British),

. . . . developed closer contact with our office and for one reason or another made frequent and long visits, often doing some of the detailed auditing with the excuse that they would have that much less work to do at the time of final audit. This practice permitted them to check our company bank books periodically and thereby incidentally keep abreast of my withdrawals. I am strongly of the opinion that this firm had more

* And also operations into Greece, Albania, Yugoslavia, and through Istanbul into Europe. See those sections below.

** The Jewish Agency in Palestine later offered to transmit, free of charge, reports from its worldwide intelligence network. OSS accepted the offer in August of 1944, stipulating that there

would be no return for the information, and no obligation to use the material in any way. The Agency at first suggested placing a representative with OSS/Cairo to handle its material, an offer which was refused. Results, in general, were almost nil, and, in April 1945, the Washington office directed that the agreement be terminated.

than a mere business interest in their close contact with our office during my stay. In the same
general sphere, it may be well to mention my
company's banks, all of whom were advised that
I was given authority to draw considerable sums
of money. These banks called me and seemed to
manifest a great interest in whether or not I
would utilize the authority granted me.*

Communications proved to be a weakness.
Once the German threat to the area ceased,
the British were interested in maintaining
control. If OSS wished to plant long-term
agents unknown to the British, radio sets
were not feasible. State Department pouch,
on the other hand, was extremely slow, that
from Teheran to Cairo often taking from two
to three weeks. State cover was permitted
in only a few locations. In others, OSS
agents had to blow their activities, because
of the necessity of entering State Department offices directly, in order to deliver reports and cables for transmittal. Agents
located at points away from State offices
had almost no method of communication,
since transportation facilities were inadequate. For instance, the only recourse open
to an agent at Dahran, Arabia, was to take
the trip all the way to Cairo to deliver his
reports.

By September 1944, SI/Cairo had infiltrated agents into the following Middle Eastern countries:

(1) *Egypt.* Members of the OSS/Cairo
staff turned in information acquired in the
course of business, including reports on
Egyptian politics and on Jewish, Armenian,
Polish, Czech and Russian activities in the
country. Further information was gathered by an agent of the Labor Desk/SI, an
important member of an Arab Trade Union,
who was able to travel throughout the Middle East as Union representative. His February 1944 tour, for instance, produced intelligence on labor groups in Egypt, Palestine, Lebanon and Syria, in particular on
Communist influence and activity in the
Arab labor movement.

---

* Returnee Report, Agent AG-110, 9 September
1944, History File 215A.

Two R&A representatives arrived in Cairo
in June 1943 and established contacts with
the Jewish Agency, the Sudan Agency, the
Sudan Government and U. S. and British
organizations. Among the most useful contacts was
                    which provided valuable information
on petroleum activities in the Middle East.
Quantities of maps, almanacs and periodicals were collected on tours of the Middle
Eastern countries. A library of information
on these areas was extensively used by approved American and British representatives
in Cairo. R&A prepared numerous reports
on political and economic developments, and
on Russian policies in the area.

An X-2 office was established in Cairo in
late 1943, for the protection of OSS and other
U. S. agencies in the Middle East. X-2/-
Cairo also served as administrative and file
center for sub-bases subsequently established in Istanbul, Beirut and Athens.*

X-2 activity in the Middle East was limited
by several factors. As for SI, personnel with
adequate backgrounds of experience and
language facility were scarce. Cover was
extremely difficult to establish, and, in Syria
and Lebanon, SI and X-2 collaborated to
limit the number of U. S. agents by joint
briefing. In addition, X-2 was prevented
from undertaking any offensive counter-
espionage operations, authorization for
these having been delegated to a British control board by Anglo-American agreement
prior to X-2 arrival. Similarly, protective
counter-intelligence ** had been well taken
care of by British agencies and by the U. S.
Counter-Intelligence Corps. X-2 was of

---

* These X-2 offices are treated further in this
section, excepting the one in Athens, which is
covered under "Athens," below.
** Counter-intelligence is the defense of one's
own agencies against enemy penetration. Counter-espionage carries the fight to the enemy, using double-agents. For further explanation of
these functions, see especially the sections on X-2
in Washington. London, France, and Italy.

service to SI and other U. S. agencies in checking prospective agents and employees against the London files, and meantime built up the facilities for presumptive postwar activity.

(2) *Lebanon and Syria* (Ten agents: seven SI and three X-2*). During the war, the French remained in control of these countries and it was dangerous for natives to travel with secret material in their possession. As a result, only two of the agents were successful in building up local chains.

Agent "Stallion," who established the first of these, had arrived in the winter of 1942. In the summer of 1943, he obtained a bona fide position with an American commercial company, a job which enabled him to travel through the area maintaining contact with his sub-sources. In December 1943, he was able to hire another OSS agent as his business assistant, and between them they operated the old chain, set up a second one, bringing the total of known sub-sources to sixty, and continued transmitting intelligence obtained by themselves. They uncovered the contact system between natives in Syria and Italian submarines operating in the Mediterranean. Sub-sources provided considerable material on smuggling and espionage activities. In 1945 "Stallion" also produced valuable intelligence on pro-Russian factions within the Armenian community and on French economic activities used to promote the French position in Lebanon, tracing the latter down to its operational center, a commercial company used as cover.

Two other agents also worked together, one a businessman, the other a female clerk in a U. S. war agency. The latter did the code work for both of them, while each sent in valuable reports on industrial installations, economic and political developments, the Syrian and Lebanese press, etc. Harbor plans of several Syrian ports were eagerly received by MID.

---

* These and subsequent totals are for the period 1942-45.

"Squirrel" arrived as Military Observer in Damascus in April 1944. There he developed a chain of about one hundred witting and unwitting informants, including six paid agents. He submitted thorough regional studies on the Druze and Jezireh territories. Most of his reports dealt with political and military developments, for which he maintained particularly good relations with British and Syrian military circles. In May 1945, during the time of the French shelling of Damascus, he received commendation from the American Charge d'Affaires at the Damascus Legation for his cool and competent coverage of the incident.

"Carat," an X-2 agent, arrived in Beirut in early 1944 as Cultural Attache of the Legation. He was assisted by an Army Public Relations Officer, also in Beirut, and by other representatives in Damascus and Aleppo. There was, however, practically no enemy espionage activity in the area. British and French services during their three years' occupation had cleaned up the remnants of the enemy systems, and the realistic Arabs had long since given up their Nazi affiliations. The X-2 agents built up files on local politicians and political movements, propagandists, potential agents and members of the British and French Intelligence Services. Studies of the growth of Russian activity in the area were of particular interest as were those on the development of the Syrian National Party. Thorough reports covered the unrest in the Alawite territory of Syria, discovering a French hand in the disturbances. "Carat's" political intelligence was well received by the U. S. Minister, who forwarded many of his reports directly to the State Department.

(3) *Palestine-Transjordan* (Six agents: five SI, one X-2). Several travelling agents briefly visited this British-controlled area, but only two set up long-term chains. These two were associated with Jewish and Arab political circles, respectively, with the result that Cairo/SI received intelligence from both of the conflicting groups.

49

(4) *Iraq* (Four SI agents). British control of Iraq insured adequate military and counter-espionage coverage. However, road reports, strategic terrain analyses and coverage of the Kurd Movement were rated by MIS as excellent work.

Two agents, "Bunny" and "Buffalo," worked as a team. "Buffalo" was a commercial dealer in U. S. goods, representing also several specific firms. His cover was not successful, however, because trade regulations, priorities and a shortage of dollar exchange in Iraq prohibited any quantity of trade. "Bunny" was
hired by the Iraqi Government to

His contacts were excellent. He knew the Prime Minister and various other high government officials, and provided OSS/Cairo with a running commentary on political developments.

In April 1944 a neutral diplomat, on his way out of Germany, gave "Bunny" a detailed report on the results of the Allied bombings of Berlin. He mentioned the Berliner attitude of doing the day's work between 2 and 5 p.m., when Allied bombers never came over. Specific commendation from the highest military authorities and from the White House rewarded this information, which was one of the first such reports to come out of the Reich. Bombing of Berlin between 2 and 5 p.m. commenced.

"Bunny" and "Buffalo" maintained close relations with the American Minister and with British Security Intelligence. They assisted the latter in uncovering and breaking several Nazi spy rings. "Buffalo" personally interrogated one agent who, after 23 hours, finally broke. The exchange of information, arranged as a result of these successes, provided OSS with future counter-intelligence files.

(5) *Saudi Arabia* (Two SI agents). Intelligence in this country was unsuccessful. Communication difficulties proved insoluble for the only two agents who could be recruited in the country; from their location,

the U. S. Legation at Jiddah was almost inaccessible. One agent did bring in several reports on trips to Cairo.

(6) *Iran* (Eight SI agents). The initial OSS purpose in Iran was to collect military-geographical information in preparation for a possible German advance through the Caucasus. A two-man team began operations early in the war, one of the men arriving in the autumn of 1941 (operating under COI), the other late in 1942. Each had previously lived in the country, engaged in research, and this activity was continued as cover. The reports were more of a scholarly than of a current intelligence nature, but the material submitted on roads, economic conditions, and popular sentiment, the press reviews, biographical compilations and analyses of Soviet and British policy in Iran formed valuable basic intelligence.

As Axis success turned to defeat, the emphasis shifted to political and economic intelligence. Two men, trained in Washington, were given commissions with the Persian Gulf Command, by arrangement between its commanding general and OSS/-Cairo. The plan was to gather intelligence on Russian internal affairs by developing agent networks among the Polish refugees in Azerbaijan. The two agents failed in their admittedly difficult task and turned to economic reporting plus a running analysis of the Russian program in Iran.

However, of two other Americans working for the Iranian Government, one acquired a particularly good sub-source in Azerbaijan. This man built up a chain and provided reports on all phases of Russian activity in the area, including military unit locations, activities of the leftist Tudeh Party, and similar intelligence. He was the only Anglo-American source of information in the area.

(7) *Afghanistan* (Two SI agents). This independent monarchy was first covered directly from Washington by the British Empire Section of SI. Two agents arrived in the fall of 1942 to work as
Inadequate prepara-

tion made the project a failure: lack of training resulted in almost worthless reports; a communications mix-up rendered criticism and direction impossible; the State Department regretted its original approval of
cover for secret activities; and the American Minister accordingly discouraged and hampered the work.

When Cairo/SI was given jurisdiction of the area in July 1943, the two agents were withdrawn and de-briefed. It was decided that the unfortunate relations which had developed with State Department representatives in the area prohibited their useful return.

(8) *Turkey*. Positive intelligence on Turkey, as on Egypt, was not approved by the Department of State, but an Istanbul office was established in April 1943 as a base for operations in the Balkans,* and some incidental reports were made by members of the staff. Officers running maritime operations at Izmir (for the delivery of agents to Greece**) turned in similar incidental information on economic affairs, industrial installations, politics and transportation.

A two-man R&A unit arrived at Istanbul in January 1944, to find that most of its collecting and evaluating functions were already being performed by State Department, OWI, IDC and British Ministry of Information services. The unit established a reference library and map collection, and prepared some analyses of political developments in the Balkans.

In the spring of 1945 an OSS Planning Board directive authorized SI to conduct, and X-2 and R&A to continue, intelligence activities on Turkey and adjacent territories. OSS/Istanbul joined in the general task of establishing U. S. peacetime espionage.

X-2/Istanbul. X-2, unlike SI, was authorized to operate in Turkey itself. This country, officially neutral, wavered back and forth in its degree of cooperation with Axis and Allies according to the relative fortunes of war.

Axis agents and sympathizers were numerous, including the large colonies of German businessmen and officials, Vichy French and White Russians. The laxity of control on the Turko-Bulgar border, travelling southward, was notorious, and the whole area served as an excellent headquarters for German intelligence in the Middle East and points south and east.

In the summer of 1943 an agent who had been recruited by the Counter-Intelligence Division of SI/Washington was dispatched to Turkey as a special intelligence agent for SI/Washington.

He had been provided with a fund of some $25,000,
by OSS.
His failure to contact OSS Istanbul left him

* See "Istanbul," below.
** See "Greece," below.

51

without colleagues, communications or liaison with the Turkish Government.

In January 1944 he was incorporated into a more prosaic and better briefed X-2 office staff, established in Istanbul at that time. Here communications facilities permitted quick reference to the Cairo files and the central files in London. British MI-6(V) in Turkey allowed X-2 free access to its personality cards, and reports were exchanged. When the chief of X-2/Istanbul first arrived, he was given a desk in the British Passport Control Office to learn procedures as they were affected by current local conditions. Close relations were likewise maintained with the Military and Naval Attaches and with CIC. The CIC representative, however, withdrew from Turkey from October 1944 until April of the following year, leaving the field to X-2.

Following the collapse of Italy, the activities of the Italian Military Attache in Istanbul were supported by funds from American and British sources. From the Italian espionage system, a small group of agents and watchers was taken over by X-2.

By early 1944 British services had the situation well in hand. Most of the key German agents had long since been identified, and many were giving themselves up for Allied exfiltration and internment. During the first days of January 1944, the British arranged the defection of Erich Vermehren, number two man of the Abwehr * in Turkey. Three more Abwehr defections in the first week of February, those of Mr. and Mrs. Kleczkowski, and of Willi Hamburger, had been accepted (without authority) by two OWI men, who subsequently asked X-2 to take over.

---

* German foreign intelligence service.

Normally, a counter-espionage organization prefers in such circumstances to persuade defectors to maintain their positions and work under control. Removing them notifies the enemy of the penetration and merely invites a fresh and better disciplined set of officials and agents into the area. The whole process must be repeated of identifying, surveying and penetrating the new organization.

In this case, however, Vermehren, Hamburger and the Kleczkowskis were suspected by the Germans and had been ordered home. It was decided to take them to Syria for the valuable counter-intelligence material to be gained from interrogation.* The effect on the Abwehr in Turkey was demoralizing. The chief was recalled in disgrace, and a complete reorganization attempted, with the Sicherheitsdienst ** (SD) making a bid to dominate. Double-agents under British/-X-2 control reported developments among the Germans, principally that of the discouragement of Pfeiffer, the new chief. The operation appeared to be a highly successful and profitable one—and, considered alone, was so.

However, the advantage given to the SD (one of Himmler's secret Nazi organizations) over the Abwehr (the old-line, partially anti-Nazi foreign secret service) was a blow to OSS/Bern operations. Penetration of the Abwehr on a high level was bringing Bern valuable intelligence, notably inside reports on all the preparations for the anti-Hitler coup of 20 July 1944.*** The disorganization of the Abwehr in Turkey gave Himmler an opportunity to push forward his Sicherheitsdienst, as part of a campaign to estab-

---

* The Russians requested the opportunity also to interrogate the Kleczkowskis. OSS stated that this was impossible but agreed to give them a prepared questionnaire and return the answers. The offer was accepted by the Russians whose questionnaire provided OSS with incidental indications of past Russian intelligence activities and clues to their intentions.
** Nazi security police.
*** See "Bern," below.

lish Nazi supremacy over the Wehrmacht. The suspicion and investigations following the defections caused some of Bern's sources to dry up temporarily.

X-2/Washington subsequently issued an order forbidding further defections from the Abwehr. The real lesson, however, was the necessity for centralization of all penetration operations. Lacking an adequate and efficient central control, British and OSS counter-espionage encouraged the Abwehr defections.*

In collaboration with the British, X-2 continued the job, principally of protecting U. S. agencies in the area (since the British, according to agreement, handled all double-agents). The two services identified some 1,500 agents, and of these, after Allied representations to the Turkish Government, about 800 were neutralized:

Confined	750 (approximately)
Extradited	25
Defected	9
Controlled	14

Among others, a German agent was uncovered working in OWI. OSS/Istanbul had had some difficulty with OWI personnel. Many of the newspaper reporters seemed to take an unpatriotic delight in hunting out, through their American connections, OSS personnel and proclaiming them as "spies" and "super-sleuths." The actual threat of spies seemed humorous to these Americans. Therefore, when an old and trusted employee, Yumni Reshid, was accused by X-2 of working for the Germans, OWI personnel ridiculed the possibility. Under interrogation, he made a full confession.

The discovery of a German group of some thirty agents, trained for the penetration of OSS and other U. S. agencies, revealed an interesting line of attack on the Allied intelligence system in the Middle East. Four of its officials voluntarily offered information through which the project was neutralized.

Twenty-nine undercover agents had been placed in the Middle East, and in all but two countries (Afghanistan and Arabia) intelligence coverage was good. As the war moved away, reports shifted from a strictly military-geographical interest to more general political and economic information. Over 500 sub-agents helped turn in, by June 1945, more than 5,000 reports.

Use of OSS services became widespread. Counter-intelligence information was constantly demanded. X-2, for instance, became the review agency for all visa applicants for the United States from Cairo, Ankara and Istanbul. It collaborated with the State Department on the "Safe Haven" project, tracking the flight of German funds from Europe. By 1945, relations with State Department representatives were close.* Mr. Wadsworth and Mr. Henderson, Ministers to Lebanon and Iraq, were emphatically in favor of the continuation of OSS in peacetime. MID frequently gave OSS/Cairo the highest rating of all intelligence sources, and specified that OSS supplied the best coverage of any agency in the area.

In general, OSS/Middle East acquired an outstanding record. Careful selection of personnel resulted in excellent liaison with U. S. and Allied agencies. The administration of agents from Cairo worked well, on the general principle that one desk-man was required to care for four chief agents in the field. Agent problems were quickly attended to, and weekly letters, with questions, criticisms and commendations, resulted in high agent morale and a steady stream of carefully evaluated and detailed intelligence.

---

* It may be noted that Himmler's advantage was short-lived. The next defection was that of Nellie Kapp, who had been in the employment of Moyzisch, the head of Himmler's SD in Turkey.

* See Memorandum "Relations Existing Between OSS and State Department Missions," 14 December 1944, History File 215b.

Part III

ITALY

In December 1942, one month after the Allied landings in North Africa, the first U. S. team in enemy-occupied Europe was placed by SI/Algiers in Corsica. The team transmitted intelligence for over six months prior to capture, and was most valuable in obtaining for OSS the support of AFHQ. In June 1943 a team was dispatched to Sardinia, but suffered immediate capture. In September, OSS missions sent to the two islands found and reported Axis forces evacuating. Corsica became an OSS maritime base for depositing agents in Italy and France.

Meanwhile, OSS penetration of Sicily prior to the landings had been prohibited by AFHQ for fear of alerting enemy forces. During the campaign there in July, August and September, OSS still had not developed its function in support of army tactical operations. The chief of SO/Sicily was captured leading a team through enemy lines.

To continental Italy, two units were dispatched by OSS/Algiers. SI/Italy's concentration on political reporting and its lack of liaison with the principal operations in Italy made its work ineffectual. Many of its personnel were returned to the United States; it was limited to political contacts in liberated areas; and its few agents in occupied Italy were turned over to the second unit.

The latter was the detachment which landed with Fifth Army at Salerno and Anzio and, during the longest campaign of the European war, developed for the first time the techniques of OSS support to ground armies. Short - range, locally - recruited agents were daily infiltrated through enemy lines, to return with tactical information out of range for reconnaissance patrols. More carefully trained teams were equipped with radios and dispatched on missions deep into enemy territory. One of the long-range missions in Rome, for example, reported the German plan for the counter-offensive at Anzio.

In June 1944 a reorganization was effected. To improve OSS's position vis-a-vis the armed forces, 2677th Headquarters Company (Algiers) became 2677th Regiment (Caserta). Italy was administratively divided into two zones, Headquarters Company being at Caserta with AFHQ, and Company D in the forward zone moving with the Allied Armies in Italy. Two detachments of Co. D operated under the U. S. Fifth and British Eighth Armies. (Eighth Army selected OSS, rather than British SOE, to run all through-the-lines operations in its sector.)

The Committee for National Liberation in North Italy (CLNAI) provided effective support of Allied forces. Company D and its army detachments, together with small OSS bases at Annemasse and Campione, on the French and Swiss borders, respectively, joined SOE in exploiting CLNAI. Guerrilla groups, trained, supplied and coordinated by OSS and SOE, sabotaged enemy equipment, harassed and delayed enemy forces in movement, took over whole areas behind enemy lines, and even held mountainous sectors of the Allied line.

A. WEST MEDITERRANEAN ISLANDS

By December 1942 the Tunisian campaign had begun. The few OSS members who had been in North Africa preparing for Operation *TORCH* were assembled to form a headquarters at Algiers with AFGH, and, besides counter-intelligence in Morocco and combat intelligence in Tunisia,* operations were begun across the Mediterranean. At the end of the month, a radio operator of *TORCH* experience dispatched a team to Corsica.

Men began to arrive from Washington in small numbers. By February, OSS/Algiers included training officers for SI and SO operatives, SI members of the Western European Division and the Labor Desk and SO representatives who were largely diverted to administrative work, but who also began establishment of an air drop packing station, as well as a parachute school for agents.

Within a week of its approval of JCS 170 ** in February, AFHQ requested personnel for the penetration of Italy, Sicily and Sardinia. The first SI agent for Italy, "Sorel", to be dispatched from Washington, reached North Africa, in February 1943.

His instructions, however, were to make only minimum contact with OSS/Algiers headquarters. It was not until late March that an SI representative arrived in Algiers to begin operations towards Italy, Sicily and Sardinia. The delay *** in his arrival meant a corresponding delay in the activation of an Italian desk in the field. The first unit of Italian SI recruits for the field was earmarked for

Sicily and scheduled for departure from Washington in February. However, the climax of the Tunisian campaign put military transport space at a premium, and the first contingent of three officers and nine enlisted men did not leave the United States until late in March. A second contingent was dispatched in June, and in the same month, after overcoming many delays in obtaining approvals for personnel, transportation and other items, SI/Italy sent its first, and unsuccessful, mission to Sardinia.

R&A, X-2 and MO representatives arrived in mid-1943 and Operational Groups, prevented from use in Sicily by lack of transportation, trained for operations in Corsica, Sardinia and the Italian mainland. Until July 1944, OSS activities into Italy continued to be directed from Algiers.*

Corsica

The first OSS secret agent team inside enemy-occupied Europe was successfully infiltrated one month after the Allied landings in North Africa. Established north of Ajaccio, Corsica, the team's clandestine radio station, PEARL HARBOR, sent its first message to Algiers on 25 December 1942, and continued almost daily contact until May 1943. Through direct liaison with the Corsican Maquis,** the team reported extensively German and Italian order of battle on the island. The intelligence was relayed to AFHQ.

The establishment of a secret radio-intelligence network in Corsica had first been at-

---

* See Part I, "North Africa," above.

** Washington Exhibit W-38.

*** His passport had been held up by the State Department because his name appeared on the Dies Committee as a Communist. This was ironic in view of his conservative political leanings which actually tended to slant his subsequent operations in Italy towards rightist political groups.

---

* The full Algiers establishment is described under "Algiers Base" in Part V, "France," below.

** "Maquis" refers to the high, dense shrubbery covering the sides of Corsican mountains, the traditional hideout of outcasts in the 19th century days of the Vendetta. The term was generally applied to all French resistance groups.

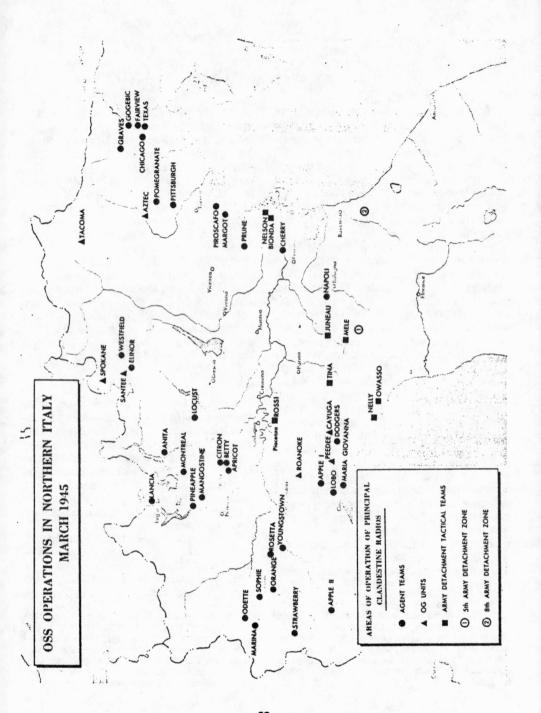

OSS OPERATIONS IN NORTHERN ITALY
MARCH 1945

AREAS OF OPERATION OF PRINCIPAL
CLANDESTINE RADIOS

● AGENT TEAMS
▲ OG UNITS
■ ARMY DETACHMENT TACTICAL TEAMS
① 5th ARMY DETACHMENT ZONE
② 8th ARMY DETACHMENT ZONE

tempted by British SIS a few days after the North African landings. Whereas SO and SOE collaborated according to the agreement of June 1942,* SI maintained its independence in North Africa.

"Tommy" was on friendly terms with the chiefs of the French Deuxieme Bureau in Algiers, and through it he obtained an officer to lead the four-man team and to direct intelligence from Corsica. Through its offices, too, he obtained the permission of Admiral Darlan and General Giraud to use the submarine "Casabianca".** AFHQ and the British Admiralty, in charge of the harbor, also gave approval for the mission, and essential equipment was furnished to ready the submarine.

To work under the intelligence officer provided by Deuxieme Bureau, "Tommy" recruited his Corsican radio assistant as operator for the mission and two other Corsicans as assistant operator and liaison agent, respectively. The submarine commander was to help "Tommy" pick the most suitable point for the group to land along the Corsican coast, and await "Tommy's" return after the landing. With three wireless sets, a million French francs and several thousand Italian lire, food, supplies and false documents, the five OSS men headed for Corsica on 11 December 1942.

The technique employed by l'Herminier, commander of the "Casabianca", for finding a landing site and putting agents ashore, became standard for subsequent missions. Upon first reaching the target area, he made a daylight periscope reconnaissance until a

suitable landing point was found—in this case, a beach at the foot of the Bay of Chioni. He then submerged and held the submarine on the bottom until after dark. This required detailed knowledge of the underwater terrain and conditions in the Mediterranean and great skill in maneuvering and handling the submarine. Shortly after midnight on the night of 14 December, the "Casabianca" re-surfaced—barely out of water, to avoid being sighted by Italian patrols—and moved to within a mile off shore. Two crew members, armed with Sten guns, landed the agents and their equipment by dinghy. The submarine returned to its original position and remained submerged for thirty hours, when a second boatload of supplies was to be taken in and "Tommy" brought back.

On this second trip, the dinghy capsized. The two crew members, stranded, remained with the agents for two months.* "Tommy" himself returned to the submarine after a perilous hour-and-a-half swim.

Although, of necessity, no preparations for the arrival of the agents had been made in Corsica itself, they were welcomed by friendly local inhabitants and aided in the unloading of supplies. From 24 December until the capture of the PEARL HARBOR station by occupation troops five months later, the four-man combination of intelligence leader, liaison man and radio operators worked with a growing number of agents to obtain and transmit information from enemy-occupied Corsica, and to establish a resistance nucleus for use in the event of future landing operations.

They found that the Italians (25,000 as of 8 December) had occupied the Island of Corsica without meeting resistance (the result of orders from Vichy), and that, although stationed in strength at beaches on the east and west coasts, they had not penetrated to

---

* See "Introduction," above.
** The 1,600-ton "Casabianca," latest type of submarine in the French Navy, had just escaped from Toulon to Algiers with its commander and full crew aboard.

---

* A subsequent submarine operation in February evacuated the two sailors and delivered the first U. S.-dispatched arms and ammunition to reach a European underground movement.

the interior except on main highways and railroads. The two brigades of the French Army in Corsica had been demobilized, and the French general placed in "residence surveillee". Italian morale was low, since the population was universally hostile to the Fascist invaders, and the Corsican gendarmes used by them were non-cooperative. For example, when the gendarmes were ordered to collect all firearms, they passed among inhabitants recommending that they hide their arms and only turn over those which were unserviceable. The inhabitants were, on the other hand, anxious to assist the OSS agents, and freely furnished information from villages and out-of-the-way places.

Security, on the other hand, was practically non-existent. Insularity, widespread inter-family connections and a united hatred of the occupying forces, meant that the Corsicans took little care to guard their speech from possible traitors in their midst. That PEARL HARBOR operated for as long as it did without enemy discovery was proof of Corsican solidarity and Italian weakness. In the summer of 1943, the chief radio operator was captured, tortured and killed. No more was heard from the other members of the team. During its period of operation, PEARL HARBOR dispatched 202 messages. Although the first OSS unit in enemy-occupied Europe, it had been considered by AFHQ a model for battle order reporting.

OSS, having as yet only slow procedures for issuing decorations, was forced simply to pay the operator's mother in recognition of her son's services. The importance of decorations and agent psychology in general was something OSS had already learned, but for which it had not yet been able to develop satisfactory arrangements with the Theater Command.

On the night of 8 September 1943, when the Italian surrender was announced, French Maquis groups rose in all parts of the Island of Corsica and seized control of towns and installations. A radio appeal was broadcast to Allied authorities in North Africa, urgently asking assistance against the Germans, who were moving onto the Island in strength from Sardinia. French headquarters in North Africa hastily prepared the Battaillon de Choc and several units of Moroccan and Algerian colonial troops, as a skeleton Expeditionary Force to aid in the liberation of the Island. AFHQ requested OSS to supply troops as a token Allied force to accompany the French.

Donovan selected one Operational Group (OG) of two officers and thirty men to carry out the mission, accompanied by a demolitions instructor for the Maquis and a small group of SI officers and trained Corsican agents from the SI/France Desk. The OSS group left Algiers with the French troops on French cruisers and destroyers, and arrived in Ajaccio on 17 September. A second group followed shortly, with an R&A officer and SI men to set up an advanced base for maritime penetration of Italy and France.

Corsica was now occupied by 80,000 Italians and a small German garrison consisting principally of radar observation and other air force technical crews. Upon the Italian collapse, the Germans decided to evacuate their forces in Sardinia, overland as far as possible, to avoid Allied air attack. Ignoring their recent Italian allies, the Germans began to move from Sardinia to Corsica, up the level east coast of that Island and across to Elba and the Italian mainland.

The size of the Allied Expeditionary Force limited it to harassing operations. The Maquis groups had been supplied with guns and ammunition from SOE and OSS by ship, submarine and plane. However, the insular Corsicans found it difficult to turn their attention from their traditional enemy, the Italians, toward the Germans who were relatively unknown to them. Furthermore, the French officers of the Expeditionary Force tended to deprecate and antagonize the leaders of the Maquis.

OSS/SI became at once the principal link with the Maquis. Within a matter of days, SI agents had organized a courier system to bring information on conditions all over the Island and particularly in Bastia, the key port of the German evacuation. OSS assisted in organizing and supplying communications for the Maquis groups holding a German feint toward Zonza in south-central Corsica. Information provided by the Maquis from all over the Island was given to Expeditionary Force headquarters and relayed to Algiers, serving as AFHQ's principal source of information on the military situation on the Island.

The OG moved northward with the French Goumiers to attack the east coast road, just south of Bastia. Bazookas were inoperative because of a shortage of fresh batteries. A three-man OG team, on an advance patrol to place mines and harass a German armored column, was killed by cross-fire ahead of the most advanced French positions.

The last German units were evacuated from Bastia on the morning of 4 October. That same day an advance group of R&A and SI officers entered the town with OG's and the first French troops. A variety of recent data on the German army was collected as well as newly manufactured items of abandoned equipment. Much recent and otherwise unavailable information on continental France was secured and sent back to Algiers for analysis. In addition, German and French documentation and equipment were assembled for use in future intelligence penetrations, and advance SI and OG bases were established.*

Sardinia

On 29 June 1942, SI/Italy dispatched its first team, consisting of a W/T operator and four enlisted men, to penetrate Sardinia. The PT carrying the agents, escorted by two other PT's, drew in close to the coast of northwestern Sardinia on the night of 30

June. The agents rowed themselves and their equipment ashore in a rubber boat, which was attached by a line to the PT so that it could be pulled back after the agents had landed.

Rough seas had disturbed navigation. Since no conducting officer rowed in with the agents, the fact that the landing was not made exactly at the selected pinpoint did not become apparent to those on the PT.* On shore, the agents, who were in uniform, did not find their bearings until the next day and were quickly captured by Italian sentries. They were not turned over to the Germans but were forced to play back their radio under control of Italian intelligence officers. In their first message, however, they covertly informed Algiers, by their prearranged danger signal, that they were captured and operating under duress. Security had been preserved, but the operation itself was a failure.**

After the Italian surrender on 8 September 1943, reports reached AFHQ that the Germans had decided to evacuate Sardinia. AFHQ requested OSS to reconnoiter the Island, report on the situation and, if possible, win over, or arrange for the surrender of, the Italian garrison. Donovan appointed three SO and OG officers to the task.

Accompanied by a British radio operator, the team was parachuted in uniform near Cagliari on the night of 12 September, where it found that southern Sardinia was already free of Germans. Bearing letters from General Eisenhower and from the newly-established Badoglio headquarters, the team contacted the Italian commander on the Island, who placed himself at its disposal. Communications were immediately established with AFHQ and reception arranged for General Theodore Roosevelt's occupation forces. The OSS team, that had been held for a

---

* See "Corsica Operations," below.

* Thereafter, conducting officers accompanied all rubber boat operations. See "Corsica Operations," below.

** For further operations by SI/Italy, see that section, below.

month as prisoners by the Italians, was released unharmed, and its radio equipment returned intact.

Sicily

Corsica and Sardinia were of minor AFHQ interest compared to Sicily. Although OSS had one team ready for dispatch to that Island early in June, AFHQ clearance was cancelled at the last minute for fear that agents entering at so late a date might alert coastal defenses.

During the campaign itself, OSS attempted line-crossings for intelligence and sabotage but was largely unsuccessful, although the task appointed and procedures developed represented a step forward from the errors of the Tunisian campaign.* One OSS agent went ashore on D-Day, 11 July 1943. This was "Sorel", who had been dispatched from Washington to act independently of OSS/Algiers.

he accompanied the first wave of the 3rd Division ashore. Speaking fluent Italian, he interrogated prisoners on the spot, obtained information on camouflaged enemy gun emplacements that were pinning down the landing forces, and himself led a charge on a pillbox and an Italian command post. From there he maintained a deceptive phone contact with Italian rear headquarters, denying the need for reinforcements in "his sector".

Donovan also went ashore on D-Day, and subsequently directed the main OSS unit for Sicily of two officers and eight enlisted men, who landed on D-plus-4, attached to G-2, Seventh Army.

It was quickly found that agent personnel recruited and trained in the United States for secret intelligence work could not be used on short-range tactical or combat intelligence missions. In contrast, selected natives, recruited, trained and briefed on the spot, had not only natural cover for line-crossing but also an intimate knowledge of

---
* See "Tunisia," above.

the terrain. However, the American-recruited agents' knowledge of Sicilian dialects and of the country made them useful both as interrogators for forward Army units, Counter-Intelligence Corps (CIC) and Allied Military Government (AMGOT), and for recruiting native sub-agents and informers in rear areas.

A few such recruits carried out through-the-lines missions, without any notable success. In late July the chief of SO/Sicily arrived and laid plans for sabotage operations behind the lines. By this time, however, enemy resistance had cracked; Palermo fell on 22 July and the Germans were retreating to the northeast. Since, presumably, OSS was the only agency at the front capable of line-penetration operations, Seventh Army G-2 directed that a mission be carried out. On 1 August, after several projects proved abortive due to the rapid Allied advance, the SO chief organized a team and personally led it towards enemy lines in the north-central sector in the mountainous region above Mistretta.

The team, consisting of three enlisted men, one radio operator and two native guides, headed towards an Italian unit whose morale had been reported at a low ebb. While crossing a stream past the main enemy positions, the radio man was seriously wounded on a land mine, which exploded and gave away the team's position to a German patrol.

The team members ahead and behind regained Allied lines; the SO chief and one enlisted man, also wounded, remained with the radio operator and were captured; the Germans left the radio man as mortally wounded. After two days, the latter succeeded in attracting a native's attention and was recovered by advance American units. The enlisted man managed to escape, after killing the German officer who was guarding him, and returned to American lines to report his observations. The SO chief was not heard from again, although several penetrations, both of agents and native sub-agents, were attempted in order to try to recover him. Having just come from the United States with extensive information on OSS plans and organization, he should not, in the interest of security, have undertaken to lead a mission into enemy territory.

In the last stages of the campaign and in the occupation period, OSS contributed substantially to the work of the forward elements of CIC and AMGOT. SI officers maintained active contacts with native resistance groups, including the "Mafia" and underground elements with connections throughout Italy. The "Mafia" was a Sicilian separatist movement which had sprung up in various parts of the Island. Extensive information was gathered about its activities and leaders, its efforts, unsuccessful for the most part, to gain popular support; and the sympathy toward it of some Allied officials, particularly in the British zone. Representatives of the Partito d'Azione, one of the stronger Italian anti-fascist resistance groups, supplied data on pro-Allied personalities and organizations useful for intelligence penetration of Italy. Reports on Fascist officials in hiding or still in office were supplied to CIC and AMGOT, but arrests by Allied authorities were slowed by the policy of avoiding disruption of local government or services. Lt. Colonel Charles Poletti, Chief of AMGOT, frequently consulted the OSS unit on civilian appointments, on the effectiveness of specific AMGOT projects or on economic matters such as transportation, resources and the developing black market.

At Donovan's direction, and in line with his desire to "get the professors to the front", an R&A representative had accompanied the OSS unit which landed with Seventh Army Headquarters. He assisted in planning OSS operations, in prisoner interrogation and in the work of the advanced AMGOT units. His principal task, supplementing that of the G-2 Captured Documents Section, was to enter major localities and to seize and assemble, from public buildings, libraries and other structures, official and strategic documentation on Sicily and Italy, of interest to OSS and AFHQ.

After the fall of Palermo, he organized most of the professors of the University there to prepare studies on various Sicilian political, economic and social problems, as well as on conditions in continental Italy. The reports proved of particular value to AMGOT officials, and, whereas data produced on continental Italy did not live up to expectations, the staff of the University, thus harnessed, became an ex-officio advisory body to assist in solving some of AMGOT's most immediate local problems.

SI/Italy, meanwhile, established a base at Palermo and sent several small missions with occupying forces to the smaller Italian islands of Stromboli, Lipari, Ventotene, San Stefano and Ponza. Many of these were penal colonies where SI interrogated (and in some cases recruited) Mussolini's political prisoners, and collected enemy documents, equipment and codes.

In Sicily OSS had acquired little experience in behind-the-lines work in support of ground armies. Most of the staff had become involved in occupation and political work. The failures, both on Sardinia and in Sicily itself, were principally those of SI/Italy, a unit whose activities were later sharply curtailed by Donovan.*

SI/Italy began from bases in Palermo and South Italy to attempt long-range agent operations and to establish political contacts. However, a new unit, including an experienced French intelligence officer, was formed to accompany Fifth Army on the campaign in Italy itself, while a third set of operations (SI and OG) were initiated from Corsica.**

---

* See "SI/Italy," below.
** See following sections.

B. FIFTH ARMY DETACHMENT

Prior to the Salerno landing, OSS had participated in no extensive military campaigns. In both Tunisia and Sicily * there had been insufficient time to develop its functions in support of ground armies. Furthermore, there were no OSS agents or informant chains yet established on the Italian mainland from North African bases. Initial contacts with Italian resistance elements had been made by the SI/Italy section in Sicily, but these were not as well developed as the active liaison between the OSS staff in Switzerland and the Italian patriot movements in the north.**

The OSS position in the Theater was inevitably that of a new agency about whose functions and relative position neither its own members, nor those to whom it was immediately responsible, were sure. Its general role had been delineated by JCS 170, and a G-3 Special Operation Section coordinated its activities with those of British SIS, SOE and other units. Nevertheless, OSS members had to develop plans and functions as each new situation arose, and then had to locate or initiate an administrative procedure to gain approval and supplies for each unorthodox operation. In areas of direct AFHQ jurisdiction, approval of an operation by G-3 Special Operations was the basic prerequisite. However, in a specific zone of combat the designated army commander was in charge. In the face of shortages of transport, facilities and supplies, army staffs were reluctant to grant allocations to units that might not produce effective results for months. This was particularly true in the early days of invasion with ship-loading space at a premium.

For OSS it was important to land at a beachhead at least with army headquarters, principally: (1) To exploit the early confusion of landing, for the infiltration of agents through enemy lines; (2) to contact friendly resistance groups for information and as an immediate source of reliable recruits; (3) to recruit from among overrun civilians or military casuals; and (4) to detect potentially dangerous overrun enemy agents or sympathizers. In Italy this importance was heightened by uncertainty over the extent of the effect of Italy's collapse on the German position in southern Europe.

In both the Sicilian and the subsequent Italian invasion, the absence of a clear directive from AFHQ to the army concerned made it necessary for OSS to sell itself directly to the field commander at the beachhead, by commitments of tactical and combat intelligence, and by undertaking or improvising any other services possible in direct support of immediate military operations. In this respect, the OSS unit at Fifth Army Headquarters in North Africa was fortunate in gaining the active support of General Clark, and landed on D-Day both at Salerno and Anzio. Special Detachment (OSS), G-2, Fifth Army could thus, through the long Italian campaign, develop for the first time the functions and techniques of an OSS unit supporting ground armies.

Fifth Army Preparations

Donovan conferred with General Clark and his G-2, Colonel Howard, at Fifth Army Headquarters in Morocco, late in July 1943, on his way back to Washington from the Sicilian landings. Clark expressed appreciation of the counter-espionage work that the OSS Detachment with Fifth Army had

---

* See "Tunisia" and "West Mediterranean Islands," above.

** See "Bern," below.

done on the Spanish Moroccan border,* and Donovan offered to place OSS resources at Fifth Army disposal for the Italian invasion. For this, the functions of the Detachment would be expanded by adding five operations specialists and research experts for tactical and strategic intelligence procurement. Furthermore, the Detachment would be put on a full military basis headed by a commissioned officer.

As reconstituted for the invasion of Italy, the OSS Special Detachment, G-2, Fifth Army was built around a nucleus of Americans who had lived, worked or studied in Europe and were fluent in one or more of French, Italian, German and Spanish. Two SI/Italy section operations officers were transferred to its staff, and key intelligence and services men from OSS/Algiers were added. American and native Italian personnel, speaking fluent Italian or with standing as radio amateurs, were recruited and trained to serve as agents, radio operators, or in supporting assignments such as clerks and interpreters. Eighteen were secured, with G-3, AFHQ approval, from U. S. Army replacement depots at Oran and Casablanca, when reinforcements from Washington were slowed by tight travel priorities. Loading space for some forty OSS personnel, attached to the invasion forces, was arranged directly with G-2, Fifth Army, with additional personnel to be made available after the end of the Sicilian campaign.

The relative spheres inside Italy of the Fifth Army Detachment and the SI/Italy section were delimited. It was decided that the latter should continue its plans for strategic penetrations from Sicily,** while the former would concentrate on tactical operations in direct support of the invasion. The two activities would serve to complement each other and would, it was planned, join forces after the capture of Naples.

Earliest OSS participation in the Fifth Army's Salerno preparations consisted of

active assistance to CIC. At the Army staging area at Bouzarea near Algiers, the OSS Detachment provided the Army's counter-intelligence staff with badly-needed interpreters from its Italian-speaking personnel. R&A/Algiers supplied comprehensive briefing intelligence on important objectives in the Naples area.

The Detachment was organized, just before D-Day, in cognizance of the integral position OSS would occupy with CIC during the Italian landings. Two advance teams, each with one officer and six agents or enlisted men, were formed and attached to CIC units with VI Corps and with the 36th Division. Another group, consisting of the OSS Detachment chief, an assistant, a radio operator and five agents, stayed at Fifth Army Headquarters. These three Detachment units were to accompany the invasion forces; the Headquarters intelligence officer, the remaining agent personnel and the services staff would follow on D-plus-2.

Organizational alignment with CIC was not interpreted to limit OSS activities to counter-intelligence. The head of the Fifth Army Detachment directed that it "stand ready to recruit, train, brief and infiltrate combat intelligence teams on missions for G-2's or S-2's" and through "contacts with pro-American and anti-Fascist organizations—recruit likely personnel for informers, infiltrators, coup-de-main groups, censorship work, guides, interpreters, translators, recruiters or organization leaders to be subsidized."*

With no organization already inside Italy that could be used as a basis for operations, the Detachment, on short notice, had to start on an assignment whose scope and nature were not yet clear even to topmost Allied echelons. It drew, for knowledge of intelligence operations, on the *TORCH* activities, on missions of counter-espionage conducted along the Spanish Moroccan border, on OSS training, and on the experience of a small

---

* See "Oujda Operations," above.
** See "SI/Italy," below.

* OSS Fifth Army Directive, quoted in field report, History File 179.

number of French officers assigned to the Detachment. Of particular value was a Service de Renseignements (SR) regular who, himself a French agent and operations officer in World War I, had actively assisted in the *TORCH* and Spanish Moroccan activities.

Salerno

The two advance OSS teams landed on D-Day (9 September 1943) near Paestum, and joined forces, as did CIC personnel, upon the convergence of the 36th Division and VI Corps. At first, they worked principally to assist CIC, which itself was engaged in duties not proper to its function. Interrogations of civilians and Italian military casuals were immediately begun for data on enemy concentrations and battle order. Information was reported by courier and OSS radio to division and corps and on to the OSS staff at Army Headquarters. Jointly with CIC, OSS representatives entered liberated towns, inspected and placed under guard municipal structures, and took preliminary steps to assure civil services until Military Government officers could arrive.

OSS teams soon began tactical line-crossing missions for ten- to fifty-mile penetrations, using natives, chiefly members of pro-Allied resistance groups, hired and briefed on the spot. "Most agents were recruited for one job and no more . . . (they) could be sold on going through the lines once or twice but very seldom more than that."* They were paid off and left behind after debriefing.

In the course of placing men through the lines, the team leaders frequently found themselves up to twenty miles ahead of forward American positions. One team entered Agropoli shortly before the scheduled American assault and accepted the "surrender" of the town, while sending back urgent messages that the town was unoccupied by the enemy.

* Field Report, History File 179.

On 15 September, two Americans and sixteen Sicilian recruits were forwarded from the SI/Italy section in Sicily. Operating as three six-man radio-equipped teams, they conducted three reconnaissance missions southward and eastward from the beachhead, to confirm the evacuation of German units above Potenza. One team then headed northward for Avellino, but was caught in an enemy cross-fire which killed two agents and seriously wounded two others. A new team was formed to penetrate Naples. Two agents of this team succeeded in reaching the city but lost communication, since they abandoned their radio to evade German road patrols.

Meanwhile the OSS unit at Fifth Army Headquarters had remained on board the transport as a reserve, to be assigned wherever needed, in view of delays in beachhead operations due to enemy resistance from the north. On D-plus-2 the Detachment leader and his men were ordered to proceed ashore at Maiori on the Sorrentine Peninsula to:

. . . report to Colonel Darby (of the Rangers) and do whatever is necessary for the security of his command, to supply him with combat intelligence and to secure specific information concerning the beaches, enemy strength and positions between Castellammare and Naples.*

The Rangers' sector was cut off from the main beachhead and needed various unavailable supporting services. At Colonel Darby's urgent request, the OSS staff improvised unanticipated functions. It helped to recruit and organize some 400 civilians into labor squads for the unloading of supplies (at fifty lire a day with rations), interrogated refugees for information on battle order and conditions in Italy up to the Swiss border and in Yugoslavia as well, held German agent suspects for CIC investigation, aided in refugee clearance and food distribution, and, in the absence of Military Government officers, helped to establish provisional government under local non-Fascist Italian functionaries.

* Field Report, History File 179.

By the time the Rangers' position was consolidated, the full efforts of the OSS staff in the sector were committed and its available funds virtually exhausted. On D-plus-7 Military Government and CIC officers reached Maiori; but they still needed the OSS unit to assist them with interpreters and guides.

OSS field headquarters were established at nearby Amalfi. Radio contacts were consolidated with the advance teams on the southern flank, with Algiers headquarters and, aided by couriers, with army, corps and division headquarters.

By D-plus-7, OSS units on the mainland, reinforced by new OSS personnel, were conducting up to eighty interrogations daily. Italian Army, Navy and Air Force officers were recruited to assist in the questioning of Italian military casuals. Italians in uniform were still free to circulate behind German lines and much of the information that was produced by these interrogations was unique in its coverage and detail. Among the refugees were Italian resistance leaders, engineers and scientists who gave extensive and authoritative information on conditions inside Naples, on German movements, and on railroads, docks and public utilities being mined or demolished by the Germans.

Naples

Upon establishment of the Salerno beachhead, Naples became the principal Detachment target. The stream of refugees from that city, and from the rest of Italy, grew as German evacuation of the city became imminent. Using fishing boats, many who chose not to risk crossing the lines sailed across the bay to the Islands of Capri, Ischia and Procida. There, all available OSS personnel joined in a general interrogation program.

The original OSS advance units with VI Corps and 36th Division were shifted from the southern flank to Capri, where a temporary Allied PT boat base had been established. In addition to interrogation work on that Island, they set up bases on Ischia and Procida, where they recruited numerous islanders, fishermen and refugees from the mainland, and briefed them for short-range penetration of Naples. A total of five teams were sent into Naples harbor by fishing boats, which also carried arms for Neapolitan patriots to organize guerrilla warfare within the city. Two teams failed to reach the mainland due to machine gun fire from the German shore patrols. Other agents, infiltrated in this manner, had orders to pass southward through the German lines and to report to OSS headquarters on the mainland.

The occupation of Naples began on 1 October. Italian civilians, recruited by OSS, served as guides for several advance patrols of the 82nd Airborne and 36th Divisions and the British 23rd Armored Brigade, as well as Colonel Darby's Rangers. OSS agents and contacts with the Italian resistance movements contributed substantially to the work of CIC and Military Government personnel. Fifth Army Detachment headquarters was moved promptly to Naples, and training, holding and communications areas were requisitioned and established.

Tactical line-crossing infiltrations by the OSS unit on the mainland were carried out and increased in number up to twenty a day. In one two-day period short-range OSS intelligence material provided objectives for nine Air Force bombing missions.

Three days after the 9 September landings at Salerno, a deputy of the Italian resistance movements (combined under the Committee of National Liberation—CLN) who had been in communication with OSS/Switzerland,* crossed the American lines seeking the OSS unit on the beachhead. He delivered significant data on the enemy situation in northern Italy and volunteered to place reliable members of the resistance at the disposal of OSS for infiltration work.

* See "Sub-bases on Swiss and French Borders," below.

68

When Naples was occupied, the Neapolitan resistance leaders offered their services. Members of various political parties volunteered to serve as agents and to supply other reliable recruits. Patriotic Italian officers and men escaped from German-held territory to join Allied forces. Aside from these, key industrialists from among Italy's largest manufacturing enterprises also appeared as volunteers. One in particular was still active in his corporation and carried a "laissez-passer" from the top German military echelon in Italy. Under code name "Carlo," he became one of the key OSS agents.

An Italian general of the illustrious Garibaldi family crossed the lines and contacted the OSS officer operating with the Fifth Army. Because of his name, it was decided to enlist his services. Previous experience * discouraged any thoughts of establishing a "Garibaldi Legion" as the general desired, but he did prove valuable in recruiting high-calibre Italians for penetrations through the lines, particularly for Anzio and Rome.

Problems of security and selection were met by improvisation. Italians who were recommended by the resistance movements were recruited with little further questioning. The resistance leaders' acceptance of responsibility for an individual, and his own willingness to undertake a mission regardless of dangers involved, were judged sufficient evidence of security, since it was impossible at that time to check adequately all individuals on the spot. As for dealing with conflicting elements outside the combined resistance movement, individual OSS operations officers followed all approaches regardless of political position—from ultra-con-

servative business interests to the well-organized Italian Communist Party—to obtain as complete intelligence coverage as possible.

Up to Naples, the Fifth Army Detachment effort had been scattered. While individual items of significant tactical intelligence had been passed on to the Army, the Detachment was repeatedly diverted to direct services for unit commanders, such as securing billets or supplies, bolstering security or Military Government staffs lacking in Italian-speaking personnel, and general interpreting and liaison details. Furthermore, no rigid distinction between the functions of personnel originally assigned to various OSS branches had been possible.

With the increased urgency of operations into northern parts of Italy and the Rome region prior to Anzio, the Fifth Army Detachment was reorganized along more functional lines, and all possible means of clandestine transport for agent infiltration explored. By 1 December, the Detachment, with headquarters at Caserta, was realigned into an intelligence staff and an operations section. The intelligence staff exploited contacts already built up with Italian political parties and armed forces in Rome and elsewhere, and recruited and trained locally obtained agents and refugees from occupied areas for new missions. The operations section recruited also, and arranged for the transport and supply of agent teams. Two forward echelons were formed—one for operations on the Fifth Army front,* the other to accompany the invasion being planned for Anzio.

Anzio

The OSS Anzio unit, consisting of two officers and two enlisted men, landed with the Rangers on 22 January 1944. It made radio contact with OSS headquarters at Caserta for the relay of intelligence to G-2 on the

---

* Upon the invasion of continental Italy and the fall of the Fascist Government, OSS had attempted to form "operational nuclei" of Italians under General Pavone. It was planned that, following training, they would enter enemy territory to organize and direct resistance groups. Lack of morale and initiative soon discouraged the attempt, and OSS subsequently used SO and OG personnel to accomplish the objectives.

---

* See sub-section on "Rome," below.

beachhead, and with OSS agents and station VITTORIA in Rome.*

Messages from VITTORIA were decoded and passed to G-2 on the beachhead as soon as they were received. Since one of the sources was an Italian "liaison officer" in Kesselring's headquarters, much of the information from VITTORIA was of great value in supplying data on the movement of German troops. Through the station, for example, came first word of the arrival of an infantry regiment stated to be the initial reinforcement of German forces facing the beachhead.

Subsequently, and until it went off the air in mid-March, VITTORIA gave regular explicit details on German road and rail movements in the Rome area, together with German unit insignia observed.

Perhaps the most significant item of information produced was the report, early in March, that the enemy planned a diversionary feint from Cisterna, prior to a heavy armored attack downward from Albano. Based largely on this information and subsequent confirmatory reports, an American armored regiment was moved from one sector of the beachhead to another. Two agents, dispatched independently on tactical infiltrations from the beachhead, returned after three days behind enemy lines and confirmed German preparations for the armored assault. Due to the timely move by the armored regiment, the German attack lost its advantage of surprise.

Twenty-two successful tactical intelligence missions through the lines were completed from Anzio by OSS/Fifth Army Detachment. The agents were, for the most part, ex-Italian officers with anti-Fascist records; others were members of the Italian San Marco (Marine) and Nembo (Parachutist) Battalions. Agents were kept at the OSS headquarters at Anzio, in an old fortress surrounded by a moat and heavily guarded. Most were sent on only one trip behind the

---

* See sub-section on "Rome," below.

lines, although two agents went on three missions each. Upon their return, they were sent to Caserta for rest.

The head of the OSS/Anzio unit attended regular conferences with G-2, VI Corps, and received specific day-to-day requests for information to be used as intelligence directives for briefing. On the first mission through the lines, the agent came back in forty-eight hours with information which indicated that four battalions, as well as tanks of the Hermann Goering Division, were being removed from Cisterna.

One agent, a former sergeant of the Italian San Marco Battalion, was seriously wounded, upon his return through the lines, by an American soldier on front-line guard duty. He was not picked up until dawn and, upon being brought to the field hospital, insisted on reporting to the OSS commanding officer before receiving extensive treatment. Periodically revived by injections of plasma, he gave a report and a rough but accurate plan of German fortifications at Littoria. A few days later, prior to evacuation to the American general hospital in Naples, he repeated his information, but by this time American dive bombers had already knocked out the enemy guns.

In April, a team of two men was sent, at the request of G-2, through the lines toward Cisterna and Cori, to report on soil conditions in order to ascertain the feasibility of using tanks and armored vehicles in the sector. The American attack that finally broke out of the beachhead followed the route surveyed by these agents.

Rome

The Fifth Army, following the occupation of Naples, gave top priority to the Rome area, and expressed additional interest in the development of intelligence sources as far north as the Swiss and Yugoslav borders. With these requests, and in view of the unprecedented opportunities for recruiting and penetration afforded the Fifth Army Detachment on the Salerno beachhead and in Na-

70

ples by the aftermath of the Italian collapse, Donovan directed that primary attention be given to placing agents in Rome, and that contacts be initiated wherever else possible within Fifth Army's field of interest. SI/ Italy meanwhile would concentrate on northern Italy.

The first strategic intelligence team was dispatched by Fifth Army Detachment across the lines on 12 October. Its target was Rome and it consisted of: "Coniglio," one of the leaders of the Neapolitan resistance; "Cervo," who had just arrived from Rome, where he had been a junior officer on the Italian General Staff and had served as Assistant Military Attache and on the Italian-German Armistice Commission; "Corvo," another leader of the Neapolitan resistance; two other officers; and a radio operator. "Coniglio", head of the team, was instructed: (1) To develop an informant service in the Italian capital; (2) to arrange for the reception of supplies and radio equipment for resistance in central Italy; and (3) to dispatch other agents and sub-agents with radio sets from Rome into northern Italy. "Cervo" had the additional assignment of finding and evacuating a certain Italian scientist and inventor.* Two men accompanied "Coniglio" across the lines on 12 October 1943; the others followed four days later.

On 17 October several high-ranking Italian naval staff officers and "Carlo", a prominent industrialist, arrived in Naples, after crossing American lines, and supplied extensive up-to-date military and economic information on northern Italy. "Carlo" immediately volunteered to return to Rome to build up a network of agents, and, after intensive briefing, was dispatched across the lines on 1 November, accompanied by two other agents and a young woman trained as a radio operator. After a successful crossing of the lines, "Carlo" was wounded by a German land mine. He dispatched one

* He was successful. See Washington section on Special Projects.

agent back to OSS headquarters at Naples, while the other agent and the radio operator proceeded to Rome. He himself was picked up by the Germans. But his knowledge of their language was sufficient to convince them, and he was carried to a hospital and given the usual first aid. During the night he escaped from the hospital, despite his wounds, and hitchhiked to Rome on a German truck. When he arrived in the capital, a friend hid and cared for him. He recovered after twenty-two days in bed, and contacted "Coniglio."

Aided by "Carlo's" acquaintances, "Coniglio" succeeded in reaching the leaders of the major political parties—Socialist, Communist, Social Democrat and Partito d'Azione— and the senior general of SIM* in German-occupied Italy. "Coniglio", however, was unable to communicate by radio with the OSS base station. It had not been possible to train his radio operator adequately in Naples, prior to crossing the lines, so that the latter was unaccustomed to the SSTR-1. A local radio technician was called in to assist but was likewise unable to make contact. "Corvo", therefore, was dispatched overland to Naples to report and to deliver the information already procured. He reached OSS headquarters on 27 November. After his departure it was found that an insufficient aerial had been used for transmitting. This defect was remedied, and from then on radio VITTORIA in Rome operated without difficulty until its capture in March 1944. By the time the front became stabilized in November 1943, initial contacts in Rome had been established, as well as a reliable means of communicating intelligence from that city to OSS and military bases farther south.

A mass exfiltration mission from Italy was carried out for the first time in January 1944. Late in December, radio VITTORIA had requested that a sea pick-up be arranged on the west coast where a safe landing point had been found near Fossa del Tafone.

* Italian Military Intelligence.

"Coniglio" and "Corvo" wished to report in person on their position and capabilities and receive instructions for further operations. Furthermore, the Italian scientist, found by "Cervo" through Italian naval intelligence channels, had to be exfiltrated. The landing point was out of range for Naples-based surface craft, and an urgent radio message was sent to the OSS advance base in Bastia, Corsica, on 31 December requesting that pick-up be made from there. Two evenings later, a U. S. PT boat from Corsica reached the pinpoint, successfully exfiltrated "Coniglio", "Carlo", the scientist; three Italian naval intelligence officers and the SIM general, all of whom were dispatched immediately to Naples by air. This operation, called RICHMOND I, was the first of a series of clandestine maritime landings successfully run for Fifth Army Detachment by OSS/Corsica.*

OSS preparations in Rome for the liberation, which was expected to come with the landings at Anzio, were made by "Pietro", a young American foreign correspondent fluent in Italian, especially recruited for the mission by General Donovan. His specific orders were to contact OSS radio VITTORIA, act as intelligence officer for the Fifth Army in Rome and give the signal for sabotage and counter-sabotage measures to coincide with the Allied landings at Anzio.

"Pietro" was landed from Corsica at the Fossa del Tafone pinpoint, on the night of 21 January, along with four other agents and a radio operator assigned to the Milan area. Exfiltrated on the same mission were several agents returning to the base and one Allied prisoner of war. In addition, there were three political leaders from the Rome underground movements, on their way to urge unity of all Italian resistance at a meeting to be held in Bari at the end of January.

"Pietro" was brought to Rome, where he immediately conferred with "Coniglio" and representatives of resistance groups from a

part of the Central Committee of the CLN. At the meetings, "Pietro" relayed the instructions of the Allied commander and alerted all groups to preparedness for an uprising in support of Allied landings at Anzio.

The five-month stalemate of the Allies at the beachhead necessitated postponement of OSS plans. The groups which "Pietro" had alerted for resistance and sabotage were transformed in February and March into a series of comprehensive intelligence networks regularly reporting specific details on the movements of German units, armor, equipment, etc. in the Rome area and to and from the Anzio beachhead. Among the sources of information tapped were the various political parties, industrialists and leading Roman citizens still enjoying German confidence, and officers on the "Open City of Rome" staff, including one actually assigned to Kesselring's headquarters.

Elaborate precautions were taken to maintain the security of both VITTORIA and a second clandestine radio transmitter, which had been set up to handle the heavy flow of traffic between "Coniglio's" and "Pietro's" agents in Rome and the armies on the Anzio beachhead. Nevertheless, in March 1944, security of the OSS stations was blown and their sole means for secret wireless traffic from Rome severed.

On 13 March the VITTORIA operator encountered by chance the same local radio technician who had been consulted in October 1943 when the station was established.* This man had subsequently entered the pay of the Germans as a spy on resistance activity in Rome. "Cervo", in charge of finding safe houses for radios, at once ordered the VITTORIA operator to hide and, with an orderly, set out to change the location of both OSS stations. By the time he reached the houseboat where one station was located, the VITTORIA operator had been denounced to the Germans by the technician-

* See "Corsica Operations," below.

* See above.

spy and had, under pressure, revealed "Cervo's" identity. Despite five days of torture, "Cervo", who knew virtually all OSS agents in Rome, revealed no single detail. He was shot by the Germans on 23 March, along with 320 other Italians, at the Ardeatine Caves, in reprisal for the attack on a German police truck in the streets of Rome. The capture of "Cervo", who managed both radio stations, cut off direct communication between Rome agents and OSS, but the remainder of the agents were still safe.

The problems of hiding against the threat of further denunciations, reestablishing intelligence chains, and reopening contact with the base were further complicated by the overlapping jurisdictions of "Coniglio" and "Pietro". "Coniglio" had received no briefing from his base about "Pietro's" mission or his status. "Pietro", on the other hand, had not been instructed that "Coniglio" was "chief OSS clandestine agent in Italy." The need for security precautions prevented their meeting in person often enough to discuss conflicting points, and communication between them was carried on only through messengers and cut-outs. After VITTORIA's capture, they found separate means of relaying intelligence. "Pietro" contacted a British SIS circuit in the area being operated by two Italians. Unfortunately, the SIS receiving base in southern Italy did not relay "Pietro's" messages to OSS/Naples until they were over a month old. "Coniglio" sent his intelligence on events in Rome by courier northward, for relay by other OSS radios in northern Italy.*

On 27 April another team was dispatched to Rome to contact agents there. The team, consisting of an agent and two radio operators, was landed on the Adriatic coast by the British. The agent utilized a forged pass, "signed" by a high-ranking German Organization Todt officer, which he presented to the German commander at Ascoli. He was immediately given a German staff car, and he and his two operators were driven safely to

* See next section.

Rome. In his briefing he had been ordered to take control of radios which, he was told, were already in Rome. · When he finally contacted "Coniglio" and learned that there was no means of direct communication, he joined with "Coniglio" in reorganizing information services, dispatching messages by courier to an OSS radio in Milan,

Friction between agents in Rome, resulting from insufficient coordination and control by OSS operations officers, had prevented the evolution of a long-range intelligence organization from a tactical mission in support of a military operation. The initiative for action inside Rome was placed in the hands of agents themselves rather than retained by operations officers at the base. The latter were inadequately informed on conditions inside Rome after the Anzio landing failed to drive the Germans from the city. Thus the officers responsible for the operations did not know the facilities and resources of the teams inside the city. When contact was lost, the agents were forced to look to sympathizers inside Rome for funds and support. Several prominent Italians virtually liquidated their fortunes to make sufficient funds available to the OSS agents.*

To contact the agents in Rome and the CLN Committee headquarters there, a radio-equipped team led by an Italian professor, a key figure in the Communist organization in Rome, was dispatched. The professor volunteered to parachute, but because of his advanced age (53) and a bad knee condition, was not allowed to take any practice jumps. He and two radio operators were parachuted in the vicinity of Tivoli, in two feet of snow. Although they landed safely, they were dropped forty miles off pinpoint and lost their radios and most of their other equipment in the snow. They reported their

* In July 1944, Donovan ordered a special committee to investigate the circumstances of the Rome operations as well as to liquidate the financial claims arising from the agents' activities.

condition by carrier pigeons which were dropped with them. Despite these difficulties, they succeeded in contacting the CLN in Rome, but only shortly before the liberation of the city.

Meanwhile, OSS agents there had passed to the Anzio and other fronts intelligence of considerable value, and had succeeded in organizing patriot forces in Rome into secret brigades for the prevention of German "scorched earth" programs. As a result, when the Allies finally broke out of the beachhead and the Germans evacuated Rome on 6 June 1944, the major electric and telephone centrals were maintained intact and one of Rome's radio stations preserved from destruction.

C. EARLY INFILTRATIONS OF NORTH ITALY

The nine months from the occupation of Naples until the capture of Rome in June 1944 were a developmental period for OSS in Italy. Strategic infiltrations were begun, and the first teams were placed in central and northern Italy. By parachute, PT boat and submarine, or by direct penetration of the front lines, agents, radio operators and supplies were delivered deep into enemy-held territory. Intelligence was received in steadily increasing volume, reliability and detail. Close liaisons were established with the principal centers of Italian resistance throughout occupied Italy and their activities progressively coordinated with the operations of the Allied Armies in Italy. Recruits, for both intelligence and sabotage work, were procured from resistance groups and from volunteers both in liberated territory and behind the lines. AFHQ, the armies in the field, the air forces and naval headquarters all became customers of OSS intelligence and research activities.

This was also a reorganization period for OSS/Italy. As the agency became steadily more integrated into the military organization of the Theater, it also reflected the duality of authority existent in the Theater hierarchy. Allied Force Headquarters itself had direct control of all areas not in the immediate zone of combat, including northern Italy, as well as Corsica, Sardinia and Sicily. 15th Army Group regarded all of Italy as under its authority. Fifth Army, a part of 15th Army Group, required and requested strategic intelligence and operations covering areas far ahead of its front lines and well into AFHQ territory, even up to the Brenner Pass. Within OSS, the SI/Italy section, based at Palermo and reporting to AFHQ, found itself overlapping strategic intelligence work undertaken by Fifth Army Detachment, particularly in air lift, clandes-tine transportation, liaison with Italian and British authorities, and recruiting. At the same time, the OSS advance base in Corsica was assigned operations by AFHQ into central and northern Italy independent of Fifth Army operations.

The OSS program called for both SI development of intelligence chains, and SO strengthening of resistance movements and accomplishment of specific sabotage operations. As a result, all bases undertook both types of activity indiscriminately. Not until June 1944 were the early agent chains coordinated under Company D (OSS) at 15th Army Group.*

1. From Fifth Army

During November and December 1943, concurrent with its overland operations, Fifth Army Detachment established liaison with the Allied air forces at Brindisi, to obtain air lift during light moon periods (most favorable to parachutage) and maritime transportation during dark moon periods. Due to the difficulty of obtaining clearances for clandestine shipping activity, contact was made through American liaison officers with the Italian Naval Ministry at Brindisi, and approvals were finally received to use an Italian submarine, the "Axum", based in Brindisi. With transport thus assured, operations and intelligence officers of the Detachment could plan for long-range infiltration and exfiltration missions in the Rome area and in North Italy.

Only two line-crossing missions north of Rome had been carried out—on 22 October and 2 December—to contact resistance groups in Florence and Milan. On 5 December, by means of the "Axum", a total of six-

---

* See "Bases in Italy," below.

teen agents and radio operators were landed on the Adriatic coast at Castel di Mezzo for missions in Rome, Ravenna, Genoa and Florence. Throughout December attempts were made to send additional radios to the agents by air and by sea, but the constant unfavorable weather prevented further long-range operations until 1944.

Early in January "Coniglio" in Rome* was designated chief of OSS/Fifth Army agents in German-occupied Italy. He was instructed to establish new radio stations in Rieti, Perugia, Florence and Milan, and to intensify his reporting of German order of battle and military movements, as well as to maintain liaison with Italian political parties in Rome. Upon further briefing, he and "Carlo" were supplied with nine radio sets and ten million lire (credited to the account of "Carlo's" company in Naples for use in enemy-occupied Italy). Along with four other agents, including a young woman, "Vera", who was assigned to the Florence region, they were landed without incident on the night of 17 January in the RICHMOND II operation by PT boat from Corsica.

Typical of these early Fifth Army missions were CASSANO, MARIA GIOVANNA and NADA, dispatched during December 1943 and January 1944.

CASSANO was originally briefed to join a resistance movement reported in the Valle di Comacchio of the Ravenna region. When the team reached Ravenna, it learned that the resistance had been mopped up by the Germans. Reporting this to base, CASSANO was ordered to Venice to establish an intelligence service in that city, from which it transmitted successfully from the beginning of the year until May. On 1 May four more agents, with supplies, were sent to the team by submarine. The landing took place at Cortelazzo near Venice, just as a Fascist patrol passed on the coast. Of the agents who had been landed, two were killed and two others captured, who, under inter-

rogation, revealed the details of the operation. The Germans attacked the original CASSANO team, killing an agent, a native assistant and a civilian passer-by. The radio operator escaped, hid his radio and ciphers, walked to the Anzio beachhead and crossed safely into American lines on 31 May.

The MARIA GIOVANNA team, headed by agent "Corvo", reached Genoa late in December. It transmitted successfully until the middle of February 1944, when it was instructed to prepare for Corsica operations RICHMOND IV and V to take place on the Ligurian coast. The team was ordered to the pinpoint to maintain an hour-by-hour contact at the beach and to act as reception committee for the landing. At the gate of the Genoa railroad station, the customs officer insisted on inspecting the suitcase containing the team's radio set. "Corvo" took the suitcase out of the hands of the radio operator and told him to escape, shot the guard and himself managed to escape over a fence into a crowd. He was forced to abandon the radio set, but sent an urgent message over another radio circuit to cancel the RICHMOND operation. Another radio was parachuted to him at a pinpoint north of Venice, which enabled his team to continue coverage of German convoys and ship movements from Genoa. In mid-September 1944, the operator and an agent of team MARIA GIOVANNA were surprised and captured by the Germans. "Corvo" was away, but his assistant and the operator were presumably killed, and the Germans took over the radio as a deception. Handling of this enemy-controlled station was turned over to X-2 officers and maintained by OSS until March 1945.*

The key member of NADA was a woman, agent "Vera". "Vera" carried a radio set in a suitcase, on a 200-mile rail trip, to the leader of the Tuscan resistance movement. She then established contact with guerrilla

* See "Fifth Army Detachment," above.

* See "X-2/Italy," below.

groups in the Spezia area and with the CLN in Florence. Through her efforts, 65 supply operations by parachute were arranged.

One of her radio operators was found untrustworthy, since he was living with a German chorus girl in the pay of the SS and had been seen boasting in public about his radio work and his cipher plan. Members of the resistance in the neighborhood abducted and executed him.

On 2 July a group of German SS men broke into the room where "Vera" and her radio operator were making contact with the OSS base. The major was wounded, and two Germans were killed by hand grenades thrown by "Vera", who succeeded in destroying the radio and escaping out of a window with the operator. They joined a patriot group a few miles outside of Florence and, within eight days, found means of reopening communications with OSS. By September "Vera", a price on her head, was obliged to escape. She crossed into American lines during an artillery battle.

An especially effective network was developed by a key agent for the Milan region who landed from Corsica in late January 1944, carrying papers prepared for him by OSS and "signed" by a German general. In Milan he built up a large network of industrial and resistance contacts extending throughout North Italy. Forty-seven sub-agents reported to him at various times. On 20 May German SS troops raided the apartment in which he and an agent were operating. Armed with Sten guns, the two men resisted capture throughout the evening and into the morning, reportedly killing over thirty Germans. In the morning, out of ammunition, they leaped from the roof of the apartment house to commit suicide. The agent was killed and the radio operator survived, although seriously injured. Another agent, "Como", a Milanese doctor who had witnessed the gun fight, secured the crystals and papers in the apartment, hid the radio and escaped into Switzerland to report and

to maintain contact with the resistance movements.*

In addition to such intelligence operations from Fifth Army, a sabotage team was parachuted north of Rome to attempt interruption of communications between Rome and Florence. The team, dropped from British planes on 13 March 1944, consisted of one officer and twelve men recruited from the Italian Nembo (Parachutist) Battalion. Poor landing conditions scattered the team and equipment over a stretch of several miles, and some of the men were injured.

By the following morning, however, much of the demolitions equipment had been recovered, and on 17 March the team set out to cut the rail line between Terni and Perugia. It was attacked by a German patrol in the village of Appennino. Several of the men were killed and wounded, while the officer was captured by the Germans and shot on the spot. A few managed to escape. According to pre-arranged plan, another radio was dropped to them, but unfortunately was broken in landing. The remainder of the team dispersed and was finally overrun in June.

Concurrent with these long-range penetrations from Fifth Army, two other units were carrying out similar operations on a smaller scale—OSS/Corsica and SI/Italy.

2. Corsica Operations

Upon its liberation early in October 1943,** Corsica was the northernmost Allied salient toward southern Europe, and became an important OSS advance base. It served as headquarters for the OG/Italy unit, as a dispatching station for SI operations into central and northern Italy and southern France, and as a forward field communications base.***

* In September 1944 "Como" became one of the leaders of the Val d'Ossola uprising. See "Italian Resistance," below.
** See "West Mediterranean Islands," above.
*** See "Algiers Base," below.

OSS headquarters were established at Bastia, the northeast Corsican seaport, 35 miles from the Italian mainland, and approximately 90 miles from the strategic Ligurian coast. Administration and communications headquarters, as well as the OG training and staging area, were located at Ile Rousse, while a supply center was maintained at Ajaccio.

Corsica served primarily as a maritime rather than as an air base. American PT's of Squadron 15 and a flotilla of British motor gun-boats and motor launches of the African Coastal Forces moved up from Sardinia and had begun to operate out of Bastia by the end of October, both for naval sorties and for clandestine operations. In addition, a flotilla of five Italian MAS boats, manned by volunteer Italian crews from Maddalena, was also made available for the latter. Although the Italian boats* had the advantages of low silhouette, high speed (up to fifty knots) and special auxiliary engines to permit silent maneuvering off pinpoints, the American PT's were used for the majority of operations. The radar of the American boats was important for defense and navigation, and their range made it possible to reach as far west as Toulon and as far south as the Tiber River.**

British SIS and SOE and the French services also opened advance operating stations in Bastia. Close coordination between the intelligence organizations was essential to prevent dangerous overlapping of pinpoints or sorties, and to plan and schedule future operations. The British senior naval officer, in command of naval forces, accepted and encouraged clandestine maritime oper-

* They were withdrawn from clandestine work in March 1944, after the crew of one boat had mutinied in the course of a joint British-French mission, killed the British and French officers and agent personnel, as well as their own officers, and sailed into an enemy-held port.

** OSS had no maritime craft or personnel of its own in the Western Mediterranean until March 1944. SI and OG officers in Corsica shared maritime operations responsibilities.

ations, and established a procedure for determining sea transport priorities between the various organizations. In addition, a joint Intelligence Pool was organized by OSS and other services to centralize and make available all operational intelligence relevant to clandestine maritime activities, and to plan details of individual operations.

A chain of observation posts was projected on islands off the Italian coast, astride the German shipping lanes, to report enemy sea and air activity. Coastal shipping was particularly important to the Germans, due to the constant interruption of land supply routes by Allied air attack.

The first operation took place two weeks after the liberation of Corsica. On the night of 16 October 1943, twelve OG's landed on the island of Capraia, north of Elba, from a British minesweeper, the only craft then available. The landing was unopposed, and the OG's remained to establish an observation post in the former Italian naval semaphore station atop the Island. Direct radio contact was maintained with OSS/Bastia. A "crack" code* permitted rapid reporting of observations to Bastia, where a direct private telephone line made possible instant relay of information from OSS headquarters to the Allied Forces War Room. Regular supply missions from Corsica maintained the garrison and rotated OG personnel.

The second post was established on the night of 8 December, when nine OG's landed unopposed on the Island of Gorgona, twenty miles off shore from Livorno. A high-powered telescope afforded direct observation of enemy port and shipping activities in Livorno. For example, considerable activity was reported at large fuel storage tanks in the harbor, believed by the Air Force to be unused. Results of successful Air Force attacks on the tanks were re-

* Using a series of letter symbols to indicate weather and shipping developments.

ported by "O.P.#1"* within two hours of the subsequent raids.

Enemy plane spotting from the O.P.'s was particularly important for the security of Allied airfields on Corsica, making it impossible for enemy pilots to take advantage of the islands as a screen against Allied radar on Corsica.** In addition, weather reports covering sea, precipitation, visibility, wind direction and velocity were sent at least three times daily.

A third observation post was established on the German-held island of Elba at direct AFHQ request. In December an SI team was clandestinely infiltrated and maintained on the summit of Mount Cappane, the westernmost peak on Elba, overlooking the harbor of Porto Ferraio. Reports were sent by line-of-sight radio direct to Bastia, and covered not only ship movements but conditions on the Island. The team was detected by the Germans after six weeks but was successfully withdrawn on 1 February.

The O.P.'s were raided repeatedly by German assault groups and strafed by enemy planes. Off Capraia, a MAS boat bringing new equipment was sunk by mines planted within the harbor during a German attack of 20 February 1944. A strong German force overwhelmed the small garrison on Gorgona on 27 March, but withdrew after destroying the semaphore station. OSS casualties were two killed and three wounded. The O.P. was abandoned but soon ordered reoccupied at AFHQ request and maintained until after the Allied capture of Elba in June.

Reconnaissance and small-scale attacks on coastal installations were carried out by

OG units. In October, November and December, a series of feints were ordered by G-3, AFHQ to draw fire from enemy coastal defenses and to simulate commando landings along the Italian coast south of Livorno, in order to give the impression of Allied interest in the region. Three such operations were completed between 28 October and 5 December.

In an attack on the coastal highway near Castiglioncello on 2 January, eight operatives blew a stone bridge near the shore. Air reconnaissance the next day showed the bridge damaged and probably unsafe for traffic.

An American pilot was forced down on the Island of Pianosa later that month. Two OG reconnaissances explored the northern tip of the Island, and a joint OG-French raiding group of 150 men overran the bulk of the Island in a night attack in March, capturing prisoners (not including the pilot) before withdrawing.

A final amphibious raid by an entire OG section in late March 1944 was the GINNY mission, ordered as part of Operation *STRANGLE* * to cut the coastal rail line south of Spezia. GINNY, consisting of fifteen operatives, was landed successfully, but the passage of German coastwise convoys forced the PT's to leave the pinpoint. The difficulty of the terrain delayed the mission, and it was discovered and captured by the Germans the next day. After "special" interrogation,** all were shot, even though they were in uniform and prisoners of war.***

Meanwhile SI/Corsica placed five strategic intelligence teams in northern Italy, principally in the Genoa-Spezia-Milan area.

---

* The Observation Posts were designated numerically from north to south: Gorgona "O.P.#1", Capraia "O.P.#2", Elba "O.P.#3".

** Planes on Bastia/Borga airfield could be dispersed or in the air five minutes after an alarm from O.P.#2 (Capraia), itself about five minutes flying time from Corsica. No radar was placed at the O.P.'s, due to lack of sufficient equipment or personnel for adequate protection from attack by air or sea.

---

* See "R&A/Italy," below.

** They revealed details on OSS explosives and training methods, and on the Allied military position in Corsica.

*** German General Dostler, directly responsible for the shooting order, was tried, convicted as a war criminal, and executed in 1946.

These were in addition to "O.P.#3" maintained on Elba, and a second mission on Elba shortly before the Allied attack on the Island.

The small staff on Corsica was supplemented by personnel from SI/Italy, and, after December 1943, liaison was maintained with both the SI/Italy section and the OSS Fifth Army Detachment.

The most active team, YOUNGSTOWN, was landed on 18 February. It consisted of an Italian officer and radio operator, who for seven weeks transmitted data on enemy shipping movements in the harbor of Genoa and details of German convoy procedure. The team had been landed with insufficient funds,* and seven attempts to land more money for it failed. The Italian officer was captured but succeeded in escaping.**

In April AFHQ sent a high priority directive to secure fresh intelligence on Elba preparatory to the French invasion of the Island. The leader of the original "O. P. #3" was re-infiltrated. His communications failed, as did three SI attempts under fire to rescue him. Although pursued by the Germans, he succeeded in observing installations and disposition on the Island and managed to escape by stealing a boat and rowing back the 30 miles to Corsica.

SI infiltration operations were carried out both for the SI/France Desk in Algiers and for the Fifth Army Detachment (subsequently OSS/AAI) in Italy. Corsica provided an excellent recruiting ground for native personnel to be dispatched to France and for Italian military personnel available from Italian units remaining in Corsica or stationed in Sardinia. Several successful maritime operations in southern France were completed in winter and spring

of 1943-44, at a time when continuously unfavorable weather conditions had grounded all air lift from Algiers for a stretch of four months. The first entailed a successful landing of two agents near Cap Camarat on 29 December. Among the last operations, in June, two agents, who had been successfully landed, radioed from their pinpoint that barbed wire and mines made it impossible for them to leave the beach without detection. They were recovered by a second maritime operation five days later.

Between January and May a series of landing operations, designated RICHMOND, were successfully conducted in support of OSS/Italy. More than thirty agents were exfiltrated and over fifteen others successfully infiltrated in a series of trips to a pinpoint north of Civitavecchia. Many of the agents subsequently operated in Rome * while others had assignments in various parts of North Italy.**

By March 1944 X-2 was added to the branches represented in Corsica, and not only assisted in protecting the security of OSS operations but collaborated with French services and American CIC in general counter-intelligence activities. Security and Special Funds, as well as Services, completed the staff in 1944.

In May and June the advance of the Allied armies in Italy and the capture of the Island of Elba sharply restricted the coast available for clandestine landings. Upon establishment of German radar installations along the Italian shore and concentration of the area covered by fast German E-boat and corvette patrols, operations became progressively more difficult. German precautions along the southern coast of France increased following the Normandy invasion. At the end of the June moon period maritime operations from Corsica were discontinued. OG headquarters moved to the Italian mainland, and the control of agent chains in northern Italy was transferred to Company

---

* In line with an economy move by the OSS/Corsica Executive Officer, and despite the protests of the SI operations staff.

** He managed to cross the French-Italian border to be overrun in the Seventh Army advance. He was subsequently dispatched on a second successful mission to the Genoa area.

---

* See "Fifth Army Detachment," above.
** See previous and following sections.

D.* By October 1944 liquidation of the remaining OSS/Corsica activities was complete.

3. SI/Italy

While the Fifth Army Detachment landed at Salerno and Anzio to dispatch short-range missions in direct support of the ground armies,** SI/Italy was directed to mount long-range operations from bases in South Italy.

In Sicily, SI/Italy had organized few through-the-lines missions and had dispatched an unsuccessful team to Sardinia. Subsequently, it committed all of its personnel to assisting occupation forces in locating enemy agents, documents and equipment, and developing liaison with local political forces such as the renegade Mafia.*** In Italy proper, it continued its political reporting and dispatched several teams, many of which were unsuccessful, to North Italy. As a result of its failures in both fields, it was reorganized in July 1944 during the general organization of OSS bases in Italy at that time.

AGENT TEAMS

Two SI/Italy agents were landed on the Island of Giglio, the night of 1 November, on an operation requested by the PT Commander at Sardinia to establish an observation post for enemy convoys. When after three weeks no signal had been received from the men, they were recovered by PT boats. Their presence on Giglio had been discovered and they had been hiding from German and Italian patrols. For radio communication the team had had only an SSTR-1, with which it had been expected to contact a similar set at the SI base in Maddalena. The SI officers had not ascertained, before the mission, whether two SSTR-1's would be

able to communicate with each other over so great a distance.

After two more months of recruiting and preparation, a series of missions were run by SI/Italy from Brindisi, using Italian submarines or Allied air lift. On 26 January 1944 the first three of these were dispatched by submarine. The PEAR team, consisting of an Italian Air Force officer and a radioman, was assigned to the Venice-Padua-Trevisa region. It reached its objective successfully and contacted the base on 9 February. The other two teams were unsuccessful: one assigned to the Trieste region fell into the custody of the Yugoslav Partisans; the other reached its destination in the Bolzano area but was captured.

On 14 February a team of three men was parachuted into the Udine area. It landed safely, contacting base on 22 February. Transmissions stopped, however, on 12 April, when the team was also taken into custody by Yugoslav Partisans.

On 21 February three additional teams were landed by submarine. RAISIN began to operate from the Bologna area on 19 March. In May this team was instrumental in arranging the recovery of five Allied general officers and an American consular officer who were subsequently ex-filtrated by "A" Force.* The second team was captured by the Germans in a raid, shortly after reaching its destination in the Florence area. The third team, LEMON, made contact on 21 March, but its transmission was irregular. Its signals were carefully watched, and it was subsequently ascertained that the team had been captured and executed, while the radio was being operated by the Germans.

On 16 March three more SI/Italy teams were parachuted successfully. The first, APRICOT, opened liaison with CLNAI headquarters, the central committee of Italian resistance for North Italy. ORANGE consisted of two Italian Air Force officers who

---

* See "Company D," below.
** See "Fifth Army Detachment," above.
*** See "West Mediterranean Islands," above.

---

* British organization for exfiltrating Allied POW's.

landed in the French Italian Alps and began regular contacts on 26 March. The third team consisted of an Italian professor assigned to the Milan area. When the Germans raided his station, he escaped and crossed into Switzerland.

On the night of 23 March three more teams were landed by submarine, assigned to Bologna, Milan and Spezia, respectively.*

Throughout these operations, there was no coordination with OSS/Fifth Army, and a problem developed when Allied Air Force bases in southeastern Italy became the principal dispatching points for air lift of secret missions. Air Force officers soon found themselves coordinating the activities of the SI group and the Fifth Army Detachment, neither of which had any knowledge of the plans of the other.

SI/Italy was preoccupied with maintaining the independence of its operations from any control except that of the distant desk head in Washington. Due to a series of actions which the staff interpreted as interference with its operations by the British, direct contact with AFHQ was avoided insofar as possible.

POLITICAL REPORTING

Meanwhile, as it had in Sicily, SI/Italy again diverted many of its resources to political reporting. When a rump Italian Government under Marshal Badoglio established itself at Brindisi shortly after the Allied landing at Salerno, a small group of officers accompanied an R&A representative to join the Allied Military Mission to the Italian Government. Liaisons were developed with available Italian leaders to obtain such political and economic information on Italy, on the situation inside Germany and on the intentions and capabilities of German military, political and economic leaders, as

*Three months later SI/Italy teams in North Italy were transferred to Company D control. See "Company D," below.

might be available through interrogations of men recently in close relation with high German authorities. R&A obtained some general information, as well as reports on Albania, Yugoslavia and North Africa, and items of technical information on Germany.

SI/Italy established liaison with directors of SIM.* While many of the regional SIM offices had defected to the Germans and the Italian "Republicans", some, including ones in Rome, Bologna and Florence, had gone underground and retained contact with the SIM chiefs who remained with the Badoglio regime. SIM agreed to supply agent recruits to SI, as it was already doing for the British. Few, however, were thus acquired.

It soon became clear that the Italian Government would not be able to move to Rome for an appreciable length of time, and that the interim regime in Brindisi had little to offer in the field of intelligence. By the end of October 1943, only an SI/Italy liaison officer remained stationed in Brindisi with the Italian Government, while other members began to develop contacts with various political groups in liberated Italy.

For this work, SI/Italy suffered several handicaps. It established liaisons with Italian political groups in connection with its principal function, the recruiting and dispatch of clandestine agents into enemy territory. This policy tended to compromise the semi-official atmosphere essential for political reporting. In addition, due to Italian sectionalism, the Sicilian ancestry of several of the SI officers was deprecated by Italian political leaders from central and northern Italy.

Furthermore, informal or semi-official contact with foreign political elements entailed an overt intelligence procurement function, clearly more in the province of trained R&A personnel. Political reports forwarded by SI/Italy might more aptly have been classified as unevaluated propaganda.

* Italian Military Intelligence.

SI/ITALY REORGANIZATION

As part of the general reorganization in July 1944,* several SI/Italy personnel were returned to the United States, and all its missions in enemy-occupied territory were coordinated under SI and SO at Company D (successor to Fifth Army Detachment). In particular, Donovan wished to eliminate the separatism and reluctance to accept control shown by some individuals and units. Several of the operations officers were ordered back to the U. S. for rest and rebriefing.

A Personnel Review Committee dispatched from Washington checked the health and morale of all available personnel, and a series of inspection and review officers toured OSS/MedTO installations. The SI/Italy section was the principal unit investigated. Its personnel, predominantly Sicilian-Americans, had tended to form a clique, reluctant to concede authority to others. Its absorption with political reporting frequently took the men into fields more the province of R&A. It was burdened with "agents" recruited in the United States for Sicily but never used in action.

As a result of Donovan's directive, the functions of the section were reviewed and all its operations ordered closely coordinated with remaining OSS operations. The responsibilities of its chief, who was to report to the chief OSS MedTO Intelligence Officer, were defined to include the handling of reports from its teams already operating and the maintenance of certain specific political intelligence liaisons. Some fifty percent of the section's personnel were returned to the U. S. for reassignment or release.

---

* See next section.

In competition with R&A, the remaining fifty percent continued political reporting from contacts with various factions and from sources inside the Vatican. Throughout the Italian campaign, in fact, there existed a duplication of overt intelligence work by SI and R&A. In addition, the division of functions between the SI staff and the Reports Board became indistinct. After the OSS/MedTO reorganization of July 1944, the staff of SI/Italy took control of the dissemination of political intelligence on Italy. This was due principally to a shortage of Italian-speaking personnel on the Board and the desire for control of disseminations on Italy by the SI section. Its reporting control necessarily compromised its own dissemination, since source evaluation was handled by the same unit actually collecting the information. Also, the SI section processed reports in the same style as secret messages from enemy territory, frequently deleting source identification essential to the proper evaluation of political intelligence. Finally, the distinction between "front-line military intelligence" and "political intelligence", adopted by the SI/-Italy staff, prevented adequate and continual political briefing of the operations officers with the armies, and forced them to divert part of their efforts to keeping themselves posted on Italian political developments.

Fortunately R&A was simultaneously covering the more productive overt sources,* and the Fifth Army Detachment was performing the proper functions of SI.**

---

* See "R&A/Italy," below.
** See "Fifth Army Detachment," above and "Company D," below.

D. BASES IN ITALY

Military echelons, from AFHQ down to corps and division, relied increasingly on OSS for intelligence and operations support. To cope with its new assignments, the agency faced the problem of adapting its organization in Italy. The units improvised for the Salerno landings, and the other groups working separately to plant initial contacts deep in enemy territory, all required centralization. The long-range had become the immediate. Individualistic pioneering needed careful coordination and direction.

The pattern of OSS development in MedTO was virtually the reverse of that in ETO. In London, the need for meticulous planning, liaison and coordination, both with SHAEF and with British and other national counterparts of OSS, had resulted generally in the formation of a large and complete overhead staff which then created a working organization to fit the specific assignments.

In MedTO, small units devoted their full efforts from the beginning to the double task of developing initial penetrations and contacts wherever possible inside enemy-occupied territory, while at the same time establishing themselves with AFHQ and the individual armies and services.

Relations with British counterparts were those of complementary services, independent in their activities. Liaisons were effected as needed by the progress of operations. Subsequently, a staff was superimposed upon the operating section to formalize the liaisons and to channel operations according to Theater directives. After the departure of the original OSS Theater chief in October 1943, succeeding high-echelon personnel, frequently new to OSS, found themselves taking over a functioning organization of progressively experienced field operatives engaged in developing intricate operations on a large scale. They, therefore,

gave the operating sections wide autonomy and served more as high-echelon liaison officers, supporting and facilitating field activities than as actual field commanders.

In May 1944, G-1, NATOUSA proposed that OSS/MedTO be designated a regiment. 2677th Headquarters C o m p a n y (Provisional) G-3, the designation established in 1943, gave insufficient autonomy to OSS in questions of tables of organization, promotion slots and supplies. On 11 May, G-1, NATOUSA recommended that OSS become the 2677th Regiment OSS (Provisional), to be assigned to Headquarters, NATOUSA, with authorization for 476 officers and 1,498 enlisted men, the "strength of this unit . . . *not* chargeable to the theater overhead allotment but . . . chargeable to the Office of Strategic Services . . . suballotted for duty in NATOUSA." Further, "Only personnel certified by the Office of Strategic Services will be assigned to this unit," and promotions, suballotment of personnel to "provisionally organized letter designated companies," could be authorized by the regimental commander. The regimental commander "is authorized to publish orders attaching units, detachments, or individual personnel of the Regiment to other Headquarters or units within this Theater, as approved by the Assistant Chief of Staff, G-3, AFHQ", and "to publish travel orders that do not obligate funds." In addition, he is "authorized to deal directly with the Commanding General, SOS NATOUSA, for the purpose of making arrangements for the local supply of the regiment or elements thereof." *

Donovan approved the proposal, and the designation "Regiment" became effective 23

---

* NATOUSA G-1 Section, 11 May 1944, History File 102.

May, with a Strategic Services Officer, MedTO, as regimental commander.* The final organization and form of the Regiment took shape only after a series of preliminary reorganizations and investigations,** ordered by Donovan to facilitate a smooth and rapid final integration of OSS into the Theater establishment.

An additional decision had to be made within OSS itself with regard to the exact form its Theater organization should take. On the one hand, the various OSS branches in Washington sought to concentrate as far as possible on the specific objectives assigned to them, and resisted the diversion of their personnel in the Theater to activities for OSS in general or for Theater customers alone. On the other hand, the Theater Command considered that no agency under its control should divert its efforts to matters apart from the immediate military situation. To meet Theater requests and priorities, it was essential that the OSS staff be sufficiently flexible to contribute wherever possible, while at the same time following or adapting original branch responsibilities as necessary or as time permitted. Under the regimental organization, the individual branches were represented at regimental headquarters, while indirect support of the army in the field was concentrated in a forward operations section, subsequently designated Company D, to function as a general OSS unit.***

The 2677th Regiment OSS (Provisional)

The Regiment was not activated until July 1944. At that time, AFHQ moved from Algiers to Caserta. Headquarters of the 2677th Regiment OSS (Provisional) was established at the former Fifth Army Detachment base in the palace at San Leucio, near Caserta, with complete responsibility for all OSS operations from the Mediterranean into France,* Italy, the Balkans and the Middle East.**

Intelligence Officer. The Intelligence Officer at Caserta was responsible for SI, R&A, X-2, MO, CD and R&D activities, for coordinating all intelligence activities, for providing intelligence and the appropriate personnel for SO and OG projects, and for planning future activities in accordance with Theater intelligence requirements and Washington plans and directives. By March 1945, the intelligence staff was reorganized into Forward and Rear Sections. The Rear Zone Intelligence Officer maintained direct control of R&A and the Field Photographic Documentation Project (IPDP).*** He shared control over SI and X-2 activities with the Forward Zone Intelligence Officer, whose headquarters were moved to Florence. The latter, in addition to sharing SI and X-2 control, directly controlled MO, R&D and CD. As in London, R&D and CD combined to form one section whose principal function was the preparation of cover material for agents. In March the documentation staff of R&D was transferred to Services.

The Reporting Board,† a part of the SI Branch, was under the Strategic Services Officer and the Chief Intelligence Officer. It entailed a staff of up to fifty researchers and editors, processing and disseminating intelligence reports received from all sources. Items from the field were carefully screened and checked. Evaluations were made for reliability of source and material. The information was edited, all indication of source removed, except for a code name or number designation, and the material disseminated in a standard form to authorized customers.

---

* Hq. NATOUSA, AG 322/310 A-O, 22 May 1944.
** See "Fifth Army Detachment" and "SI/-Italy," above.
*** See "Company D," below.

---

* Transferred to ETO in the fall of 1944. See "West Front," below.
** OSS/Cairo was designated 2791st Provisional Operations and Training Unit.
*** See Washington section Field Photographic.
† Also designated SI Reports Division.

An additional Reports responsibility was periodic consultation with customers, both to obtain evaluations of the significance and form of the information, and to secure direction and recommendations on improving the intelligence coverage or reporting technique.

Much of the material received by the OSS/MedTO headquarters Reporting Board at Caserta emanated from France, either directly or by courier via Madrid or Switzerland. Subsequently, items from the Balkans and Central Europe also arrived to be processed. A large volume of intelligence on all topics was received from OSS/Washington and the field missions or from Allied intelligence agencies for dissemination according to inter-agency agreements.

Military intelligence, and such data as was of immediate and direct value to the armies in the field, was disseminated directly and as rapidly as possible. This included principally information on enemy movements, order of battle, installations and emplacements, and targets for bombing or sabotage. To expedite the handling of such items, Reporting Board officers were stationed with forward detachments as well as at OSS Theater headquarters. Thus the Reporting Board was represented in the original Fifth Army Detachment which landed at Salerno, and, after July 1944, a Reporting Board staff was attached to Company D headquarters. In addition to direct dissemination to armies, corps and sometimes divisions, military information was also reported to AFHQ and Army Group headquarters.

Operations Officer. The Operations and Training Officer was responsible for the activities of SO, MU, Schools and Training, Operational Supply and Field Photographic (before its transfer to Intelligence). His responsibilities included planning and coordinating SO and MU operations, and establishing and maintaining adequate training sections for all types of instruction except communications. With the concentration of the control of actual field operations in Company D, the function of the Operations and Training Officer at Caserta became largely one of liaison.

Operational Groups. The OG's had, by August been organized as the 2671st Special Reconnaissance Battalion Provisional (Separate), with its own headquarters and table of organization. It was felt that, since the OG's in effect constituted tactical military units, they should not be obliged to adapt themselves to the modified military procedure governing the remainder of OSS. Furthermore, since in enemy territory OG personnel operated in uniform, it appeared more appropriate that they be kept separate from other clandestine activities, in order better to justify their treatment as prisoners of war should they be captured. A total of nine OG missions was dispatched to work with North Italian patriot groups. Actually, in the final phases of the Italian campaign, the centralization of operations under Company D did not always permit specialized use of OG personnel distinct from other American OSS personnel activities behind the German lines in support of resistance or patriot groups.

OG headquarters were in Caserta. Of its subdivisions, "Company A", assigned to Italian operations was originally in Corsica and subsequently moved to Siena. The two other OG companies, "B" and "C", included OG personnel in France and the Balkans, respectively.*

Signal Officer. All communications were under the control of the OSS Signal Officer. His responsibilities included maintenance of signal facilities and message center, supervising all agent signal traffic, frequencies, procedures and ciphers, signal security and the communications training of all agent and operator personnel.

* See "Greece," "Yugoslavia," and "France, OG's," below.

The expanding OSS installation in Italy entailed an overloading of communications resources in the Theater. By September 1944, it took up to three days for a message from clandestine radio inside North Italy to reach Company D. Clandestine radios maintained contacts with the communications base station at Bari, which relayed messages to Caserta, where they were decoded, translated and passed on to Company D. In October direct communications were arranged between Bari and Company D, and, early in 1945, between agents in North Italy and Company D.

Services Officer. The Services Officer was responsible for all matters relating to supply, transportation, billets, properties, mess and duplication or reproduction facilities and operations.

Changes in Theater Boundaries

The progressive reorganization of the entire Mediterranean Theater entailed redrawing Theater limits to include the former Near East Theater of Operations. With southern Italy secured, the most ready approach to the Balkans was across the Adriatic instead of from bases in Egypt and Libya. Under the new 2677th Regiment, activities were channelled into three main efforts—to southern France, up the Italian mainland and toward the Balkans. Four OSS Companies, A, B, C and D, were established.

Company A. This unit originally included all OSS personnel committed to the southern France invasion. On 1 November, it was rearranged to include only personnel remaining in Algiers; personnel in France was transferred to ETO. The Company was de-activated on 17 January.

Company B. This was an administrative unit with jurisdiction over all OSS operation mounted from the area of Bari and Brindisi. Activities from Company B into the Balkans and Central Europe were controlled directly from Regimental Headquar-

ters.* At Brindisi, an OSS operational supply detachment was assigned to the British packing station preparing air drops flown from airfields in the area. Several training and holding areas were also maintained under Company B administrative control.

Company C. This originally included all OSS personnel at the advance base in Corsica.** After the French campaign and the German withdrawal to the Gothic Line in the fall of 1944, the Corsica base was closed and personnel transferred to Italy or southern France.

A second Company C was activated in March 1945, when a major air operations center was opened in the Cecina area near Leghorn. American bomber squadrons were assigned to operate from Cecina to complement the RAF squadrons from Brindisi. The proximity of Cecina to the front meant new highs in tonnages dropped to Italian partisans, and greatly facilitated agent dispatch. Holding areas for agent personnel, both for Italian operations and for operations into Central Europe, were maintained in the area and the radio school was moved up from Brindisi. Both Company B at Bari and Company C served to implement air operations planned and directed by Company D, while activities relevant to penetration north of the Alps were under regimental headquarters control. A Maritime Unit base was established briefly at Leghorn, but served more in a supply capacity when Leghorn became a major port for American supplies. A supply depot was established to handle material consigned to OSS.

Company D. In February 1944, G-3 Special Operations Section of 15th Army Group took over coordination of all Allied Special Operations into enemy-occupied Italy.

---

* The Independent American Mission to Marshal Tito was a "special detachment" reporting to the Regimental Commander as Theater Strategic Services Officer, and also to the Director of OSS. See "Yugoslavia" and "Belgrade," below.
** See "Corsica Operations," above.

"Special Ops" was to allocate air lift and supply drop tonnages, and prevent overlapping or duplication of contacts with resistance groups. The OSS/Fifth Army Detachment was raised to Army Group level and re-designated OSS/AAI. As such, it represented all OSS branches on "Special Ops".

Company D, activated in July, was assigned jurisdiction over all OSS activity within the area previously prescribed as the jurisdiction of OSS/AAI. Its base moved first to Siena and then to Florence, accompanying AAI Headquarters. Following the pattern set in OSS/AAI, OSS branch lines remained subordinate to Company functions. The Detachments with the Fifth and Eighth Armies were maintained, and a third unit, established near Ravenna by MU personnel, conducted maritime operations with Italian naval personnel.

Control over all agent personnel inside enemy-occupied Italy was concentrated in Company D. The activities of the agents in organizing partisan resistance groups and operations were delegated to the Company operations officer (who after January 1945 was himself the Chief of SO in the Theater). Direction of intelligence agents, dispatched both by the former OSS/AAI group and by SI/Italy, was assigned to the Company Secret Intelligence officer, while an attempt was made to concentrate in Company D the original agent dispatchers of the other units. Various officers were responsible for MO, Reports, Communications, Services, Security, Special Funds and X-2.*

1. R&A/Italy

The first R&A representatives reached North Africa in the spring and summer of 1943 to collect documentation, to exploit new intelligence sources in liberated territories and to support AFHQ, air forces, armies and the operations branches of OSS itself with

---

* See "Company D" and "Italian Resistance," below.

research assistance. With the liberation and conquest of additional areas and the consequent emergence of problems of military government, relief and rehabilitation, emphasis shifted to economic and political intelligence for R&A/Washington and support to American missions and agencies, both military and diplomatic, in preparing and implementing post-hostilities and occupation programs. At its peak, the R&A staff numbered some fifty officers, civilians and enlisted men.

Target Analysis. Operational programs were developed both for OSS operations branches and for the Mediterranean Air Force and various AFHQ sections. In the planning of specific OSS operations, both background information and detailed topographic data were collected and analyzed.

Direct assistance was given to strategic and tactical air forces by the preparation of ·target programs for air bombardment. At various times after November 1943, a small staff of six to ten officers from R&A was assigned directly to MAAF Headquarters, first at La Marsa, Tunisia, and subsequently in Italy, to serve as a target analysis group within A-2, and to act as liaison to MAAF from the Enemy Objectives Unit.* The group followed the effects of bombings and the program of enemy reconstruction. Air photo cover was used, and, in the process, the photo-interpretation system for strategic air targets was modified. From photographs, other intelligence and general evaluations, priority lists of targets were drawn up and nearly always used without change by Fifteenth Air Force. In addition, significant specialized air target intelligence was collected by an R&A team cooperating with CSDIC staffs on detailed interrogations of prisoners of war.

The work of the unit brought about a sweeping revision in strategic bombing pro-

---

* See "R&A/London," below. This unit served in fact as an important coordinating link between the respective programs of ETO and MedTO air commands for the strategic bombing of Germany.

cedure in MedTO. In March 1944 the Air Force began Operation *STRANGLE* to prevent German supply from reaching the front overland.

Air Force bombing policy called for continuous high-altitude attacks on freight yards, sidings and repair shops. This, however, served principally to reduce local or civilian transport, as German supply trains were made up inside Germany, and, in addition, only served to attack the strongest link in the enemy rail system, since European rail equipment production exceeded the rate of destruction.

For *STRANGLE*, R&A prepared a program for railroad interdiction, urging the simultaneous blocking of all rail lines by the destruction of bridges and tunnels—points of maximum repair difficulty—together with blanket cratering of rights-of-way in as many places as possible. Three belts of interdiction were selected and specific targets pinpointed. When the attack began, in the third week of March 1944, the combination of bridge and open line bombings kept Italian rail lines between the Apennines and Rome cut until the Germans were driven north of the Arno.*

Maps and Cartography. R&A Map Division men were active in the Theater, collecting and assessing various foreign cartographic material, located in North Africa, France and Italy, or brought in by OSS personnel on field missions. The Map Division assisted the Reporting Board in the location and verification of geographic references in intelligence dispatches. In particular, precise map overlays were prepared for material on southern France, summarizing information on order of battle and German installations along the southern French coast prior to the Allied landing there.

---

* A similar program of interdiction was later adopted in support of the Normandy invasion. This consisted in destruction of the bridges over the Seine and Loire in order to isolate northern France prior to the landings.

In 1945 geographic coordinates, photo interpretation and general target direction on Italy were given to the Intelligence Photographic Documentation Project (IPDP)* undertaken jointly with the Field Photographic staff. IPDP aimed to provide detailed protographic cover and analysis of strategic regions in Europe; it stressed coastline, terrain, transport, urban features and industrial installations.

Document Collection. One of the original directives of the R&A field staff called for the procurement of items of detailed documentation lacking in the United States and available abroad, particularly in regions once under enemy control. Principal targets included specialized official and private files, libraries, archives, research institutes and universities. By the end of 1943, R&A men had covered North Africa, Sicily, Corsica and southern Italy. Liaison was maintained with the AFHQ G-2 Document Collection Section; in this way, effect screening of relevant items could be effected. Extensive shipments of documentation were dispatched to OSS in Washington while, at OSS/MedTO headquarters, an "intelligence library" was maintained for the use of OSS as well as of AFHQ and the State Department.

In 1945 all City Teams included in their directives the procurement of specific documentary materials to supplement the work of the G-2 S-Forces.** In Italy the chief items of interest were on German, Italian and Japanese industrial resources, and matters affecting Italian economic and social readjustment after VE-Day.

Aid to Civil Affairs. Early in 1944, R&A officers were called upon by G-5, AFHQ to supply economic information and political details on France and Italy, and to participate actively in the training and briefing program for Civil Affairs to be assigned to

---

* See Washington section on Field Photographic.
** Similar to ETO T-Forces. See section on "Liberated France," below.

newly occupied territories. Prior to the invasion of southern France, the R&A staff in Algiers provided extensive assistance in the form of studies on civilian post-liberation requirements and on the industrial potential of regions still under enemy control. After the landings there, two R&A officers, assigned as political intelligence officers for G-5, Seventh Army, in Marseille, prepared specific reports and analyses for the Civil Affairs staff on such problems as the French political return to democratic methods and the administrative organization of southeastern France.

After July 1944, when the principal R&A Theater activities were moved to Rome, G-5 received additional assistance in preparation for the occupation of northern Italy. R&A estimates on the supplies necessary to maintain specific civilian ration levels, and on the appropriate shipping requirements, formed the basis for the briefing of American officers of Allied Civil Affairs staffs and the Allied Control Commission.

Overt Political Intelligence. In late 1943, the R&A staff in Algiers had begun, on a small, experimental basis, selective reporting and analysis of current social and political conditions in Italy and France. This intelligence, not strictly military in nature but of more direct interest to Military Government, to the Allied Control Commission, to the political and economic sections of AFHQ and to the State Department, was disseminated principally to higher Theater echelons, at their request, rather than to armies in the field. Such material was also forwarded to OSS/Washington for the information and use of political analysts.

The Italian situation differed from the French in the relative political "truce" that prevailed throughout the war. Although jockeying for power, the major Italian political groups active behind enemy lines cooperated under the Committee of National Liberation (CLN). This unification strongly influenced party representatives in liberated Italy, who nevertheless made political information readily available on all sides, in their eagerness to broadcast their particular views and plans. The problem became less one of reporting than one of discretion in the evaluation and use of information obtained.* It was, nevertheless, a pressing one, due to lack of adequate State Department staff in Italy.

After the capture of Rome, political reporting on Italy was systematized. Emphasis was placed on overt sources not readily accessible to accredited American military or diplomatic representatives. To maintain an informal atmosphere, an apartment was rented in Rome for meetings with prominent Italians. In this way, supplemented by observation of daily political and public developments, extensive information on political thinking and intentions was obtained and periodically disseminated to R&A/Washington and to Theater customers in the form of digests or general reports. R&A officers did not adopt any cover but represented themselves as attached to AFHQ and concerned with Italy. All spoke fluent Italian and were well-grounded in a knowledge of Italy and Italian political affairs.** By the spring of 1945, political reporting was established as an essential function of city teams. After VE-Day, overt political reporting by R&A became a major OSS activity, and filled a vacuum in general American intelligence coverage between the liquidation of wartime intelligence agencies and the arrival in the field of permanent State Department representatives.***

2. X-2/Italy

In the Mediterranean Theater, as in the European, X-2 worked in intimate liaison with its British counterpart, and originally

---

* The task was shared by SI/Italy. See that section, above.

** A similar British political reporting unit, active in Rome, had the advantage of a staff of older, higher ranking officers, all of whom had been long peacetime residents of Italy.

*** See section on "The Liberation of Europe, Italy," below.

acted principally as a complement to the British effort. This tended to produce within OSS a lack of confidence in the Branch's "security", particularly on the part of SI/Italy, confronted with apparent British resistance to the development of independent OSS clandestine networks. SI argued that separate and unrelated clandestine intelligence chains were indispensable to the security and protection of both British and American operations, and feared that close X-2 relations with the British would jeopardize this separation. In addition, the development of initial SI agent chains required close personal supervision by operations officers, who were not at first appreciative of the X-2 system of control through close coordination and lateral liaison between field stations all over the world.

These objections were not overcome until after the capture of Rome in mid-1944, when the relative positions of British and American intelligence were defined, and when the X-2 staff and facilities became adequate to fulfill their assigned OSS functions of vetting SI agents and protecting OSS clandestine operations in the field.

SICILY

The first X-2 station in the Italian zone was in Sicily. An X-2 operative reached Palermo in August 1943 as a field representative reporting directly to X-2/Algiers. His activities were hampered by inexperience and by the hostility of the SI/Italy staff. The latter took strenuous exception to X-2 criticism of the close relations built up by SI during and after the Sicilian campaign with such native groups as the renegade Mafia. In North Africa and Sicily, the part played by X-2 was relatively negligible, and, except for the fact that an X-2 observer had been sent into Italy with a British intelligence field unit, X-2 had no experience on which to base a mobile unit's operations.

NAPLES

In December 1943 a forward X-2 station was opened in Naples. As the unit grew, numerous organizational difficulties had to be overcome. X-2 was operationally autonomous within OSS, and only relied on OSS Theater headquarters for administration and services. At the same time X-2 was, in the military sense, attached to Fifth Army, but had to work with the Counter-Intelligence Staff of 15th Army Group to complement its intelligence plan for the whole of Italy. This dual control confronted all phases of OSS activity and was only rationalized in the July 1944 reorganization. As with the rest of OSS, X-2 at first received from the military authorities, both British and American, little confidence, and consequently no responsibility for any but minor cases until it could show proof of its capabilities.

Between January and May 1944, progress toward recognition of the unit's usefulness was gradual but sure. In Naples, the principal function of the X-2 staff consisted of assistance in the clean-up of stay-behind agents for the Army, but in addition good starts were made toward longer-range counter-espionage operations. A small group of X-2-briefed tactical agents were put through the lines by Fifth Army Detachment, with the result that some fifty agents in the area north of Monte Cassino were identified and captured before the fall of Rome.

The first exclusively CE* operation undertaken was the running of a double-double-agent in support of an important double-agent being run by the British. The technique applied here was to "blow" the American-run agent—to have him send to the Germans his W/T signal that he was under control—in order to give the Germans the impression that the Americans were so new

---

* On the distinction between defensive counter-intelligence (CI) and offensive counter-espionage (CE), see Washington section on X-2.

at the game that they would not know about such signals, and that, therefore, all German agents who had not sent the signals were operating freely. Consequently, the German evaluation of the British-run agent rose, and they accepted his reports, chiefly because they differed from those of the "controlled" agent. The field experience of handling this type of case was valuable to the unit in its later work, and also won X-2 most useful recognition in Allied intelligence circles.

In cooperation with MO/Naples, leaflets in the form of funeral memorials were prepared, giving the names and identifying details, including pictures, of Italians who had worked as agents for the Germans and had been captured and executed by the Allies. Large numbers of the leaflets were dropped into enemy-occupied northern Italy, and subsequent reports from many sources testified to their deterrent effect on the enthusiasm of Italians for work with the German Intelligence Services and on the morale of those already assigned missions. By 1944 there were virtually no cases of Germans crossing the lines. The short-range agents were almost always Italians who tended to accept the training and money given them, but who, for the most part, when captured, told all they knew. Throughout the Italian campaign, a large percentage of the Italian agents working for the Germans surrendered immediately on crossing the Allied lines.

ROME

In May 1944 an S-Force, consisting of British and American intelligence groups of both positive and counter-espionage sections, was formed for the Allied entry into Rome. The chief of X-2/Naples directed all OSS personnel attached to this Force. The turn of events at Anzio, which delayed the Force's arrival in Rome until 4 June, gave the group that much more time to coordinate targets.

After the disorganization resulting from the defeats at Sicily and Salerno, the German Intelligence Services had made use of the period preceding Cassino to set up schools for training agents in Rome and Florence, and to send saboteurs for training to Scheveningen in Holland. Valuable information as to the exact location, organization and personnel of these schools was gained from captured agents before the S-Forces went to Rome. This information helped considerably in the planning of definite targets for the occupation of Rome, resulting in the capture of 47 principal stay-behind agents and 17 wireless sets in the first three weeks.

REORGANIZATION—THE SCI/Z

In the July 1944 reorganization of OSS/MedTO,* X-2 was placed under the administrative control of the Regimental Intelligence Officer. X-2 Theater headquarters, however, were established in Rome, due to the volume of work involved in exploiting the hundreds of targets in that city and the fact that Rome was the logical center for future Italian operations. Only a liaison officer was stationed in Caserta, who covered the Naples area as well.

A small station was opened in Bari on 16 August 1944, as a dispatch point for X-2 activities in the Balkans.** Similarly, a station in Siena with Company D began, in November 1944, to brief outgoing OSS agents and to interrogate those returning. The arrangement served to maintain OSS security, and, incidentally, was a valuable source of counter-espionage information.

Direct intra-branch communications through OSS channels were opened between X-2 offices in MedTO, ETO and Washington, for strictly X-2 operational traffic. This made possible close cooperation between Rome and London, where X-2 was represented in the SHAEF CI War Room.*** In fact, for security, all army CI staffs in Italy were only permitted to communicate with

---

* See "Bases in Italy," above.
** See sections on "Yugoslavia" and "Belgrade," below.
*** See "X-2/London," below.

the War Room through either X-2 channels or those of the British counterpart, MI-6(V).

At the same time, X-2, which had been operating in Italy throughout the first part of 1944 without any formal place in the Theater intelligence pattern, was assigned, under AAI with the designation SCI/Z,* to a status corresponding to that of the British SI(b) field units, and under the coordinating control of the Assistant Chief of Staff, G-2, CI, AAI. This clarification of X-2's position in Italy placed it on an equal competitive footing with other counter-espionage agencies, enabling the unit to operate on a much larger scale in the following year.

After July 1944, X-2 began to vet all OSS strategic agent personnel through security checks against local and London X-2 files. After the capture of Florence agent personnel and native employees of OSS were vetted, as well as those of Military Government, CIC and later of the State Department.

FLORENCE

During the summer months of the Allied advance from Rome to Florence, SCI/Z collaborated with British SI(b) teams and with G-2 and 15th Army Group in the capture and interrogation of over 500 persons. SCI/Z also provided information for the pinpoint bombing of German Intelligence Service headquarters in North Italy. In addition, SCI/Z participated in X-2 activities on the French-Italian and Swiss-Italian borders that began after the southern France campaign.

In August and September 1944, preparations were made in London and Rome for SCI participation in the Florence S-Forces operation. Despite the difficulties incident to the occupation of Florence, extensive detailed information was obtained on German intelligence operations. By 15 September the last of the Florence targets had been

eliminated, and the emphasis of X-2 work changed to the collection of target information on northern Italy and Austria. The SCI/Z staff in Florence became the advance base for further X-2 operations.

By this time the X-2 technique in Italy had developed its final form. SCI/Z in Florence consisted of two separate units. One was located with the British team and with CIC in the Piazza Signoria, servicing CIB, 15th Army Group. This unit handled interrogations of special CI interest. After a captured agent was turned over with a preliminary interrogation report, the unit made out an arrest form for the AMG jail, then notified SCI/Z Rome and 15th AG of the preliminary information. Rome cabled London for traces, and, on the basis of this accumulated information, Florence concentrated on a full interrogation. The end result was sent then by Florence to SCI/Z Rome where the final report was mimeographed and disseminated to army groups, armies, SCI, CIC, British FSS and French DSM, as well as AFHQ.

The second group of SCI/Z Florence was located in OSS headquarters and handled offensive counter-espionage. Because the armies were stalemated in early 1945, there were numerous penetration and double-agent opportunities and it was this section which briefed, interrogated and vetted OSS agents, and supervised penetration and double-agent operations.

OPERATION OF CAPTURED OSS TEAMS

SCI/Z worked closely with intelligence and operations branches of OSS under Company D in watching the security of agent circuits in the field. It collaborated on the briefing of all agents dispatched to partisan areas. In addition, certain agents were assigned specifically to collect counter-intelligence information. Further, X-2 observed all agent communication traffic and took direct supervision of such OSS teams as were ascertained to be definitely operating under German control.

---

* Corresponding to the Special Counter-Intelligence units in France. See "X-2/France," below.

The outstanding case in Italy of an OSS clandestine station being doubled and forced to play back for the Germans was MARIA GIOVANNA.* Another team in Genoa, ZUCCA, occasionally made use of the MARIA GIOVANNA radio. When a Gestapo plant succeeded in becoming one of ZUCCA's informants, a series of arrests were carried out among members of that chain, and papers were found revealing the identification and location of MARIA GIOVANNA. At the same time, German D/F-ing pinpointed the MARIA GIOVANNA radio and made it possible for the Germans to capture one agent and the radio operator, together with codes, crystals and transmitters. The leader, "Corvo", was away at the time and eluded arrest. However, contrary to his briefing, he had not destroyed any of his back traffic files, which, along with his procedure tables, were seized.

The Germans decided to play back the station, since all the necessary data were at hand and the radio operator professed himself willing to collaborate. The first controlled message was sent in late September after a week's radio silence. This lapse was not considered abnormal by the OSS control station, as the operator explained that he had been encountering radio difficulties. MARIA GIOVANNA did not have a prepared signal to send to indicate that it was being played back. The operator, however, whose code radio name was "Falco", commenced signing his name as "Falso" on all messages. Unfortunately this was considered to be an error in transmission by OSS Communications Branch, which corrected the name each time in the decoded message before it was passed to SI.

The first message transmitted from the OSS base station, after MARIA GIOVANNA came under control, contained a security breach which entailed serious consequences. An agent, connected to both MARIA GIOVANNA and ZUCCA, had returned through

* See section on "Early Infiltrations of North Italy" from Fifth Army, above.

the lines to report. He drew up a message to inform all future OSS line-crossers of proper methods and routes, and gave the name of a certain priest who would arrange for guides. Thus, the Germans were able to close down the escape routes and arrest the priest in question.

At least one parachutage of materiel was sent MARIA GIOVANNA in good faith, but, after about a month, the station began to arouse OSS suspicions. The station was coming on the air more frequently than in former times, details in intelligence messages declined and messages contained an inordinate number of requests for information, additional agents and supplies. Certain personal questions were framed and transmitted to MARIA GIOVANNA. The controlled agents recognized these questions as tests, and managed to answer them erroneously, thus indicating to SI satisfaction that they were being played back.

In late November, as soon as German control had been definitely established, X-2 took over operation of the case as a triple-cross. This was continued for some three and a half months, with the basic object of endeavoring to secure the dispatch of German agents back across the lines. From the post-VE-Day interrogation of German officers connected with the playback, it was ascertained that the Germans never recognized the case as a triple-cross.

It was AFHQ's desire that the cross be maintained until after the winter Allied offensive in Italy. Finally, some indiscreet messages were sent to the Germans which might have indicated to them that an offensive was being contemplated. AFHQ became alarmed at the risks inherent in the triple-cross and requested that it be closed down. A last OSS message was sent to MARIA GIOVANNA in February 1945, instructing it to discontinue sending, as it had been discovered that the signal plan was insecure. The Germans believed that OSS had finally discovered the playback, but considered that "Corvo" had probably managed to inform his superiors of the doubling operation.

After the circuit was cancelled, the radio operators were placed in a concentration camp, and were set free when the camp was overrun by Allied forces.

GERMAN INTELLIGENCE SERVICE "KEYS"

In the fall of 1944, SCI/Z began the publication of an extensive series of reports, called German Intelligence Service "Keys." These were expert summaries of all available information on the German services in general and on the specific divisions of the SD and Abwehr in the areas ahead, targets giving the locations of all GIS schools and establishments in northern Italy, and lists of all known SD and Abwehr members and of their relationships. These handbooks, periodically revised, gave a nearly perfect record, from all sources, in a form usable by the lowest echelons of the army CI staffs in the field, and provided fully cross-referenced data for the use of CIC and British FSS interrogators. In this way it was possible for SCI/Z to uti-

lize the services of over 200 interrogators in the accumulation of still further data from the rapid interrogation of captured enemy personnel.

For these "Keys", considerable source material came from the exploitation of the Italian Intelligence Service itself. Although Italy ultimately had the status of a co-belligerent, all of its services had worked hand-in-hand with the Germans for a long time. X-2 had access to the complete Italian counter-espionage files, which included not only information on German intelligence personnel and operations, but also on those of the services of other countries all over the world. The data, in addition to those obtained from the British, French and Norwegian services, gave X-2 a wealth of information to supplement that which its own units were able to obtain in their short period of wartime operation.

3. MO/Italy

Morale Operations into Italy began in 1943 from the Algiers base. JCS 170* had appeared too early to treat MO functions, and, in accordance with a directive signed by Eisenhower on 7 February 1943, all activities in the field of psychological warfare came under the "control, coordination, and direction" of the Psychological Warfare Board, AFHQ. MO representatives, sent in early 1943 to contribute to the psychological warfare program in North Africa, were attached directly to PWB to form a collection and evaluation center, working closely with OWI, FCC and the British PWE and MOI. For the first year, OSS/MO personnel devoted themselves almost entirely to conducting open propaganda.

Following the division of COI into OWI and OSS in June 1942, however, the distinction between "white" and "black" propaganda had been developed.** During a trip to Sicily in July 1943, Donovan worked out

---

* See Washington Exhibit W-38.
** See Washington section on MO.

an agreement with PWB according to which MO personnel would continue work within that AFHQ unit, but would concentrate on collection, evaluation, psychological intelligence and "black" propaganda. OSS would contribute $15,000 monthly to PWB. Finally, in January 1944, an MO/PWB agreement granted autonomy to the OSS Branch (subject to PWB coordination) to conduct "black" propaganda through subversive radios, newspapers, leaflets, letters and rumors.

During the period when MO was still under the complete control of PWB, some subversive projects were undertaken. The most notable of these was the establishment of the first MO "black" radio in Tunisia in late June 1943, just prior to the invasion of Sicily. This was "Italo Balbo", so-called because the famous Marshal had been anti-Mussolini, and many Italians believed him to be still living. The objective was to undermine Axis military capacity by promoting discord and dissension between Fascists and Nazis and between Fascists and the Italian civilian population, urging resistance against the Germans and against those Italians who had "sold out to the Nazis." The speaker himself was an Italian recruited in Tunisia. Allied monitors reported enemy "jamming" of the station on at least five occasions and numerous Italian prisoners of war, upon later interrogation, were surprised to hear that the station was not authentic.

"Italo Balbo" faded out after the conquest of Sicily, and a new "black" radio was established briefly at Anzio until subjected to artillery attack.

In central Italy, where adequate radio facilities were not available, emphasis was placed on the preparation and dissemination of printed material. MO instituted a poster campaign with the slogan "Wie Lange Noch?" (How much longer?) to provide evidence that a strong underground movement operated inside Germany. A series of sixteen leaflets, posters and stickers, using a large "W" as its symbol, was placed in Ger-

man vehicles, on walls, on doors and windows, in books and other appropriate places, by agents operating behind enemy lines.

The most ambitious program in this field was the underground newspaper "Das Neue Deutschland".* This purported to be the instrument of a German peace party the aims of which were to end the war, liquidate the Nazi Party and set up a new German state on democratic principles. Its platform included educational, religious, reconstruction and veteran planks, all couched in semi-religious language. In general, the doctrines of the movement reflected liberal principles which sounded quite specific but which were, in fact, so broad as to appeal to men of widely differing political beliefs.

"Das Neue Deutschland" produced a sharp reaction from the enemy. A special warning to German troops was published in Information for the Troops ("Nachrichten fur die Truppe") in October 1944, and Himmler's publication "Das Schwarze Korps" carried a front page denunciation of it.

Another MO leaflet was designed for German frontline troops on the Eighth Army front in August 1944. It took the form of a Feldpost (V-mail letter or circular) purporting to come from a "League for Lonely Women". Soldiers on furlough had only to pin an entwined heart symbol (given in the leaflet) on their lapels to find a girl friend. The missive ended with the "reassuring" admonition: "Don't be shy. Your wife, sister and sweetheart is one of us. We think of you, but we think also of Germany."**

These leaflets were delivered to the Maquis in France and the partisans in North Italy for dissemination by them. Italian agents and SAUERKRAUT *** missions infiltrated through the lines to distribute them in forward areas. Three days after the first infiltrations, copies were found on German POW's in Italy and France. G-2 believed

---

* See Washington section on MO.
** The leaflet is included in History File 306, Section X.
*** See below.

97

them to be authentic German documents, and gave the information to "Stars and Stripes". "Time" magazine and many newspapers also carried the story, believing it to be true.

The greatest difficulty which faced MO was that of distributing printed material, for no matter how cleverly calculated its subversive propaganda, its effectiveness was nullified if it could be traced to Allied sources.

Usually such material was passed to resistance groups or to Allied agents by secret air drop. Partisan units at the front lines could often make it possible for MO to exploit an immediate tactical situation:

An example of a precision morale operation was a joint PWB/MO job on Italian fascist divisions fighting for the enemy. SI at Siena first reported the appearance of the Monte Rosa Division at the Brenner Pass, and the desertion of several hundreds the moment the train struck Italy. It was made up of Italians interned by the Germans in the Balkans and given the alternative of slave labor or the Army. Their morale obviously was soft, yet the Germans needed them badly and intended to use them on the lines.

I took this tip to PWB at AAI. SI and SO followed the Monte Rosa, and later the San Marco, Littorio, and Italia divisions until they settled near La Spezia. PWB opened up with aerial leaflets; and through a Partisan band nearby, MO surreptitiously distributed a "pass" from a self-styled "Patriots' Committee" inviting them to join the Partisans. (Actually we didn't know whether the Partisans would honor that pass, but we didn't give a damn; the idea was to make the Italians completely useless to the Germans.)

The effects were cumulative. The appearance of the MO leaflets aroused the German suspicions. Kesselring was forced to interlard the Italians with German units he badly needed elsewhere. When the Italians reached the front lines, they deserted in whole platoons armed with surrender passes dropped to them by PWB. They were withdrawn in 15 days.*

Mo improvised another effective way of reaching German soldiers in a given locality at a given moment. The SAUERKRAUT operations utilized carefully screened POW's who were infiltrated in German uniform behind enemy lines. This plan was first used

* Field Report, 10 March 1945, History File 140c.

following the attempt of 20 July 1944 on Hitler's life,. when MO wished to post a forged military announcement by General Kesselring to the effect that he was resigning his command, knowing that the "war is lost to Germany", and that senseless slaughter would be the only result of Hitler's Last Stand Order. The usual method of agent infiltration by parachute drop was dismissed as too slow for this purpose, and the SAUERKRAUT teams were quickly recruited, briefed and dispatched. The operation was highly successful, and Kesselring found it necessary on 13 September to deny authorship of the proclamation. Subsequent fakes were equally effective and provoked strong German counter-measures. None of the POW's used in these operations were captured by the Germans nor, so far as is known, were any of them "turned" against MO. In addition to their distribution of subversive material, the agents brought back valuable tactical intelligence. A.C. of S., G-2, Fifth Army, recognized the contribution, requesting that further operations of a like nature be undertaken.

A third device for the infiltration of "black" propaganda was the CORNFLAKES project, which exploited the disruption of the German postal system resulting from Allied bombing of the railways. Fake German mail bags were made and filled with copies of "Das Neue Deutschland" and subversive letters stamped, postmarked and directed to real addresses taken from directories. These were dropped by the Fifteenth Air Force in strafing missions over marshalling yards and railroad stations, in the hope that they would be picked up as stray mail bags scattered from wrecked railroad cars, and sent on through the regular mail. In twenty sorties, 320 mail bags were dropped.

By the close of the campaign the MO print shop had turned out some 30,000,000 items. An attempt was made to evaluate the effectiveness of "black" operations through investigations conducted among German prisoners of war. Conclusions were that about half the German POW's had heard of the "Das Neue Deutschland" movement; the CORNFLAKES project to infiltrate the Nazi mail system had not been suspected; German troops had deserted in tens and twenties to the partisans all over northern Italy during the last phases of the campaign, and Italian Fascist troops had deserted in blocks numbering up to 400, most of them carrying MO pass notes. The total of known desertions directly affected by MO subversion was estimated at 10,000.

It was, however, impossible to evaluate the net over-all effects of "black" propaganda. Demoralization was cumulative, resulting not only from propaganda, but also from bombings, hardships, defeats and from countless other conditions and events. To add to these, and in many cases to bring them to a head, the "black" propaganda supplied by MO constituted a significant supplementary weapon in Allied hands. The frequent and violent German reactions to specific MO themes and plants formed perhaps the best concrete measure of MO effectiveness.

4. Company D

On 3 July 1944 OSS/AAI moved to Siena,* immediately upon the capture of that city, and on 20 July was activated as Company D. The OSS advance detachments with Fifth Army, VI Corps and X Corps were reorganized into twin forward detachments with the Fifth and Eighth Armies respectively, directly responsible to Company D. In addition the Maritime Unit, with its Italian San Marco personnel and equipment, operated on the Adriatic end of the front, and OG personnel and teams were made available both for missions to patriot groups in enemy territory and to direct partisan units at the front.

Twenty-eight long-range OSS teams were active inside northern Italy at the time of

---
* And to Florence in January 1945.

Company D's activation in July 1944. A total of 63 agents had been infiltrated, not including teams or personnel on short-range tactical operations immediately behind enemy lines. With the front stabilized on the Gothic Line, the distinctions between operating and strategic agents generally disappeared. Originally both the detachments with the Fifth and Eighth Armies dispatched their tactical operations across the lines, instructing agents either to report by courier or to return through the lines at an established place and time. The nature of the terrain and the static front made these operations progressively more difficult, however, and detachment agents soon parachuted in the same manner as strategic agents, communicating by radio either directly to the detachments or to the OSS base radio station.

Control over both agents and resistance groups immediately ahead of the lines was turned over to the detachments. Longer-range operations into northern Italy were directed from Company D headquarters.

In the two months of Allied advance from Rome towards Florence, extensive intelligence was obtained at the front from overrun agents and partisan groups, many of whom were recruited on the spot for further missions into North Italy. In addition, numerous key figures from North Italian resistance groups, prominent scientists, engineers and businessmen crossed into Allied lines to volunteer their services. Those recruited were at first sent to Caserta for training and briefing. Later, personnel were sent to OSS training and briefing areas near Brindisi for instruction in parachuting, intelligence, sabotage and communications.

A few early individual sabotage missions were dispatched. EAGLE, for instance, consisting of three American officers, was sent on 3 August 1944 to block approaches to the Brenner Pass. The officers were active inside northern Italy, despite unusual difficulties, for a period of four months. Subsequently, the leader of the mission ordered his two colleagues to return through the lines while he made a final attempt. A supply drop to him was arranged through an OG mission late in December. He did succeed in blasting one section of an escarpment approaching the Pass, and completely blocked traffic for several days. Shortly thereafter, however, he was captured and, though uniformed, was tortured and killed.

In September, plans for further ground sabotage operations were suspended at the request of the Air Force, on the grounds that if intelligence agents could be infiltrated to report on targets for sabotage, the sabotage itself could be more effectively accomplished by subsequent bombing than by individual clandestine demolitions operations.

Teams were placed inside enemy-occupied Italy throughout the winter 1944-45. The flow of intelligence increased progressively, and in February over 2,000 items of information were received from teams in the field, covering order of battle, bombing targets, transport, lists of collaborators and war criminals and economic and political data. Teams were placed or reinforced in the regions of Venice, Udine, Bolzano, Milan, Como, Turin, Genoa and Lake Garda.

Among the numerous reports received were those of mid-December which warned of a contemplated German offensive on the sector held by the 92nd Division, new to the front. Subsequent reports of German movements gave confirmation. When the attack actually came on 26 December, the 92nd Division recoiled, but, as the Germans began to advance, resistance groups on either side of the German spearhead attacked the flanks. The Germans, fearing a trap, withdrew. Had they effected a break-through, the entire Allied position, due to the lack of reserves on the Fifth Army front, might have been seriously threatened.

Several OSS teams sent regular weather reports, as well as intelligence data, to the Twelfth Air Force throughout the winter.

On 11 December the latter reported:

Poor weather prevents frequent photo-reconnaissance of Brenner-Tarvisio and Postuni lines. Air Force therefore largely depends on your reports on damages, repairs, and by-pass routes.*

Master "Safe Area" maps** were also disseminated and a program was inaugurated of regularly forwarding all changes.

FIFTH ARMY DETACHMENT

The Fifth Army Detachment of Company D had a staff of ten at the time of activation. At its peak, it included forty officers and enlisted men and forty additional personnel regularly assigned, together with another thirty temporarily attached or on loan from the OG 2671st Special Reconnaissance Battalion. It reported to G-2, Fifth Army, for direction.

Until the capture of Florence, the Detachment's main activity consisted in mounting short-range intelligence penetrations ahead of the lines for tactical and combat intelligence similar to operations begun after the Salerno landings. Further data were received from refugees and resistance members who crossed the American lines or who were overrun in the Allied advance.

Agents were placed in enemy territory either by plane through Company D channels or by direct line infiltration. Several of those parachuted had radios in direct contact with the Detachment's mobile radio station. In July, two such teams were dropped to points north of Pisa, near Spezia, from which point they retreated northwards with the Germans, reporting details of enemy movements, supply dumps, headquarters and strategic emplacements. Subsequently, additional teams were parachuted northwest of Spezia, south of Cremona and near Parma. At one time, four agents teams were reporting directly to the Detachment, and frequently answering specific questions from G-2, Fifth Army.

---

* Cable, that date, Caserta to Bern, OSS Archives.
** Similar to those prepared for Yugoslavia. See that section, below.

100

For infiltrations through the lines, agents were trained and briefed by the Detachment, then usually escorted to points forward of advance American positions, sometimes accompanied by a reconnaissance patrol. The agents then made their way alone, and either returned across the lines or were recuperated by patrol. Other agents remained in hiding until overrun. Several teams, to remain for brief periods behind enemy lines, were dispatched using carrier pigeons to report intelligence.

An OSS doctor contacted local medical personnel, dispatching them through Fifth Army lines to exchange medical supplies for intelligence.

Prior to 1 August 1944, the II and IV Corps of Fifth Army also infiltrated agents for front-line intelligence. On that date, however, G-2, Fifth Army placed responsibility for all agent infiltrations across Fifth Army lines under the OSS Detachment. When the front became stabilized before the Gothic Line in the fall of 1944, control over the numerous Tuscan and Ligurian resistance bands near the Fifth Army front was turned over to the Detachment by Company D. Fifth Army interest in the active use of these partisan bands on a thinly protected front created for the OSS unit the function of partisan direction and control, which quickly became its major assignment.

By 16 October all partisan activities in the Fifth Army sector were assigned by G-2, Fifth Army to the OSS Detachment for coordination. OSS was to provide partisan patrols both for combat and reconnaissance, as well as guides, litter bearers and ammunition carriers when needed. Furthermore, partisan activities behind the enemy lines—from building road blocks to mounting full-scale attacks on enemy concentrations—were to be directed via Fifth Army Detachment. Through it would be channeled all information on the enemy turned in by the partisans.

In October, IV Corps requested that an OSS unit be specifically assigned it to afford more immediate control of partisans in the Corps area. OG personnel was loaned to Fifth Army Detachment for this purpose.

II Corps attempted to maintatin control over partisans in its sector until December. At that time the Corps G-2 admitted that he had a minimum of information on the situation behind enemy lines facing his Corps, and requested an OSS unit at least to procure prisoners of war for interrogation. The II Corps unit for work with the partisans was absorbed into OSS and, within a matter of days, the reorganized and re-supplied partisan formations were sending in, not only extensive intelligence on enemy dispositions, but a steady stream of prisoners of war. During the winter, additional OSS Fifth Army units were stationed with the 92nd Division, the Brazilian Expeditionary Force and the 10th Mountain Division.

Supplies to partisan units behind enemy lines proved difficult to deliver throughout the winter.* The Tactical Air Force supporting the Fifth Army flew numerous small supply drops, despite the dangers of such operations so near the front. However, the most active sector for the partisans was that before IV Corps lines, in mountainous country where the topography added to the difficulties of air drops. Mule team supply trains were organized, and, using several hundred animals, over a ton of supplies could be delivered on each trip. Despite difficulties of weather and supply, several thousand partisan effectives were thus maintained in the IV Corps sector alone, and in some sectors were relied upon to cover several miles of the front.**

EIGHTH ARMY DETACHMENT

The Eighth Army Detachment of Company D consisted of one officer and four enlisted men at the time of its activation. It remained a small unit in comparison to the Fifth Army Detachment, with a complement at peak not exceeding four officers and fifteen enlisted men.

---

* See "Italian Resistance," below.
** Ibid.

The unit had developed out of the original OSS X Corps Detachment formed during the Naples campaign and redesignated Eighth Army Detachment when Eighth Army moved to the Cassino front in March 1944. After its activation under Company D, it reported to G. S. I., Eighth Army, for direction.

The front covered by this Army, including the Adriatic coast and the approaches to the strategic Po Volley, was static and strongly held by the Germans. The most successful technique of obtaining tactical intelligence proved to be the dispatch of carefully selected field missions by parachute or by clandestine maritime landing on the Adriatic coast, with radios reporting either directly to the Detachment or to the main OSS station in Italy. OSS agents joined active resistance groups and were able to give the Eighth Army comprehensive tactical intelligence coverage as far north as the Venice area. In the taking of Ravenna, for instance, the Detachment set up a mobile radio station in the British V Corps area to work directly with two of its radio teams in the tactical zone. The speed of transmission of intelligence enabled the Corps to use the station as a means of locating targets and directing artillery fire.

Field missions were supplied either through Company D facilities or through means improvised by the Detachment itself. Four Italian Air Force planes, manned by Italian personnel, were directly assigned to the Detachment for short-range supply drops. On "dark moon" nights PT boats under the Maritime Unit were used, particularly to supply patriots around the Valli di Comacchio.*

An indication of the success of the Eighth Army unit can be obtained from the fact that the British concentrated all clandestine line penetration activities in their sectors under the Detachment instead of under SOE. At one point they recommended that the OSS Detachment commander be incorporated into Eighth Army G-3 as "Special Ops" officer. This was not effected, however, particularly since there was no parallel in Fifth Army organization.

MARITIME UNIT

In February 1944 an arrangement had been concluded between OSS and the Duke of Aosta to make available to OSS the techniques and services of the Italian San Marco Battalion, an "elite" corps of Italian naval personnel specializing in amphibious operations and maritime sabotage. A volunteer group of five officers and fifty men from the Battalion was assigned to OSS, along with the latest items of Italian maritime equipment. Included were swimming gear, two-man "mattresses" with silent electric motors to permit clandestine landings, and other assault, reconnaissance and demolitions equipment.

The San Marcos were placed under the direction of OSS Maritime Unit Branch personnel. In May they were based at Fasano, south of Bari, subsequently moved to Falconara, north of Ancona, and, after the capture of Ravenna in December 1944, set up an advance base near that city. U. S. PT's and British MTB's were used alternately with Italian MAS or MS boats,* under British Navy control. By the spring of 1945, the MU staff had been reconstituted as the Maritime Detachment of Company D, and had added various locally procured fishing craft and speed boats to its equipment.

The first mission took place on 19 June 1944, a sabotage operation which succeeded in blowing a railroad bridge along the coast one hundred miles behind enemy lines. A second such operation was carried out late in July. In the August moon period, the first operation for intelligence purposes was run, at Eighth Army request, to exfiltrate agents and an Italian with plans and photographs of a section of the Gothic Line in the

---

* See below.

* For a discussion of the relative merits of these boats see "Corsica Operations," above.

Pesaro region. Several carefully briefed partisan guides and San Marco officers were infiltrated and returned successfully four days later. The material reached Eighth Army four days before its attack on the Gothic Line in the Pesaro sector.

A total of ten clandestine maritime patrols on Lake Comacchio were accomplished, several small islands in the lake occupied, and a series of small offensive forays run against the enemy-held northern shore of the lake. By mid-April partisan groups south of Chioggia were contacted and, with the more clement spring weather conditions, rapidly supplied both by air and by sea.* Several other operations were run jointly with the Eighth Army Detachment to infiltrate and recover agents and couriers.

---

* See "Italian Resistance," below.

E. SUB-BASES ON THE SWISS AND FRENCH BORDERS

LUGANO

OSS/Bern's first channels into Italy were established in December 1942, through contacts among political refugees living in the neighborhood of Lugano, just across the frontier from Italy. These men formed the nucleus of the committee, representing the major underground parties, which was secretly established as the CLNAI in Lugano in May 1944.*

The cleavage in Italian diplomatic and consular ranks, as a result of the fall of the Fascist Government, opened a broad field for the penetration of Italy through official channels. Many of the high-echelon personnel were pro-Allied. Those who were not were either dismissed or assigned to unimportant posts. SIM, the Italian secret service, not only became an SI source, but served as a medium for the release of Italian military personnel interned in Switzerland. Prisoners thus freed were sent back to Italy to organize SI chains, and to act as liaison with the partisans. Several of the smaller Italian consular posts afforded valuable cover for SI and SO operations, and at OSS insistence they remained open, despite initial orders from the Badoglio Government to terminate them.

At first, OSS/Bern was hampered in organizing its activities in Italy, both by the lack of Italian-speaking personnel and by inadequate cover. An American, resident in Lugano, was made OSS representative.

Since his status was unofficial, he had periodic difficulties with the Swiss, who on several occasions virtually terminated his operations. Since diplomatic cover was essential, the State Department authorized, at the end of 1943, the establishment of a Vice-

* See "Italian Resistance," below.

Consulate at Lugano. Although the OSS representative could now operate more securely, sub-agents continued to be hindered by unpredictable Swiss controls. But the Vice-Consulate protected caches of arms and supplies and a clandestine press for printing identity cards and passes.

From 1943 on, a series of well-organized intelligence chains into Italy sent to OSS/Bern a constant stream of couriers with documents, maps and the latest data on German movements and fortifications.

On 28 January 1944, a "revolution" was staged in the Italian enclave of Campione, a small village across the border from Lugano and peacetime gambling center for visiting tourists. In the "revolution" (which was unopposed) Campione declared its allegiance to the Badoglio Government, and an OSS base was established on Italian soil.

At OSS suggestion, it was determined that the Commune should be placed under the control of the Italian Legation in Bern, which by this time was cooperating with the Allies. The Swiss agreed to insure the food supply for the 600 inhabitants. Swiss francs replaced the lire. It was also decided that OSS would assume Campione's expenses until the Italian Government could again meet them.

Campione at once became the base for operations difficult or impossible to conduct from Lugano. In December 1944 a radio station was installed, and some of the intelligence which had formerly been routed through Bern was radioed directly from Campione to Caserta. Efforts were made to maintain contact with the resistance forces in the Como region, using small sets with a limited range, but, due to technical difficulties, the system never functioned reliably.

To coordinate air targets and air supply and to handle the volume of Italian intelligence coming from Bern, a Swiss Desk was established at 2677th Regiment headquarters in Caserta in July 1944. The speed and importance of Swiss intelligence rose sharply with the establishment of radio contact on 28 August, and the opening of the French-Swiss border for pouch delivery. By 31 September, pinpoints, complete with ground signals and BBC call phrases, were on the air supply schedule for Italy.

The need for further coordination became apparent with the premature partisan uprisings, such as those in the Val d'Ossola and the Val d'Aosta.* While these effected a temporary diversion of German troops, nevertheless the gain from the abortive attempts was not considered equal to the loss of well-organized resistance centers deep in enemy-held territory. In addition, the chief of OSS/Bern desired strongly to shift Italian contacts from inside Switzerland to Annemasse ** and Campione in order to avoid Swiss annoyance and to preserve the operations into Germany. Frequent border violations, both by partisans and by OSS agents, emphasized the need.*

In November it was decided that all operations into North Italy would be under Company D control, and that OSS agents there would not contact OSS/Switzerland except in emergencies or when full information on their operation had been given to its chief. Lugano would maintain operating courier and supply routes into North Italy, but these would be coordinated by a Company D liaison officer established there in January 1945. Wherever possible, patriot groups or intelligence chains would be supplied with radios to report to OSS/MedTO, direct rather than by courier through Switzerland, in order, not only to concentrate operations, but also to expedite the transmittal of intelligence to Allied forces in Italy.

---

* See "Italian Resistance", below.
** See below.

ANNEMASSE

At the time of the campaign in southern France, the extensive coverage of German order of battle along the French-Italian frontier by the partisans and the Piedmontese resistance groups kept Allied forces informed of all German military movements which might have constituted threats to the Seventh Army flank. The PAPAYA mission of nineteen men was dispatched to the region of Annemasse, just inside France, to contact these patriot organizations.

PAPAYA occupied an anomalous position between theaters. It was supplied by OSS/France, operationally controlled by OSS/Switzerland, and administratively handled by OSS/Caserta. Operational material for delivery to the partisans was dispatched to PAPAYA from Italy. Its position was further complicated by French annexationist aims across the Italian border. The French resented any potential interference with, or observation of, their plans to obtain possession of the Tenda and Briga regions, and feared that political reports sent out from the area would place their activities in a bad light.

PAPAYA reached Annemasse in the last week of September. The mission leader did not wait for the "proceed" signal, but crossed the border into Italy on his own initiative, accompanied by several other mission members. All were quickly captured by German border patrols and interned as prisoners of war.* The remainder of the mission stayed on the French side of the border, and was subsequently reorganized into an advance supply base for North Italian operations.**

Like the base at Campione, it assisted the detachments at Fifth and Eighth Armies and the Maritime Unit on the east Italian coast in the exploitation of Italian resistance to support Allied forces.

---

* Fortunately the Germans did not interrogate them closely.
** And for operations into Germany. See "Bern", below.

F. ITALIAN RESISTANCE

1. Air Delivery

Air drop was the principal method for agent penetration and the only means of delivering supplies in any quantity into enemy-held territory. Infiltration by sea had become progressively difficult as the front moved up the Italian mainland, while maritime operations on the west coast were impracticable after June 1944.* The east coast had been heavily mined offshore and operations, such as those of the Maritime Unit on the British Eighth Army front, entailed a considerable element of uncertainty and, at best, could transport only limited quantities of supplies.**

Air containers and packages for partisan groups were prepared at a British-operated base near Brindisi. The OSS packing station, established in Algiers, had been dismantled after the South France invasion and the closing of the OSS base in Algiers. To meet the urgent supply requirements in North Italy, a new OSS packing staff was assembled, and its nucleus initially assigned to assist the British complement.

Air dispatch was effected by long-range RAF planes based in the Brindisi area. Due to the distance from the Italian front, weather factors frequently forced cancellation or postponement of agent and supply operations from Brindisi, despite reports of perfect conditions by the resistance groups. In addition, with RAF planes serving both the British and OSS, it frequently appeared to OSS officers that partiality in priority allocations was shown at times to British over OSS operations.

When weather prevented operations from Brindisi, the Twelfth Tactical Air Force, based near the front at Cecina and in the Arno Valley, was often able to carry out small-scale operations to fill immediate requirements of the Fifth and Eighth Army detachments.

Special Operations Section of AAI (15th Army Group) began its task as coordinator of all special operations into North Italy in February 1944.* To this Section was delegated responsibility for the equitable allocation and control of airlift for personnel and supplies. In effect, the dispatch of all missions, both for operations and intelligence purposes, required clearance from "Special Ops" whether infiltrated by air or by sea.

The liaison officer to "Special Ops" from Company D was recognized as representative for (1) the former OSS/AAI operations which were arbitrarily classified as OSS/SO, (2) the operations of SI/Italy which remained designated OSS/SI and (3) the Operational Groups. Strictly secret intelligence missions, that is, the infiltration of teams for clandestine intelligence, in contrast to supply drops and missions to contact partisan or resistance groups, were not under "Special Ops" control, except for the scheduling of transportation, and in cases of suspected overlap with British SIS projects.

At first, "Special Ops" attempted to set up British and American spheres of influence in North Italy and arbitrarily to establish the ratio of supplies to be dropped between these zones as two-thirds of the total monthly lift to the British zone and one-third to the American. This ratio approximated the number of resistance contacts that had been made in North Italy thus far by SOE and OSS. However, SOE had been more able to initiate long-range operations into North Italy, beginning immediately after the Salerno landings, basically because it was ac-

---

* See "Corsica Operations", below.
** See next section.

* See "Bases in Italy", above.

107

cepted as an integral part of the British military effort and did not have to divert part of its efforts to establishing its role in the Theater. Only by mid-1944 was OSS in a position to embark on a full-scale Special Operations program for North Italy. It protested vigorously the ratio, as working to prevent the adequate development of OSS contacts among resistance groups.

The allocations of spheres of influence was also questioned, as it would have entailed OSS' abandoning many of its more firmly established resistance contacts, such as in Genoa, Milan, Turin and Spezia. The matter was referred to AFHQ and the decision made that existing contacts of OSS and SOE should be maintained, overlaps should be apportioned equally between the services, and that, for a period of ninety days, both OSS and the British services would have equal monthly supply drop allocations.

The effect of this was to raise the monthly allocation from the original one for the month of March 1944 of 45 tons for OSS and 90 tons for the British, to an allotment of 142 tons for each agency in August. The July OSS quota had been set at 84 tons, but due to a diversion of planes to Italy when it was impractical to fly them elsewhere, a total of 141 tons was actually dropped for the agency in that month.

In September, all available long-range aircraft in MedTO were diverted from Mediterranean targets to Poland, in a Strategic Air Forces move to support the underground inside Warsaw. This severely affected the partisan supply program in Italy at a crucial moment, preventing adequate re-supply of several major partisan groups suffering under concentrated German mopping-up campaigns.*

In October, a wing of American four-motored bombers arrived at Brindisi to supplement the RAF, but weather conditions held up all but fourteen percent of the scheduled 1,600 ton drop for that month. On the few good days, mass drops were attempted,

but although increased tonnage was lifted, the margin of error in this method was great and the material was scattered over a wide territory. Out of 223 tons delivered, only 92 were recovered in usable condition.*

Throughout the winter, OSS and SOE bent all efforts to deliver as many supplies as possible despite unfavorable weather and despite the Theater Commander's order to the partisans to "lie low".** Total tonnages dropped were 149 in November, 350 in December, approximately 175 in January and 592 in February.

In March 1945, the American four-motored bombers were moved up to Cecina, where a field had been specially prepared during the winter. The bulk of installations relevant to Company D operations were then transferred from Company B in the Bari-Brindisi area to a newly activated Company C in the Cecina-Leghorn area.*** With American planes, improved weather, and the high output of the OSS packing station, which exceeded all schedules, new highs were reached in successful missions and amounts of supplies delivered to the partisans. The March allotment of 700 tons had been flown by the 23rd, and 190 more were delivered by the end of the month.

In the spring of 1945, OSS had more clandestine radio circuits successfully in operation and active liaisons with a greater number of effective resistance groups than did its British intelligence and operations counterparts. In the last two months of air supply, the OSS allotment was set higher than that for the British, and by VE-Day the total of American supplies, handled by the OSS packing station and successfully delivered inside North Italy, appreciably exceeded corresponding SOE totals.

While it is significant that OSS, once established and recognized in the Theater organization, could overtake its British

* For similar experiments with mass drops see section on "Supply" in France, below.
** See next section.
*** See "Bases in Italy", above.

* See next section.

counterparts in a relatively short period of time, the degree of resistance organization and activity inside northern Italy had by then reached such a pitch that it became less a matter of claiming credit for individual partisan groups than of relaying as effectively as possible the directives necessary properly to coordinate partisan efforts with the impending final Allied offensive.

2. Resistance Aid to the Armies in North Italy

Partisan bands, which had developed spontaneously to resist the German occupation of Italy, grew stronger and more united after the capitulation of the Italian Army in September 1943. This was particularly true in North Italy, where Italian anti-Fascist as well as anti-German sentiment was at its strongest. Many former Italian Army officers joined the civilian resistance groups and imparted to them the formal organization of military units. Early activities were principally in the form of aid to Allied airmen who had bailed out, passive resistance to occupation directives, minor acts of sabotage, and service as intelligence sources for the Allied secret agents whose presence became known to an ever-widening range of partisans.

In North Italy the six principal anti-Fascist political parties, Partito d'Azione, Communist, Socialist, Christian Democrat, Liberal and Republican, banded together to form a unified resistance movement with headquarters in Milan. This organization became known as the CLNAI (Comitato di Liberazione Nazionale per l'Alta Italia), and was both a political and a military organization. Its president was Pietro Longhi, a prominent banker and former president of the Credito Italiano of Milan. Its military activities were concentrated in the CVL (Combattenti Volontari di Liberazione).

By April 1944 CLNAI had constituted itself the supreme authority for resistance in North Italy, and, as it gained in strength, it

assumed the stature of an underground government. Contact had been made with the Rome headquarters of the organization in the winter of 1943–44 by OSS agent chains there. In September 1944 a combined SI/OG mission, MANGOSTINE, was dispatched from Company D to serve as the permanent liaison between OSS and the northern headquarters of CLNAI. Two of the three officers had charge of intelligence and operations respectively. (The team leader was killed shortly after arrival.)

In November 1944, several of the CLNAI leaders (including President Longhi, Ferruccio Parri, later Premier of Italy, and Raimondo Craveri, son-in-law of Benedetto Croce), were exfiltrated through Switzerland and brought to Caserta for conference. They sought a tripartite agreement with the Allies and the Italian Government, to supply them with the funds necessary for their operations and to extend to them recognition as the de facto government in North Italy. They proposed placing into the field 90,000 partisans, and estimated the monthly expense per man at 1,500 lire, which, combined with a further sum necessary for couriers, transportation and the relief of bereaved families, came to a total of 160,000,000 lire a month. The sum was to be distributed to partisan groups all over Italy, according to regional priorities established by the Allied Command, but only to units under the control of CLNAI. This would avoid the passing of Allied funds to unauthorized or brigand groups, and would serve to unify patriot activity.

On 7 December 1944 an agreement was signed under SACMED authority whereby OSS and SOE would each allocate 80,000,000 lire per month for five months to CLNAI.* This money would be repaid to the British and American Governments by the Italian Government after the war,

---

* The total was raised in March 1945 to 350,000,000 lire, still shared by SO and SOE.

Air drops were not to be used. No other Allied funds of any size were to be given to individual resistance groups without specific approval from CLNAI.

The Italian Government was at that time in a political crisis from which it did not emerge until shortly before Christmas, when Bonomi became Premier. On 26 December Bonomi signed an agreement recognizing CLNAI as the provisional government of North Italy, which would subordinate itself to the central Italian Government upon the liberation of North Italy. The CLNAI delegates were successfully returned on 29 December.*

In the summer, fall and winter of 1944, OSS was instrumental in harnessing resistance groups throughout North Italy and forging them into a weapon that created a major diversion of the German military effort on the Italian front. In the interior, partisan bands were equipped and trained, and their operations were coordinated for maximum effectiveness in driving the Germans from whole areas and in making German movement, except in large convoys, dangerous at best. On sectors of the front itself, partisan support made it possible for thinly spread Allied forces to hold the line.

As the Allies advanced, partisans were organized by OSS to operate directly in support of the U. S. Fifth Army. This presented certain problems with respect both to partisan groups at the front and to those overrun by the advance. Food, clothing and equipment for hundreds of men were provided initially by supplies forwarded from OSS supply depots. Subsequently, through the cooperation of army, corps and divisional supply units, supplementary standard items of equipment were obtained. For clothing, the partisans were given GI uniforms dyed a dark green. A hospital for partisan wounded was established near the Fifth Army front.

The principal organized resistance group in the Florence region had early been contacted by OSS agent "Vera" of the NADA * team. A series of supply operations had permitted the partisans in the resistance group to equip themselves and, by means of their communication with OSS headquarters, to carry out operations of immediate aid to the armies. For instance, an enemy staff car carrying Japanese naval and military attaches was demolished at a road block, and highly classified papers were seized and delivered to OSS. When Allied troops entered Florence, the operations of this group alone accounted for some 500 German casualties and the blowing of seven major highway and rail bridges to impede the German retreat.

On 10 June two leaders of another resistance movement in the Apuan Alps, northeast of Genoa, crossed into American lines and supplied extensive, detailed information on the German Gothic Line. They immediately volunteered for a second mission and refused parachute training as being too time-consuming. After demolitions and communications briefing, they were parachuted "cold", late in August, to the FAUSTO resistance group, which at that time was reported to number 4,000 men and to have captured 450 German prisoners.

The group operated between Genoa and Piacenza, and in September captured a German courier carrying top secret documentation from Kesselring to the German commanding officer on the front facing the Fifth Army. The papers, weighing over 100 lbs. in their cases, were brought through the lines and delivered to OSS. Considered highly significant by 15th Army Group, they also included identification of German espionage agents in Italy which proved of interest to CIC.

---

* Parri, future Premier of Italy, was arrested by the Germans one week after his return. OSS/Bern, however, arranged for his release in March 1945. See "Secret Surrender Negotiations," below.

---

* See "Early Infiltrations of North Italy," from Fifth Army, above.

110

The Germans began a major assault on the guerrillas in August with the objective of clearing Route 45 between Genoa and Piacenza, in a drive which extended through early September. Just at this time Warsaw resistance priorities diverted air lift from Italian operations and it became impossible to provide adequate re-supply.* Axis forces cleared the highway, and subsequently opened a second offensive on the partisans, who had withdrawn into the hills. The resistance dispersed after an appreciable diversion of German troops had been accomplished, and soon re-formed on the Fifth Army front along with other patriot groups of the Tuscan resistance, which had remained active north of Spezia.

When the general German retreat from Rome to the Gothic Line was at its height in the summer and fall of 1944, several major partisan groups deep inside North Italy, supplied with communications and weapons by OSS, engaged in open warfare against the Germans, aided by OSS/OG teams sent in to coordinate and lead specific units.

One of the principal uprisings was in the Val d'Ossola, where a large group of partisans, one of whose leaders was OSS agent "Como",** attacked German garrisons along the Lago Maggiore and sought to clear the enemy from a stretch of the Swiss-Italian frontier. "Como" had frequently contacted OSS/Switzerland and had established a supply base at Campione. From there he made frequent trips into Switzerland to procure equipment and arms and transport them across the border to the Italian patriots. On 11 August an OG mission, CHRYSLER, consisting of two OG officers and three enlisted men, parachuted to join the partisans, along with seven tons of supplies.

Early in September the Germans were reported to have committed up to two divisions to eliminate the Val d'Ossola bands. On 9 September they occupied the town of Can-

nobio. Two weeks later, the guerrillas notified OSS/Switzerland that they could recapture the town if they could be supported by Allied air attacks on certain specified targets, including enemy barracks and lake boats being used as transports.

Bern relayed the message to Caserta on 22 September, and on 25 September, the day of the partisan attack, the Tactical Air Force bombed as requested:

The bombing was a complete success. Landing stages at Luino were destroyed and six lake steamers damaged at the pier. A large steamer carrying 500 Fascist troops was sunk . . . the bombing took place at the same time as the partisan attack, the re-capture of Cannobio being successfully accomplished. The partisans are now in control of the whole region to a point north of Intra. As a result of this operation, morale has been greatly raised in all of North Italy.*

The news that a partisan operation had been successfully supported by Allied air operations was considered by the Germans a severe blow to their military prestige. They staged a heavy counterattack, and the partisons requested further Allied air support for an additional drive to be staged in October. However, with Allied aircraft diverted to support the Warsaw resistance,** it was impossible to comply, or even to deliver adequate supplies. Thus it was inevitable that the German attack should succeed.

"Como" made a final trip to Switzerland, obtained a quantity of Swiss arms and ammunition and loaded them secretly on a freight train. When the Swiss border control discovered the contraband, he took over the train, crashing it across the frontier into Italian territory occupied by partisans.

His operation was embarrassing diplomatically, and the Swiss took direct exception to it, particularly in view of the fact that the smuggled arms were of Swiss manufacture. "Como's" wife, who served as his assistant in Switzerland, was arrested, but

---

* See previous section.
** See "Early Infiltrations of North Italy" from Fifth Army, above.

* OSS cable, Bern to Caserta, 27 September 1944. OSS Archives.
** See previous section.

made her escape from jail by tieing sheets together and letting herself out of a window. Because of his connection with "Como", the OSS representative in Lugano lost his passport, and his travel from Lugano was restricted. "Como's" departure, not only from Switzerland but from Campione, became imperative, but considerable subterfuge was necessary to get him, via Geneva, into France and back to southern Italy, where he was detained for the duration.

Meanwhile on 10 October the Germans had recaptured Cannobio, and most of the valley was again in their hands. The remainder of the resistance dispersed or retreated into the hills. The OG CHRYSLER team, along with numerous resistance members, crossed into Switzerland. Two key OSS operations officers were dispatched to Switzerland from Company D to obtain a firsthand report of the situation and to establish procedure for supporting North Italian operations near Switzerland.*

An additional uprising, although on a somewhat smaller scale, took place in the Val d'Aosta, but, before appreciable supplies could be delivered by air to reinforce the partisans, the German mop-up had forced them to disband.

On the eastern end of the front, Ravenna partisan groups were contacted in September and supplied in a series of night maritime landings. A radio, BIONDA, served as liaison between the partisan group and Eighth Army headquarters. Both the intelligence supplied through BIONDA and the guerrilla operations of the partisan group were of direct material assistance in the capture of Ravenna.

On the western coast, meanwhile, another Allied action was supported by partisan action. When the 92nd Division attacked towards Spezia in October, the "Apuan patriots", located in enemy territory, struck at the enemy from the rear, making it possible for the 92nd to overrun Massa, while another partisan brigade actually occupied Carrara. Partisans continued to support the Division in its drive for Spezia, while an additional brigade operated to the north and east of the Division's right flank.

For the Brazilians, the partisans acted chiefly as an advance unit to report German attack preparations, and held mountainous sections of the line on a par with regular troops. At the time of the IV Corps Christmas offensive, the commanding general of the Corps credited OSS-directed partisan groups with having prevented a far-reaching enemy break-through.

Further operations and OG teams were dispatched throughout the winter, and liaison was effected with the major organized centers of partisan resistance. Conferences were held in the fall with commanders of the two leading resistance movements on the French Italian frontier, and a program was outlined to pass supplies to these groups both by air and through Annemasse.* The two leaders were re-infiltrated by parachute to their respective groups.

In November two members of the resistance command in the Parma zone, one of them a priest, came out through the lines to contact the Pope and the Italian Crown Prince. The priest had been charged by the Bishop of Parma with informing the Pope of the activities of the Church in the clandestine movements in North Italy, and obtaining ecclesiastical authority for the Bishop to appoint chaplains upon request from partisan bands. Until late 1944, the Vatican had discounted the resistance movement, first because it considered it dominated by revolutionary and anti-clerical elements, and second, because of unfamiliarity with its effectiveness and strength. It was significant that, shortly thereafter, the Vatican reversed its position, and religious leaders were encouraged to support the patriots.

---

* See "Sub-bases on the Swiss and French Borders", above.

* See "Sub-bases on the Swiss and French Borders", above.

All OSS teams were briefed to assist in the exfiltration of Allied airmen shot down over North Italy. Coordination of such operations was the responsibility of the Escape and Exfiltration Section of Twelfth Air Force. In January the latter reported that the assistance to its program by OSS and the use of OSS facilities had raised the number of downed airmen rescued from 10% to 17%. By winter, five out of every nine Americans rescued were evacuated through OSS channels.

In November the Theater Commander issued a directive to all partisan groups in North Italy to "lie low" for the winter. The extended stretches of bad weather, that had repeatedly made flying impossible, and the danger of further diversion of Theater aircraft aroused fears that it would not be possible to give adequate supplies to the partisans during the cold months, particularly in view of the fact that open resistance groups would have to be fed, clothed and equipped. The effect of this directive on partisan morale was naturally depressing. OSS, SOE and AAI vigorously protested these measures, and all efforts were made to deliver as many supplies as possible.

The Germans capitalized on the "winter lull" by conducting another series of severe counterattacks and mopping-up operations. An interesting commentary upon their respect for partisans came to light from prisoner of war interrogations, when it was learned that German soldiers had to be given special inducements for days of service in anti-partisan operations (Baenderkampftage). Nevertheless, the combination of supply shortages and German counter-measures forced many of the partisan groups to disband for the winter.

Starting in December, however, the Maritime Unit undertook to organize other partisan groups in the Po Delta. The entire Po Valley had proved the most difficult part of enemy-occupied Italy for agent infiltration, due to the heavy concentration of German forces in this highly populated area.

In the Comacchio region radio BIONDA * and partisan leaders from Ravenna were re-infiltrated, and a partisan group of several hundred Italians was maintained and operated in close liaison with the Eighth Army Command. Weather conditions throughout the winter made re-supply at times extremely difficult. Nevertheless, the intelligence produced through BIONDA remained an effective and important source both for Eighth Army and, more specifically, for the Polish Corps.

By March the weather had lifted, and the flow of supplies successfully dropped to partisans exceeded allocation schedules.** Groups that had dissolved in the winter re-formed in numbers stronger than ever. At this point AFHQ, however, desired to prevent expansion of the resistance movement, to avoid repetition of the bitter post-liberation experience in Greece. Again OSS, SOE and "Special Ops" protested, requesting instead 1,200 tons as the monthly allotment. They argued that the strain on the resistance throughout the winter made it unwise, as well as a breach of faith, to withhold supplies just when the partisan effort was reaching its full potential for the final drive in North Italy. The directive was revised. Recognizing the wide potential strength of the partisans in support of the final drive, AFHQ decided that there should be no limit on supplies to partisans in the Apennine area, whose activities formed a part of 15th Army Group's tactical plan. Supplies to partisans in other areas, however, were limited to 250 gross tons, and an increasing percentage of non-military supplies, such as food, clothing and medicine, would be included in supply drops.

To avoid the difficulty feared by AFHQ, special American Liaison Officer Teams (ALOTS) were formed to assist in maintaining partisan discipline. They were to enter specified areas and establish liaison with the local or zonal partisan command, in order to

---

* See "Company D", above.
** See previous section.

113

TRANSLATION

Telegram from C-in-C, South-West.

To: 1. Supreme S.S. and Police Chief in Italy.

2. Commander, 14th Army.

3. Commander, Army of Liguria.

Date: 26th February '45.

Activity of partisan bands in the Western Appennines, and along the Via Emilia, particularly in the areas of MODENA, REGGIO and PARMA, and south-west of them, as well as near the neighborhood of PIACENZA, has spread like lightning in the last ten days. The concentration of the partisan groups of varying political tendencies into one organization, as ordered by the Allied High Command, is beginning to show clear results. The execution of partisan operations shows considerably more commanding leadership. Up to now it has been possible for us, with a few exceptions, to keep our vital rear lines of communications open by means of our slight protective forces, but this situation threatens to change considerably for the worse in the immediate future. Speedy and radical counter measures must anticipate this development.

It is clear to me that the only remedy, and the one which is unavoidably necessary to meet the situation, is the concentration of all available forces, even if this means temporary weakening in other places. I request you therefore to combine with 14th Army and the Army of Liguria, in carrying out several large scale operations which will nip in the bud the increasing activity of the partisan bands in Northern Italy. Please let me have your proposals as to when these measures can be carried out, and with what forces.

(Signed) KESSELRING

coordinate and assist in operations and act in an advisory and instructional capacity, as well as transmitting directives from 15th Army Group. In addition, each ALOT was given specific plans of action, both positive and counter-scorch,* to be executed in support of the Allied spring offensive. But the principal assignment, from the point of view of the Theater Command, was to prevent friction with and between partisan bands. Four of these teams were prepared for dispatch in the spring.

In April 1945, when Allied Armies in Italy unleashed the final offensive across the Apennines, there were over 75 OSS teams active behind enemy lines, working with resistance groups, organizing sabotage and harassing operations, planning counter-scorch measures, and sending intelligence by radio to Company D or to the detachments with Fifth and Eighth Armies. Entire regions in North Italy were actually cleared of German troops, and the German Commander-in-Chief admitted that movement, except in large, heavily armored convoy, was impossible.

So close was partisan cooperation with individual army units that coordinates for artillery fire were frequently reported to corps, division or battalion headquarters. At other times, partisan groups established road blocks on German supply routes behind the front, and sent word by radio of the development of German traffic congestion, to permit bombing and strafing by Army Air Force planes.

On 5 April all partisan units in tactical positions immediately ahead of American lines were alerted by General Clark to support the impending Allied offensive. On 9 April the Eighth Army attacked in the east, and on 14 April the Fifth Army opened its offensive in the center toward Bologna. The army detachment teams were quickly overrun. Six agent teams, reporting directly to the Eighth Army Detachment, were able to furnish sig-

nificant tactical information to the British on conditions along the east coast as far as Venice and up the Po Valley as far as Bologna. Additional teams were sent into enemy territory both for Fifth and Eighth Army detachments. Fifth Army teams were parachuted as far north as the area east of Lake Garda to observe movements along strategic enemy retreat routes, and all stations reporting to the Detachment were ordered to transmit bulletins every four hours instead of on the former schedule of once a day.

MU personnel on the Adriatic continued offensive patrols on Lake Comacchio and carried additional supplies to partisans along the entire coast from the Po to Venice. Between 22 and 27 April, OSS officers, with personnel from the San Marco Battalion and from SOE, coordinated the general rising of partisan groups to liberate a stretch of fifty miles of Italian coast including Chioggia on the Venice Lagoon.

OG teams, operating in the area south of Piacenza and Parma, organized successful road blocks on the key transport routes in their region and conducted extensive harassing operations against German columns and concentrations.

Orders to the partisans included not only the immobilization of enemy columns but the cutting of potential enemy escape routes to the north and the prevention of demolitions, particularly of municipal, industrial and transport installations. Specific missions ordered by "Special Ops", including orders to march on Parma and Fidenza, were carried out by over 4,000 patriots active in the region. Fidenza fell on 23 April three days before the arrival of troops of the American 34th Division. The German 148th Infantry Division was trapped through partisan operations between Pontremoli and Parma, and surrendered to the Allies on 29 April. Direct support, in the form of a strong road block and sudden flanking movement, was given to the 92nd Division in the capture of Pontremoli.

---

* Preventing enemy destruction of vital installations.

Allied Liaison Officer Teams and OG's took the lead in organizing partisan groups to cut potential enemy escape routes. Missions in North Italy were not alerted by 15th Army Group for all-out attack until 25 April, and, with the rapidity of the Allied advance, it was not possible to develop the full partisan potential before the attack order. Nevertheless Route 38, leading from Lake Como northeastward to the Brenner, was cut and held near Stelvio Pass and a by-pass route east of Sondrio, Route 39, was closed at Colle d'Aprica. Route 42 leading to Bolzano was also closed. Other teams operated successfully in the regions north of Udine and near Belluno.

Several widely separated counter-scorch operations were notably effective. An OG unit, directing 15,000 partisans in the Genoa region, interrupted German demolitions of the city's roads and took 3,000 German prisoners. AFHQ and the Allied Control Commission placed great importance on this operation, since it had been planned to use Genoa as a principal port for bringing food and supplies to North Italian cities. By the time the American 92nd Division reached the port, order had already been restored in the city, and enemy prisoners and equipment were turned over to Fifth Army. Other teams in the region between Lake Garda and the Swiss border were directly instrumental in preserving from destruction several key dams and power plants which provided twenty percent of the electrical supply of Milan. One team captured intact a large German communications center at Corvara.

Perhaps the most spectacular counter-scorch operation took place in Venice where team MARGOT, in liaison with the CLNAI, opened contact with the German commandant of the city, and received a guarantee that installations in Venice, threatened with destruction by the Germans, would not be touched, in exchange for a promise by the partisans not to attack or molest the German garrison prior to Allied arrival. In addition, using the partisan threat, MARGOT secured plans of mine fields in the harbor and nearby waters.*

---

* For OSS/Bern negotiations leading to the Axis surrender in North Italy on 2 May, see "Secret Surrender Negotiations," below. For post-liberation activity in North Italy, see "Italy" under Part VIII, below.

Part IV

SMALL EUROPEAN RESISTANCE MOVEMENTS

OSS joined British services in organizing, supplying, directing and exploiting resistance movements in Greece, Albania, Yugoslavia, Czechoslovakia, Denmark and Norway. (Underground groups in Belgium, Holland and Poland were handled principally by the British with OSS/SO support at the London base.)

In five of the six countries, the SO/SOE agreement gave SOE control of coordinated operations in connection with resistance, and guerrilla groups had long been organized. SI, SO and OG's helped SOE to support, and to gain intelligence from, the various groups, in some cases establishing liaison with resistance units which had refused British overtures. In the Balkans, U. S. personnel soon became involved in the internal political conflicts, often disagreeing with British policy. In Scandinavia, on the contrary, where resistance was unified, native agents were principally used, and SO worked in closest coordination with SOE.

In Czechoslovakia alone, no large resistance group at first existed, and there was no SOE preemption. In August 1944, according to arrangements by the Czech Government-in-Exile in London and Moscow, Czech Forces of the Interior began an insurrection with headquarters at Banska Bystrica. Apparently no arrangements for supply had been made, and OSS/MedTo rushed to dispatch quantities of its Cairo stocks, but was largely prevented by bad weather. At the same time, Russian forces failed to break through to the resistance group as promised. The result was a disaster to resistance and OSS personnel.

A rough estimate of enemy forces detained through 1944 by these small-nation * resistance groups would total, together with the continuous losses in German war materiel and soldiers, some forty divisions.

* Not including Belgium, Holland, Poland, and Czechoslovakia.

A. GREECE

Between August 1943, when the first two SI agents disembarked from a submarine, and November of the following year, over 300 OG's and SI, MO and SO agents were infiltrated to Greece and the Greek Islands. These were dispatched by air from Italy and Cairo, by land from Turkey, or by sea from Turkey and Italy. Special operatives worked with guerrillas in harassing German troops, destroying vital installations, and reporting enemy battle order. Agents worked undercover in Greek cities, running extensive chains to collect political, economic and military intelligence. They gathered many of the shipping reports which made it possible for the RAF to clear Axis shipping from the whole Aegean. From 1943 on, OSS provided the State Department with the only independent American information on Greek political affairs and the moves and intentions of other powers in that country.

Two OSS representatives had arrived in Cairo in April 1942 to survey possibilities for operations across the Mediterranean. In December JCS approved establishment of a base, and in March 1943 the first SO officers for Greek operations arrived, followed in May by the first SI officers. The SO/SOE agreement * gave SOE in Cairo direction of SO operations, and SO teams were ordered to use British communications under the command of the senior SOE officer of the area of operations. Since it coordinated air transport over the Balkans, SOE similarly attempted to assert control of SI activities. The independence of U. S. intelligence was however maintained, although SI thenceforth had to rely chiefly on sea transportation.

On the other hand, SIS offered every kind of advice and material support to SI, includ-

---
* Signed in London, June 1942. See "Introduction", above.

ing all documents from 1943 up to the outbreak of the Greek Civil War at the end of the following year. SIS furnished also money (gold), arms and maritime conveyance for SI teams, until OSS/Cairo was able to supply these services independently. In return, OSS afforded considerable assistance with the clandestine boat service it later built up. SI agents penetrated several areas on which British coverage had been insufficient (e.g. Evros, East Thessaly, Corfu and Euboea), supplementing Allied order of battle intelligence.

Assistance also came to OSS from the Hellenic Information Service of the Greek Government-in-Exile; HIS recruited all service personnel for the SI/Greek Desk, as well as some agents. In return for this, OSS supplied HIS with selected intelligence reports on political and economic conditions inside Greece.

Recruiting and Training

Agents were recruited principally in and around Cairo, although some arrived from the United States. They were mostly Greeks at first, but it was early decided to use Americans to lead the teams. Reasons given for the decision were: (1) That American agents would provide less biased intelligence coverage; and (2) that native agents would find it more difficult to gain the necessary respect and assistance from guerrilla groups.

Initially, agents received rudimentary instruction from the desk heads only, but, by August 1943, a training school was in operation, originally out in the desert at Ras el Kanayas, later on the outskirts of Cairo. A nine-day briefing course for English-speaking agents included instruction in order of battle, reporting, cover, code, maps, escape and security. Sixty-eight agents, who were to parachute in, went to the British school at Ramat David in Palestine, where in ten days they made six day-jumps and two night-jumps. Here, also, they received British training in demolitions, field craft, close combat and associated arts. Radio operators went on field trips to other cities in Egypt, for practice in setting up clandestine sets and operating unknown to the control authorities. Finally, the agents waited in the holding area at Ras el Kanayas, taking refresher courses, pending the laying on of transportation.*

Infiltration

The greatest handicap to operations from Cairo was inadequate transportation. Parachute training, followed by the long wait on the priority list of the Balkan Air Force, took months. The question of a small air unit under OSS control was unsuccessfully raised. MTB's were requested repeatedly but never arrived. Of the means available, Greek caiques, which usually transported agents in about one and a half months, proved to be the fastest.

Caiques were small fishing and cargo vessels, from two to eighty tons, manned by crews of from two to six men. The larger ones were fitted with antiquated auxiliary engines, producing a speed of three to four knots. Thirty-six of these boats were at one time or another operated, first by SI, later by OSS/Maritime Unit. The port of Alexandria was embarking point from Egypt; from there, the larger (fifty to eighty ton) caiques sailed to Karavostasi on the northwest coast of Cyprus Island, where OSS hired crews and built up a large store of supplies. The next stage, accomplished in twenty to forty ton caiques, went to Kusadasi, Turkey, and the final jump-off post was Rema Bay, Turkey, whence the smallest of the vessels transported agents to occupied Greece.

SIS facilitated the organization of this service, not only in the charter of caiques

and the supply of the Cyprus base, but also in making arrangements with the Turkish secret police for permission to operate U. S. caiques in Turkish waters and ports.

Secret Intelligence

Between May and October 1944, 30 SI teams totalling 80 U. S. agents left the bases at Cairo, Bari and Istanbul, a maximum of 23 teams being in Greece at one time. Of these 23, 5 were performing liaison with guerrilla groups (four with EAM/ELAS in Thrace, Thessaly, Euboea and the Peloponnesus, one with EDES * in Epirus), while 18 were undercover in enemy-controlled territory, including Athens, Salonika, Khalkidike, the Dodecanese and Aegean Islands and Corfu.

The only British or American mission to reach EAM headquarters was SI team PERICLES, which accompanied this Hq. from 29 April 1944 almost to the outbreak of civil war at the end of the year. Through its connections with the Greek labor movement in Cairo, the Labor Desk/SI had established contact with EAM and arranged for the reception of three men (one U. S. Army officer, one Greek naval officer, and one Greek labor leader) to act at liaison. PERICLES' principal contribution consisted in independent U. S. political intelligence on EAM, its composition, strength and leadership, its reactions to the Greek unity conferences in the Middle East, its organization of a National Council in April 1944, and similar information of value to the State Department. PERICLES also signalled the unexpected arrival of a Russian Mission in July 1944, at a time when the British were contemplating denunciation of, and withdrawal of all their missions from, EAM; PERICLES provided exclusive news of the personnel and apparent purpose of the Russian drop, and of its reception by EAM.

---

* These training facilities were also used for agents destined for Yugoslavia.

* EAM and its army, ELAS, formed a leftist resistance group, eventually taken over by Communists. EDES was a smaller anti-Communist resistance group. See below.

Of all the SI teams, probably the most successful was the three-man HORSEBREEDERS, whose leader, prior to his enlistment in the U. S. Army, had been in British employ as an agent in Crete. HORSEBREEDERS was assigned the penetration of Volos, an important port from which little, if any, worthwhile intelligence had been produced. SIS had particularly requested this penetration, inasmuch as it was not satisfied with the SOE agent there and did not wish to compete directly with him.

Establishing himself in Kerasia, a village near Volos, the leader of HORSEBREEDERS established a network of some 500 sub-agents, covering Volos and the Thessaly plain northward. Recruiting a second radio operator, it provided a radio and set him up on Skiathos Island to report ship traffic on the important Pireaus-Salonika route through the Straits of Skiathos. Using this information, combined with intelligence from U. S. and British agents in Piraeus and Salonika, squadrons of the RAF joined the Royal Navy in clearing the Aegean of German shipping.

Two other radio operators were trained in the field, one to assist the original operator, and the other to establish a set near Lamia. The job was facilitated by the help of the EAM organization outside Volos, which provided contacts over the whole area.

Some idea of the operation of this extensive undercover chain may be obtained from the returnee report of its leader:

The network was composed of cells. Each cell consisted of about ten to twenty men who were working into a certain area. The organization plan of two cells was about as follows: Number 15 and number 23 were the cut-outs, that is, the persons to disappear in case of accident to some near person in the cell in order to cut the connection between the cell and central agent and not permit the enemy to pass from one side into the other. In that case, the reconnecting agent, number 07, would help in reaching the other central agent by going backwards through the other cell. The first organizer, number 01, was only to pass on the mail and follow the work of the cell in general. The numbers 02, 03, 05,

and 06 with their helpers a, b, and c were doing the main work, and I was corresponding with them and the first organizer. The helpers were to report and receive orders and instructions each one from his superior. A central agent was in each town, where the mail from all cells was concentrated, on the same day of the week or when there was something urgent, and from there it was forwarded to me. . . . Each report had to have in succession the number of the cell, the number of the agent and helper, its evaluation and the date of the information. For instance, 1605b5619 meant that in the 16th cell, the helper denoted by the letter b of the agent 05 saw with his own eyes (5) so and so to happen on June 19th.

In a special branch belonged persons who held positions very close to the enemy intelligence as interpreters, generally to German officers. They could inform us when the Germans suspected Greeks or were going to arrest certain people. In this way we could protect the network. Sometimes they also had the opportunity of obtaining valuable information or dealing with the Germans themselves. In this way we were able to buy secrets and to make sabotage against their army. . . . In addition, to this same branch belonged persons who gave shelter to other members of the organization in time of emergency or when they were passing through their villages.

I answered each of their reports and remarked on each point of information they sent me. I also specified what else I needed and gave them instructions on how to obtain the additional information. . . .

In addition I established five observation posts with which I was in direct touch by phone. Thus I knew immediately every shipment into Volos Port and from Euboea Island to the Thermaic Gulf. Two of the above posts were also observing car movements on the road from Volos to Larissa and from Volos to Almyros and the railroad line from Volos to Larissa. . . .

Agents had been put at all entrances of each town to observe what enemy war material was going in or out of the town. The same thing was done in the ports and aerodromes and railway stations. I had reports of all enemy transportation or movement with exact times everywhere in my area. The reconnaissance men were reporting about the quality and quantity of the enemy war material, and men were sending plans of the aerodromes, ports and every other enemy installation on the coast. . . .

The branch of sabotage also did a very good job. My agents were putting sand and emery dust in the grease boxes of the trains passing along the main railway between Lamia and Pir-getos. . . .*

It should be remembered that HORSE-BREEDERS operated under the advantageous conditions of an occupation, where there is less danger of being given away to the government than in neutral territory, and more recruits available than in an enemy country. Nevertheless, the accomplishments were spectacular.

Every method was employed by the occupying forces to capture such teams. Fifteen Germans tracked down an SI agent at Calchi, took hostages in the village and demanded his surrender. The agent secured his ciphers and documents and killed himself.

Morale Operations

MO meanwhile carried on operations to terrorize German garrisons, discourage collaborators and bolster resistance in Greece. Several media were used. From Cairo, in January 1944, the "black" radio MORSE broadcast in Morse code four times nightly to Greece and the Balkans. The programs consisted of newscasts, interspersed with rumors which MO wished planted, some of which were published in underground newspapers. The cover used for German broadcasts was that of a Nazi wireless operator giving the "inside story" to his fellow operators; for Greek, Hungarian and Rumanian broadcasts, it was an underground station sending out the truth to resistance groups.

In August 1944, the "black" radio station BOSTON was set up near Izmir with the cooperation of the Turkish secret police. It transmitted on a daily schedule of six ten-minute programs; the voice posed as a "reformed" Greek collaborationist, trying to convince his former partners of the folly of continuing their collaboration. This station was the target of a Nazi sabotage attempt and jamming operations. All radio broadcasts were discontinued after the liberation of Greece and the invasion of the Balkans in October 1944.

* The entire report is in History File 215.

MO also dispatched special missions to Greece and Crete. One such team was infiltrated in June 1944 to Volos, under HORSEBREEDERS' care, for the purpose of distributing subversive MO material. The two men printed a Greek newspaper designed to bolster Greek morale, and distributed pamphlets urging resistance. They sent out poison-pen letters, posted fake military orders and spread rumors.

MO originated a campaign to convince German troops that their commanders believed the war was lost and that soldiers should be saved to rebuild Germany. The British had kidnapped General Kreipe, German commander in Crete, and MO circulated the story that he gave himself up in protest against the "useless slaughter" of his troops. When General Krech was killed by Greek Andartes near Sparta, MO's version was that the Gestapo killed him while he was·trying to escape to a British submarine; according to MO, he left a letter justifying his escape by pointing out that Germany had lost the war and that it was criminal to sacrifice further lives, and stated further that he was taking this action in conjunction with General Kreipe. This campaign was implemented by rumors, "black" and "white" radio, planted letters and newspaper releases.

Special Operations

SO and OG sabotage was coordinated and directed by SOE according to the SO/SOE agreement.

The first SO sabotage operation was a dramatic one. At the request of the U. S. Joint Chiefs of Staff, following a letter from Secretary Hull,* SO undertook to cut the flow of crome ore from Turkey. R&A furnished important information on bridges in the Evros district. A four-man team crossed into Evros from Turkey on 29 March 1944, and walked five hours to the local EAM Hq. There it stayed two months, training and equipping (with parachuted arms) a force of 220 guerrillas and warding off attacks by

* See JCS Memo 816 in OSS Director's files.

122

troops of the quisling Greek Government. Bridges on the only two rail lines were selected:

Svilengrad bridge (Bulgaria) : 210 feet long and twelve feet high. Two U.S. officers and 170 guerrillas. 1,400 lbs. of plastic explosives.

Alexandroupolis bridge (Greece): 100 feet long and 45 feet high. Two U.S. non-commissioned officers and fifty guerrillas. 550 lbs. of plastic explosives.

On 27 May the detail for the first bridge arrived at the location.

Our plan was: (1) To place sufficient guards to eliminate any interference from the German guard post of ten men and the Bulgarian post of 21 men; (2) to prevent any reenforcements from reaching there in time; (3) cut all telephonic communications; (4) carry out the demolition of the bridge.

The first step was very easy because the Germans were caught napping and did not interfere until the last five minutes of the operation. They fired a flare and opened up with a machine gun and sub-machine guns in the general direction of the bridge. Luckily the bridge was already mined and we were making the connections with prima-cord. Steps two and three were easily carried out. . . . After the demolition of the bridge we began our forced march, crossing the Arda river at 0400 hours. There a German post noticed us and notified the reconnaissance battalion.

The next evening the reconnaissance battalion was hot on our trail. . . . Captain——, Lt. —— and the sabotage crew broke away from the main body and proceeded south to get the news of the southern bridge leaving a Greek officer in charge. This young officer after three days of maneuvering finally ambushed the CO of the German battalion and his staff and killed all of them.*

The detail for the Alexandroupolis bridge was equally successful, and the economic sabotage mission completed.

OSS activity was complicated by Greek politics. The strongest resistance group was the Communist-led EAM, with its army, ELAS, consisting in 1944 of an estimated 20,000 regulars and 10,000 irregulars. Next was the Socialist EDES, with an estimated 6,000 regulars and 4,000 irregulars. British

policy maintained consistent support of the Government-in-Exile in Cairo, at the same time sending military supplies to both resistance groups. U.S.-British relations were complicated by the constant appeals of EAM/ELAS and EDES to U.S. agents for assistance in combatting British influence in Greek affairs.

In this connection, a major SO achievement was the negotiation of the so-called "Plaka" agreement of February 1944 between EDES and EAM. This temporarily ended internecine fighting between the two guerrilla forces and directed their combined energies against the Germans, allotting different areas of combat for the two groups. The senior American officer on the Allied Military Mission to Greece * was credited by the British Mission Chief with major responsibility for the agreement.

Other SO operations included train hold-ups and road-mining, accompanied frequently by skirmishes with the Germans. A total of 25 SO agents entered Greece between September 1943 and November 1944; most of them were attached to guerrilla bands (principally EAM), leading them in sabotage operations, arranging for supplies by air and sea and for evacuation of U. S. fliers.

The first 4,800 pounds of military equipment arrived at a secret airfield on 21 October 1943, the same plane evacuating the first 10 airmen. Using guerrilla labor, SO completed four clandestine airfields, at Paramathia (EDES territory), Neohorion, Grevena (Macedonia) and Mavreli; these served through 1944 as supply and evacuation points. An over-all agreement was finally made for EAM to deliver all U. S. fliers to Euboea, whence they would ship out on OSS caiques.

The climax to Allied sabotage in occupied Greece carried the code name *Smashem*. According to plans of the SO/SOE Allied Military Mission, *Smashem* was to be the

* Report of the Evros Mission, p. 3, History File 215.

* Joint SO/SOE Mission to Greek resistance, commanded by an SOE officer.

123

final and operational phase of activity, with OG's and British Commandos cooperating with guerrillas to hamper the German troop withdrawal.

Beginning 23 April, 190 OG's, in groups of from three to fifteen, entered Greece by caique and joined guerrilla bands at strategic points. September 8 was fixed as the opening date for *Smashem,* with orders to sever rail lines and highways to impede the German withdrawal northward toward Yugoslavia. One Operational Group, stationed thirty miles from Lamia, near the Athens-Salonika railway, blew up over 7,400 yards of track. Another cut the Larissa-volos line, causing a seven-day interruption of train service. OG's ambushed convoys and trains, destroying locomotives, trucks and cars, and fighting numerous actions with German garrison troops. They were withdrawn in November 1944, having accomplished the following:

(a) Trains ambushed—14
(b) Bridges blown—15
(c) Trucks destroyed—61
(d) Railroad lines blown—6 miles (total)
(e) Enemy killed—349 (definite count)
(f) Enemy wounded—196 (definite count)
(g) Estimated killed and wounded—1,794 *

An unusual SO feat was the establishment of a clandestine hospital in Greece by a dental officer, who parachuted into Greece in December 1943. By June 1944, it had grown so large that 134 mules were required to move it from one location to another. The staff was international, consisting in that month of four Americans, three Russians, four Greeks and two Italians. The hospital cared for, in the following priority: (a) Members of the Allied Military Mission (U. S. and British); (b) EAM guerrillas; (c) local civilians. Following a drive against EAM, in the course of which the Germans burned 127 villages, the hospital provided 800 pounds of typhus and typhoid vaccines, sulfa drugs, atabrine, bandages, etc. This material had been flown in for the purpose and was distributed through Greek doctors.

Between the time of the arrival of the first SI agents in Greece in July 1943 and the outbreak of civil war in December 1944, OSS had undertaken extensive operations, handicapped to some extent by the absence of any faster transportation than the one to two month caique service. Supply of guerrillas by SO, and the delaying operation *Smashem* by OG's aimed at detaining as many German troops in Greece as late as possible. SI networks gathered information on enemy battle order, shipping, rail and other communications, and industrial production in Greece. SI also supplied the State Department with its only on-the-spot American intelligence on the national and international political developments in Greece.

Ambassador Lincoln MacVeagh wrote that OSS had:

. . . at all times been of great assistance to me in the conduct of this Mission. In addition, the number of written reports to which the Embassy has been accorded access has given it precious assistance in its attempts to evaluate conditions correctly in the enemy occupied countries to whose Governments it is accredited.*

UNRRA and FEA offered similar appreciation. At the outbreak of the civil war on 3 December 1944, extensive OSS networks were well established and afforded the State Department independent American coverage of military and political developments and, in particular, of EAM-British relations.**

---

* OG History of Operations in Greece, Part I, gives the breakdown of these statistics, History File 184.

* MavVeagh to OSS/Cairo, 14 October 1944, History File 214, pp. 112-3.
** See "Athens," below.

B. ALBANIA

The German occupation aroused resistance, as it had in neighboring Greece and Yugoslavia, from several Albanian guerrilla groups. Because the latter spent much of their time and equipment in civil war, U. S. policy was early decided against the supply of weapons. While no SO unit therefore entered the country, SI sent five teams for purposes of intelligence only. By November 1943, when the first arrived, the Communist-led FNC * controlled most of the country, and it was to FNC units that the five OSS teams were attached.

The first SI representative arrived in Cairo in June 1943 to begin operations into Albania, but found no suitable recruits with facility in the language. In November the desk moved to Bari and began dispatching agents originally recruited in the United States.

The first SI team, TANK, was smuggled ashore at night by British motor boat on 17 November 1943. The British SOE mission in Albania had refused to cooperate with OSS agents, unless they accepted British command and used British communications. The three men therefore, with FNC support, established themselves independently in a cave by the sea. They built up a network of agents and, by January, were radioing German battle order, economic information and intelligence on the strengths of the rival guerrilla groups. Among other services, they aided the return of a plane-load of 26 Americans forced down over FNC territory; this party (including eleven nurses) was helped by representatives of SOE, SIS and SI to reach the coast, when an SO team evacuated them by sea. A German drive through the Shushica valley, combined with the ill health of the team members, forced evacuation of TANK by British boat in February.

In March the BIRD team took over the same area. Surviving a month-long attack by 800 occupation troops specifically detailed for its destruction, the team remained until July 1944, and provided reception points for three further teams.

The first of these parachuted in March, the other two in July 1944. Despite repeated German attacks, they remained with their FNC guerrilla units, maintaining intelligence coverage. Upon the German withdrawal in October 1944, one team entered the capital, Tirana, while the other two worked up into northeast Albania, radioing military developments and data on industrial destruction. All three stayed in the country, giving economic and political coverage and serving as liaison for State Department and other U. S. agencies until the establishment of a city team in Tirana in February 1945.*

Perhaps the principal difficulty encountered by SI/Albania was its lack of control over transportation. Air supply of teams in enemy-held territory depended upon the closest relations and identity of interests between those responsible for the teams and for the required air operations. Support of U. S. teams by the Balkan Air Force (British) was unreliable throughout. After months of waiting had beset several missions, the head of the Albanian Desk unsuccessfully proposed, as had section chiefs in other areas, the establishment of an OSS air unit to obviate such delays.

---

* National Liberation Front.

* See "Tirana", below.

C. YUGOSLAVIA

Fifteen Reichswehr divisions, aided by some 100,000 well-armed native occupation troops, were detailed to maintain order in Yugoslavia against the large-scale resistance activities. It was of importance to Allied forces in Italy, confronted by twenty-six German divisions, that the fifteen in Yugoslavia remain there. SO teams, with OG aid, joined British forces in effecting military supply of resistance groups by sea and by air, while SO and SI liaison officers attached to guerrilla units radioed enemy battle order, bombing targets and other strategic intelligence to bases in Bari and Cairo.

U. S. officers were recruited in Washington and Cairo to act as uniformed liaison with units of the Partisan (Tito) and Chetnik (Mihailovich) resistance groups. They parachuted from Balkan Air Force (British) planes and were received by British groups already operating with the resistance. Trained in SO, they were to lead guerrillas in the destruction of strategic installations.

Arrival in the field soon showed that the Partisans already had efficient officers (many of them Communist), not disposed to U. S. leadership, and desirous only of the weapons to work with. The SO men became in effect intelligence officers and were instructed to send in enemy battle order, economic information, and political and military intelligence on the resistance.

Lack of SI training was evident on political and economic reporting. In general, the SO officers had little conception of economic intelligence, and sent none. Their political appreciations compared unfavorably with those prepared by their British colleagues. Understandably, they usually supported the groups they were living and fighting with. Liaison officers with the Chetniks favored the Chetniks, while those with the Partisans supported the Partisans. Even more unreliable were agents of Yugoslav descent, who usually were predisposed to one side or the other and reported the situation in moral black and white.

But military intelligence was valuable. The Partisans at first knew little of battle order reporting and needed the aid of OSS liaison officers to build up efficient and widespread intelligence units with each Partisan Corps.

The first officers were flown from Cairo and parachuted 18 August and 22 August 1943, to the headquarters of Mihailovich and Tito, respectively. As in Greece, both were SO officers attached to the British missions already there and had to use SOE communications and SOE code.

Using British facilities meant British control plus unnecessary delay in transmission of messages. However, the agreements signed in London in June 1942 between SO and SOE gave the latter the right to coordinate SO activity in the area.* Furthermore, the British in Cairo controlled air transportation to the Balkans, and had the network in the field which must arrange for the arrival of new agents. Considering, perhaps, that their own organization was successfully carrying out the job required, or for other reasons, they opposed any independent SI operations in Yugoslavia—the Americans would be under British command in the field and would have to remain at base in order to wire through British radio. SO teams arrived successfully, once having agreed to use SOE communications, while SI teams found it difficult to obtain air priority from the (British) Balkans Air Force.

Donovan's trip to Cairo in November 1943 established the right of U. S. operatives in the Balkans to independent communication.

* See "Introduction", above.

Later, during the summer of 1944, SO personnel in Yugoslavia were redesignated SI (thus releasing them from the restrictions of the SO/SOE agreement), and, in September, command of OSS teams in the field was transferred from the British Military Mission to the Independent American Military Mission to Marshal Tito.

On 26-27 December 1943 the first two OSS/Yugoslavia teams (ALUM and AMAZON) to carry their own radios were dispatched to Slovenia by SI. Faulty navigation resulted in the parachutage of three of the seven men directly into a camp of White Guards (pro-Axis native troops). Fortunately, the White Guards concluded that an Allied air invasion was upon them, and the three were able to make a quick retreat, returning later at considerable personal danger to retrieve their secret code books.

ALUM sent in volumes of intelligence collected by the two teams. While the political information lacked balance (the leader of ALUM was of Yugoslav descent and 100% pro-Partisan), the military reporting was excellent. Locations of anti-aircraft fields, interceptor fields and locator points in Slovenia were cabled out. Battery sites, gun calibres and serial numbers were given. From a captured German, the men obtained the complete AA and locator system of southern Austria. They worked out two safe flight paths, one northeast to Wiener-Neustadt, and the other northwest toward Munich.

During 1944 the group expanded to fourteen men, a fifteenth being killed when his parachute failed to open.

A spectacular achievement was the crossing of an advance section of the group, consisting of one American and two Partisans, over the border of the Greater Reich. Arriving on 23 June 1944, the section survived 44 days. The men constructed a bunker of logs, cut by themselves, on the side of a hill overlooking the main rail line from Zidani Most to Ljubljana. Transmitter, battery and pedal generator were installed underground and the whole camouflaged, so that it was invisible from ten yards. Villagers, contacted by the Partisans, left food baskets nearby twice a day. Railroad workers turned in daily manifests of traffic on the line and also on the Zidani Most-Maribor line.

A railroad guard discovered them, and they moved several times, continuing to transmit daily railroad intelligence. After 5 August 1944, they were not heard from.

SO's and OG's worked together with British forces to supply the Partisans. Following the Italian surrender in September 1943, Tito's forces had advanced and occupied the whole Dalmatian coast, opened up the port of Split and appealed for an Allied landing and/or military aid. On 5 October, a mission from Tito arrived at Algiers and was contacted by members of the Yugoslav Desk from Cairo. On 11 October, one of the Americans reconnoitered Vis Island (where the Partisans proposed to unload military supplies), in a Royal Navy gunboat provided by the Allied Naval Command and camouflaged as a fishing smack. On 15 October, at OSS initiative, the first load (200 tons of coal), provided by the same Command, left for Vis on board a Partisan vessel.

OSS organized the shipping operations at Bari, negotiated for the supplies and obtained the ships. By 25 October, there were 25 vessels smuggling goods the 120 nautical miles to Vis; and by 31 December, there were 40. These consisted of small vessels owned by the Partisans, and of ships in Italy, formerly belonging to the Royal Yugoslav Government.

Following the German raid on Bari in December, the base moved to Monopoli. Normally the ships left Monopoli at daybreak and arrived at a checking station at Manfredonia at 2000. Here they lay until 1300 the following day. The Italian Adriatic could be traversed by daylight. By nightfall the ships would enter the danger zone, and by 0300 be at Vis, in time to be camouflaged before daybreak brought German air reconnaissance.

In January 1944 the British, who had contributed all the military supplies, took over the operation. During the period of OSS direction, the following had been accomplished:

Number of loaded ships sailed from Italy	155
Total tonnage shipped	11,637 tons
Partisan troops shipped *	2,000
Partisan wounded evacuated *	700
Partisan refugees evacuated *	20,000
Number of ships repaired and operated	44

* Partly by Royal Navy vessels. These figures are taken from "Final Report on SBS Supply Line to Partisans", 20 May 1944, History File 137.

It is estimated these supplies made possible the activation of 30,000 guerrillas.* Two thousand Yugoslav guerrillas were equipped in Italy and shipped into Yugoslavia.

On 20 December the Germans diverted three divisions (the 1 Mountain, 114 Light and 755 Infantry Divisions) to clean up the coastal activity. They recaptured all the Dalmatian Islands but Vis, which was defended by a large force of Partisans, British Commandos, and 211 OSS OG's. Fifteenth Air Force bombings of Mostar Island and of the ports of Zara and Fiume assisted its defense. The holding action was intended to maintain the flow of material, but the three Reichswehr divisions directed against the supply line closed off the coast.

OG's and Commandos remained to harass enemy forces on other Dalmatian Islands and to obtain enemy battle order there and on the coast. Operations included:

(a) Destruction of the German garrison on Solta Island and capture of the town of Grohote by OG's and British Commandos.

(b) An attack on Brac Island. British troops, to which OG's were attached, forced

---

* For breakdown of supplies sent in, and above estimate, see publication "Partisan Supply Operation," p. 25, History File 199f.

the enemy into an inner defense ring, inhibiting his movement.

(c) Destruction of an enemy patrol on Hvar Island.

(d) Attack on Korcula Island. OG's and Partisans cleared two-thirds of the Island.

(e) Repeated reconnaissance to obtain battle order on the islands of Mljet and Lagosta, and on the mainland.

A typical attack was that on Solta Island, carried out by a force of 600 troops, principally Commandos, but including an OG detachment of 150. A landing on the southern coast was effected from LCI's at 2400. Troops proceeded to move into position around the town of Grohote under cover of darkness. Due to the extremely difficult terrain, positions were not taken up until 0600 and the presence of Allied troops was prematurely disclosed to the enemy, who opened fire. Troops moved up under fire to assault positions, and at 0700 the RAF dive-bombed the town with P-40's, according to plan. The bombing accomplished its purpose of softening up resistance, the enemy was attacked and the town taken. The enemy garrison of approximately 110 men was killed or captured. American casualties were one killed and five slightly wounded.

This and other operations were commanded by the much larger British force, and served mainly as initiation for the OG's in preparation for action in Greece, Italy, France, Norway and the Far East. The Group was withdrawn in July 1944 upon the retreat of German occupation troops.

Meanwhile, on the mainland, the U. S. network in Partisan country spread. Along with its British counterpart, the Yugoslav Desk had moved, at the time of the shipping operation in October 1943, from Cairo to Bari. There Serbo-Croatian-speaking agents could be recruited in greater numbers than in Cairo. A training school was established. In April, control of OSS operations in Yugoslavia and Central Europe, was transferred from Cairo to AFHQ, MedTO.

By October 1944, forty OSS officers and men were running fifteen intelligence teams, attached to the various corps of the Partisan army. Intelligence included daily battle order cables, with map locations of important targets. The teams served as liaison to coordinate air attacks with Partisan operations.

In December 1943, the two-man Air Section had moved up from Cairo to Bari to take over the job of transmitting Partisan bombing requests to the Fifteenth U. S. Air Force. Since targets were cabled without integration from American and British officers accompanying all Partisan corps, some priority system was necessary. Conference with Marshal Tito's representative in Bari produced a decision to use only those bomb requests approved by him. Target bombing in support of Partisan offensives commenced in late March 1944, and, besides offering tactical assistance, served to raise Partisan morale.

The Fifteenth Air Force was of considerable assistance to the Partisans in late May. The Germans attacked Tito's Hq. at Drvar on 25 May, with glider troops landing in the area itself, and with armored columns closing in on all sides. Due to the surprise of the attack, request for air support was not cabled out until the 27th. On 28 and 29 May, B-17's, B-24's, P-38's and P-47's of the Fifteenth Air Force bombed and strafed German troop concentrations around Drvar, and, on the following day, the Partisans broke through German lines to the South. Marshal Tito noted this in an order of the day: "American and British prestige is now equal to that of the Russians."

The Air Section of OSS/Bari also served A-2, Fifteenth Air Force, in preparing a basic map survey of rail and water communications in the Balkans, and in selecting interdiction points, using OSS, Photo Reconnaissance and other intelligence sources.

Drops of men and supplies were carried out by the Balkan Air Force, which had earlier moved from Cairo to South Italy. The actual task of parachuting to guerrilla groups in Nazi-controlled territory was complicated and dangerous, the average experience being something like that of SPIKE team:

After being recruited in Cairo by Major —— —— the first of March 1944, we moved up to Bari, 7 April 1944. At Bari we expected to stay only a few days before taking off for our job in Macedonia.

We made our first attempt to enter the country 25 April 1944. This attempt failed due to the plane having to turn back before reaching the pin point because of bad weather. We turned back that night and arrived in Bari being greeted by a bit of anti-aircraft fire, as the pilot thought we were over Brindisi and came in unidentified. We made several more attempts to get in until the night of 23 June 1944. We jumped into the British Mission "Burlesque," headed by Major Saunders. This was a bad night for all. Major —— hurt his ankle, Sgt. ——, his leg, and radioman ——, his back, in a fall from the tree he landed in. I drifted several miles away from the drop zone and after four or five hours of wandering around the mountains found some Partisans, and later the British Mission. . . . After being chased around the mountains by the Bulgarians, we made our way to Vueje.*

Four secret meteorological stations, staffed by OSS, radioed weather reports every six hours, sending measurements taken with technical equipment which had been parachuted in; balloon runs, for example, were made daily. The transmission of weather intelligence received special handling, and reached the 19th Weather Squadron at Cairo on the average of seven minutes after it had been put on the air in Yugoslavia.

Escape routes for U. S. fliers were organized. Partisans, under OSS direction, brought in downed fliers, and housed them in barracks near fields they had constructed. Working with the Air Crew Rescue Unit (Fifteenth Air Force), OSS arranged for planes to transport the men periodically. By VE-Day about 1,600 had been safely flown out.

---

* Report of SPIKE team, 9 August 1944 to 14 November 1944, p. 1, OSS Director's File 15,868.

The first "Safe Area" maps to be issued by any U. S. Air Force in any theater were prepared by the Air Section for the guidance of airmen over Yugoslavia. These showed areas under Partisan control, toward which downed fliers should attempt to make their way, and were reproduced in 500 copies for distribution to the Fifteenth and Twelfth Air Forces, the Desert Air Force (British), the Balkan Air Force (British) and MACAF. First issued in January 1944, they assisted in the recovery of 467 airmen during the first four months of use. Beyond this concrete effect, they fortified air crew morale during operations over Yugoslavia, Bulgaria, Austria, Rumania, Czechoslovakia and northern Greece.

From August to October 1944, an X-2 unit was active in Bari, briefing SI agents destined for Yugoslavia and Albania. Results were, however, small compared to those obtained by liaisons in London, and from the documents and personnel of the Italian services that came under Allied control after the surrender of Italy. In October the unit began to close, and two of the personnel entered Yugoslavia with the Independent American Military Mission.*

Subversive propaganda was sent in by MO. Specially packed leaflets, pamphlets and posters were dropped to U. S. representatives with Partisan forces. These were intended to demoralize German garrisons and terrorize native collaborators. An MO officer concluded, however, that the results were smaller than in more highly educated countries. The illiterate half of the population not only was unaffected, but could see little reason for risking lives to get the leaflets to the enemy. Many of the three million pieces delivered found other uses.

MO was also criticized by the Partisans for distributing surrender leaflets, which brought German deserters and German satellite troops flocking to Partisan strongholds. Inasmuch as the Partisans had in-

adequate food and clothing, no place to keep the prisoners, insufficient personnel to guard them, and a degree of inimical sentiment toward them, they shot them. The MO leaflets had the net effect of stiffening German soldier morale.

Meanwhile, of the two competitive resistance groups, the Chetniks had lost favor with the Allies. OSS liaison officers at the two Hqs. had submitted reports respectively favorable to the group to which they were attached and unfavorable to the opposing group. Allied policy was eventually settled in favor of Tito, and, in early 1944, all U. S. and British representatives with Mihailovich were withdrawn.

U. S. airmen, however, continued to bail out over Chetnik territory, where they could not be contacted and evacuated by U. S. agents. Further, it was felt that the U. S. should maintain intelligence units in all sections of Yugoslavia. With the support of Ambassador Robert D. Murphy, General Eaker (MAAF) and General Twining (Fifteenth Air Force), the point was finally won. On 3 August the HALYARD team parachuted to Pranjane, eighty kilometers south of Belgrade, where Mihailovich had collected, housed and fed 250 U. S. fliers. The three members of HALYARD directed 300 laborers, using sixty ox-carts, in the construction of an airfield 600 yards long and thirty wide. On 9 and 10 August, C-47's evacuated all 250 airmen. On 26 August, 58 additional U. S. fliers and two British came out. By the time the team left in November 1944, the total was over 400.

A six-man mission, intended for the acquisition of intelligence in Mihailovich territory, parachuted successfully to the air rescue team on 25 August 1944. This move proved to be an unfortunate one. The Chief of Mission, a Lt. Colonel, explained to General Mihailovich that his assignment was purely to collect military intelligence, and that his presence did not constitute political support of the Chetnik Government.

_____
* See "Belgrade", below.

Nevertheless, an imaginative leaflet in Serbo-Croatian appeared, reading in part:

The delegates of the Allied American Government and the personal representatives of President Roosevelt, the tried friend of freedom loving small nations, have arrived.

Immediately, upon his arrival, Colonel —— and the members of his mission went to the headquarters of the Supreme Command. On this occasion he presented a written message from President Roosevelt. . . . The whole meeting and the discussion at the headquarters of the Supreme Command was photographed by an American photographer, who was chosen to be present at this important event as an official war photographer for Fox Movietone News.*

The false claims made by this leaflet had just the effect on the Partisans which the British had wished to avoid. Tito, who had not been consulted, took the opportunity (coinciding as it did with the arrival of the Red Army) to cease active cooperation with U. S. and British liaison officers. One after another, teams at the various Partisan corps reported they were tied down to headquarters, could not travel without Partisan "guides," and received, together with their British colleagues, only the skimpy daily Partisan communiques. English and American representatives duplicated the radioing of this intelligence, and were able to collect little else.

On 1 November 1944, a month after arrival, the Mission returned (to submit reports favorable to Mihailovich). The Partisan attitude, however, never changed,** and OSS, unlike the British Military Mission, had few bargaining points. The British were able, as before, to obtain concessions from the

---

* Copy in the Director's Files, File 13,860, OSS Archives.

** To a certain extent, members of the mission to Mihailovich encouraged misunderstandings by speeches at Chetnik meetings and over the Chetnik radio. It may be argued, on the other hand, that Marshal Tito would have found some other opportunity, if this one had not occurred, to cease cooperation with the Western Allies.

Partisans due to their strong position: they had direct radio contact with the Balkan Air Force, and were able to produce air support for Partisan military operations more quickly and more often than could OSS teams; this same contact insured efficient air supply of British teams; finally, the British (like the Russians) spoke as official representatives of their Government, which the American agents did not.

To remedy this last weakness, the Independent American Military Mission to Marshal Tito arrived in Valjevo 9 October 1944, and took command of all U. S. teams formerly attached to the British Military Mission. Negotiations with Marshal Tito, to improve intelligence coverage with greater freedom of movement for U. S. teams, proved relatively unsuccessful. Difficulties in obtaining permission for entry and movement of U. S. personnel continued on a smaller scale.

The Mission prepared medical, economic and battle order reports, including one of the first American war intelligence reports on the Russian Army's combat methods. On 20 October, with Belgrade still half in German, half in Russian, hands, the Mission entered that capital and became a City Team, gathering political and economic intelligence, and acting as U. S. liaison until State Department representation arrived.*

Prior to the Mihailovich set-back, OSS/Yugoslavia had turned in some outstanding successes. Continuous relay of German battle order was important to the armies in Italy. The coordination of air bombing with Partisan activities helped detain fifteen German divisions in Yugoslavia. It was always difficult to evaluate in tangible form the results of secret intelligence and operational activity. But the equipping of tens of thousands of guerrillas and the evacuation of some 2,000 downed airmen were concrete accomplishments.

---

* See "Belgrade", below.

D. CZECHOSLOVAKIA

Lack of contacts in German-controlled Czechoslovakia hampered both British and U. S. subversive operations. Only two OSS units penetrated the country, the first in late 1944, when a Slovak resistance movement momentarily appeared, the other in 1945.

Encouraged by the Russian advance in Hungary and Ruthenia, two divisions of the Slovak Independent Army revolted. Aided by partisan groups, they seized Banska Bystrica in late August, set up their Hq., and broadcast appeals for help over the local radio station. Contact with the Czechoslovak Government-in-Exile had been established by the insurgents in the planning stage, and it was through Czechoslovak Army Hq. in London that OSS made arrangements for the infiltration of a liaison group and an air crew rescue unit. The Slovak Army, together with the partisans, prepared the Tri Duby airfield (ten km. south of Banska Bystrica) for B-17 landings, and arranged recognition signals.

On 17 September 1944 six OSS personnel were landed at this airport by the Fifteenth Air Force. Five tons of military supplies for the partisans accompanied them. Thirteen U. S. fliers and two British were evacuated.

On 7 October six B-17's landed sixteen additional OSS personnel together with twenty tons of Marlins, Bren guns, bazookas, ammunition, explosives, medical supplies, food and clothing. On this trip 28 U. S. aviators were evacuated.

The OSS purpose was to act as U. S. liaison with the Czechoslovak Army and the partisans, to arrange for their supply by air, to train them in the use of American weapons, to evacuate U. S. fliers in partisan care, and to collect intelligence on German and partisan battle order, industrial targets and military, economic and political developments.

The mission was attached to Czechoslovak Army Hq. at Banska Bystrica and commenced cabling reports. Between 13 and 20 October, for instance, it cabled out over 1,000 words a day of enemy battle order and target information.

But the Germans could not risk the continued sabotage activity so close behind front lines, and commenced, in September, a powerful drive to wipe out Czechoslovak resistance. The commanding officer of the first six OSS men, realizing the danger, had wired an urgent request for increased supply of military materiel. He asked for only one more man, a radio operator. Five separate teams, however, had been prepared in Bari for reception at Tri Duby (SI, SO and medical survey teams plus agents for Hungary and Austria). These teams were ready to fan out independently of the original team, and the first group had agreed to receive them, with the understanding that it could not be responsible for their safety. One of them, the Hungarian pair, was successful. But the others were caught in the partisan flight before the German advance.

As the German troops closed in on the insurgents, resistance became increasingly disorganized. On 26 October the Czechoslovaks evacuated Banska Bystrica in favor of Donovaly. The American group of 37 men (OSS agents and U. S. fliers) divided into four sections to accompany separate units in the hope that casualties would be smaller. From then on, a nightmare, panicky retreat began, as the completely disorganized partisans threw away their weapons, stole the American supplies and fled through the snow-covered mountains toward the Russian lines. The Czechoslovaks starved and froze. On one day 83 of them, waiting for the return of a reconnaissance patrol, died of cold.

Reunited, the OSS group, losing men one by one, traversed the mountains. On 6 November, one OSS member and five U. S. aviators on patrol were captured. On 11 November, all the airmen, together with two OSS officers elected to stop in a village and surrender. On 26 November, one OSS man was surprised on a food-purchasing visit to a small village. On 12 December, two more OSS personnel were captured. At Christmas, the remnant OSS group had been for several weeks at a mountain hotel near Velny Bok, two of them sleeping in a house nearby. On the day after Christmas, 250 German and Hlinka guards attacked the hotel, on information supplied by a partisan guard. All the OSS personnel in the hotel were taken, sent to Mauthausen concentration camp, tortured for what information they could give, and executed on 24 January 1945. The other two OSS men, aided by a partisan girl, successfully escaped some fifty miles to the Russian lines.

The principal difficulty appears to have been incomplete planning on the part of the resistance movement and of its Allied supporters. Supplies and a swift military advance had been guaranteed by the British and the Russians respectively. As it turned out, the Russians took two months to get through the Dukla Pass, for which they had allotted two weeks.* Finally, in mid-October, the Russians flew in to Tri Duby airfields two brigades of Czechoslovaks trained in Russia. Unfortunately these were almost unarmed, and once landed, could only join in the general flight toward the Russian lines. Meanwhile the British apparently made no effort to help the insurgents. OSS rushed material from Cairo to Bari, but bad weather prevented most of the supply sorties.

One other OSS agent, "Cottage", penetrated Czechoslovakia. He was a native, with contacts in Prague, trained in Italy and parachuted near Prague in late February 1945. He never established radio contact, due to a faulty or possibly sabotaged set. He did, however, organize a small resistance group and participated in the Prague insurrection of 5 May.

---

* This failure was not for lack of trying, inasmuch as some 120,000 men were reported lost in the attacks.

E. NORWAY AND DENMARK

Secret operations in Norway and Denmark differed markedly from those in any other Nazi-dominated territory, resistance in both countries being well unified and the native intelligence services in effective control. Since the principal effort from London was directed toward France, OSS attempted no large-scale coverage.

It was the task of SO and SOE to arrange for supplies, training and communications with the resistance groups, and for this purpose SO and SOE base offices in London were integrated after 1942 in an organization later known as Special Force Headquarters (SFHQ).*

SFHQ/Scandinavia, though theoretically a joint operation, was in the main British-run, SOE having supported Danish and Norwegian resistance movements for over two years before SO set up an operating establishment in London. The agents were native Norwegians and Danes, under the orders of the Norwegian Government-in-Exile or of the Danish Freedom Council. They were recruited in the area of operation, over 100 being secretly brought to England for training in SOE schools. SO and SOE cooperated in arranging for supplies and transportation.

An exception to this British control of the operation was the advance SFHQ base in Stockholm. Although it was directly under SFHQ/London, it had to be separated, for purposes of cover, into British and American units. Activities of the American unit, WESTFIELD, began with the arrival of the chief in November 1943, and supplemented those of the SOE mission, which had been in Stockholm since 1940. By July 1944 there were eight SO staff members, Some 70 sub-agents were employed.

SHAEF's directive to SFHQ called for a two-fold task, first a counter-scorch effort to preserve installations, and second, sabotage of transportation to delay the German troop movement southward. During 1943 and early 1944, SHAEF had requested little action in order to avoid reprisals and useless waste of lives. But on 26 October 1944, extensive rail sabotage was authorized, and on 2 December 1944, as the West Front advance slowed to a halt, SHAEF requested the strongest delaying action possible.

Both WESTFIELD and SFHQ/London were divided into Norwegian and Danish sections: *

Norway

Except for a small Communist resistance group, operating in southeast Norway, all resistance was centralized under the national "Milorg". Section F. O. IV of the Norwegian High Command in London controlled "Milorg", and it was with F. O. IV that SFHQ cooperated. By January 1944, nineteen teams of from two to six Norwegian agents each had been equipped with W/T in England and dispatched by air and sea to lead resistance groups in Norway. By VE-Day there were 62. (See map.)

SO worked with SOE in supplying these teams. When one-half of the Norwegian fishing boats, used to transport agents from the Shetland Islands, were sunk by enemy action, OSS procured in November 1943 the use of three 110-foot U. S. subchasers, which operated from then on without loss. SOE had been unable to supply its teams by air during the summer months due to the length

---

* See section on SO in "London Base", below.

* A third section of WESTFIELD became active in September 1943 in the dispatch of agents to Germany. See "Stockholm," below.

of the Arctic day. In 1944, however, OSS obtained the services of Colonel Balchen of the USAAF, who, with six B-24's based at Leuchars, Scotland, volunteered to risk the long daylight hauls of summer. Americans in SFHQ also developed, in early 1945, the use of double hessian bags for drops of clothing, bandages and other soft materiel. The bag cut container weight by 100 pounds, and the use of light flare parachutes, also developed at that time, produced a further decrease in the auxiliary load.

In Sweden, the SO WESTFIELD mission initiated the supply of resistance groups north of the 62nd parallel, an area which the SO/SOE agreement assigned specifically to SO. Three supply and communications bases, code-named SEPALS, were established along the far northern Norwegian frontier. Swedish permission was obtained, with the excuse that they would serve as weather stations.

First W/T contact with a SEPALS base was received by London on 9 August 1944. From this date, the fifty Norwegian agents manning the bases worked across the border, leading local resistance groups, establishing supply caches in Norway for their use, gathering intelligence and fighting off attacks from German frontier patrols. Sabotage operations included the demolition of one regimental supply depot filled with highway construction machinery, nine German border guardhouses and barracks, two mountain snow-ploughs, one 17-truck highway ferry, a smaller ferry and a 1500-ton Finnish steamship.

The demolition of the supply camp, for instance, was carried out by a party of five men on 12-13 January. The purpose was to prevent the construction by the enemy of a new road between Storfjord and Theriksrosen, to be used for the withdrawal of German troops from northern Norway and Finland. The party left base in the early afternoon of 12 January, and reached a sheltered position near the depot three and a half hours later. Here they waited, and per-

formed a final reconnaissance. At 2345 hours the group cautiously approached the camp, placed explosives and escaped. The first charge detonated in ten minutes, and the others followed. Later intelligence, furnished by the Swedes, disclosed that the entire supply depot had been destroyed, and the road construction abandoned.

The SEPALS parties organized and armed a northern resistance group of some 6,000 men. This group supported OSS operations, and was of considerable assistance after VE-Day to the 1,200 Allied troops who invested Norway to take control of the 130,000 German troops still there. Members of the resistance also gathered intelligence for cabling through the bases back to London. They covered the German escape from Finland and movement to Narvik, shipping activities, laying of minefields, and other military and naval developments during the last six months of the war. The bases also provided meteorological data for use by the British-based air forces and by ATC.

SO activities in South Norway supported SOE activities with the resistance groups there. WESTFIELD sub-agents provided safe addresses. Both sea and land routes to the Oslo area were worked by the British and American groups. An SO chain of some 400 agents in Oslo distributed over half a ton of propaganda material prepared by OWI and MO.

---

* Some of the supplies also went to Denmark and to resistance groups in southern Norway.

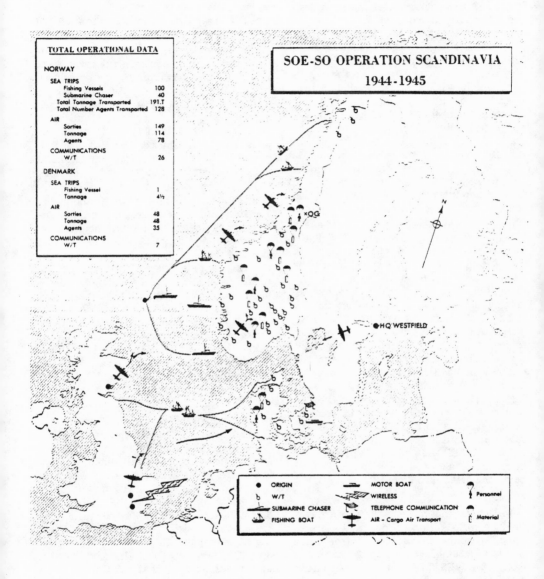

TOTAL OPERATIONAL DATA

NORWAY

SEA TRIPS
Fishing Vessels	100
Submarine Chaser	40
Total Tonnage Transported	191.T
Total Number Agents Transported	128

AIR
Sorties	149
Tonnage	114
Agents	78

COMMUNICATIONS
W/T	26

DENMARK

SEA TRIPS
Fishing Vessel	1
Tonnage	4½

AIR
Sorties	48
Tonnage	48
Agents	35

COMMUNICATIONS
W/T	7

SOE-SO OPERATION SCANDINAVIA
1944-1945

×OG

●HQ WESTFIELD

● ORIGIN		MOTOR BOAT		Personnel
W/T		WIRELESS		
SUBMARINE CHASER		TELEPHONE COMMUNICATION		Material
FISHING BOAT		AIR – Cargo Air Transport		

WESTFIELD also sent five men into Norwegian territory to receive an SFHQ mission. The RYPE team consisted of twenty American OG's, dispatched from London on 24 March 1945 to cut the Nordland rail line at two points in the North Trondelaag area. The purpose was to prevent German re-deployment of 150,000 troops in northern Norway, which was being accomplished over these lines at the rate of a battalion a day. Fourteen members of RYPE landed at the reception point at Laevsjoen, while the fifth plane lost its course, and the men were mistakenly ordered by the pilot to parachute into Swedish territory. An arrangement with the secret police, however, soon released them from internment, and they crossed the frontier to rejoin the main body of the team. Further efforts to reinforce the group from London resulted in two plane crashes and the death of ten OG's.

Trekking on two long trips through the snow, RYPE carried out both of its rail-demolition tasks successfully. The first, involving the blowing of the 18-foot railway bridge at Tangen, was accomplished on 15 April. And on 23 April, the group, reinforced by the returnees from Sweden, blew up a 2½ kilometers of rail with 240 separate charges of plastic. Although attacked by German rail guards, they escaped without losses. The two operations reduced the German rate of troop movement south from one battalion a day to approximately one battalion per month.

Like the SEPALS parties, RYPE was also of service in taking over control on VE-Day, being the first Allied troops in the area.

Denmark

In Denmark, even more than in Norway, SFHQ directed all operations, and the area remained under the British control which had been established prior to the arrival of OSS. The WESTFIELD mission carried out some independent work, including management of the only clandestine boat service (bi-weekly) carrying agents, supplies and microfilmed messages between Malmoe and Denmark, and conduct of the only wireless telephone link from Haelsingborg to Denmark. The mission further handled from Sweden all radio communication from SFHQ teams in the field.

When the Germans terminated local self-government in Denmark in the summer of 1943, the Freedom Council was organized, with a headquarters in Sweden. SFHQ worked through the new Council, cleared agents (all Danish) with it and exfiltrated only a few to England for training. Supplies were parachuted by Britain-based planes, or carried by boat from England and Sweden. Between January 1944 and April 1945, SFHQ parachuted 268 tons of supplies.

SHAEF requests for increased sabotage of transportation, in October and again in December 1944, resulted in a large-scale effort. The railroad attacks between 25 January and 12 February were particularly effective, blocking completely, for that period, the main eastern railroad in Jutland. Movement southward of the 233 Reserve Panzer and 166 Reserve Infantry Divisions was considerably delayed. Other sabotage was directed against industrial targets. For example, on 2 January eight guerrillas attacked and destroyed the Charlottenlund factory making radio parts for V-2; the factory was subsequently abandoned.

An unusual example of air support for a resistance movement was the bombings of Gestapo files. In October, German counter-intelligence had been taking a serious toll among members of the resistance, particularly in the Jutland region. On the basis of urgent W/T requests, SFHQ arranged for the bombing of Gestapo and Sicherheitsdienst headquarters in Aarhus to destroy the files on resistance activities and men. Twenty-five Mosquito bombers, dispatched on 31 October, demolished the headquarters, and it was reported that 150 German Gestapo and counter-espionage officials were killed in the attack. Similar operations were repeated at Copenhagen on 21 March and at Odense on 17 April.

In general, individual credit could not be divided between the SO and SOE organizations. Since SOE had been operating for some time prior to SO arrival in London, maintained a much larger staff in SFHQ, and had actual, if not nominal, control of all the operations, the larger share of credit for the accomplishments of SFHQ should go to SOE.

In Norway, the signal accomplishment was the organization, in cooperation with the Norwegian Government-in-Exile, of a resistance group counting 31,980 effectives. These were armed with 450 tons of equipment, delivered by parachute drop from the British Isles, boat from Scotland and Sweden, and cross-country gun-running from Sweden. Some fifty agent teams, trained in England, provided leadership and communication with the London base. About 200,000 German troops occupied Norway until February 1944, when the Germans started to move southwards for the defense of the Continent. When, in October 1944, SHAEF requested delaying sabotage in Norway, in order to ease the situation on the West Front, "Milorg"/SFHQ sabotage of rail lines, roads, boats and port installations was so effective that on VE-Day German forces in Norway still numbered over 100,000 men, composing twelve divisions.

In Denmark, the total effect produced by SFHQ was the organization and arming of a resistance group numbering by VE-Day some 13,000. The flat terrain of Denmark made the suppression of resistance a much easier task than it had been for the twenty German divisions in mountainous Norway. Nevertheless, in March 1945, Denmark still held 35,000 Nazi troops, constituting three and one-half divisions.

In general, all these operations were British-directed. The principal SO activities were those involved in effecting radio communication, obtaining supplies and documents, packing them and laying on air or sea transportation.* The attached exhibit

---

* These activities are described in some detail in the sections on SO in France, below.

gives some idea of the quantity of supplies dropped to Denmark by air alone.

SUMMARY OF AIR OPERATIONS
Denmark

	Successful	Unsuccessful	Agents successfully dispatched	Radio sets delivered	Tonnage
1941					
December	1	..	2	..	.
1942					
January	..	..	..	..	..
February	..	..	..	..	..
March	..	..	..	..	..
April	1	2	2	..	..
May	..	..	..	..	..
June	..	..	..	..	..
July	..	..	..	..	..
August	1	..	..	..	.75
September	..	..	..	..	..
October	1	1	1	..	..
November	.	..	..	..	..
December	..	2	..	..	..
TOTAL	3	5	3	..	.75
1943					
January	..	2	..	..	..
February	1	5	3	4	.50
March	1	..	4	..	.50
April	2	..	..	2	1.00
May	..	..	..	..	..
June	..	..	..	..	..
July	4	..	3	..	1.50
August	6	..	..	..	6.00
September	..	..	..	..	..
October	3	..	..	..	2.00
November	..	4	..	..	..
December	3	1	3	..	1.00
TOTAL	20	12	13	6	12.50
1944					
January	..	..	..	..	..
February	4	2	2	..	3.50
March	..	..	..	..	..
April	6	4	3	..	6.50
May	4	..	..	..	5.00
June	..	..	..	..	..
July	..	..	..	..	..
August	10	5	2	..	10.00
September	26	17	..	..	30.50
October	24	15	9	,.	32.75
November	65	32	1	..	86.00
December	6	11	..	..	7.00
TOTAL	145	86	17	..	181.25
1945					
Jan.-Feb. 23	46	31	1	..	65.00

Part V
FRANCE

The principal OSS effort of the European war was directed toward France. Large OSS bases at London and Algiers provided extensive R&A, X-2, CD, R&D, Communications and other services. By the time of the invasions, OSS had gained some three years of experience, less than any foreign espionage agency, but sufficient to produce a creditable performance.

SO operations from London and SI operations from Algiers presented a striking contrast. The support and exploitation of resistance, directed from ETO, were conceived to be paramilitary tasks. SO recruiting, training, dispatching and servicing were handled in a military and largely impersonal fashion, apparently modelled on SOE procedures. SO and SOE officers and men, many of them in uniform, parachuted into France and organized resistance groups, trained them, arranged for the large air drops of supplies, directed sabotage and incidentally transmitted intelligence. On and after D-Day, resistance was coordinated with the advancing Allied armies by an additional 276 personnel dispatched as liaison, and by SO/SOE detachments with each of the armies in the field. Generals Eisenhower and Patton, among others, paid official tribute to the remarkable resistance effort in causing diversions, covering undefended flanks, disrupting enemy communications, protecting vital installations and delaying and harassing enemy troops in transit.

For a variety of reasons, SI/London failed to mount any extensive espionage operations into France. In mid-1944 one large-scale operation, *Sussex*, was carried out jointly with SIS, involving the mass training and dispatching of over fifty teams to areas not covered by the resistance. Despite the late start, some valuable intelligence was obtained.

Algiers, while serving as an advance SO/SOE base, served principally as an SI operation center and produced the outstanding direct intelligence record of the war. In contrast to agent processing at OSS/London, Algiers agents were recruited, trained, dispatched and serviced on a personal basis, in an effort to make each man in the field feel that some one man at the home desk would do everything possible to support him. From early 1943, extensive radio-equipped chains were built up, supplemented by the exceptionally large courier chains operated out of Bilbao and Barcelona, Spain. By D-Day, a mass of data on locations of almost every enemy company, every installation and every fortification, real or dummy, in South France, had been passed on to Seventh Army with an accuracy and coverage which amazed General Patch and his G-2, particularly when the campaign itself provided the acid test.

Finally, the SI unit in Algiers formed the Seventh Army Strategic Services Section, and again developed methods of civilian infiltration which set the OSS field detachment record for the European war.

A. BASES

1. The London Base

The OSS establishment in London served not only as the base for clandestine activities in northern, western and central Europe, but also as a collection and dissemination center for intelligence of interest to U. S. and Allied agencies in Washington and London.

Early administrative arrangements were characterized by informality, since no elaborate chain of command was required.* During 1943 and 1944, however, the base expanded to meet growing commitments, and administrative procedures became more complex. By mid-1944, OSS/London was an elaborate organization which included more than 2,000 personnel and 14 branches. All branches reported directly to the Deputy Strategic Services Officer, and through him, to the SSO. The chain of command represented a departure from the Washington arrangement, where the Director, OSS, controlled the various branches through three deputy directors for intelligence, operations and services. In London, the SSO and Deputy SSO were also supported, at the planning level, by a Plans and Operations Staff and a Secretariat.

Secret Intelligence

In June 1942, when OSS succeeded COI, little division of function existed within the SI Branch in London. A small staff located in the U. S. Embassy disseminated intelligence reports from British air, military and naval offices and from a few refugee governments in London.

First specialization within SI/London took place in September 1942, with the establishment of a Labor Desk. Because its activity was distinct from other SI divisions in

---
* See "Introduction", below.

its emphasis on labor channels, the Desk enjoyed, until the end of the war, a status separate, with the exception of the Training Division, from the rest of SI.

Counter-espionage, which had first been considered a function of SI, was on 15 June 1943, transferred to the new X-2 Branch, in order to work more closely with the British in that highly specialized activity.

To extend liaison facilities and to improve lateral intelligence procurement, SI established individual geographic desks for France, Belgium, Poland, Yugoslavia, Norway, Italy, Holland and Czechoslovakia. In addition to regular liaison duties with the various exile governments,* the desks were charged with the recruitment and briefing of agents for eventual operations in these countries. They were unable, as a result, to devote much time to the growing number of intelligence reports from other agencies arriving in London by cable, pouch and courier. To process and disseminate such intelligence, a Reports Division was established under SI in the summer of 1943.**

By September of that year, when an Administrative Officer/SI was appointed to direct supplies, personnel, orders, etc., SI/London included the Chief, Assistant to the Chief, Executive Officer, Training Officer, Labor Desk, Washington Desk, geographic desks (see above), Reports Division and Administration Office.

The Training Section began activity in the fall of 1943 in connection with the *Sussex* and *Proust* plans, but did not report directly to the Chief of SI until April 1944. Thereafter, it worked closely with the country and Labor Desks to prepare agents for opera-

---
* See "Liaison with Foreign Intelligence Services", below.
** See that section, below.

tions on the Continent, and supplied equipment and facilities for other Allied missions. The Section was replaced by the over-all OSS Schools and Training Branch, established in ETO on 14 October 1944.*

Morale Operations

Initial difficulties in obtaining recognition from PWE, COSSAC and SHAEF, as well as jurisdictional conflicts with OWI and SO, rendered MO relatively inactive until December 1943.** Only then was the Branch finally given a role in COSSAC's psychological warfare program.

When SHAEF took over control of this program, with the creation of PWD early in 1944, MO was integrated into the new organization and given responsibility for de-development of PWD's "black" *** propaganda. Although MO continued to work within PWD throughout the war, making contributions of personnel and equipment, particularly for combat propaganda in France, the Branch was authorized to act more and more on its own in "black" production. By the summer of 1944, PWD retained no more than the right to coordinate MO activities. The OSS Branch thus had an independence similar to that possessed by British PWE, with which MO collaborated on numerous projects.†

Special Operations

In June 1942, OSS/SO and SOE had entered into an agreement which spelled out the basic terms of cooperation between them.†† As early as April 1943, there was a realization of the need for a joint SO/SOE headquarters in London to coordinate American and British teams in the field. The proposed headquarters must have responsi-

---

* On the SI reorganization for the infiltration of Germany, see "Direct Penetration from London", below.
** See "Introduction", above.
*** For a discussion of MO activity, see the Washington section on that Branch.
† For its operations in France, see "MO—West Front", below.
†† See "Introduction", above.

bility for the dispatch of agents and the supply and direction of resistance groups. It was estimated that sixteen SO/SOE officers would be required for the headquarters, eight of whom would be detailed to an Operations Room.*

On 4 September 1943, SO/SOE representatives met to discuss unification. Recognition of the need for additional personnel resulted in a statement of responsibility for D-Day procedure for the Operations Room "including the participation of OSS". On 7 September, SO pointed out that OSS representation ought not to be restricted to the Operations Room, but should include full responsibility for operations in U. S. sectors of the future front. The British accepted the suggestion, and also admitted American personnel to the controller staff in the Operations Room, where they would have charge of cables, incoming and outgoing, and responsibility for certain cases which had been inadequately handled by the country sections.

By December 1943, the combined headquarters of SO and of the London Group of SOE had virtually been established. Official recognition of the new arrangements was given in two documents, dated 10 and 14 January 1944.**

The first, addressed to the regional directors and section heads of SO and SOE, originated from the SO/SOE headquarters, London, and was signed by the American chief, SO and the British chief, SOE. It stated that "integration between the London Group of SOE and the SO Branch of OSS, ETOUSA, has taken place". It went on to underline the joint aspect of the integration in the following provisions: (1) Duties would be assigned to officers irrespective of their American or British allegiance; (2) certain sections, of equal concern to both SO

---

* The controlling center, where maps, charts, messages, and other data pertinent to all SO/SOE operations would be maintained.
** SO War Dairy, Vol. 12, p. 33 and p. 111, respectively, History Files.

and SOE, such as Air Operations and Planning, would be run jointly; (3) in the event of an operation of concern to only one of the two agencies, the officer of the organization concerned would make the decision; in the event of an operation of equal importance to both organizations, a disagreement would be submitted for decision to the Director (British) or the Deputy Director (American) of the joint headquarters.

On 14 January 1944, SO and SOE signed a document entitled "SOE and SO London Operational Arrangements", constituting official recognition of the combined headquarters. It was divided into two sections: A. "Outline of Purposes", and B. "Conduct of Operations from London".

Section A outlined current and estimated capabilities in support of D-Day planning. Section B stated that SO, while maintaining its own administrative offices at the headquarters of OSS/London, would coordinate all operational matters through SOE.

SHAEF approved the integration·on 24 January. The principle of dual control and equal responsibility between SO and SOE was thus effected, and SO became fully merged with its British equivalent. It was, however, physically impossible for OSS to assume partnership on an equal basis, due to the lack of personnel. Thus, joint control at the top, rather than full partnership down the line, characterized the operation. The Director of SO became Deputy Director of SO/SOE. Responsible to him, and through him to the British Director, were the Planning Section, manned jointly by American and British Army personnel, and two Executives—one American and one British—who both operated at the planning level exclusively. The more important desks and the Training and Air Operations Sections were manned jointly and were directly responsible to the Deputy Director. Desks with a lower priority, such as those for Iberia and Spanish Morocco, were manned by either British or U. S. personnel alone.

SO/SOE was designated Special Force Headquarters (SFHQ) on 1 May 1944—a change in title which had no effect on the functions of the organization. The new designation clarified the relationship to the new Special Force Staff Detachments, SO/SOE units to be attached to the armies in the field.

Operational Groups

In ETO no provision was made for a large OG Command like that in NATO. Recruiting and training of OG units for missions into Scandinavia, and possibly France, from the U. K. base were arranged with some SO/SOE support. But only in May 1944 was a separate OG Command established under SFHQ and SHAEF for operations in support of *ANVIL*.

In December 1942, the chief of SO/Washington had come to London to obtain Theater approval for JCS 170,* and had attempted, at the same time, to sell the idea of "operational nuclei" for guerrilla warfare in occupied territories. SOE was inclined to discourage such operations, and the Chief of SO talked instead to a Norwegian general, interested in forming a basic unit of the OG type for use in sabotage operations in Norway.

The "Norwegian" OG's were activated in April 1943, under the direction of SFHQ, and in liaison with the Norwegian military attache. Seventy-nine Norwegian-Americans (10 officers and 69 enlisted men) were recruited from U. S. Army units and given preliminary training—including mountain climbing, skiing, and amphibious operations—in Colorado and Massachusetts. The "Norwegian" OG unit arrived in Scotland in December 1943, with headquarters, after January, near Inverness, and under SFHQ/Scandinavia command. It completed, at SO and SOE bases and schools, an intensive sabotage and combat training program in: (1) Demolition of rail lines, high bridges, power installations, telephone and telegraph

* Washington Exhibit W-38.

145

communications, etc.; (2) weapons, map reading, compass and Morse code; (3) scouting and patrolling; (4) unarmed combat; and (5) parachuting and rubber boat assault exercises.

Realistic field problems were carried out for an SO/SOE amphibious coup-de-main attack on Norwegian mining and loading machinery. The actual operation, however, was dropped when neither motor torpedo boats nor submarine chasers could be released for the specialized OG mission. In view of British restrictions existing vis-a-vis Norway, the OG's were transferred in May from SO/Scandinavia to a separate OG command directly responsible to SFHQ, for post-D-Day operations in France, preparatory to the invasion from the Mediterranean.

In June 1944, OG/ETOUSA was increased by the arrival of four groups of "French" OG's from Algiers. To supplement the little paramilitary training received by these men in the U. S., they were drilled thoroughly in paramilitary techniques, particularly demolitions, and instructed in W/T procedure and foreign weapons. Little parachute practice was provided, since they had received this training in Algiers. The "French" OG's participated with the "Norwegian" OG's in seven parachute missions into France in August and September 1944.* Members of the "Norwegian" OG's also participated, in March, in an SO mission for Norway.**

Transport

Air transport filled the greatest part of the demands for dispatching agents and supplies. The Maritime Unit in London ran into one difficulty after another. Established in December 1943, the Branch had planned a number of operations in collaboration with DDOD (I), its British opposite number. All MU projects, however, were ultimately abandoned because of equipment failures, disapproval of targets, and discovery that the water was too cold to permit efficient underwater swimming operations in the invasion area. Subsequent MU activities were limited to ferrying two teams to enemy points on the French coast in July 1944, and, later, to operating a "water-taxi" service for OSS personnel crossing the Channel.

Efforts to obtain U. S. Army aircraft for agent drops began in October 1942 and continued unsuccessfully for a year. A shortage of planes made Eighth Air Force priorities difficult to obtain, even though both Admiral Stark and Ambassador Winant supported the requests. It was not until October 1943, when JCS approved the allocation of aircraft for the support of the Polish underground, that the Air Force agreed to supply air lift, and it was not until January 1944 that it became available. From that point on, however, squadrons of specially converted B-24's, and later A-26's, stationed eventually at Harrington, carried out agent and supply drops for SI and SO, along with similar planes pooled by the British. By March, some 200 flights were being run per moon-period.

———————————

London was the center of numerous other activities for the support of the various operations undertaken by OSS/ETO against the enemy in France. A trained Security staff protected the organization; a Medical Services unit watched over the personnel's health, and a Special Funds Branch handled the disposal of unvouchered funds for certain projects and staff members. In addition, a Services Branch had been established in September 1943, and, within six months, a fiscal section handled routine finances, a supply section was available for obtaining or shipping equipment, a motor pool was in operation, and mess and billeting facilities were being run for hundreds of OSS enlisted personnel.

The ensuing seven sections cover some of the larger base activities of OSS/ETO.

———————————

* See "OG's in France", below.
** See "Norway and Denmark", above.

(a)   R&A/LONDON

During most of the war, London was the focal point for R&A activities conducted in ETO. The Branch undertook political and economic analyses on European subjects, conducted surveys and compiled reports for SHAEF, the various armies and army groups, the U. S. Embassy, Civil Affairs units and American and Allied intelligence agencies. It prepared extensive studies on psychological warfare for OWI, MOI, PWE and the MO Branch of OSS. One unit of R&A developed new, effective techniques of target analysis, and worked in closest collaboration with U. S. air forces. The Branch compiled maps for the armies, the Military Government officials and for OSS operational purposes.

In addition, R&A maintained such standing headquarters services as biographical files on European personalities and a library of background materials on all appropriate areas. Finally, R&A centered in London an exhaustive and all-inclusive document procurement service which routed to Washington and other OSS bases throughout the world a steady stream of foreign books, maps, newspapers, magazines and other periodicals either in the original or in microfilm reproduction.

At its start in May 1942, R&A/London was designed merely to service Washington with materials gathered in Britain. The original two-man staff screened what intelligence could be harvested from informally developed London contacts, and procured appropriate material for the program of the Interdepartmental Committee for the Acquisition of Foreign Publications (IDC).*

It was immediately apparent that the IDC procurement program called for the closest working relationship with the British. Arrangements were soon made with the Ministry of Information, the Foreign Office and H. M. Stationery Office, for access to the volume of newspapers, periodicals and books from the Continent available to these British

---
* See Washington section on R&A.

agencies and unavailable in Washington. A further agreement with the British Association of Libraries and Information Bureaus (ASLIB) provided facilities for microfilming these materials for transmission to Washington. Additional materials of an intelligence character—maps, guide books and reports—were obtained from agencies such as the Colonial Office, the Admiralty, the Inter-Service Topographical Department and the Crown Agents for the Colonies.

These relationships, on the whole, worked smoothly. Two complications, however, had to be overcome. First, the initial R&A emphasis on procurement alone meant that the Branch could offer little in return to the assisting British agencies. By the end of 1942, however, shipments of reports from the Washington headquarters furnished the London office with materials for exchange. Second, the British wanted opposite numbers to deal with, and, in R&A's case, other U. S. agencies had either reached the scene sooner or corresponded more closely to the British conception of a counterpart. For instance, R&A attempts at close liaison with PWE, for research in psychological warfare, met steady opposition during 1942, for the British considered OWI the proper channel. It was not until 1943—after arrangements had been made in Washington for R&A-PWE collaboration on developing the Civil Affairs handbooks for occupied Europe—that the situation improved.

Relations with the Admiralty's Inter-Service Topographic Department (ISTD) were particularly close, following an R&A contribution of five geographers to that agency in December 1942. Not only were the intelligence resources of the Admiralty constantly at the service of R&A, but the connection served as a general introduction to other British agencies. The hope of all British agencies for personnel reinforcements also, in many cases, served R&A interests.

Relations with some U. S. offices were more complicated. The Economic Warfare Division was the designated U. S. opposite num-

147

ber of the British Ministry of Economic Warfare. R&A had early conflicted with EWD, when it attempted to deal directly with MEW. The Branch shortly thereafter tried to do air target analysis for the Eighth Air Force. EWD, which was already doing this work, brought pressure at highest levels to prevent further R&A incursion. The result was a compromise, whereby an Enemy Objectives Unit was established under EWD authority, but staffed jointly by both EWD and OSS personnel under an R&A Chief. The new group produced remarkable achievements in the fields of target selection, damage assessments

The controversies with EWD were the direct result of the shift in emphasis from procurement to operational research, accompanied by a switch from servicing Washington to servicing the Theater itself. Early in 1943, R&A, with a staff increased to six professionals, began doing target research for SO/SOE. For some time, R&A evaluated POW interrogations for G-2, and entered upon a long series of reports on French morale for ETOUSA. In March, the Branch began an analysis of German and Italian files captured in North Africa, and uncovered, among other items, important Mareth Line blueprints.

The R&A staff performed research for Civil Affairs Section G-1, ETOUSA and contributed teaching materials and personnel to the CAS training program. The Branch undertook regular contributions in the political, social and economic fields to the weekly intelligence summary of G-2, ETOUSA, from which there developed, in December 1943, a similar summary for the Embassy.

An additional service for the Theater was the creation, in October 1943, of a Biographical Records Division and the enlargement of the R&A Library. By the end of the year, the latter was supplying 39 U. S. and British offices with R&A/Washington reports, and served, for numerous branches of ETOUSA, as the sole access to British materials.

Meanwhile, procurement activities continued. The microfilm service transmitted 10,000 newspaper pages of military obituaries and a series of German timetables. In the course of its regular work, it reproduced, by July 1943, 1,000,000 photos of newspapers and periodicals. A newly established Stockholm outpost supplied the Branch with 136,500 photos of periodicals unobtainable elsewhere.

In the first half of 1944, R&A/London grew from 21 to over 200 members. Emphasis shifted from research on specific requests to studies originated within the Branch. At the same time, efforts were made to shift research emphasis to the post-hostilities period.

This program was exemplified by the transformation of the over-all R&A weekly, designed to meet customer's needs, into the European Political Report, an interpretive periodical prepared under independent Branch editorial policy. The Branch now concentrated upon support to G-5 (Civil Affairs) and USGCC, and turned out a quantity of handbooks, reports and administrative maps for occupation authorities, covering biographical data on 7,500 German and Austrian personalities, food situation studies, reparations capabilities, Soviet reparations intentions and practices in liberated areas, disarmament of defeated powers and minority problems.

Vetting forms, for use throughout Germany, were edited and printed, and charts showing detailed make-up of various Nazi organizations furnished. Most important of all was the groundwork laid for the establishment in Germany of an OSS-staffed area to train some 900 German nationals, to be used by G-5 as a nucleus for internal German administration.

Concurrent with these activities directed toward immediate post-hostilities problems, R&A continued service to the more operational armed forces. The Branch produced reports on the Axis ball-bearing industry, the machine tool industry in Yugoslavia and Greece and on German police and air raid defense systems. Maps were prepared on the flooded areas of Holland, the woodland areas of France and the power lines in the Ghent-Lille area.

Soon after D-Day, R&A personnel were attached to T-Forces,* which entered newly occupied cities with the Allied armies to secure important documents. In September 1944, an outpost for OSS/Paris was dispatched. Others were arranged for Brussels and Eindhoven, and preparations were undertaken for units in Germany itself.

Meanwhile, R&A began to give SI direct support in appraising and editing secret intelligence. Similarly, after the liberation of France, R&A/London analysts collaborated in briefing SI agents for the long-range penetration of Germany.

During the fall of 1944, the London office's services were geared more and more to the needs of such agencies as UNRRA, USGCC, ACC, G-5, CAD and USES. The Economics Division provided UNRRA, in late 1944, with statistical information on the food and clothing situation in areas to be occupied. Early in 1945, friendly POW's were interrogated on locations where important documents might be found, and T-Force targets were worked out accordingly. For USGCC, 113 maps were prepared on administrative areas in Germany. Displaced Persons maps were made for G-5. In April 1945, Branch resources were concentrated for an elaborate study of the so-called "Redoubt", on the chance of a German last stand in West Austria.

* See sub-section on T-Forces under "Liberated France", below.

Meanwhile, the R&A Far East unit increased its collaboration with X-2.* Much information on Far East installations was obtained from X-2's insurance company connections, and the unit developed an extensive program for the collection of documents on the Far East in Germany.

Most of the R&A staff for Germany moved to Paris, during April, and within two months the rest of the contingent left London for Wiesbaden. R&A/London's functions dwindled to the procurement of personnel, dispatch of supplies and maintenance of communication facilities for the forward bases.**

(b) X-2/LONDON

A Counter-Intelligence Division of SI, organized in March 1943, became the Counter-Espionage (X-2) Branch of OSS by June of that year. Despite the late start, by 1945 the United States had acquired an experienced group of professionals in the complicated techniques required for the protection of U. S. services abroad.

The British Services

From the beginning of the war the British had urged creation of such a service either in OSS, or jointly between OSS and the FBI. After it had been formed, the British carried out a thorough policy of offering the new section complete access to files in London, sources, secret methods, procedures and

* See next section.
** See "Liberated France" and "Central Europe", below.

knowledge of the personnel, organization and operations of what was probably the world's most experienced and efficient, and therefore most carefully safeguarded, security system.

Characteristic of the apprentice training offered OSS by the British was that given to some X-2 members in the double-agent section of MI-5 (B). These officers were assigned desks in the offices of that section and had free access to the files of double-agent cases, to the traffic of current ones, and to the officers who had directed or were directing such cases. Normally, in the course of their study, they met both double and controlled enemy agents whom the British were operating, helped to gather the "chicken feed" which was to be transmitted to the Germans, and learned the relationships between the sections to which they were attached and the other intelligence organizations which shared the exploitation of double-agent networks. One American officer was given a desk in the room of the director of the double-agent section, and was made party to all conversations and conferences on problems arising in connection with the management of current British cases, some of which were of a long-range character and therefore involved the highest security. When the secret methods of the British agencies were fully understood, the importance of the security risk they took was appreciated as overwhelming.

It was on this basis that X-2/London opened offices adjoining those of the British, and began in March 1943 to learn the job. It early became obvious that London would have to be the center of X-2 operations in Europe, North Africa, and the Middle East, due to the presence in London of other Allied counter-espionage services and the sources of intercepted material which were available only there.

ton CE files had grown from liaison sources, and from X-2's own subsequent field operations, to something like the quantity of those in London, action on cases of American interest would have to be handled by the group stationed in England.

This decision was not intended to, and did not, stop the flow to the United States of CE material of all classifications. The accumulation of CE files in the OSS Registry by the end of the war attested the steady and voluminous flow of CE reports and studies from the London desks to those in Washington. It did mean, however, that, on the whole, such material would be of use there chiefly for information purposes and for organization into a basic American registry of CE intelligence relating to areas outside the Western Hemisphere.

Other Liaisons

The prime necessity of maintaining a direct and close coordination, not only with the British but with other Allied CE agencies, was another important consideration in centering American overseas CE headquarters in London—at least until the last stages of the war. The headquarters, files and staffs of the Free French, Norwegian, Dutch, Belgian, Polish, Czech, Greek and Yugoslav Governments were located in London, as were those of the French Service de Securite Militaire. The eagerness of the chiefs and officers of these services to cooperate with the Americans provided an opportunity that no American CE group could disregard.

Liaison with the French was closer than that with other agencies, although it never reached the level of that with the British. British counter-espionage agencies were unwilling to admit the French services, and reserved joint operation to X-2 only.

Source material came not only from Allied counter-espionage services but also through liaison with SHAEF Evaluation and Dissemination Section, Combined Services Detailed Interrogation Center (U. K.), London Military Documents Center (the earlier Military

Intelligence Records Section), War Department, War Office, War Crimes Commission, SOE, Admiralty, FBI, ONI and U. S. Army Central Registry of War Criminals and Security Suspects.

Training

CE schooling of the more formal kind supplemented the apprentice training. From the earliest days, English and French officers, from London headquarters or from the field, shared their experiences with X-2 personnel in frequent formal training talks. The subjects of these talks ranged from notes on communications, office procedures and the like, to analyses of the over-all CE situations in certain areas. One series illustrated the interrogation methods of the Germans (by men who had been interrogated by them) and of the English (by men who had conducted the interrogations of enemy agents). Such English establishments as central registries, interrogation centers and training schools were open to X-2 officers for observation .visits. Another principal element in the X-2/London training was the schooling that grew out of the day-to-day association with colleagues in the British and other Allied CE services.

Desks

X-2 was first organized on a regional basis (1) The Western European section was established with three main desks, French (including Belgian and Dutch), German and Swiss; (2) the Iberian section included Spanish, Portuguese, Italian and—through 1943—North African desks; (3) the Scandinavian; and (4) the Middle Eastern sections (established during the first quarter of 1944) handled the affairs of their areas under an arrangement of one desk each. American CE interests in Eire were covered by an officer who made visits to Dublin at regular intervals

In May 1944, Reports section was added to these and placed under an officer whose responsibility was the supervision of all X-2/London reporting procedures.*

The work of these desks comprised the bulk of X-2 activity: carding, collating and interpreting all reported items of CE information in terms of the centralized intelligence available in and through the London registries; preparing notes for the field based on these studies, embodying information, suggestion and direction; answering specific inquiries of field officers; preparing, for Washington and the field, handbooks and other over-all studies of the CE situation, enemy organizations and enemy methods; disseminating relevant intelligence items to other Allied agencies; and conducting liaison with other OSS, American, British, and Allied offices.

X-2 also personally checked SI agents against the British files, as well as employees of other U. S. agencies. Such vetting had disturbed SI/X-2 relations for some time, because SI feared that the tracings would reveal its agents to the British services. Growing recognition by the other branches of OSS that such revelations could be avoided, and that the benefits received from that service were valuable, enabled X-2 to carry out more fully the directives of the Joint Chiefs of Staff and of the Director, OSS, to safeguard the undercover operations of the other branches in the field. Further evidence of profitable cooperation between SI and X-2 was the preparation by the X-2/French Desk, in July 1944, of CE briefs used for SI agents who were dispatched into five areas in France during that month. As the armies advanced, X-2 also conducted interrogations of SI agents who had been overrun by the armies and had been returned to England.

———————

151

Preparing Special Counter-Intelligence Teams (SCI)

In preparation for the invasion of Europe, the X-2 intelligence sections for the areas to be occupied had two main tasks: the gathering of as great a store of basic counter-espionage files as possible from the registries of the British and other Allies; the preparation of a machine, consisting of Special Counter-Intelligence teams,* for work with the invading armies, and a headquarters War Room to support their operations.

These tasks were clearly parts of the one main purpose: the liquidation of the enemy intelligence and subversion services. The earlier operations, from neutral countries and newly gained footholds in Africa and on the Continent, aimed at drawing a tight intelligence ring about the periphery of enemy occupied and dominated Europe; those that accompanied the attack of the armies applied in the field the stores of intelligence so far gathered toward the neutralization and control of enemy services.

There was in London a startlingly large and accurate mass of data on individual enemy agents and their organizational relationships, on channels of communication, and the like; it was possible not only to list and map enemy offices and operational stations, communications chains and training schools, but also to pinpoint the location of individuals and of related groups of the German satellite undercover agencies. This information had been gathered from the activities of Allied CE stations in neutral countries, the surveillance of known enemy chains, the operations of double-agents and controlled enemy agents, the interrogation of defected or captured enemy agents, censorship sources and various other means. The SCI teams carried this information to the field with them—information, which they, and the CIC teams of the armies, exploited with results that expanded at times

in almost geometrical progression: the swift capture and interrogation of one pinpointed agent led to the identification and location of one, two, or three others, who each might yield like identifications in his turn.

Members of the SCI teams to accompany American armies in the field were trained and briefed in the X-2/London office, and, for a group of selected officers, in the double-agent section of MI-5 (B). The training consisted of formal lectures on enemy organizations and their relationship; the study of CE files of invasion areas; classes in codes and communications procedures; work with desk personnel in the preparation of SHAEF cards, target lists and the like; and discussion and study group meetings with experienced British and American officers.

---

* See "X-2/Italy", above and "X-2/France", below.

War Room

In late April 1944, the training of the SCI units and the Western European Desk's arrangements to serve them, were tested in a three-day field exercise carried out, together with SI and SO units, at Horsham under simulated battle conditions. An analysis of the weakness of the liaison and communications methods, brought out under this test, indicated the need of more standard procedures, which were accordingly prepared and published in May. The document fixed the terms under which a joint British and American headquarters' Western European Desk, to be known as the SCI War Room, was to operate, and defined the relationships between SI, SO, and X-2 with respect to the handling of agents, the interchange of information and the interrogation of certain categories of persons. The plan established two separate organizations in COSSAC. One of these was the Evaluation and Dissemination Section (EDS) to compile, analyze, edit, and distribute (a) the semi-overt type of counterintelligence (on collaborationists, police, political papers, etc.), and (b) such secret intelligence   furnished it for production and distribution in the form of handbooks and pink SHAEF cards. The other was the so-called SCI War Room, an unofficial arrangement

for the purpose of servicing SCI units in the field and EDS in London.

The SCI War Room contained master maps pinpointing all known German agents and espionage centers, including "national" sub-agents of Allied-controlled G e r m a n agents. It was a headquarters desk, geared to serve as the operational and intelligence base for the units with the armies. In the period before the liberation of Paris, it handled all requests, even for supplies, from the field.

Besides the normal desk work of receiving, processing, carding and distributing the mass of information from all sources and preparing target lists and studies for the units, it answered queries for checks on arrested or suspect agents, assisted with fuller information for field interrogations, and arranged with the field units for shipment to the U. K. interrogation centers of enemy agents of importance or special promise as double-agents.

Until a special Vetting Desk was set up at the end of 1944, the War Room had also the task of carrying through security tracings on an increasingly large number of SI agents recruited in the field as military operations progressed.

Reorganization

In early March 1945, a reorganization of the War Room and desk system was accomplished, which (a) made of the War Room a broader and less secure agency, and (b) gave to the desks the job of handling double-agents. The desks were now organized, not according to countries within the SHAEF area of responsibility, but according to branches of the G e r m a n intelligence services.

The new SHAEF G-2 Joint Counter-Intelligence War Room was to work directly for the SHAEF Counter-Intelligence Branch (CIB) staffs during the last phase of military operations and through the liquidation period that would follow the collapse of Germany.

153

The French services were also admitted to participation.* The Director and Deputy Director were attached to SHAEF and were not responsible to their respective Services. The War Room had no concern with the running of agents, although it did receive relevant information produced from such operations; nor was it responsible for German activities outside the SHAEF area except for Austria, which, by special agreement, was to be the concern of the War Room during the occupational phase.

The new War Room was looked upon by the CIB staffs as part of their own machine, and they had recourse to it constantly for information on the German intelligence services, and guidance in the conduct of their operations. This relationship made for a diffusion of information on enemy intelligence personnel and organizations to lower field units, which had hitherto known little or nothing about them. The War Room assisted in training and briefing interrogators assigned to the American Interrogation Center, a number of whom came to London for study and conference. It also sent to the field over-all studies on enemy sabotage activities and methods, although none was prepared on such general topics as types of agents employed, missions, cover stories, etc.**

Desks were also relieved of the manual work of producing or amending SHAEF cards, by an arrangement that had all checking and processing, as well as the making of new entries on cards, done by a staff of expert women at the Registry. The translation, evaluation and distribution of all incoming captured documents were managed by a single section under the direction of an experienced officer, who supervised the production of English precis of relevant documents and of accession lists of all documents for the officers of the interested desks. That officer also supervised Registry action on his material. Such work as over-all studies, including the London weekly survey of the CE situation for SHAEF, was taken care of by a small section of expert editors.

The most striking of the new features, however, was that the desks were assigned, not to the study of the GIS in certain areas, but to that of highly particular sections of the Abwehr or the Sicherheitsdienst themselves. Thus the several desk officers could become final experts on assigned sections and sub-sections of the GIS. Given that concentration of specialty, an officer could have at his command all the information available on his subject, and could, therefore, handle more business more effectively in a day than he could if his interests were more dispersed and the necessity of refresher reading on various kinds of scattered cases necessary. Such functional arrangement of targets was an ideal one for a CE agency since the targets were, not areas, but enemy undercover agents and operations themselves. Normally the area desk was the only workable solution to the problem of world coverage; the final integration of data had to take place in general study sections working with the registry files. In 1945, however, the enemy undercover agencies were concentrated in a small enough area to permit desk specialization.

An X-2/London Desk

A typical desk history, through the various reorganizations, was that of the German

---

* The SCI War Room had previously maintained liaison with MI-5 and with the French through one officer from each of these services.
** Reports on the extreme vulnerability to enemy saboteurs of Allied supply lines were unfortunately ignored by Services of Supply.

Desk, which began its work in January 1944. As was true of all the London desks, its first activities centered chiefly on the job of building up its basic file of records from the large accumulations of the counterpart British desk. It focussed on the enemy undercover organizations in Germany, which for the purposes of the Desk, included Austria.

In August of 1944, the Polish, Czechoslovak and Swiss desks were incorporated into a German Desk, in preparation for a German War Room to service SCI teams and the field stations, before and after the German surrender. Actually, no such War Room came into full operation for the reason that the joint X-2/MI-5/MI-6 SHAEF G-2 Counter-Intelligence War Room came into being in time to deal with the mass of work on the arrests, interrogations and the like, that came with the decline and collapse of the German military strength. The new arrangement left to the Desk the management of all special cases, and the processing and distribution to Washington of the reports transmitted to it by the War Room on German cases. Lists of suspect persons, organization studies of the GIS, area target lists and similar material, made in preparation for the support of the field teams in Germany, were, despite the change, distributed to the field.

Target lists, worked out from sources ranging from top secret material to German telephone books, were found to be highly useful to T-Forces and CIC teams, which went into towns and cities with the first army units. Such raids yielded in turn, from captured documents and the speedy interrogations of captured GIS personnel, fuller and more recent information of targets ahead. A staff of the German Section in the Paris office worked on this project exclusively. Its lists, produced and distributed at top speed, were, when time allowed, supplemented and corrected by cabled and pouched notes drawn from the London files of the German Desk and of the War Room. Headquarters could, by this time, draw on fully checked and detailed interrogation reports of captured or defected German officers and agents of high grade. Toward the end of the fighting and after, only the more highly placed and more knowledgeable members of the GIS could be given thorough interrogation. They would yield more information of the significant personnel in the echelons below and above them, with the least expenditure of time and energy.

The German Desk collaborated with the War Room, not only in making target lists, but in the preparation of studies and reports on the methods and techniques of German intelligence services, recent changes in the relationships among branches of the various German services, their plans for long-range resistance, sabotage and intelligence operations and related activities.

During the period of settlement after VE-Day, the Desk served the X-2 staffs at Wiesbaden, Frankfurt, Munich, Salzburg, Berlin, Stuttgart and Bremen. All special cases handled by these stations were directed by the London German Desk.

The SHAEF War Room aimed at as rapid a self-liquidation as possible. By the end of the summer of 1945, the German intelligence services had disappeared as organizations. By that time, too, the CIB staffs were in a position, with the information provided by the War Room, to take over much of the work hitherto done by that unit. In September 1945, it was terminated, and X-2/London remained the controlling center of U. S. counter-espionage operations in Europe.

The War Room had been an arrangement for the servicing of the mobile CE units that mediated between the London registries and the CIB staffs with armies and at army groups. However much CE data on X-2 field unit might carry with it, it was unlike SI or SO field units in its continued dependence on the central registries. Swift recourse to the full information in the central files was a prime requisite for counter-intelligence and counter-espionage operations. Control had to rest at the center in which the registries were located.

The only serious division of authority occurred in September 1944, when a Paris office was established to coordinate, under London direction, U. S. counter-espionage in France. Despite the difficulties inherent in this division, the office and the SCI teams offered an excellent opportunity for many of the X-2/London personnel to test independently, in actual field operations, their extensive British training.*

(d) LIAISON WITH FOREIGN IN-
TELLIGENCE SERVICES

One of OSS/London's more important intelligence responsibilities lay in maintaining relations with the non-British foreign services also operating in ETO. As the center for most of the exiled governments, London was a giant "marketing place" for all intelligence activities. The various foreign services offered, not only a wealth of information from their own underground sources, but also a rich reservoir of personnel and contacts for agent operations. The return, to be given for these assets by OSS/London, was in money, equipment, facilities, techniques and the exchange of appropriate OSS-gathered intelligence.

There was no set pattern for OSS relationships with these foreign services. Some of the contacts were initiated through General Donovan at the highest level. Others were arranged by the Strategic Service Officer through the good offices of the Embassy or armed forces. Some simply grew out of informal personal relationships at branch or sub-branch levels.

As a result, there was rarely any particular coordination and often some confusion. For example, trouble arose when—as in the case of liaison with the Poles—two uncoordinated OSS contacts were in touch with two different political factions of the foreign service.

At times, efforts were made to integrate liaison more closely, but none was particularly successful, since many of the informal contacts were on a personal basis which brought a quicker, more satisfactory service than could be obtained through channels. The advantages of informality and ready access outweighed the disadvantages of inconsistency and duplication. Qualified analysts were available to sift and weigh conflicting intelligence, and any irreconcilable conflicts could always be handled on a case-by-case basis by the Commanding Officer.

French

The French were the first of the foreign intelligence agencies with which OSS/London developed liaison. Contact was arranged through the U. S. Embassy in July 1942, and, by 1943, SI was in close touch with BCRA (the de Gaullist secret intelligence agency), various French officials of the FFI, and numerous individuals outside the de Gaulle movement. Most helpful, outside of the political intelligence obtained, were the ground reports of bombing results in France for A-2 and the information on names, descriptions and locations of Allied airmen who had been shot down. OSS/London's closest relations with the French were in the development of the SI *Sussex* and SO *Jedburgh* plans,* but, throughout the period of preparing for the French landings, other liaisons were maintained by such OSS units as R&A, MO, X-2 and the SI Reports Division. There were difficulties, particularly when de Gaulle occasionally evinced displeasure at Anglo-American policy by cutting off all intelligence contact. Relations, however, were always somehow reestablished and continued throughout the war.

Polish

Contact with the Poles began in August 1942. SI soon developed a Polish Section for liaison with both the Polish Intelligence Service, which concentrated on military intelligence, and the Ministry of Interior, which handled political, psychological and social intelligence. From the latter source, SI received intelligence reports on conditions in Italy, Rumania, Bulgaria, Yugoslavia and Germany. Simultaneously, SO made connections with London representatives of the Polish resistance program through a liaison officer at SOE. Meanwhile R&A was in touch with some of the leftist Poles in London.

---

* See "SI/North France" and *"Jedburghs"*, below.

In the summer and fall of 1944, SI requested information for G-2 on the Russian-Polish crisis. Polish dispatches, however, proved to be so heavily slanted against Russia that they were often valueless. Moreover, the Poles were so divided among themselves that information on any subject varied according to which Pole had provided the data. Finally, it became apparent that the Poles were not only sometimes using resistance supplies against the Russians, but were inflating their share of available materials through identical requests made simultaneously of OSS/London, OSS/Washington and the British. The OSS Polish investment, in the long run, appears to have been largely unproductive, but justified by the necessity of playing all possibilities.

Dutch

Although occasional reciprocal services were performed by OSS and Dutch intelligence officers, after the dispersal of the latter's network by the Nazis in the summer of 1942, regular contact between OSS and the reconstituted military (MID) and secret intelligence (BI) branches of the Dutch service was established only in October 1943. Relations were greatly facilitated by the intelligence OSS could offer on Far Eastern areas, where the Netherlands had an interest.

Five elaborate maps on coastal defenses in Holland were made available by the Dutch to SI and turned over to ONI. Summaries of W/T reports from Holland on German battle order were supplied SI regularly, and, after June 1944, on the same day they were received from Dutch MID by BI. Via this rapid relay of Dutch W/T messages, SI received information on German plans to inundate Holland, and, for the Army Air Force, on V-bomb sites, bombing results, etc. Two complete maps were prepared from aerial photographs, showing all areas in Holland of actual or probable inundation and results of daylight bombing attacks. They were sent to Washington. Documents and personal articles, currently in use in

Holland, were also made available for SI agent use by the Netherlands services. This close liaison eventually made possible the development of an advance OSS base at Eindhoven.* As a result, SI could recruit prospective intelligence agents to be sent to the rear for training, and prepare the MELANIE field mission into Holland in late 1944.

Belgian

Belgian intelligence officials were first contacted by OSS/London in August 1942, in order to discover, for the Eighth Air Force, civilian reaction to Allied bombing in Belgium. Further intelligence from this source was sporadic and disappointing; the Belgian services were bound, by an agreement with the British, to limit relations with other Allied organizations.

SI did arrange, in early 1944, to receive from the Belgian Surete raw military intelligence reports—Air, Naval and Battle Order—simultaneously with the British. Cabled spot intelligence began arriving in February 1944. These cables, in increasing numbers,** reported V-1 and V-2 emplacements and other vital military targets, of special interest to the Eighth and Ninth Air Forces. Through initial contacts, SI was able to establish at Brussels, in September 1944, its ESPINETTE outpost which recruited agents for the penetration of Germany.***

R&A obtained from the Belgians a wide collection of clandestine newspapers and a large volume of economic and administrative material including, later in 1944, information on Lithuania, Esthonia, Poland and D e n m a r k. Twenty-four administrative maps of occupied Belgium were prepared by R&A in collaboration with Belgium intelligence representatives.

* See "Belgium and Holland", below.
** SI was receiving a peak load of one hundred operational cables a week from Belgian sources in September 1944, just prior to the liberation of the Low Countries.
*** See "Belgium and Holland", below.

Norwegian

Contacts with Norway's intelligence services and with the Foreign Minister were first made by SI in September 1942. Until a year later, however, when arrangements were made for SI to receive directly secret military intelligence from Norway, rather than through the Military Attaché at the U. S. Embassy, little other than occasional political-economic reports were received. Following this clearance, SI procured reports on submarine bases and activity in Norwegian waters, as well as ground estimates of AAF bombing results on Norwegian targets, and reports for COSSAC on supply and transportation needs there. Access to the files of the "E" office of the Norwegian Royal Ministry of Defense assured up-to-date data on shipping, defense installations, etc., in that country. SI reciprocated with supplies for British-Norwegian intelligence teams, and with underground intelligence reports from Sweden of interest to Norwegian officials.

Czechoslovak

In July 1942, OSS replaced the U. S. Military Attache as sole American liaison with the Czechoslovak Intelligence Service. CIS had no intelligence sources of its own in Europe, until 1944, and its reports, although regular, were often duplicated elsewhere or of dubious value. In July 1944, however, CIS teams began operating in Czechoslovakia, and SI was able to receive prompt answers to requests by the War Department, SI Labor Desk, R&A, X-2 and OSS/Washington on such items as rocket experiments on Rugen Island, mining operations in western Bohemia, an underground arms factory and air targets in Slovakia. Through contacts with leading Czechoslovak political figures and the Political Intelligence Section of the Ministry of Interior, SI obtained information on political developments, economic data on Central Europe and dossiers on individuals in the underground—Poles, Austrians, Hungarians and Sudeten Germans.

Both SI and R&A were in touch with Danish, Yugoslav and Greek officials. Liaison was carried on with the last two for OSS/MedTO. The intelligence flow from all these sources, however, was scanty, and no agent operations directed toward them were mounted from London.

Throughout the period, OSS/London attempted in vain to develop closer relations with the Russians. During the spring and summer of 1944, a few selected intelligence items were submitted to them by SI, and the Reports Division developed an informal contact with one Russian source. Nothing important, however, was ever received in return, and the tenuous relationship finally dissolved.

(e) REPORTS DIVISION/SI

In the early days of OSS/London, when the flow of intelligence was small and the list of customers short, items were handled by the appropriate geographic desks, and, on urgent occasions, by the Strategic Services Officer, ETO. But with the gradual shift in emphasis from service for Washington to support for the Theater, intelligence specialists came into demand, and, in the summer of 1943, the Reports Division/SI was established to process and disseminate intelligence. At the end of 1944 the Division included over one hundred personnel.

By July 1943, material was being processed from British and other Allied intelligence sources, from OSS offices in Algiers, Stockholm, Bern, Lisbon, Madrid, as well as Washington, and from other OSS branches. Later, many of the sources were OSS espionage agents reporting directly to London from behind enemy lines. The intelligence from all these sources poured into the Division by cable, pouch or courier.

On arrival, the material was broken down by subject matter and processed by military, political, economic and scientific experts. These specialists first evaluated the information on the basis of source and other known intelligence concerning the subject. The material was then translated, if necessary, edited, mimeographed and distributed to all interested agencies within the Theater. These included the Theater Command, the various armed forces, U. S. State Department representatives, numerous British and other Allied intelligence agencies, such U. S. units as EWD, OWI and OSRD, and joint services like PWD, CAD and ACC.

Adequate dissemination to all these customers without duplication, contradiction or embarrassment was complex and delicate. For instance, the greatest care had to be taken to keep OSS intelligence, hostile to an ally, from falling into its hands. Such material was classified "Control", signifying that dissemination must be restricted to U. S. customers. Particular caution was also required in disseminating material received from one ally concerning the internal affairs of another.

Likewise, special precautions were needed to prevent material originating with an ally from returning to it or one of its own customers via OSS channels. Such an event not only made for duplication but also might lead to false confirmation—an apparent, but actually unjustified, affirmation of intelligence previously received. Similar care had to be taken that OSS material should not reach customers via some shortcut before expert analysis, editing and evaluation by the Reports Division. In this event, aside from the risks of duplication and false confirmation, there was the collateral danger of two contradictory reports emanating from OSS at the same time.

Security posed another problem. Some items could safely be disseminated to some customers but not to others. For example, special care had to be taken, in April 1944, on disseminations of certain psychological warfare material to OWI, which that agency sometimes revealed to the Germans in propaganda broadcasts. All the material involved was useful to OWI analysts, but some of it was too confidential for broadcast purposes. The Reports Division worked out with OWI a system of special symbols on disseminations, indicating which material forwarded them could be used on the radio.

Speed was another problem. Occasionally information arrived of such urgency that the usual Reports procedure had to be by-passed. On these occasions, the Chief of Division and the SSO usually went personally to the interested customers and indicated that a regular dissemination would follow. During the invasion of France, a special teletype machine was installed to relay hot items direct to the appropriate military Hq.

A by-product of its work in disseminating information was the Reports Division's important role in intelligence target selection. From 1943 on, the Division's customers submitted lists of new subjects in which they were interested. In turn these requests were noted and passed on to operational desks for relay to other bases or agents in the field. In 1944 the Reports Division, on its own initiative, took up the work of collecting lists of such intelligence objectives, and in the fall became the Division of Intelligence Direction, selecting targets for and briefing German agents. In this way, the Division developed closer liaison between the various SI Desks and outside agencies.

(f) CLOTHING AND DOCUMENTS

While an agent's positive record depended on such personal factors as ingenuity, he could not be expected to succeed without such basic essentials as clothing and documents, correct to the minutest detail. Furthermore, agent morale depended to a considerable extent on confidence in cover, in the authenticity of clothing, suitcase, cigarettes, matches and the like.

It was decided, in Washington, that the most efficient operation of R&D and CD must necessarily be at the operations center of London, rather than in Washington. Representatives of both Branches arrived in April 1944. Theoretically, CD would collect the requisite data, while R&D would manufacture the items. In practice, the two pooled their resources.

R&D in Washington had compiled a list of equipment and machinery necessary for a complete printing, lithographing and photoengraving plant, to be delivered to London as soon as possible. However, the delay in arrival of the equipment was so great that, to all intents and purposes, the Branches had to equip themselves on the spot, on either a loan or a purchase basis.

The work could not have been carried out at all without considerable British cooperation. One British company supplied a lithographing press which was installed on 4 July. Another plant loaned, privately and without charge, a photoengraving camera and a routing machine, with the sole proviso that the machines be marked as the property of the company—to be returned at some future date. At the end of May, suitable arrangements were made with a British firm for the purchase of paper of the most specialized nature. The mill's output was only nine tons a week, but it produced under ideal security conditions. CD/R&D concluded that it was already working for SOE, which agency had quietly permitted OSS to benefit from the mill's experience.

In April 1944, the two Branches began combined operations with a staff of five. The number increased steadily, so that by the end of the year there was a total of thirty-six personnel, including five civilians. By that time the procedural pattern was set. In two separate buildings near the OSS/London office, CD/R&D handled the production of clothing and documents.

Clothing

For the clothing shop, OSS supplied a tailor, while Polish Intelligence furnished a cobbler. Relevant clothing data came from careful study of actual examples of the uniforms to be duplicated. For example, a trip to a British POW camp produced valuable information not only on enemy uniforms, but also on articles suitable to be carried in an agent's pocket. At various times (14 October represented the first such mission), personnel were dispatched to the Continent to obtain German uniforms, accessories and equipment.

In clothing, complete anonymity was desired, but it was hard to locate inconspicuous garments. An additional hazard was provided by laundry marks, which proved almost impossible to remove. The British applied a cleansing method, but this affected the dye of the cloth so that a suspiciously light spot remained.

No detail was too insignificant to escape notice. Buttons had to be sewn on by threading the holes in parallel instead of criss-cross fashion. Inside pockets were fitted on each side, and, if the suit were tailored to order, a tailor's slip would be on the inside of the left pocket. Sometimes a strip of cloth matching the material of the suit would be placed along the rim of the inside pockets of the jacket. Normally, plain bone buttons were used, but suspender buttons were sometimes marked "elegant" or "for gentlemen" or "mode de Paris", as was found to be customary on both German and French clothes.

Accessories were varied in origin. For example, shoelaces were German, handkerchiefs were British imitations, and towels were made in Ireland. Since the stock of genuine articles was insufficient, a Camouflage Section was established in August 1944 to manufacture additional accessories, as well as lead pencils to be used as concealment devices, belt buckles for the same purpose, letter drops and the like.

In the fall, when the SI demand turned to German equipment, field trips to the Continent produced sufficient material for use as models. The stock of second-hand items soon gave out, and CD/R&D resorted to the normal British methods of manufacturing clothing and subsequently soaking, dirtying and subjecting it to several cleanings and pressings.

Documents

In May 1944 CD/R&D began the production of rubber stamps and documents. BCRA furnished background intelligence,

while OSS/Washington sent blank documents. In addition, field detachments, other American agencies and T-Forces * supplied valuable data and blanks from time to time.

The problems of letterpress, lithographic press and photoengraving equipment were early solved, but the question of print was recurrent. Continental type was varied and its supply was short. The solution lay in printing from photoengraved plates. A suitable photoengraving plant was established, which could turn out work of a refinement and character necessary to produce plates that would duplicate enemy documents perfectly. It was, of course, often hard to find an original document that was not faded or discolored, and R&D had to develop various chemical processes to sharpen outlines.

Papers, even when perfectly matched in form, color and texture, differed greatly when examined under ultra-violet light. This difficulty was never corrected, but appears not to have been discovered by the enemy. Watermarking, it was found, must be effected simultaneously with the actual manufacture of the paper, a procedure with which the British paper mill, mentioned above, was familiar. Unfortunately, perfection required time; SIS had spent, on one occasion, two years to produce a single document, but, since time was important, perfection often had to be sacrificed to expedience. In such duties as paper matching, filling in by hand and matching colors, the fatiguing detail and accuracy required was extreme. Nevertheless, CD/R&D achieved notable success. A very small percentage of agents were discovered because of unsatisfactory papers or clothing.**

(g) COMMUNICATIONS

Message Center

Prior to the establishment of an OSS Communications Branch, radio traffic for all

---

* See "Liberated France", below.

** See ensuing sections on France and Germany.

OSS sections in London was handled by the Message Center. This central routing point was formed, after the OSS/OWI split in June 1942, from the staff of the original COI code room, which had been established at the U.S. Embassy in December 1941. It moved, on 1 September 1942, to OSS Headquarters on Grosvenor Street.

Through teletype links (for local purposes), and cable lines and wireless (for long distance), the OSS Message Center maintained contact with other official agencies in London, both U.S. and foreign, and, after August 1943, with points all over the globe. Where it did not have its own facilities—such as cable channels—OSS arranged to use State Department, Army or commercial circuits. The first OSS link was over a commercial trans-Atlantic varioplex circuit to Washington which served the increasing amount of administrative traffic.

Because the major portion of all messages passing through the OSS communications center in London was classified, each network had a special cipher system—double transposition, confidential machine, etc.— depending on the nature and extent of the traffic.* Cryptographic procedures and other security precautions at the Message Center were strict. Incoming messages were given a prefix number indicating, for cipher clerks, the code system employed. The deciphered text was then paraphrased before distribution, to prevent comparison by enemy interceptors of the clear text with its coded counterpart and possible compromise of the cipher system itself. The original coded text and deciphered copy thereof were filed for permanent reference in the code room. Outgoing cables, sent through the OSS Message Center, had to be encoded exactly as received, a paraphrased version being returned to the originator for filing.

----
* A Bern-Algiers-London-Washington net, for example, had a transposition type of cipher, and used U.S. State Department wireless and cable facilities. For a discussion of codes and ciphers, see Washington section on Communications.

Efficiency of London-Washington traffic was increased considerably with the addition, in January 1944, of an Army teletype scrambler. This unit enciphered messages at the same time that they were transmitted to the mouth of the trans-Atlantic cable, thus avoiding two time-consuming processes; encipherment and paraphrasing. Its high security permitted its use even for top secret messages.

Meanwhile, arrangements for large communications bases to accommodate prospective field operations were being worked out between OSS officials and the British in London. SIS and SOE already operated independent secret networks in many parts of the world. As in similar discussions involving OSS and these organizations, SO and SOE—admittedly restricted to wartime duration—were anxious to pool their resources and experience, while SI and SIS guarded the independence of their respective long-range secret intelligence networks. During the summer and fall of 1942, it was agreed that SO should handle its commitments through British-controlled communications links, while SI might establish its own station on a separate site.

Station CHARLES

On 22 September 1942, an OSS Communications Branch was officially established, and, soon afterwards, projected OSS W T arrangements in London received G-2 and Signal Corps approval. A new station— 53C, or CHARLES, the third radio base in SOE's London network—would be built, equipped and staffed by American personnel.

By November 1943, Station CHARLES could begin operation. Intended at first to cover only the northern, or Scandinavian, sector of the three into which the British had divided Western Europe for communications purposes, Station CHARLES was given, as Normandy invasion plans were formed, responsibility for SO/SOE operations in France as well. To prepare for its more extensive commitments—which were to include *Jedburgh* agent teams and mobile detachments with armies and army groups—Station CHARLES called for more personnel and field equipment, tied in its training with the highly-developed British programs at SOE stations 53A and 53B, and set up a Technical Maintenance section devoted, among other things, to experimenting with new radio equipment and techniques. Since the personnel problem remained unsolved, the British loaned 36 high-speed radio operators and 50 additional female personnel to CHARLES until an allotment of Americans could take over, and permanently assigned 22 skilled cipher clerks. By 1944 the station was manned by 300 personnel.

In February 1944, Station CHARLES began a series of trial exercises to prepare field and base operators alike for actual operations. And on 13 March, it undertook its first "live" commitments—Norwegian teams, transferred from SOE Station 53A. By the end of March, procedures had evolved in the radio rooms, and new trainees were gaining confidence in the techniques of indicating call signs, "break-ins", requests for frequency and schedule changes and other signals. The field exercises were continued with *Jedburgh* and mobile unit personnel, so that, by D-Day, the operators at CHARLES were familiar with, and could work simultaneously, three types of commitments, each with its special problems. They learned for instance, never to repeat coded messages in full, always to map out and rotate schedules (skeds) on an hour-to-hour basis, and to tune transmitters over wide frequency ranges (usually high during the day and low during the night).

Profiting from all that was learned of internal procedures, routing of messages, etc., in the first seven months of its development, Station CHARLES, just prior to D-Day, was physically remodeled to ensure the greatest efficiency. At that time its six principal departments consisted of:

Radio operators (Received and transmitted)

Coders (Enciphered and deciphered; trained clerks for other theaters)

Perforators (Prepared call signs and broadcast tapes, for routine or mass signalling)

Teleprinters (Contacted SO/SOE Hq. and other stations)

Registry (Kept message files, logs of contacts, etc.)

Technical Maintenance (Maintained receiver and transmitter sites, tested, repaired and experimented)

These departments reported to a centrally located Control Room and a directing Chief Signalmaster.

Garbled or indecipherable messages were reduced almost totally by a system of interpretation, in which the duty signalmaster and skilled cipher supervisors joined to analyze problem messages on the basis of Morse (transmission) errors, context, agent's language faults, past messages and other data. Repetition was rarely requested. Code groups which had been missed entirely, due to static or other causes, were provided either by recordings or by monitoring reports from other SOE stations (made on contacts where the operator was not highly proficient). If an operator's capture by the enemy were suspected, his transmissions were "fingerprinted": during a contact undulator tapes were run to obtain a visual picture of the sender's "fist", and checked with tapes at headquarters made by the SO or SOE agent prior to dispatch.

After the cipher system to be used had been determined, different signal plans were prepared for each agent group by OSS and SOE planning boards. Each plan included: the operating frequencies to be used for both regular and emergency contacts (selected from lists of workable frequencies provided by SHAEF, after consideration of the location of the agent in relation to London and other agents, season and anticipated ionospheric conditions); contact times; call signals (variable or fixed three-letter groups); a signal system for arranging alternate or additional skeds, using a Day Indicating Table for the day of the week and a Transposition Table for hour and minute; base broadcast periods; and the "Q" signal system of three-letter combinations with specified meanings to facilitate and shorten contact time.

An early and elaborate plan was that for the Norwegian agents, who were scheduled to make at least one contact every other day, always at a different time according to a prearranged schedule, and never on the same frequency. Frequencies could be changed during a contact, by either the base or the outstation, by so signalling in accordance with the signal plan's tables and codes. Contacts were limited to one hour—not for security reasons alone, but because the number of agents to come on the air each day were closely scheduled.

The later *Jedburgh* plan was simpler, allowing two daily contacts at different times on odd and even days. Frequencies could be changed but, because of a limited 8-channel arrangement, agents were requested not to ask for different schedule times. Each *Jedburgh* plan was, nevertheless, provided with one of two 24-hour emergency channels, to be used when communication outside the regular sked time was urgent. Nightly broadcasts from CHARLES to all *Jedburgh* teams were also listed on the plan. Although many *Jedburgh* communication links were weak, comments of returning agents were generally favorable. All frequencies, and particularly the emergency frequency, on which 832 contacts were passed, were satisfactory.

At the SO/SOE Army Detachments, the heavy units (RCA dual channels and SCR-399's) were allowed 24-hour contact, while the lighter jeep-mounted SCR-193's with mobile army units were allotted one hour in every three. A fixed three-letter call sign for the base and a three-letter variable call sign for the field units were changed each day.

Station CHARLES worked altogether 64 *Jedburgh* teams, 24 mobile circuits and more than 32 Norwegian commitments. Heaviest traffic during July and August was with the mobile army units. Upon the liberation of France, main traffic at CHARLES reverted to the Scandinavian sector. By the middle of October, CHARLES had closed, the few remaining *Jedburgh* and detachment channels being transferred to SOE Station 53A, and the Norwegian commitments to 53B. Station CHARLES personnel moved to the Far East, to the Mediterranean, to the new OSS base in Paris or to SI station VICTOR.

Station VICTOR

In the attempt to meet priority needs of the SO/SOE stations, Theater allocations of specialized communications equipment, personnel and frequencies for an independent SI station were postponed. Station VICTOR (SI) was not established until March 1944, at which time it undertook responsibility for half of the joint SI/SIS *Sussex* missions and for four mobile detachments. In April, there were already several W/T-equipped SI teams in France, while only temporary base facilities existed to serve them. All operations at VICTOR, until well after D-Day, were conducted during a period when permanent installations were still in the process of assembly, and an adequate complement still being acquired. By July there were as yet only 100 personnel. The consequent differences in performance of Stations CHARLES and VICTOR were, under the circumstances, not surprising.

In contrast to the SO/SOE base, Station VICTOR did not constitute a self-contained unit. Although carrying on its own radio contacts with the field, it relied for ciphering and distribution on the main Message Center in London. The Center deciphered and sent, via its numerous teletype circuits, VICtor intelligence direct to BCRA, SIS, X-2, Eighth Air Force, Director of Intelligence of the U. S. Strategic Air Force and G-2, SHAEF. The actual work with VICTOR was handled by a special operations staff at the Message Center. Only in July 1944 was this "ops" section, with its cipher facilities, moved to the VICTOR site, to permit greater speed in the coding and decoding of VICTOR messages.

Station VICTOR was handicapped in other ways. A month after its activation in March, and only a few weeks after its one large field exercise had been completed, actual operations were begun by *Sussex* agents in France. In addition, owing to an SIS security ruling, agents in training might not contact the same base with which they would be communicating from the field. VICTOR operators, as a result, did not have the benefit of the trial-and-error experience, and the knowledge of personal idiosyncracies that CHARLES personnel were able to acquire before working their agents in the field. Furthermore, the late start of the *Sussex* program caused SI/London to dispatch some agents before they had completed training.

Signal plans used at VICTOR, for *Sussex* and *Proust* agents, called for one scheduled contact every other day, each on a different frequency, at a different time, and using a different call sign. Alternate contact times, frequencies and call signs were provided *Sussex* plans which were operated on five channels, four for normal schedules and broadcasts, and one for emergency use. These were rotated except for the low-frequency channel which was used exclusively for VICTOR's two nightly broadcast periods directed toward all agents.

Of the many complaints that came back to VICTOR from *Sussex* operators, most could be attributed to VICTOR's unfamiliarity with the agents and to inadequate *Sussex* training. Furthermore, SI agents lacked the resistance protection on which most SO agents could depend. For this reason, the former were often forced to set up aerials in locations that were physically secure, but unsatisfactory from a communications standpoint. When signals were not actu-

ally weak from these combined causes, they were frequently interrupted by enemy jamming.

Better luck was experienced with the light and heavy Special Signal Detachments with Allied armies and army groups. Standard U. S. Army Signal Corps equipment and procedures were used from positions of relative safety, and good atmospheric conditions permitted a high average of successful contacts. The SI/X-2 staffs operated, as did the corresponding SO/SOE units,* on a 24-hour basis in the case of the heavy sections at Headquarters, and on hourly skeds in the case of the light detached units.

2. Algiers Base

Algiers was planned to serve as the major MedTO base, corresponding to that in London, for operations into Europe. In London were centered the main headquarters of OSS Branches X-2 and SO. SI and R&A also maintained large staffs there for liaison and intelligence correlation. Various other operating and supporting branches brought the London personnel total close to 2,000.

OSS/Algiers, on the other hand, was staffed by not more than one-third as many. R&A and X-2 activities were limited, and SO did not begin support of SO/London until early 1944. For SI, on the contrary, Algiers offered greater opportunities than did London. Most important of its advantages was its location in a U. S.-controlled theater, where British services, in particular SIS, could not hamper SI operations, and where American units were more apt to give OSS the necessary supply, quarters and transportation support. For the penetration of France, SI could also find many suitable recruits, some of them fresh out of France, in the French colonies of North Africa.

According to JCS 170 ** (approved in principle by the Theater Commander on 7

* See above.
** Washington Exhibit W-38.

166

February 1943), the following OSS activities, among others, were authorized:

SI activities in . . . south and southwest Europe . . . to the eastern boundary of Italy, and the islands adjacent thereto; SO activities in Italy, Sicily, Sardinia, Corsica, France, and other places as are required by the North African Theater Command.

Counter-intelligence and counter-espionage in these and certain other areas were also authorized.

Secret Intelligence

For operations into Europe, SI was divided into desks—French, Italian,* Labor and, later, Spanish.**

Activities of SI/France began with the arrival of its chief in late February 1943. Attention was first directed toward the struggles of the major rival French factions in North Africa. OSS officers associated by necessity with all political factions, Giraudist and de Gaullist, but principally with patriotic anti-German elements who had assisted OSS in preparations for the North Africa landings. The weight of information from these sources on various detailed aspects of the de Gaulle-Giraud conflict in the summer of 1943 frequently caused OSS reports to conflict with those of State Department representatives. That Department took strenuous exception to OSS political reporting on North Africa, as overlapping the work of its representatives on the scene, who were normally charged with such activity.

Donovan at the time placed less importance on political reporting than on military intelligence in direct support of the armies in the field, and ordered SI/France to redirect its emphasis accordingly. Thereafter, the SI/France staff trained, briefed and dispatched its agents strictly to obtain military and order of battle intelligence from inside enemy-held territory.

A Labor Desk was also established under SI, designed for eventual penetration of Germany through contacts with underground refugees in North Africa and France. Approvals for agent transport proved difficult to obtain, however, and the staff of the Labor Desk was transferred in March 1944 to Bari, Italy, for infiltrations through Yugoslavia.

The Chief Intelligence Officer controlled, in addition to these sections, the Reports Office. With the arrival, in November 1943, of specialists in battle order and coastal defenses, the first technical direction of intelligence was possible. The Algiers staff could then be divided into Operations and Intelligence and increase agent efficiency accordingly.* Toward D-Day (15 August), liaison was established on a high level with AFHQ and Force 163 and specific suggestions, inquiries and criticisms were freely exchanged on incoming and outgoing reports.

X-2

Counter-espionage work in North Africa had first been carried out by OSS/Oujda,** and its commanding officer had established the X-2 unit in Algiers, reporting to X-2/London.

In June 1943 a new chief, previously briefed in London, arrived and reconstructed several of the informant agent chains he had previously used during the *TORCH* operation in Tangier, Araboua, Rabat, Casablanca, Fez and Oran. As of July 1943, the old OSS stations in these areas and at Oujda reported their CE activities to X-2. The central files in Algiers were organized to incorporate the scattered CE intelligence there, as well as that which began to come in from the field stations. In September, X-2 and the Communications Branch coordinated their activities for D/F-ing enemy stations.

Relations with the French were productive. All French counter-intelligence and police reports were made available to X-2 through the DSM liaison. X-2 units, particularly the Oujda group, worked with them in several successful operations against enemy parachutists in the Department of Constantine.

---

* See "Italy", above.
** See "Trans-Pyrenees Chains", below.

* See "Agent Processing" by SI/Algiers, below.
** See "Oujda Operations", above.

The new officer had, however, the difficult task of establishing close relations with British   While the latter received volumes of CE material from SIS, X-2 could not offer in exchange a similar quantity from other OSS sources.

However, small X-2 units were eventually dispatched to Italy and France, where they were able to engage in independent operations. In early 1944, the North African stations were transferred to Washington control,* while the units across the Mediterranean continued to report to X-2/London.

Research and Analysis

The first R&A representative reached Algiers from Washington in May 1943 and established liaison with various U. S. military units interested in intelligence, as well as with representatives of the U. S. Treasury, PWB and the North African Economic Board. From the short-handed days of 1943 until the close-down of the Algiers office late in 1944, R&A worked integrally with the Reports Office to translate, process, evaluate and disseminate raw intelligence reports for various customers in the Theater.

Special Operations

A small SO group arrived in Algiers in January 1943. Because of the shortage of OSS personnel in North Africa at that time, most of these men had to undertake administrative and housekeeping duties at OSS headquarters in Algiers. Lack of adequate leadership and planning at this stage, plus depletion of SO personnel through assignment to other work, appreciably delayed the start of SO operations based on North Africa.

According to the London SO/SOE agreement, activities of these two organizations in North Africa would be joint, and coordinated by SO.** So well entrenched, however, was SOE in the Theater—including primary access to transportation, recruits and

---

* See "Africa", above.
** See "Introduction", above.

equipment—by the time OSS officers initiated their discussions, that SOE's acknowledged superiority in North Africa gave SO little opportunity to expand independently beyond its auxiliary contributions of administration, training and Operational Groups.

Massingham was the organization SOE established in Algiers, following the Allied landings, for operations into Europe. In accordance with negotiations between London and Washington, it was to be a purely British endeavor; however, OSS, with theoretical command of Special Operations in the North African Theater, might and did send an OSS observer.

At the *Massingham* camp at Ain Taya, the OSS representative assisted as an instructor. After understudying British SOE officers, he began training young recruits from the Corps Franc d'Afrique in demolitions, the handling of Sten guns and hand grenades, and· unarmed combat. The instruction lasted from 9 December 1942 until Christmas, when Darlan's assassination by a student of the Ain Taya camp brought activities there to an abrupt close.

Liaison, already established during the Tunisian campaign continued throughout the war in the form of a joint program of parachute training and supply packing operations at the OSS-organized Club des Pins school, near Sidi Ferruch, west of Algiers. Under the direction of experienced OSS officers, classes ranging from ten to seventy Spanish, Italian and French recruits were trained weekly for SOE, SIS, Deuxieme Bureau, Bataillon de Choc, and OSS missions. Their intensive instruction included practice parachute jumps into unfamiliar territory and paramilitary training, close combat, demolitions, small arms, etc. In mid-September, first recruits for the newly-formed Operational Groups * began training at the Club des Pins parachute school.

A packing station was also established. Parachutes for personnel and supplies were rigged and various types of containers tested

---

* See below.

in experimental drops. This remained a joint British-American program until March 1944, when OSS set up its own independent supply and packing facilities. Modifications of American aircraft, once planes were obtained, were developed in various experimental tests to attain maximum efficiency in dropping both personnel and supplies.

A small independent SO training area (Station "P"), established in January 1944 near Algiers, was reorganized and moved in April to Chrea as an enlarged OSS paramilitary school. Here, until July, approximately fifty SO agents and saboteurs—mostly French recruits—were trained each month as organizers, instructors, and members of French Commando units. Courses at Chrea included: small arms, map reading, field craft, security, demolition, communications and industrial sabotage.

SPOC. In early 1944 it was agreed between SHAEF and AFHQ that the support and control of all resistance activity in southern France would rest with SHAEF. Responsibility for this function was delegated by SHAEF to SFHQ,* and, under SFHQ, a joint American and British headquarters, known as G-3 Special Project Operations Center (SPOC) was established on 1 May at Algiers to conduct operations in France.

Prior to this centralization of control, SO/North Africa ** had arranged with French Army headquarters in Algiers to obtain the services of a limited number of French officers and enlisted men. In return, SO undertook to provide paramilitary and parachute training for a much larger number of French Army personnel. SO personnel in Algiers were rarely fluent in French or familiar with any special part of France. For this reason, it was felt in Algiers that SO operations before D-Day, be-

cause they involved living under an assumed name, with false papers and in civilian clothes, could be performed more effectively by Frenchmen.

Pursuant to this agreement, about one hundred Frenchmen were recruited and trained in Algiers for work as SO agents in France. These men were made available to SPOC, and it was arranged to procure 200 more. Six French Operational Groups and 25 *Jedburgh* teams sent from London came under the tactical control of SPOC, as did the SO Packing Station in Algiers, which had been established in March. An Air Operations Section, similar to that at SFHQ/London, was created to work with the Bomber Group which provided the air lift for body and supply drops from North Africa.

A total of 212 American SO and OG personnel were infiltrated into southern France by SPOC during the summer of 1944. Of these, 9 were SO agents, 21 were *Jedburghs*, and 182 made up the 14 combat sections into which the Operational Groups were divided for work in the field.* In addition, 30 French SO agents worked for SPOC in France.

At the time of the *ANVIL* invasion (15 August 1944), G-3, SPOC controlled 10 Inter-Allied Military Missions, 17 *Jedburgh* teams, 10 Operational Group missions, a British Paramilitary Group, and special counter-scorch teams in the ports of Sete, Marseille and Toulon. Since 20 May, the SPOC Air Supply Section had dispatched more than 1,500 tons to Maquis and undercover Allied groups. At least seven Lysander and Dakota moonlight landing operations had been successfully completed in southern France, carrying heavy weapons, infiltrating Allied leaders for consultation with FFI chiefs, and exfiltrating agents, resistance leaders and Allied airmen.

A special staff known as Special Force Unit No. 4 (SFU-4) represented SPOC with the Seventh Army during and after the *AN-*

---

* See "London Base", above.

** SPOC's responsibility covered the South France area assigned to General Cochet by General Koenig, Commanding General of EMFFI. See Exhibit in "Resistance Aid to *OVERLORD*", below.

---

* See "Building French Resistance", *"Jedburghs"* and "OG's in France", below.

VIL invasion. Its purpose was to coordinate the activities of the various SPOC teams with FFI and with the Seventh Army and 6th Army Group in the field, and to provide a central wireless link between them and the Algiers base. SPOC agents in France sent situation reports, supply requests, etc. to Algiers via the SFU-4 link at Seventh Army Hq. or via advance OSS units with the Seventh Army. Upon the completion of their missions, agents contacted SFU-4 officers with the Army for further instructions, or proceeded to rear bases at Grenoble and Avignon for de-briefing and repatriation.

By early September, FFI action against the enemy had virtually ceased in most departments. However, Algiers continued to supply resistance groups covering the Allied flanks against by-passed enemy pockets in the southwest and on the Italo-French border. Lyon was taken by Seventh Army and FFI forces on 4 September, thus ending the need for further SPOC operations in southern France. The organization was officially liquidated on 9 September 1944.

Operational Groups

Donovan anticipated inclusion of radio-equipped guerrilla-type units as part of SO in the Mediterranean Theater, when he sent, in January 1943, the Chief of SO to discuss with Theater authorities the use of "auxiliary operational groups".

OG recruits were volunteers from U. S. Army units who spoke the language of the country where they would operate. Consisting normally of four officers and thirty enlisted men, each group was divided into combat sections comprising, as a rule, two officers and thirteen enlisted men, including a radio operator and a medical technician. They were trained at camps in the United States.*

The first Italian-speaking OG recruits did not reach North Africa until late July 1943. The men were incorporated into an Operational Group command as Company A, and

---

* See Washington section on OG's.

given final SO training and briefing for operations in Corsica, Sardinia and Italy. OG's for France, sent from Washington in February and March 1944, were organized in Algiers as Company B and used pursuant to SHAEF plans for the June and August invasions.

Communications

Following D-Day in North Africa, the OSS Communications staff consisted of a small group of Frenchmen, most of whom had assisted with preparations for Operation *TORCH*. The OSS station in Algiers provided the sole radio link with Gibraltar from North Africa and transmitted all Army and State Department messages there until an AFHQ Signal Corps unit was established at Algiers.

By March 1943, all Frenchmen had been replaced by American personnel. The small coding, transmitting and receiving office had expanded to include a message center at SI headquarters in Algiers, and a large Communications headquarters—including base radio and main receiving stations—at Cap Matifou, about twenty kilometers away. A communications school, where agent-operators were trained separately for clandestine radio work, was located some distance from the other bases. By May 1943, OSS/Algiers was in direct contact with OSS offices at Casablanca and Tangier, with clandestine stations in Corsica (PEARL HARBOR) and southern France (MEXICO), with the SOE/*Brandon* post at Le Kuif, Tunisia, and with a seldom-used but important station at Madrid. Besides those direct contacts, the Message Center also handled messages, through State Department and Army channels, to and from OSS bases all over the world.

An important sub-station was established at Ile Rousse, Corsica, in October 1943. This was used for servicing OG operations and as an alternate base for agent circuits in France, when Algiers could not be reached from the field.* Forty percent of incoming

---

* Corsica was about 300 miles from the average French circuit, compared to Algiers' 600 miles.

field messages from France in the pre-invasion days of 1944 were relayed to Algiers via Corsica, which continued to serve as a substation until October 1944.*

Transportation

After the official activation of Experimental Detachment, G-3 (Provisional),** OSS requisitions were subject to the same priority system governing other combat forces in the Theater and, as such, depended on allocation from the Theater Command. Personnel was restricted by the need for Theater Command approval of all persons entering the Theater for duty. Similar transport difficulties were encountered. The first agent mission to Corsica had been shipped by the French.*** Subsequently, Donovan arranged with General Eisenhower for OSS to go direct to the RAF command for aircraft, so that it no longer had to apply through British SIS, which was often slow in cooperating.

According to the provision of JCS 170, the Chief of Staff, AFHQ, agreed to ask the Mediterranean Air Command to set aside for OSS "three bomber type airplanes" for use during each moon period. By May 1943, the priorities of Allied air operations were still preventing their release. British Halifaxes could be requested through SOE, but these could not be counted on for all occasions or on short notice.

In June 1943, Donovan persuaded General Curtiss, A-2, U. S. Strategic Air Force, to agree to assign a few planes for special operations. It was not until August, however, that two B-17's, a C-47 and seven B-25's were released to OSS and airmen transferred from

regular bomber units to the OSS Parachute School. At Club des Pins,* trap doors were installed in B-17's and experimental night landings made from the C-47 on improvised runways. B-25's, too fast for personnel drops, were adjusted for container and package use.

An experiment was attempted in March 1944, modelled on the successful British system of "Lysander" mail pickups. B-17's and C-47's were tried, but, because they stalled at low speed, could not be used for aerial pick-ups. Clandestine fields for receipt by air of documentary intelligence, "burnt" agents, etc., were, nevertheless, prepared by SI agents in France and a few serviced at infrequent intervals by British "Lysanders".

Finally, USN PT Squadron 15 was made available by AFHQ for agent deliveries from Corsica.**

———————

In June 1943, Experimental Detachment, G-3 (Prov.), became 2677th Headquarters Company (Prov.), still attached to G-3, AFHQ. Sub-bases for the Italian campaign were established at Bone (Algeria) and Bizerte (Tunisia). As operations into the Continent grew, the original members of the small *TORCH* operation were replaced by administrative officers. In November 1943, a new commanding officer was appointed.

All of OSS/Algiers, except the units concerned with the southern France operations, was shifted, in July 1944, to Caserta, Italy. Remaining in Algiers until September 1944 were the staffs of SPOC, SO supply, French and North African SI, R&A and Communications. By 1 November, all but the SI stations at Casablanca, Tangier, Oran, Tunis and Algiers,*** concerned for the most part with CE activities, had closed down or moved to bases on the Continent.

* For a description of the circuit established to supply the 15 August invasion fleet with up-to-the-minute intelligence from the French coast, see "Intelligence for *ANVIL*", below.
** On 1 April 1943. See "Tunisia", above.
*** See section on Corsica under "West Mediterranean Islands", above.

* At Sidi Ferruch, see sub-section on SO, above.
** See "Corsica Operations", above.
*** See "Africa", above.

B. EARLY INFILTRATIONS

1. Algiers Intelligence

The first clandestine network organized by OSS for intelligence in metropolitan France was established three months after the North African landings and without benefit of any SI organization as such. Radio operator "Tommy", who had served Operation *TORCH* and run the OSS operation in Corsica (the first in enemy-occupied Europe),* was assigned the task. Because he had both experience and extensive personal contacts in France, "Tommy" was asked, at the same time, to take radio sets and to re-establish W/T contact for SOE, whose station near Nice had been broken up by the Germans. In return for British air lift, OSS performed these services.

The mission proceeded in the first week of February via Corsica in the same French submarine, "Casablanca", that had carried "Tommy's" Corsican team a month previously. By the end of February, "Tommy" had succeeded in setting up a clandestine station for the Deuxieme Bureau in Marseille, a new British sabotage post in the Alps, and the beginnings of an OSS intelligence network and W/T station, MEXICO, in Toulon. He was given virtual independence in the recruiting and training of OSS agents and operators; security and on-the-spot policy were, for all practical purposes, in the hands of one man. Necessary as this delegation was at the time, lack of complete control from Algiers made for complications later on.

Although officially working in liaison with the Giraud-backed SR intelligence service, whose Marseille station he had organized, "Tommy" quickly contacted key figures in

* See "Operation *TORCH*" and "West Mediterranean Islands," above.

the underground movement. These patriots, fervent supporters of General de Gaulle and opponents of Giraud, were among the first to volunteer their whole-hearted cooperation to the OSS cause in France, and it was with their help that "Tommy" set up his secret radio station, MEXICO, in Toulon. An experienced radio operator was supplied him through the leader of all underground resistance in the Provence region. These same securely organized patriots volunteered to protect the new OSS station and construct a network of agents to provide it with information, military, political and economic, throughout the south of France, for transmission to AFHQ, Algiers.

In addition to maintaining contact with these competing French followers of Giraud and de Gaulle, "Tommy" kept in touch with the secret station of British SOE. For the sake of security, all three sources had to be kept separate and ignorant of each other. "Tommy" organized "Comite OSS". This was a liaison organization made up of SR and OSS agents, designed for exchange of information between the two organizations and nominally giving SR supervision over OSS activities. In actuality, SR claimed information from OSS sources as its own, and the main purpose of "Comite OSS", as far as "Tommy" was concerned, was to ward off SR suspicions of his other underground contacts.

Station MEXICO, operating clandestinely in enemy-occupied territory and receiving the cooperation of hundreds of individuals, ran grave risks every day of being blown. "Tommy", insofar as he was capable under the complicated conditions in which he operated, took precautions. A special committee of high officials supporting the underground movement was appointed to ensure the physical protection of the OSS station

173

at Toulon. The committee consisted of a former counsellor of the prefect of Var, the police chief of Toulon, the head of the Toulon arsenal, a local pharmacist, and two police inspectors. When "Tommy" suspected in mid-April that SR officers were attempting, for political reasons, to dispose of MEXICO and its personnel, he organized a second radio station some sixty miles north of Marseille as a reserve base.

Despite these precautions, "Tommy's" three-way contact with rival organizations in a single limited area, however disguised, could not help in the long run but arouse suspicion and jealousy. Strained relations between SR and "Tommy" were a natural result of his extensive connections with the de Gaullist underground. The official liaison between SR and OSS in France, "Comite OSS", was discontinued although "Tommy" still obtained secret reports via one of his agents employed at the SR station.

Another blow to MEXICO's security came in early May when the newly-formed SI/France desk in Algiers decided to send a mixed mission to French, British and U. S. stations alike. "Tommy", who was to signal the submarine in and return with it to Algiers, made arrangements for the landing party and for the security of his own men. He gave instructions on the handling of the French, the British and the new OSS agents (the first to be sent to France by the SI desk at Algiers), and on bringing the new arrivals to Marseille with the least possible contact between them.

On his first return trip from France to Algiers, "Tommy" brought bulky information, such as maps and documents, which could not be communicated by radio. Of chief interest to G-2 and the Air Force in North Africa was the full plan of AA defense in France, including the secret signal code which had been obtained from a German major in exchange for gold.

During the initial three-month period under "Tommy", MEXICO sent almost 500 mes-

sages to Algiers. While Allied forces were then active in Tunisia, they needed, for future operations, the intelligence which came to them on defense preparations, political opinion and Axis movements generally in France. MEXICO's detailed coverage of enemy shipping activity from Marseille to Toulon was especially appreciated by G-2, and resulted in the Allied torpedoing and sinking of at least five enemy ships attempting to leave for Tunisia.

Back in Algiers, "Tommy" worked with the new executive officer of OSS/Algiers on plans for sending badly-needed supplies into France. At the same time, it was decided that sample U. S. weapons might be distributed to resistance groups, already organized, for later use. The method to be employed for getting the various supplies to the Maquis who could use them was the parachute drop.

"Tommy", who again would lead the expedition, took a parachute course at British SOE headquarters and became thoroughly grounded in the use of secret weapons, grenades, mortars, Sten guns, and the like. Between 12 May and 19 June, OSS/Algiers attempted without success to obtain from the American Air Force at Constantine (Algeria) a plane for OSS use. Eventually it turned to the British. Coincidentally, the SOE station in France had just been captured by the enemy. In agreeing to provide transporta-

---

April 5, 1943

FROM MEXICO
NO. 132
UN CERTAIN NOMBRE D'AVIONS BOCHES
ETAIENT TEMPORAIREMENT A ISTRES LE
TRENTE MARS X IL Y AVAIT DES MESSER-
SCHMIDTS DU DERNIER MODELE CENT DIX
X IL Y DEUX PIECES ARTILLERIE DE MARINE
DE CALIBRE 305 X X A PEYROLLES IL Y A
DEUX PIECES BOCHES DE 280 SUR WAGONS
ILS SONT SUPPORTES SUR LES WAGONS PAR
SEPT TRETEAUX X X TOUS LES DEUX JOURS
ON DEPLACE UNE DE CES PIECES
Received April 5, 1943
(Message from Station MEXICO, giving miscella-
neous battle order intelligence.)

tion for the OSS parachute mission, SOE asked "Tommy" to carry over radio sets and money to rebuild its station. On the same flight, "Tommy" was to drop an OSS agent who was to go, with underground assistance, to Switzerland and northern Italy. And he himself was instructed to set up additional intelligence stations for OSS in southern France, arrange secret landing places for future parachute drops and plane and submarine landings, extend his French underground contacts, and supply them with arms and other necessary equipment.

On 19 June 1943 at 2200 hours, "Tommy's" party left Algiers in a British Halifax, and parachuted to a reception group of Maquis agents near Mont Ventoux in the Vercors region at 0120 hours. So secure were the preparations at the landing point that "Tommy" was able to stay on for twelve days and start a new station—BOSTON—for sending intelligence to Algiers. "Tommy" then reinstalled the British SOE station, and supervised its operation and two supply drops over a period of two months.

From July to October 1943, "Tommy" worked at building up his OSS intelligence network under the nose of an increasingly active Gestapo, and without any additional supplies being furnished. The latter fact was attributable partly to bad weather, which made parachute drops difficult, and partly to OSS dependence for transportation on the British. OSS promises to "Tommy's" agents of money, weapons, food and personnel were broken on more than one occasion, and had the unhappy effect of losing much Maquis support.

In the midst of these difficulties, OSS station MEXICO was captured. "Tommy", much disturbed by what he considered the unsympathetic attitude of new OSS administrators toward the work he had done, blamed the incident on SI insecurity. His accusations may not have been entirely unwarranted; the SI/France Desk (being organized in Algiers) was admittedly laboring under a handicap of limited and inexperi-

enced personnel in its first efforts at intelligence chain-building in France.* Whether it was the attempt of the new and insecure SI agent to contact MEXICO that put the Gestapo on the trail is not certain. However, it was not long after this agent's arrival at the OSS station in Toulon (in disobedience of order from Algiers), that the Gestapo moved in, and that this same agent was killed.

Fortunately, by the time of the loss of MEXICO, "Tommy" had secured experienced operators, agents, and radio sets for two new stations: TEXAS at Carcassonne, and YORK at Toulon. Soon after these were established, when lack of money and food made further operations next to impossible, "Tommy" set out for Algiers via Spain. A projected schooner pick-up was deemed inadvisable, and he crossed the Pyrenees alone on foot to reach the U. S. Consulate at Barcelona. Here he found a message instructing him to return at once to his OSS stations with new codes and signal plans and one million francs. All three bases had become badly disorganized from lack of supplies and support, and were in danger of being seized by the Gestapo. YORK in Toulon was abandoned or caught, after the operator had cabled futilely for enough money and food to keep himself alive.

Taking money, crystals, and new codes, "Tommy" went first to Carcassonne where he moved TEXAS' position, changing its name to DARTMOUTH, and then to BOSTON in the Vercors, whose position had become endangered as a direct result of the Gestapo's capture of the YORK operator. BOSTON was moved just in time to escape capture. Several of OSS' most faithful agents were arrested during this period and not heard from again.

Early in September, "Tommy" received orders to return to Algiers via Spain. This he did, after leaving one of his best Spanish-speaking agents at Barcelona for future

* See "SI/Algiers Chains", below.

liaison between OSS/Barcelona and France. Word was received a month later, via members of de Gaulle's intelligence organization, that the Vercors station was in desperate straits, because promised parachute drops had not materialized. The capture of the station followed shortly.

A new operator working the DARTMOUTH radio in Carcassonne was detected in Algiers on 5 November 1943. Despite "Tommy's" assurances that the new man was one trained under his own orders, the DARTMOUTH operator was later discovered to have been captured and replaced, for one week, by a German attempting to get information of Allied invasion plans. The circuit was continued, after the original operator had been "persuaded", so cleverly by the enemy, that suspicions of the Algiers operators were not again fully aroused. DARTMOUTH worked for nearly a year in France under enemy control and, following D-Day in South France, for six more months in Germany. During the period, the doubled station successfully arranged to receive four teams, which were of course captured on arrival.* The date and place of ANVIL was never given to DARTMOUTH.

This type of deception was frequently employed by Axis and Allied counter-espionage units,** but DARTMOUTH was the only OSS station worked back by the enemy for such a long period of time without detection. Two factors contributed to its success: (1) A double violation of communications security on the part of OSS—having an operator who was recruited in the field without being briefed at home base, and who was in turn allowed to recruit substitute operators without the knowledge of OSS/Algiers;*** (2) the German ruse of making comparatively slight use of the circuit for apprehending OSS agents of whom they were undoubtedly

aware, and pretending to cooperate with OSS/Algiers to the extent of allowing two key French underground officers to pass through their station carrying important papers. As for their messages, a subsequent X-2 analysis stated:

The intelligence reports sent in from the DARTMOUTH station were regarded by SI/Algiers as being fairly accurate and of good quality on the whole. There was nothing in them which, at the time, would have led SI to believe that (the operator) was under control.*

The number of "Tommy's" losses brought accusations and suspicions at the Algiers base. French SR's charges of "Tommy's" complicity with the Axis did not help his position and lent weight to suspicions that he himself was a double-agent. "Tommy" proceeded to London in February 1944, at his own request, to clear himself of charges which he regarded as unjust. Here, he was, to a large extent, exonerated by American and British personnel who had first-hand knowledge of "Tommy's" work in the field. Suspicions of "Tommy" have however never been cleared, although X-2 later reported capture of a German Intelligence Service document which

. . . tends to confirm that, apart from the doubling of the W/T operator at DARTMOUTH, the chain was not blown through penetration, but rather through a combination of successful D/F-ing and the arrests of agents which produced information leading to the location of others.**

"Tommy's" personal insecurity may have contributed to the high rate of losses in personnel. Where as a double-agent normally reserves his knowledge of agents and agent networks for cautious sale, "Tommy" had an excitable garrulous temperament and his talk was loud and free.

* See "SI/Algiers" and "Direct Penetration from Italy" of Germany, below.
** See "X-2/France", below.
*** It should be noted that there was in this case no pre-arranged system of signals for reporting capture.

* X-2 study: "Penetration of OSS by Foreign Intelligence Services", p. 8, in CIG Files.
** X-2 file: "Penetration of OSS by Foreign Intelligence Services", pp. 49-50. Communications officers have since determined that D/F-ing was never as effective as feared. See "First 'Joan-Eleanor' Operation", below.

Notwithstanding the ambiguity of the evidence: (1) His were the first OSS stations to be established in enemy-occupied territory, and (2) reports reaching Algiers from the networks were prolific and in the main accurate, evoking high praise from G-2, AFHQ.

2. SO/London

The principal task of SO/London, upon its establishment in early 1943, was to join its British counterpart, SOE, in building a strong and effective resistance force in France.

The first elements of such resistance were the Maquis—young men who had gone to the hills and woods to avoid being mobilized by the Vichy Government or deported by the Germans for forced labor. They and others had formed separate groups such as the Forces Francaise de l'Interieur (de Gaullist), the Francs Tireurs et Partisans (controlled by Communists), Organization de la Resistance dans l'Armee (followers of Giraud) and the Armee Secrete. Of these the strongest was de Gaulle's FFI, directed from London by the Bureau de Renseignement et d'Action (BCRA). However, to achieve the unified strength desired by Allied military leaders, the various underground groups required training, arms, supplies, money and, above all, organization and direction. First Allied assistance to this end came from British SOE, established for the purpose in 1939.

At a series of meetings held in London from March to September 1943, representatives of SO, SOE and the Free French drew up plans for the work to be done by resistance groups in France. It was agreed that the main effort before D-Day should be directed toward sabotage of factories, power plants and fuel storage dumps, so as to decrease and delay the flow of war materials to the Germans.

Since France had been an Allied country until it was overrun by the enemy, and since the overwhelming majority of its population was known to be pro-Allied, American and British planners desired to effect this reduction with the least possible loss of French lives and property. SO and SOE agents in France would direct the sabotage of targets designated by SHAEF and disable industrial installations and communications, without the killing or wounding of French civilians or destruction of their homes which almost inevitably resulted from bombing attacks by Allied air forces. The management and workers in French factories would be induced to cooperate with the saboteurs, either by direct appeals to their patriotism, or by blackmail in the form of threats of wholesale destruction by aerial bombing.

The SO and SOE officers in London determined that the resistance movement would be most effective if it limited its operations to those traditionally associated with guerrilla warfare. They believed that small underground groups could successfully carry out sabotage, hit-and-run raids, and attacks from ambush, while any attempts on their part to take and hold ground would be self-defeating. They also were concerned lest action by resistance groups, undertaken at random, hinder the operations of the American and British combat forces on and after D-Day. In order to meet the necessity of control and coordination of the resistance by the Allies, SO and SOE agents were instructed to organize, direct and restrain the resistance elements in France. Their position as representatives of the Allied High Command, their W/T communication with SHAEF through SFHQ, and their ability to obtain and distribute arms, ammunition and other supplies gave these agents considerable authority.

In February 1943 the SO/French Desk began its work. Plans were made to contribute individual operatives, recruited by SO in the United States, to SOE teams already in France or preparing to go there, and to form similar teams composed entirely of SO personnel.

Like OSS/Algiers, SO/London initially suffered high casualties. On 13 June 1943 with SOE approval, "Alfred", the first SO agent to go to the field, was parachuted into France to organize a circuit known as SACRISTAN in the LeMans-Nantes-Laval area. Contrary to practice subsequently adopted, "Alfred" was sent to a region where he was well known and could make use of his family and friends.* "Narcisse", his W/T operator, was sent to join him on 20 August.

"Alfred" was successful in organizing a resistance network to carry out day-to-day sabotage operations and to gather intelligence. But on 21 December his courier was arrested and talked, causing forty-five arrests and the blowing of the whole circuit.

On the 23rd December seven of the Gestapo came to the house where Narcisse was staying, during dinner, and arrested him and his host. They handcuffed him and while they were doing this he threatened one of them with his revolver (according to Captain ———, he kicked him in the groin with both feet), upon which the man shot him in the chest. He pretended to be dead and three of them immediately bundled him off in a car leaving the other four to deal with his late host. Two sat in front discussing the affair, the third was with the "body" in the back. They had searched his trouser pockets but after he dropped "dead" they had not searched his jacket, in the pocket of which he still had his revolver. While in the car he managed to ease this out of his pocket and shoot in rapid succession the man beside him and the two in front. The car went into a ditch, whereupon Narcisse abandoned the car and made his way to the house of some friends nearby, intending to warn Alfred as soon as he was sufficiently recovered.

On the following day, early in the morning, Alfred was in the garden of his house when several men whom he took to have been Gestapo appeared on the garden wall, brandishing revolvers. Within a few minutes the house and garden were surrounded. On the fourth side there was a fairly high wall which the Gestapo evidently thought was too high for escape, but Alfred managed to scramble over this unobserved and made his way to the same friends where Narcisse had taken refuge with the object of warning Narcisse. They thus found themselves together and able to compare notes. Realizing that the game was up, they decided to leave.

At Laval they contacted a Free French group through whom they sent their messages to London.**

---

* This policy was proven too insecure by "Alfred's" experience and was discontinued.
** SO War Diary, Vol. 3, Bk. II, pp. 17-18, History Files.

These two SO agents escaped via Spain and arrived in London on 25 February 1944. A few months later, on 6 May, they both returned to France, to a section of the country where they were not known and had no contacts, on a more successful mission.*

SO began in October 1943 to contribute to the work of the various SOE sections. An American SO officer with the DF Section undertook a mission to exfiltrate a group of twelve pilots and to test the escape route he would use. He crossed the Channel in a torpedo boat, transferred to a smaller boat off the coast of Brittany, and made successful night landing. Proceeding to Paris, he established contact with an SOE agent who told him that the RAF pilots had been arrested by the Germans. Instead he was asked to take out an American airman and an SOE agent who was in danger. The SO officer conducted these two men to a safe house near the coast to await transportation to England. Following receipt of a radio message specifying the time and place of departure, the group went to the beach. Because their S-phone did not work, they were unable to communicate with the boat offshore, and the attempt failed. After a second rendezvous was arranged, the group used a lamp to signal the boat and was picked up successfully.

An example of early 1944 operations by the F-Section was the MARKSMAN circuit in the Departments of Haute-Savoie, Ain and Jura which helped to organize and arm more than 1,000 Maquis troops in the mountains, and directed their activities. "Gael", the SFHQ officer who had been sent to that circuit in October 1943, described the life of the Maquis:

Some days we ate in the Tour d'Argent, on others our meals consisted of a contemplation of the good meals we had had, and imagination flavored the saliva called forth by those recollections. Extremely rarely we slept in a bed. More often on a floor, and sometimes in a nice warm cowshed, or when weather permitted, under the

pines, wrapped in a parachute for lack of blankets. Once or twice we lived in a chateau, but we found it had a bad effect on our morale. More often we didn't sleep, especially during moon periods. We were perpetually on the alert, and from that point of view the life was a strain, as there was not, as for the normal soldier, a possibility of repose behind the lines. We were always in the front lines, and more, for we did not know from which side an attack might come. . . . Barely a week went by in which the Maquis was not attacked.

Saboteurs of the circuit disabled the Schmidt-Roos ball-bearing factory at Annecy and the power station at Ambrouay. They repeatedly cut railway lines, derailed trains, disabled locomotives, turntables and control cars, blew up bridges and sabotaged machine shops throughout the area. Their operations were so extensive that German reprisal began early in February and increased steadily. The guerrilla tactics of the Maquis made enemy losses many times greater than they themselves sustained. The enemy used planes, cannon and mortar, as well as small arms, in their counterattacks, burned villages and shot many civilians. The lack of sufficient ammunition seriously handicapped the Maquis, and they were often forced to yield ground. Yet the MARKSMAN circuit succeeded in completely disrupting railway communications in the assigned sector. As more and more German troops were employed to combat these attacks, enemy capabilities in other directions were correspondingly reduced.

Besides taking part in operations from London, SO provided a W/T link between London and Geneva for a newly-organized French resistance g r o u p, and supplied money to a number of others in the mountains along the Swiss border through agents employed by OSS/Switzerland.* Through such direct and indirect links, OSS/SO grew to equality with SOE in the organizing for D-Day of an effective armed French resistance of some 300,000 men.**

---

* See "Building French Resistance", below.

* See next section.
** See "Operation OVERLORD", below.

3. Bern Chains

Headquarters were established in Geneva under OSS/Bern * for the penetration of France, and to bring aid to the French resistance forces. A French lawyer acquaintance of the mission chief arrived in Geneva clandestinely, to establish contact on behalf of the French resistance. The mutual confidence which resulted from this old friendship was put to good advantage.

In March 1943, the lawyer gave OSS a detailed picture of the French underground. Shortly thereafter, the commander of the largest Maquis in France, that in Savoy, slipped across the border to give information on conditions in this region, and to request material and financial aid. In April, SFHQ/London authorized the financing by OSS/Bern of resistance forces in specified areas, according to allocation worked out between London and Algiers.

Despite innumerable difficulties and delays, the work was slowly organized and expanded. With the tacit consent of the local Swiss authorities, a secret French resistance mission was established in Geneva, and later three to four members were permanently located there. Through them the bulk of the work with the resistance in France was carried on. An efficient courier service operated over the border carrying intelligence from all parts of the country. Millions of French francs in currency were smuggled across, and supplies were sent to the resistance in the mountains of Savoy. During the latter half of 1943, Bern inaugurated the regular transmission of messages from the delegation in Geneva to London and Algiers.

Swiss assistance was particularly helpful in the maintenance of contacts across the frontier.

Without this assistance the casualties among

* See "Bern", below

those who constantly crossed the frontier illegally would have been much higher, since there was a concentration of Nazi agents in the Geneva area.

Experience proved that the easiest way to fool the Germans was to provide agents with a supply of silk stockings, soap and other materials rare in France. If they travelled through safely, these goods were the best currency they could have on the French side of the border. If captured, they passed themselves off as simple smugglers and received a nominal sentence, or more often evaded the issue by keeping their mouths shut and giving their captors the goods they were carrying.

Occasionally, "agents provocateurs" were found in Switzerland pretending to work with the resistance movement. By giving such agents fictitious missions in France, OSS could lure them into the hands of the resistance, where they would receive summary execution.

OSS/Bern intercepted the orders for the scuttling of the French fleet at Toulon in November 1942, and this information was promptly reported to the proper services. A wealth of data was supplied on German submarine bases, both on the Atlantic and Mediterranean coasts.

For battle order intelligence, considerable guidance was required. At first, the French chains were prolific with reports on political and economic conditions but, since it was common knowledge that German troops were all over France, failed to see the importance of reporting on their movements, insignia and similar items in this specialized field of intelligence. They learned in time, and battle order information forwarded by Bern which, during 1943, amounted to only about ten percent of its reports, by 1944 constituted some fifty percent of the total, and was rated "timely and of value" by MID. It included the designation and location of units, troop movements and transportation of material and food, by road and rail.

In addition to the channels operating through the organized French resistance, other lanes into France were developed. Two former friends of the mission chief, who had been officials of the League of Nations, had close liaison with political leaders in France and placed all their sources at his disposal, acting as intermediaries. In particular, these men developed contacts with members of the Radical Socialist Party, and, together with other items, developments within the scattered remnants of the Party were immediately reported to Switzerland. Through a trade union representative, OSS/Bern helped to finance the resistance movement in labor and Socialist circles in France and received current information concerning their activities.

Valuable reports were also received from an official in the Paris office of the SNCF (national railroad trust). Over a period of nearly a year prior to VE-Day, he sent information on railroad conditions, rail traffic and bomb and sabotage damage. Beginning in September 1943 and through the winter, he sent a series of special reports on troop movements in France. In this way, the direction and magnitude of the latter could be plotted with precision. OSS/Washington gave an "A" evaluation to this source, and considered his reports the best information on French railroads obtained from any field office. The courier who handled the railway information service was unfortunately apprehended on one of his trips back to France, deported to Germany and not subsequently heard from.

In October 1943, several resistance representatives came to Geneva, and, in a series of conferences, they presented detailed information on resistance potentialities and listed its essential requirements. In November, a complete plan was forwarded for resistance sabotage of railway communications throughout France and, ultimately, for paralyzing traffic on D-Day.

Before the Allied invasion of France in June 1944, OSS/Bern had means of ascertaining the day-by-day developments in the Vichy Government through a channel which went to the immediate entourage of Marshal Petain. Through other sources it received copies of the important messages sent by the German diplomatic representatives in both Vichy and Paris. It had eight separate networks, with hundreds of agents, working into France, and was able to identify and locate all of the important German military units there.

C. AGENT PROCESSING

Agent processing by SFHQ/London, compared to that of SI/Algiers, illustrated the different approaches of SO and SI work. While the provision of documents, clothing and cover stories was a complicated but relatively standardized job, that of recruiting, training and handling agents left room for wide variation in method.

SO/ETO had the paramilitary task of directing resistance forces in large-scale support of the Allied invasion. A series of screening, training, processing and holding areas were established, w h i c h handled agents on a relatively mass-production military basis. Recruits were mostly officers and enlisted men of the American or British Armies, and were treated according to rank or rating. Their job in the field was to lead men already committed to resistance. High in Allied priority was the job of maintaining maximum discipline among resistance forces, in order not only to offer the most coordinated support to the invasion, but also to avoid post-liberation political difficulties.

SI/Algiers, on the other hand, dispatched, not resistance leaders in U. S. uniform, but native French intelligence organizers. A reverse policy was pursued of selecting a few highly qualified individuals with excellent contacts in the target area, who would be expected to build up networks of hundreds of agents covering large intelligence fields. The SI/France establishment was maintained apart from OSS/Algiers and the few agents, once chosen, were treated as personal friends by the members of the SI desk, so that they entered the field assured of strong backing, based on a close personal relationship. Their desire to perform creditably, based originally on patriotic, psychological or other motives, was strengthened by the personal one. The bravery required to infiltrate enemy territory was often accompanied by unusual psychological characteristics. The SI/Algiers approach to these men as individuals proved to be most successful.*

SO/London and SI/Algiers were the two most notable examples of SO and SI methods of agent processing, generally standard for OSS in Europe.**

1. SFHQ/London

SO personnel dispatched from London were recruited in the United States and the United Kingdom from the ranks of the U. S. Army and Navy. Perfect French accents were not required, since the men would mostly be working with resistance groups. American officers in American uniforms were expected to carry more prestige with the Maquis and to be able to assume command more easily than would French-speaking civilians.

Training

During 1943, an arrangement was made with SOE for the reception of American recruits in England. Students who had already received some instruction in the OSS schools in the United States were also sent to SOE schools for additional practice. New arrivals were given a tentative duty assignment with some branch or section, then went to Franklin House, the SO reception center at Ruislip, outside London. Here they re-

---

* See "ANVIL", below.
** One notable exception was SI/London, which appears to have followed largely the policies of its larger SO counterpart in London. Agents were handled on a mass scale and on a relatively impersonal and military basis. The results did not measure up to those of SI/MedTO. See "SI/North France" and "Direct Penetration from London" of Germany, below.

ceived a limited amount of introductory training in the use and care of various small arms, map reading, compass use, field craft and close combat. An obstacle course provided conditioning for parachute work. Facilities for recreation included football and baseball fields, volley-ball courts, a swimming pool and movies. While students were at Franklin Hall, their security was checked by SOE.

After security clearance had been obtained, recruits were sent to the SOE Student Assessment Board, where they were given a four-day course designed to test their motivation, intelligence, aptitudes, emotional stability, initiative, discipline, leadership, self-confidence and physical coordination and stamina. The findings and recommendations of the Board were reported to the SO Training Officer, who passed them on to the branch or section concerned. For example, of 61 prospective *Jedburgh* officers who took the course, only 43 were approved for work as agents in France. Those rejected were transferred to other branches, given routine non-operational duties within the organization, or released from OSS. A majority of the failures were due to lack of sound motivation, which was regarded by the Board as the first and most indispensable qualification of a successful agent.

After study of the Assessment Board's report, arrangements were made for further training of satisfactory recruits. SO agents usually went first to one of the paramilitary schools for a five-week course, which included instruction in weapons, unarmed combat, demolitions, guerrilla warfare, basic W/T operation, intelligence, use of small boats, and organizing and equipping resistance groups.

Upon completing this course, students went to parachute school for training, which lasted from four to six days, depending on the weather. In this short time they took special exercises on the ground, made four practice jumps, three by day and one at night, and learned the correct and safe

method of parachuting. The students were then ready to attend one of the finishing schools, where the course consisted of three weeks' instruction in all phases of agent activities, followed by a 96-hour field problem. The latter was designed to give each student as close an approximation as possible of clandestine life in enemy-occupied territory, and to provide an opportunity for instructors and section representatives to judge the student's grasp of what he had been taught and his ability to use it.

Most students attended one or more of the specialized schools operated by SOE. Radio operators went to the Wireless Training School at Thames Park. Here they were first tested to determine their speed and accuracy in receiving and dispatching messages in Morse code. According to the results of this test, students were placed in one of four classes and taught to send and receive correctly. On reaching 20 words a minute, students went to a laboratory where they were taught the construction of simple receivers and transmitters, the location and correction of faults in a set, and the use of codes. Once proficient in this work, students began to practice sending to and receiving from a fixed or mobile set at a distance from the school, then were taken to an "out-set" to practice sending to and receiving from base, and were finally sent to some large city in England where they set up and operated a clandestine radio.

Instructors kept all the sheets of paper used by students in their cipher work, because it was found that W/T operators had a tendency to repeat the same mistakes, especially in the field working under stress. Badly garbled cables could often be decoded by the instructors who were familiar with each agent's typical mistakes.

Instructors were also accustomed to each man's way of sending Morse code and were familiar with his particular "fist". At one time, for example, messages from the field were received purporting to come from an SO agent, "Liontamer", who had not been heard from for some time. Headquarters first noticed that the words and style of these messages did not sound like his own. His W/T instructors were called in, and they recognized at once that the person sending these messages was not "Liontamer". He had been captured, and the Germans had evidently obtained his code and were sending messages in his place. An additional security measure was adopted, in recording, before his departure, a W/T message from each agent.

At other specialized SOE schools students received instruction on Foreign Weapons; Mines and Booby Traps; Industrial Sabotage; Propaganda; Reception Committees; Street Fighting; and the use of Lysander and C-47 planes to land or pick up men and material in enemy-occupied areas.

After a student had completed the required combination of courses, he went to an Operational Holding Area where he remained until he left for enemy territory. While waiting, he was given "refresher" instruction in all the subjects he had studied with a view to correcting any faults or misconceptions previously acquired. He took part in field problems designed to present conditions and difficulties similar to those he would face on his operational assignment.

After a student completed his training, he became operationally available to his parent section, which then began to prepare him for infiltration.

Cover and Documents

A cover story, as watertight as possible, and adapted to his background and personality, was carefully built up and drilled into each agent. False papers were prepared for use in the event he was picked up by the French Milice or by the Gestapo, and French clothing and money were obtained for him.

Several of the agents that SOE had previously infiltrated into France had been captured because of defective documents and cover stories. Agents had always been given identity papers from the same few towns in France, and SOE eventually had to send

agents into France to gather more identity papers which could be duplicated. In February 1943, a new French Documents Section was therefore organized, under an SO officer, which tried to collect all the samples of French papers it could and to build up files on schools, prison camps, bombings, etc., so that satisfactory cover stories could be written. Specific details on bombings were important since agent papers would indicate residence in a town whose files had been destroyed by air attack.

At one time the Germans devised a new French identity card for police inspectors, which briefly baffled SFHQ. Each card had a nine digit number and the French police could tell at once by looking at that number if the identity card was authentic. It did not take long, however, to discover its significance. Each prefectural city in France had a number which was represented by the first three digits. Five other digits gave the date, month and year of the bearer's birth, and the last one, whether it was even or odd, indicated whether the person was male or female. An SOE agent obtained a complete list of all the cities in France and their corresponding numbers.

Papers had to be aged. This was sometimes done by rubbing them in ashes or in a powder made of crushed rock and by rounding the corners with sandpaper. Alternately, training officers carried documents in their hip and shirt pockets till they were suitably sweated.

The reports of the Royal Patriotic School (where all foreigners entering the U. K. in any capacity other than diplomatic or military had to be screened) were used for piecing together cover stories out of the lives of other individuals. From the date of the organization of the new French Documents Section, no SO agent was reported caught in France on account of faulty papers or cover story. These were filled out and memorized in the greatest detail. One agent, for instance, was arrested because the Germans did not believe that he was a repatriated prisoner from a German concentration camp. When questioned by the Gestapo, he gave a complete description of the camp where he was supposed to have been, as well as the name and description of the commander of the camp and of the doctor. A German soldier who had been a guard at the camp was called in to verify his story, and was forced to admit that every detail was correct. The Gestapo released the agent after apologizing for suspecting him.

The best cover that could be given to an agent was one corresponding to his real profession. One SO agent, "Aramis", a civilian over sixty years old and an artist by profession, spent most of the time he was in France painting, and was never suspected of other activities, partly on account of his age. "Aramis" made numerous paintings in Paris on the Left Bank of the Seine and was thus able to make a plan of all strong-points fortified by the enemy. Unfortunately, the paintings were rarely completed, since sabotage groups used him to watch the bridges while they were preparing the charges. This system involved the one weakness in "Aramis'" cover. He never succeeded in selling any of his paintings and, if he had been questioned, would have found it difficult to explain his source of funds.

An occasional error was the repetition of cover stories once a good one had been found. "Aramis" reported being picked up in a raid in Paris and discovering that the man who was questioned before him told the same story he himself planned to use when his turn came.

For French clothing and equipment, SOE early developed its own especial manufacture, and, even after North Africa became a possible source of such items, SOE and SO continued the processes. As a result, agents reported that they could easily recognize another SO or SOE agent in France because they all wore the same type of clothes and carried similar suitcases. Apparently the Germans never noticed this, but it was dis-

covered later that in Paris the Gestapo had learned to identify SO/SOE wrist watches.

A final SO refinement was to have all dentistry originally obtained in the United States done over in French style.

Briefing

Each agent was briefed on the area where he would operate, on the contacts he should make there, and on the targets he was directed to attack.

SOE policy was to build up an agent's confidence by not passing on discouraging information. He was assured, for instance, that his papers were in perfect order, even when the French Document Section itself had doubts as to whether they would pass and whether the stamps on them were correct.

Many agents, on returning from the field, complained about this deception. One agent, "Ludovic", resented having been sent to the field as an organizer without being told that his predecessor had been arrested and the circuit blown. The possibility remains, nevertheless, that without so much self-assurance, he might not have accomplished his mission successfully.

Infiltration into France

Arrangements were next made to infiltrate the agent, usually by air. Other means of infiltration, infrequently used, were night landings from small boats, and crossings of the French border inland from Spain or Switzerland, either by night along remote mountain paths or by boldly presenting false papers at frontier posts. In a few areas, resistance groups were able to clear secret landing fields. Lysanders and C-47's made night landings on these fields to deliver agents and to pick up others. The most common procedure, however, was to drop the agent by parachute at night to a reception committee, at a pinpoint and time arranged by means of radio messages between SFHQ in London and men already in the field.*

---

* When necessary, agents were dropped "blind" with no reception committees to meet them.

The parent section made arrangements for a flight to carry the agent, usually accompanied by his W/T operator, their personal equipment, and supplies for the resistance groups or SFHQ personnel in the area. Priority among proposed missions was determined by American and British officers of the Western European Directorate of SFHQ, with the object both of meeting the long-range requirements of the over-all program, and of filling the most urgent current needs reported from the field. In accordance with the allotted priority, the parent section submitted a request for air lift to the Air Operations Section of SFHQ, which was responsible for liaison with the British Air Ministry and the squadron (British or American) which would mount the operation. The final decision as to the feasibility and timing of a proposed air operation was made by the RAF, which had accurate information on terrain, weather conditions and presence or absence of anti-aircraft defenses at the target area. When a flight was approved the Air Operations Section notified the country section concerned, which then brought the men, equipment and supplies to the airfield, and sent out a pre-arranged radio signal to alert the reception committee.

A signal was also designated for the reception committee to use when it heard the airplane in the area. In daylight smoke-fires were most clearly visible. At night a series of lights would be placed in a pattern so as to form a letter which the pilot could observe from the sky. At one point, London gave instructions that bonfires should be used instead of lights, which were thought to be too small. This method proved unsatisfactory from a security standpoint because: (a) The fires could be seen for some distance laterally; (b) they were hard to put out; and (c) the traces they left on the ground were difficult to conceal. Flashlights were used in the great majority of cases.

In addition, a lamp sometimes served to flash an identifying letter in Morse code.

When available, S-phones were used to enable a member of the reception committee to talk to the dispatcher in the plane. A similar reception technique was used to guide the planes to the field and to signal all clear.

When the target area was reached, the pilot located the pinpoint by means of the ground pattern formed by the flashlights. In early operations it was customary to wait for a blinker signal indicating all clear. The pilot usually made a trial run to test the wind. Meanwhile the dispatcher alerted the men who were to be dropped. If the ground signals were favorable and the wind not dangerously strong, the pilot made a second run over the pinpoint and the dispatcher gave the word to jump.* The pilot then circled the field again and dropped the containers and packages on a subsequent run.

2. SI/Algiers

Recruiting

Of those who applied or were recruited by SI as agents or radio operators, only those with special qualifications could be used. Unlike OSS/London, SI/Algiers chose to run the risk of dispatching agents to localities they knew well, where they could depend on the most contacts. As a security measure, however, agents generally must have lived in France since the German occupation. Because of the dearth of such persons in North Africa in 1943, this factor was waived if the agent had been in a locality over a long period of time and knew many people on whom he could count for help.

Few men possessing these qualifications for undercover work in France were available to OSS in Algiers, and the recruiting and handling of agents by SI was never on anything but the smallest scale. In view of the fact that new missions would in the future

---

* Several agents reported that after they left the plane, it took them some time to get their eyes accustomed to the darkness and to recognize landmarks. One agent suggested that they be given dark glasses to wear inside the plane, to avoid this difficulty.

be subject to long-range planning—sometimes as long as four or five months—it was fortunate that this was the case. The late entry of SI/France into the field, in comparison with the British and French intelligence services, meant that the most suitable agents had been preempted. In addition, the Eisenhower-Giraud agreements * gave the French Army primary access to the best men. This was particularly true in the case of radio operators who were rapidly being siphoned off by the new French Army being formed in North Africa.

The prestige acquired by OSS, as a result of its work with Frenchmen before the North African landings, opened channels to an otherwise closed market. Some of SI's best technicians and most successful agents were drawn from this source. Men who had worked for the United States in Operation *TORCH* and had become accustomed to the irregular and exciting aspects of clandestine existence wished to continue the same work for OSS in France. It was from this small handful of experienced men that SI picked its first French recruits and proceeded to clear them officially for OSS intelligence operations.

Training

The first physical training for the new recruits was a ten-day course in parachute jumping and small arms practice. This was easily arranged by virtue of the fact that OSS officers were responsible for setting up the parachute school at the British training area, and had, since operation *Brandon*,** been training recruits for British, American and French services alike.

OSS established its own finishing school in the Atlas Mountains of Algiers. It was planned that agents who had completed their parachute course should go there for intensive 15-day instruction in intelligence operations. Under a staff consisting of four officers and five enlisted men, small groups

---

* See "SI/Algiers Chains", below.
** See "Tunisia", above.

of French recruits in GI uniforms became theoretically acquainted with the rules of clandestine living and intelligence procurement.

More important than the subjects taught during this period were the relations established between the agents and the men responsible for directing their intelligence operations. Working, as they did, with only a few recruits at a time, the SI organizers were able to study at close range the inherent weakness or strength of each recruit, and reject or retain accordingly. During this time, too, the men, who were to be working far from base under lonely and perilous conditions, developed with their leaders a sense of personal dependence and mutual confidence indispensable to their morale and to the success of their mission.

As a test of the degree to which clandestine technique and radio signals had been learned, a field trip was added to the final preparations of each agent-operator team. On these trips, the two men learned to work in close harmony with each other and practiced transmitting intelligence as though actually in enemy territory. They secretly established themselves in Morocco or Tunisia, and reported Allied troop movements or harbor traffic by code to the Algiers base. SI/France would usually tip off American military police and CIC to the suspected presence of "enemy" agents in this area, thus providing a practical test of their ability to work safely under cover.

Cover and Documents

At the same time that agent and operator were learning their work, a cover story was established for each, and as many security problems as possible anticipated and arranged for. Given fake identities, the agents were persuaded to use as many real details in their personal backgrounds as possible to give coherence and validity to their fabrications. One, who was actually tubercular, posed as a patient undergoing rest treatment. Carrying an X-ray and accompanying letter signed by a doctor, he could ascribe his civilian status and frequent travelling between contacts to his condition and the necessity of consulting physicians. His operator-assistant selected the profession of a salesman of agricultural machinery—an occupation that had been granted exemption from the draft by virtue of its high priority.

Clothing, made in France after the German occupation, was obtained from refugees and other sources in North Africa, by exchanging GI uniforms or American civilian clothing. British clothing was too well made and thus avoided for agent use inside France. Blank documents—identity papers, travel permits, ration coupons, etc.—to supplement the men's efforts to pass as French civilians, were unsuccessfully requested from Washington, and OSS/Algiers was never able to obtain complete facilities for this important phase of intelligence work. Even after the arrival of a few R&D personnel in May 1944, OSS continued to rely on the more elaborate services of the British

French SR put at the disposal of SI/Algiers up-to-date models of important papers and the proper methods of using them. From them too, OSS learned of the Vichy system of registry, by which all papers could be checked instantly with the police. False papers could serve only as temporary expedients for getting into the country and should be replaced, as soon as cover was established, with ones legally issued by local authorities. An agent located in one city attempted usually to acquire documents of another city to avoid detection. Thus, a man working around Marseille might use Lyon identification papers, relying on bureaucratic inefficiency or severed communications to prevent a long-distance check by Vichy or German officials.

From SOE's instructive insistence on last-minute precautions, SI/France adopted the technique of the mock police interrogation. A steady stream of inquiries was directed at the agents in an effort to break down their cover stories. In this way, the latter could review in their minds the most salient facts of their assumed identities, and were forced to defend them down to the minutest details.

Dispatching

Most SI missions were planned as "blind" drops to regions which both team members knew well. The pinpoint was usually a place close to the first contact the agent wished to locate. Reception committees were used instead of "blind" drops when agents were unfamiliar with the territory or when they knew of no contact in the immediate vicinity. These consisted of friendly persons, usually agents from a chain already established in the area, who were previously informed of the mission and who made arrangements of signalling in the landing and assisted in making first contacts for the agents after their arrival. Since this system involved criss-crossing chains and threatened security, "blind" drops were used whenever possible. Subsequent supplies, of necessity, were parachuted to ground reception groups prepared by the agents receiving the new equipment.

SI/France placed principal reliance for agent infiltration on air drops: (1) A single plane flying over France from the Mediterranean coast was rarely contested by the enemy who usually did not consider it sufficient excuse to reveal flak positions; (2) security of agents was relatively assured by landing on isolated inland plateaus sparsely occupied by the enemy; * (3) alternate landing spots in the general vicinity of the target could be used at the last minute in the event that one was found for any reason to be insecure.

Sea operations were thought to entail more risk: (1) Enemy coastal patrols main-

* In drops made in the Massif Central region of central and southern France, no Germans were ever encountered by SI agents.

tained a close watch; (2) "zones interdites" established in coastal regions made for stricter controls than in the interior. However, three teams were landed and one recuperated by PT boat from Corsica,* when prolonged bad weather and inability to secure planes threatened indefinite delay. Although not considered as safe as air drops, this type of clandestine maritime mission served as an alternate infiltration method during dark-moon periods or under other conditions unfavorable for flight.

In the interests of visibility, parachute missions were made during a full moon period.** To make the pilot's job easier, salient physical characteristics recognizable from the air were considered in the selection of pinpoints: a forest clearing, river, dirt road, lake, or bend in a rail line.

SI operations officers acted as "joe-handlers", and administrators of details of supply and transport for specific missions. "Joe-handlers" attended to the many personnel problems—material and psychological—involved in preparing agent recruits. They accompanied agents through their training routine, their "holding" period, and

---
* See "Corsica Operations", above.
** Some dark moon drops were successfully made by OSS, at a later date, in both France and Germany.

aided their departure, even to the point of making last-minute financial, legal, family and other personal arrangements. They also dealt with G-3, Special Operations, AFHQ, to obtain necessary air priorities, secured American equipment—medical supplies, radio sets and weapons—and personally supervised the packing of material to be parachuted before every mission. Thus each agent had one man at home base on whom he could depend for support and care, both before and after his departure to the field.

Last-minute checks on equipment, clothing, documents, etc., often revealed minor errors that, if discovered by the enemy, could blow the operation. This led SI/Algiers to draw up a check-list to be used with all intelligence agents just before dispatch into the field. Under headings of Pinpoint, Cover, Identity Card, etc., items were listed and checked to prevent neglect of any detail. Among the things that had to be remembered before departure were such particulars as: all necessary legal arrangements, local newspapers, thread (for measuring distance between buried equipment and a recognizable landmark), danger signals, money, poison (in case of capture) and alternate means of communication (letter drops, rendezvous points, etc.).

D. OPERATION OVERLORD

1. Planning for D-Day

During 1943 SO/London became a full partner in a joint American-British enterprise. Integration with SOE was formally approved in January 1944, and in May the partnership was designated Special Force Headquarters (SFHQ). Directly under SHAEF command, SFHQ was given responsibility for coordinating all underground resistance in France in direct support of the forthcoming Allied invasion.

Integration of SO and SOE, plus the steadily growing SO contribution as more men and more supplies arrived in England, gave added weight to American views on policy. The SO proposal for large-scale paramilitary resistance, supported by delivery of a maximum amount of arms and other supplies, and culminating in an all-out attack on the Germans on D-Day, was the plan eventually adopted. On and after D-Day, plans called for disruption of enemy communications, attacks on troop movements and supply convoys, and raids on enemy headquarters in order to hinder and lessen German resistance to the Allied advance. During the German withdrawal from France, the Maquis were to prevent enemy demolition of installations needed by the Allies.

Specially trained SO and SOE agents would help Frenchmen to accomplish these objectives. Their secret circuits, developed in France for more than a year prior to D-Day, would serve as nuclei for an eventual uprising of resistance at the time of the invasion. To supplement these, almost one hundred three-man inter-Allied *Jedburgh* teams, equipped with W/T, would be dropped in, to help in the coordination of resistance activities with the needs of the invading armies, to train men at new resistance centers following the landings and to direct the delivery of additional supplies by air. Intelligence would be transmitted by them, as well as by SI teams dispatched to towns and cities not covered by resistance groups. In addition to these, French-speaking Operational Groups, together with similar British airborne (SAS) troops, trained and armed for guerrilla warfare, were held in readiness to carry out special demolitions or counter-scorch activities and to act as operational nuclei in areas where open warfare between resistance and Germans might break out.

SO/SOE planned to provide resistance with arms, ammunition, demolition materials, radio equipment, clothing and medical supplies. As early as October 1943, OSS/London had received ETOUSA approval for the establishment of a storage, packing and dispatching center and assignment of two or more air squadrons to drop the supplies and bodies.

In order to prevent disclosure of SO and SOE participation in the resistance movement, it was agreed that American and British agents should be attached to local groups rather than to a central headquarters, and that the groups to which these agents were attached should be controlled directly by the Allies in London instead of by higher headquarters in France.

A reorganization, favored by SO, and eventually concurred in by the British, provided that the French should not only be given an equal voice in the direction of resistance in France but should be given administrative control as well. Accordingly, in May 1944, a tripartite staff, manned largely by SO/SOE personnel, was set up under SHAEF as Etat Major, Forces Francaises de l'Interieur (EMFFI) to deal with all matters concerning French resistance. French General Koenig in London was appointed, on 6 June,

Commanding General of organized French resistance forces, reporting to SHAEF. SFHQ continued to serve SHAEF, through EMFFI, as the agency responsible for air and sea transport, the packing of operational supplies, and the provision of W/T communications with FFI in France and with the SF detachments with the armies in the field.

Special Operations Center (SPOC), formed in May 1944 at Algiers, served as an SO/SOE base under AFHQ to coordinate resistance in South France. Thereafter, 25 *Jedburgh* teams went to North Africa from the United Kingdom to prepare for operations in southern France, and "French" Operational Groups stationed there were readied for missions in support of the forthcoming invasions.

Shortly before D-Day, staff detachments, composed of SO personnel, were attached to the General Staff Section of each American army and army group headquarters. These Special Force (SF) detachments, consisting of approximately fifteen officers, 35 enlisted men and a radio signal section, acted in an advisory capacity to the commanding general of each army and army group, in coordinating the activities of French resistance with the strategic and tactical plans and operations of the military organization concerned. The staffs also transmitted enemy intelligence furnished by French resistance to the proper staff section of the military headquarters. These detachments came under the operational command of EMFFI, while remaining under the direction of the military headquarters concerned.

Following a radio appeal from General Eisenhower at the time of the invasion, a large proportion of the male population of France, and many women, sought to join the Maquis. Few of these could be used because of their lack of training, organization and discipline, and also because the amount of material available was naturally insufficient for such numbers. The excessive zeal of the response brought disastrous consequences in some parts of France where the

enemy was able to take effective countermeasures. In some instances, the hordes of eager recruits hampered the operations of resistance groups which had been preparing for months to attack their targets.

This confused situation made even more difficult the work of the American and British agents and W/T operators, who had been slowly building up small groups of capable Frenchmen and training them to carry out attacks on strategic targets. SFHQ-EMFFI representatives—American, British and French—succeeded, nevertheless, in instructing large groups of Maquis in weapons and guerrilla warfare, and in organizing them into units whose support to the invading forces was subsequently recognized by Allied leaders.

2. Building French Resistance

Eighty-five OSS officers, enlisted men and civilians worked behind enemy lines in France in 1944, as part of SO/SOE circuits.

This small group, augmented after D-Day by the *Jedburghs,* helped SOE to organize, arm, train and lead some 300,000 Frenchmen against the enemy. It arranged for the delivery, reception and distribution of supplies for the use of these men, and provided communications and liaison between their leaders and Allied headquarters, making it possible to coordinate resistance behind the enemy lines with the plans of the American and British commanders.

During the first six months of 1944, F-Section * circuits and resistance groups in contact with SO and SOE agents in France sabotaged more than 100 factories producing war materials for the Germans. Some were disabled on brief secret raids carried out by saboteurs trained and equipped by F-Section agents. Others were put out of action with the complicity of the management or of the workers. Agents pretending to be travelling salesmen, completely equipped with forged documents showing that they were legiti-

* See "Early Infiltrations", above.

mate representatives of existing French firms, called on the managers of a factory, requested that they permit the sabotage of certain machines, and threatened Allied bombing of the plant if they did not agree. Compliance was usual, since it saved the lives of countless French civilians, and prevented the destruction of the entire plant. For the Allies, successful operations of this kind meant that vital parts of important factories could be disabled with a large economy of men, aircraft and materials, and with the greatest precision.

When the management refused to cooperate, the matter was immediately referred to SFHQ in London, where representatives of the French trade unions were called in and told what was wanted. They then approached the workers in the factory, and were usually able to obtain their help. If this approach also should fail, the factory was bombed from the air.

French production of war materials was further reduced by the continuous sabotage of the high. tension lines carrying hydroelectric power from southern France to the industrial consumers in the north. This operation was combined with a successful effort to reduce the coal stocks in France by cutting the rail and canal systems carrying coal from the mines to industrial centers, and by instigating frequent short strikes in French and Belgian coal mines. Because of the shortage of hydro-electric power, greater use was made of steam plants, forcing consumption of coal reserves which became increasingly difficult to replenish. In a short time, many factories had to close down for part of each week because of the lack of electric power.

The disruption of rail communications was carried out by workers and managers of the Societe National des Chemins de Fer (national railroad trust), as well as by resistance groups and F-Section saboteurs. These men repeatedly cut rails, sabotaged turntables, blew up control towers, derailed trains and disabled locomotives. More than

1,000 engines were put out of action, and five repair shops were successfully attacked, by Frenchmen under SFHQ direction, during the first six months of 1944. By repeatedly destroying or damaging locks in various canals, resistance groups and saboteurs, working with SO or SOE agents, paralyzed traffic for long periods of time on 36 of the inland waterways of France. The day-by-day work of French industry, and German military operations in France, were further hindered by intensive and continuous sabotage of the French underground telephone system.

After 6 June, SO agents quickly established contact with Allied commanders moving forward into France, and made available to them large resistance groups which were then used to facilitate and support the advance of army task forces. Maquis frequently protected roads, bridges and other installations needed by the Allies, from destruction by the Germans, and themselves took many towns before the arrival of army units. Also, under SO leadership, they often took part with American, British and French army troops in combined operations against the enemy.

Illustrative of the accomplishments and difficulties of SO circuits in France, were the STOCKBROKER, UNION and BEGGAR teams:

STOCKBROKER

In April 1943, an SOE agent had gone to the Belfort - Montbeliard - Besancon area along the Swiss border in East France to organize STOCKBROKER, which became one of the most successful circuits. Its saboteurs destroyed transformers at the Peugeot works at Montbeliard, the Leroy Foundries at Ste. Suzanne, and the Usines Winmer at Seloncourt; disabled locomotive turntables and engines, and derailed trains loaded with German troops and equipment; and blew up the Usines Maillard in the Doubs, the Koechlin works at Belfort, and the telephone exchange at Dijon, as well as hangars containing German Army supplies at the airdrome near Vesoul, loading cranes at Montbeliard and Nevers, and a steel railway bridge over the Haute Saone canal.

In December 1943, the SOE agent was shot and wounded in a brush with the Feld-gendarmerie, and escaped to Switzerland. In April 1944 an SO agent parachuted into the area to take over the circuit.

This agent arrived safely in the hands of a reception committee and spent the first night at X's house. The next morning at seven o'clock, Mademoiselle X was leaving the house in order to go to the school where she was a school mistress, when she was stopped by German soldiers in uniform and brought back to the house. The family was awakened and the SO agent, assuming (wrongly) that the Germans had come for him, jumped out of the kitchen window and was in the process of climbing the wall about ten yards away when he was shot through the head by one of the Germans. He was taken to the hospital at Montbeliard and died some hours later without regaining consciousness. The "X" family was immediately removed to the local prison.

In May, two SO officers came in to take his place. They were "Alfred" and "Narcisse" on their second mission to France.*

They had at their disposal almost no arms and very few explosives. Forced to improvise, they soon developed a cheap method of sabotage. Stopping a train about three kilometers from the tunnel near the Montbeliard station, they persuaded the mechanics and other personnel to leave, got up steam and started the train off on its own. The latter collided with a stationary train in the Montbeliard station. This was the first "phantom train", an operation which was subsequently widely used throughout the region. In early June, for example, STOCK-BROKER derailed a train in the Baume les Dames tunnel, and a few hours later a second piled on top of the first.

* For first mission, SACRISTAN, see "Early Infiltrations", above.

At the time of the arrival of the Allies, the Maquis of the region comprised 3,200 men, led by "Alfred". Of these 1,800 were well-armed and had considerably damaged the forces of the German retreating eastward.

UNION

UNION, one of the first tripartite teams to the Maquis, went into the field in January 1944. The American, British and French officers of the mission quickly established liaison with the regional Maquis headquarters at Lyon, and with the military chiefs of the Departments of Vercors, Savoie, Drome and Isere. They found an extremely confused administrative situation in the area, where several resistance organizations with divergent political views and loyalties were working independently and often at cross purposes. The team leader reported to SFHQ the number of effectives in the area, the state of their morale, training and equipment, and their needs. He found that lack of transportation and money were serious problems, and that security at the regional and departmental levels was poor. UNION used its influence to coordinate the activities of the various groups. It set up a network of W/T operators and couriers which provided communication between the four Departments as well as with London.

The Maquis threat to German occupation forces grew proportionately. In Vercors in January, two small Maquis units were attacked by three hundred Germans in trucks. The enemy lost twenty killed and the Maquis three. Maquis leaders stated that they could have wiped out the Germans if they had had sufficient arms. In February, the Germans attacked the Maquis in Vercors with three mechanized battalions and light tanks. These attacks increased in number and strength. Eventually two German divisions were used against them, with disastrous results. In May, the UNION chief estimated that a force of seven thousand men would be required to hold Vercors against the Germans. Although these were available, it was not possible to arm and equip such a large group.

Vercors is a mountainous region with an average altitude of 3,600 feet. It is surrounded by three rivers, the Isere, the Drome and the Drar, and is difficult of access. The passes, roads and woods, leading to and around the Vercors area, were mined by the Maquis, who daily strengthened their position, trying to transform the Vercors plateau into a resistance fortress. The majority of the Maquis were young men and boys who had almost no military experience. According to their French chief, they could fight in hit-and-run actions, but were not likely to stand combat lasting several hours. A great handicap was the lack of field equipment such as blankets, mess kits, raincoats, boots and uniforms. The situation in Vercors before and after D-Day illustrated the error of attempts on the part of the resistance to take and hold ground in the face of enemy counter-measures and showed the danger of having too large a resistance force, insufficiently armed, in one area.

To supplement UNION's work in this vital region, two new units were dispatched after D-Day. On 28 June, OG section JUSTINE, consisting of two American officers and thirteen enlisted men, parachuted to a reception committee near Vassieux in Vercors. Their mission was to strengthen the Maquis and to conduct guerrilla warfare against enemy supply lines and communications. They trained men of the local Maquis in guerrilla tactics, and instructed them in the use of American and British weapons. On 6 July, the SO EUCALYPTUS mission was dispatched to assist the UNION agents.

At this time the Maquis consisted of 2,000 men. All were armed, but heavy equipment, such as mortars, essential in mountain warfare, and heavy machine guns, were short or lacking. A few bazookas were on hand. The general mobilization of all Vercors took place on 11 July. This called to the colors over a thousand men, bringing the Vercors forces to 3,200, plus an additional 600 labor-

ers who were working on the Vassieux airfield. On 12 July the Germans were on the move. La Chapelle en Vercors was bombed on 12 and 13 July.

On 14 July at 0800 hours, a drop by some 85 Allied planes of 1,457 containers took place at Vassieux. The inhabitants ran out in the streets shouting and waving to the fliers as the fortresses circled over the roofs. Thirty minutes later the Germans started bombing and strafing the town. This continued from morning to evening and prevented the men from collecting the containers. Only at night was it possible to gather some 200 of them. The Germans started the destruction of La Chapelle en Vercors. From 1400 hours until 1700 hours explosives were dropped; from 2000 to 2130 hours incendiaries. The town was ablaze, and the planes machine-gunned people endeavoring to save their belongings from their houses.

On 19 July 1944 at 0900 hours, 21 German gliders landed at Vassieux, and some 450 SS men entrenched themselves in the ruins of the town. Led by the OG's, the Maquis attacked the enemy four times in three days, surrounded them completely and killed some 250 men. They failed to effect a surrender, however, for lack of artillery and mortars. While the Germans continued to receive reinforcements and supplies via glider and plane, the Maquis had used up all its reserves. The SS massacred some one hundred civilians at Vassieux, often killing whole families on sight. Of 120 houses in the town, only seven remained inhabited.

By 20 July, Vercors was bottled up. Bombing of the whole plateau lasted until the 23rd. All passes and roads were guarded by enemy troops equipped with artillery. On 21 July there was a general German attack. Land, Meaudre, Autrans and Villand de Lans were occupied. Hostages were shot; several farms were burned. Resistance losses in Vercors, out of 3,200 fighting men and 600 laborers, were from 600 to 700 killed.

Throughout these operations, the OSS W/T officer of the EUCALYPTUS mission kept London informed of the situation and was, for a long time, the only link between Vercors and the Allies.*

The OG section moved from Vassieux across the Borne and on to the Plateau of Presles above Saint-Marcellin. Here it learned that the entire Isere Valley was guarded by enemy troops posted fifty meters apart. The Germans intended that no one should escape from Vercors. When 400 German troops moved into Presles, the section took to the woods. For eleven days it remained there, while German patrols scoured the woods and fired into the underbrush trying to scare the Maquis into the Isere Valley, where many were shot trying to escape. During this time the men ate nothing but raw potatoes and occasionally a little cheese. They were never allowed to speak above a whisper. Not more than one man moved at a time, and then never more than fifty feet.

Finally one of the Maquis guides with the section went into Saint-Marcellin and stole a truck. With this transportation the section moved down the west side of the Isere Valley into the Chartreuse mountains above Grenoble. It then crossed the Isere and moved into the Belledonne mountains. At this time the section was in poor condition. Three of the men were unable to walk, all had lost weight, and many had severe cases of dysentery. Two weeks later, they all moved into Grenoble to join the American troops already there. They learned that

22,000 German troops had been diverted against the Maquis in Vercors during July, including the 9th Panzer, the 189th and part of the 157th Divisions.

BEGGAR

BEGGAR consisted of one SO officer, "Ludovic", and two enlisted men. They were parachuted on 11 April 1944, to organize a sabotage circuit in the area north and slightly west of Paris, comprising Clermont, Beauvais and Pontoise. They were met by a reception committee, and, after spending two days in the house of a game keeper, went to Paris.

"Ludovic's" first task was to establish himself as a member of the community and to make his cover story foolproof. He first walked for days through the streets of Paris becoming accustomed to Paris life. He bought collaborationist newspapers and ate on the black market. He procured all the items which he thought a Frenchman would have in his pockets: he purchased tickets for the Loterie Nationale; he had someone write him at his address in Paris and kept the letter in his wallet; he obtained newspaper clippings and acquired photographs; in the telephone directory he found people whose name was the same as his assumed name, went to see them and figured out with them how they must be related, thus acquiring distant relatives who could say that they knew him.

At the time, one of the most important documents to have in one's possession was a Certificat de Travail. When the police arrested a man, they often telephoned the employer to see whether the man actually worked where he claimed to. Through one of his new friends, "Ludovic" was put down on the pay roll of this man's factory. He worked there for a day in order to familiarize himself with the plant. He refunded every month to his friend the check he had received as salary.

These security precautions proved to have been necessary in "Ludovic's" case. He was arrested twice. The first time was in Paris,

---

* The French considered this agent one of the heroes of Vercors. It is interesting to note that, shortly after his arrival in France, he was almost caught when he went to a town outside Vercors to the post office to buy stamps. He was a stamp collector and showed great interest in the Petain stamps, which he had never seen before, although they had been in common use in France for the last three years. This attracted the attention of a man standing behind him who could see at once that he had not been long in the country. The girl at the post office winked at the agent, who then realized that he was attracting attention. He left the post office hurriedly with the man following him, and had a great deal of trouble in getting rid of his pursuer.

when approximately a hundred persons were taken to the Commissariat of Police and interrogated in the presence of the Feldgendarmerie. They telephoned his employer and, having found that he actually was registered and supposed to be working there, released him. The second time was after there had been some sabotage on a road in the neighborhood, and the police were trying to catch those who had done it. "Ludovic" ran unexpectedly into a spot control, but, after being questioned and searched, was released. The Germans never did discover that he was the man they were seeking.

As an organizer, "Ludovic" was not expected to participate directly in any kind of sabotage or other activity. He did, nevertheless, take part in many attacks, both on railroads and telephones, in order to show his men that he was not asking them to accomplish anything he feared to undertake himself. Most of the time, however, he was establishing rendezvous, making plans, trying to improve sabotage methods, teaching the use of explosives and stressing to his men the importance of security. The local resistance group had no knowledge of his identity. No member of his organization knew where he lived.

"Ludovic" had no original contacts in the area, and had to recruit. Step by step, he built up an effective circuit. By 5 June, he had 91 men working for him, divided into eight units: seven sabotage groups and one reception committee. By 31 August there were 505 men organized, trained and equipped by the BEGGAR team.

They began to sabotage communications in the area in June. Railway and telephone lines radiating from Creil, Senlis and Beauvais were cut repeatedly, and several trains, one of them loaded with tanks, were blown up. "Ludovic" also sent in valuable military intelligence. On 12 June, he reported the presence of 500 well-camouflaged Tiger tanks in the Foret de Bez, where they were awaiting night-fall before moving toward Clermont. On 24 June he reported the existence of depots of pilotless planes in the quarries at Neucort and St. Leu d'Essereu, and underground airfields at Creil.

STOCKBROKER, UNION and BEGGAR typified the early SO/SOE effort in organizing and directing French resistance. Supplementary to these were the Operational Groups, the air supply program to arm guerrillas and the *Jedburg*-Field Detachment arrangement for coordinating resistance on and after D-Day with the advancing Allied armies.

3. Supply

Up to September 1944, OSS made available to a growing number of French resistance groups substantial deliveries of equipment, ranging from munitions and weapons, such as carbines and bazookas, to medicines, clothing and shoes. Combined deliveries by SO and SOE, under SFHQ and SPOC, amounted to some 10,000 tons of supplies before and after D-Day.

The British, in 1943, planned to organize resistance into small, secret, self-contained cells directed from London by W/T communications controlled by SOE. They wished also to limit the amount of supplies sent to France because of their belief that rival resistance groups would use them to fight each other instead of the Germans, and that political control might in this way be seized by undesirable elements. SO/London believed, on the contrary, that resistance should be developed along paramilitary lines on a national scale, the French to share leadership equally with the Americans and the British. It advocated a substantial increase in the quantity of arms, ammunition and other supplies sent to France, in order to increase participation in the underground movement, and to assure maximum military effectiveness of the resistance forces on D-Day. Believing in accomplishing the invasion of France quickly and with the least possible losses, SO naturally gave less weight than the British to possible political consequences. With the growth of the OSS contribution, the American view was finally accepted.

SO's first air deliveries, in the month of January 1944, amounted to 96 containers as against 570 from the British. Thereafter, the American deliveries from the United Kingdom increased steadily to a peak surpassing British totals in June, July and August, after which the urgency of resistance needs declined:

Month	Containers*	Packages**
January	96	20
February	228	58
March	391	170
April	988	649
May	1,139	742
June	4,024	968
July	8,357	3,069
August	6,059	2,273
September	5,382	2,370
TOTALS	27,164	10,319

* Containers, holding up to 220 lbs. (net weight), were fitted with parachutes and released.
** Packages were dropped free. Holding up to 100 lbs., they were used for non-breakable items (i.e., uniforms, packaged food rations).

Necessary containers and packages were prepared by trained personnel and prisoners of war at separate SO and SOE packing stations in both the United Kingdom and in North Africa. The SO base at Holme, England, servicing North France, employed a staff of 326; SO supplies to South France were handled by a staff at Algiers numbering 142 persons. At the U.K. base, OSS prepared approximately 50,000 containers in nine months time—double the output of the similarly manned British station. Both operated on a 24-hour basis after May.

Actual delivery was planned jointly by SO and SOE in direct radio contact with resistance groups, and carried out by modified USAAF or RAF bombers with specially trained crews. Allocation of procured supplies was also jointly decided on the basis of over-all tactical and strategic considerations. Quotas were established in line with SHAEF needs. The resistance group requesting supplies by secret wireless suggested safe dropping zones measuring at least two miles square. Proposals for delivery of specified quantities of various items to designated pinpoints originated in the country sections of SFHQ. If the project were approved and a priority allotted, the country section notified the Air Operations Section. Standard containers already packed with arms, ammunition, explosives, demolition devices, rations, clothing, shoes and medicines were allocated, and special packages were prepared for such items as W/T sets and crystals.* On the day before the drop, BBC broadcast the code name of the zone selected. Confirmation was radioed immediately by the resistance group involved, which, meanwhile, had a reception committee ready to give proper identification signals and to receive the supplies. Radio contact was constantly maintained in case of last-minute changes in conditions, such as the appearance of German patrols. Once a hard-pressed resistance group safely received supplies dropped into a large clearing in which a company of Germans camped for the night.

On supply drops, unlike most body drops, several planes were frequently used on a single operation, and completion of a program for a target area often required a series of flights to one or more pinpoints. In addition to regular night missions, air units were called upon to make a few large-scale daylight operations, delivering huge quantities of material to critical centers of open resistance or where active support was desired for specific military campaigns.

The first of four such missions was carried out on 25 June 1944, when French resistance, in open combat with German troops, demanded large additional deliveries of arms.

* W/T sets often arrived broken, even though various methods for improving the packing were developed.

It involved successful sorties by 180 Flying Fortresses of the 3rd Air Division (Eighth U.S.A.A.F.), with fighter protection. Seventy-two plane-loads went to the Haute Vienne region; 36 loads each were flown to the regions of Ain, Jura and the Vercors plateau. Another mass flight, the largest, took place on 14 July (Bastille Day) and consisted of 349 Fortresses with escort. On that occasion, 320 of the huge air fleet dropped to six open resistance centers, including Vercors, in broad daylight, 3,794 containers holding 417 short tons of equipment, enough to arm more than 20,000 men.

Although larger and psychologically more effective than night supply missions, this type of operations in areas where resistance was both extensive and overt tended to cause severe enemy reprisals.* Because of heavy fighter protection during these daylight sorties, however, the bombers rarely encountered flak or air opposition in flight. Of the planes that were unable successfully to drop their loads, mechanical trouble and parachute failure were most often to blame. Approximately 98 percent of the supplies dropped on daylight missions were successfully recovered.

Not all regions could be supplied as adequately as planned. In Indre, for example, the Germans were extremely active, and reception difficulties caused repeated cancellations of air deliveries. The Pyrenees area, at the extreme range of both Britain and North African-based bombers, was most difficult to reach. In the vital sections, however, of the Massif Central and along the Rhone Valley, established supply quotas were either met or exceeded.

From January through September 1944, SO parachuted more than 3,500 tons of supplies from England, and approximately 1,500 from Algiers **—representing, in all slightly

more than fifty percent of the total SO/SOE contribution to French resistance.

4.   Jedburghs

Between June and September 1944, 276 *Jedburghs* were parachuted into France, Belgium and Holland. Of these, 83 were Americans, 90 British and 103 French. They made up three-man teams consisting of two officers and one radio operator, wore Army uniforms and prepared no cover story. If captured, they were to give only name, rank and serial number, claiming prisoner of war treatment according to military law. *Jedburgh* teams were supplementary to the SO circuits, and helped organize and arm part of the large number of recruits who joined the resistance movement in response to the Allied call to arms and to the impetus provided by D-Day. They did not assume command functions, since the French had their own leaders, but they suggested, helped to plan, and took part in sabotage of communications, destruction of fuel and ammunition dumps, attacks on enemy pockets cut off by the advance of the Allied armies and the procurement of intelligence. They subsequently provided liaison between American and British task forces and the Maquis, as various areas were overrun.

During June and July, eight American SO officers and six radio operators parachuted behind enemy lines as part of nine *Jedburgh* teams. Most of these entered Brittany, together with units of the Special Airborne Service, the British counterpart of OSS OG's. Initially, each team established contact with the local resistance leader, began radio communication with SFHQ in London, and arranged to arm and equip the Maquis in its area of operations.

The *Jedburgh* teams in Brittany armed and organized more than 20,000 men. Under their direction, these men kept railroad tracks cut, derailed trains and destroyed engines, paralyzing all railway traffic throughout the peninsula. On the roads, they at-

---

* See account of UNION team under "Building French Resistance", above.

** An independent SO packing and supply station was not established in Algiers until 15 March 1944.

tacked German troop and supply movements from ambush. As a consequence of this Maquis activity, a major part of the German forces in Brittany was diverted to fighting resistance groups. Due to the mobility of the Maquis, their superior knowledge of the terrain and their extremely high morale, they were able to inflict losses many times heavier than they suffered themselves. The principal difficulties were those of coordinating activities and supply requisitions with local SAS forces, and of explaining to the Maquis why SFHQ occasionally failed to drop the arms requested.

During August and September 1944, 69 additional American *Jedburghs* parachuted into France. They, too, concentrated on organizing attacks on railways, roads and bridges, and on cutting electric power, telephone and telegraph lines, thus hindering German commanders in moving troops, bringing up supplies and communicating with one another. The Paris-Beauvais-Dieppe railroad was cut ten times during the last two weeks in July; the Paris-Orleans-Limoges line was kept unusable from June onward. There was frequent railroad sabotage in and around Bordeaux and Toulouse. The Paris-Berlin long-distance cable was cut for two weeks in July, and the Paris-Lyon and Paris-Mulhouse cables were repeatedly interrupted.

Jedburgh teams organized ambushes, attacks against German garrisons and convoys, and small-scale actions to mop up bypassed or isolated enemy units. They also deployed resistance forces to immobilize German troops trapped for lack of supplies or inability to reopen escape routes. On 29 July in the Cahors region, for example, a *Jedburgh* team and seventy men of a resistance group attacked a German column of 26 vehicles, damaged six armored cars and two 108 mm. guns, and inflicted 29 enemy casualties to every one of their own. On 2 August in Brittany, a team with thirty FFI men held a road ambush on the main Paris-Brest road for two days and fought off a German anti-aircraft battalion. Escaping with only two casualties, they were instrumental in the capture of the Germans by advancing U. S. troops the following day.

Counter-scorching was an important phase of *Jedburgh* work. After the Allied break-through from the Normandy beachhead, it was realized that the Germans were in rapid retreat and might attempt a "scorched earth" program. *Jedburghs* were instructed wherever possible to carry out widespread minor demolitions and sabotage, rather than to destroy major installations which, when captured, would be important to the Allies. Upon the approach of Allied armies, they worked to protect vital bridges and power plants. In some cases, assistance of SAS units or OSS Operational Groups from England or North Africa was requested by radio. Usually, however, *Jedburghs* and resistance forces were sufficient to prevent scorching. For example, on 17 August 140 Germans with twelve AA guns holding a power plant in Aveyron surrendered to a *Jedburgh*-led resistance group when all escape routes were closed. The power plant, rendered useless to the Germans through repeated sabotage of high tension lines and pylons in the vicinity, was taken undamaged.

Probably no single *Jedburgh* operation could be regarded as wholly typical of the miscellaneous functions performed by these units. An account of two of the teams follows:

HORACE

On the night of 17-18 July 1944, team HORACE, consisting of a U. S. and a French officer, and a U. S. radio operator, was dispatched from the U. K. to Finistere, westernmost Department of the Brittany peninsula. They were to contact two *Jedburgh* teams and SAS elements already in the area, and to assist in coordinating large resistance forces, particularly around the German-controlled port of Brest. Their purpose was to create the greatest possible diversion of German strength from attacking invasion forces, and to prevent their escape from by-passed pockets pending their capture by the Allies.

The men, followed by containers and packages, were parachuted, as planned, into a field some forty miles southeast of Brest. Moving by night and hiding by day, they made arrangements for safe houses, guides and contacts, with the aid of local Maquis. Contact with London was quickly established. News of their arrival spread rapidly and the Germans offered a reward of 1,000,-000 francs for information leading to their capture dead or alive. Warned by resistance leaders of strong German repression in Brest, team HORACE, nevertheless, decided to proceed there themselves, when efforts to make contact via messenger with *Jedburgh* team GILES and northern Maquis groups failed.

German restrictions were tight in the Brest area. Every town and village had its German patrol or garrison, and defenses were extensive. Vehicular traffic was restricted to a few individuals—doctors with special passes, civilian drivers of trucks carrying supplies to the Germans, etc. Bicycles, if used, were automatically confiscated. Curfews were strictly enforced.

With the aid of two Frenchmen—later learned to have been sent by the FFI leader of the Brest Arrondissement, at the request of the French commandant of resistance in Finistere—the three members of the team were cached in emptied wine barrels and driven, as part of a truckload of wine for the Germans, to a wood five miles north of Brest. Spending the night in a foxhole, they proceeded the next day in the same manner to a safe house in a valley near Lesneven. The driver was stopped many times by German patrols. When a flat tire developed, a German patrol helped him change it.

Headquarters and guards were set up, never far from the Germans, and satisfactory communications with London maintained. Messengers were employed by HORACE to pass SFHQ instructions to resistance leaders, who, in turn, forwarded them to their men by word of mouth. In this way, groups were formed to prepare dropping grounds and to act as reception committees for supplies and Allied personnel.

There were no organized Maquis in Brest. All had been killed, captured, or forced to leave by strong German repressive measures. Resistance consisted of a few leaders driven underground and some 5,000 unarmed civilian partisans. Many worked for the Germans in arsenal and dock areas and, because of special passes, carried small arms in without being searched. To provide arms for the others, team HORACE prepared small ammunition dumps in the surrounding countryside, each known to groups of ten to twelve persons only. Containers and large weapons were transported from dropping grounds under hay in horsecarts or in civilian trucks carrying supplies to the Germans.

Many fields selected by HORACE for dropping were rejected by London because of flak or presence of German troops. The few parachutages attempted were successful, and, by the time the Americans attacked Brest, arms for 1,500 men had been supplied. Weapons captured from the Germans were distributed to arm the remainder.

On 29 July, team HORACE radioed intelligence, supplied by a French dock worker, that the Germans were planning to sink two 14,000-ton tankers to block the port of Brest. These ships were destroyed by Allied bombs on 8 August.

On 2 August, HORACE received SFHQ instructions to complete resistance plans in preparation for an Allied attack on German-held pockets in Brittany. Resistance leaders were instructed to procure intelligence on enemy troop disposition, defenses, German headquarters, etc. and were given, as a top priority assignment, the preservation of bridges, tunnels, viaducts, and all major works on the Lamballe-St.Brieux-Morlaix-Brest railway line.

With the approach of American troops on 7 August, team HORACE was attached to

G-2, Sixth Armored Division (U.S.) serving as liaison between G-2 and FFI. It turned over to divisional intelligence officers a suitcase of maps and detailed reports on permanent coastal installations at Brest, collected over the whole period of German occupation by French patriots. When the Brest resistance leader was driven into hiding and lost contact with his companies, the *Jedburghs* worked directly with the resistance groups.

Thirty Frenchmen were chosen to bring information on enemy defenses out of Brest. Upon encountering American troops, they were to give the password "Angouleme" and act as guides. Resistance combat forces protected the exposed flanks of the Sixth Armored Division through security patrols, and, when this Division pulled out, acted as a counter-reconnaissance screen between Point de Corsen and St. Divy to prevent enemy patrols from discovering the fact that some 30,000 German troops were faced by only two battalions of American infantry.

In mid-August, the signal was given for all-out French attack on the area. Resistance units ambushed the enemy where they could and freed many villages. Actual fighting by resistance in the area was slight—their main value lay in protecting flanks, procuring intelligence and repulsing German patrols in undefended areas. Resistance forces did attempt to attack a strongly fortified area, but were defeated with heavy casualties. Thereafter, they concentrated on containing enemy positions until properly equipped troops could move forward.

A strong German coastal position at St. Pabu, north of Brest, was surrounded by resistance until the arrival of the Americans. The German commander threatened the French with local reprisals if they did not withdraw. G-2 countered with a threat to turn over some 2,500 German prisoners to resistance guards unless they surrendered. The Germans agreed to surrender to the Americans, and two members of HORACE were sent by G-2 as part of a group to interrogate the commander and receive the capitulation of the St. Pabu garrison.

With the beginning of the VIII Corps attack on Brest, small FFI containing forces were relieved, and HORACE began working with G-3 to coordinate resistance forces with the Second Ranger Battalion in cutting off German forces west of Brest and capturing the le Conquet area. The French *Jedburgh* officer continued to work at FFI headquarters, assisting the civil affairs department and translating French intelligence reports. The two U. S. members of HORACE participated in front-line combat as guides, while 300 Rangers and a like number of FFI silenced the four 280 mm. coastal guns of the important Graf Spee battery, and attacked 2,000 Germans in heavily-mined, concrete emplacements.

On 9 September, the battle ended with the capture of six fortified concrete positions and 1,250 prisoners. Le Conquet peninsula was turned over to FFI. Team HORACE returned by air to England on 15 September.

ALEXANDER

ALEXANDER, the 29th *Jedburgh* team dispatched to France from the U. K. base, consisted of a U. S. lieutenant, a French lieutenant and an American sergeant who acted as radio operator. They were dropped on the night of 12 August, with thirty SAS men, to contact a SPOC mission in the Creuse region, to assist in arming and coordinating resistance there, and to help harass enemy movements on the Perigueux-Limoges-Chateauroux and Toulouse-Limoges-Chateauroux roads and rail lines.

Although headquarters of the mission in charge of resistance operations at Creuse had recently been subjected to heavy German attack, this group was in complete military command of underground operations and was conducting successful ambushes on all roads leading from the main German strongholds. ALEXANDER was assigned, by the EMFFI military delegate in the region, to contact and coordinate the efforts of rival Maquis leaders of the Armee Secrete (AS) and the Communist-controlled FTP in northern Dordogne. South of Perigueux, which had just been liberated, the *Jedburghs* contacted the mutually suspicious Maquis leaders "Rac", 28-year old regular army man, and "Louis", ex-mechanic and Communist. Each commanded some 4,000 men, only half of whom were armed. Besides the need for arms and munitions, both groups lacked gasoline. Contrary to popular belief, the French Maquis were highly dependent on motor transport, and were forced to use unreliable charcoal-burning vehicles known as "gazogenes". Team ALEXANDER repeatedly requested the necessary supplies; however, an administrative mix-up prevented their receipt.* It had therefore to improvise, leading guerrillas in foraging raids for enemy equipment.

The Germans in the area varied from 20,-000 to 45,000. Following a crushing defeat north of the Loire, their movements were divided between rapid retreat to the north and east by most units and a determined opposition on the part of others charged with holding the Atlantic ports of southwest France, including Royan and La Rochelle.

The FFI continued to harass them by ambush and open engagement, and, on 27 August, prepared to attack Angouleme, held by an estimated 2,500 Germans. For the concerted FFI movement against Angouleme, AS and FTP forces were brought into active liaison, stimulated considerably by local pride engendered by the entry of guerrillas from the neighboring Departments of Haute Vienne and Vienne.

Preparations were ingenious. Fifty men who knew the town were infiltrated via the

sewage system. The parish priest of Torsac provided the means of arming resistance within:

Looking extremely solemn and chanting Latin incantations, he would lead a mournful funeral procession into the cemetery in Angouleme, where the coffin would be interred with much loud weeping. The coffin, of course, contained arms and would be disinterred during the night by the resistance.*

A coup was carried out just before the attack, in which an AS group exfiltrated from Angouleme 300 Italians, willing to surrender with their arms, which included anti-tank and heavy machine guns. The Maquis advanced. However, the German evacuation made the occupation less of a victory than a foregone conclusion.

After Angouleme ALEXANDER lost touch with "Louis" (who moved to the La Rochelle front) but continued to work closely with "Rac" until the end of the mission late in November. They pursued the Germans toward the garrison at Royan, and, after various engagements around Saintes in which at least three Maquis and an estimated hundred Germans lost their lives, were stopped along a line on the Seudre River guarding the approaches to the port which the Germans intended to hold.

During this time, ALEXANDER procured a sizable amount of jettisoned German arms. From other Allied missions and agents in the region they collected, in late September, some 100,000 rounds of much-needed .303, and, from a trip made north of the Loire for the purpose, a requisition of 5,000 gallons of gas from Brittany. By October, no more supplies could be secured through such scouting techniques, and large dumps of unused German munitions were forbidden them by SHAEF order. Two members of ALEXANDER went to OSS/Paris and London to arrange for seven parachutages, which came through in two flights at the end of October.

---

* SFHQ operations had by this time grown to such a scale that administrative errors might be expected. Agents in France alone were numbered in the hundreds, not counting those in other parts of Europe. In this particular case, the agents apparently should have sent their messages in French rather than in English, and had entered a sector of France covered by a different desk than that which dispatched them.

---

* From ALEXANDER Report, SO War Diary, Vol. 4, Bk. IV, History Files.

ALEXANDER also cooperated in obtaining the first intelligence received by London on a new German secret weapon, V-4. A Polish soldier under the German command at Royan gave himself up to the FFI for interrogation. A former officer in the Polish Army, he had been one of a section handling the new weapon, still being perfected. Detailed plans and specifications of the anti-infantry V-4 (employing a compressed air principle for a devastating blast effect, to a range of 2,000 meters) were drawn up by the Polish officer and flown to London. He was then taken by members of team ALEXANDER to Paris to be questioned by Ordnance Intelligence, SHAEF. This officer remained until the end of the war the chief Allied intelligence source on the German V-4.

Jedburgh teams were recalled from the sector at the request of General de Larminat early in November. On returning to London, ALEXANDER left, at the OSS/Paris office, a detailed map of German dispositions in the Royan area with exact indications of German defenses. Although the stalemate at Royan still existed at the *Jedburgh's* departure, FFI forces at the time numbered seven regiments of 12,000 men against 11,000 Germans, and reinforcement by regular French troops under de Larminat's Cognac headquarters was imminent.*

———————

HORACE and ALEXANDER, like the other *Jedburghs*, were, in conception, liaison teams dispatched to exploit to the maximum resistance forces already built up by earlier SO/SOE efforts and by Frenchmen themselves. Many arrived too late for any behind-the-lines action, and nearly all of those who were dispatched in time, stated that two to six more weeks would have permitted more successful operation.

Results were, however, highly praised by Allied commanders. With well-trained, capable radio operators, the *Jedburghs* represented, wherever they were, a strong radio link between FFI leaders and other Allied groups in the field, such as SAS, and headquarters in London. When other recourse failed, *Jedburgh* officers personally visited higher echelon staff members to voice the needs of the Maquis. Besides the all-important task of making available, by all possible means, arms and supplies to the resistance and preparing landing and dropping fields, they acted as translators and interpreters, assisted in surrender arrangements, helped lead sabotage and ambush operations, provided intelligence on resistance and enemy strength and other information as well, and worked to coordinate separate resistance forces under a unified command.

Overrun by advancing Allied armies, most *Jedburghs* served in division or army headquarters as sources of local intelligence, as guides and as organizers of intelligence activities immediately ahead of the lines. They also continued as links with the local resistance to help establish civil administration and to arrange FFI assistance in guarding supplies and installations.

5. OG's in France

Operational Groups were sent into France between June and September 1944, either to operate alone or to direct resistance groups in actions where large units of American behind-the-lines agents were deemed necessary. These "French" OG's were based mainly in Algiers as Company B; no staff of any size had been established at the U.K. base. Some OG missions were completed from London, however, at a late date, by two groups sent from Company B, Algiers, and by two "Norwegian" OG's diverted to France for lack of an immediate Norway program.*

Fourteen sections,** based on Algiers, parachuted into France between 8 June and

———————

* For further OSS activity against the German pockets in West France, see "Liberated France", below.

* See OG's under "London Base", above.
** An OG section consisted, usually, of 15 men, including a radio operator and a medical technician.

2 September 1944. They were armed with automatic rifles, machine guns, some heavier weapons such as the bazooka, and supplies of demolition explosives, mines and booby traps. Working with Maquis they protected the flanks of Allied forces driving in from the beaches, ambushed German columns and blocked their progress, destroyed enemy supply and communication lines and forced the enemy to divert troops for their protection. In addition to this sabotage and guerrilla warfare, OG's arranged supply drops, armed and equipped resistance groups and instructed them in the use of American and British explosives.

The OG's in London, consisting of both "French" and "Norwegian" OG personnel, started late, but undertook successfully seven missions between 1 August and 9 September 1944. They reinforced Maquis to harass and ambush German units, saved from destruction by a retreating enemy two important hydro-electric plants, and protected, for subsequent Allied use, lines of communication and transport.

Another important OG contribution was the raising of morale among the French population. The arrival of American squads (two to a section) in uniform in areas far in advance of the Allied armies, heartened and reassured the people. Maquis leaders told the OG's that, even if they had not carried out a single tactical operation, their presence alone was of enormous value.

Recorded achievements of all OG engagements in France included: cutting of 11 power lines and communication cables, demolition of 32 bridges on key railway lines and highways in the Rhone valley, mining of 17 roads, and the destruction of 2 trains, 3 locomotives and 33 vehicles. In the course of their various expeditions, OG's killed 461 Germans and wounded 467. By exaggerating their strength and threatening attack, OG sections demanded and received the surrender of enemy units totalling more than 10,000 prisoners. Casualties among the OG

sections in France were: five killed, twenty-three wounded and one missing in action.

EMILY, the first OG section in France, parachuted to a reception committee in Cantal on the night of 8 June 1944. Its mission was to deny enemy use of railway lines and to harass enemy movements on the main roads in the Department of Lot. Working with Maquis officers, the OG's made plans to attack a steel railway bridge over the Cele River at Conduche. Riding in a five-ton wood-burning truck and accompanied by a guide provided by the Maquis, the section approached to within one kilometer of the target on the night of 11 June. A reconnaissance showed that the bridge was not guarded. OG security guards were dispatched to patrol the road approaches to the target, and a Maquis, armed with Bren guns, took up outlying positions. The OG demolition squad then placed eight 30-lb. charges on the bridge and cut fuses for 15 minutes. After the security guards had been withdrawn and accounted for, the fuses were ignited and the entire group left in the truck. The resulting explosion badly twisted the steel bridge, making the doubletrack rail line between Paris and Toulouse completely unusable.

In July, section EMILY arranged a supply drop and distributed arms and ammunition to the Maquis in Lot. It set up a firing range and instructed the men of the Maquis in the use of American small arms, mortars and bazookas. Through the Maquis, section EMILY arranged to have the foreman of the railroad yard at Capdenac disable 28 locomotives by removing the bronze injectors, which were impossible to replace. Several men of the section, assisted by a Maquis, carried out a demolition which caused the 100-meter steel span of the Madeleine bridge south of Figeac to drop into the Lot River, thus eliminating use of Highway 140. Early in August, section members with Maquis protection knocked out a 64-meter steel section of the double-track viaduct at Souillac.

On the night of 23 July, a second OG section, LOUISE, blew up a highway bridge across the Rhone and a railway bridge across a highway near Viviers in Ardeche. The former, which was a suspension bridge, dropped into the river, making it impassable for barges carrying gasoline for the Germans, and breaking all communication and power lines. The railroad bridge dropped onto the highway below and blocked vehicular traffic for several days. Six days later, section LOUISE ambushed a column of 400 Germans at Lesbans, killing approximately one hundred. One tank and six trucks were destroyed by bazooka fire and Gammon grenades. On 1 August, men of this section derailed a train carrying sixteen tanks and five box cars loaded with enemy supplies.

Two weeks later, four 37-mm guns were parachuted to the section. All were damaged during the drop, but three were assembled, and two proved usable. With these guns, the OG's and a Maquis of forty men took up positions on a hill overlooking Chalons, which the Germans were evacuating. In one day they killed some two hundred Germans as they moved out of the town.

On 31 August, four members of section LOUISE learned that a German column was in the valley near Chomerac. They drove to the village of Chambonte and demanded the surrender of the German garrison. The German major in charge would not assume responsibility for surrendering, and asked the Americans to speak to his commanding officer. An hour later this officer, a colonel, arrived. LOUISE informed him that he was surrounded by elements of the American and French Armies, and that, unless he surrendered, the Allies would take no prisoners. The colonel asked to see the officer in command of the OG's and to confer with his battalion commanders. These officers came down one by one from their positions in the hills. After the conference it was decided that all but one of the battalions would surrender to the OG's as prisoners of the Allied armies. At this instant, firing began nearby, and in a few minutes a French tank appeared. An OG officer, seeing that the tank belonged to an Ally, ripped off his white undershirt, took a riding crop from the German colonel, and waved his hastily made flag violently. The firing ceased. All the battalion commanders now decided to surrender. The OG's and some Maquisards took them to their positions to bring down their troops. By this bluff, the OG section received the surrender of a German regiment, and took 3,824 prisoners.

On 9 August, six OG's of section BETSY and a small Maquis blew up a double-track bridge southwest of St. Etienne, Department of Loire. This not only cut the railroad but blocked a main highway. On 13 August, section PEG destroyed a railroad bridge between Carcassonne and Rivesaltes which had been in continual use by German supply trains. The next night this section destroyed three stone arch bridges, completely cutting Route Nationale 117. A few days later, one officer and four men of BETSY, with eighteen Maquisards, were sent to prepare a road block on the highway near Couiza, Department of Aude. While setting the charge they learned that a force of 250 Germans was approaching. The charge was set and blown hurriedly, and did not do sufficient damage to block the road. The group withdrew into the hills, while the officer and one sergeant remained behind to delay the enemy advance with fire from their automatic weapons. During the engagement which followed, the OG officer was killed and the sergeant wounded. The former was hit four times by machine gun fire before he fell, but continued to fight until a German officer emptied his pistol into his head. The sergeant fought on alone until his right hand was shattered by an explosive bullet and his left foot hit, and then managed to withdraw under the protecting fire of the other OG's who had taken up positions behind rocks on the hill overlooking the road. He was later awarded the Distinguished Service Cross for this action.

Section PATRICK, consisting of 4 American officers and 21 enlisted men, was sent from England to the Department of Indre to seize the important dam and hydroelectric power station at Eguzon and protect it from destruction by the Germans. The OG's, and a Maquis of 200 men, moved into positions about one kilometer outside Eguzon. Three OG officers and a Maquis agent met with the officer commanding a French unit which had been sent by the Vichy Government to help the Germans hold this installation. He stated that he had orders to defend Eguzon against any attack. The OG leader replied that he had orders from General Koenig of the FFI to take and hold Eguzon for France. He added that he was ready to attack with paratroops, leading the French officer to believe that a substantial American force had come to Eguzon for that purpose. The latter then agreed that his objective and that of the OG's were identical, and undertook to inform the German commander that he and his men would not be attacked if they withdrew at once without carrying out any demolitions. The Germans completely evacuated Eguzon the next day, leaving the plant intact. It would have been impossible to prevent damage to the installation in the event of combat.

With respect to equipment, all OG sections reported the need for more long range weapons and the frequent inadequacies of the Marlin. The American bazooka and the British Gammon grenade were found to be invaluable in ambushing enemy tanks and vehicles. It was felt that each section should be supplied with light machine guns and B.A.R.'s. The training received by OG's prior to their actual operations was found to be more than adequate. Many remarked that what they faced in the field proved easier than the problems continually worked out during their practice period. Factors which they wished had been stressed more were: (1) Thorough briefing in French military nomenclature; (2) maintenance and repair of radios for radio operators; (3) operation and maintenance of all types of foreign vehicles and weapons.

Operational Groups were the most military units in OSS. Their job was to carry out hit-and-run sabotage raids or to protect vital installations from destruction by the fleeing enemy. Always in U. S. Army uniform, they had to depend on the protection of resistance groups and on their own ingenuity to avoid capture.

Following successful operations in Yugoslavia, Greece, France, Italy and Norway,* the Operational Groups were withdrawn for action in the Far East.

6. SI/North France

It had been early determined by Donovan that SI, unlike SO, would avoid close collaboration or integration with its British counterpart.** SI bases in Cairo, Algiers, Italy and neutral countries developed their own intelligence methods and operations, and in many areas outstripped SIS coverage. In London, however, the Branch found it difficult to obtain facilities, priorities and approvals for independent operations.*** It insisted on retaining its independence, but sought SIS cooperation on an equal basis in order to benefit from the latter's experience and superior position in London. SIS, however, appeared to wish to hamper the development of its counterpart, raising, for example, constant objections to SI attempts to establish liaison with foreign intelligence services in London. Finally, in May 1943, SIS offered to enter into a joint operation, *Sussex,* to dispatch 120 agents to France. This was accepted by SI in June 1943. However, preparations took nearly a year, and the large majority of *Sussex* agents entered France in June and July 1944, shortly to be overrun.

---

* See those sections, above.
** See "Introduction", above.
*** Ibid.

Until late 1944, when SIS had to admit a degree of failure in the penetration of Germany,[*] SI's only independent operations were the VARLIN team (Labor Desk) of January 1944, and the mid-1944 *Proust* operations, both in France. The former was unfortunately cut off without communications, and the latter missions were largely unimportant, since priority tasks were always given the joint *Sussex* project.

VARLIN

The VARLIN mission to Paris in January 1944 was the first operation to be dispatched anywhere by SI/London. As such, its real significance lay not so much in the assigned task but more in its value as a first experience and its consequent importance for later operations.

VARLIN was originally designed by the Labor Desk as an organizing rather than an intelligence mission. Two agents, and an SOE sabotage expert added at the last minute,[**] were dispatched to work with the CGT [***] in directing sabotage and psychological warfare among French laborers being deported to Germany. A W/T operator was to follow.

Lack of communications from the beginning rendered the mission impotent, although the original sabotage directive from London was passed on to the CGT. The initial error, from which VARLIN never recovered, was to dispatch the agents without the W/T operator. The expectation had been that the latter would arrive from the United States within the month, when he could join his colleagues in the field. Because he was a national of an occupied country, however, he was never cleared by State Department

---

[*] See "Direct Penetration (of Germany) from London", below.

[**] The Air Force had agreed to postpone bombing of the SKF ball-bearing factory at Ivry, if saboteurs could disable it without large loss of life to French civilians. On 17 May, the SOE agent accomplished his mission, with labor union assistance and VARLIN aid in arranging contacts.

[***] Confederation Generale du Travail, the largest French labor organization.

---

and finally traversed the Atlantic as a Belgian seaman. Meanwhile, the agents in the field were compelled to use BCRA pouch facilities. When the W/T operator was finally dispatched, he lost his gear in the landing operation. He spent 6 July to 20 July establishing definitely that his equipment had disappeared, and at that point made contact with the W/T operator of one of the *Sussex* [*] teams, only to find that the latter was himself unable to communicate with London, due to a signal plan mix-up. The difficulty was finally cleared up in August, via BCRA channels.

In the brief period that remained before the liberation of Paris, VARLIN was instructed to concentrate on German military intelligence exclusively. The W/T operator transmitted, thereafter, information on enemy troop and materiel movements.

VARLIN pointed up the advantages of careful communications planning. It demonstrated that failure to send agent and W/T operator simultaneously, and failure to take every conceivable precaution with respect to equipment, might well render useless any mission dispatched to the field.

Sussex

The joint SI/SIS *Sussex* plan, submitted to the Theater Commander in outline form on 5 July 1943 and developed in detail in November, was designed to supply strategic and tactical military intelligence to the Allied armies upon their invasion of North France, through a group of 120 agents organized in two-man teams. Each team was to consist of a French observer and radio operator, trained in England in a joint SI/SIS school and dispatched to France by parachute to cities and towns not covered by SO/SOE resistance contacts.

By the end of 1943, about three-quarters of the SI/London staff was devoting the greater part of its time to preparations for *Sussex*. The operation marked the beginning for SI/London of large-scale intelli-

---

[*] See below.

---

gence procurement through its own agents in the field, rather than through Allied intelligence services in London.* At the same time, it represented the greatest contribution made by SI/London to the military operations involved in the invasion of the Continent and the liberation of France.

SHAEF listed, for SI and SIS, key points in France to which teams should be dispatched. These included communications and railway centers, sites of main motor transport parks, enemy headquarters, airfields and repair centers and crossings over the rivers Seine and Loire. Targets were divided equally between American (*Ossex*) and British (*Brissex*) teams. An American radio station, VICTOR,** was established to communicate with *Ossex* agents in the field. SI field detachments would transmit to the armies in the field all intelligence received from *Ossex* agents and other sources via SI/London, and would relay to SI/London, for transmission to agents in the field, all requisitions for intelligence received from the army G-2's.***

The United States was early rejected as a possible source of recruits, since personnel there was felt to be too long out of touch with conditions in France. Agreement with BCRA afforded two possible areas for recruits recently escaped from France: England and North Africa. SI instituted rigorous screening procedures in both areas, and obtained a mass of promising agent material of varied background.

The training program, operated by SI and SIS jointly, went into effect in November 1943, when the *Sussex* school opened, and lasted until June 1944. The first teams were fully trained and briefed in time for their dispatch on 9 April 1944. Instruction consisted of:

* See "Liaison with Foreign Intelligence Services", above.
** See London "Communications", above.
*** See next section.

Conditioning course... 2 weeks.
Parachute course...... 1 week.
Basic course .... 6 weeks. (Or 4 weeks depending on the student's aptitude. This included W/T, map reading, close combat, and the like.)
Field problem .... 1 week.
Leave.................. 1 week.
Finishing course...... 1 to 6 weeks. (This comprised review of subjects, pending dispatch.)

When time permitted, agent and operator were each given training in the tasks of his team-mate, in case a casualty should necessitate lone operation.

The most valuable element was the field problem, similar to, but longer than, that of SO/SOE training.* Operating for one week undercover in England, teams had to acquire and transmit secret intelligence on assigned targets. Local police were warned of enemy agents in their areas, and trainees, if caught, were subjected to severe grilling. Should they break down and reveal their actual identity and activity, they were not used on *Sussex* operations. The field problem did more than could any training course to familiarize agents with clandestine procedures and to give them the all-important self-confidence required.

As the training period of the first group of agents drew to a close, they were supplied with French identity papers, provided largely by the British. They were briefed in detail on their areas of operation, generally localities where they were not too well-known, since chances of recognition and consequent insecurity would be too great.** Although the original scheme had been to drop agents "blind", *Sussex* planners concluded that prearranged contacts on the ground should be provided in the interests of safety

* See "Agent Processing, SFHQ/London", above.
** This policy contrasted with that of the SI desk in Algiers, which sent agents, whenever possible, to the areas they knew best, where they might have the most contacts. SI/Algiers produced better results, but these may be attributable to other policies and advantages, including its early start.

209

and of the morale of agents in unfamiliar territory.* To this end, a pathfinder team was dispatched, consisting of four agents, including one woman.

Pathfinders. On 8 February 1944, a British plane dropped the pathfinders "blind" into an area with which they were familiar, near Chateauroux in the Department of Indre. Through personal contacts they were to locate, for *Sussex* teams, parachuting pinpoints, temporary and permanent hideouts, emergency shelters capable of housing a radio operator and as many well-placed informants as possible. They had specific instructions to complete their mission without the assistance of existing SO/SOE French networks.

The team was partially successful in its mission despite initial and continuing difficulties. Bad weather delayed dispatch, and the dropping operation, through an error, omitted most of the supplies. Of the personal acquaintances they were to contact, the majority had moved or been arrested. This contingency, together with the fact that contact with resistance groups was precluded, made progress slow. As the Allied landing became imminent, with some sectors still unorganized, the chief of the team ignored instructions and made reception arrangements with various local Maquis.

Safe dropping points provided by French resistance groups had the disadvantage of forcing many teams to travel considerable distances to reach their working areas. With the reception details thus arranged for, however, the pathfinders were able to concentrate on locating permanent hideouts. Covering most of northern France, from the Loire to the Belgian border and from the Atlantic to Alsace-Lorraine, they succeeded, despite their late start, in arranging for re-

ception and conveyance to safe houses of many, though not all, of the *Sussex* teams.

The Teams. Between 9 April and 31 August 1944, SI/London dispatched 26 two-man teams to France.* Since these were to operate in support of D-Day operations in Normandy, activities were directed principally toward the northern sector of France with a particularly heavy concentration in the Paris area. Of the 52 agents dispatched, six were executed, including the only woman, and one was deported to Germany.**

From the moment of dispatch, *Ossex* teams lost their bipartite character and reported back to SI headquarters via VICTOR, the SI station. They sent in a total of 1,164 intelligence items of battle order material, data on V-1 sites, bombing results, locations of Luftwaffe dumps and similar intelligence.

Frequent and vigorous field exercises in communications were an integral part of the training program. Nevertheless, returning agents frequently complained of "unsatisfactory radio contact", "serious radio difficulty", and the like. • Teams PAPIER, CENDRILLON and MADELEINE complained that the base failed to answer, either by normal contact or by emergency channels. In general, agents reported that Station VICTOR was slow in responding to calls from the field, and that signal plans were often mixed. In part, this was because Station VICTOR was in the process of establishment during the operations, receiving always priority second to station CHARLES.*** In part, it was because SI/London occasionally decided, in view of its late start, to dispatch radio operators to the field before completion of training.

Many teams, however, did transmit large quantities of intelligence, and the general quality of *Ossex* reports was commended by

---

* SI/Algiers, on the contrary, preferred to drop its agents "blind" in order to avoid crossing chains and thus threatening security. The briefness of the *Sussex* operation made such a precaution less important.

---

* An equal number were dispatched by SIS.
** Six, at the completion of their missions, were re-dispatched on MARQUISE, one of the *Proust* operations. See below.
*** See London "Communications", above.

the G-2's of First Army, Third Army 12th Army Group and SHAEF. G-2, First Army is quoted as saying:

The boys (pilots of medium bombers) liked them because whenever they went to bomb a target chosen from *Sussex* intelligence there was always a big explosion; in other words, a dump was there.[*]

Certain teams were singled out by SHAEF for special commendation. They were VITRAIL dispatched to Chartres on 10 April, JEANNE to Orleans on 10 April, FOUDRE to Juvisy on 7 June and DENTELLE to Alencon on 7 July.

On D-Day, 6 June 1944, there were ten *Ossex* teams in France. Team VITRAIL was one of them, having parachuted to the Chateauroux resistance group on 10 April. This was in accordance with the final pathfinder arrangement to effect reception through already existing resistance facilities. The reception committee of six men appropriated the weapons dropped for them in return for their services, and conducted the *Ossex* agents to the temporary shelter where "Jeannette" of the pathfinder mission gave them a permanent address. The latter had been forwarded through London from another pathfinder, and had the wrong street number. After various attempts to locate the correct one, VITRAIL turned to the local organizer for an alternate safe house. The chief of the pathfinder team came to it there with the word that its outstanding equipment would be parachuted in the next moon period.

While waiting for this equipment, the team located six sub-sources: two railway stationmasters, a railway engineer, an employee of the prefecture and workers at two separate airdromes. The two agents assisted at *Sussex* drop operations in the hope that each would include VITRAIL equipment. In the meantime, because he had assisted at intervening drop operations, the operator could utilize equipment slated for other teams until his own came. When the

set finally did arrive at the end of May, it was damaged in parachuting, so that, for his entire period in the field, the W/T operator was forced to use the equipment of other SI teams.

Of the fourteen messages transmitted, G-2 stated:

The series of reports transmitted to G-2— SHAEF by OSS from Chartres in the early stages of operation *OVERLORD* were exceptionally able and useful.[*]

These included messages on enemy troop movements, airdromes, bombing targets and bombing results. Beyond this, VITRAIL more than justified its existence by the identification of the Lehr Panzer Division, on maneuvers in western France immediately prior to D-Day:

An officer at 21st Army Group is reported to have told Colonel ——— of FUSAG that a *Sussex* agent was the first to identify the movements of the Lehr Panzer Division, and that the value of this piece of information alone was sufficient to justify all the work that had been put into the *Sussex* project, even if nothing else were accomplished.[**]

He was arrested on 10 June while identifying a convoy. After eight days of torture he sent out word via the prison barber that he could hold out no longer and advised his accomplices to change residence. At his trial on 26 June he completely incriminated himself, the chaplain reported, but gave away nobody else. "You can say that I died like a Frenchman and a good Christian—Long live France".

Team JEANNE, dispatched together with VITRAIL on 10 April, sent the record *Sussex* total of 170 messages, of which 127 contained intelligence. The reporting was concise, the encipherment perfect and the transmission, according to the operators at VICTOR, the clearest.

JEANNE demonstrated great energy from the beginning in overcoming difficulties. Like VITRAIL, it had to wait one month for

---

[*] SI War Diary, Vol. 3, Bk. I, p. 217, History Files.

[*] SI War Diary, Vol. 3, Bk. I, p. 12, History Files.
[**] SI Progress Report No. 33, 15 June 1944, History File 3.

W/T equipment * and used this interval to build up an effective network. The agents were forced to find their own safe house because the one provided was too small. One of the pathfinders came to them there and briefed them on local conditions and targets.

Furthermore, the observer was incapacitated most of the time, first from a broken ankle and then from recurrent bouts of malaria. Despite these various handicaps, during five months he built from two original contacts a network of eighty informants.

The closest security was observed. At no time did the observer disclose his address to any of his sub-agents. He made contact either by designated rendezvous or via letter box. Both men made a special point to be in the company of a girl when they were on the move looking for information. They used two girls to effect liaison every morning before 10 o'clock. They took particular pains not to spend money, since that might give rise to questions, and did not go to public places such as movies or restaurants. This careful policy had excellent results. None of their informants was arrested.

JEANNE's messages were so frequent and so detailed that Station VICTOR warned the operator to curtail activities for his own safety. He ignored the warnings and turned in an impressive record. SHAEF commended JEANNE repeatedly for reports on troop movements and on general communications conditions in the Orleans area. Certain specific messages resulted in immediate action. For example, JEANNE reported traffic moving through the area, explaining that the only way to stop it was to bomb the railway bridge at Vierzon over the Loire. Two days later, B-24's completely destroyed the bridge. On another occasion, the operator reported to London the location of a munitions train being loaded between Or-

leans and Les Aubraies. Three hours later, Thunderbolts arrived and blew it up.

Team JEANNE followed enemy movements up to the liberation of Orleans, where it assisted Third Army with a detailed report on German defenses.

Team FOUDRE was parachuted in the region of Fontainebleau on 7 June. The reception committee consisted of fifteen Maquisards whose principal concern was the arms and munitions which the team had brought. Although one member permitted the team to spend the first night at his house, the committee was of no assistance in finding a safe address or means to transport the equipment to such an address if found. The team made these arrangements on its own. The address that London had provided was good, and, after contact was established, the observer reported that the "mission went off without a hitch".

FOUDRE followed the routine procedure with respect to dispatch and field operations. At the same time it demonstrated that a team can fill requests for tactical intelligence in time for appropriate action. Generally, *Sussex* agents gathered intelligence on their own initiative; however, in some cases, specific items would be requested through an SI field detachment by the army G-2 to which it was attached. Such a request would be relayed via headquarters in London to those *Sussex* teams in the best position to answer it. On 10 August 1944, a G-2 representative requested information on a factory behind the German lines at Le Bouchet, suspected of producing chemical warfare material. Coordinates and installation details were required to render a possible air attack reasonably accurate. FOUDRE supplied them.

Team DENTELLE was parachuted to Alencon on 7 July after two abortive attempts on the nights of 6 and 8 June when the ground signals did not appear. On this occasion the reception committee marked the field backwards in an attempt to avoid mishaps which had occurred in previous

---

* The identical experience of VITRAIL and JEANNE, both dispatched early in the *Sussex* operation indicates that W/T delay was one of the initial errors attributable to lack of experience.

parachute operations when the pilot came in from the wrong direction. This time the pilot followed the markings correctly, and the observer sustained an injury.

Despite overshooting the mark, DENTELLE established contact with the reception committee. The address that London had provided proved false, and the team could not obtain an alternate because the electric power in the area was too weak to establish effective radio contact more than once or twice, and no safe power source could be found for recharging the batteries. In desperation, the operator made contact with a British major who was able to conduct him to a Maquis south of Alencon, which provided the necessary batteries and security to send messages. The operator, with Maquis assistance, set up shop in a nearby farm. No sooner had he done this, than 150 Germans with automotive equipment moved in, and, since his cover was that of a harvest worker, he had to curtail his activities and remain until the Germans left. He subsequently moved out with the Maquis. The observer had no difficulties in maintaining his cover, presenting himself as a Parisian on a rest cure and a black market operator.

DENTELLE was in the field a little over a month when it was overrun by the Allied armies. Due to the brevity of the operation, only eleven intelligence messages were sent, but these were of such high quality that they merited SHAEF commendation, particularly reports on installations and tank movements in the Alencon area.

The procedural pattern for all the *Sussex* teams was similar. In order to cover, the volume of items on which SHAEF desired information, the agents needed assistance in establishing themselves speedily. This had been one of the assigned tasks of the pathfinders and this, because of the time element, the latter had often been unable to effect, with the result that agents had to rely on resistance groups or on themselves.

The success of a team depended upon its ability to build an effective informant organization. For this reason, teams VITRAIL and JEANNE were outstandingly successful. JEANNE had eighty sub-agents for the bulk of the five months that it was in the field. Although VITRAIL had only six informants, these were sufficiently competent to provide good results.

Difficulties were generally occasioned by injuries sustained on landing or by a dispatching error which resulted in dropping agents at a field where no reception was arranged. Despite such accidents, the occasional communications failures and the late start of the project, intelligence produced warranted the following over-all estimate by G-2, SHAEF:

The results obtained in the reports from the *Sussex* operation have been very helpful. Not only was the information useful, but compared with the great volume of CX reports * received the level of accuracy has been gratifyingly high. The manner in which the operation has been carried out reflects the obviously excellent training which the intelligence teams had been given.**

Proust

The *Proust* project served as an auxiliary to Sussex to build up a reserve pool of agents for any unforeseen exigencies of the post D-Day period. Some fifty agents (including six returned from *Sussex*) were dispatched on missions varying widely in nature. With the exception of the VARLIN team, which had gone to France in January 1944, *Proust* was the only independent SI/London project for agent infiltration into France. The joint SI/SIS *Sussex* program was already in preparation, and, as a result, *Proust* had considerable difficulty in obtaining priorities for personnel, training, equipment and transportation. Furthermore, in May and June many of the personnel were transferred

---

* SIS reports.
** SI War Diary, Vol. 3, Bk. I, p. 14, Memo 27 July 1944, from Brig. Gen. J. T. Betts, GSC, D/AC of S, G-2, SHAEF.

to *Sussex* and to the newly formed field detachments with the armies.*

French BCRA participation in *Proust* included the furnishing of recruits to be trained as agents and the assignment of French officers to instruct and to act as liaison between the French students and the American supervisors. BCRA, however, did not supply its highest calibre agents and, on certain occasions, withheld agents who had already been recruited for *Proust* by OSS/Algiers. As with *Sussex*, returning agents frequently complained of communications difficulties.**

Teams began leaving on missions to France early in June. Dispatch was effected by parachute, with the exception of two teams transported by OSS/Maritime Unit PT boat to the Morlaix and Ploermel areas. The agents carried out low priority tasks. For example, when MONKEY was activated at the request of Third Army and FUSAG, it was stated specifically that the relatively low priority of the mission did not merit the use of "superior, highly-trained *Sussex* men", hence *Proust* agents would do.

MIDIRON was a typical *Proust* operation. It comprised eight one-man teams dispatched to act as intelligence liaison with Maquis groups and to build up existing intelligence networks. These French sources supplied material mainly of a tactical nature to be used in support of the ground troops. MIDIRON personnel transmitted to station VICTOR a total of 151 messages, of which more than one hundred came from one agent, "Noir". Intelligence included information for Third Army on German troop movements during the retreat toward the Belfort Gap, reports for distribution to the Seventh and Ninth Armies and coverage of FFI and FTP military and political activities.

"Grenier" was an accomplished W/T operator, who achieved excellent results. He was in the field for a period of forty days, and during that time his contact with VICTOR

* See next section.
** See above.

was uninterrupted. He sent in detailed reports on his area: bridge locations, troop movements, strength of armament, identifications, convoys, rail and road movements and bombing results. For a two-week period, he repeatedly requested bombardment of the area because of heavy troop movements. As a result, the area was twice attacked, with German casualties as high as 2,000 dead and heavy destruction of materiel.

Agent "Poil", upon returning, made several criticisms regarding his equipment. For example, a Canadian captain of his acquaintance in the field commented that he was wearing a "spy shirt". (Shirts supplied by SI/London had collars with long tips, whereas French shirt collars had short tips.) Similarly suspect were his razor blades because they had no markings at all, his shorts because they were of a type never seen in France and his cigarettes because they were of a pre-war make on which manufacture had ceased. "Poil" further commented that the agents should receive not only appropriate equipment, but also adequate briefing on the customs of the country; e.g., the French smoker kept his cigarette butts in a bag or in his pockets for use in making new cigarettes; persons bicycling through French towns were required to have both hands on the handlebars, etc. Despite these difficulties, "Poil" achieved a substantial measure of success. He accomplished several reconnaissance missions of which the most important resulted in the machine-gunning by Allied aircraft of 5,000 Germans whose presence in the area he had reported.

Other *Proust* teams performed similar odd jobs. MARCEL, for instance, consisted of three American officers, whose W/T operators never arrived (when their plane missed pinpoint). The three officers found a Maquis, set up a base, and directed harassing activities. Intelligence gathered was sent by line-crossers to Seventh Army forces. When the team was overrun, it was able to provide a complete picture of German strength in the Epinal area four days before that city was taken. MONKEY and GIRAFFE, dispatched by PT boat to the Brittany area at the request of Third Army and FUSAG, collected tactical intelligence in preparation for the Normandy landings. MARQUISE, which included six *Sussex* agents who had completed their missions, comprised six two-man teams dispatched to eastern France with concentration in the Vosges area. MARQUISE sent little intelligence to London, using instead sub-agent couriers to the field detachments with the armies.

Proust had served as a source of agents for intelligence demands which might arise after D-Day in Normandy and which could not be covered by *Sussex* teams. Various such exigencies appeared and were covered by *Proust* agents, often with excellent results. Casualties were low: out of some fifty dispatched, only one operative was killed. Trainees still at the *Proust* school at the end of August were sent either to the new OSS continental base at Paris or to the field detachments.

7. Army Detachments in North France

As plans for the Normandy invasion developed, it became apparent that some mechanism was needed to insure the full benefit of resistance support for the advancing Allied armies. Intelligence from SI teams had to be disseminated quickly. CE items had to be forwarded immediately to those most directly concerned. At the same time, opportunities for new operations had to be promptly and expertly exploited.

The most effective way of insuring full utilization of OSS support obviously lay in placing OSS representatives with the armies and army groups themselves. Such personnel could then form an effective link between the field's requirements and the London base, where the various supporting activities behind enemy lines were controlled and serviced. Accordingly, a series of arrangements was worked out early in 1944 for the attachment of separate SO, SI and X-2 units to the invading forces.

SO was the first OSS branch to request authorization for special detachments to operate with the armies.

Permission was sought as early as September 1943, and SHAEF approval obtained in January 1944, authorizing the attachment of "Special Force Detachments" (of SFHQ) to G-3 of each of the armies and army groups operating out of ETO. The specified duties of these special units, which became generally known as "SF Detachments", were: (1) To provide a channel for advising the armies and army groups as to the potentialities of resistance; (2) to relay to London specific requests for intelligence or resistance aid; (3) to aid in picking up overrun agents or members of resistance organizations; (4) to provide the armies and army groups with intelligence obtained through resistance sources.

On the basis of this directive, three SF Detachments were organized: SF Det #10 for the First Army, SF Det #11 for the Third Army, and SF Det #12 for the 12th Army Group. To these three, SF Det #13 was afterwards added for the Ninth Army, which did not become active until late in 1944.

Meanwhile, SI had also obtained approval for the attachment of special units to the various armies and army groups. On the theory that men with experience in handling espionage agents would be better equipped to interpret, evaluate and analyze intelligence from undercover sources, plans were first laid for SI Field Detachments in the summer of 1943.

On 10 February 1944 ETOUSA approved the project. SI Detachments were authorized to operate under G-2 of the First and Third Armies. The specified duties of these detachments were to disseminate *Sussex* * material, to forward intelligence targets named by the local G-2's, to recover agents, to recruit agent prospects, and to serve as

* See previous section.

215

liaison where needed. Additional SI Detachments were later authorized to work with the First Allied Airborne and Ninth Armies in the same capacity. A similar SI Detachment was activated in May to operate under 21st Army Group, but early in August, after less than two weeks on the Continent, was liquidated. Difficulties of operating an independent U. S. secret intelligence unit entirely surrounded by a British army proved insuperable.

Arrangements in the meantime had been worked out for X-2 representation, when in February 1944 SHAEF authorized the attachment of "Special Counter-Intelligence (SCI) Units" to the various armies and army groups. These SCI units were to operate under SHAEF's responsibility and control. They were instructed "to distribute and interpret CE information received from London and advise as to use", and were also to serve as the sole channel for handling such material between the various forces in the field.*

First Army

First elements of SF Detachment #10 reached the Continent on D-plus-4. Developments quickly proved that the Detachment could offer more immediate assistance to forces in the field than that originally contemplated through liaison between armies and resistance via London.

It was apparent that the urgency of battle conditions ruled out the delays involved in coordinating FFI support through W/T to London, and Detachment members were soon in direct personal contact with the Maquis. The uses of such resistance help also exanded rapidly, as the advantages of Maquis aid, in mopping up, in patrolling lines of communications and in guarding exposed sectors, became obvious.

The most significant discovery was the enormous importance of French resistance as a source of accurate tactical intelligence.

---

* The activities of the SCI units in France and of X-2/Paris are covered in "X-2/France", below.

The Maquis role in this respect had originally been contemplated as incidental, but it proved to be a major contribution. Tapping this intelligence was one of the functions which most occupied the First Army SF Detachment. It culminated in the Detachment's development, together with SFHQ/London, of the *Helmsman* plan. Under this plan, overrun resistance agents were given SF Detachment briefing on tactical intelligence targets, then flown over to the U.K., whence they were parachuted back into France at points about fifty miles behind the enemy lines. These agents then had the job of recruiting sub-agents, briefing them on required tactical intelligence, and sending them back to the Allied lines with what information they could pick up along the way.

One such agent, parachuted into the Avranches region, succeeded in recruiting and sending back 28 sub-agents just before the St. Lo break-through, with excellent coverage of German artillery placements, tank units, troop dispositions and the condition of strategic bridges.

Meanwhile, the Detachment continued its more orthodox role of liaison between First Army and supporting FFI units. Its first mission after landing was to relay a First Army request to the Maquis for more phone-wire slashing behind enemy lines. The objective was to force German units to use radio, which would enable easier signal interception.

Later, the Detachment arranged with the FFI for a series of actions designed to paralyze enemy rail transport in certain designated areas behind the beachhead. As a result, German reserves, stationed as close as Brittany, arrived to reinforce the enemy units in Normandy only after days of marching on foot. Similarly, when the First Army moved into high gear after the capture of St. Lo, the Detachment arranged for pressure-easing attacks by the FFI on Nazi units operating west of the Avranches-Domfort line.

Meanwhile, the SI First Army Detachment had also moved into action. From the start, however, its activities were hampered by two factors. First, the Detachment arrived on the Continent in only piecemeal fashion, its full complement not landing until 23 June, almost two weeks after the arrival of a harassed and overworked advance unit. Secondly, the Detachment was, from the start, under a shrewd but unsympathetic G-2, who objected to such an irregular unit outside the normal framework of military command.

Without the support of the G-2, the First Army Detachment's position deteriorated rapidly, dependent as it was for equipment, personnel movements and authorization for all activities. Finally, on 3 August, the Detachment was removed to the 12th Army Group level, on the grounds that it did nothing which could not be done equally well by CIC or some other integral part of the Army.

During its abbreviated career, the First Army Detachment handled some 330 *Sussex* messages, plus 80 OSS messages from other sources. However, G-2 considered only 25 items satisfactory for its daily intelligence summary. The Detachment's one significant operational achievement was an ably executed terrain study of the Coutances area just before the St. Lo break-through.

Third Army

SF Detachment #11—the SO field unit attached to Third Army—arrived in France on 7 July, but became operational only on 1 August along with the rest of the Army. Most of the Detachment's day-to-day activities followed a pattern similar to that of First Army. In addition, however, the Detachment played an important role in guarding Third Army's southern and western flank during its sweep through France.

When Third Army turned eastward beyond Avranches, the Detachment was requested to organize resistance forces into a screen to protect the right flank from enemy harassing action. By 26 August, 3,400 FFI men were disposed on the Merzillac-Nantes-

Angers line. Tightly coordinated radio contact with London enabled frequent parachute drops of arms and ammunition to these irregular units. After the flank was extended to embrace Tours, 2,500 men were added to the screen. Later, units totalling 7,000 more Maquisards took their place when the line had been stretched to Bourges. In its final form, this flank guard totalled eighteen different resistance groups, including 25,000 FFI, and extended all the way to Chatillon. While it is questionable whether the enemy at this point could have effectively smashed the attack, there is little doubt that Third Army's remarkable speed was considerably assisted by its ability to ignore the right flank.

Resistance units working with the Third Army Detachment offered, as elsewhere, a valuable source of intelligence. For example, on 8 September the Detachment relayed one report from an agent at Baccarat which revealed 200 German tanks unloading there. The report led directly to a 2nd French Armored Division action which knocked out 65 of the tanks and apparently upset German plans for a counterattack.

The SI Third Army Detachment arrived in France on 3 July, and, like its SF counterpart, became operational along with the rest of the Army on 1 August. Unlike the SI First Army Detachment, relations with G-2 proved excellent from the start. The Detachment's only early trouble was the failure of the original plan of activity, since, by the time of its activation, the *Sussex* agents had mostly been either overrun or were offering information of little use to Third Army. At first, Detachment personnel sought out military requests for intelligence targets, and worked up elaborate situation maps for quick presentation of items.

Soon, however, the Detachment found itself making valuable and uncontemplated contributions on short-range tactical intelligence. Results from the *Sussex* teams had been disappointing. Recruiting for further long-range strategic missions proved unfeasible, due to lack of time for preparation and to lack of interest on the part of Third Army. But combat intelligence remained a vital and unprovided necessity. The SI unit turned to launching numerous infiltrations immediately behind the German lines with quickly recruited and untrained native agents. The latter would work their way back to the SI Detachment with whatever information they could gather.

More than one hundred such missions, all hastily improvised, gave results where carefully laid plans requiring long preparations had proved useless. For example, a mission south of the Loire supplied battle order information which encouraged Third Army to depend on FFI protection (coordinated by the Third Army SF Detachment). A mission to Metz in early September made possible the destruction of a long-range gun which was shelling Third Army Headquarters at Nancy. Another Metz team prevented the destruction of important bridges by quick relay of information on the unexpected weakness of their guard. A mission to Dienze supplied information which enabled the Air Force to blow up the dam there and further hinder the German retreat.

The Detachment grew from 23 persons in July to 80 by the end of September. Personnel, many of whom were young French officers experienced in intelligence and familiar with the terrain, operated not only at army level, but in teams at corps and division as well. When OSS/London sought to withdraw the unit, following the First Army Detachment's failure, Third Army Headquarters approved its Detachment's request to remain.

Ninth Army

Both the SF and SI Detachments were activated along with Ninth Army in Brittany on 5 September. The French campaign was almost over and little was accomplished at that time. SF Detachment #13 worked with French resistance on the German coastal pockets during September. After

several weeks in Rennes, the SI Ninth Army Detachment moved with the rest of the Army to Arlon, Belgium. It disseminated occasional intelligence messages from London, but made no infiltrations during the French campaign.

12th Army Group

SF Detachment #12 was originally activated in June 1944 mainly to carry on staff functions in support of the more operational units working directly with the armies and resistance. After the St. Lo break-through, however, there were so many intelligence needs to be filled that th Detachment concentrated on a more operational role.

Agents were dispatched to cover areas behind enemy lines, where they obtained tactical intelligence. Close contact with the FFI was also maintained, and the Detachment served to tone down French resistance enthusiasm for rash projects, so that personnel could be used with least possible waste. The SF Detachment furthermore, developed into the chief funnel for de-processing overrun SO/SOE agents.

SI's 12th Army Group Detachment resulted from the unexpected removal of its First Army Detachment.* After reassembling at army group level, the Detachment gradually reorganized its activities. Among other items, it originated a photographic project, covering strategic installations along the northern French coast.**

The Detachment continued to carry out a small role in procuring tactical intelligence, such as an infiltration mission into the Mortain pocket, using gendarmes on bicycles to cover the Alencon district. But it was mainly occupied in headquarters intelligence functions. Much agent de-briefing work was carried on as the Allies advanced, and thirty to forty interrogations were carried out weekly. During August the unit

---

* See above.
** This later developed into the Intelligence Photographic Documentation Project. See Washington section on Field Photographic.

also disseminated some 450 processed reports, forwarded from OSS/London, 57 of which were used in the 12th Army Group, G-2 Intelligence Summary.

Typical of the headquarters work done by the 12th Army Group Detachment during the liberation of France was its rush procurement, for the first Allied units entering Paris, of an over-all report from OSS/London, giving all available information on the location and stocks of enemy depots in the Paris area.

———————

During the four-odd months of the French campaign, OSS/ETO had learned the techniques * for field detachments attached to army headquarters. The job was carried out as originally planned: Intelligence from London was disseminated to the local headquarters and requests forwarded; overrun agents and Maquisards were interrogated; Maquis elements were coordinated to serve army needs, in some cases with unexpected success (e.g., the defense of the Third Army right flank along the Loire).

But the new task which had been discovered by both SF and SI detachments was that of sending civilian agents across the lines for tactical intelligence. While regimental S-2's could rely for some reports upon patrols carried out by U. S. soldiers, OSS could recruit local civilians, overrun agents and resistance personnel for penetration a few miles behind the lines. Recruits could either walk through the lines or be parachuted from planes based in England or France. Once they arrived, they could recruit sub-agents, assign targets for observation and send them back through the lines to report their information to the local OSS unit. Such intelligence complemented that of army patrols and in many cases was of considerable use (e.g., the report of 200 German tanks at Baccarat).

———————

* Techniques which were earlier developed by the Fifth Army Detachment (see "Italy", above), and later perfected by the Seventh Army Detachment (see that section, below).

By the end of the campaign it had become obvious that a combination of the various branches in the field would save communications, manpower, supplies and facilities, provide centralized administration and cut down on overlapping activities. When, on 1 October, the SFHQ units, lacking resistance contacts in Germany, were broken up, SO and SI personnel merged, together with the various supporting services, to form OSS Field Detachments under the direction of OSS/Paris.* It was now clear that the greatest contribution to the Army advance could be made by infiltration of civilian agents behind the lines, and the new units turned to the difficult task of finding German-speaking recruits.**

8. Resistance Aid to Overlord

A total of 523 American officers, enlisted men and civilians of the SO and OG Branches of OSS worked behind the enemy lines in France during 1944. Of these, 85 were SO agents and radio operators in F-, DF- and RF-Section circuits, 83 were *Jedburghs,* and 355 made up the 22 sections into which the Operational Groups were divided for work in France.

The casualties among these three groups are shown on page 220.

Throughout France, before and after D-Day, SFHQ supplied, directed and communicated with the Maquis in the largest resistance uprising in history. F-, DF- and RF-Section circuits had, during the year preceding D-Day, built up the resistance movement from London headquarters. Just after D-Day, an additional 276 operatives were formed as tripartite *Jedburgh* teams to coordinate the resistance activities in London with the moves of the advancing Allied armies, and to send in tactical intelligence gathered by the Maquis for army use. Large quantities of supplies were dropped by B-24 and B-17 squadrons detailed to SFHQ.

* The X-2 units, performing highly specialized duties, remained autonomous. See "X-2/France", below.
** See "West Front", below.

	Killed or Died of Wounds		Missing-in Action or Taken Prisoner		Wounded or Injured	
	Number	Per-cent of Total	Number	Per-cent of Total	Number	Per-cent of Total
SO	3	3.5	10	11.8	5	5.9
Jedburgh	5	6.0	3	3.6	6	7.2
OG	10	2.8	4	1.1	40	11.2
TOTAL	18	3.4	17	3.3	51	9.8*

* No over-all figure for OSS casualties behind enemy lines has been prepared. However, the ten percent figure of SO/France would not be far from average. SI/North France ran approximately seven percent casualties and SI/Germany about five percent. SI/Austria suffered nearly fifty percent but with only a small number of teams. In general, casualties were high on the first infiltrations of 1943 when the Allies were not so clearly winning the war and when OSS had little or no experience, and low in the subsequent missions, progressing to almost complete safety as VE-Day approached. In assessing this tentative ten percent figure it may be noted that, of the total killed, wounded, captured and MIA, the number killed (and tortured) represented a higher percentage than those of normal combat. Few agents became prisoners of war.

Special Force Detachments were sent in with the armies, for liaison with SFHQ representatives behind enemy lines, and to handle overrun agents and Maquis, while SAS and Operational Groups led bodies of FFI in sabotage, combat and counter-scorch operations.

Resistance, as organized for the Battle of France, represented a tremendous striking force—open and covert—in support of the Allied armies. Of inestimable assistance to U. S. and British troops, their civilian army was a source of constant fear to the Germans, who refused on many occasions to surrender to FFI troops and often avoided action altogether in areas where Maquis had been sighted. Through controlled sabotage, ambush and irregular combat, resistance groups impeded the movement of German reinforcements toward the original Normandy beachhead and guarded the flanks of the American armies driving to the Seine in the north and to the Vosges from the south. They harassed the enemy behind his lines, destroying his transport and communication lines and diverting whole divisions from the front. They supplied continuous tactical and strategic intelligence on the enemy situation, prevented German demolition of vital installations, and assisted in isolating and mopping up enemy troops by-passed by the Allied advance.

The full strength of the French resistance, as it had been built up by SO and SOE, was called into action by SHAEF on D-Day. The destruction of 800 strategic targets, ordered by SHAEF, was, with few exceptions, accomplished within one week. Thirty-five strategic telecommunication centers were attacked successfully in France on the eve of the invasion, and thirty industrial sabotage operations in both France and Belgium carried out. SFHQ-organized resistance bands procured plans of enemy coastal defenses and U-boat pens at St. Nazaire and contained important enemy pockets on the Atlantic coast at Lorient, St. Nazaire, La Rochelle, Royan and Pointe de Grave. Unassisted by any of the regular Allied troops, FFI liberated all of France south of the Loire and west of the Rhone, forcing the surrender of 20,000 Germans unable to escape. The underground in Belgium and Holland preserved the ports of Antwerp and Rotterdam for Allied use.

Through continued controlled sabotage of bridges, waterways, rail and communication lines, ambushing of enemy troop trains, isolated garrisons, etc., and actual engagement of troops, large sections of German military manpower and materiel were delayed or diverted from opposing the Allied advance across France toward Germany.*

* "Twenty-first Army Group have stated that, in their opinion, the over-all action of French Resistance has resulted in an *average* delay of 48 hours being imposed on movement of German formations to the bridgehead area." (From report on "French resistance during the first ten days of the operations in Normandy" in History File 49.)

The SS "Das Reich" Panzer Division was first reported (by OSS/Algiers) moving north from the Bordeaux region on 8 June. SFHQ directed resistance groups along the route to harass it. The Division was still at Dordogne on 20 July. Other divisions were similarly delayed and decimated. It was several weeks before any sizable amount of artillery or armored equipment could be brought up to Normandy. The result of this action by resistance groups in France was summed up by an official SHAEF communique, which credited

French Resistance with the remarkable feat of preventing Rommel's regroupment of forces for a full four weeks after D-Day.*

After the Third Army break-through at Avranches, 7,000 Maquis, armed with bazookas, machine guns, rifles and mortars, deployed along the banks of the Loire River and protected the northern peninsula route to Brest, particularly the Morlaix Viaduct. When the Army turned eastward, these same forces, at the command of General Patton, accomplished the mopping up of by-passed Germans, including the rounding-up and turning over of prisoners. South of the Loire, patriotic groups protected the exposed right flank of Third Army in its advance on Paris.

At least 5,000 enemy troops were deployed to disperse resistance at Correze during

---

* SO War Diary, Vol. 5, Bk. II, p. 88.

June. Between 15 July and 13 August, 11,-000 Germans (including 2,000 artillery and 400 glider troops) engaged in the heavy attack against the Vercors plateau, after a mass Allied daylight supply drop to that strong open resistance center was carried out.

The cutting of all field telephone lines, in fulfillment of General Bradley's order, forced the Germans to use radio. Through this means, their messages were intercepted, their codes broken and their movements revealed.

Strategic and combat intelligence, not accessible to regular army patrols, was provided by resistance members from incidental observation or as a result of line-infiltration missions under the guidance of SF and SI Detachments. Reports of enemy artillery, tank or troop dispositions coming from Maquis agents and observers resulted in Allied bombing which served, among other things, to stem a projected German attack at Baccarat, and to hamper their retreat at Dienze.

Combined resistance in France, under Special Forces direction, accomplished the following reported results from sabotage and open fighting with the Germans:

	June	July	Aug.
Rail cuts	109	691	85
Telecommunications cuts	35	77	28
Road and waterway cuts	10	41	24
Industrial sabotage	7	25	12
Locomotives destroyed	50	269	3
Convoys attacked	2	8	14
German aircraft shot down	2	5	..

ALLIED EXPEDITIONARY FORCE

Office of the Supreme Commander.

31 May 1945.

Before the combined staff of Special Force Headquarters disperses I wish to express my appreciation of its high achievements.

Since I assumed the Supreme Command in January, 1944, until the present day its work has been marked by patient and farsighted planning, flexible adaptation to the operational requirements of Supreme Headquarters, and efficient executive action during operations. In no previous war, and in no other theatre during this war, have resistance forces been so closely harnessed to the main military effort.

While no final assessment of the operational value of resistance action has yet been completed, I consider that the disruption of enemy rail communications, the harassing of German road moves and the continual and increasing strain placed on the German war economy and internal security services throughout occupied Europe by the organized forces of resistance, played a very considerable part in our complete and final victory. In DENMARK and NORWAY the commanders concerned have already reported on the great help which they have received from resistance forces in maintaining law and order during the early stages of liberation.

The combination of certain sections of your two organizations . . . was the means by which these resistance forces were so ably organized, supplied and directed. Particular credit must be due to those responsible for communications with occupied territory. I am also aware of the care with which each individual country was studied and organized, and of the excellent work carried out in training, documenting, briefing and dispatching agents. The supply to agents and resistance groups in the field, moreover, could only have reached such proportions during the summer of 1944 through outstanding efficiency on the part of the supply and air liaison staffs. Finally, I must express my great admiration for the brave and often spectacular exploits of the agents and special groups under control of Special Force Headquarters.

I would be grateful if you would convey, as a personal message, my thanks to everyone at Special Force Headquarters for their work. And through you I would like to express my gratitude to the two parent organisations, without whose cooperation and help the great success of Special Force Headquarters could not have been achieved.

Sincerely,

/s/ DWIGHT D. EISENHOWER.

Director OSS, UK Base,
ETOUSA.

E. OPERATION ANVIL

1. SI/Algiers Chains

With the official recognition of OSS Experimental Detachment, G-3 (Prov.), AFHQ, on 4 February 1943,* the situation with regard to intelligence work from the Algiers base became at once more critical and more clear. The establishment of an SI desk for the penetration of France from Algiers was one of the earliest results of the JCS-approved North African Mission. On 23 February, the newly-appointed desk head was directed to lay plans for an intelligence program to cover all of that region which before November 1942 had been "Vichy France".** Specifically, he was charged with recruiting, training and dispatching agents for new radio-intelligence networks to transmit all possible information of interest to the planners of a possible Allied invasion of South France.

During 1942, no over-all plan had been instituted for gathering and evaluating intelligence from France. The executive director of OSS/Algiers, appointed in January 1943 to supervise all branches, had depended for intelligence largely on "Tommy". The trial-and-error efforts leading to the first OSS secret radio stations for intelligence in enemy territory have already been described.*** These were remarkable not only for the intelligence produced, which was considerable, but for the mere fact that chains of agents were established and radio contact made with Algiers in a period when lack of transport, personnel and supply made all plans limited and haphazard in the extreme.

* See "Algiers Base", above.
** North France was covered by SI/London. See that section, above.
*** See sub-section on Corsica in "West Mediterranean Islands" and "Early Infiltrations", above.

"Tommy's" activities opened underground channels of penetration in France and laid part of the groundwork for intelligence operations of a similar nature. Theoretically, "Tommy's" chains should have served as wedges for the entry of SI into South France. Actually, in view of their insecurity, it was decided to keep the new chains as separate and distinct as possible from those already associated with OSS.

Difficulties, encountered from the start by SI/France, continued throughout the spring and summer of 1943 to hamper their plans. Large obstacles were its lack of submarines and planes, and its dependence on the French and British for documents. In addition its experience was limited. The ways and means of conducting intelligence operations, known only through the unsatisfactory medium of the classroom, had to be learned gradually by the SI/France staff through its own efforts and with considerable assistance from other sources.

"Tommy's" OSS stations PEARL HARBOR (Corsica) and MEXICO (France) automatically became the responsibility of the new desk, but there was relatively little interference from SI/Algiers with what these networks did, except in major questions of policy affecting intelligence for AFHQ as a whole. For instance, OSS continued to cooperate with French SR in the operation of PEARL HARBOR until disagreement as to the treatment of an agent who had been "burnt" prompted SI/France to take over control.

Independent as SI/France may have wished to remain, it had repeatedly to rely at first on the professional experience of the British and French services, and in times of emergency, on "Tommy's" stations. From working PEARL HARBOR with SR officers, SI received important lessons in the handling and instruction of agents. It learned, for one thing, the method of asking, via pre-arranged secret code, for specific details without revealing to the agent the complete nature of the information desired. In this way, the broad scope of AFHQ's plans could be kept secure even if the agent were captured and tortured.

OSS station MEXICO was used by a French SI agent when he forgot his signal plan and had no other means of contacting Algiers. DARTMOUTH, another of "Tommy's" stations, was approached in 1944 by several SI agent-operator teams when their radio sets were damaged by parachute drop, or when no other means of rapid communication existed. The results of these contacts were catastrophic: agent and station were both blown in the case of MEXICO; at DARTMOUTH, the Gestapo established secret control and subsequently arrested agents of three SI chains. These incidents served as bitter confirmation of the principle that intelligence chains should overlap as little as possible, if ever.

RELATIONS WITH THE FRENCH

Service de Renseignement (SR), the intelligence section of the French professional secret service (Deuxieme Bureau) had established itself in Algiers shortly after the North African landings. SR personnel had escaped from metropolitan France where they had been in close touch with G-2 and OSS officials at Vichy. This fact, plus their long-term experience in secret operations against the German Wehrmacht, made SR extremely valuable as a potential OSS ally. Friendly relations, established by Donovan with the SR representative in Washington during the *TORCH* preparations, and contacts with the chief of SR in Algiers in connection with the PEARL HARBOR station in Corsica, solidified the association between the organizations. In all but the matter of recruiting agents, which became a question for the Army to settle, the utmost cooperation was given OSS/Algiers by

SR officers at a time when the American organization had little to offer in return. It was probably realized by SR even then, however, that cooperation with the American intelligence service would be the best way to reestablish itself following the disorganization at the time of the French Army's collapse in 1940. This contact was maintained, in spite of minor differences, even after General de Gaulle set up his own intelligence organization.

The arrival of de Gaulle's BCRA in North Africa in May 1943 gave rise to a dilemma as to which faction OSS should deal with. De Gaulle demanded equal status with the Americans for operations in France, as provided for in London. SI/Algiers insisted, because of fear of political involvement and lack of security in the de Gaulle organization, on independent operations. In deciding to continue its well-established relations with SR, OSS benefited from the latter's superior operational experience. On the other hand, the decision alienated the rapidly rising BCRA faction; * and, when de Gaulle finally replaced Giraud as head of the Army, the release of Frenchmen to the Americans was ended. However, the adverse effect the whole feud had on agent morale and on relations among members of the SI/France staff was of more moment than the halt put to the recruiting of Frenchmen.

Aside from the disadvantages imposed by the late entrance of OSS into the Theater in relation to competing services of other countries, there were the circuitous conditions of the Eisenhower-Giraud agreement. This was an understanding, reached in January 1943, to clarify the status of Frenchmen working for OSS. Under its terms all French nationals of draft age

---

* This BCRA-SR breach was not healed until October 1943 when the rival intelligence systems were merged under a single head. A second decree on 19 November, following the resignation of the original chief, fixed the merger under the major influence of de Gaulle.

working for the Americans had first to be inducted into the French Army, if not already mobilized, and then detached by special permission for service with OSS. Few Frenchmen with the necessary qualifications for intelligence work—widespread contacts, recent residence in France, etc.—were likely to be released by the French under this plan. Radio operators were in constant demand by the French signal corps, and most of those allowed to work for OSS had therefore to be under draft age.

The January 1943 agreement did have its more fortunate aspects, however. It established a clearly defined official relationship between OSS and the French agents working for it. The security represented by official French recognition of U. S.-employed agents, following their release, made it possible for OSS to count on the loyalty of its French agents even at the height of the tension represented by the SR-BCRA confusion and during the most secret days preceding the invasion.

RELATIONS WITH THE BRITISH

The groundwork for good relations between OSS/Algiers and the British had been laid early and well, particularly with SOE, which had established the *Massingham* mission in North Africa for extensive operations into France. SOE had represented the British in the OSS-State Department preparations for *TORCH*. Its officers had worked closely with OSS in the Tunisian campaign, as well as in the establishment of a parachute training school at SOE's North African Headquarters. "Tommy's" setting up for SOE of a secret radio station in France and reestablishment of its radio connections after the station was destroyed by the Gestapo helped to assure a continuation of OSS/SOE cooperation during the operational phases of the French/SI Desk.

The head of SOE's *Massingham* detachment in Algiers, who had himself parachuted into France on secret missions, freely advised OSS intelligence officers on training and infiltration procedures. In this way OSS men with theoretical knowledge only were given the benefit of hard-won practical experience. The desire to cooperate with OSS displayed by leaders of SOE's North African detachment was extended to include equipment as well as ideas. When transport facilities and documents could not be obtained from American sources, *Massingham* arranged with London for Halifax bombers to parachute OSS intelligence agents into France, and gave access to false papers—identity cards, ration coupons, travel papers, etc.—to complete cover stories. These latter services, when discovered by SIS, as usual led to considerable disagreement and discussion, both as to SIS/SOE relations and as to the part OSS would be allowed to play in France.

It was in June 1943, on the occasion of French/SI's preparation of its first parachute operation, that SIS became involved in OSS plans for the penetration of France. Britain's senior intelligence service was displeased with SOE cooperation with OSS on two counts. SOE, it maintained, had overstepped authority in offering facilities for an American SI mission without clearing operations with SIS. It was equally displeased to learn that OSS planned independent intelligence operations in France side by side with its own carefully built-up networks. It expressed, in later discussions, fear (1) that inexperienced OSS agents would "burn" British agents, since it was difficult for agents working in the same area not to know each other, and (2) that OSS would affect the recruiting market unfavorably by paying agents more than did the British.

On 27 July 1943, Donovan met with Sir Stuart Menzies, Chief of SIS, to discuss the problems raised by the SIS-OSS misunderstandings. In a confirming letter to Menzies the next day, Donovan wrote:

. . . It was agreed that in the future, as far as SI activities in North Africa directed toward France are concerned, they will be fully discussed between the chief representatives of the two organizations in North Africa and forwarded in the form of recommended plans to London, where, if they meet with the joint approval of SIS and OSS headquarters, arrangements will be made for their implementation. . . . This arrangement shall in no sense be interpreted as impairing the complete independence of either of the services concerned, but is intended to achieve what at this time seems a necessary coordination, in order to avoid possible confusion or duplication . . .*

Despite the "complete independence" proviso, SI/France construed the agreement as an attempt by the British to place OSS operations under their control. At that time, however, and until October when OSS had its own planes, it did little more than recognize an existing state of affairs. For, as the Executive Officer of Experimental Detachment, G-3, (Prov.) admitted in a memo on 2 August 1943,

. . . so long as the British control the only feasible means of transport into France from North Africa they control our operations there.**

At the suggestion of G-3, AFHQ, an attempt was made to circumvent the reference of plans to a joint OSS/SIS committee which would have crippled OSS operations considerably. For the next mission in September, SI simply requested air lift for a certain date from SIS/Algiers. SIS complied, and no attempt was made in this or later operations to enforce the Donovan-Menzies agreement. In the words of the Chief of the French/SI Desk:

We were never able to ascertain whether this was due to the friendliness of SIS/Algiers, whether the agreement was not circulated through all the SIS/London sections, or whether SIS simply realized afterwards that it would be impossible for them to enforce the agreement.***

Grateful as SI/France was for the valuable assistance rendered by its French and British counterparts, the Algiers OSS staff looked forward to the day when it could be a completely independent organization with its own sources of supply, transport and services. Establishing a valid place in the AFHQ scheme (Experimental Detachment, G-3, Prov. was not officially activated until 1 April 1943), and procuring the personnel and supplies needed for permanent training areas, maritime, air and motor pools, and other pertinent administrative branches, were to be painfully slow.* The newly-authorized OSS Detachment had first to prove itself to the American Hq. to which it was attached. Determined to do the best job possible with what was at hand, SI/France undertook the difficult task of recruiting ** and prepared to launch its first missions.

THE FIRST ATTEMPTS

Pending the time-consuming process of having the first few recruits detached by the French Command, there came to AFHQ, Algiers, three promising escapees. These were "Truc", an independent French agent, his radio operator and an assistant. These men claimed to have left behind in France an operating intelligence chain of some proportions which they offered to turn over to American intelligence authorities.

This was the second week of April 1943, and it was considered important to begin operations. SI's decision to use these men at once was further influenced by the fact that they had documents of their own to cover their entry. In a matter of weeks, devoted to finding transport and drilling the operator in clandestine radio techniques, SI/France had prepared separate plans for infiltrating the men into France. The radio operator was to proceed alone by French submarine to find friends at Toulon and make W/T contact with Algiers. The other two were to go as a team, by U. S. Navy PT boat, to a point off Malaga, just outside Spanish waters, meet friends and

* Director's File No. 12,133, OSS Archives.
** Ibid.
*** Report from Algiers, by Chief of SI/France, History File 182a.

* See "Algiers Base", above.
** See "Agent Processing", above.

work their way over the Pyrenees into France.

Both plans failed—one avoidably, the other for more fortuitous reasons. Operator "Bollo", only partially proficient in his radio work, insisted at the last minute on being received by the "Tommy" group in Toulon in order to be assured of a safe headquarters. This was agreed to with reluctance, on condition that contact would not be maintained after arrival. SI/France warned him to eschew contact with the MEXICO station and advised him to return to Algiers in case of trouble. "Bollo" landed safely near Cap Lardier and reached Toulon after escaping police control on the train. He was never able to make contact over his own radio, and first word came from him to Algiers via MEXICO. It was shortly after this that the station was captured and "Bollo" shot.

From the unhappy results of the mission came the realization that "it does not pay, humanly or practically, to send off agents who are not completely prepared".* When the safest means of transport—i.e. parachute and plane—were denied, the only alternative, a submarine supplied by French SR, was used despite the insufficient time that remained for preparing the operator. The crossing of agent networks was also recognized as a dangerous risk. It was determined that, without complete, tested training, missions were usually not worth undertaking at all. Although the base could not anticipate all contingencies, a self-assured agent, made psychologically and physically secure by reason of complete technical efficiency and unhurried training in an atmosphere of mutual confidence, could overcome any number of odds in the field.

Less disastrous was the failure of the "Truc" mission to southern Spain. Twenty-four hours after landing on the coast, the two OSS agents were picked up by Spanish

* Chief SI/France: Report from Algiers, History File 182a.

police, jailed and questioned. Their cover story, that they were escaping from North Africa because of their anti-American activities (in proof of which they produced false police summonses), held. Both men were eventually released and turned over to Allied authorities at Gibraltar without having divulged anything of their secret mission. An unforeseeable accident had prevented the completion of an operation, but, due to satisfactory briefing and documentation, security was not violated and no lives were lost.

PENNY FARTHING

By 1 May 1943, SI/Algiers still had no agents of its own in France. However, the first official French release of four agents and three operators for OSS employment came through at this time. By splitting the group into two-man teams, consisting of an organizing agent and a radio operator, it was hoped before long to send a pair to establish intelligence chains in each of the three main areas through which an invading army would have to move: Rhone Valley (southeast), Massif Central and Garonne Valley (southwest). In contrast to the hurried atmosphere in which the first three agents had been dispatched, the next mission was not carried out by the French Desk until three-and-a-half months later.

During the long weeks of preparation, complicated many times by formal requests to AFHQ and SOE, cancelled promises and lack of OSS priority, SI/France became thoroughly familiar with the many details of planning that precede a successful intelligence operation.

Late in June, word came from SOE/London, via *Massingham*, that a British plane would be available for an OSS parachute operation from London during the July moon period. The Chief of SI/France accompanied his first team, PENNY FARTHING, to London, whence it was to be flown to its pinpoint in northern France. SOE officers cooperated fully in the final

227

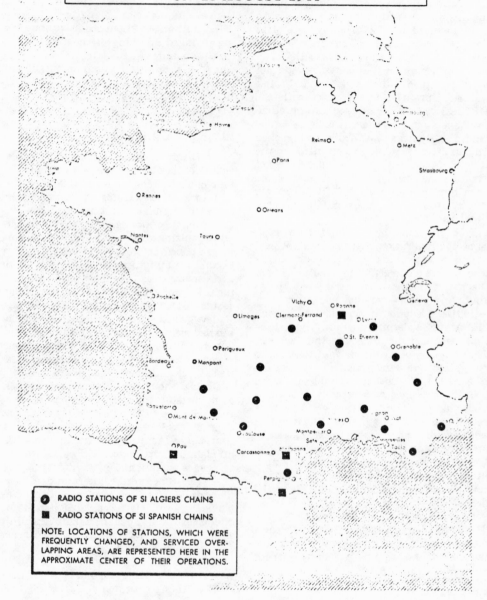

SI RADIO COVERAGE IN SOUTHERN FRANCE ON 15 AUGUST 1944

● RADIO STATIONS OF SI ALGIERS CHAINS

■ RADIO STATIONS OF SI SPANISH CHAINS

NOTE: LOCATIONS OF STATIONS, WHICH WERE
FREQUENTLY CHANGED, AND SERVICED OVER-
LAPPING AREAS, ARE REPRESENTED HERE IN THE
APPROXIMATE CENTER OF THEIR OPERATIONS.

preparations of the mission. Complete documentation was provided the OSS agents in London, a pinpoint selected and a final test interrogation made. Just before departure, the agents were briefed in the innumerable details of their mission—its over-all purposes, the kind of intelligence they were to obtain, known characteristics of the region where they would work and other important data.

The first pinpoint selected for PENNY FARTHING had to be changed when enemy flak installations were discovered on the route to the dropping place. An alternate pinpoint was rejected by the agents because they had no friends there with whom they might establish a safe house. SOE, aware of the insecurity involved, nevertheless consented to let the two men parachute to a reception group of SOE agents. They were to be received on the field, obtain the latest information on travel regulations, procure July food coupons and leave the reception committee the next morning. As the plane circled the target and the men prepared to jump, the signal lights of the ground committee went out. They did not go on again, and the plane returned to an airport in the north of England. Later, it was learned that the whole reception committee was arrested by the enemy in the act of signalling in the plane.

Bad weather for the rest of the July moon period postponed PENNY FARTHING until the following month. The let-down in morale suffered by the agents, following this, was considerably lessened by their knowledge that, had it not been for the British navigator's precaution in not permitting the jump, their capture would have been certain.

On 17 August 1943, PENNY FARTHING parachuted "blind" to a spot near Clermont-Ferrand. With Lyon as headquarters and main radio base, "Jacques", the team leader, chose sub-agents from Clermont-Ferrand and Lyon to act as chiefs of networks in other areas. Radio operator

"Toto", with a wide wartime acquaintance among French Army radiomen, was able to recruit and train operators in clandestine radio procedure. The new operators were used to relieve "Toto" at Lyon, and subsequently to work new radio circuits for the growing needs of the PENNY FARTHING chain. Those who did not remain at Lyon to work directly with "Jacques" and "Toto" were dispatched to work for networks being established under a former French Army officer in the Clermont-Ferrand area and in the southeast under two young student volunteers. Communications and liaison between the new stations and Lyon were maintained via couriers and by frequent trips made by "Jacques" and "Toto" themselves.

"Jacques" and "Toto" learned the elements of battle order reporting and proceeded to instruct their key agents in the finer points of efficient military observation.* Not all agents benefited from this instruction, and reports reaching Lyon from various branches of PENNY FARTHING were not equal in quality. This "Jacques" attributed to the background of the agents chosen—it was discovered that, even with a good briefing program, it was better to use men who had first-hand knowledge of military life for procuring military intelligence. In the course of training agents for his various chains, "Jacques" distinguished three categories into which recruits might fit according to their competence and possibilities: (1) Those who could devote their entire time to the work and were intelligent enough to be used in obtaining military information; (2) those who, although they might have considerable free time, were better used as liaison and courier agents; (3) those who could not devote all of their time to the job but who were able to find rooms, locations for radio sets, places of refuge, etc.

---

* A special section for battle order briefing was established as part of the SI/France Desk in September 1943. See "Algiers Base", above.

The initial PENNY FARTHING station, RAVINIA, sent its first message to Algiers on 15 September 1943, as arranged one month previously. A second station, ALPINA, began functioning on 13 December. Just before ALPINA was set up, RAVINIA operators became aware of German D/F-ing. To combat this danger, PENNY FARTHING laid down certain rules: (1) A station once suspected of being D/F-ed should cease operation; (2) any network must have at its disposal a number of different stations; (3) the signal plan for each station should be as dissimilar as possible from any other in the same network; (4) control of more than one station by the same operator should be avoided or carefully disguised by manipulating the key differently; (5) frequencies and times should be changed as often as possible.

The greatest blow to the PENNY FARTHING chain came in April 1944 with the capture of "Toto", radio operator and assistant organizer. He and a liaison agent of the southeast network were arrested by German agents during a rendezvous in a Lyon cafe. How the leak occurred could not be determined with certainty, although it was believed that "Toto" was betrayed by a subagent. The chiefs of the network were notified and all agents warned to observe the strictest security precautions. Meanwhile, a liaison agent who had not been alerted was arrested, as well as one of the chiefs of the southeast chain.

News of the incident came to Algiers by cable on 17 April 1943:

TOTO ARRESTED BY GESTAPO UNDER CIRCUMSTANCES THAT ALLOW NO HOPE. RECORDS CODES AND MOST OF MONEY SAVED. HASTINGS (southeast radio station) OFF AIR. ALL TRAFFIC HENCEFORTH THROUGH CARTHAGE.

"Toto" conducted himself ingeniously during his interrogation and succeeded in escaping, though condemned to die. Because of his advanced knowledge of radio, the Germans considered him an important prize and sent special interrogators from

Berlin to question him. Throughout the questioning, "Toto" managed to say nothing of importance while giving the impression that he was revealing accurate information. On the contrary, he obtained valuable information on German D/F-ing methods, given him undoubtedly in the belief that he would soon be dead. Having established a tacit understanding with one of his interrogators, "Toto" managed to avoid torture and delay execution until after D-Day (South France) with the constant excuse that he had much more information to divulge.

On the 24th of August (1944), a few hours before he was to be shot, his Gestapo guard and a Nazi colleague grasped him as if taking him to his execution and, as soon as they were in the car, untied his hands and declared themselves to be his prisoners and handed over their guns. "Toto" drove them around the German lines to a Maquis some 40 kilometers from Lyon. His odyssey ended, he immediately put himself at the disposition of an American division for intelligence missions through the lines.[*]

On 21 September 1943, the second SI/France team, MUTTON PORK, was dropped from an Algiers-based British plane in southwestern France. After a month's hiding in an attic, due to immediate spotting by German D/F, the pair emerged to organize three chains and two radio stations for intelligence out of Bordeaux and Toulouse. This network sent in a growing volume of valuable information (sixty-four messages) until the end of March, when a Gestapo penetration of the Bordeaux branch resulted in arrests which ended this network's effective coverage of the southwest area. The chief agent managed, nevertheless, to reorganize the untouched elements of the chain, and, through contact with an OSS/Spain source, continued to send pouches of information through Spain to Algiers.

It had taken seven months for SI/France to establish itself and its first opera-

* From "Jacques'" Story, Report from Algiers, History File 182a.

tive chains. In this time the Desk came to know intimately the detailed factors of mounting and directing intelligence operations—from the initial problem of finding recruits, through the period of training, to the critical moment of infiltration, and the best ways of meeting the needs of agents in the field. They learned, too, the importance of time: that an agent's preparation is at least a two to three months' process, with even more time required for W/T operators, and that a team cannot be expected to be productive for a month or so after its dispatch.

Although new missions were planned in the latter months of 1943 by SI/France, bad weather prevented any more from being carried out until January 1944. By this time the critical period of initiation for SI/-France was over. On 10 January 1944, AFHQ invited the Desk to form a part of Task Force 163, the planning staff for the invasion of southern France.

Eleven new missions were infiltrated by air and by sea into France between January and May 1944. Although not all succeeded—at least three were compromised by the Gestapo-controlled station DART-MOUTH *—they augmented the program of complete intelligence coverage already begun, and, together with the Spanish chains into France, contributed notably to the success of the Allied armies in the southern France invasion.**

2. Trans-Pyrenees Chains

While SI/France was seeking to establish its first successful intelligence teams from Algiers,*** the organization of chains for intelligence in southern France was already under way from OSS bases in Spain. As early as January 1943, a few agents were being surreptitiously organized in key cities in central and southern France at the insti-

gation of SI chiefs stationed at Barcelona and Bilbao. By October, ten chains, evolved from these first penetrations, were producing important intelligence. They developed, under careful direction, to the point where, in May 1944, fifteen chains with some 1,400 agents were furnishing more than fifty percent of all raw strategic intelligence reaching AFHQ from France.

Because of the limited personnel and other curtailments imposed by the Hayes-Donovan agreements * of November 1943, no large-scale organization for agent recruiting, briefing and dispatching was established at SI/Spain bases similar to that which the Algiers office was developing. Recruits consisted principally of Frenchmen who had escaped over the Pyrenees and were anxious to join the Allied cause. To equip these men with the necessary documents, the Barcelona office made its own arrangements, paying local engravers and printers for clandestine copying work. Vichy police badges exemplified the more important and more difficult of the deceptive articles reproduced under OSS direction in Spain.

Radio contact between agents in France and bases in Spain was impossible since there were no experienced radio operators, training areas or other facilities available to OSS/Spain. Communication took the form of personal contacts, mail, letter-drops and over-the-border agent-couriers. The main disadvantage of this method of communication was its slowness. The large number of persons who had to be involved in transmitting the pouches from field to base was another. It proved ideal, however, for the delivery of maps, overlays, documents and similar material which could not otherwise be communicated. It was for the purpose of getting this type of intelligence to Algiers that the North African-based networks first came into contact with the Spanish overland chains. Infrequent liaison was made

---

* See "Early Infiltrations", above.
** See "Intelligence for *ANVIL*", below.
*** See previous section.

---

* See "Spain and Portugal", above.

only in cases of emergency, or when SI/-France agents with no other means of transport were escorted to Barcelona by agents of the Spanish chains.

The courier system that was evolved to meet the early communication needs of the OSS trans-Pyrenees chains, despite its drawbacks, worked well. Crossing the border with papers of military importance and even articles of food and clothing was, of course, illegal, Spain being a "neutral" country. Couriers—one or more for each chain—traversed the Pyrenees at night, at regular intervals, carrying messages between agents and organizers. Crossings were continued even after stringent anti-Maquis measures enforced by the Gestapo after March 1944 made such journeys increasingly dangerous.

According to a pre-arranged schedule, contact between agent and courier was made in small towns or cities like Perpignan, not far removed from the border. A leading agent of the HIHI chain reported:

During a period of eighteen months C. crossed the border every two weeks. Sometimes he made the crossing even more often, since he also went to get the mail that arrived from Barcelona. This is how he would be notified of the arrival of the mail: C. lived at Bourg-Madame (France) and had some cousins who lived on the opposite side of the border, in Puigcerda (Spain). When the mail arrived from Barcelona, the family in Puigcerda hung up the wash, consisting of large white sheets, in the garden. Armed with a pair of binoculars, C. scanned the horizon every day; from his window he was able to see his cousins' garden. When he saw that the sheets had been hung out he left the same evening, crawling through the countryside for one kilometer and fording a river. . . . This he did even in the coldest weather. The return trip had to be made by the same route and the same dangers faced once again.*

"Dead letter drops" were also used, especially when it was necessary to use another chain's route for delivery of a pouch, etc. These consisted of pre-arranged locations—building, receptacle or other inconspicuous place—where secret material could be deposited by one agent and picked up by another without personal contact. In this way, security of the chains could be maintained by insulating sub-agents from one another. At secret meetings between agent and courier, or by way of letter boxes, reports collected by various members of the chain were exchanged for new coded instructions, money and supplies.

The AKAK chain had a particularly reliable courier system and was used many times to service other chains which had broken down because of insecurity or enemy capture. When a chain with headquarters at Perpignan became insecure, for example, AKAK served as its communication link to Barcelona until it could be reorganized. Another, OPOP, was never able to establish a dependable communication system of its own, and relied on AKAK to carry its intelligence reports back to base. AKAK had two reserve routes for alternate use in case the original were "blown". Using five men, it was able by May 1944 to transport three voluminous pouches a week over the 160 miles between Toulouse and Barcelona. In contrast, another chain in the Rhone Valley region, although an exceptionally valuable source of intelligence, could not send pouches more often than twice a month.

The first agents for these intelligence chains were recruited in January 1943. An individual whose security and contacts were well known was usually selected by OSS to build and direct a chain in a region of strategic importance. This leader, who often acted as courier for the chain as well, chose sub-agents from among his friends to act as sector chiefs and organize smaller networks of agents to procure intelligence in particular areas. Each agent was given a code name or number by which he was known to his superior and which could be used in all secret correspondence. Sub-agents, in turn, recruited others to help them. In this way the network grew.

---

* Report of HIHI Chain, History File 185a.

Security required that an agent be known to the one who originally contacted him and to as few others as possible. For example, the network chief was in touch with each of his personally appointed sector chiefs, while they themselves were kept separate from each other. In turn, agents employed by them were kept ignorant of the chief and he of them. Occasionally, one highly trusted agent might be used by the chief as his alternate for liaison or courier duties.

Even before the Gestapo in France began to curtail seriously the movement of all persons in occupied France, prior to the Allied invasion from the north, personal liaison between agents was dangerous. Overland travel had to be as inconspicuous as possible, usually by bicycle or train. Search of rail passengers by the Gestapo was a common occurrence and new methods had always to be devised on these trips for concealing documents or other compromising materials. The method of recruiting agents, the extensive financial arrangements, and the amount of travelling involved in building up a chain of any proportions were described in a report by a key organizer in the HIHI chain:

C. (courier-agent) gave me 10,000 francs and told me to get in touch with my friends at Le Puy, to find an agent and to go to Toulon and get in touch with Mme. F. . . . C. asked me to get the address from Mme. B. and gave me the addresses of Dr. C., Dr. G., Colombe, and a baker by the name of. . . . . who lived at Cannes. . . . He gave me another 10,000 francs for Mme. F. and an intelligence objective.

Mme. F. arrived . . . I explained to her that she would have to get in touch immediately with our correspondents in Toulon. . . . I gave her the intelligence objectives and added that I would notify her by postcard of the date of my return: that the text of the card would be "Bon souvenir," signed Camille, and that the date of my arrival would be the date I used on the card. . . .

I went to le Puy . . . there was the deputy mayor who was in a position to give us the most useful information. . . . Not only did he inform me of troop movements, but gave me the names of German officers, reported on the state of the airfields, on industrial production, on German requisitions, etc. . . . From le Puy I left for Per-

pignan . . . I found C. We arranged to meet at Perpignan every 10th and 25th of the month . . . he gave me 50,000 francs for the chain in general.

On my way back I stopped at Alex . . . where my cousin A. begged to become a part of the chain. I gave him the registration number 5-3 and asked him to establish a network in the entire Rhone Delta. He agreed, and I appointed him sector chief.*

The greatest care was taken to maintain good relations with the agents and at the same time to improve the quality of their intelligence. Agent questions to OSS/Spain were answered promptly and financial requests were given particular attention.

Initially, agent chiefs received through their various contacts all types of information concerning the German occupation of France. In proportion to the influence and ingenuity of the agents employed, both general and specific intelligence on enemy policies, troop movements and military preparations, were turned over with a minimum of technical coaching from their supervisors. In the best chains, various persons in high official positions were employed to relay all items of importance available. They notified their chain links, among other things, of the presence of armored units in Marseille, of German plans to build submarine bases in various locations, and of developments at a number of key rail junctions (schedules of German trains, movements of troops, military insignia, etc.). A particularly valuable sub-agent established cells in all the ministries of Vichy, and developed contacts with police and railroad officials. Through his access to confidential telegrams coming to Vichy from all parts of France and to other documents which he stole, copied and returned to the ministries, intelligence of high political and military import reached the Allies.

As plans for invasion were begun, the demand for detailed intelligence on specific areas became greater. One chain in particular, HOHO, whose experienced chief had

---

* Review of Chain 1942-HIHI, History File 185a.

given his sub-agents extensive briefing, was transmitting reports of unusual accuracy and neatness. Several of HOHO's "ideal reports" were photostated and sent as samples to heads of each of the other chains. Miniature printed booklets were dispatched as well, giving instructions for reporting enemy battle order, and the identification of enemy materiel. As a direct result of this program, the quality of agents' reports, after January 1944, on such items as troop description and location, battle order and coastal defenses, improved considerably.

From this system of "remote control" briefing, it was a natural step to begin sending from Spain specific directed intelligence requests based on the needs of the Allied invasion forces. By April 1944, SI/Spain had achieved with the trans-Pyrenees chains reasonably balanced coverage throughout southern France. Of the nine chains from Barcelona and five from Bilbao, some remained small and only slightly productive, while others had become complex networks extending as far north as Paris, Brittany, and the Belgian border. Most adequately covered was the region between Modane (in the Alps) and Bordeaux south to the Pyrenees and the Mediterranean. The reliability of the pouched intelligence reaching AFHQ in Algiers—averaging one hundred separate reports a week—was recognized by high G-2 source and content ratings.

Two plans were developed for maximum exploitation of the chains for operation *ANVIL*. In order that Spanish chain agents might be used by advancing units, each was given the pass word "Racine" and a code number. Specific intelligence objectives were assigned for each to carry to the local OSS unit or G-2 upon being overrun. In fact, this project produced few results, due to the unexpected speed of the Seventh Army advance.

A more successful plan was to supply the trans-Pyrenees chains with W/T sets and operators by air from Algiers, to implement

the slow-moving (two to three weeks) strategic intelligence, coming by pouch through Spain to AFHQ, with quick, efficient tactical intelligence. As radio equipment and operators were both scarce, a skeletal distribution of available W/T sets to Spanish chains was designed to provide the most efficient service in terms of priority intelligence needs of the invasion forces.

Before W/T sets, personnel and other supplies, such as money, arms, medicine, etc., could be parachuted into southern France, suitable pinpoints had to be selected by the chain leaders themselves and relayed via Madrid to Algiers. These reception fields were to be chosen not only from the viewpoint of strategic radio coverage but also as dropping points for supplies and, in a few cases, as landing areas for SO or OG teams. Chain leaders arranged, too, for reception committees at each field, appropriate messages to be used for signalling committees in advance of operations and a light signal. All other operational preparations were the responsibility of the SI/Spanish Desk in Algiers.

Staff members of French and Spanish SI/- Algiers secured scarce W/T equipment, recruited agents and operators, and trained, briefed, and handled them up to the time of their dispatch. Because of the difficulties in securing French personnel in North Africa,* French-speaking Spaniards were found and given special radio instruction at the Algiers communication school. Necessary personal equipment, including articles of French or European manufacture were provided new recruits. All of this was done in a relatively short time, for, unlike the preparations undergone by agents of French SI teams, these men were to be received by persons already well-established in enemy territory. A temporary cover story was given each operator and agent, with instructions to devise a more permanent identity and cover immediately after

---

* See previous section.

arrival in France. Besides preparation of personnel, SI/Algiers made arrangements with the British and French for one-line messages to be broadcast over BBC and "Radio Alger" as signals to ground reception committees. They arranged with SO and Army officials for parachute packing and air transport from the Blida airfield near Algiers.

On 6 April 1944, the Spanish Desk in Algiers, requesting G-3 operational approval, reported a minimum of ten operators who would be ready (pending receipt of frequency allocations from OSS/Communications) to be parachuted by the end of the month. To supplement these, chain leaders selected certain of their agents to be instructed in radio techniques by the Algiers-trained operators in the field. At least six parachute pinpoints had been forwarded by chain leaders via Madrid and had been approved by MAAF in Algiers; and fourteen actual operations—supply, personnel, and combined—were tentatively planned as "blind" or reception committee drops during May.

Exchange of instructions and other details involved in the operations was made difficult by the necessity of planning every phase in both Spain and Algiers. The arrangements for landing fields, signals, and time schedules were complicated still further by the unwieldy courier communications system. The radio station at OSS/Madrid, with insufficient materiel and only one operator, could monitor the important Algiers broadcasts only at set hours—never on a 24-hour basis. No matter how important the coded messages and telephone calls received from Barcelona and Bilbao, their transmission to Algiers had to await the hour set by radio Madrid's limited schedule.

The parachute operations themselves were subject to the same hazardous system of communications. The variability of the weather often led to last-minute cancellations of flight plans, but, because of the red tape governing the broadcast of signals over military-controlled BBC and "Radio Alger", these changes could rarely be relayed to awaiting reception committees in time. Furthermore, plans to fly the same operation the next night could not always be complied with by agents in the field.

Nevertheless, reception fields were prepared and supplies and personnel dropped to many of them during the moon periods of May, June, and July. By D-Day, 15 August 1944, four radio circuits had been established and were operating a daily schedule to Algiers. These were well spaced for sending intelligence from areas of military importance and for supplementing the seventeen W/T stations being run by SI/France.[*]

3. Intelligence for Anvil

The long and tedious efforts of SI in South France—beginning with "Tommy" in December 1942 and the simultaneous first penetrations from Bilbao and Barcelona, through the organization of the French Desk in Algiers and its coordination with agent networks directed from Spain—culminated in Operation *ANVIL*, the invasion of South France.

Working in closest liaison with AFHQ and Seventh Army's Force 163, SI/Algiers relayed G-2 requests and criticisms to its agents in return for detailed observations in the main areas of enemy concentration: along the Mediterranean coast from Perpignan to Nice; in the southwest or Pyrenees region; and along the vital rail networks linking South France with battle areas in the north. Double, triple, or even greater coverage [**] was maintained at key junctions along the Garonne and Rhone valleys—Bordeaux, Toulouse, Lyon, Avignon—and around Sete, Toulon, and Marseille, chief ports guarding the southern approaches to France. Confirmation of all urgent data

---

[*] For intelligence results, see next section.

[**] OSS/Spain listed over thirty known agents and sub-agents, belonging to seven separate chains, in the city of Toulouse alone.

was possible through this system. In addition, enemy movements could be checked from various vantage points and at various stages of relocation or dispersion. This feature of SI intelligence coverage was exceptionally important during the rapid shifts of enemy troops between and after the *OVERLORD* and *ANVIL* landings.

From 5 May 1943 to 15 September 1944, OSS/Algiers made available to G-2, AFHQ more than 8,000 separate intelligence reports, the greater part of which were duplicated for interested sub-sections of the Army, Navy, and Air Forces. Of these, more than half emanated from Spanish-based chains; at least a quarter of them came from chains controlled by French SI in Algiers. Supplementary intelligence reached Algiers by cable from chains in France operated by Bern and London.

The earliest long-range intelligence to concern the *ANVIL* Planning Staff was the German system of defense, particularly along the Mediterranean where the armies would meet their first resistance. Coastal defense emplacements, minefields, entanglements, roadblocks, anti-aircraft guns, searchlights, etc., represented a relatively static sort of intelligence which could be reported early and still have significance at the time of invasion.

Most reports from southern France chains reaching Algiers in 1943 were of a general, strategic nature: Location of airfields in the Lyon-Clermont Ferrand-Avignon triangle, condition of Rhone bridges, construction of submarine pens at Bordeaux, bombing damage to rail yards at Cannes, capacity of repair shops at Oullins, and the like. First notes on coastal defenses east of Marseille were brought to Algiers by "Tommy" in February 1943. With the gradual extension of enemy Mediterranean fortifications in 1944, the mushrooming of camouflaged artillery emplacements, pillboxes, casements, and anti-tank walls, as well as the laying of underwater obstacles such as mines and blockships, were accu-

rately reported with accompanying drawings by a growing number of spotters.

Because of the detailed technical aspects of defining complicated defense structures, this type of intelligence came via pouch through Spain in the form of scaled drawings, sketches, and map overlays. The first-hand observations of on-the-spot agents permitted the reporting of details not visible from the air, and thus augmented to a large extent Army aerial photographs. One of the most valuable services performed by SI agents in this regard was the distinction of fake from real defense installations.*

One of the first and best coastal defense reports was compiled by an agent, landed in France by PT boat in December 1943, who sent it (within a month, as requested by AFHQ) by pouch via Spain to Algiers. It consisted of overlays at 1:50,000 from Avignon south to the sea and east to the Italian border. Another agent gained the confidence of German naval officers commanding nineteen batteries at Port St. Louis, east of Marseille. Besides confirming positions and calibres of guns already reported, he gave their range and setting, and details on their crews and supply arrangements, as well as their command and observation posts. So complete was OSS intelligence on enemy fortifications by August that when AFHQ requested "data on the wall at Frejus" (one of the landing points), SI was able to provide factual data ** from thirty separate agent reports.

---

* The indispensability of ground intelligence to the success of Allied aerial observation and action was clearly illustrated in:
(1) The ability to distinguish between "active" and "dummy" camouflaged defenses;
(2) Provision of immediate indisputable evidence of unit identities through detailed descriptions of uniforms, insignia, etc.;
(3) The checking of local movements on a day-to-day, hour-to-hour basis; and
(4) Continued observation under weather conditions adverse to air operations.
** Down to the sand content of the concrete, and the name and address of the Italian engineer who had started the wall in 1942.

After the beginning of the Allied assault in Normandy, intelligence became more tactical in nature. Agents were asked to concentrate particularly on enemy supply lines, communications and transportation. In this, SI cooperated closely with A-2 to locate and frequently recheck storage points and troop concentrations along highways and railroads. Asked by AFHQ to signal targets for bombing by the Eighth and Fifteenth Air Forces, SI responded, in the seventy days between *OVERLORD* and *ANVIL*, with map coordinates of 29 gasoline dumps (at least five million gallons), 12 ammunition dumps, and 45 transport bottlenecks.

Apart from special G-2 and A-2 assignments, highest priority was given, and most radio time devoted, to order of battle. The German Army in South France, following the occupation, consisted of the First Army covering the Atlantic area from Bordeaux, and the Nineteenth Army commanding the Mediterranean sector, with reserve areas at Clermont-Ferrand and Grenoble. During the first months of 1944, SI turned in increasingly clear reports of troop locations, unit identifications, reorganizations, and movements. By May 1944, the trial period with Seventh Army's Force 163 was completed, and G-2 recognized OSS chains as having supplied the major part of the plan of enemy troop concentrations and defenses. While some reports could not be counter-checked, 72 percent of their intelligence had been confirmed.

Of prime interest to G-2, after the June landings in the north, were the number and identity of any of the sixteen armored and infantry divisions, in the enemy's two army areas in southern France, moving toward the Normandy beachhead. Covering all railroad and deployment centers in the First Army area, "Jerome's" PENNY FARTHING chain was able to spot, on 8 June, the Das Reich (2 SS) Panzer Division—originally reported by him on its arrival from Russia in February—and follow, when all other services had lost track of it, its initial movements toward the north. The information was cabled promptly to Algiers, from where it was forwarded to London. Both SHAEF and AFHQ expressed appreciation of the timeliness, detail, and accuracy of the reports, which resulted in bombing of the tank convoys by the Air Force and delaying sabotage operations by the Maquis in the region of Brives.* Transfer of three infantry divisions northward was similarly reported between 24-26 June. A typical PENNY FARTHING cable read:

MOVEMENT 43 TRAINS. ORIGIN BAYONNE. DESTINATION SAINTES AND BEYOND. RATE AT LEAST 12 TRAINS 24 HOURS. CARRYING INFANTRY DIVISION. LOADED AS FOLLOWS: 3 TRAINS AT ST. JEAN DE LUZ, 3 AT HENDAYE, 5 AT ST. VINCENT DE TYROSSE, 7 AT CAMBO, 7 AT BAYONNE, 10 AT LABENNE, 5 AT PEYREHORADE, 1 AT PUYOO, 2 AT USTARITZ. CODE NAME KLATSCHMOHN.

These movements were checked and confirmed by aerial photography, and subsequently bombed, strafed, and sabotaged.

Arrivals of replacements were noted throughout July. Constant cross-checking by various chains continued, even after D-Day, to keep the Army informed of troop positions and relocations, often in advance of their actual movement. From the scattered deployment of enemy divisions, it was plain that the Germans remained unaware of the location selected for the Allied landings.

An ironic and illustrative sidelight to the enemy's bewilderment was the special commendation given by G-2 to SI station MENADO for its coverage of the target area east of Toulon. Unknown to SI/Algiers, this station was operated under German control throughout July and was cabling seventy-five percent accurate information ** on coastal artillery and the port of Toulon. In this case the high percentage of good intelligence was bait to uncover the place and

---

* See "Resistance Aid to *OVERLORD*", above.

** This was not an unusual average for SI/-Algiers chains. G-2 commended the station because the area became a landing point.

time of the Allied landing. SI policy, drawn from French SR experience, fortunately prohibited informing agents in the field of such high security plans, and OSS/ Algiers, in spite of its ignorance of enemy control of MENADO, revealed neither the urgency of the Toulon information sought nor any details of the invasion plans.

Under a special communications arrangement, intelligence from southern France in the week before D-Day was made available not only to G-2, AFHQ but also to intelligence officers on General Patch's command ship afloat. Since approximately seventy percent of OSS clandestine circuits fell within the general target area, an elaborate "blind" network was set up earlier to cover the heavy increase of radio traffic during the landings. The dummy broadcast circuits operated on a 24-hour basis from 13 July to 9 August. Thereafter, actual traffic was inserted into the continuous stream of dummy messages. The headquarters ship afloat received, at three positions, messages via Algiers from the stations in the field. Of 94 messages sent by SI/Algiers to the invasion fleet on its way to France, Signal Intelligence reported all were received, and only one garbled. This was better than any other net operating to the ship. On D-plus-three, a link was established, according to plan, with the advance army section in France, and the one-way traffic to the ship was discontinued.

Through this unprecedented communications system, urgent inquiries of the invading forces were relayed quickly to agents in critical tactical areas, and responses readily returned in the same fashion. A special request 36 hours before the invasion elicited an immediate report on antiparachute pickets at Le Muy, an area where American paratroopers were scheduled to land. On 13 August, a final survey of the target area was made by an OSS agent who bicycled from Cannes to Hyeres. His cables, received by the incoming command ship, included information on occupied (not dum-

mied) defense emplacements, with their calibres and coordinates.

Earlier strategic intelligence also had its value. A landing strip not under German observation, a detailed plan of which had been supplied a Spanish chain agent by a Marseille police official, was used by Allied troops. And information regarding the placement of fire power at Toulon and Marseille influenced the Allied decision to take these cities from the rear.

Following the landings on 15 August, G-2, Seventh Army could report: "D-Day dispositions (of German troops) confirmed advance information in every particular." As for the intelligence on defenses submitted by OSS agents, Lt. Gen. Patch paid personal tribute to its "extraordinary accuracy". A G-2 memorandum of 30 October 1944 stated:

Intelligence provided for operation DRAGOON (ANVIL) was probably the fullest and most detailed of any provided by G-2, AFHQ in a series of combined operations commencing with TORCH. . . . A rough estimate of the proportion of accepted ground Intelligence supplied by the three Allied agencies shows that 50% was provided by OSS, 30% by the S.R. (French) and 20% by I.S.L.D. (British). . . .*

Another G-2 report on ANVIL credited OSS sources with 79% of all battle order material used by the invading forces.

SI agents behind German lines continued, during and after the assault, to transmit messages to Algiers. Others, upon being overrun by divisions of American Seventh and French First Armies, were able to supply intelligence officers with on-the-spot tactical intelligence.

By September, except in certain southwest sections of France and in the ports of Toulon and Marseille, few of the areas covered by SI agents remained in German hands. The gathering of tactical intelligence in advance of the attacking Allied forces devolved upon OSS units attached to army divisions in the field.**

---

* See exhibit attached.
** See next section.

238

ALLIED FORCE HEADQUARTERS

OFFICE OF THE ASSISTANT CHIEF OF STAFF, G-2

30 October 1944.

Memorandum: for D/A. C. of S., G-2.

Subject: O. S. S. Contribution to Intelligence Collated for Operation DRAGOON.

1. The intelligence provided for Operation "DRAGOON" was probably the fullest and most detailed of any provided by G-2, AFHQ in a series of combined operations commencing with "TORCH".   The GOC, 7 U. S. Army himself paid a personal tribute to its "extraordinary accuracy".

2. The material collated by G-2, AFHQ came from a variety of sources but the very considerable contribution of O. S. S. merits special emphasis, not only on account of its intrinsic worth but because the results obtained provide a signal example of what can be done by an agency of this kind when it consents to work in closest cooperation with the Operational Headquarters which it is serving.

3. A rough estimate of the proportion of accepted ground Intelligence supplied by the three Allied agencies shows that 50% was provided by O. S. S., 30% by the S. R., and 20% by I. S. L. D.

4. The French Desk at Algiers maintained daily contact with the O. I. Section at AFHQ.   All the members of it were indefatigable in their efforts to secure the information requested.   Nothing was declared to be impossible.

A full and accurate picture of the static situation in Southern FRANCE was gradually built up and when the events of July and early August threatened to confuse the whole issue by setting the whole enemy lay-out in motion, a phenomenally accurate check on troop movements was maintained with the result that we were not only able to keep 7 Army in possession of an up-to-date picture but also to provide SHAEF with information in advance of any other source.

5. I have had not inconsiderable experience of intelligence planning and am very fully aware of the patience and meticulousness required of both planners and intelligence agencies.   I consider that the results achieved by O. S. S. in respect of Southern FRANCE before DRAGOON so outstanding that they should be brought to the attention of interested authorities, together with the names of our principal collaborators.

/s/   H. B. HITCHENS, Col.,
/t/   H. B. Hitchens,
Colonel, G. S.,
G-2 Section, O. I.

4. Seventh Army Detachment

Early in the planning of *ANVIL*, Seventh Army's Force 163 requested OSS to supplement its SI chains with tactical intelligence teams to accompany invasion forces. A separate OSS unit was established in April 1944 as the Strategic Services Section (SSS) under the "direct supervision and control of A. C. of S., G-2, Force 163." *

SSS began with a considerable lead over the field detachments being prepared in England to accompany the European Theater armies. While the latter had almost no SI operational experience, SI/Algiers had procured, and continued through 15 August to procure, the intelligence data which was principally responsible for making operation *ANVIL* the "best briefed invasion of the war." While the northern detachments were constituted of individuals from the OSS/London offices and from new arrivals, SSS consisted, in the main, of the same group which had been running French intelligence operations from Algiers for over a year. Finally, as a result of its excellent intelligence record, SSS had the strong favor of the Seventh Army G-2, who gave the unit both support and leeway for action. These two factors, experience as a unit in SI work, and G-2 assistance, largely accounted for the SSS record as the outstanding OSS army detachment of the war.

SSS was divided into two sections. To organize long-range intelligence missions and to handle administration and liaison with the Army, headquarters would move with Seventh Army G-2. The decision to carry on this work from the highest level was based on past experience in Tunisia,

* Although, for administrative purposes, SSS was given official responsibility for all OSS activities with the Seventh Army, its main function remained that of intelligence. All other operations were undertaken by SPOC, which was nominally under SSS, but actually free to organize its own program in conjunction with G-3, Seventh Army. See "Algiers Base", above.

Sicily, and southern Italy where OSS men were used for non-OSS functions.*

A second single unit was originally planned to be located closer to the front lines for tactical infiltrations. When it became apparent, however, as early as D-plus-two, that the campaign was to be one of rapid advance, with forward elements radically separated from the main Army CP, SSS representatives were assigned to form permanent units with each of the Seventh Army's divisions—3rd, 36th, and 45th.

Liaison was maintained with French and other agencies, and these organizations worked for Seventh Army in much the same way as did SSS. Because of G-2's desire to avoid jurisdictional confusion and overlapping of intelligence, SSS alone was granted full-time recognition on the staff at Seventh Army Hq., and information coming from French agencies was left largely to the discretion of the SSS liaison officer as to what and how much could be used to supplement OSS agent reports. Gradually, even greater administrative autonomy was given SSS to the extent, eventually, of its being consulted incident to the planning of subsequent Army operations.

SSS forwarded all locally-obtained French reports, indicating their source but under its own letterhead. However, when the large number of inaccuracies was noted, especially in the case of the numerically preponderant but virtually untrained FFI agents, SSS adopted the practice of sending under its letterhead only those reports submitted by its own agents. G-2 confidence in SSS reports rose considerably thereafter. SSS was given a permanent place on division situation maps, and its material was reproduced with increasing frequency in Army Periodic (daily) Intelligence Reports, which were distributed down to the smallest forward echelon combat units.

The clandestine circuit of pre-invasion days was continued. The base at Algiers

* See those sections, above.

received messages from agents in enemy-occupied France which were relayed to advance Army Hq. on the command ship afloat * and during its progress on the French mainland; it also passed specific Army requests to these same SI agents.

The transmission of intelligence from Algiers to SSS Hq., and by courier to the divisions, was speeded up when radio sub-stations were installed at the forward SSS units. The bulk of intelligence received from behind-the-line-agents via Algiers was of decreasing value, however, as the Allies advanced. The time involved in transmitting information from the field to Army Hq. via Algiers ** often cancelled its usefulness. And, too, the agents supplying behind-the-lines intelligence by radio were overrun too quickly to be of real tactical or strategic assistance. By September, all SI chains were absorbed by the Allied advance, and the rear echelon base at Algiers moved to Marseille.***

Contact with advance SSS units from Hq. was maintained by courier or mobile radio jeep at each of the divisions. When the lines tightened and the various CP's concentrated in a comparatively small area in the Vosges region, courier jeeps between divisions and Army headquarters saved more time than wireless messages which required coding and decoding.

Occasionally, SSS received direct requests from various Army units for information not locally available; these were relayed to other OSS bases. When the Engineers of the Seventh Army requested on 3 November an accurate description of the cables anchoring German pontoon bridges on the

Rhine, the inquiry was radioed to Bern and a full report received shortly thereafter. In addition to such specially radioed intelligence, pouches arrived regularly from Paris and Bern containing miscellaneous material, compiled by R&A, on political, economic and social conditions of interest to planning and control sections at Army headquarters.

Two distinct phases marked the progress of the Allied armies in their drive from the beaches on the Riviera near St. Torpez to their junction with Third Army on the Moselle at Epinal and their arrival at Germany's western defenses. The first six weeks were characterized by unexpectedly weak enemy resistance: by 4 September (D-plus-20) two divisions—the 3rd and the 36th—had raced some 170 miles to Lyon and the 45th was nearing Vesoul a hundred miles farther north; by the end of September, they had reached the Moselle River. So rapid was Allied progress up to this point that SSS' greatest problem was to maintain agents abreast and in advance of divisions in order to secure fresh information of value to the Army.

With the crossing of the Moselle on 21 September, mobility of the front decreased. Opposition became increasingly fierce as the Meurthe River in the Vosges region was approached, and the relatively stationary front became more dangerous to penetrate.

During the first period, all activities were adapted to the immediate situation on a trial and error basis. Moving with the armies from one town to the next in quick succession—often from twenty to seventy miles a day—SSS tapped all available sources for enemy intelligence.

Lacking adequate French-speaking personnel, G-2 called upon SSS men to mediate with the local populace—civilians, refugees, Maquis, etc.—as interrogators, and interpreters. Local officials were often exceedingly helpful in providing useful intelligence. It became common, upon entering a town, to contact the Bureaux of Water

---

* See previous section.
** This was necessitated because small agent battery sets were capable of operating under long-range conditions, but were not equipped for short distances.
*** This latter location was used as a small headquarters for receiving SSS personnel and supplies until they came under the Field Detachment Headquarters (FIDES) established in Paris in the fall.

and Forests, Roads and Bridges, etc., for the kind of technical data they could provide about the region. Besides maps and documents, they donated the services of engineers and consultants. Through them, too, access to an extremely important group was gained—the forest wardens. These men were not only exceptionally loyal but were ideally adapted as local guides.

To supplement the incomplete, and often inaccurate, reports obtained from local residents and organizations and the delayed and rapidly dwindling intelligence of the SI networks, SSS prepared its own short-range, through-the-line missions. The divisional units, consisting at first of no more than three or four men under a team captain, set up operational bases close to the division CP's, assigned liaison officers to division G-2, and proceeded to fit their activities to the immediate needs of their respective units.

The original SSS staff of 23 on D-Day was augmented at intervals until some 150 men represented SSS in one capacity or another in France. This was a remarkably small number considering the extent of the SSS program, and very few could be assigned to the divisions. The effect was that the SSS units never became departmentalized; they worked as highly versatile units to solve the simultaneous problems of organization and operations. As one SSS officer reported:

In Col. ....'s Seventh Army unit . . . branch affiliation seemed to have practically no bearing on the nature of duties performed. This was particularly so with the division teams where everyone had to perform all functions—Hq. liaison, planning, recruitment, briefing, infiltration of agents, and reporting—at one time or another.*

Tactical intelligence was to be concerned with areas "just behind the fighting zones". As such, it was distinguished from "combat intelligence" gathered directly on the bat-

tlefront, which was considered more appropriate for military patrols than for SSS.

Most recruits for the missions were locally chosen for their knowledge of the terrain or for their ability to perform a particular job in keeping with their "natural cover". These included, besides agents, guides (to direct agents through difficult or unfamiliar territory), couriers (to act as cut-outs or go-betweens in the transmission of reports), passeurs (to carry incriminating supplies, such as radio sets, to safe hiding places in enemy territory), and, occasionally, fausseurs (persons capable of equipping agents with false identification papers and other documentation).

Agent material, although more exacting in its standards, was plentiful. Where, as was often the case, able-bodied young men were not available, boys, girls, and women volunteered to go through the lines, singly or in teams, to procure needed information about the enemy. Women were found to be especially successful for this short-range intelligence work. In the first place, they attracted less suspicion in enemy territory than men, who were apt to be searched and drafted by the Germans. Secondly, although they usually lacked the necessary background for reporting technical data, they were often able to extract from enemy officers knowledge of their military intentions not otherwise available.

The FFI also provided considerable assistance. Local leaders of the strongly organized Maquis regions provided names and addresses of numerous persons willing to run every risk in order to aid in the liberation of their country.

Because their value was often limited to given areas, few volunteers could be used more than once. Even when the days of rapid advance were over, security precautions forbade, in the case of "open" assistants such as woodcutter guides, repeat performances. Agents who were found to be eminently suited for clandestine intelligence work were, however, used over and

---

* Field Report, Vol. III, History File 140c.

242

over again. These, and certain of the experienced SI agents who were overrun, were assimilated as part of the SSS units to form permanent agent "pools". They proved invaluable when the stiffening of the lines and an indifferent population near the German border stemmed the tide of volunteers at a time when they were badly needed.

Little or no difficulty was encountered in the handling of agents in the first phase of the advance. Inspired by patriotic motives, they worked willingly and strenuously, refusing monetary rewards. It became customary to recompense agents participating in this hazardous through-the-lines work with clothing, cigarettes, coffee, or other sorely needed or highly-prized items. On occasion, bonuses were paid for successful missions.

Because of the speed with which the armies moved and the general absence of enemy counter-intelligence, agents required a minimum of service and cover precautions. Moving through territory in which food and friends were plentiful, they blended with the population and shifted for themselves. It was a rare case during this period when agents had to be billeted in the same place on two successive nights. Only when the poorer and less secure regions of the Vosges were reached and the Army's advance slowed to a standstill did SSS operations officers have difficulty in contending with the problems of housing, feeding, and morale of their agent personnel.

Briefing, always one of the most important phases in the preparation of an agent, was subject to the same exigencies of time and space as other SSS activities. While the lines remained fluid or non-existent, time was of the essence and there was a minimum of coaching. Agents sent to penetrate enemy-occupied territory were asked to report everything that might be considered of importance to the divisions. As the fluidity of the front decreased, agents were infiltrated to obtain specific details on the defenses of particular towns, enemy troop

dispositions and strength, road and bridge conditions, artillery emplacements, river fords, etc. Persons found suitable for intelligence work were simply and briefly trained in precise observation and quick reporting techniques, including use of map overlays and pinpoint coordinates. When the agents had no previous experience, they were given limited objectives. A few salient questions about the Seventh Army targets—a bridge, a town, etc.—were emphasized and related directly by means of maps to the area which the agent would cover. This area was usually one with which the agent was familiar; if not, a guide was provided. Although not specifically briefed, guides and couriers who accompanied agents were also closely questioned on their return for the information gleaned from personal observation in important military areas.

The first and simplest type of operation attempted by SSS division units was "civilian reconnaissance." This required that persons knowing the countryside, and capable of moving about near the front under a logical pretext, be infiltrated some ten miles behind enemy lines, scout the area on foot or bicycle, and return within three or four days. Objectives generally were: (1) To report presence of enemy in and around towns in advance of the Allied line of march; (2) to determine amount of expected resistance or defense on routes being used; (3) to guard flanks of divisions by reporting any and all enemy troop deployment and movement encountered.

In the first weeks of rapid Allied advance, the enemy, intent on retreating, had little time to devote to effective physical obstruction or counter-intelligence. Comparatively few casualties were recorded during this period. Using the simplest of cover stories adapted to their surroundings—e.g. fleeing from the Americans, visiting neighbors, etc.—agents, if captured, were usually released at once with little questioning. Of those who were not released, most managed to escape and find their way back to the American side. Danger to agents' lives from cross-fire and the threat of capture were, however, always present. Precautions and careful preparations became increasingly imperative for this type of operation.

Where extreme looseness of the line existed and disorganization of the enemy permitted, agents freely penetrated enemy lines without benefit of guide or escort. The usual procedure, however, was to have an SSS conducting officer accompany the agent or agents through no-man's-land to a point opposite the enemy outpost selected for infiltration.

For this phase, SSS was dependent on its liaison with advance sections of the Army and with various resistance organizations. Places penetrated successfully by other SSS units or by the French services were coordinated through consultation with liaison officers at staff Hq. FFI representatives were often able to suggest secure persons in enemy areas who could be of assistance. They were helpful, too, in providing agents with lists of safe houses, weak points in the enemy lines and secure routes of passage.

The divisional CP was notified of each operation and a likely sector chosen. Smaller advance CP's were likewise informed and consulted by the SSS officer in charge of the mission, and the sector to be penetrated studied in detail on situation maps in the light of all that was known from patrol reconnaissance and other combat intelligence operations in the area. A meeting was sometimes arranged with the platoon commander on the afternoon preceding an operation. Presence of the agents themselves at regimental and company CP's was avoided; they were taken directly to the front and a final check on the route to be taken made during daylight with the guide, SSS escort, and agent present.

The crossing took place at maximum darkness, according to the moon-phase, planned so that a safe house in enemy territory might be reached easily before daylight. When the enemy was in particular evidence, armed military patrols were used to conduct agents to the point of infiltration.*

Exfiltration, like infiltration, presented few problems to begin with. After circulating behind enemy lines as an ordinary civilian, the agent returned in the same inconspicuous manner in which he had penetrated the lines. SSS officers discussed with the platoon commander the probable route of the agent's return and the approximate hour at which he might be expected to appear at the American outpost. The agent was instructed to ask to be taken to SSS Hq. upon encountering American soldiers. The agent was retrieved at once, regardless of the place or hour. If it was believed that the mission could be accomplished in a short time, an SSS escort might await the agent's return at an agreed-upon rendezvous near the front. Or, as was often done, a hotel in a liberated town might be selected as a rendezvous point to which the agent or his courier would return with his report.

So many of the agents were overrun soon after they had succeeded in reaching their objective, that, rather than return through the lines, they waited for the division to catch up to them. A list of hotels along the probable line of advance was given the agent; he made contact with a member of the unit at the one in the town most recently liberated.

The emphasis on speed which characterized all SSS intelligence operations led to development of techniques designed to increase the efficiency of transmission of "civilian reconnaissance" reports. Instead of returning themselves through the lines or waiting to be overrun, agents employed

* Missions did not follow an exact pattern, of course. Each was planned and conducted in relation to the factors peculiar to the particular situation.

244

couriers to run the lines. Where a team of two or three was involved, a stagger system was often used. A courier was sent back with the first day's intelligence, one agent returned the next day with the second day's findings and a copy of the first report, while a final report and copies of the preceding ones might be carried by the original agent.

Another communication system was attempted without success. An agent with the 45th Division unit near Baccarat dropped messages into the Meurthe River to be picked up near Chenevieres. This proved too uncertain—the distance was great and a coincidental flooding of the river swept away the nets which had been constructed to receive the messages. Radio sets were requested, but did not prove practicable until after the lines had become stabilized in one vicinity. For technical reasons, they were not available, at any rate, for short-range intelligence until later.

Slow and uncertain as were the methods of "civilian reconnaissance", they were the best that could be devised under the haphazard conditions that prevailed. In addition to the fast pace which rendered so much costly intelligence obsolete, SSS was hampered by another factor. This was the frequent shifting and crossing of division objectives resulting from high echelon rearrangement of forces. On 26 August, for example, the Seventh Army was given the area north of the Durrance River, instead of the region west of the Rhone to Lyon. This meant a complete change of direction for all SSS units and a great loss in time and personnel. This happened not once but often, with a division's objectives changed as many as five times in a week. Data gathered by one division could be transferred to another or to the French First Army, when it was a mere case of replacement; but, more often, the work accomplished in one sector was nullified, since such changes ordered on short notice caused the abandonment of carefully prepared projects. Because the direction and use of agents for intelligence was such a personal matter, they could not be handed back and forth at will.

In spite of handicaps and mistakes, intelligence of high value was obtained by SSS and sent to those who needed it. At the 3rd Division, for instance, a team of six boys and another of three men scouted approaches to Vesoul and reported light defenses. The wife of a Vesoul police official walked fifty kilometers through a heavy barrage all night to that city and returned with an overlay of defenses, two hours before the assault began. On 14 September, G-2 requested reconnaissance of an area where FFI had reported the presence of 100 tanks. Three agents were infiltrated the night preceding an attack and found the report false.

At the 45th Division, a team of four young people was assigned the mission, on 10 September, of covering the town of Baume-les-Dames. They were briefed, given maps, and each told to report on one quarter of the town and surrounding fields and to return before dawn. Under heavy American artillery fire, they entered the town over garden walls.

Marianne entered the hospital in the center of town, spoke with some German soldiers and nuns and came back with the information that the town's garrison consisted of twelve men and non-coms billeted at the hospital, and four officers and a few enlisted men at the Kommandantur a few blocks away. . . . We were able to get back without being challenged and report the findings to Bn . . . we recommended that a patrol be sent in to capture the twenty men, and the CO agreed to this proposal. . . .

Leading the patrol across the fields, we entered Baume as light was breaking. Two Germans were seen in the street but they escaped before they could be shot. . . . We reached the hospital some distance ahead of the patrol and Marianne again entered . . . this time shaking the Germans out of their sleep and telling them to surrender for the Americans had arrived. They did. . . . Since it was then dangerous to stay in the town which was open from the north, or to take the time necessary to capture the Kommandantur, orders were issued to return with the prisoners. . . . We had no difficulty in driving back to the American lines, where we immediately reported the additional information that the Germans had tank and troop concentrations about four kms. north of Baume on the road to Lure. . . .*

Routes of enemy retreat and withdrawals were disclosed, accurate information on strongpoints, roadblocks, mines, and blown bridges obtained, and important service rendered on such items as:

River fordings
3rd Div. team gave a complete report on 24 September of all possible fordings of Moselle R. between Remiremont and Le Thillot. The list of seven places where the river might be crossed and which were used by American troops included minute description of river bed and banks. "From Rupt-sur-Moselle to Le Thillot, the river generally is ten meters wide and averages only thirty cms. in depth. The only place where it is believed fording is impossible is in the vic. of Saul, which lies SE of Ferdrupt 269320 at approximately 270317. The bridge at Saul was destroyed in 1940 and has not been rebuilt".**

Defense of towns
SSS teams were able to provide G-2 with the defense plans for such cities as Aix, Marseille, Valence, Lyon. The 36th Div. team performed outstanding service in getting the plans for Lyon. The SI PENNY FARTHING chain in the area was contacted—agents were put through the lines near Grenoble to report on defenses, airports, etc., resulting in the city's seizure by the Allies the next day with a minimum loss of life.

Supply and evacuation establishments
During the 24 hr. period of 5 September, 28 trains, averaging fifty cars each, moved from Belfort to Mulhouse, including two hospital trains, one train of seventy cars carrying robot bombs and apparatus, 7-8 supply trains and the remainder, troop trains. . . .***

Incidental taking of prisoners
The leader of the 3rd Div. SSS team in seeking contact with one of his returning agents, learned of the presence of forty Germans in the nearby woods. After protracted negotia-

* Team captain's report on 45th Division, SSS, History File 194.
** From Periodic Report No. 36, 21 Sept. 1944, of G-2, 3rd Infantry Division, History File 194.
*** From Periodic Report No. 22, 7 Sept. 1944, of G-2, 3rd Infantry Division, History File 194.

tions with their veteran sergeant-leader, the SSS officer persuaded them to surrender.

The tightening of the lines, after the Moselle was crossed, made it far more dangerous for agents posing as civilians near the front. In the face of mounting casualties, SSS attempted fewer operations, took greater security precautions with regard to cover, documentation, etc., and began to replace "civilian reconnaissance" missions with agent chains and teams with radio sets for direct, short-range communication.

An interesting incident foreshadowed this turning point which, although it at first weakened G-2's confidence, ended by strengthening the position of SSS. A 36th Division unit agent, "Gaston," reported:

A movement from Gerardmer toward Le Tholy during 25 September, of more than sixty pieces of 105 mm artillery, accompanied by 100 to 200 horse-drawn wagons.

Such massing of enemy strength was totally unexpected and higher army echelons warned against "wildness" in reporting intelligence. Checking missions were launched. Two SSS agents were captured and killed by the Germans; two were conscripted in a German forced labor draft. Heavy enemy shellfire followed shortly to corroborate conclusively the accuracy of "Gaston's" original report.

An unusual mission undertaken, in an effort to build up an agent chain, was that of "Joe-1912," a clergyman recruited by the 36th Division unit. Wearing his clerical garb and a Red Cross brassard, and carrying holy oil, "Joe-1912" was to proceed with a forest ranger guide to enemy-held Bruyeres and St. Die. He was to recruit and instruct sub-agents for intelligence work in these cities and to establish chains of informers over the mountain passes and into the Alsace plains. If apprehended, his story was that he was hurrying to the next town where the ranger's friend was dying. After extensive reconnoitering of areas under fire, the SSS conductor released the team at a point west of Bruyeres where there was good wooded cover. The passage through the forest and the cover story worked. On 30 September, the forest ranger returned with his own personal observations and a report from "Joe-1912's" first sub-agent, giving excellent and detailed coverage of the Bruyeres region. "Joe-1912" succeeded in organizing a chain * as far as St. Die and returned on 8 October, after the anti-clerical attitude there prevented further exploitation of his cover.

The use of secret radio was worked out gradually. Radio sets constituted an added risk in penetrating enemy lines, since an agent caught with one was liable to immediate execution. The type of battery set (SSTR-1) used by SI agents with their long-range networks was not adapted for short-range intelligence reporting on the Seventh Army front. Nor were the ciphering and monitoring techniques developed in pre-invasion France suited to the close combat conditions encountered. SCR-300 "walky-talkies" were obtained. SCR-300 was a frequency modulation "line-of-sight" device chosen for its short-range possibilities and because little training was required. It was limited to short ranges, could operate only under certain atmospheric conditions and had to be placed on high ground with no obstruction between sending and receiving sets. Although used eventually by all SSS divisional units, it was at the 36th that this set was first adapted with unusual success in conjunction with the MAYFAIR team.

MAYFAIR was composed of an experienced SI agent, who had previously been parachuted behind the lines as part of the *Proust* operations,** an FFI lieutenant who

had completed successful missions for the detachment, and a guide recruited locally through the FFI. The SSS leaders devised a practical plan to adapt the limitations of the SCR-300 to agent work. A simple verbal code was contrived; seven possible points of transmission on high ground behind enemy lines were charted; two receiving sets were placed on hills near American positions, so selected that, between them, they could cover by "line-of-sight" whichever of the seven points in enemy territory the agents were able to use. Instead of fixed contact times, the receiving operators listened on prearranged varying frequencies during a given ten-minute period of each hour from 8 a. m. to 7 p. m., and the desired one or two daily contacts could be made at such times as the exigencies of the agent's situation permitted. Besides giving the agent freedom of time and place in transmitting, the plan provided for intelligence of unusual freshness. No report would be more than thirteen hours old; most would be less. And an item of sufficient importance could be secured, transmitted, and received in a matter of minutes.

The first attempt at infiltration was made on the night of 5 October near Herpelmont. Troop movements delayed the operation, and the agents returned after having crossed the lines, since they found they would not have cover of darkness until they reached a safe house. An attempt was made in another sector the following night, but the party returned when one of the agents was wounded by a booby-trapped grenade located between the lines. An experienced replacement was quickly briefed, and the team was successfully dispatched near Fays the night of 7 October.

The first message was received the following day, giving the calibres and coordinates of the locations of 54 pieces of enemy artillery (105 mm, 88 mm, and AA). Between 9 and 25 October, 25 messages were received, containing, among other information, precise locations of guns and ammuni-

---

* These agents were eventually incorporated into the "Lulu" chain formed by the 36th Div. unit in early October between Bruyeres, St. Die and the passes of the Vosges. Couriers from eight sub-agents of the "Lulu" chain supplied, until overrun in late October, ten complete reports, including map overlays, and 170 items of intelligence on the region from Raon l'Etape to Fraize.

** See "SI/North France", above.

247

tion dumps. When the agents complained that no action was being taken on their reports, it was discovered that the Division Artillery Commander had not been informed that these were radioed on-the-spot reports. American artillery went into action, with MAYFAIR not only sending new positions but assisting the direction of fire by reporting on its accuracy. On 24 October, the counter-battery officer of VI Corps stated that the reports were the most accurate intelligence of the sort available from any source. MAYFAIR changed location on the same day to prevent capture, after the Gestapo dispersed the Maquis who were actively assisting them. The next day the radio set was damaged by American shellfire, and the agents returned through the lines to the SSS unit for a final oral report.

A team was dispatched jointly on 28 October by SSS officers of the 3rd and 36th Divisions, to find the "lost battalion" of the 141st Regiment. This was another case where the hoped-for SSS distinction between "combat" and "tactical" intelligence was ignored, due to the urgency of the mission. It did not succeed. The SSS trio was ambushed, a French agent killed, and two Americans wounded and captured.*

Incidents such as these continued, after October, to take a toll of SSS personnel, and attempts were made to withdraw battle-weary men. In the two months following D-Day, the 3rd Division unit had infiltrated 111 missions, handled 178 reports, and fur-

_____

* Because they were wounded, they were routed through medical channels (having hidden incriminating equipment), and were not subjected to the interrogation and torture which would normally have accompanied their capture. Both lived on in prison camps until liberation.

nished the Division with a total of 868 separate intelligence items (exclusive of vague or minor ones). Units at the 36th and 45th Divisions had established similar records. The joint losses of the three at the end of October were 10 killed, 15 wounded, 39 captured. Many of those captured were ultimately recovered.

Meanwhile, XV Corps, with two new divisions was transferred from Third Army to Seventh Army, demanding SSS assistance. Attempts to withdraw personnel from other divisional teams and to recall the SSS unit with the First Airborne Task Force * were blocked by the military authorities in charge of these units. Certain personnel were transferred, however, at the end of October, to the 79th and 44th Divisions, along with members of the recently disbanded SFU-4 (SPOC)** organization.

By the time the Allied armies reached the German-speaking Alsace region, SSS division methods of short-range infiltration were no longer practicable. The tactical intelligence units were withdrawn in November and new arrangements made for strategic and tactical intelligence in the Reich. Airdrops became the safest method of infiltration, controlled by SSS at Seventh Army Headquarters. In Germany, too, SSS produced the best results of all the field detachments on the West Front.***

_____

* SSS/Seventh Army administrative control of the unit with ABTF passed at this time to the OSS Detachment with the 6th Army Group. Other outlying SSS units—one at Toulouse for counter-intelligence in southwest France, and one at Pontarlier for liaison and facilitation of intelligence exchange between Army and OSS—were placed under Sixth Army Group also.
** See "Algiers Base", above.
*** See "West Front", below.

248

F. X-2/FRANCE

Because of the extreme mobility of the armies, it was essential that a plan be devised whereby expert counter-espionage assistance could be rapidly forwarded to the counter-intelligence staffs in the field. For this purpose, small groups of X-2 personnel were attached to field armies and army groups under the operational control of the Army Chief of Staff, G-2 through the Chief CIB. These Special Counter-Intelligence (SCI) units were directed to:

(1) Handle distribution of counter-espionage information, advising on its proper use in order to assure maximum security;

(2) Provide information regarding secret enemy intelligence organizations, personnel and activities, suggesting, on the basis of this knowledge, counter-espionage objectives and methods of dealing with them; and

(3) Help in the examination of captured enemy documents and captured enemy agents of intelligence interest. These services were primarily to assist the CIC staffs in the field, but also had a long-range value, in that the intelligence headquarters was in a position to obtain on-the-spot information for use in other areas and in piecing together the over-all pattern of enemy intelligence organizations. Other duties of the units were more closely tied to the general function of X-2 itself, protecting OSS sources of secret information in the territories invaded behind Allied and enemy lines, and supervising the play-back of controlled enemy agents (CEA's).

Only trained personnel could be expected to fulfill these duties, and it was for this reason that SHAEF approved the plans for SCI submitted by OSS in October 1943. The Counter-Intelligence Corps had neither the qualified personnel for this work nor the authority to handle all sources necessary for the complete coverage of CE cases. However, since CIC did have the executive authority which SCI lacked, the closest cooperation between the two groups was practiced, with the understanding that prisoners taken or documents captured would be available to SCI units.

Security reasons, coupled with the fact that much of the SCI material required previous special training, led to the maintenance of a mobile communications system separate from the army. In addition, direct lines between units and their headquarters considerably expedited the transmission of information needed for fast identification of captured agents and for the direction of operations. Each unit was equipped with its own files on CE personalities and targets, and personnel had been indoctrinated in all material pertinent to the area involved.

Two SCI groups landed with the armies in France in the north, and one in the south. The 31st SCI unit arrived with the U. S. First Army on Omaha Beach on D-plus-three. The 62nd SCI unit went into Normandy with Third Army in early July. Both units were incorporated into the 12th A. G. Target Force for Paris, and arrived there on the 25th of August 1944, before the Germans had been completely cleared from the city. The group divided, half to continue forward with the American armies, and half to remain in Paris which became headquarters for all SCI teams in France.*

Meanwhile, the 69th SCI, attached to Seventh Army, had landed on D-plus-five

---

* Total Paris and field X-2 personnel in France averaged approximately 150, and, of that number, the work in Paris engaged about sixty.

and later at various points on the southern French coast. Seventh Army advanced rapidly, leaving large areas behind it which required X-2 coverage. In October, the group was transferred from the jurisdiction of AFHQ to that of X-2/Paris and split into the 11th, 55th and 88th units, covering respectively the southeastern, southwestern and Seventh Army operational areas.

It had been found that control of counter-espionage operations could not efficiently be divided between various small units, and the consolidation of authority in Paris was an attempt to remedy this fault. Even this move, which still permitted a certain degree of confusion between the London * and Paris X-2 offices, did not approach the British counter-espionage policy which had maintained the tightest control in London, centered around the all-inclusive files and maps in the War Room.

The mere existence of a subordinate central office caused certain difficulties. A lack of reproduction facilities at the time of establishment of the Paris Office necessitated sending all the London files on France to Paris. Since agent cases had often to be checked against items of counter-espionage information on other countries, there was a degree of inefficient checking in both Paris and London, each of which lacked a complete file with all possible cross-referenced data.

The Paris unit entered that city on the evening of 25 August 1944.

The work was coordinated with that of the related sections of SHAEF, particularly the section which was responsible for approving all material transmitted by controlled enemy agents. X-2 also worked in conjunction with the French CE services, to which it eventually turned over most of its operations. It vetted all agents and employees hired by OSS in France, all visa applicants at the U. S. Embassy, and exchanged, with the two FBI representa-

* See "X-2/London", above.

tives at SHAEF, information on the cases of renegade collaborationists and on espionage leads affecting cases being handled by FBI in the Western Hemisphere.

Operations and Research and Intelligence Sections were established, the first being divided into two desks, one for tracing and handling the general run of Axis agents in France, the second for the operation of double-agents.

The Research and Intelligence Section, building up card files and sending out reports to the field and to interested agencies, created the principal control problem vis-a-vis the London office. It produced (chiefly from recently captured documents) target lists of cities and areas for the use of the CIB staffs, and did so at great speed. However, the London desk interested in such matters often had additional data, and had constantly to send out corrective lists, compiled in the light of the latest information available in full at headquarters. That information made it clear that the intelligence drawn from the captured documents—on the location of enemy intelligence offices, homes, training schools, etc.— was often no longer true or accurate. From this experience, X-2 again learned the importance of centralizing counter-intelligence and counter-espionage operations.

A counter-sabotage unit was directed from a special desk in the R. and I. Section. This desk coordinated all information on enemy sabotage agencies, personnel, methods and operations, and distributed this material to its officers who had been assigned to the G-2's of the different base sections on detached service from X-2. One of its chief aims was the protection of the oil pipe-line that supplied the armies, which was the target of many parachuted or line-crossing enemy sabotage agents. The counter-sabotage unit also handled the cases of all defected or captured enemy sabotage agents, several of whom supplied much valuable information on German methods and post-war plans. The mass use, during the German drive toward Liege and the Meuse of December 1944, of sabotage and subversion agents trained by Skorzeny, chief of the sabotage section of the Reichssicherheits-hauptamt, presented the unit with a major problem, both in the number of agents used and in the fact that they were dressed in American uniforms. However, nearly fifty percent of the number reported to have been used were captured.

Although the Paris job was largely one of directing operations of the SCI teams, several agents were captured in and around the city. A large number of enemy agents and espionage officials, captured in the area by X-2/Paris or turned over by other authorities, had to be given at least preliminary checking, and in some cases had to be sent to England for the more thorough Camp 020 * interrogations. By the end of September, X-2/Paris had in hand six enemy W/T agents, either operating or preparing to operate under its control. The secure housing, feeding and guarding of these individuals, apart from the intelligence aspects in the handling of their cases, presented difficulties of bothersome detail in the badly disorganized state of Paris at that time.

Numerous informants of varied—Allied or enemy—intelligence background provided, during those days, quantities of information, or leads to information, of a CE nature. One of these was developed into the greatest single source of information on the various German intelligence organizations and operations in France. Others proved to be the means to achieving profitable penetrations of the German organizations in several areas.

These investigations were carried out in some cases independently and in others jointly with the French and British. Particularly close liaison was maintained with the French, and no action involving French nationals was taken without consultation with the official French agency.

* See "X-2/London", above.

As in other countries, the role of X-2 in France was largely advisory. The executive work of X-2/Paris was normally done by the Counter-Intelligence Branch, SHAEF, or the local Army command. There were cases, however, when executive action was taken by local X-2 units or by the French DSM or by one of its successor agencies, the Bureau de la Surveillance du Territoire (in civilian counter-espionage cases).

One of the most fruitful captures was that of a German non-commissioned officer (X-2 code name, "Jigger") of Abwehr II (sabotage) headquarters. Because of his two years with that section and his contacts with German intelligence personnel during that time, "Jigger" was able to supply SCI with an impressive mass of detailed notes on the Abwehr II organization, its personalities and methods, as well as extensive records which he had removed from the files of the Paris ("Lutetia") headquarters. He made journeys with officers of the Sabotage Unit for the purpose of locating sabotage dumps, of which 1,000 were believed to have been left in France by the German armies, and located a large number of such caches. In return for his services, he was furnished room and board by SCI, but no pay. "Jigger's" value to the Allies was appreciated by the Germans. A captured agent under interrogation at the 12th Army Group revealed the fact that agents had been dispatched by the Germans to assassinate him.

From a theoretical standpoint, one of the most interesting cases was the play-back of a German agent in Paris, for six months after his death. "Keel", an SD agent since 1940, gave himself up to X-2 on 28 August 1944, three days after Paris was liberated. He had been left by the Germans as a "sleeper" agent, and X-2 decided to use him. One month later he was killed by French citizens, taking justice into their own hands, for his previous informing activities during German rule.

An American sergeant thereupon took over the operation of "Keel's" W/T set, explaining the changed "fist" by a fictional severe accident to the dead agent's right arm. A French CE officer checked the new messages for correctness of idiom and tone. Although the German base maintained contact with the sergeant until April, no agents or supplies were ever parachuted to him. However, three paymaster agents were captured, all of whom had been told to find "Keel" and determine whether or not he was a double-agent. Each carried 200,000 francs for him.

Such controlled enemy agent (CEA) operations as these supplemented the headquarters and liaison activities of X-2/Paris. A much larger quantity of double-agent cases was meanwhile handled by the SCI units with the armies, acting under London and Paris coordination. Three such cases are described below:

DRAGOMAN

DRAGOMAN, a Spanish national living in Cherbourg, was the first Abwehr W/T agent to be captured after the invasion of France who was susceptible of exploitation as a controlled enemy agent. He thus became the first American SCI case to be run on the Continent.

As was true of most of the German agents subsequently captured, DRAGOMAN agreed immediately to work under control. Attempts to contact his base were commenced on 13 July 1944, and contact was successfully established on 25 July. DRAGOMAN was almost continuously on the air for more than nine months, until early May 1945. During this period he worked as an interpreter for an American Army office in Cherbourg and lived at home. His W/T transmissions were made from an SCI installation and supervised by SCI officers.

Another German agent, named DESIRE, was sent to contact DRAGOMAN in late August and, through the latter's cooperation, was arrested by SCI. As a result of the capture, another stay-behind W/T

agent, who was working near Granville, was arrested within twenty-four hours. He became the SCI-controlled W/T agent, SKULL.* DESIRE was not doubled.

The notional employment of DRAGOMAN presented to the Germans was as similar as possible to his true position. He stated that he was working as an interpreter in an American Port Office. In this capacity he could be presumed to learn of certain local plans involving the use of French labor, equipment or property, but could not be expected to learn much of troop movements. He would be able to gather some material from direct observation of the harbor, but no more than could be seen by German reconnaissance planes. The fact that he held an all-day office job could creditably be supposed to limit the amount of his observation.

With these limitations in mind, messages which could be transmitted by DRAGOMAN, in answer to the German questionnaires which he received, were approved by the appropriate SHAEF authorities. This material consisted of censored facts, which, by omissions, were made purposely misleading to the Germans, who were forced to draw certain conclusions from them.

At German request, DRAGOMAN made several notional trips around the Cotentin Peninsula to report on specific targets, and even went to visit SKULL in order to pick up money from the Germans in payment for his services. He was also instrumental in keeping SKULL "alive" over an initial three-month period, when the latter notionally was unable to establish contact with his base because of damage to his radio set. DRAGOMAN's detailed reports of SKULL's supposed difficulties were followed by the Germans with the keenest interest.

DRAGOMAN sent, in all, 238 messages to the Abwehr, and, in conjunction with SKULL, whose messages he often confirmed or supported, largely controlled information reaching the Germans from Cherbourg and

---
* See below.

252

the Cotentin Peninsula in general. In short, data concerning this strategic area which reached the Germans was only that which the Allies considered it safe or advantageous for them to know.

Specifically, as part of a plan to show strength against the possibility of a German attack from the Channel Islands, Special Plans, 12th Army Group, requested that DRAGOMAN identify, for the Germans, 12th Armored Division patches in Cherbourg. When questioned about the pipeline out of Cherbourg, DRAGOMAN represented it to the Germans as so formidably guarded that, presumably, the Germans were discouraged from large-scale attempts to sabotage it. He was able to build up a picture of American armed naval strength in Cherbourg in order to discourage submarine attacks on incoming convoys in adjacent waters.

As proof of German confidence in DRAGOMAN, he received, in a parachute drop made to SKULL, new radio equipment, crystals and a new signals plan.

Interrogation after the war of both DRAGOMAN's German case officer and the CO of Leitstelle I-West, to whom DRAGOMAN's messages were passed, revealed that the Germans considered DRAGOMAN as one of their best stay-behind W/T agents in France and never considered the possibility that he was working under control.

SKULL

At the time of the invasion of North France, seven agents were in W/T contact with Le Havre under the direction of Friedrich Kaulen, an official of the I. M. Division of the Abwehr. When his position at Le Havre became dangerous in mid-June 1944, Kaulen moved his establishment to Arcachon, south of Bordeaux, where he added an eighth member to his chain. Because of the swift Allied advance, his station was soon organized into the Front-Aufklaerungskommando 60 to be withdrawn to Holland. This withdrawal of the directing agency from the area of actual operations left the I. M. agents of Kdo. 60 free to cease working for Kaulen. Whether these agents, left on their own in France, meant to continue working for the Germans if they had not been captured by the Allies, is hard to tell. However, the first of the group was arrested 26 August 1944, and, by 10 December, all but two were in Allied hands.

These members of Kaulen's network were more than eager to transfer their affiliations—simply for the purpose of saving their skins, if for no other reason. By December 1944, five members of the I. M. chain had resumed their operations under Allied control. SKULL and one other agent were put on the air under American auspices, with the French and British together running three others. A sixth was considered too dangerous to risk and caused several difficulties.

Shortly after his arrest on 26 August, SKULL was sent to England for interrogation. The trip, which required considerable time, coupled with the difficulties encountered in trying to find a set similar to the one he had used previously, delayed his return to the air for three months. Fortunately this lapse, which might have caused his German employers to become suspicious, was covered by DRAGOMAN.[*] The enemy base accepted the statement that SKULL's set was in need of repair, but asked that DRAGOMAN go to St. Pair (where SKULL was notionally located) to inquire further. This tended to connect the two men more closely than SCI would wish. Should the Germans discover that SKULL was controlled, they would almost immediately suspect the other Normandy agent, and the latter's value to the Americans was far greater in Cherbourg than was SKULL's value in St. Pair.

A second problem in the launching of the SKULL case was that the sixth member of the group captured was a confirmed Nazi and therefore a bad risk for use as a double-

---

[*] See above.

agent. The Germans would realize that he was under arrest, unless some adequate explanation could be given for his going off the air. Since he had by far the most dependable character in the network, they would expect him more than the others to carry out his mission. It was known both to the enemy and to SCI that he had a great weakness for women, so a story was transmitted by DRAGOMAN to the effect that the man had disappeared with a new "friend", and that SKULL had stayed off the air, not only because of his damaged set, but also for fear of being compromised by this action of his colleague's.

In the meantime, a suitable W/T set and location had been found for SKULL at St. Pair. Contact was established on 27 November 1944, and was satisfactorily maintained until 2 May 1945. The situation had been extremely delicate, and a single false step might have brought disaster both to the SKULL operation and to DRAGOMAN in Normandy. The latter case was well on its way to being one of the most successful in the then strategic Cherbourg area, and SKULL was only intended to be a short-range operation. It was soon discovered, however, that this linking of agents would have been essential anyway, since the Germans were unable to pay their agents without using them interchangeably as paymasters. Later, SKULL himself became the trusted paymaster for all German agents in France, and this position made it highly desirable for SCI to continue his case, even though, from a military point of view, his area was unimportant.

On 1 February 1945, the first drop to SKULL was made by a mail plane en route from Germany to the Channel Islands. The success of the drop was more than could have been anticipated. Along with the money for distribution to other agents, new crystals and new signal plans had been sent. Shortly after this, Kaulen himself arrived in the Bordeaux sector to expand his network. Bordeaux was at that time a German pocket; and he asked SKULL to meet him there for consultations. This approach offered the Allies a perfect opportunity, and Operation TRIPOD was inaugurated. If Kaulen could be captured alive, he might be persuaded to give X-2 information, not only on the German intelligence plans for France, but details of the stay-behind network then being formed for the North Sea coast of Holland and Germany. In addition, he might have information on the post-war intentions of the German services. Since Kaulen had already requested a rendezvous with SKULL, the operation would, on the surface, appear to be relatively simple. However, the possibility that SKULL would be blown, should the scheme fail, had to be considered in the light of his importance as paymaster and key to the German network in France. This consideration was weighed against the probable value of a successful TRIPOD operation, and it was finally decided that the controlled agent should meet the German near Bordeaux. A meeting place was designated, and arrangements were made for a reception committee to be stationed there ready to capture the two men. Any persons accompanying Kaulen were to be taken or killed. A story would appear the next day in the Bordeaux papers stating that a Frenchman and a German officer had been killed by the FFI, and the rest of the party could be truthfully reported as either captured or killed. This would bring to a dramatic close the careers of Kaulen and SKULL, and the latter's notional death would preserve the rest of the French operators from suspicion.

On 6 April 1945, SKULL, accompanied by SCI officers and a large group of heavily armed French and American soldiers, proceeded to the appointed field adjacent to the point on the bank of the Gironde where Kaulen's boat was to land. SKULL flashed the prearranged signals to guide the German party in, and, on the pretense that he must get his valise, drew Kaulen into the field with him. Unfortunately, his light accidentally flashed fully on the face of an American sergeant, and, in the ensuing confusion and shooting, a soldier nearly strangled SKULL. Despite directions that all firing was to be low, Kaulen was shot three times and died within a few minutes.

Despite this unfortunate turn of events, much was gained from the operation. One of the achievements credited to SKULL in connection with the TRIPOD operation was that, since he was more trusted by the Germans than any other agent in France, the instructions found on Kaulen for him contained many valuable details. It was noted that in these very complete instructions every agent mentioned was already under control, or at least neutralized, by the Allies.

SKULL's career under the 31st SCI unit in northern France was an unusually safe counter-espionage operation. His job for the German Intelligence Service was that of errand boy. As a result, X-2 could gain extensive CE information, while offering in return almost no intelligence.

WITCH

On the night of 26 October 1944, a German plane carried out the double mission of supplying beleaguered German forces on the French coast and parachuting en route a French agent and W/T operator. Their mission was to procure intelligence on Allied troop identification in the Verdun area, to report their findings by W/T and to return across the German lines within eight days.

The two agents were captured separately by local French authorities, within a few hours of landing, and turned over to SCI officers through the American CIC. The fact that the W/T set and radio data were recovered in good condition, and that the men appeared willing to work for the Americans, warranted consideration of the use of at least the W/T operator as a controlled agent.

Although the men had been sent on a short-term mission, it was felt that, if con-

tact could be successfully established with the Germans, they might be persuaded to allow the agents to stay indefinitely behind Allied lines. The batteries for the W/T set could not be expected to last for more than a month; so the enemy would also have to be persuaded to supply new batteries or a hand-operated set within a few weeks. Since the information-gathering agent would be only an encumbrance in a controlled W/T operation, it was decided that WITCH, which was the code name given to the radio operator, would report to the Germans that he had not seen his companion after the jump and that he had presumably been killed or arrested.

WITCH was installed in the 12th Army Group Interrogation Center jail in Verdun, and managed to make contact with his base on 4 November. He was the first controlled W/T agent to operate in northeastern France. A logical explanation was supplied the Germans concerning WITCH's difficulties after parachutage, in order to explain the eight-day delay in opening contact.

In the event that the Germans should insist that WITCH return, it had been decided to gain at least one counter-intelligence advantage out of the case, by forcing the Germans to suggest the easiest route across the lines, so that American security authorities could be notified of the loop-holes. Thus on 10 November, WITCH asked his base to "advise places favorable for passage", in case he had to return. The enemy replied that, because of events at the front, return was not favorable, but that the most auspicious time and place would be announced as soon as feasible.

While WITCH was operating in the vicinity of Verdun, his traffic had little tactical significance. Arrangements were made with the proper authorities to clear material of a type which allowed WITCH to make a pretense of work, while he was maneuvered into a position to assume a more serious role.

In two messages, received on 26 November and 1 December, the Germans finally proposed to WITCH several alternative routes for his return through the lines. These were promptly communicated to CIB, Third Army, and steps were taken to tighten security controls on these routes. At the same time, it was decided to have WITCH notionally attempt to try to return by one of these routes in order to prove his good faith. He warned his base that if he failed he would return to Verdun, and requested that they listen for him for the next ten days.

During the ensuing week, the local G-2 at St. Avold, a town on one of the routes, cooperated in simulating the supposed arrest and escape of WITCH. Although the capture was not enacted, the 80th Division public address system was used in St. Avold to announce the arrest and escape of an alleged enemy agent, whose description was given in detail. This was done for the benefit of any German informers or line-crossers who might have been in St. Avold in a position to report back to the Germans.

After the passage of sufficient time for WITCH to make his way notionally back to Verdun, he sent a bitter message to his base, reporting his failure and berating the Germans for their inefficiency in choosing escape routes. The base replied apologetically and instructed WITCH to establish himself in the Metz-Thionville area. Thus WITCH had been ordered to a strategic spot and could now be handled on a long-term basis. This occurred just in time for the Battle of the Bulge. Metz was a most critical point along the lateral lines of communication and a spot where an uncontrolled agent could, with reasonable accuracy, observe the entire American plan of unit shifts unfolding to meet the Ardennes crisis. The movement of WITCH and another SCI-controlled agent to that city tended to build up agent concentration to the saturation point, so that the Germans would consider it fully covered and not feel compelled to send in additional agents who might be able to work uncontrolled.

During this time, a system of communications and tactics was worked out with G-2, which functioned so smoothly that SCI was able to report events and units to the enemy within a few hours after the units were known to have been committed and so no longer required secrecy as to their movements. Although this was known information, the time lag in transmission was so small that it looked as though WITCH were doing a fine job of reporting. During this period the movements of six divisions were covered. The Germans were so pleased with the tactical information that they awarded WITCH the Iron Cross—the first of three Iron Crosses American-controlled W/T agents were to receive from the enemy for their outstanding work. The advantage to American security in controlling enemy espionage in the area was, of course, inestimable.

In addition to tactical intelligence, requests for money and complaints that his batteries were about to wear out constantly appeared in WITCH's traffic, in an endeavor to force the Germans to send a courier. During the month of January, his pleas for assistance were finally answered, and his base sent detailed questions relative to the arrival of a parachute-courier. Elaborate plans were made for a safe rendezvous, but, due to an error in navigation, the Luftwaffe plane dropped the courier and eight other agents fifty miles off pinpoint. With one exception, all these agents were in custody within twelve hours, due to excellent Army security measures.

WITCH's courier, who was given the cover name of WIZARD, had a W/T set, batteries, a new signal plan, spare radio parts, 125,000 francs and $120 for delivery to WITCH. On landing, he buried all his equipment and part of his money, which immediate search by Allied agencies failed to locate. Since, however, batteries were by this time notionally essential to WITCH, he reported that

WIZARD had brought the batteries and part of the money, and had left to fetch the W/T set and the new signals plan. This explained to the base why the new plan was not put immediately to use. The next step was to get rid of WIZARD without arousing enemy suspicion. This was easily accomplished inasmuch as WIZARD had been instructed to return to Germany. WITCH reported that, having failed to find his cache of equipment, WIZARD had left on his return trip, and was not heard from again.

Meanwhile, WITCH's traffic continued from Metz with renewed volume. He was asked by the Germans to visit the Sarrebourg-Saverne area (an indication that the enemy had no agents there) but demurred.

A hint, on 24 February, that a co-worker might be sent to WITCH aroused SCI hopes that another agent might be trapped, but these hopes never materialized. At about this time, WITCH was given notional employment in the American Red Cross Club in Metz, where he supposedly would be able to observe a wide variety of shoulder-patch unit identifications and to pick up any sort of military gossip deemed fit for German ears.

WITCH lost contact with his base for three weeks in March but regained it again on 3 April. Contact was sporadic during the month, and the base was last heard on 29 April. For many weeks after the close of the war, WITCH's schedules were monitored in the hopes that some remnants of German intelligence might attempt to reach him, but results were negative.

In post-war interrogations, the CO of Leitstelle I-West and the CO of the Kommando to whom WITCH reported agreed that WITCH was one of the four outstanding German stay-behind agents in France and, in fact, came to be considered the best agent of all by I-c Oberbefehlshaber West, because of the tactical information which he furnished.

These cases illustrate the type of work performed by X-2 in France.* The Branch had only been organized in 1943 and had had to find the manpower and equipment to establish a complete foreign counter-espionage organization later than had other large branches. This disadvantage was offset, however, by remarkable British assistance and tutelage, with the result that, by the time of the French campaign, X-2 was able to contribute teams of trained personnel, who could carry on the counter-intelligence and deception job independently and competently.

In early April 1945, SCI moved forward, when 12th Army Group left Verdun for Wiesbaden. Jurisdiction over French cases was then left to the French, with an SCI liaison officer reporting to both SCI headquarters Paris and to the SCI unit with 12th A.G. in Germany.**

---

* A similar job was carried out by the SCI team in Italy. See "X-2/Italy", above.
** See "Central Europe", below.

Part VI

INDIRECT PENETRATION OF CENTRAL EUROPE

From three neutral capitals, OSS attempted the most difficult kind of positive intelligence work. Normal agent operations involved sending to the target area a quantity of observers to collect information which could be heard, seen, bought, or stolen. The process was a straightforward one, subject to relatively direct control. Less predictable was the indirect approach, by which intelligence operatives attempted, often from outside, to obtain information from a few highly-placed members of the target community. Through them it was possible to gain high-level intelligence of a type which could rarely be obtained by agents operating directly on a lower echelon.

Bases were established at Stockholm, Istanbul, and Bern, the first two with staffs approximating fifty personnel, the last with less than twelve Americans.

Poor direction in Istanbul resulted in almost complete failure. All contacts in Central Europe, instead of being operated individually by OSS/Istanbul, were handled through one sub-agent, whose activity was penetrated by the Gestapo. Stockholm and Bern, on the other hand, produced excellent high-level intelligence. One Stockholm item in 1943 was rated by British SIS "the find of the year", and one Bern agent "the best intelligence source of the war". German authorities unsuspectingly conducted a Stockholm agent on a one-week tour of the German synthetic oil industry. Bern's greater quantity and quality included contacts in the German underground group which engineered the 20 July 1944 attempt on Hitler's life, and accurate reportage on German scientific developments in atomic and bacteriological warfare, and on the V-bombs, including both their assembly and firing locations.

Control of such operations was a far more delicate task than that involved in the direct approach. Security and communications presented peculiar difficulties. Years of preparation, and experienced personnel would have increased the chances of success, but even then the risks were great. After Pearl Harbor, it became evident that the United States had few men trained in such work and little time for the long-range preparations which are normally essential to its success. Mistakes and losses (as was apparent in Istanbul) were inevitable; the achievements (particularly those of OSS/-Bern) were surprisingly high.

A. STOCKHOLM

Like Bern and Istanbul, Stockholm provided a neutral base close to German-controlled Europe. Here OSS interviewed refugees, sailors, travellers, officials, and businessmen from Germany, Denmark, Norway, and the Baltic countries, and reported infringements of Swedish-German agreements. Some of the best intelligence finds of the war were acquired through liaison with representatives of Baltic countries in Stockholm. From Swedish sub-bases in Malmoe, Haelsingborg, and Goeteborg, OSS agents penetrated Norway, Denmark, Finland, Lithuania, and Germany. Bases along the Norwegian frontier dispatched supplies across the border to Norwegian guerrilla groups.

SECRET INTELLIGENCE

The first agent (dispatched by COI) arrived in March 1942 to lay the groundwork for further intelligence activities. By the end of the year there were three men, including the prospective mission chief,

The State Department had the controlling decisions in the entry of new OSS representatives, and also in communications. It was therefore with some misgiving that the new OSS mission chief listened to the U.S. Minister's first ultimatum. A week after his arrival, the Minister called him in to inform him that any espionage activity for the U.S. on his part would result in the Minister's personal request for his recall.

Relations, however, slowly improved. State Department cable facilities were used, with the Minister retaining the right to inspect all outgoing messages.

And in mid-1944, following the SKF affair,* it was the strong stand taken by the Minister vis-a-vis the Swedish Government that allowed OSS to remain in that country. As the Axis defeat became more obvious during 1944, and Swedish cooperation with the Allies improved, the Minister made high-level arrangements through the Swedish Under Secretary of State for meetings between OSS and the Swedish secret police.

Three _____ established in Malmoe, Haelsingborg, and Goeteborg, received OSS agents as _____ in the summer and autumn of 1943. These ports line the Kattegat sea-lane between Denmark and Sweden, and provided excellent vantage points for (a) interviewing sailors, refugees, travellers, officials, and businessmen coming out through Denmark, and (b) spot intelligence on German traffic to and from Norway. By contacting leaders of transport workers in these ports and in Stockholm, OSS procured the first consistent flow of accurate information on the German transit traffic to and from Norway through Sweden. The information showed that the personnel and materiel traffic was far heavier than the Swedish-German agreement permitted, and than believed by the U.S. State Department. OSS reports covering the shipment of troops resulted, in late 1943, in the suspension of the Swedish Government's permission for German troops to be moved through Sweden.

Nevertheless, it was the

---

* Described below.

at Malmoe who collected, from a Swedish official in the seamen's union, the most telling evidence on German troop movements via Oresund, Sweden.

Through contacts with the Danish resistance, he also recruited two young men who were dispatched to Denmark. They came back some weeks later with intelligence on German troop movements, installations, and morale, and returned again to Denmark. By the time of their second return, the Swedish secret police had learned of their activities and arrested them. Through the tacit assistance of a Danish-born police officer, however, they were released and returned to Denmark, whence one of them went to Germany to return eventually with more German military intelligence.

Other agents were subsequently dispatched on round trips to Denmark from Stockholm. In the same way, travellers from Goeteborg established networks of SI agents in Norway, Finland, and the Baltic states. An SO contact with a Gestapo group in Norway produced, in early 1945, the number and location of German divisions there, including those which had just moved in from Finland.

An outstanding espionage accomplishment was the coverage of SKF ball bearing shipments to Germany. During early 1944, one of the main objectives of the strategic bombing program was the destruction of the German ball bearing industry. As the supply of enemy ball bearings became more stringent, due to the success of the air program, acquisition of Swedish ball bearings became increasingly important to the enemy. Despite strenuous efforts by the Economic Warfare Divisions of the American and British Governments, including extremely liberal preclusive buying arrangements with SKF, it was estimated that five to seven percent of the total German supplies were coming from SKF Goeteborg, with the percentages running considerably higher for certain types of bearings.

During 1943, the OSS in Goeteborg obtained from his transport worker contacts the approximate tonnages of ball and roller bearings leaving the harbor, the names of the ships loading bearings, the times of departure, and ports of destination. This intelligence, wired to London, caused the sinking by air attack of one such ship.

In order, however, to gain even more accurate information, the SI representative contacted through cut-outs, an individual, "B", who was working in the SKF shipping office in Goeteborg. "B" had considerable moral misgivings, being divided between loyalty to his company and his government on the one hand and, on the other, belief in the Allied cause. He would accept no payment.

From December 1943 to May 1944, he supplied reports on the ball bearing shipments, serial numbers and quantities; also on the export of ball bearing tools and machinery, such as the lathes made at the SKF subsidiary plant in Lidkjoeping and shipped to Schweinfurt. To avoid discovery, the OSS cut-outs were constantly changed, but on 13 May 1944 "B" was arrested by the Swedish secret police.

The data he had supplied showed that the exports were larger than the Swedish Government had admitted. In May, a U.S. Economic Warfare Mission arrived in Stockholm, and, using these figures, extracted an agreement to stop all ball bearing shipments. Agent "B" was given a three-year jail sentence, lost his position in his firm, and for some time his rights as a Swedish citizen.

Agent "Red", recruited in Washington, acquired some excellent intelligence. An oil dealer, he had been blacklisted early in the war for trading with the Germans. He was given a chance to prove innocence and went to work for OSS in Stockholm. As a Swedish citizen, he affected a sympathetic interest in maintaining the German oil supply. He pretended to plan a synthetic oil plant in Sweden and contacted August Rosterg, who owned the controlling interest in the German firm of Wintershall. From him he obtained considerable information on German oil manufacture and supply.

In October 1944, he arranged a week's tour of the synthetic oil industry in Germany, visiting and inspecting many plants. His subsequent report received favorable comment from British MEW and American experts. In particular, the information on the Ammendorf plant was considered valuable. German officials finally became suspicious and avoided further contacts with him.

The Japanese next approached "Red" independently, in the fall of 1944, with a proposition that he buy ball bearings for them. He accepted the assignment and actually bought some. In the meantime, however, the Russo-Japanese negotiations for shipping the bearings via Russia broke down, and the Japanese began laying plans for smuggling them into Germany. The Swedish secret police uncovered the negotiations, and the attempt was given up, but not before "Red" had obtained valuable evidence of the types and amounts of bearings most desired by the Japanese, incidental information on Japanese and German personalities and activities in Sweden, and clues which helped the Swedes arrest a group of smugglers. Through VE-Day, the Japanese continued their close relations with "Red", who exploited them for much counter-intelligence information.

One double-agent, "Phillip Morris", was taken on by OSS/Stockholm. He presented himself to SI in April 1943 and offered information on members of the Italian Intelligence Service and bombing targets in Italy. A Washington report (based on information from the British, the FBI, and X-2/Italy) described "Phillip Morris" as one who would sell his services to the highest bidder or bidders. The chief of mission,

however, elected to hire him and laid on an operation to take place in Italy. The agent was unfortunately arrested for espionage by the Swedes in late 1944, and escaped with German assistance to enemy territory, where he reported the contacts given him in Switzerland and in Italy.

The best intelligence of all came from liaison with foreign services in Stockholm. The intelligence service of the Polish Government-in-Exile in Stockholm gave OSS top priority in reports, in return for assistance in supplies, transportation, etc. A notable item was its report on a new underwater detection device ("schnorkel") installed on German U-boats. X-2 rated highly Polish counter-espionage material. A similar liaison with the Hungarian Minister in Stockholm began in December 1943. Esthonian, Latvian, Lithuanian, Belgian and Dutch refugee groups provided further intelligence. In return for an OSS/Stockholm pledge not to establish independent networks in Denmark, British SIS and SOE relayed all their reports on the area.

Good relations with the Swedish Government proved remunerative, particularly after the termination of German transit traffic in the fall of 1943.

The release from jail of several SI sub-agents was secured.

The First Secretary of the Soviet Legation approached an SI official in late 1943 with a proposed barter arrangement. In return for SI reports on Baltic shipping, the Russians would supply certain Japanese information. SI soon discovered that this exchange was a one-way street, and the relationship was converted into a social one. It was suspected that the Russians hoped merely to ascertain the extent of American penetration into Finland.

The Finns were at war with Russia and Britain and had no relations with the British in London. In Stockholm, however, OSS approached the Finnish Military and Naval Attaches.

The Labor Section/SI cultivated labor and social-democratic groups in Stockholm for political and economic intelligence. Through the International Transportworkers Federation, several German sailors were contacted who supplied reports of bombing results and shipping activities. A Swedish sailor, signing up on a German ship, was dispatched by the Labor Desk to stay in Hamburg and gather intelligence for some time prior to working his way back. He left on 24 February and arrived safely at Hamburg, but was not again heard from.

Labor Desk attempts at direct infiltration through Denmark were complicated by British refusal (through SFHQ) to permit use of their Danish lines for passing leftist agents to Germany. Labor/SI had to buy from Danish resistance headquarters in Sweden, safe passage for one social-democrat agent, "Herbert".

"Herbert" landed in Denmark and was conducted through the country to the German border. His mission was to contact local ITF and other union groups in and around Hamburg. Stockholm heard nothing from him until May, when the British found him in a Hamburg prison awaiting execution as a spy.

In general, the most successful SI infiltrations were the indirect ones like agent "Red", while SO handled the bulk of direct penetrations.

SPECIAL OPERATIONS

Sweden offered possibilities of direct infiltration by boat either to the North German ports or through Denmark. Since the time was short, however, OSS/ETO maintained in London the facilities already established there. A document section was, for instance, never set up in Stockholm, with the result that agents had to wait long periods for the arrival from London of papers, which were often outdated by that time. A Labor Desk agent, "Goethe", could not leave when his documents came two months late and incorrectly prepared. No air transport was available. At the same time, Swedish ships ceased traffic to Germany in late 1944, when insurance companies withdrew their coverage. This left OSS only two possibilities, German ships to Germany and Swedish fishing boats to Denmark.

The latter route proved simpler, since Danish resistance contacts offered a degree of safety in the trip to the German border. The WESTFIELD Mission,* SO, sent one team through Denmark, but at a time when the SFHQ lines had just been blown, and most of the members were hiding out.

---

* See "Norway and Denmark", above.

The team was divided into two sections. "Birch", the leader, who had friends in Berlin, was to go in first alone, establishing, if possible, a safe route through Denmark and Germany. The radio operator and one assistant were to follow as soon as they had word from him outlining the route. A courier had deposited two radio sets, explosives, cameras, film, food, cigarettes, and liquor for them in Berlin. Pending the arrival of his radio operator, the leader would use the bi-weekly courier service.

"Birch" left Goeteborg by Swedish trawler on 22 February 1945, but had to turn back because of Gestapo seizure of the fishing hamlet in Denmark where he was to land. On 5 March, a second attempt succeeded in landing him at Skagen. Here he arranged for transportation by car, through a Danish resistance agent, known to the fishing group which had brought him ashore.

From Skagen, he was driven to Aalborg, where he contacted a dentist as a safe address for his two assistants. He took a train to Kolding, passing several control searches, and in Kolding contacted a fish dealer, one of the members of the old SFHQ underground.

The fish dealer took him across the German frontier between Krusaa and Flensburg at midnight, 13 March; midnight was the usual hour for a delivery of fish, and the controls were not too strict. They drove to Hamburg, where "Birch" went to a safe address provided by SFHQ, and arranged for the trip of his successors. Moving on to Bergedorf, he looked up a gasoline dealer, whose name had been given him by the fish dealer, and made similar arrangements.

At Bergedorf he met a Danish chauffeur who agreed to take him to Berlin in return for American cigarettes and coffee, plus gasoline from the dealer. "Birch" was in Berlin by 15 March.

Living with friends in Bernau, a few miles northeast of the capital, he prepared a report which he sent back

He slowly legalized his status, obtaining the various necessary papers, licenses, and ration cards. He recruited a noted physician, who treated, among others, Ribbentrop and Goebbels; the doctor provided, besides intelligence, two guns with ammunition, and lodgings in both Berlin and Potsdam.

Subject to constant Anglo-American bombing, and eventually to Russian artillery, "Birch" covered the whole Berlin area and sent back, three more reports. He took a car trip to Hamburg in early April, principally to see if his two followers had yet arrived. His trip took him within six miles of the front, where he found and reported the degree of disorganization and wreckage. Returning to Berlin, he spent nearly all of the last half of April in an air-raid shelter with the rest of the starving Berlin population. The Russians entered his sector of Berlin on 2 May, and he was returned to the U. S. occupation zone on 20 May, carrying one of the first reports on conditions in the Russian zone.

The radio operator and assistant, who were to follow along the underground route to Berlin, never arrived. The two men did traverse Denmark in late April, aided by fake documents, cigarettes, and pornographic pictures. Crossing the German border on 2 May, they spent four days in Luebeck, surrounded by British troops. When they were overrun on 6 May, they supplied counter-espionage and tactical information.

"Birch" was the only successful direct infiltration from Stockholm. Even this mission came too late for the reports, relayed by courier, to contain any outstanding items. OSS/Sweden did not have the facilities (documents, transport, staff) available in London * for such direct operations.

* See "Direct Penetration from London", below.

MORALE OPERATIONS

A two-man MO unit arrived in April 1944, and, using OWI equipment, began production of black propaganda. Some 250,000 pamphlets, leaflets, stickers, posters, letters, and seductive booklets and postcards were turned out. The unit produced and distributed the Harvard Project News Letter, *Handel und Wandel*. This was a weekly business publication containing largely financial news, together with editorial matter frankly angled from a German industry viewpoint. Its purpose was to hold out the hope to German businessmen that if they acted to throw out the Nazi leaders, Allied business interests would cooperate with them in building a bulwark against Bolshevism. Limited distribution of this publication * was made mostly through SO agents in Norway, Denmark, Sweden, and Germany, the bulk being distributed through OSS/Stockholm, the remainder through Lisbon. One pamphlet in late August 1944, following the Finno-Russian armistice, was distributed among the German troops in North Finland urging them to escape to Sweden. Swedish officers stated that a large number of soldiers deserted, many of them carrying the leaflet. Rumors were also spread in Stockholm, some of them reaching, through friendly news reporters, the front page of Swedish papers.

X-2

The three-man X-2 unit, under State Department cover, performed the only U.S. counter-espionage in Scandinavia.

Upon arrival in April 1944, the first X-2 agent was presented by SI with visa information (including photos) on every German citizen who had entered or left Sweden for the previous several months. SI fur-

---

* Comments on *Handel und Wandel* are in the section on MO/Washington. To propagandize for a "bulwark against Bolshevism" was not then part of Allied policy; MO, however, was free to do so, since its publication pretended to emanate from enemy sources.

ther assisted in the penetration of two embassies: a Bulgar contact furnished regular coverage of developments, personnel and reports in the Bulgar Legation; through a Sudeten-German trade unionist, a representative of the SI/Labor Desk contacted a code clerk in the office of the German Military Attache, and, from March 1945 to the end of the war, obtained copies of German cables even before they were sent. With such SI aid, and in cooperation with the British, Swedish, Norwegian, Danish, Dutch, and French counter-espionage services, X-2 acted to protect both Sweden itself and U.S. agencies in Sweden from Axis espionage.

Maximal attention was given to the technological field, in view of Sweden's outstanding industrial and scientific achievements and their possible use by the enemy. The best defense being offensive penetration, information was collected on the intelligence services, of the northern European states at home and of the external intelligence organizations active within each of these countries. Penetration of these services, including those of underground movements, pseudo-governments, and governments-in-exile, was carried out through controlled and double-agents. X-2 gave valuable assistance in the neutralization of over 150 active German agents (all confined or executed) and the identification of over 3,000 agents and officials of intelligence interest. Of paramount importance in mid-1945 was the information obtained on the collaboration between German and Japanese intelligence organizations and between the Axis and neutral countries.

X-2 also frustrated enemy activities directed at the United States. It was initially responsible for keeping out of the United States several technologists, formerly in German espionage, who could have greatly endangered the security of the U.S. scientific program, particularly in the field of nuclear physics, and numerous others who, on the basis of CE files and the X-2 vetting interviews, were found to be more than undesirable. Toward the end of hostilities, the number of visa applicants increased to such an extent that, by early summer 1945, the Stockholm office was handling close to 1,000 monthly.

In conjunction with the British, X-2 ran several double-agents into Germany to obtain information on German rocket developments. For the State Department, in addition to vetting all visa applicants, it checked its non-American employees (with a resultant dismissal of five), and helped on "Safe Haven" work.

———————————

From its staff of three in 1942, OSS/-Stockholm had grown by September 1944 to 35 members.

An R&A representative arrived in the fall of 1944 to collect periodicals for IDC. An MU unit made a tactical study of the Kiel Canal with a view toward possible sabotage. Upon the liquidation of other branches, according to State Department policy, in the summer of 1945, the one branch remaining active through September was X-2.

SO, MO, X-2, and R&A all contributed to SI collection of secret intelligence. From these and other sources, OSS/Stockholm had obtained during the war:

(1) Reports by travellers from Germany on military, industrial and political developments, particularly harbor reports.
(2) Nearly all U.S. information on Finland after the rupture of relations.
(3) First authentic information (from a German soldier) on location and nature of the 8th Mtn. Div.
(4) Economic, political and military coverage of Denmark and Norway.
(5) German visa material (leading to arrest of German networks).
(6) German troop transit information (leading to abrogation of Swedish-German agreement).
(7) Finnish code-breaking successes and sales.
(8) Russian Navy coverage.
(9) SKF ball bearing export information (leading to stoppage of these exports).
(10) Direct information on synthetic oil production.

B. ISTANBUL

Istanbul provided an unparalleled opportunity for the gathering of intelligence on Central and East Europe. Through Turkey travelled the main body of Jewish and other refugees from the Nazi regime. A stream of businessmen and government officials passed back and forth. Some seventeen foreign intelligence services were active, while the city itself teemed with professional international informants. Provided U. S. activities were not directed against the Turks themselves, the Turkish police was willing to cooperate in every way, even providing hotel and border registration lists. OSS/Istanbul, handicapped by unsatisfactory personnel, failed, with a few exceptions, to exploit this rich field of intelligence.

The first agent in Turkey was "Rose", an American businessman recruited in New York in April 1942, while on a trip home. The chain he established in and around Istanbul operated into 1945, gathering intelligence from important local residents and from travellers arriving from Europe. A contact in the Rumanian Embassy furnished him copies of the political and economic reports pouched to and from the Rumanian Foreign Office. Another sub-agent obtained a copy of the Reichs Telegram Adressebuch, listing telegraph addresses of all German firms. The majority of "Rose" intelligence, however, came from a newspaper reporter, turned international agent, and was unreliable rumor. An exception was the information on Rumanian oil developments and output, gained from "Rose's" excellent contacts in that business.

A year later, in April 1943, an OSS representative arrived to establish a mission for (1) organized interrogation of travellers, (2) counter-espionage, and (3) operations into Hungary, Bulgaria and Rumania. His cover of Lend-Lease representative was supported by his previous experience as an American banker. By mid-1944, the mission consisted of 43 members under State Department, FEA, Military Attache, business, press and other covers.

Besides the above-mentioned "Rose" chain, other local informants were picked up in Istanbul and Ankara. In December 1943 a special mission, recruited in the United States, held conversations with the Bulgarian Minister in Turkey and opened discussions for getting Bulgaria out of the war. A subsequent one-man team arrived to gather intelligence available on the Far East through the Turkish merchant marine. From arrival lists obtained by bribery of the Turkish police, OSS interviewers picked out the most important and likely persons; the interviews resulted in military targets, economic data and political coverage of developments in the various Central European countries.

Operations into Europe itself were channelled through agent "Dogwood." "Dogwood" was a Czech engineer, who had previously worked for British services in Istanbul and had been handed over to OSS by them. He became chief agent of the CEREUS circle of elderly well-connected individuals resident in Istanbul, and was given charge of all subsequent contacts passed on by the American Military Attache office and other units.

CEREUS consisted of the president of an Istanbul firm, an Austrian businessman (in radio), a rich and idle Austrian with many social connections in his home country, a German professor of economics—friend of Franz von Papen, another German professor with widespread connections among German Junker families, and a Hungarian nobleman—manager of an American oil firm in Istanbul. It established contacts in four

Nazi-dominated countries—Austria, Germany, Hungary and Bulgaria:

AUSTRIA

The Austrian businessman of the circle talked, in September 1943, to the assistant general manager of the Semperit Corporation (operating seven rubber and buna manufacturing plants scattered from Duisburg to Krakow). The assistant manager volunteered at that time fuel and construction details of V-2, its exact size, speed and range, and the locations of various plants manufacturing or assembling the weapons, including Peenemuende.* He gave similar details on synthetic rubber production, e.g. on the manufacture of experimental rubber plates to cover submarines in an attempt to nullify Allied radar. His information received special commendation from SIS/London.

Through this man, OSS communicated

"Cassia" was a member of the Secret Committee of Fourteen, organizing an Austrian resistance movement. He maintained an intelligence network all over Central Europe through the personally picked managers of over twenty warehouses. On his trip to Istanbul in January 1943, "Cassia" turned in valuable industrial information, outlined the organization of Austrian resistance, and made plans for the reception of OSS liaison agents.

From these Austrian industrialists also came the first indication that the Messerschmitt factory complex at Wiener-Neustadt had largely transferred to Ebreichsdorf, Pottendorf and Voslau. Fifteenth Air Force photo-reconnaissance checked on this hint and verified it.

GERMANY

Helmut, Graf von Moltke, a leader in the plot against Hitler, sent a message to OSS/-

* Reported three months earlier by OSS/Bern. See next section.

Istanbul through a member of the CEREUS circle. He requested arrangements to confer, during his December 1943 trip to Turkey, with any of three pre-war acquaintances. Of the three with whom he would feel safe in discussing the anti-Hitler plot, only U. S. Ambassador Kirk in Cairo was available.

An OSS representative carried the message to the Ambassador, who refused to meet von Moltke and sent an unsigned note to the effect that he saw no reason to renew the acquaintance. OSS arranged for a meeting with Brigadier General Tyndall, U. S. Military Attache in Turkey, who talked with the Count for an hour and a half on 17 December 1943. The latter, however, felt too insecure to give any information, and returned to Germany, where he was arrested in February and subsequently executed as a ringleader in the 20 July attempt on Hitler's life.*

HUNGARY

In September 1943, a CEREUS contact was approached by a well-known Hungarian double-agent with a proposal from the Hungarian General Staff for an exchange of liaison officers. OSS/Istanbul was aware of the character of the contacting agent, and suspected an attempt at penetration. The obvious course was, nevertheless, to effect the exchange, maintaining the closest security, gaining what intelligence was possible, and revealing nothing.

That each party might be assured the other was bona fide, code signals were broadcast over the Algiers and Budapest radios at stated hours on a given day.** An OSS agent of Hungarian nationality was infiltrated to Budapest, and a new Hungarian Military Attache arrived in Istanbul in No-

* OSS maintained close contact with other members of this opposition group through Bern. See next section.

** The Germans broke the code broadcast, since OSS/Istanbul sent the preliminary messages to Algiers without adequate communication security.

vember and contacted OSS through "Dogwood." The Attache, the Hungarian double-agent, and other Hungarian agents served as couriers.

As suspected, the operation turned out to be an attempt to infiltrate OSS. Although some of the Hungarian General Staff seriously wished to negotiate, on satisfactory terms, with U. S. representatives, the German Gestapo had the situation in hand. For instance, the new Hungarian Attache in Istanbul was, privately, also in Gestapo pay. Due to insufficient OSS security, the Hungarian agents gained knowledge of other Istanbul contacts, and caused the subsequent collapse of CEREUS operations.

BULGARIA

Through a traveller, "Dogwood" recruited an agent resident in Sofia. Border control was too tight to permit the dispatch of a trained radio operator carrying his set, and OSS had to be content with sending the crystals. The agent recruited an operator with a radio, but satisfactory communication was never established.

Besides providing these contacts in Europe, circle CEREUS picked up occasional intelligence in Turkey. For instance, a Czech engineer, who had directed the construction of many of Bulgaria's water systems, supplied detailed industrial and tactical information with expertly prepared maps.

Through the latter half of 1943 and early 1944, CEREUS submitted over 700 reports from some 60 sub-sources on battle order, industrial targets, production data, political opposition and allied subjects. Although SIS in London rated a few items highly, all of the intelligence was undependable and much of it planted.

Since the mission chief exercised no control over "Dogwood", the latter would not reveal his sub-sources, merely assigning them various code names on his reports. The Reports Office in Cairo was therefore unable to evaluate the intelligence material.

The large majority being vague hearsay, the Cairo Reports Officer at one point refused to process or disseminate the material as intelligence at all.

A further weakness in the intelligence resulted from the centralizing of operations through "Dogwood." Since the latter was not a member of the OSS office, he could not have available the facilities and data necessary for briefing and training. CEREUS members and contacts received therefore almost none, and their intelligence reports showed the lack. Had they been operated directly by OSS instead of through a doubtful sub-agent, many would have been released after X-2 vetting, and others might have been developed into excellent sources.

The careless handling of agents eventually resulted in the arrest of many of the OSS/Istanbul contacts in Europe. On 19 March German forces occupied Hungary, arresting all members of the General Staff and all OSS agents involved in the negotiations who had not previously committed themselves to German control. Two days later, the Gestapo apprehended "Cassia," _____ and leader of the Austrian resistance.

It was unfortunate for some members of the Hungarian General Staff that their group had been penetrated by the Gestapo. But the arrest of other OSS contacts was due to insecure OSS handling. There were two main possibilities. Agent "Dogwood" may have been German-controlled, in which case all operations were blown from the start. Alternately "Dogwood" was not a double-agent, but his self-confident garrulity, unchecked by the mission chief, was responsible. Both knew that the Hungarian negotiations involved double-agents, might be an attempt to infiltrate OSS, and required carefully insulated handling. Yet "Dogwood" had such extraordinary self-assurance that he apparently thought he need only take a double-agent into his confidence in order to gain his support. The mission chief exercised almost no control over him, and meanwhile himself gained fame around Istanbul for his talkativeness. Despite the presence of an X-2 representative from October 1943 on, the mission chief supported "Dogwood" in his refusal to allow X-2 vetting of CEREUS recruits.*

In the end, the enemy-controlled Hungarian double-agents knew all about the Hungarian and Austrian operations, and the arrests followed.

There were other security violations. The Turkish Intelligence Service, after relations with the U. S. organization had improved, informed OSS that: (a) Two chauffeurs, one assigned to the mission chief's car, were in Russian service; (b) the X-2 chauffeur reported regularly to the Turkish police on X-2 activities. A further notable penetration of OSS was effected by one Mrs. Hildegarde Reilly, reputed to have been the most successful female agent working in Istanbul during 1944 and 1945. Mrs. Reilly came in contact with an OSS officer, and, although she was known to be a double-agent, the mission chief approved the association, hoping that some information on German activity could thus be acquired. The project backfired, inasmuch as Mrs. Reilly is known to have reported to the Germans on OSS personnel and activities. Other similar penetrations were accomplished by various female spies in the city.

In June 1944, a new chief arrived in Istanbul to salvage what of value remained. There were by then no contacts in Europe.

---

* This affair provided one of the main reasons for the OSS directive of 19 June 1944, requiring that all agents hired in the field be vetted against X-2 files.

A detailed investigation was undertaken, and members of the CEREUS circle, including "Dogwood", were summarily released.

Relations w i t h British agencies improved.* An over-all rise in the quality of intelligence acquired from European travellers followed the creation of a Joint Interrogation Board with members from OSS, the U. S. Military Attache's office, British Naval Intelligence and SIS. A system of negative checks was evolved to avoid U. S.-British competition for, and dual use of, agents, without revealing the actual employees of either party to the other.

Two men were infiltrated into Bulgaria and Rumania in July. But communication lines were cut by the rupture of Turco-Axis relations in August. The two city teams for Sofia and Bucharest were prepared and dispatched in September 1944, and OSS/Istanbul itself became the equivalent of a city team.**

The CEREUS operation illustrated the multiple pitfalls of this type of intelligence. Disasters were likely to slow the early steps of a new agency in a treacherous field. Yet attempts had to be made somehow to acquire experience in indirect operations, one of the most remunerative approaches to strategic intelligence collection.

---

* Various British intelligence officers had privately voiced criticisms of the insecurity of OSS/-Istanbul during the CEREUS operation. In May 1944, a meeting of representatives from all British agencies had decided to minimize relations with the mission, pending some improvement in security in both business and personal activities.
** See sub-section on Turkey under "Middle East", above.

C. BERN

In both World Wars, Switzerland was the main Allied listening post for developments in European enemy and enemy-occupied countries. Switzerland's geographical position and its neutrality made it the happy hunting ground for the intelligence services of all the belligerent countries. In this respect, it was chiefly of use to the Allies since Switzerland opened no doors to the outside world for the surrounding Axis forces. British, French, Polish, Czech, and many other services had long been established and had combed the field for useful agents, and there were few high calibre men equipped for this work who had not already been impressed.

OSS, too, exploited the espionage opportunities of Switzerland. An exceedingly small staff located there succeeded in producing the best OSS intelligence record of the war. Some one hundred chief agents, many of them leading chains with hundreds of sub-agents, provided early information on such items as V-1 and V-2, atomic and bacteriological research, the German counter-offensive at Bitche and the planning for the 20 July attempt on Hitler's life. Members of the staff handled negotiations with various satellite governments and for the surrender of Axis forces in North Italy on 2 May 1945.

Intensive planning in OSS/Washington for the establishment of an office in Bern began in the spring of 1942, and, in May, the first representative of OSS left for Switzerland, where he was attached to the U. S. Legation. An assistant was dispatched a few months later, and, in November 1942, a third member arrived to take charge of the mission. Several additional persons had been chosen to assist him and were to follow shortly, but, with the Allied invasion of

North Africa, the Germans moved into southern France, and the last remaining channel of access to Switzerland was closed. The mission chief himself arrived at the border a day after it was closed, and it was only due to the assistance of individual Frenchmen, in defiance of orders from Vichy, that he was put across the border into Switzerland and escaped threatened internment.

The Swiss mission therefore started with three men, but, by borrowing certain persons from other U. S. agencies and by use of a few Americans who had been caught in Switzerland by the German invasion of South France, a small unit of less than a dozen key individuals was organized.

An office was opened in buildings occupied by OWI, where OSS enjoyed diplomatic immunity. Meetings with sub-agents were held, after blackout, at the mission chief's house, where surveillance was almost impossible. Sub-bases were established in Geneva, Zurich, Lugano, Ascona and Basel with similar security precautions. Knowing that telephones were tapped by the Swiss, no secret information was passed over the phone.* No messages of a secret character were sent by Swiss post. In conjunction with the Legation, a courier service was arranged with the outlying sub-bases.

As all mail or courier communication between Switzerland and the outside Allied world was cut off, OSS/Bern had to rely solely upon commercial radio over the Legation stamp, supplemented for certain pur-

---

* This rule was violated once in a crisis which left no alternative, and the agent involved, to whom a rendezvous was given, was picked up by the Swiss within a few hours.

poses by the trans-Atlantic telephone.* The first and most serious communication difficulty was a mechanical one, namely the task of enciphering the multitudinous reports which had to be sent every day to Washington, and often to London and Algiers as well. Two of the key members of the staff, who were vitally needed for other work, had to spend their entire time in ciphering and deciphering. Fortunately, relief came from the skies. As American aviators made forced landings in Switzerland, permission was obtained from the Swiss to attach a certain number of these aviators to the Legation staff. Soon the OSS mission had six or seven of them working as cipher clerks on a 24-hour shift.

During the period of Switzerland's isolation, attempts were made, from time to time, to get pouch material through to London or Algiers. These efforts were largely unsuccessful until the liberation of Corsica in October 1943, when a complicated but nonetheless reliable scheme was worked out. Maps, drawings and the full texts of reports were microfilmed in Bern and sent to Geneva, where they were given to a locomotive engineer on the Geneva-Lyon run. The film was hidden in a secret compartment built over the firebox. If the train were searched by the Germans en route the engineer had only to open a trapdoor at the bottom of the box and the film was immediately destroyed in the flames. In that event, the engineer would notify OSS on his return to Geneva, and a duplicate film would be given him. At Lyon, the film was turned over to a courier, who took it by bicycle to Marseille. Here it was entrusted to the captain of a fishing boat bound for Corsica, where, finally, it was picked up by plane

* Four to five times weekly, the mission chief telephoned ten-minute summaries of news to Washington. While the conversation was scrambled and not easily intelligible to the Germans, it was heard in clear by the Swiss, and the messages were limited to general political and economic information.

from Algiers. Over this involved route, only ten to twelve days elapsed between Bern dispatch and Algiers receipt of the film.

In November 1944, after the French border had been opened, a clandestine radio post was established at Bern. Up to this time, the use of commercial channels had lost time and limited the stations which could be reached, since the messages had to pass through diplomatic or consular offices. Earlier efforts which various of the foreign missions in Bern had made to establish clandestine radios had always been balked by the Swiss. They had no difficulty, of course, in D/F-ing them, and their practice then was to interrupt transmission by cutting off the electric power at the appropriate moment. If this hint were not taken, formal diplomatic action would follow. By the end of 1944, however, OSS/-Bern had established such good relations with Swiss intelligence that it decided to try out a radio post, and was not molested.

While deeply attached to maintaining their own neutrality, the Swiss really had one serious fear, invasion by Germany. In 1940 the Germans had been poised to strike France through Switzerland. It was only the quick break-through in the north which had avoided this. In March 1943, the Germans again came near to invasion to open up better rail communications with Italy, for the purpose of provisioning their hard-pressed armies in North Africa.

To avoid possible incidents, Switzerland had passed stringent legislation directed against any persons operating in its territory in the interests of any of the belligerent powers. This legislation, of course, did not apply to the official representatives of the belligerent powers, except insofar as they might be found guilty of suborning Swiss nationals or residents. Allied intelligence officers, therefore, had to exercise the greatest care and circumspection. Those directing the various Allied services were officially attached, under various covers, to their diplomatic missions. The agents whom they employed, to escape the scrutiny of the Swiss police, had to use ingenuity and guile and observe the rigid rules of security, both in their contact with the officials for whom they worked and in carrying out specific missions.

OSS/Bern, however, established close relations and personal friendships with many Swiss officers, particularly in the intelligence service. An exchange of information was initiated on German troop movements, in which the Swiss were particularly interested, and the U. S. secret radio station was allowed to operate.

Joint OSS/OWI operations were worked out in the field of propaganda warfare. The OSS mission had early established contact with a Frenchman, known under his cover name of "Salembier", who had been one of the French Deuxieme Bureau's chief propaganda artists in World War I. He knew his trade, and was set up in business, operating from Geneva, by OSS and OWI jointly. Millions of pamphlets, leaflets, cards, postage stamps, and every form of literary propaganda were printed and smuggled into Germany and Fascist Italy. When the Frankfurter Zeitung was suppressed by Hitler, a small edition was printed in Switzerland and sent into Germany. Much material was also dispatched to the French resistance to aid them with their own publications. The speeches of de Gaulle were reprinted in vast quantities and smuggled into France.

OSS/Bern also maintained close contact with the intelligence operations of the diplomatic staff and of the Military Attache's office. There was a free exchange of battle order information between OSS and the latter, and, at one time when he was not permitted to communicate other than to G-2, Washington, a certain amount of his material was incorporated, with clear source indication, into the reports sent by OSS/Bern to SHAEF.

Relations were established with several prominent dissident diplomats of satellite states. They included the Hungarian and Bulgarian ministers to Switzerland, Baron Bakach-Bessenyey and Georges Keosseivanoff, and the former Rumanian Minister, who had severed official relations with his country and was living in retirement in Geneva. The anti-Nazi elements in Hungary were particularly anxious to make contact with the Allies and, in September 1943, maneuvered the transfer of Bakach-Bessenyey from Vichy to Bern, and from that time on, he was in secret contact with OSS. These sources provided considerable economic and some military intelligence, but their reports were especially interesting for the light they shed on their countries' political dilemmas.

Another valuable channel of information became available as early as December 1942, when the French Embassy in Bern, upon the total occupation of France by Germany, ostensibly terminated its military and naval information services. The well-trained and long-established Deuxieme Bureau personnel, which, over the years, had developed a large network into Germany and had as well prime contacts in France, was threatened with disbandment for lack of funds. OSS/-Bern agreed to finance the service under its old head, a French major of long training in the Deuxieme Bureau, and the latter managed to retain his position at the Embassy. Working in cooperation with the American Military Attache, the Deuxieme Bureau service was maintained and expanded. In order to give its personnel the feeling that they were working for their own Government, the material they collected was sent by radio through OSS channels directly to the military services of the French in Algiers. From this source, OSS received weekly some one hundred pages of intelligence on Germany, France, Italy and the Balkans.

Such was the general background in which the small unit at Bern operated. Some of its more interesting activities follow:

HUNGARY

In February 1943 Kallay, the Prime Minister of Hungary, sent an emissary to Switzerland to establish contact with OSS. His purpose was to give information on the position of his country, and to request the initiation of informal and confidential conversations between Hungary and the United States. While the Hungarians were apprehensive of an open break with Germany, they feared the Russians far more. In July, the emissary informed OSS/Bern that his Government was prepared to liquidate its existing commitments toward Germany and refuse to enter into new ones, thereby attaining a de facto state of neutrality, contingent, however, upon certain guarantees from the United States regarding Hungary's frontiers and assurances concerning Russia's Hungarian policy.

Although discussions of this nature were out of the question, Bern felt that Hungarian good faith might be tested by requesting cooperation in an operation. It was suggested that the Hungarians make arrangements to receive an American agent, whom they would furnish with military information, for transmission by a secret radio to be sent in by Swedish courier from OSS/-Stockholm.*

SPARROW, as this project was called, might have been successful if it had not taken almost eight months to put into effect. The Hungarians were in agreement in principle, but, for various reasons, stalled for several months before actually getting down to details. Innumerable difficulties had to be ironed out with OSS/Algiers. It had been decided to send a team of three men, and considerable time elapsed before the qualified personnel could be found. Finally, on 15 March 1944, SPARROW, consisting of a colonel, a major and a lieutenant, parachuted into Hungary close to the Yugoslav border.

* The radio arrived. See "Stockholm", above.

Plans had been worked out with the head of the Hungarian intelligence service, General Ujszaszi. The agents were to be treated as prisoners of war, and go through the routine questioning by the military authorities. Then, instead of being interned, they would be taken to a secret hideout from which they could operate their transmitter.

At first, all went according to schedule. The men gave themselves up at the nearest village. Shortly thereafter an English-speaking major appeared, stating that he had been waiting for them for several days. Together with their equipment, he took them by stages to Budapest, where they arrived on the evening of 17 March. They were then taken to General Ujszaszi, who received them cordially, and apologized for the necessity of keeping them in jail. The two cabinet ministers SPARROW had come to see were out of town for a few days, but he would arrange an interview as soon as they returned.

Less than 48 hours later the Germans occupied Hungary, and the men were turned over to the Wehrmacht. For two weeks they appeared to be getting away with their cover story, that they were on a mission to the Yugoslav Partisans when their plane was hit by anti-aircraft fire, and that they had been forced to bail out. Then the Gestapo took over with interrogations lasting for six weeks. During one of them, the colonel was shown a twenty-page signed statement by General Ujszaszi which told the whole story. The men had no recourse but to admit the obvious details, but were able to conceal the OSS origin of their mission. Eventually they were returned to the jurisdiction of the Wehrmacht, interned in Germany and liberated by the American forces nearly a year later.

AUSTRIA

The effect in Austria of the Moscow Declaration furnished excellent proof of the value of psychological warfare. The announcement, in October 1943, that the United Nations would guarantee the independence of Austria, encouraged the growth of resistance. In December 1943, OSS/Bern was contacted by envoys of an underground organization claiming a membership of 5,000 made up largely of Socialists and Communists. They wished to set up a channel through which to send intelligence and receive instructions.

At about the same time, relations were established with the coordinating committee of the Austrian resistance movement. This group had already contacted OSS/Istanbul, and had been given a transmitter and code for communicating with Algiers. However, on their return from Turkey, the couriers had been forced to abandon their radio in Sofia. As communications were far easier to maintain with Switzerland, the group had sent two envoys to establish a link there. Plans were worked out with Algiers to send agents and a transmitter, but the project fell through when the Germans occupied Hungary, where much of the activity was centered.

The leader of the group, "Oysters", came to Switzerland in March 1944, where he had a wide variety of contacts in industry, government, commerce and police, even to topranking Gestapo officials, and was able to give Bern a quantity of valuable information. To counteract Russian influence, "Oysters" was anxious to have the Allies undertake a radio propaganda campaign directed at Austria. Fifteen to twenty experienced Communist agents, he reported, were being parachuted every month into Austrian territory.

Due to OSS indiscretions in Turkey,* plus data secured by the Germans when they occupied Budapest, many of the Austrian resistance leaders were arrested, including "Oysters". Although an Austrian by origin, "Oysters" was a naturalized Brazilian. Bern therefore initiated steps to have him exchanged for a German in Brazil.

This was never effected, but the negotiations served to stay his execution, and he was taken over by the Russians when they occupied Budapest.

Bern had numerous other channels into Austria, and one source, an Austrian industrialist, was of particular value. It was he who first gave OSS/Bern the location of the V-bomb laboratory at Peenemuende,* and much of the technical information on the rockets.

Late in 1944, the Austrian resistance established a secret post in Zurich, and arrangements were made for a courier service between Zurich and Vienna.

"K-28

considered himself an envoy of the resistance, an operations man, although he was willing and did furnish Bern with some of the best intelligence obtained on Austria during the last months of the war. The fact that SI and SO operations were handled by the same U.S. organization, rather than by two as in the case of the British, proved a great advantage. OSS/Bern could fit "K-28" into its scheme of operations without any difficulty, and used him both for SI and SO activities.

"K-28" travelled back and forth frequently, from Switzerland to Milan and over the Brenner to Vienna and back, disguised as a German courier. In 1945, in order to check details on the Austrian underground organization, Bern arranged with OSS/Paris to send with "K-28", to Vienna, an Austrian agent who had been working

---

* See "Istanbul", above.

* See below.

with the exile group in Paris, to the great mutual advantage of both parties. Those inside were encouraged with the knowledge that they had outside help, and the exiles were strengthened by establishing this direct contact with internal resistance.

GERMANY

Intelligence on Germany, from the end of 1942 when the Swiss mission was established, was gathered from a wide variety of sources. It came from officials in confidential positions inside Germany; from businessmen who occasionally visited Switzerland; from political and labor leaders once prominent under the Weimar Republic, who had fled to Switzerland after Hitler came to power and who maintained contacts with Germany; and from various church organizations.

This work had an unexpected measure of success, largely because of two circumstances: (1) A highly placed agent working inside the German Foreign Office gave OSS/-Bern unstinted cooperation for eighteen months, and (2) the German military foreign intelligence service, the Abwehr, contained anti-Hitler elements.

The Foreign Office Contact. The best of all Bern's sources was established in August 1943. "Wood" held a most confidential post in the German Foreign Office. He had entered the foreign service before Hitler's rise to power, and from the beginning had been a staunch opponent of the Nazi regime. Despite his refusal to become a Party member, because of his abilities he was attached to several German diplomatic missions abroad. After the outbreak of war he was recalled to the Foreign Office, where he was rapidly promoted to a position which gave him access to the most secret information.

The inside view "Wood" thus obtained increased his opposition, and he embarked on his underground career. Since he was unable to leave Germany to make personal contact with the Allies, he had secured the

cooperation of a member of the French resistance, an Alsatian doctor. Through this channel he had sent information to both the French and the British. Finally, with the help of a woman who had charge of the Foreign Office courier service, he received permission to make the trip to Bern as official courier. The initial contact with OSS was made through a friend of "Wood's", resident in Switzerland.

"Wood" brought with him several copies of top secret Foreign Office cables, and, from copious notes he had made in Berlin, gave OSS/Bern many additional items of vital information. Secret and top secret messages were being mimeographed in several copies for various German Foreign Office bureaus, and it was "Wood's" task to destroy the copies which came to his office. The liaison position of his bureau provided him with the most important ones. At the first meeting, "Wood" told OSS/Bern that it would be possible for him to secrete the significant messages and to arrange either to bring or send them to Bern from time to time.

For several months, "Wood" managed to go to Switzerland every few weeks. Soon he was bringing cables by the pound, officially packaged and sealed by him in the Foreign Office. The problem of handling this periodic flood of material was a staggering one. The security angle alone was perplexing enough, and the task of translating and encoding took the time of the entire staff at Bern for weeks after each batch of telegrams was received, until the frontier opened in September 1944 and the material could be sent out in bulk.

Toward the end of 1944, both because of the increasingly difficult conditions in Berlin and to facilitate transmission, "Wood", furnished with an OSS camera, began to photograph his documents and send long rolls of film. He sent this film to OSS in an envelope addressed to an imaginary Swiss sweetheart, by German couriers who had no idea of the material they were carrying. The photographing of these messages was generally done in the basement of a hospital in Berlin with the help of the Alsatian doctor. During the frequent air raids, the work had to be done with flashlights.[*]

As Allied interest shifted to the Far East, the material received from the German Air Attache in Japan became increasingly important. Bern lacked any established route for passing to "Wood" the urgent requests from OSS/Washington. Deciding that the simplest and most direct way was least likely to cause suspicion, OSS/-Bern dispatched a post-card from the Swiss sweetheart. On the reverse of an Alpine scene was a message, stating that one of her friends, prior to the war, had kept a shop selling Japanese trinkets, toys, etc., and had found a considerable market for them. Now her friend could get them no more. In view of Germany's close alliance with Japan, was it possible to find any of this Japanese material in Germany, or to get it through Germany? Her friend wanted more of it. This tip was all that "Wood" needed. The next batch of material contained dozens of up-to-date reports, direct from the German Embassy in Tokyo.

Over a period of a year and a half, OSS received from "Wood" more than 1,600 true readings of cables to and from the Foreign Office and some forty German diplomatic and consular missions. They included reports from the military and air attaches in Japan and the Far East, data on the structure of the German secret service in Spain, Sweden and Switzerland, and espionage activities in England and in the British Embassy in Istanbul. Each step in the German efforts to bribe wolfram from Spain, to squeeze more raw materials and commodities from satellite states, and to get more manpower from France was laid bare. "Wood" also informed Bern about Allied codes which had been broken by the Germans.

Until his escape to Switzerland some months before VE-Day, "Wood" was never suspected. British SIS rated him the best intelligence source of the war.

The Abwehr Contact. Through contact with members of the Abwehr, OSS/Bern maintained close touch with the underground elements in Germany who plotted the overthrow and the assassination of Hitler.

Early in 1943, direct contact was established with one of the chief Abwehr personnel in Switzerland, Hans Bernd Gisevius, Vice-Consul in the German Consulate General in Zurich.

At one of the first meetings between the mission chief and Gisevius, the latter, who had just returned from Berlin, drew from his pocket the texts of several secret telegrams which had been sent by the American Legation in Bern. The Gestapo had broken the State Department code, which, because OSS was so under-staffed, had been occasionally used for long reports from that office of a political nature.

One of the enemy-deciphered cables was a report, based on information previously furnished by Gisevius, on the political situation in Italy, and mentioned that certain leading Fascists, including Ciano, were possibly open to approaches from the Allies. This cable had been shown to Hitler, who promptly forwarded it to Mussolini. A few days later Ciano was removed from his post as Foreign Minister.

To what extent the cable may have been responsible for his dismissal has not been revealed by any Axis documents thus far uncovered. The information brought by Gisevius was immediately passed on to the American Minister, and the code was gradually discarded. To have ceased using it

---

* One of "Wood's" more trying experiences occurred when Himmler requested a file which, at the moment, was being filmed. "Wood" had to rush back to his office and pretend to pull out of his files what he was actually extricating from his coat pocket.

abruptly would have aroused German suspicions, and naturally it was used only for innocuous reports, or to furnish the Germans with misleading information.

This initial proof of good faith marked the beginning of a long and close association. Gradually Gisevius revealed the names and the plans of those involved in the plot to overthrow Hitler, to which Bern gave the code name "Breakers." Until Gestapo suspicions were aroused, nearly a year later, Gisevius constantly travelled back and forth between Zurich and Berlin and kept OSS currently informed regarding "Breakers." When, finally, it became unsafe for him to return to Germany, his place was taken by another Abwehr conspirator, who also operated under the cover of Vice-Consul in Zurich.*

"Breakers", as Gisevius revealed it during the eighteen months preceding 20 July 1944, comprised a group of high German officers, the chief of the Abwehr and some of his staff, Foreign Office officials, Goerdeler—former Mayor of Leipzig, and Socialist and trade-union leaders.** They were anxious to enlist American support for their plans, and even proposed to cooperate with American forces behind the German lines. In particular, they wished to secure American and British collaboration against Russia. "Breakers" was always told, however, that, while Washington was glad to know that there were Germans who were trying to oust the Nazis, and sympathized with this aim, it was first up to the Germans themselves to take action against Hitler. Moreover, under no circumstances would America break faith with her Russian ally.

Gisevius returned to Berlin about the middle of July 1944, and took part in the abortive putsch on the twentieth. He escaped the Gestapo dragnet after its failure, and for six months remained in hiding in Berlin. He informed OSS/Bern of his whereabouts, and, to help protect him, OSS circulated the rumor that he had escaped to Switzerland. The Gestapo combed the country for him. Finally, with a complete set of Gestapo papers prepared by OSS/CD in London, Gisevius did make his escape to Switzerland in January 1945.

Industrial Intelligence. "Breakers" and "Wood" were the two most striking of the operations of OSS/Bern directed against Germany. There was, however, a constant flow of intelligence from many sources. Important German industrialist centers were penetrated, and detailed information regarding production in various lines of German industry, particularly aircraft, was forwarded to Washington. Swiss industrial circles were in close touch with German business, and, by discreet contact with pro-Allied members among them, it was possible to obtain the most detailed information on the German situation. The German Legation and most of the German Consulates were also thoroughly penetrated, and little went on there which was not known.

Among other items, Bern reported on the midget or "beetle" tank, a year before it made its short-lived appearance at Anzio on the Italian front. Much information on the locations of aircraft factories was also secured, including data on the first jet-propelled planes.

Bern gave a considerable amount of intelligence on the factories manufacturing parts for the rocket bomb, including the Rax Werke at Wiener Neustadt, which was raided toward the end of 1943. The first inkling of the nature of V-1 came from a Swiss industrialist, who, as early as February 1943, informed OSS/Bern that the German secret weapon was possibly some sort of aerial torpedo. It was not until the end of May that Gisevius reported that the

---

* The position of the Abwehr in Germany was badly upset by various defections from its service engineered by British and U. S. counter-intelligence in Istanbul. See sub-section on X-2/-Istanbul in "Middle East", above.

** "Breakers" leader, Graf von Moltke, also contacted OSS/Istanbul in late 1943. See previous section.

Germans had developed what he understood to be a new heavy missile employing the rocket principle. This, he said, was already in limited production somewhere in Pomerania. At the end of June, Gisevius and another source brought details on the rocket, and an Austrian source fixed the location of the assembly plant and testing ground at Peenemuende. Finally, on pinpoints furnished by Bern and checked by air reconnaissance, Peenemuende was raided by the RAF in the summer of 1943.

Hitler had hoped to have his rockets over England at the end of 1943, setting 30 November as the deadline for "Program A-4", as the Germans called it. The raid on Peenemuende upset the timetable, and the first rockets did not appear until June 1944.

Information on the rocket bomb installations was one of the major items covered by the French chains during the spring and summer of 1944. The first such reports reached Bern late in 1943, and, months before the Allied air forces took action, many of the launching sites, especially in the Pas de Calais region, had been pinpointed. One chain obtained valuable photographs of the emplacements themselves.

Until the launching sites were overrun at the end of 1944, OSS/Bern continued to receive intelligence from Germany and France on the characteristics of the V-bombs.

Washington showed great interest in some Bern reports on bacteriological warfare and urged Bern to push investigation. However, while a certain amount of data was collected, no conclusive evidence was uncovered that the Germans were preparing for this type of warfare, although there were many indications that they had ample supplies of poison gas.

An outstanding Swiss physicist provided information on his fellow German scientists who were working on atomic development. This project in the United States was then so secret that what was going on in this field in other countries was not even assigned as a target to Bern. The only evidence Bern received that its cable had caused quite a stir in Washington was the immediate instruction to reclassify it as top secret, closely followed by a detailed questionnaire as to the location and activities of a long list of German scientists. From then on, contact with the Swiss physicist was closely maintained and much information sent.

Ascertaining that the headquarters of German atom splitting activities had been moved from the Kaiser Wilhelm Institute in Berlin, Bern was given the task of finding out where the German atomic energy scientists were really working. The first clue received on their hideout in South Germany came from several letters mailed by one of the atomic scientists to a Swiss friend in touch with OSS/Bern. None of the letters were mailed from the exact place where the scientific laboratories were established, but the telltale postmarks from little towns all near together in a particular locality, taken in conjunction with other information, enabled OSS to pinpoint the laboratory's location. Sabotage was planned and an agent sent to Bern for the purpose. Unfortunately, he was picked up by the Swiss, due to indiscretions on his part, before Bern could get him into Germany. However, information acquired through Bern and other sources had already satisfied atomic experts in Washington that the Germans were far behind in the race.

West Front Intelligence. In September 1944, when the French border opened, OSS established a sub-base at Annemasse,* just over the frontier from Geneva, for penetrations of Italy and the Alps. Two productive chains were also operated from Annemasse through Switzerland into Germany. Later, a base was established on the northern frontier of Switzerland, first at Pontarlier and then at Hegenheim in Alsace. Through it, operational military intelligence from

_____
* See "Sub-bases on the Swiss and French Borders", above.

Switzerland could be supplied directly to the 6th and 12th Army Groups.

The post was first used to relay directly to the 6th Army Group daily reports on the Rhine water level readings. Preparations were then being made for the passage of the Rhine, and it was feared that the Germans, as soon as Allied forces attempted to lay down pontoon bridges or to use river landing craft, would blow up some of the dams either on the Upper Rhine or on its tributaries, and create a temporary flood to wash away the facilities established.

Here speed was important. A flood, started in the Upper Rhine between Lake Constance and Bale for example, would take several hours to reach the critical points in the middle and lower Rhine, where U.S. forces might be trying to cross. Direct radio signals were worked out so that Bern could get this information through to 6th Army Group in a matter of minutes. In addition, the Army wished to be informed on any particular flood conditions in the Rhine arising from natural causes, and for this reason requested the daily readings. It desired them taken at various points along the river, which was not easy. Several Bern agents were picked up when the mysterious telephone calls, from points along the Rhine to Bern, were intercepted and analyzed. Readings at Bale, however, could be taken and communicated with relative ease. The OSS/Bale representative would merely take an early morning stroll across the Rhine bridge, read the gauge, and telephone his observations to Bern. A few minutes later 6th Army Group would have them.

A Labor Desk was also opened in Bern, after September 1944, for the direction of labor union and similar contacts. Labor Desk policy was based on the experience that more useful results were obtained by taking advantage of the trade union and socialist elements who already had contacts in Germany, or the possibility of traveling to Germany, than by attempting to bring in outsiders to infiltrate them through Switzerland.

Union leaders produced useful recruits who had regular occasion to cross the border, and, by feeding them directives, equipment, and money, developed chains within enemy territory which produced regular and useful intelligence. In general, the attempts to bring in outsiders and pass them over the German border without the knowledge of the Swiss resulted in a high percentage of failures. Swiss counter-intelligence was extremely efficient, and the German frontier well guarded on the German side. At the end, travel within Germany was surrounded with so many confusing and ever-changing restrictions that it required a large staff to follow them and to keep the travel papers, passports, food cards, and the like, up to date. The Swiss, with all their facilities and their firsthand knowledge, were naturally much more quickly informed than any of the other intelligence services possibly could be.

German preparations to flood the Belgian and Dutch coastal areas were reported by Bern, long before similar information reached Washington and London from other sources. Sufficient reliable information was also collected to forecast the German offensive in the Bitche-Wissembourg sector, launched on 1 January 1945. OSS/-Washington was later assured that this information was of great assistance in stemming the tide of the German break-through in that area.

JAPAN

Despite the distance between Japan and Switzerland, the latter was nevertheless a good base for obtaining Japanese intelligence. The current information obtained through the German Foreign Office by the

"Wood" contact was an example.* In addition to that, there was a German refugee industrialist in Switzerland who had close contacts with the Japanese Navy and continued throughout the war to be in touch with high Japanese naval officials, both in Japan and in Germany. He proved a useful source of information, being out of sympathy with the war party in Japan.

As the war drew to a close, two Japanese officials, attached to the Bank for International Settlements, established, through a neutral member of the Bank, running contact with OSS/Bern. Prior to the Potsdam Conference, information came through this source, indicating Japanese willingness to surrender on the basis of the territorial integrity of the four main Japanese islands, provided the Emperor and certain basic features of the Japanese constitution be maintained. The whole background of Japanese reasoning, influenced as it was by the chaotic conditions of Germany resulting from its fight to the bitter end, was set forth in submitting this proposal. It was deemed of such importance that, at the request of Assistant Secretary of War McCloy, the mission chief took the information to Secretary of War Stimson, at the Potsdam Conference in July 1945.

X-2

Until the Swiss frontier opened, OSS/-Bern had no one to assign specifically to X-2, and an attempt was made to cover it incident to SI operations. A trained X-2 officer, however, reached Bern late in 1944 and took charge of this work. With the Legation, he handled various phases of the "Safe Haven" operations. As hostilities in

---

* See above.

Europe drew to a close, he worked on the identification of the Japanese networks in Switzerland, Germany, and occupied countries. He was also put in charge of the general security of the OSS office.

Operating on a careful but semi-overt basis as American intelligence representation in the area, OSS/Bern, with a remarkably small staff, turned in the outstanding SI record of OSS.* Among other achievements, it developed what British SIS called the prize source of the war. The success was partly due to the strategic position of Switzerland from an Allied viewpoint, partly to American prestige vis-a-vis other Allies, and partly to the excellent pre-war contacts of the mission chief. Full credit must also be given to the mission for attracting a steady inflow of good informants by its reputation for security and experienced skill.

---

* OSS/Bern operations in France and in North Italy are covered in "Bern Chains" in France, "Sub-bases on the Swiss and French Borders" and "Italian Resistance", above. The negotiations for the surrender of the Axis forces in North Italy are in "Secret Surrender Negotiations", below.

Part VII

THE GREATER REICH

In late 1944, possibilities for agent communication were greatly expanded by OSS development of "Joan-Eleanor", a small radio unit with which an agent could speak directly with an OSS representative in a correspondingly equipped plane thirty thousand feet above him. J-E was available only in small quantity before VE-Day and was shared between the OSS detachments on the West Front and SI/London.

The penetration of Germany had long been postponed by both British and American services, in the hope of German surrender when France fell, and in view of presumptive high agent casualties. Army detachments on the West Front had to shift targets rapidly, seeking German-speaking staff personnel and suitable German agent recruits. In this difficult task, Seventh Army maintained its outstanding record.

American and British services began extensively to infiltrate long-range teams from London into Germany and from Italy into Austria, in the fall of 1944. In Germany, casualties were unexpectedly low, due to the disorganization there. However, SI/London recruited, trained, and dispatched agents on a mass-production and insufficiently personal or selective basis. Out of 34 teams safely infiltrated, only seven came on the air.

Austria, on the other hand, was being built up as the final Nazi "Redoubt" and had become the most tightly controlled enemy territory in Europe. OSS casualties ran close to fifty percent, but, of only thirteen teams from SI/MedTO, five provided AFHQ with valuable Brenner Pass and "Redoubt" coverage.

The Allied successes in France had prompted OSS/Bern to urge the early dispatch of SHAEF representatives to wavering German generals, a policy which was not followed. In September, however, OSS sent an apparently successful mission for AFHQ to persuade the Hungarian Regent to cease support of the Axis war. Finally, during March and April 1945, OSS/Bern handled the negotiations which led to the premature surrender of German forces in North Italy on 2 May.

A. THE FIRST "JOAN-ELEANOR" OPERATION

An essential of successful espionage is good communications. As the final battle against Germany opened up in the fall of 1944, the Reich presented problems which largely nullified all previous agent communication techniques. OSS solved these through the development and use of a communications device known as "Joan-Eleanor" (J-E).

Excellent results had been achieved in France with W/T sets, operated from safe houses and shifted frequently. It was impossible to follow this procedure in Germany. A hostile population and tighter security controls made the W/T set dangerously conspicuous to carry around and extremely difficult to hide. The need for codebooks, aerials and power supply entailed further insecurity.

The most serious handicap was the more efficient direction-finding activities which were feared in the Reich itself. W/T signals were easy to pick up, and, although this danger was minimized in France (where the W/T set could be moved from place to place), in Germany the absence of sympathetic contacts made precautions more difficult.*

Finally, breakage often rendered worthless the parachuted W/T sets. This made less difference in France, where the short flying distances and reception committees made drops of additional sets or parts comparatively easy. But such compensating factors were not present in Germany, and the smashing of seven out of twenty-two W/T sets dropped into the Reich by one SI

desk meant that the teams concerned were useless.

These difficulties were overcome with the development of J-E during the fall of 1944. J-E was a two-way communications device which enabled an agent on the ground to talk directly with an appropriately equipped OSS representative flying in a plane above him. J-E's compactness and light weight (4 lbs.) made for easy portability and concealment. Its use of small, long-life batteries eliminated the need for an outside power supply. A plane flying at 30,000 feet could be in constant touch with little danger to the agent of interception. The high frequency and vertical cone-shaped directivity virtually nullified enemy D/F-ing.

J-E offered other operational advantages. Mistakes were minimized by having the agent in direct communication with an operator in the plane who could get repeats or clarifications on confusing points. As a double check, all conversations were recorded. The direct two-way voice communication also meant elimination of the delays and dangers of code garbling. It further enabled spot briefing to be given the agent, with the additional advantage of an immediate reply. Perhaps most important of all, it meant that as much data could be exchanged in a twenty-minute contact as could be carried out in days of normal W/T communication.

To fly J-E missions, three British "Mosquitoes" were obtained during the fall of 1944. The tail-sections were remodeled to include complete oxygen systems, secondary inter-communication, direction indicators and emergency lights and to provide space for the J-E operator and his equipment. Special training was given the crews to perfect them in the precision techniques that were required for the operations.

---

* The Chief of Communications, OSS/ETO, later commented that D/F-ing had been greatly feared in Germany, but that subsequent investigations had failed to show that any OSS agent had ever been caught in this way.

287

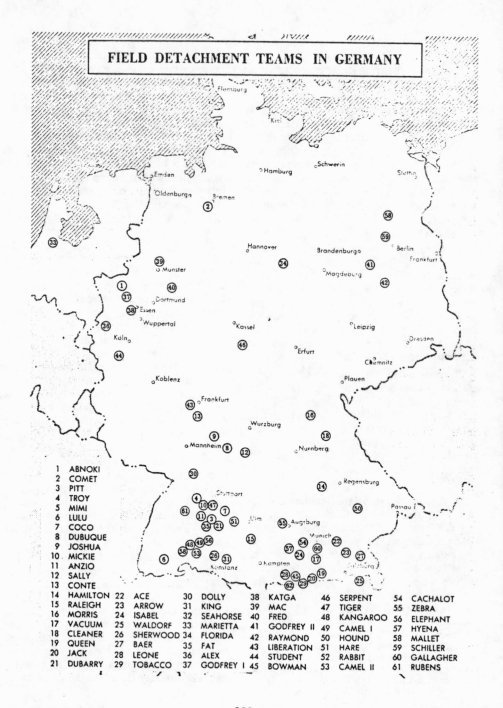

FIELD DETACHMENT TEAMS IN GERMANY

1	ABNOKI								
2	COMET								
3	PITT								
4	TROY								
5	MIMI								
6	LULU								
7	COCO								
8	DUBUQUE								
9	JOSHUA								
10	MICKIE								
11	ANZIO								
12	SALLY								
13	CONTE								
14	HAMILTON	22	ACE	30	DOLLY	38	KATGA	46	SERPENT	54	CACHALOT
15	RALEIGH	23	ARROW	31	KING	39	MAC	47	TIGER	55	ZEBRA
16	MORRIS	24	ISABEL	32	SEAHORSE	40	FRED	48	KANGAROO	56	ELEPHANT
17	VACUUM	25	WALDORF	33	MARIETTA	41	GODFREY II	49	CAMEL I	57	HYENA
18	CLEANER	26	SHERWOOD	34	FLORIDA	42	RAYMOND	50	HOUND	58	MALLET
19	QUEEN	27	BAER	35	FAT	43	LIBERATION	51	HARE	59	SCHILLER
20	JACK	28	LEONE	36	ALEX	44	STUDENT	52	RABBIT	60	GALLAGHER
21	DUBARRY	29	TOBACCO	37	GODFREY I	45	BOWMAN	53	CAMEL II	61	RUBENS

288

J-E OPERATIONS

The first J-E mission was dispatched early in November 1944, to Ulrum, Holland. From then until VE-Day, a total of fourteen J-E teams were dispatched to Stuttgart, Berlin, Munster, Regensburg, Munich, Landshut, Leipzig, Plauen, Straubing and Bregenz.

Successful J-E contact was established with only four teams—located at Ulrum, Regensburg, Berlin and Munich. Of the remaining ten missions, one was lost with its plane in the course of the dropping operation, another had its equipment smashed on landing and the rest were prevented by various factors, principally time and inexperience, from making contact. Thirty-eight J-E contacts were made with the four teams which established communication. Sixteen of these were with the mission dropped to Ulrum, which, during most of the time, was operating under German control. Only one contact was made with the Berlin team. Forty-seven other J-E flights were flown which failed to contact any team at all.

However, the percentage of successful contacts increased greatly with experience. Furthermore, results received from even the few missions contacted were on the whole so valuable and promising, relative to those from W/T equipped teams, that they more than made up for the failures.* Finally, the "know-how" accumulated, and the possibilities revealed, indicated that J-E was a large contribution to the science of long-range intelligence penetration.

"BOBBY"

"Bobby" was the first J-E equipped agent dispatched. Parachuted from London into Ulrum, Holland, on 10 November 1944, his job was to lay the foundations for an underground railroad along which subsequent OSS agents would be infiltrated from Holland into Germany. "Bobby" was also instructed to report such intelligence as he

---

* For account of W/T and J-E teams in Germany and Austria, see ensuing sections.

might incidentally gather in the course of his mission.

The J-E plane, operating in accordance with a prearranged schedule, made first contact with "Bobby" on 21 November, and regular communication continued until 30 March. "Bobby's" early contacts yielded such items as information on German preparations to flood the Polder River, enemy troop movements at Arnhem, erection of water barriers between Ens and Winschoter Diep and results of Allied air raids on the Gaarkeuken docks.

Early in February, "Bobby" was taken by the Gestapo and, from 10 February until he went off the air, his J-E broadcasts were controlled by the enemy. "Bobby's" capture was not the result of German D/F interception and was in no way due to any security weakness of his communications equipment. He was the victim of a mistake in identity, which, in the end, curiously enough saved his life.

The Germans got on to "Bobby" early in February, when they arrested an assassination party of Dutch underground workers who were on their way to kill him. This assassination team had confused "Bobby" with another Allied agent, also called "Bobby", who had turned traitor. The Gestapo interrogated the captured team and arrested the intended victim. On being informed by the Germans that the underground was out to assassinate him, the latter—although realizing that there was an error in identity—feigned indignation at such "treachery" and soon was "helping" the Gestapo.

On 10 February, the Germans began playing back "Bobby", who immediately flashed his prearranged control signal—frequent use of profanity in the course of his message. He stressed the fact that he did not want any additional assistants, reporting that he thought the Germans had one of the "other" J-E sets being used by his men (there were no such other sets). "Bobby" mollified the suspicions of the Gestapo

289

unit by pointing out that the Americans would be less likely to believe that he himself was under control if he flavored his broadcasts with cautions.

OSS had caught "Bobby's" control signal, and SI/London cooperated with X-2 in the standard operation for keeping captured agents alive and feeding misleading material to the enemy. Finally, in mid-April, the Germans used "Bobby" to carry a message back through the lines to open negotiations with OSS for a joint OSS-Gestapo operation to be directed at penetrating Russia and Japan.

During the entire period of his captivity, "Bobby" maintained the appearance of cooperation, but at the same time never gave any important operational information of OSS organization or techniques which the Germans could not be expected to know already. While he had been unsuccessful on his assigned mission, he had served as the trial J-E operation of the type subsequently to be mounted in some numbers in Germany.

B. WEST FRONT

By the end of September 1944, France was liberated and the Allied armies, together with their supporting OSS field detachments, were pressing forward into Germany itself.* For the next seven months, the various OSS field units mounted short-range penetrations behind enemy lines, screened and recruited agent possibilities for long-range espionage missions based on London and disseminated appropriate information forwarded from other OSS bases.

The new German target offered greater difficulties. There was no longer any organized resistance to tap for help on intelligence or sabotage. The front was no longer fluid enough to encourage infiltrations through the lines. Security controls set up inside the Reich were tighter than those enforced in the occupied areas. An example of what the detachments were now up against appeared when none of the 12th AG units' 23 infiltration attempts in September succeeded.

Lessons learned during the French campaign were applied. The 6th Army Group and Seventh Army Detachments were switched from Caserta to Paris control, to conform with the rest of the units on the West Front. And the whole field detachment (FIDES) system was reorganized late in October. Responsibility for operations was centered with the Chief of OSS/Paris, and the duty of servicing and coordinating the detachments' administration was delegated to a FIDES office in Paris. The distinction between SI and SO detachments was formally abolished. All personnel were consolidated into over-all OSS units assigned to each of the various armies and army groups: 12th AG with unsuccessful units at First, Third and Ninth Armies; 6th AG with a most successful unit at Seventh Army; and units in Belgium and Holland and with the First Allied Airborne Army.

12TH ARMY GROUP

Throughout the fall, the 12th AG Detachment worked principally as liaison between 12th Army Group G-2 at Verdun and OSS/-Paris. In this capacity, the Detachment wired daily situation reports to the Paris Reports Board and received, in return, information Paris considered useful to the Army Group. Examples of the latter were the daily Rhine water-level readings, which G-2 specifically requested and which Paris obtained from OSS/Bern.* Meanwhile the front had so tightened that the Detachment tried only two agent infiltrations between 1 November and the German counter-attack in mid-December. Neither agent was ever heard of again.

Relations with 12th AG had always been somewhat uncertain, ever since First Army ejected its OSS unit in Normandy.** In the latter part of the summer the Detachment had redeemed OSS standing by some valuable work during the French campaign. However, during the fall's operational lag, 12th Army Group suddenly suggested in November that espionage could be more useful if conducted from bases like Paris and London than from the field.

The issue was still undecided when First Army, which had always led objections to OSS field units, discovered an OSS Third Army outpost operating in its territory at Ettelbruck during early December. 12th

---

* On field detachment activity in France, see sections on "Army Detachments in North France" and "Seventh Army", above.

* See "Bern", above.
** See "Army Detachments in North France", above.

AG Detachment arranged for the outpost's withdrawal, but the situation was still simmering at the time of the Ardennes counteroffensive.

The sudden assault hit First Army, the only army without an OSS unit. The unexpected effect was to solidify the reputation of OSS field detachments, and their role with the armies was not openly questioned again.

"Sleepers." Once the offensive was under way, OSS developed a plan at 12th Army Group and SHAEF request, which called for numerous stay-behind agents, to be placed in the expected path of the German advance. These teams, generally known as "sleepers," consisted of an observer and a wireless operator. They were to obtain and send intelligence on order of battle and troop movements generally, in the event their locations were overrun by the enemy. SHAEF directed that the plan be immediately implemented by OSS and SIS in collaboration with French DGER and the Belgian Surete, and supplied a list of intelligence objectives and localities, in priority order, which included important rail centers and sites previously used by the Germans for panzer formations and large troop concentrations.

The personnel provided by DGER were French, some of whom had been former *Sussex* * agents. They received a general briefing in Paris, and were dispatched to the OSS field detachments for final briefing and placement. They were to communicate with Paris via Station VICTOR in England and also directly with the field detachments.

The 12th Army Group unit coordinated OSS' contribution to the "sleeper" operation, directing the placement of agents recruited by all the various OSS field detachments. By the end of December, Ninth Army Detachment had three Belgian and two Dutch "sleepers" in position; eight more teams had been placed in Third Army and French First Army areas; and four

teams had been placed with Seventh Army. In addition, ESPINETTE, the SI/Belgium mission,* and its British counterpart had recruited thirty more "sleepers," which were held in readiness. To assist in recruiting, the OSS FAAA Detachment ** was also sent to the battle area.

The teams dispatched to the Third Army zone ran considerable risks: both were sent to towns where the German language was more common and where pro-German elements, who would not have hesitated to turn the newcomers over to the Germans, were numerous. The field detachment with the Seventh Army was more successful in providing safe houses, contacts and documents. The arrival of these teams was therefore inconspicuous (in one case it coincided with the arrival of a group of 500 refugees), and, furthermore, the contacts were able to provide jobs or additional cover for several of the agents.

None of the teams were ever activated. Before it was necessary to use them, the American counterattack had succeeded, and the Germans were slowly retiring to the Westwall. This was fortunate for OSS since only three weeks had been allowed to recruit, train and brief the "sleepers", and, with such short preparation, casualties would have run high. The teams were withdrawn by the end of February. However, it was recommended by SHAEF that sufficient personnel be retained to be used in the event of a similar emergency.***

Following the Battle of the Bulge, the 12th AG Detachment's role changed, from initiating operations, to supporting the activities of other OSS field detachments attached to armies in the Group. It at-

---

* See "SI/North France", above.

* See "Belgium and Holland", below.
** See below.
*** "Sleeper" agents, employed in considerable quantity by the Germans, were seldom used by OSS in Europe inasmuch as American reverses were few. Agents placed in Eire, Spain, Portugal, Africa and the Middle East during 1941-43 were expected to serve as "sleepers" should the need arise.

tempted to develop alternative forms of air lift for agent drops. London-based B-24's proved undependable: the shortage of planes proved a constant bottleneck; sending agents all the way to Britain to be flown back to the Continent caused more unnecessary delay; the size and slow speed of the planes made low flights impossible where there was heavy flak; lack of radar equipment meant drops were possible only on dangerous moonlit nights.

The Detachment worked out with two advance Ninth Air Force units arrangements which eliminated many of the difficulties. The 155th Night Photo Reconnaissance Squadron offered two A-20's, and the 422nd Night Intruder Squadron made available an A-26.

These planes were equipped with radar, which permitted accurate drops in dark periods, and had the speed necessary to carry out operations even where heavy AA fire would be met. VE-Day intervened before full use could be made of the possibilities these new aircraft offered. On the basis of the experience gained, however, operations officers felt that the A-26 was the best plane yet found for agent drops.

Ninth Army. Ninth Army Detachment at Aachen was the northernmost of the OSS units directly supporting the armies in the field.

The Detachment had been transferred from Brittany to the Westwall in September 1944, along with the rest of Ninth Army. Against the new German target, it soon faced the same troubles that other OSS field units suffered that fall. The solid front and tight enemy control rapidly brought penetration activities to a standstill. Operations dwindled in October to interrogations of refugees who had drifted through the lines and to disseminations of OSS intelligence forwarded from Paris.

Aside from cooperation on planning "sleeper" teams during the Battle of the Bulge, activities through most of the winter were equally unsuccessful. A few teams

were infiltrated during December, in collaboration with the British, but no intelligence was received. From January to early March, only one agent—without communication facilities—was dispatched. Activities picked up in the spring with the final great Allied advance. Near the end of March, two teams were infiltrated across the Rhine on "water-lilies", small, semisubmersible British craft designed especially for subversive operations. Two more agent teams were parachuted into the Oberhausen and Munster areas. In mid-April, two additional missions were dropped with sets near Bruck and Juterborg. Wireless contact was established with most of these teams, but all were overrun before being able to send back any intelligence of real value. The front, in fact, had so liquidated by the latter part of April that agent missions ceased to pay dividends, and the Ninth Army Detachment ceased active operations as of 1 May.

First Army. Following the Ardennes counter-offensive, a detachment was reinstated at First Army, but, in the short time that remained for organization and operation, it was able to infiltrate only one team behind enemy lines. This mission penetrated eight miles, and no intelligence was received. The unit's operational failure, together with the continuing lack of any real support from First Army G-2, finally led to early disbandment of the Detachment in April 1945.

Third Army. As the battle line tightened during the fall of 1944, OSS Third Army Detachment at Luxembourg ran into the same difficulties as did its counterparts at Ninth and First Armies. The static front stymied any productive infiltrations during the early winter.

However, when the Allies launched their spring drive into the heart of Germany, activities expanded. One mission was dropped during the last week of March, and several operations followed in early April as the lines became fluid once more. Six missions were infiltrated by boat across the Rhine: one wirelessed back useful information on enemy troop movements near Frankfurt; intelligence received from two of the others helped Third Army on its crossing of the Rhine between Wellmich and Kaub.

Three more missions—two of them equipped with S-phones—successfully penetrated enemy lines during the last days of April, but by then the advance was moving too fast for productive intelligence results. The missions were all overrun before obtaining any useful information.

6TH ARMY GROUP

The OSS 6th AG Detachment differed in concept, activity and size from its northern counterpart. Outgrowth of a small liaison unit that had moved in with the Army Group on Operation *ANVIL*, the Detachment never veered much from its original purpose.

Activities were limited to providing OSS intelligence disseminations and serving as a channel for any intelligence target requests G-2, 6th AG, might make of OSS. The unit did not in any way coordinate or supervise activities of the Seventh Army Detachment, nor did it conduct any operations of its own.

Seventh Army. Southernmost of the OSS field units was the Seventh Army Detachment. This Detachment—located successively at Epinal, Luneville, Strasbourg, Saarlautern, Kaiserslautern, Darmstadt and Augsburg—was the most successful of the OSS units directly supporting U.S. armies in the final assault on Germany. It parachuted a total of 44 missions behind enemy lines between January and May 1945, with results of great value to Seventh Army. Experience as a unit, and support from a sympathetic G-2 who had worked with it before, gave the Detachment distinct advantages over other OSS field units.*

---

* For its similar excellent record in France, see "Seventh Army", above.

By late fall, it had clearly overcome the problems of locating and infiltrating agents who might operate safely in the Reich. Despite a SHAEF order, strictly adhered to by the British, not to use German nationals for Allied intelligence work, the Detachment decided that only by ignoring the order could a successful penetration of Germany be effected. Poles, French and Alsatians were rejected as potential agents, because their accent was not authentic and they would be subject, as foreign workers, to curfews and other restrictions of movement.

To get vital information for the air forces on locations of motor pools, food and armament dumps, German headquarters, etc., the Detachment turned to POW camps. These offered recruits with the requisite assets for the difficult job of operating behind German lines. As natives, they knew the Reich and its controls thoroughly. Cover was usually simple to establish on the basis that the men were separated from their units, discharged from hospitals or on furlough. Often they already had enough documentation.

Security was, of course, always doubtful and an elaborate screening process was devised to insure maximum agent reliability. The German proclivity for methodical detail made the task easier. Instead of the simple dogtag, each German soldier was equipped with a basic military book, the Soldebuch, giving information on his religion, political background and military record. From them, OSS was able to weed out three POW types who might be disaffected: (1) Catholics; (2) Bavarians and Austrians; and (3) soldiers of the shock troops, particularly those of the punitive Straf Battalionen, who had been sent to the front lines because they were politically doubtful.

Agents, recruited from POW camps, were trained in a secluded mountain spot, Station "O", and treated with friendliness but with strict discipline. They were given convincing arguments that German defeat was inevitable and that their best interests lay in helping to bring it about quickly.

Documents and individual cover stories were provided by a CD unit which had moved from London to Strasbourg in February. Models of completed documents were obtained from POW cages or G-2 at Seventh Army CP, and blanks were either captured or obtained from CD in London. A rubber stamp factory and a printing firm in Strasbourg did the technical work for OSS. An ex-German clerk assisted in the draftsmanship of Soldebuecher, Wehrpassen, etc., and a former Austrian of a Gebirgs-Jaeger regiment advised on German procedures and executed travel papers. Most recent regulations regarding their use were secured at POW cages, and all necessary changes in dates were made just before agent departure.

Once pinpoints were chosen for Air Corps approval, the battle order information necessary for creating military cover was supplied by officers at Seventh Army CP in charge of missions. At Station "P", near the agents, documents were finally prepared, over a period of two days, to fit specific missions. Papers were aged, photographs of proper size and pose for various papers made, and ration tickets for soldiers and civilians supplied. Miscellaneous supporting documents were given the agent, including personal letters, photographs, etc. If time allowed, he was urged to adopt a second identity, under which he might circulate should he be captured and escape. Fully prepared agents were then guided through the lines, where they would pretend to be returning from hospital, training or furlough. Arrangements for the agents to return were made with G-2. They were to appear either at dawn or at twilight with hands raised and carrying a white flag. Once in contact with G-2, they were to be turned over to OSS authorities.

The first POW mission was undertaken in December by a young ex-officer of the German Navy who had been reduced and placed in a punishment battalion because of anti-Nazi sentiments. The agent was infiltrated through the lines in Alsace and penetrated to a point 20 to 30 miles behind the front; he returned a week later with useful order of battle intelligence. The results of the experiment encouraged Seventh Army Detachment to expand on the POW type of tactical mission. Of approximately thirty German soldiers used, only two were captured and not one turned double.

Meanwhile the Detachment was trying to work out a successful technique for getting agents in and out of enemy territory with minimum casualties and maximum information. Mines and machine gun fire had taken an increasing toll of line-crossers during the fall, and the rigidity of the forward areas made it difficult to penetrate far enough behind the German areas to turn up useful intelligence.

The "tourist" type of mission for tactical work was developed. G-2, Seventh Army would draw up an itinerary of travel behind enemy lines. An agent with appropriate cover would parachute in, gather certain information along the predetermined route— talking to soldiers waiting for trains was especially productive—and return to Allied lines when his tour was complete. At that stage, he would be routed back to OSS and report on the targets he had covered.

Originally, it had been hoped that the "tourists" could still be occasionally infiltrated through the lines. However, in January and February only 10 out of 21 such missions succeeded in getting beyond the front. Mines took a heavy toll. Use of aircraft insured that the "tourist" could get sufficiently far behind the lines to obtain the kind of intelligence that was needed. The task of covering the selected itinerary was facilitated by a good air drop record for accuracy. Furthermore, the risks of line-crossing were halved, since the parachuted agent crossed the lines only on his way back.

Stimulated by POW recruiting and the "tourist" technique, Seventh Army Detachment activities increased in January and February. Twenty out of thirty-one penetrations were successful. Fourteen agents had completed their itinerary by the end of February. All covered their target points; five, additionally, brought back important new German battle order information.

Operations hit a peak during March and April. Twenty-six "tourists", including four women, were dropped during these months. Seventh Army Detachment continued until May to obtain tactical information through "tourist" operations. The final report, an item on enemy dispositions in the Inn Valley, came through just before VE-Day.

UNITS IN THE LOW COUNTRIES

The OSS First Allied Airborne Army Detachment was originally activated in August 1944, when preparations were under way for the *MARKET* airborne operation directed at Eindhoven, Nijmegen and Arnhem. A two-man SI team (together with an SFHQ unit) went in with FAAA when the attack was finally launched on 17 September. Two of the SO personnel were lost at Arnhem, and the SI team was put out of commission when its radio was smashed during the landing.

The Detachment next saw action during the Battle of the Bulge, when FAAA units were thrown into the fight to help stem the Nazi advance. It concentrated on recruiting "sleepers" * and locating safe houses for them. The tide turned, however, before it was necessary to activate any of these projects.

The Detachment made its final effort when FAAA units were called on to support the British Rhine-crossing operation in March 1945. Four teams, all of which were unsuccessful, went in via glider. Personnel of one team was wounded and its German car smashed while landing. A second team failed to move into enemy territory at all.

---

* See above.

The final two groups were overrun before they could obtain any valuable information.

In September, two missions entered Belgium and Holland to gather intelligence from the local intelligence networks, to recruit agents for the infiltration of Germany from London and to dispatch teams through the lines.

ESPINETTE, the mission in Belgium, sent some six teams through the lines, each consisting of locally-recruited observers and W/T operators. Total casualties were three, two men and one woman. MELANIE in Holland dispatched one agent, "Marietta", through the lines by canoe. "Marietta" contacted Dutch intelligence chains already operating, and transmitted valuable tactical information until she was overrun by the advancing Allied armies. The best results came, however, from liaison with the Belgian and Dutch intelligence services, and, from this source, MELANIE provided the most extensive reportage on any sector of the West Front.*

The purpose and organization of field detachments had been worked out during the campaigns of France and Italy. While large OSS bases dispatched long-range agents deep into enemy territory, and while regimental S-2's obtained intelligence from front-line army patrols, field detachments recruited local civilians for penetration a few miles behind enemy lines. Their primary purpose was to cover marshalling points, communications centers, concentrations of troops and similar developments of importance to ground armies.

When the lines were fluid, line-crossing involved the least difficulties. With a static front, a safer method was to parachute "tourists" behind the lines, expecting them to work their way back.

Given air superiority, "Joan-Eleanor" was by far the safest communications device for West European conditions. Agents in en-

---

* See "Belgium and Holland", below.

emy territory also sent back couriers carrying bulky reports, maps and other material which could not be radioed.

In friendly country, willing agent recruits were plentiful. In enemy territory, disaffected citizens and soldiers could be found. Seventh Army personnel noted, in this regard, the importance of offering agents American decorations and the best American medical care.*

Of the nine OSS units on the West Front, that at First Army was handicapped by a late start and an unsympathetic G-2; the FAAA Detachment was given intermittent opportunities for action, but never had time to acquire experience; two of the units were at Army Group Headquarters, and two depended on local intelligence services; of the remaining three, however, two, Ninth and Third Army units, failed, until late March and April, to obtain any agent intelligence at all. One, Seventh Army Detachment, maintained an outstanding record, infiltrating some 45 agents between December and May.

The difference was largely one of experience. By late 1944, OSS had developed a small number of personnel expert in recruiting, training, dispatching and handling foreign civilian agents. Those personnel, occupied in bases in Cairo, Italy, Spain and elsewhere, had, for the most part, to continue their tasks. OSS/London, hampered by the predominance of British SIS, had accomplished few agent infiltrations. Of the few men in London who had acquired experience, most remained to carry out the program for dispatching long-term agents to Germany. The only large and expert SI staff available for operations in France was the French Desk/SI in Algiers.

OSS/ETO had to prepare four army detachments and one army group detachment. Personnel were perforce largely men with SO or no experience. In the main, they had not previously worked as units and were unfamiliar with the army staffs, in particular the G-2's. The Algiers French Desk/SI, on the other hand, went in as a unit with Seventh Army. Its success in building up chains of agents in South France over a long period had produced close cooperation from AFHQ. SI/Algiers had worked with G-2, Seventh Army in planning Operation *ANVIL*, a landing which had been called "the best briefed invasion in history". As a result, it had at all times the strong support of the G-2, and at the same time was left to conduct operations independently. Given these advantages, the OSS Detachment with Seventh Army acquired an outstanding record.

---

* An item notably absent during the South France campaign. See "Seventh Army", above.

C. MO — WEST FRONT

The function of MO under the Psychological Warfare Division/SHAEF was to spread dissension and to create disorder in enemy or enemy-occupied lands; to encourage resistance and revolt; to subvert enemy occupation forces; and to assume the role of franc-tireur in the war of nerves. MO worked for these ends through "black" as distinct from "white" propaganda.* Its main channels were radio broadcasts, rumors, faked newspapers, news letters, official proclamations and other written materials. It was able to exploit to good effect enemy war weariness and eagerness for real news of any kind, the cleavages between Wehrmacht and SS and between Wehrmacht and Nazi Party bosses, as well as such dramatic occurrences as the 20 July attempt on Hitler's life.

RADIO

Radio was of course one of the most effective MO weapons, particularly in the European Theater where excellent facilities for establishing powerful transmitters existed. Initially, MO's radio activities were limited to collaboration with British "black" stations which had already been established.

"Soldatensender". Thus MO made important contributions to the programs of "Soldatensender". This station had a 600,000 watt transmitter with directional antennae which gave even greater localized power. It began broadcasting in 1943, purporting to be a freedom station operating clandestinely within Germany. For a while it was known as "Soldatensender Calais" and was supposedly operating from France.

After the fall of Calais it adopted the name "Soldatensender West".

In April 1944, the British asked MO for advice and suggestions with regard to "Soldatensender" programs. After considerable study, MO proposed that the entertainment be an integrated program calculated to win and hold a large enemy listening audience, rather than a desultory fill-in. The British requested MO's assistance in preparing such a program, and MO took charge of the whole of the station's entertainment. Entertainers in England were selected and scripts and music prepared there, in addition to recordings which were made in New York and flown over to England.* MO also provided some intelligence materials for the program.

The decision was made that at first no risk should be run of losing enemy listeners by including propaganda in the entertainment. Later, when MO felt confident that its entertainment had been accepted, it began the process of weakening the enemy's will to resist, appealing to nostalgia, homesickness and war weariness. These emotional appeals were made through music, sentimentality, dramatic episodes and maudlin verse. Prominent entertainers of German or Central European origin made records in New York for these programs, including Marlene Dietrich, John Hendrick, Greta Stueckgold and Greta Heller. Other recordings were made, and "live shows" staged in England. The music consisted chiefly of American jazz, and special German lyrics were written for MO. Some had purely entertainment value, some were of a nostalgic character and some contained satire against Nazi bosses. The station was extremely popular with the German soldiers

---

* For background on "black" propaganda, see MO/Washington. On its relation to PWD in SHAEF, see the section on MO, under "London Base", above.

* See Washington section on MO.

and disturbed the German Army Command to the extent that it issued, on 26 August 1944, a lengthy publication entitled "Dangerous Enemy Propaganda—Warning Against the So-Called Soldatensender-Calais."

"Volksender Drei". In late August 1944, MO received PWD/SHAEF permission to establish its own "black" radio station in Paris. The Nazis were planning a "scorched earth" program, and MO's intention was to capitalize on the natural German fear of impending destruction of family and home by spreading rumors of terror already achieved and by creating hope for a possible way out through internal revolt.

"Volksender Drei" broadcast in German, the chief speaker purportedly being commander of an undesignated town in the path of the Allied advance. The commander had supposedly been instructed to force German soldiers, retreating before the Allies, to turn around and advance, even if he had to use machine guns to make them do so. He reported that he had refused to obey the order and that his troops had taken over the town to end useless slaughter and to preserve order until the arrival of the Allies. Later, after the Allies had presumably captured the town, "Volksender Drei" appeared on a different wave-length, the speaker being "Comrade Hoffman", "son" of General Hoffman who signed the Brest-Litovsk Treaty in the last war. He and other leaders of the movement had determined to carry on their work in the interior of Germany, had formed a "German Freedom Party" and were to continue their broadcasts from a secret transmitter in the heart of Germany.

Judging from its effects behind Allied lines, the program achieved a high degree of authenticity. It was headlined in all French newspapers. Two thousand German POW's who heard the program believed it meant the end of Germany. The U. S. 12th Army Group monitors picked up the program and considered the news of the purported revolts so important that high-ranking officers in the American Army, including General Bradley, were aroused from bed to discuss the new development. (For security reasons, G-2, SHAEF had not notified any army echelons in advance of the broadcasts.) The continuous jamming the program received indicated that the Germans feared its effectiveness.

Voices. The fall of Aachen provided a psychological moment for widening the gap between the German people and the Nazi Party. At this time, MO resurrected Colonel General Beck who had been officially reported dead following the attempt on Hitler's life in July 1944, but who could not be proven dead. The voice was that of a German POW, and the speech, carefully phrased in language that Beck himself would have found natural, argued, in essence, that Hitler and the Nazis had lost the war by interference with German High Command strategy, that a war so surely lost should be discontinued, and that Hitler and his Nazi hierarchy should be liquidated. Preparations for this broadcast were thorough. Rumors were planted in advance to the effect that Beck was really alive, and, at intervals before "Beck" went on the air, listeners were urged to tune in at that time to hear a most important announcement. BBC reported that German transmitters had jammed this program more quickly than any other broadcast from England. The jamming of the wave length was continued for nearly two weeks in anticipation of the return to the air of "General Beck".

MO also produced "Hagedorn", supposedly the representative of a German underground movement, who attempted to induce the Germans to abandon the struggle in order to avoid complete annihilation. Interrogations after the war indicated that "Hagedorn" had made a great impression on many Germans.

"Annie". Another major "black" radio contribution was Operation "Annie" * which broadcast from Radio Luxembourg, one of the most powerful transmitters in Europe. Since Radio Luxembourg had been one of Goebbels' chief outlets, not only were the Germans unprepared to jam it, but German radios had been fixed to tune in to its wave length. Operation "Annie" was the first occasion on which "black" radio had been used to contribute to tactical military operations.

Station "Annie" purported to come from within the Rhineland, to be run by a group of Rhinelanders, and to address first and foremost the Rhineland region, at that time the immediate objective of Allied military operations. To begin with, it was not outspokenly anti-Nazi. Its chief bait was quick and accurate news from the battlefields of the west. Broadcasting between two o'clock and six-thirty in the morning, at a time when few other stations were on the air, it gave the military story of the day in painstaking detail with much local color. The front line was drawn in such a fashion that a battalion commander could keep his situation map by listening to "Annie". Later interrogations show that a number of German battalion commanders did so.

When the Moselle break-through occurred, "Annie" began faking news, carefully at first with reference to small regions, and in such a fashion that its reports were impossible to check. As the break-through grew, "Annie" got more flamboyant, putting armored columns miles ahead of themselves, telling of lost battles and imaginary surrenders, thus instilling a feeling of futility within enemy ranks. After the crossing of the Rhine, "Annie" created a hypothetical resistance movement, made up of Germans anxious to halt the senseless destruction of their country and the suicidal wastes of their last reserves of manpower.

---

* See History File 65b; Annex H in this file contains a number of reports on reaction to Station "Annie".

Local groups were created, given a platform and instructions for immediate action, and finally presented with a plan for the future.

PUBLICATIONS

MO made important contributions to the British publication, directed at the German Army, entitled "Nachrichten fur Die Truppe." This was originally to be primarily an MO venture, but the late arrival of MO personnel led British PWE to commence publication on its own, before MO was ready to bear its share. "Nachrichten fur Die Truppe" started as a two-page, one-sheet paper. Its first edition (numbered ≠9 to confuse German authorities) appeared on 25 April 1944. Two hundred thousand copies were dropped every night until D-Day, when a million copies were printed. In the week after D-Day, the paper's size was increased to four pages, and between six hundred thousand and one million copies were printed daily. Previously, "Nachrichten fur Die Truppe" had been devoted almost entirely to straight news. However, the larger edition allowed room for the inclusion of material of a distinctly "black" nature.

Leaflet production was also effective against enemy troops. In one instance, MO leaflets managed to force out of business "Skorpion West", the German counterpart of PWD, 12th AG. Intelligence revealed that "Skorpion West" handled not only propaganda directed at Allied troops, but also propaganda to its own troops. For wide and quicker distribution it used aircraft to drop its leaflets on its own frontline troops. This serious mistake provided MO with an unparalleled opportunity to distribute faked "Skorpion" leaflets on a large scale. Many such leaflets were produced and the German "Skorpion" was dissolved, its last leaflet being devoted to countering MO's forgeries.

The so-called Ludendorff Surrender Leaflet produced by MO/ETO was conceived around General Ludendorff's justification for his decision to escape to Sweden in the last hours of World War I, when he stated that "it is more important to save officer personnel for future wars than to die in a battle that is already lost. Soldiers are easily found but officers are a rarer commodity." This pamphlet was part of a general program designed to encourage the creation by German forces of soldiers' committees to resist "last stand orders", to cause disaffection between SS and Wehrmacht, SS and Luftwaffe, and soldiers and officers. The leaflet purported to be instructions to the officer corps from the German High Command with a notation that it was to be read by officers only, as it might, if read by the soldier, lead him to revolt. It was distributed along the Western Front by agents of an MO field team, and was dropped on German troops sparingly (four copies by each pilot) by the 9th Air Force in a routine operation, the effects of which were "black", since, in the confusion of retreat, the soldier was not likely to realize that the pamphlet was faked.

An MO Field Unit briefed German-speaking agents who were dispatched into the enemy lines carrying subversive leaflets. In addition, the same unit disseminated a substantial amount of propaganda in Holland for use by the Dutch resistance forces. These operations were generally effective, though small in scope. The problem of adequate distribution of "black" printed materials was never satisfactorily solved.

RUMORS

One of MO's standard subversive weapons was the planting of rumors, or sibs as the British called them. These were built on half-truths or exaggeration of known truths. Although it was unlikely that any one rumor could do much harm, a continuous stream of subversive ideas was bound to have some effect. Produced by PWE or MO, they were passed on by word of mouth, repeated over the "black" radio or found their way into neutral and Allied as well as "black" publications.

The creation and planning of rumor campaigns were among the earliest activities of MO/Washington,* and from its formation, MO/London was also active in this field. In late 1943 and early 1944, an effort was made by MO/London to change the emphasis of total sib dissemination. It was felt that the British were concentrating too heavily on sibs of a high political character, about German leaders and diplomats. MO believed, rather, that more attention should be paid to general sibs on conditions inside Germany, to be contrasted with other sibs about conditions in England and America. Emphasis should also be given to specific attacks upon the morale of the German women left at home. The production of the MO Sib Committee in London, which soon amounted to half or more of the total British and American dissemination, was directed largely along those lines.

The Underground Propaganda Committee under British chairmanship, on which MO was represented after May 1943, was the initial clearing house for sibs. After approval by UPC, a sib was sent to the Foreign Office and then to the Inter-Services Security Board on which SHAEF was represented. At first, all dissemination of the Committee's production was through British channels, either through agents in Stockholm, Lisbon, Cairo, and Istanbul, over "Soldatensender", or in the pages of "Nachrichten fur Die Truppe". As MO missions were established in neutral capitals, they undertook dissemination as well. After the Normandy landings, SO/SOE agents in France, and later in all occupied zones in Europe, were briefed by radio on sibs. Dissemination by agents became particularly important after July 1944, when communications with Germany from all neutral countries, except Sweden and Switzerland, were discontinued. MO arranged for SI/

---

* See Washington MO section.

302

Labor Desk and SO agents to be regularly briefed.

MO missions were established in the neutral countries Portugal, Sweden, and Turkey. The Istanbul mission, which seemed at first most promising from the viewpoint of penetrating Germany, lost much of its effectiveness when diplomatic relations between Turkey and Germany were severed. The TAURUS mission to Lisbon was operating in an area where the British had been recognized to have complete jurisdiction, and its activities were limited to collaborating with the British on the preparation and dissemination of rumors. It appeared that little contribution could be made in this field, which the British had well in hand, and the mission was removed. In Stockholm, however, the MO mission (SIOUX) did prove itself useful and offered effective means of approaching Germany.*

---

* See "Stockholm", above.

It is particularly difficult to assess the value of "black" propaganda operations. In order to do so with any expectation of making even a rough estimate, careful and extensive interrogation would have to be conducted, both after the cessation of hostilities and, so far as possible, by on-the-spot interrogation of enemy POW's and American front-line troops immediately after the operations. Such interrogation was possible only to a very limited extent.*

It is not believed that there is adequate data on which to make any reliable estimate. The confusion, dissension, and war weariness which can be fostered, if not created, by morale operations, is not subject to precise measurement. It is sufficient to say that MO, starting under heavy handicaps, did its job well enough so that many front-line soldiers and skeptical G-2's were finally persuaded of its worth.

---

* See "MO/Italy", above, for an estimate of desertions attributable to Morale Operations there.

D. DIRECT PENETRATION FROM LONDON

Direct infiltration of Germany was regarded by both American and British services as an exceedingly difficult task, with a high casualty rate to be expected. The first American unit to cross the Reich frontier (from Partisan Yugoslavia) had been wiped out on 5 August 1944, after a stay of 44 days.

Indirect intelligence began to flow in early in the war through SI/Labor Desk relations with labor and political groups in Europe, through high-level contacts maintained by OSS units in Bern, Istanbul, and Stockholm and through liaison with other intelligence services. Meanwhile direct penetration was delayed. The new U. S. espionage agency, arriving and organizing overseas during 1942 and 1943, directed its resources principally toward intelligence collection by agents in neutral countries and toward liaison with resistance groups in European countries occupied, but not won over, by the Axis.

The liberation of France did not produce the immediate collapse of Germany, and it was only then that ETO personnel and facilities were directed principally toward the Greater Reich itself. The late start was a considerable handicap to subsequent operations.*

British agencies stressed the almost prohibitive difficulty of direct penetration without the assistance of resistance groups * and friendly local populations. As it turned out, total casualties of all SI/London teams in Germany ran slightly under five percent. Disorganization had reached such a state in the Reich during the last eight months of the war, that many of the agents stayed for months without once having to show their papers. Groups of foreign workers offered excellent cover, as did the streams of refugees constantly on the road, or camping in the fields. Almost any travel orders, days or weeks out of date, were sufficient authorization on the disorganized railroads. At least one agent escaped after capture when a wall of his prison was bombed out.**

The surprisingly low casualty rate, however, followed the surmounting of many difficulties not encountered in the penetration of other more friendly territories. Of these, the principal one turned out to be neither recruiting nor reception, nor in fact the maintenance of cover from the famed Gestapo. The main problem was communication.

(a) *Recruiting.* Whereas the populations of occupied countries provided a large field of willing recruits from which to select the most suitable agents, there were few strong anti-Nazis among the Germans. The use of Communists was, for several months, prohibited by political policy. It was also decided in ETO to avoid German prisoners of war, as too unreliable to war-

---

* SI/MedTO joined, on a smaller and more successful scale, in direct penetration, while maintaining its North Italy and Balkan activities. Most of its agents went to the far more tightly controlled Austrian area. A few teams were also dispatched from OSS bases in Sweden and Switzerland. See the subsequent section, and "Stockholm" and "Bern", above.

---

* Special Operations (SO) were not conducted in Germany because of the absence of resistance groups, and because material destruction could well be accomplished by air, when civilian lives were not considered as important as in friendly territory.
** See below.

rant the risks and screening time involved.* Finally, able-bodied young Germans could not be used, since they would be liable to induction into the Wehrmacht. In sum, the total quantity of anti-Nazi and anti-Communist Germans, not former prisoners of war, too old or too infirm to be draftable and yet strong enough to parachute, was small. OSS/ETO infiltrated principally German-speaking non-Germans to pose as foreign laborers. These, too, were scarce, and the German agents were perforce of a lower average calibre and turned in a lower average performance than those of other OSS experience.

(b) *Reception.* There were no known resistance groups in the Greater Reich. All infiltrations had therefore to be "blind", except when one team, already in, received another, an operation which was possible in only five cases. Furthermore, given successful arrival, there were still few safe addresses. Some had been obtained from SIS, and, through the Labor Desk/SI, from labor, political, and refugee groups, but the majority of these were so old as to be unsafe. By the time OSS agents arrived, many of the residents had been bombed out, had simply left, or had been arrested. Nearly all agents dropped "blind" and without safe addresses.

(c) *Maintaining Cover.* Living in Germany, acquiring intelligence, and maintaining communications equipment were expected to be difficult tasks. Again, however, the difficulties were overcome. A remarkably successful document section provided agents with papers which passed hundreds of police inspections. Even when an agent was taken to headquarters on suspicion, the Gestapo had no files to check with, since most documents showed agent origin in cities whose archives had been bombed out.

(d) *Communications.* Losses ran to less than five percent. But only twenty percent

of the teams ever sent a radio message back to headquarters. And only one of 21 U. S. agent W/T sets in Germany proper ever came on the air. W/T power problems proved virtually insoluble. Only in Austria, where several agents found small guerrilla bands to protect them, could they maintain their W/T sets in operation without fear. Without such protection, sources of power could rarely be found which would not reveal to the Gestapo the W/T location.

J-E * was a partial answer, but before VE-Day there was time only to put ten sets into operation. Even J-E turned out to be insufficient. The team had to place principal reliance on J-E for routine contacts; but if the J-E pinpoint (and alternate pinpoints) should be blown, W/T was necessary to notify home base of a new location. Lacking W/T, the HAMMER team in Berlin was "lost," after its J-E point became a military staging area.

During the last nine months, 34 teams were safely parachuted, a total which amazed SOE and SIS; these services together sent to Germany one-third as many. Of all 34 teams, however, only seven accomplished direct communication. Whether more time would have permitted additional teams to solve the problem was of course undetermined. Of the seven, three were in the mountainous regions of West Austria, where German forces were in general unable to locate them. These three teams used W/T sets. The only four teams communicating from Germany proper used J-E equipment.

	Germany	West Austria	W/T	J-E
Total London Teams Infiltrated with Radio Equipment **	28	4	25	7
Total Teams Communicating	4	3	4	4

* See "The First 'Joan-Eleanor' Operation", above.

** Two of the 34 teams, safely dispatched by London, had no radio equipment, and were to communicate by pouch. One, "Downend", sent two pouches out through Switzerland. The other, "Ruppert", sent none.

---

* Both Seventh Army and SI/MedTO later used German POW's successfully.

Out of seven J-E teams, safely established in Germany proper, four communicated successfully, one from Berlin itself. But only one of the 21 W/T teams in Germany ever came up on the air. All four teams in Austria had W/T equipment; three of these, protected by Austrian partisans hiding out in the Alps, cabled out during the last weeks some excellent intelligence.

Agents were recruited by SI/French, Belgian, Dutch, Polish, German, and Labor Desks in the United States, England, France and the Low Countries. DGER (French Intelligence) supplied some, as did the Polish Government-in-Exile in London. The ESPINETTE and MELANIE missions picked up willing agents from the Belgian and Dutch services, respectively.* A small OSS unit, TRIANGLE, recruited agents and collected cover stories and documentation items near Maastricht, Belgium, for SI espionage missions. Additional recruiting was done, during the early winter of 1944, by a nearby base, FRANZ, originally an MO installation but reconverted for SI purposes in the late fall.

While the Labor Desk had been working on German penetration since 1943, the German and Polish Desks were not organized until July 1944. The Labor Desk parachuted the first agent on 1 September, and infiltrated two more in early November. But by that month, it was clear that the Wehrmacht could maintain a slow retreat through the winter, and that the clandestine penetration of Germany would require the closely coordinated effort of all available SI personnel.

As of 29 November, the Division of Intelligence Procurement (DIP) was assigned control of all SI projects initiated by the Labor section and the French, Belgian, Dutch, Polish, Czech, Scandinavian, and German Desks. Each of these sub-sections remained responsible for recruiting agents

through contacts with the respective governments and nationals, and also for supervising the course of the agent through the various training and processing centers operated by DIP. DIP directed all the facilities necessary for the preparation, dispatch, and operation of the agent missions, and reviewed the target selections of the Desks. It also coordinated similar activities on the part of the field detachments. SO and MO worked to transfer all available personnel to DIP, and DIP received priority over the field detachment infiltrations.

Recruits arriving in England were routed, by the desk involved, through an X-2 security check to the training school at Area F. Here they received two months of basic SI and operational training, weapons and combat, map reading and sketching, a one-week parachute course, W/T, battle order, and photography. An excellent feature of the program was the placing of some prospective agents for a few days in a POW camp. There the agents passed as regular POW's and, besides gaining experience and confidence in maintaining a cover, picked up the latest slang and information on current regulations and general conditions.

For briefing on recent developments in the town or area to which an agent was assigned, and for checking of documents, clothes, and cover stories, the 28-man BACH section * cooperated with the CD and R&D Branches. BACH developed, with the appropriate desk head, the agent's cover in every detail, then checked it with an extensive imitation of a Gestapo interrogation. Representatives of the section accompanied the field detachments on the Western Front, and established bases in Sweden and Luxembourg for the sole purpose of picking up documents, clothing, and, from interrogating German POW's and civilians, informa-

---

* See "Belgium and Holland", below.

* This included eight briefers, two document analysts, seven researchers, four in library and files, four secretaries and translators, and three executives.

tion on regulations, conditions, recent local events, and other data.

Although the section had been built up with SIS and SOE aid, by December 1944 both British agencies were coming to OSS for help on documents and briefing. The papers, ordered from the CD Branch of OSS and checked by the section, passed every German control.* One man, recovered by U. S. troops, was even unable to convince the interrogating officer that he was an OSS agent. When he produced his documents and stated that they were forged, a captured German official, called in as an expert, testified that they were genuine.**

Following their BACH section briefing and checking, plus a stop in the contact office to arrange their code signals on BBC broadcasts, the agents would proceed to OSS holding areas near any one of three air bases, Harrington (England), Dijon (France), or Namur (Belgium). The areas offered the greatest luxury available and every facility or service an agent might request. The purpose of this "babying period" was to give him the feeling of substantial support.

The Dijon base, for instance, was an impressive and comfortable chateau, where the arriving agents were dined and wined at their leisure, during the days they might wait for suitable flying weather. Music, reading, and various kinds of games were provided, and OSS personnel were available at all times to perform personal services, play cards, or listen to the agent during his last few days before departure. Here the equipment received a final check and was repacked. At night, both in and out of the

* With one exception. See MARTINI story, below.

** From the 85th Army Corps (German) in an Order of the Day dated March 12, 1945 came the following compliment: "The enemy forges identity papers so perfectly that only trained experts of the Security Police can recognize the falsification."

moon-period,* planes, from a squadron specially trained in the U. S. and never used on bombing missions, flew the agents to their "blind" pinpoints.

The sum of these facilities and arrangements represented probably the highest technical calibre OSS attained during the war. Physical establishments (training, documenting, briefing) had reached a level approaching perfection. Air dispatch was not handled by an OSS air unit, but the next best service, that of a specifically assigned squadron, was available.

Only one failure might be noted, an inadequate appreciation of the value of a few carefully chosen agents handled on a highly personal basis. In this respect, it had been planned that agents be guided through the whole processing establishment by the individual desks. Some of the desks, however, showed no appreciation of the personalized nature of espionage. The Polish Desk, for example, recruited sixteen teams of lowerclass laborers (who were supposed to fit into the slave labor of Germany) from the Polish Army in London, and gave them massproduction military training. Not one of the sixteen ever came up on the air.

The first OSS agent in Germany was "Downend", parachuted on 1 September 1944, overrun more than seven months later. "Downend" was a German, member of the International Socialist Kampfbund, an underground political group which opposed Communism, capitalism, liquor, meat-eating, tobacco, etc. He had been recruited in March by the Labor Desk, through ISK representatives outside Germany. As part of a joint operation with SOE, "Downend" would (a) gather intelligence for OSS, (b) build resistance for SOE, and (c) organize political groups for ISK.

"Downend" was parachuted "blind" on 1 September, to a field just over the Dutch

* "Blind" dropping caused six teams to parachute anywhere up to fifty miles off target, but was necessitated by the time factor.

border in Germany, near Sogl.* He carried the papers of a construction foreman.

Taking a train to his home town (Bochum), "Downend" went to live with a married couple, whose address had been given by ISK in London. During his seven months in the Ruhr, he organized a group of seven men, each of whom had contact with two to five other men, who were shop stewards or union organizers in the Ruhr. He established sources in Essen and Witten also, including the director of a mining firm, a director of the Deutsche Bank and a high official in Krupp. These men were used to collect information, pass on propaganda, and foster slow-downs and sabotage. Thus "Downend" had fair coverage of all military and industrial developments in the region, knew immediately the effect of bombings and frequently could find out the reconstruction plans of damaged factories. He gained information also from ISK couriers from Hamburg, Bremen, Hanover, Berlin, Goettingen, Kassel, Darmstadt, Ulm, and Frankfurt-am-Main.

This excellent network, based on the ISK underground contacts still remaining after the 20 July assassination failure, was, unfortunately, of little value, having only pouch communication. J-E equipment was not ready as early as September. "Downend" found a suitable field outside Bochum

* This agent was no less afraid than those who followed him, and had an interesting reaction to fear. During the plane trip, he slept for two hours. Upon landing, near the edge of a wood, he lay down and again slept for two hours, leaving himself wide open for discovery. Upon waking, he buried his jump-suit and parachute. At this moment, he reported, "I experienced a period of extreme despair and a very strong temptation to give up there and then, realizing, or rather magnifying, the difficulties ahead of me." He thereupon lay down and slept until 8:30 a. m., when he got up and walked to the Sogl railway station. Boarding the train, he again fell so nearly asleep, that when the ticket collector came through, he passed him his ticket, saying "You want this?" in English. The remark went unnoticed.

and organized a fifteen-man reception committee for the parachutage of a radio operator and set, plus supplies and arms. The location, however, was pronounced unsafe by SOE. The alternatives proposed by SOE were unacceptable to "Downend", since one of them was near an SS school, and the other was a training ground.

The total intelligence from this mission, therefore, was limited to two pouches carried by courier to Switzerland. One, received 18 October, contained news of the development of "Downend's" political organization, and the other, carried by his wife, who made the round trip from Switzerland in February, included lengthy reports on industrial, transportation, and political developments in the Ruhr. "Downend" was overrun on 9 April, at which time he provided G-2 with tactical information and the names of pro-Allied contacts in the Ruhr.

Communication difficulties similarly depreciated the value of most of the teams infiltrated into the Greater Reich. The four successful teams in Germany (using J-E) were:

HAMMER	Berlin
PICKAXE	Landshut
CHAUFFEUR	Regensburg
LUXE I	Weilheim

The three successful teams in Austria (DOCTOR, VIRGINIA, and GEORGIA, using W/T) all worked with an Austrian band of guerrillas, discovered by DOCTOR, the first team to enter.

DOCTOR consisted of two men, recruited by the ESPINETTE Mission in Belgium from the Belgian Surete. OSS and the Surete agreed to split expenses and share intelligence, while OSS would have operational control. SI/London trained and equipped them, supplied documents and cover stories, and dispatched them to the Dijon holding area, whence they were flown, on 23 March 1945, to their dropping point. This was a mountain slope, some twelve kilometers south of Kufstein in the Austrian Alps.

The drop developed one of the stranger coincidences in OSS experience. Parachuting in clear moonlight into five feet of snow, the two agents were spotted by a group of three men who immediately came to meet them. These three, it appeared, were deserters from the Wehrmacht who were starting a mountain resistance movement, and who, only the night before, had spread a large Austrian flag on top of the same mountain on which the two agents had dropped. They had hoped to attract the attention of Allied flyers, to obtain assistance for their movement. The two DOCTOR agents did not disabuse them of their admiration for the speed of the Allied response.

Moving their equipment to a mountain hut, DOCTOR joined the three deserters in building up a network of intelligence and sabotage agents throughout the area. By the end of the 45-day stay, it had contacted and aided underground groups in Kufstein, Kitzbuehel, and the small villages of the region. It had supplied these groups with arms, ammunition, explosives, and incendiaries, binoculars, cigarettes, sugar, and propaganda. Four radio sets were established in various villages, using local power. In this way, spot intelligence could be transmitted quickly at any moment. Three German D/F-ing trucks were put out of action by guerrilla hand grenades.

All supplies were parachuted in two missions, 14 containers on 2 April, and 12 on 24 April. The second drop, on a field prepared and lighted by DOCTOR with fifteen guerrillas, brought two additional SI/London teams. VIRGINIA and GEORGIA consisted of two Dutchmen each, recruited by the MELANIE Mission in Holland by arrangement with the Dutch Secret Service. These two teams separated from DOCTOR a week after arrival, and went to live under cover in the cities of Kitzbuehel and Kufstein with the local resistance leaders. From these cities, they too cabled intelli-gence to London and directed resistance activities.

Intelligence sent by the three teams totaled 66 messages, including: locations and plans of a heavy mountain infantry and training battalion in Kufstein; new AA reinforcements in the Inn Valley; location of Hq. of the Nazi Werewolf organization in the Tyrol; oil depot in the Halle area and defenses of the Inn Valley; location of a train load of gasoline; and location of a jet plane base on the Autobahn near Munich.

The intelligence, mostly from guerrilla sources, was of good quality. The last-mentioned item, for instance, was rated by A-2, USSTAF, "of great value". Local villagers, warned by the agents that non-cooperation would result in Allied bombing, also supplied good information.

With guerrilla aid, the agents removed charges from bridges all through the area, persuaded the military commanders in Kitzbuehel and Kufstein not to resist, and, upon the arrival of U. S. forces on 9 May, helped find local Nazis and Nazi arms caches. In this latter connection, the commanding officers of the 26th and 42nd Divisions testified that Kitzbuehel was more thoroughly purged of military and political undesirables than any section of Germany they had seen up to that time.*

These were the only three SI/London teams in Austria to come up on the air. The four London teams in Germany proper who were successful in communicating had no partisan protection, but all had J-E equipment.

LUXE I consisted of two Germans, motivated by the hope of receiving U. S. citizenship should they return. They parachuted blind to Weilheim in southern Bavaria on 4 April. LUXE I built up a chain of informants in the town of Raisting, with contacts in the countryside and in other towns. Intelligence cabled out from 4 to 29 April (when the team was overrun) included the

* SI War Diary, Vol. 12, Bk. II, p. 167, History Files.

location of an Me 262 aircraft works in an underground tunnel on the Olympia Highway to Munich, Weilheim troop and traffic movements and defenses around Landsberg. Among its other accomplishments, LUXE I acted as pathfinder for LUXE II, receiving the team on 26 April at 0005 hours, and coming on the air with J-E at 0100 hours to report safe arrival.

PICKAXE in Landshut, near Munich, had nine J-E contacts. The two agents reported rail traffic in Landshut, road traffic, the pinpoint of a communications Hq. near Achdorf, and troop movements and locations, identifying many units by describing their shoulder patches and other markings.

A third successful team was CHAUFFEUR, dropped near Regensburg on 31 March. CHAUFFEUR was one of two OSS teams in Europe carrying both J-E and W/T equipment. This double communication precaution proved to be an excellent practice. A shift in the pinpoint, necessitated by enemy use of the area involved or by removal of the team to some other location, could be announced over W/T. J-E contacts could then be resumed. Discovering a dairy which employed ten Belgian and French POW's, the two Belgian agents of CHAUFFEUR moved in and obtained the support of all the workers, including the manager, a non-German. Here they set up the only W/T set to communicate out of Germany proper. Using the milk delivery trucks, the agents, aided by the POW's, gathered considerable intelligence on defenses, troop movements, and target locations.

One of the two agents met two French girls forced to work in a German brothel; these agreed, without compensation, to draw their customers out on military subjects, and, for four days, the agent sat in a closet with a chair, a table, and a small light, taking notes two or three hours a day on conversations overheard. From these and other sources, CHAUFFEUR transmitted nine W/T messages and two J-E contacts; it gave, among other information, artillery emplacements between Irnsing and Marching, location of a fuel dump and the flak defenses of the Danube bridges near Neustadt. One J-E contact located the General Staff as a precision target:

The German General Staff is at Regensburg, Hotel Du Parc, Maximillianstrasse, the street facing the station, first house on the left.

That CHAUFFEUR successfully used W/T equipment in Germany was remarkable. It had luck in finding a source of power in the country where the unusual wattage demands could pass unnoticed, and where the equipment with antennae was easier to conceal. Furthermore, the good fortune which led the men to an isolated dairy, operated by ten sympathetic co-nationals, could not be expected to be repeated by other teams.

Besides PICKAXE, LUXE I, and CHAUFFEUR, the only other U. S. team to communicate out of Germany was HAMMER in Berlin. The two HAMMER agents were Czech Communists, recruited by the Labor Desk/SI from the Free Germany Committee in London. They had known one another for ten years, and had worked together in a Czech underground movement. Their cover and documentation identified them as Czech tool-makers (which they were) fleeing before the Russian advance (which they were not).

Parachuting blind on 2 March 1945 to a field near Alt Friesack some fifty kilometers northwest of Berlin, the two agents walked to town and took a train to the capital. There they went to the home of the parents of one of the agents. The agent's sister and brother-in-law joined in the gathering of intelligence, as did two contacts provided by the Free Germany Committee. Two other contacts, given OSS by the Committee, also proved reliable and joined in the work. These people walked around Berlin, talking to soldiers, going out to military areas and industrial plants, and generally picking up what information they could. For instance, they spent a week writing a report on tank factories still producing in Berlin, following a special request over the BBC for this intelligence, but had no chance to transmit it.

The documentation of the agents proved satisfactory. Once, when they were returning home with a satchel and sack full of maps and reports, an SS man stopped them, checked their papers, and demanded to look in the bags. They took out the dirty laundry they always carried, and he did not ask for more. This was fortunate for all concerned, since their custom was to cock their pistols while shuffling for papers.

Again a communication difficulty diminished considerably the value of the mission. HAMMER had J-E equipment, but no W/T. With J-E the agents could make contact, provided they were at the appointed reception spot. When this point became a Wehrmacht and SS staging area, they had no method of arranging with London to establish a new pinpoint.

As a result, only one contact was made on 28 March:

Against a background of considerable interference and with consequently poor understanding on both sides, the contact continued for a considerable time. Hammer reported that the Klingenberg power plant on Rommelsberg lake was fully functioning and was furnishing electric power to factories. He commented on the location of two important factories which were still operating and then went into a long request for supplies. Most of the supplies were simply food but others were more interesting. Hammer said: "We need medicine that soldiers can take in order to become ill. We need four pistols and three knives. Also food stamps and blanks or paper on which papers can be forged." During the message the Hammer team said: "Please give our regards to our wives and children." Hammer ended up by saying that the city railroad was the only system of transportation in working order in Berlin, that if that could be interfered with all traffic would stop. They also located the position of the main postoffice and telegraph office for the J/E operator and reported on location of freight yards full of 26 freight trains and eighteen passenger trains.*

---

* SI War Diary, Vol. 6, Bk. II, pp. 437-8, History Files.

On 24 April, the Russians came upon HAMMER fighting to prevent some 30 Wehrmacht troops from blowing a bridge.

The communication problem, in this case too, made the placing of a team in the capital of Germany a theoretical success, with few practical results. Of all 34 radio-equipped teams infiltrated from London, these were the only seven to come on the air. Others tried but either could not find sufficient power in a concealed location or handled their equipment incorrectly.

German clothing, provided the agents by OSS/London, was universally satisfactory. So were the documents, with only one exception. The aftermath of that exception (papers of agent "Adrian" of team MARTINI) is described below:

Adrian's Story *

After leaving his radio operator, he proceeded to Augsburg to the Eisenbahn Bureau to seek work in his line. Arriving there he inquired for work and said that he was from Poznan and was sent to Augsburg to work on the railroad. There they checked his papers and sent him to another office where he immediately saw that he was dealing with the Kripo (Criminal Police). There they checked his story and demanded a Marschbefehl (Travel Order) which he did not have. He explained that he had lost the paper and when asked why he did not lose the other papers he explained that he kept that paper separately in another pocket because it was always demanded of him wherever he went. He explained again that he was from the Poznan office and they seemed to be satisfied with the rest of his papers, and sent him to the railroad office at Halle. They issued him railroad tickets to proceed to Halle and threatened him that he was to report to Halle immediately—if he did not do so he would be punished. Instead of going directly to the railroad station he went around the city and some time later to the railroad station and then on a platform to take a train to Ulm, to inform his teammate of his whereabouts. On entering the train for Ulm he was stopped by the two men from the Kripo and his story was checked again and he was put on the train with two other Kripo men who accompanied him to Halle. They brought him near the railroad office at Halle where they left him and let him go up to the

---

* SI War Diary, Vol. 12, Bk. III, pp. 301-05, History Files.

office alone. At the railroad office, he said that he was sent from Poznan to Halle to work. The official there pulled out a list of all railroad workers registered in Poznan. His name was not on there. The official immediately threatened to turn him over to the police but he asked him if it was possible to put him on the list since he didn't want any trouble with the police and to which the official agreed for a sum of 1000 marks. The official had given him papers to go to work in Altenburg and upon leaving the building he was again accosted by the two Kripo men who demanded to see what disposition the railroad office had made of him. Seeing that his papers were in order they escorted him to the railroad station and put him on a train for Altenburg. Arriving at Altenburg, he reported to the railroad office to work and was told to report to the police to register. His papers were checked and he received ration cards and was told to report to the Wehrmeldeamt (Draft Board) because his soldiers book had expired. Arriving at the Wehrmeldeamt they checked his papers and in looking over his Wehrpass they noticed that his physical description was not entered. Also they noticed that he had a citizenship which could be revoked and it was impossible for a person of such status to be an official on the railroad and also the fact that he was 41 years old, still single and had not been in the service. They immediately called up the police. When the police arrived and were told his name they immediately pulled out a slip of paper and stated that they had a telephone (sic) from the Kripo to keep an eye on him and seeing that some of his papers were not in order took him into custody. They took him to the police station where he was searched and was there four days when four Gestapo men arrived to take him back to Halle. Previous to the trip to Halle he was able to dispose of small items of incriminating evidence which he had on him but did not destroy a large sketch of an airfield which he had in his possession. Seeing the four Gestapo arrive he knew his game was up and on the train he chewed that sketch bit by bit. Arriving at Halle he was taken to the Gestapo headquarters where they told him to take off his shoes and they cut them up layer by layer. They then took all of his clothes and ripped them to pieces but could not find anything. After checking his body, they gave him a hypodermic in the arm and in the hip and then gave him a glass of solution which he refused to drink. Upon refusal they hit him over the cheek with the butt of a rifle knocking out five teeth and he was forced to drink the solution in the glass which made him very nauseated and he vomited. Seeing that he did not vomit everything, they used two cylindrical rubber rollers which were pressed against his body and rolled from his knees up to his ribs. This process was continued until he had vomited everything out of his stomach. During this process he was hit on the back a few times with the butt of a rifle. Then the contents of his stomach were examined with a large magnifying glass and parts of paper were found. They accused him of being a spy. He explained the presence of paper due to the fact that he had eaten a caramel from which he could not take off the paper. They beat him with rubber clubs and again accused him of being an agent or a deserter. Six to eight hours a day for the next five days the beatings continued but he did not divulge anything. He was given no food and was only given a little warm water with salt. On the sixth day he was told that he was either going to be shot as a spy or was to be sent to Buchenwald, as a deserter. That morning American fortresses came over Halle and bombed the town. One of the bombs dropped near the prison and blew out the doors of his and other cells through which he escaped with two other men since everyone was underground during the raid. He ran in his weakened condition quite a distance until he reached a small forest where he collapsed from exhaustion. He slept there until the following day. After waking up the following day, he met a group of Russian and Polish slave workers who gave him a little food and a place to sleep with them. He explained his condition by telling them that he was beaten up by SS men because he was a deserter from the Army.

On 15 April the American Forces arrived and he met a Major Clark who immediately believed his story seeing his condition. He gave him information about enemy troops regarding the direction they were fleeing and their numbers. The major made arrangements to evacuate him to the rear. Immediately a CIC detachment learned about him and requested that he be allowed to stay and work with them. Working with the CIC he assisted in the capture of about twenty Gestapo members. Among the captured Gestapo men he recognized the two men who had tortured him. Seeing them he pulled out a pistol from one of the nearby soldier's holsters and fired two bullets into each of them. He worked with the CIC until 4 May when a doctor had checked his condition and ordered him to be sent to the rear. He was transferred to the OSS Detachment at Weimar and from there he was brought to Base X Luxembourg.

OSS/London, during the last eight months of the war, dispatched 28 teams, of which four were killed en route, or were never heard from. Excellent documentation and briefing, plus the disorganized condition of the Reich, accounted for a ninety-five percent survival ratio. Communication without J-E equipment was difficult, and this equipment was available in quantity only sufficient for the supply of seven teams dispatched by VE-Day. These teams, for the most part, went in too late to have time for the careful establishment of headquarters and the building up of agent networks. However, these difficulties were also faced by SI/MedTO, where a more selective and personal approach produced good results in a more tightly controlled area.*

* See next section.

314

E. DIRECT PENETRATION FROM ITALY

Operations into the Greater Reich from Italy were principally directed at Austria, although two teams went to South Germany. The famed German last "Redoubt" encompassed the whole area and was far more tightly controlled than any part of Europe (including the rest of Germany) previously attacked by OSS.

The Germans were building up defenses, moving their highest headquarters and constructing underground factories and storehouses to form a last fortress where the Nazi leaders and their elite troops hoped to hold out till the Russo-American war began. They instituted the tightest security control. For example, numbers of fake Allied agents were parachuted in Austria by the Germans, complete with agent equipment, to seek safe houses and friendly contacts in the area: if any such were found, they were liquidated. As a result, Austrians were too terrified to offer much assistance to real Allied agents.

British SOE lost its last team in Austria in November 1944, and it is not believed that SIS had any W/T-equipped agents there.* OSS again surpassed the British performance, placing twelve teams, of which seven transmitted by W/T.

Casualties ran close to one hundred percent. Two sets were played back by the Gestapo, and more than half of the teams were captured. Of the twelve teams, results were:

Killed 1
Captured 7
Fled to Yugoslavia.............. 2

Of the remaining two, one was overrun by the Russians almost immediately after ar-

rival, while the other entered only on 25 April. Prior to capture or escape, however, several teams transmitted quantities of excellent intelligence on Nazi preparations for the "Redoubt", of value to AFHQ planners, and on Brenner traffic, of value to the Fifteenth Air Force.

In addition to the unusually difficult target, several problems in preparing the operations confronted SI/MedTO. Few German-speaking personnel were available, excepting POW's, who had to be carefully screened. Due to lack of early planning in Washington, there were no training officers; agents were sent to various holding areas where they were visited by the appropriate desk heads for training and briefing.

For infiltration, OSS was at first dependent on the British 334th Wing and on Partisan bands near the Austrian border. The former method often involved three months of stalling, with priorities given to British operations. The Partisans, on the other hand, were non-cooperative and permitted neither of the two teams sent to them to cross the Drava. Eventually, an American air unit was transferred to Italy which carried out OSS operations with daring and success. Even then, bad weather often prevented photo reconnaissance of possible pinpoints, which, in any case, were hard to find in the mountainous area of the "Redoubt". The resulting delays prompted several agents to volunteer to go without photos of the dropping areas. Finally, many of the projects were held up for approval. X-2 opposed the use of POW's and some of the ranking officers at OSS/Caserta believed it was certain death for any Americans who parachuted in.

The Labor Desk/Algiers, as it had been in ETO, was the first unit in MedTO to prepare teams for the Reich. By July 1943, it had recruited sixteen persons, the majority

---

* SIS never cooperated extensively with OSS, and its security was so effective that it was rarely possible to determine with assurance where its agents were located. In this case, no intelligence was made available to OSS/MedTO which might indicate any direct SIS sources in Austria.

SI/LONDON TEAMS IN GERMANY AND AUSTRIA
1944-1945

Flensburg

⑬

Kiel

Schwerin

Hamburg

Stettin

Emden

Oldenburg

Bremen

㉙

③

②

Hannover

㉓

Brandenburg

Berlin

Frankfurt

㉑

Munster

㉕

Magdeburg

㉔

㉔

⑳

Dortmund

①

Essen

Wuppertal

Kassel

Leipzig

Dresden

Köln

⑲

Erfurt

㉒

⑯

Chemnitz

Koblenz

⑤

Plauen

Frankfurt

⑰

Wurzburg

⑯

Mannheim

Nurnberg

⑭

Regensburg

⑦ ⑩ ⑨

㉖

㉗

Passau

㉘

Stuttgart

Ulm

Augsburg

④

⑮

⑫ Munich

㉛㉝

⑧

Konstanz

Kempten

Salzburg

⑪

㉚

⑤

㉛

1 DOWNEND			
2 RUPPERT			
3 HAMMER			
4 PICKAXE			
5 FARO			
6 DOCTOR			
7 CHAUFFEUR			
8 PAINTER			
9 FARMER			
10 BALTO			
11 BOYARD			
12 SULTANE			
13 GAULOISE			
14 SIDECAR	18 DAIQUIRI	22 PINK LADY	26 ZOMBIE	30 VIRGINIA
15 MARTINI	19 OLD FASHIONED	23 PLANTER'S PUNCH	27 SINGAPORE SLING	31 GEORGIA
16 MANHATTAN	20 HIGHBALL	24 CUBA LIBRE	28 HOT PUNCH	32 LUXE I
17 EGGNOG	21 ALEXANDER	25 ORANGE BLOSSOM	29 TOM COLLINS	33 LUXE II

from the British Pioneer Corps. During late 1943 and early 1944, all Labor projects failed to receive the necessary approvals. Many of the recruits had been Spanish Loyalists. Also the name "Labor Desk" appears to have encouraged some misunderstandings on the part of commanding officers in OSS and British intelligence.

Finally, over a year later, a Labor team parachuted into Yugoslavia in August 1944. This three-man unit, ORCHID, was to be aided by Tito's Partisans in traversing the southeast Austrian frontier, and, if possible, contacting resistance groups there. On 25 October, ORCHID crossed the border into the mountainous Eisenkappel region. Here the team commenced sending intelligence by W/T, including bombing targets and information on German preparations for the Russian advance. The Partisans with them refused to move further without a large supply drop from OSS. To press their point, they politely withheld permission for the team to cross the Drava River without them. In December, one member of ORCHID was evacuated, due to bad health. After January 1945, the other two were not heard from. The Partisan unit is presumed to have been wiped out by German forces.

Meanwhile a Central Europe/SI unit had been organized, with headquarters at Caserta, to include Q-section (for operations through French contacts, particularly POW's) and the German-Austrian desk.

Q-section achieved virtually no successes at all. Four teams were dispatched, of which two were in too briefly to produce any intelligence.* The most disastrous, however, was agent "Dartmouth", who had operated as an Algiers agent in France for over a year under German control.**

When the Germans left Marseille, they instructed "Dartmouth" to cable Algiers that he had an opportunity to go to Austria

as a member of the Todt organization. OSS approved the operation, and, in October, he moved to the Feldkirch area, continuing to send misleading information and to request additional agents. On 16 February, he received a supply drop. On 10 April, a two-man team was dropped to his Gestapo reception committee and has been presumed killed in action. This made a total of four teams sent to him (including three previous ones in France). "Dartmouth" was a successful German counter-espionage operation.

Q-section also studied methods of exploiting what few active and potential resistance groups there were in Austria. Plans were prepared for the use of French deported workers, the Austrian Communist underground, and the small Austrian resistance group (P. Oe. N.), contacted by OSS/Bern.* An AFHQ directive, however, forbade the support of guerrillas in Austria, on the grounds that a second "Greece" or "Yugoslavia" was to be feared and that Austrian guerrillas might prove easier to arm than to disarm.

Meanwhile the German-Austrian desk recruited, trained and dispatched seven teams. The first of these, DUPONT, parachuted on 14 October some 40 km. south of Vienna on the northeast fringe of the Neusiedler See. The four men (one U. S. officer, the leader, who spoke little German and three Austrian POW's) dropped successfully; however, their radio equipment was parachuted into the lake. Although the three Austrians had many contacts, all of the latter were afraid to provide more than a night's lodging. They did, on the other hand, offer good intelligence. By the time of capture, DUPONT had complete data on the entire Southeast Wall—the exact location of fortified hills, anti-tank ditches, barbed wire and mine fields, pillboxes, artillery sites, etc.—and also some excellent targets, including a locomotive factory and a secret

* One overrun by the Russians, one arriving only on 25 April; see above.

** See "Early Infiltrations" from SI/Algiers, above.

* See "Bern", above.

airfield. Lack of communications once again nullified the value of this information.

On 25 October, after shifting location from day to day, DUPONT found a farmer in Schutzen who kept the agents in his hayloft. Gestapo suspicions were unfortunately aroused by one of the POW's who fell in love and bought his girl a diamond ring. In November, the four men, with the farmer and his family, were captured at home by eight plainclothesmen. The leader of DUPONT was tortured, but refused to use his cipher pads for transmitting over the radio provided by the Germans. He was sent to Mauthausen 1 April, and would have been executed had not a Czech clerk burned his execution orders. He was recovered by U. S. forces on 5 May, having lost 50 of his 165 pounds.* The three Austrians were recovered after VE-Day.

Agent "Deadwood" also fell under German control. "Deadwood" had been dropped near Innsbruck in early April 1945, with plans to proceed to Munich and set up anti-Nazi groups of five men for use by the military police when the American forces arrived. He was arrested on the train from Innsbruck, having aroused the suspicions of a German soldier by expressing the apparently unorthodox view that the prospects of the war were unfavorable to Germany, by taking undue interest in military installations, and, finally, by the use of American matches to light a cigarette. A W/T set was found in his suitcase.

The Germans ordered "Deadwood" to contact his base, intending to use him as a double, but, on first contact, he successfully gave his control signal and was recognized as a playback. The deception material of a military nature, which the enemy instructed him to send, was carefully screened by SI and X-2. On the advice of

the Gestapo, he set up his five-man groups in Innsbruck, composed entirely of Gestapo men who, in this way, considered that they would be able to penetrate the American military authorities upon their arrival.

When U. S. forces reached Innsbruck, "Deadwood" turned over his five-man groups for what they were, and, because of his close association with the Gestapo, helped track down many more of its members who had gone into hiding in the area. His mission was an unexpected success.

The most productive OSS/MedTO team in Austria was GREENUP. Two OG-trained skiers and one Austrian deserter parachuted, on 25 February 1945, in the mountainous Tyrol region of West Austria. Two pairs of skis were lost on the drop, and two of the men crawled through the snow, while the third skied, dragging the equipment to a mountain resort near the dropping point. There friends received them and helped install the W/T equipment. Contacts in the neighboring villages supplied them with intelligence, and eventually led them to a resistance group of about 1,000 men. Through these, they gained intelligence on Nazi preparations for last-ditch defense in the "Redoubt". They located aircraft plants at Jenbach and Kematen, signalled the arrivals of Mussolini and Daladier, the establishment of Himmler's Hq. and other information.

They reported that the Germans had been timing the Fifteenth Air Force bombing of the Brenner Pass and were running their rail schedules accordingly. The Air Force consequently varied the timing of its raids and repeatedly produced train wrecks which blocked the pass completely.

One of the two Americans operated in Oberpfuss, a suburb of Innsbruck. Obtaining a German officer's uniform and fake papers indicating he was under hospitalization, he moved about freely and set up a network of anti-Nazis, who gave him details of train schedules, freight and troop

---

* This man returned, nevertheless, a few weeks later to collect data on Mauthausen. His testimony at the Nuernberg trial was a large factor in the execution of the whole SS group stationed there.

movements and factory production. He maintained radio contact with OSS/Italy.

The Germans caught him finally when one of his own agents, a black marketeer, betrayed him. The Gestapo gave him "special questioning", i.e., they beat him about the body and head for four hours, "making a pulp of his face", and bursting an eardrum with a blow from the cupped hand of a torture expert. The American stuck to his cover story, until he was confronted with his agent, the black-marketeer. He still refused, however, to reveal the location of his two confederates. The Gestapo tried, among other methods of gaining information, hanging him upside down from the ceiling and pouring water up his nostrils and into the ear which had been perforated in the earlier beating.

Torture continued for two days. It was about this time that "Deadwood" concocted a story that the GREENUP agent was a notable in OSS circles.* The interrogation ceased and the prisoner (a technical sergeant) was led to the Tyrolean Gauleiter. The two agreed to enter into surrender negotiations, and the agent sent a radio message to headquarters relaying the German offer.

As U. S. forces approached, the Gauleiter changed his mind and planned to broadcast an appeal to his district urging a last-ditch stand to defend the Nazi "Redoubt". Thereupon the OSS agent returned to the Gauleiter's office, and persuaded him that resistance was hopeless. He then drove through the lines to meet officers of the 103rd Division and to inform them that Innsbruck was an open city.

Neither "Deadwood" nor GREENUP were classic operations, but their success was conspicuous. A member of the latter obtained

---

* "Deadwood" (see above) was shown a photograph of the GREENUP agent and at once, according to the Germans, became very excited and told them they had made a good catch. This man, he said, was an extremely important U. S. head agent of very high rank who would be invaluable for exchange purposes.

the surrender of Innsbruck without bloodshed. The former assisted CIC in tracking down all the Gestapo agents with whom he had associated.

An unfortunate administrative error caused the capture of two SI agents. The five-man DILLON team had changed its control signal at the last minute before departure and this change evidently had not been recorded in the home base Communications Branch. DILLON dropped to Klagenfurt in December 1944. In late February 1945, one of the men was captured and forced to talk. He led the Germans to the others, and the team leader was killed in the shooting that followed. The Germans then played back the operator, while the latter sent his revised control signal thirteen times in three weeks. It was, of course, not recognized.

Meanwhile, the German-Austrian Desk, disappointed with the low calibre of DILLON'S reports, decided to send two additional agents to improve them. DILLON tried to indicate that further agents were unnecessary, but, under Gestapo surveillance, could not emphasize the point. The two men were received in April by a German reception committee. Fortunately no casualties ensued with the Germans using the new team to initiate surrender negotiations by radio. An airfield was cleared to receive an Allied plane, but AFHQ decided not to accept the offer.

Other SI/Central Europe teams parachuted to Klagenfurt, Styria and Innsbruck. Two worked with local resistance groups they located upon arrival. Only one was killed after several weeks' work with the P. Oe. N. in Innsbruck.

Despite the tightest of enemy controls, the "Redoubt" area was successfully penetrated. The casualty rate was high, but could in at least three cases be attributed to careless security on the part of the agents in the field. No less than five of the twelve teams had come up on the air independently.* Agent "Deadwood" and a member of the GREENUP team had turned capture into success. And both GREENUP and ORCHID has transmitted, for a period of

months, volumes of intelligence of importance to AFHQ. Although British services had largely failed to infiltrate the same area, OSS had proved that penetration was possible in this most tightly controlled region.

* Two more were played back by the Germans.

F. SECRET SURRENDER NEGOTIATIONS

The existence of an undercover agency provided a logical channel for secret negotiations. Wavering enemy or satellite leaders and groups could thereby make known their desires to appropriate Allied authorities without incurring the prohibitive risk of public exposure. Such authorities, in turn, could probe vulnerable points in enemy morale without the possibility of official embarrassment.

OSS, in Bern and other areas, received frequent feelers of this nature from 1943 on. Acting as a secret channel only, it reported the instances to the appropriate authorities, and in view of the "Big Three" unconditional surrender formula, took no affirmative steps to continue negotiations. Early attempts, therefore, did not lead to peace negotiations or satellite defections; it was not until late in the war that two of these feelers were, with the approval and participation of policy-making authorities, carried to successful conclusions.

The availability of an organization such as OSS made it possible to extract valuable results, however, from many abortive negotiations. In the first place, the knowledge that certain leaders or factions had been driven to the point of contemplating surrender, revolt or negotiation constituted valuable intelligence in itself. Allied authorities could thus gauge the morale of the enemy and the effect of military operations, at the same time finding a basis for the direction of its political attack. In the second place, OSS could, while holding out no offers of negotiation and making no promises, exploit the weakening leaders and groups for purposes of intelligence and subversion.

Several early negotiations were handled in the Balkans. In 1943, OSS/Bern had suggested to Washington that a distinction be drawn between Germany and its satellites in applying the unconditional formula. In November of that year, JCS authorized efforts to encourage the detachment of satellites from the Axis, and high level contacts were developed in both Hungary and Bulgaria. The negotiations were handled from OSS/Istanbul and both came to nothing.*

On Germany itself, OSS/Bern felt that there had been a serious Allied over-estimate of the German will to resist. Extensive effects might have resulted from following up sudden Allied military successes with agent surrender missions to enemy commanding generals. Bern reported evidence, dating from the early months of 1944, and cumulatively as the Normandy and South France invasions progressed, of a real opportunity to drive a wedge between the Hitler-SS group and the old-line military forces of the OKW. Full information was forwarded on the plots against Hitler, and on the defections in the higher ranks of German army and intelligence (Abwehr) services.** No encouragement was, however, received from Washington to use the defecting contacts to split the Germans.

In the fall of 1944, Bern urged on 12th Army Group, and later SHAEF, a concentrated program to induce certain German generals on the West Front to surrender. General Bradley and his G-2, General Sibert, expressed great interest in this project and gave it their support. A member of the staff of the Bern mission went to 12th Army Group and then to London and was given access to certain German generals who were POW's. Several were selected for

---

* See "Istanbul", above.
** See "Bern", above.

possible use in contacting pliable German generals on the West Front.

The project however, was dropped at the time of the Ardennes counter-offensive, and, by December 1944, the opportunity to effect a surrender on the West Front had largely been lost. The Battle of the Bulge was, in fact, evidence that it was already too late to act. The attack, spearheaded by SS Panzer divisions, confirmed final seizure of control by the Nazi Party. Most of the OKW generals on this front who might earlier have been willing to surrender, including Rommel, Kluge, Schwerin and Stuelpnagel, had been removed, executed, or had committed suicide, and had been replaced by fanatical Nazis and SS.*

In two instances, however, OSS agents were used in ultimately successful negotiations with enemy leaders. In Hungary, an OSS agent carried a message from AFHQ which apparently prompted the Regent to take the anti-Nazi decision he had been considering. In north Italy, the SUNRISE negotiations made possible the surrender of Axis forces on 2 May 1945.

HUNGARY

On 7 October 1944, the SI/Central Europe Desk in Italy dispatched to Hungary two agents, "Moly" and "Cora". These men were flown by plane from Bari to Banska Bystrica in Slovakia, as part of a mission to the Czech·partisans. They were escorted by partisans south to the Hungarian frontier and crossed it four days after arrival. A simultaneous attempt to infiltrate a six-man team into Hungary from the south through Yugoslavia, in September 1944,

___

* After the end of the war, General Schwerin, who had been in command of the German forces at Aachen, stated that he had waited for several days to surrender the city to American forces under General Patton, which were then only a few miles away but held up because they had outrun their fuel supply. Before he could establish communication with Patton, Schwerin was replaced by an SS general, and the city was defended until it was reduced to rubble.

failed due to obstruction of passage by the Yugoslav Partisans.

Agent "Cora" was assigned to infiltrate a factory in Hungary and attempt to start an underground movement; he was not heard from after 19 October, when he was seen by "Moly" in Budapest, starting out for western Hungary.

"Moly" was

carrying messages from AFHQ, and from certain dissident Hungarian diplomatic ministers in Rome and elsewhere, to Admiral Horthy, Regent of Hungary. His mission was to urge the Regent to turn Hungarian forces against the Germans and capitulate to the Russians in eastern Hungary

'Moly' reached Budapest by train on 13 October. Upon arrival, he discovered that Monsignor Luttor, Hungarian representative to the Vatican, had heard of him through Hungarian diplomatic circles in Rome and had denounced him to the Hungarian Foreign Ministry. A personal friend, however, arranged for an interview with Horthy the following day, at which occasion "Moly" delivered the letters and attempted personally to persuade the Regent to take action against the Germans.

Horthy, who was already in touch with the Russians delivered his "Armistice Declaration" the day after "Moly's" interview. The "Declaration" was quickly followed by mass arrests by the Gestapo and a large diversion of German troops to maintain tight control.

"Moly" went into hiding, gave himself up to the Russians in February and was evacuated to Italy in March 1945, bringing with him intelligence on Hungarian conditions and a firsthand account of the Russian occupation.

"Moly's" mission capped several earlier and unsuccessful OSS negotiations with

Hungarian leaders.* Previous ones had lacked the background of Allied success and the authority of specific messages from Allied commanders. "Moly" had these supporting factors, as did OSS/Bern in greater degree for its North Italy negotiations.

NORTH ITALY

In November, an OSS team in Venice reported a German feeler indicating a desire to surrender. This was the first of a series of such feelers received throughout the following month both by Company D and OSS/Switzerland. Elaborate requests for conferences were made by the Germans and extensive conditions set for surrender. Late in January, all teams were warned that no terms could be offered except unconditional surrender to competent Allied commanders and that no negotiations could be entered into by the teams themselves, but that Company D would be prepared to transmit to the Allied Command all requests as received from the field.

On 25 February 1945, a Swiss intelligence officer conveyed word to OSS/Bern that an Italian industrialist wished to establish contact with the Allies on behalf of SS General Karl Wolff. When contact was established, Baron Parrilli, the industrialist, stated that Wolff was ready to arrange the surrender of the German and Fascist forces in North Italy.

A meeting was held on 3 March with two of Wolff's emissaries, at which it was emphasized that Allied policy required unconditional surrender. At the same time, the release of two Italian POW's was stipulated as evidence of good faith. Ferruccio Parri, resistance leader and later Prime Minister, and an Italian officer, one of the key OSS

agents in Milan, were shortly delivered to the Swiss border.

The next meeting held was between Wolff himself, the OSS mission chief at Bern, one other OSS representative and a Swiss intermediary. At that time, Wolff confirmed his understanding that only unconditional surrender would be considered by the Allies, and stated that he believed Field Marshal Kesselring could be won over to this position. He further asserted that he was acting entirely independently of Himmler.

Washington, London and AFHQ agreed to the OSS/Bern proposal that, if Kesselring were prepared to sign, AFHQ representatives should be present. OSS was informed that two staff officers were preparing to leave for Switzerland.*

At this point, Wolff ran into his first serious difficulties. Kesselring had been summoned to Hitler's headquarters and it appeared unlikely that he would return. Kaltenbrunner, head of the SD, had heard of Wolff's trip to Switzerland and had ordered him to break off all contacts there. Wolff asserted nevertheless that he was prepared to carry out his plan, agreed on further meetings and appeared on 19 March at Ascona, a town a few miles from the Italian frontier. At this time, he met first with the Bern mission chief and later with the Allied generals. He reported that Vietinghoff, Kesselring's successor, would be difficult to win over, and felt that this could best be achieved by obtaining the backing of other Wehrmacht officers. He proposed a trip to the West Front to see Kesselring.

After Wolff departed on this trip, a period of twenty days passed, during which he returned to Italy but failed to appear in Switzerland. Himmler had forbidden Wolff to leave Italy and indicated that he would

* The Hungarian Government apparently wavered throughout the war, initiating discussions with the Western Allies for possible mutually satisfactory agreement. On distinct contacts made through OSS/Bern and OSS/Istanbul, beginning in 1943, see those sections.

* Major Generals L. L. Lemmitzer (U.S.) and Terence Airey (Br.) arrived in Bern under the assumed identity of two OSS sergeants—probably the only occasion of the war when OSS was used as cover.

check on Wolff's presence there almost hourly. In view of this development, the Allied generals returned to Caserta. To maintain dependable contact, however, Wolff offered to hide a radio operator at his headquarters. A young Czech "Wally", who could pass for German and had been trained at the OSS school at Bari, was picked from an OSS advance outpost near Strasbourg. With his radio and ciphers, he was smuggled into Milan and lodged with Wolff's aide, Zimmer. One of "Wally's" messages gave the location of Vietinghoff's headquarters with an obvious invitation to bomb it. This was promptly done, and Vietinghoff nearly lost his life. A few days later, "Wally" radioed that Mussolini was in Milan, lodging a few blocks away. He again suggested a few bombs, but asked that care be taken not to drop one on himself. The invitation was not accepted.

By mid-April, the news from Wolff was slightly more encouraging. He was in telephonic communication with Kesselring, and a Luftwaffe General had joined his group. At this juncture, two "agents provocateurs" turned up, one in Bern, the other in Italy where he tried to get in touch with Vietinghoff. As a result, Vietinghoff grew fearful and doubly cautious. Himmler ordered Wolff to report to him in Berlin. Wolff stalled as long as possible, but finally decided to go. This disturbing news, brought to OSS/Bern by Zimmer on 17 April, seemed to spell the end of SUNRISE. It was followed, on 21 April, by a message from Washington, instructing Bern in the most definite terms and from the highest authority to break all SUNRISE contacts.

On 23 April, however, Wolff, his adjutant, and Vietinghoff's envoy arrived in Switzerland to sign the surrender, but were informed that orders from Washington still prohibited any contact with them. Wolff, after waiting for two days in Luzern, finally departed, stating that he could not take responsibility for the actions of German or Fascist forces if he were not in Italy to keep

them in line. He delegated full authority to his adjutant to sign.

On his return trip, Italian partisans surrounded the villa in which Wolff had taken refuge and made him a prisoner. OSS/Bern realizing that, if he were shot, the surrender, even if authorized by AFHQ and Washington, could not be implemented, decided he must be released. Accordingly, a rescue party was organized to persuade the partisans to free him. This was effected and Wolff, now in civilian clothes, reached the new headquarters at Bolzano on 28 April. On the same day, his two assistants left for Caserta to sign the surrender.

At this point communications became crucial. "Wally's" radio location at Bolzano was poor. Caserta, in the hope that "Wally" could pick up the signals, sent out the text of the signed surrender. "Wally" received the message, but for some reason was only able to decipher the first 65 groups. Wolff became suspicious of "Wally", and the latter's position was not strengthened when Allied bombers shortly thereafter dropped a bomb not many yards from Wolff's headquarters. Caserta repeated the message. Its arrival coincided with the return to Bolzano of the two assistants with the signed surrender documents.

It was now 1 May. Only 24 hours remained to put the terms of the surrender into effect, and still no confirmation came from Bolzano. AFHQ sent an urgent message to "Wally", and Wolff kept promising a reply within a few hours. Finally, in a message which reached Caserta only on the morning of 2 May, Wolff explained that, as a result of betrayal, Vietinghoff had been removed from his command, but that, at long last, the order for the cessation of hostilities had been given and would take effect at the stipulated time, 2:00 p. m. on 2 May.

The negotiations carried out through OSS/Bern for the surrender of the enemy armies in northern Italy and southern Austria had underlined one of the unique contributions an undercover—and hence quasi-official—agency could make in the course of modern war. With OSS personnel in Bern operating under cover, preliminary dealings could take place clandestinely without risking embarrassment to the U. S. Government. At the same time, OSS had the advantages of prompt access to the White House, the JCS, the State Department and high military authorities in the Mediterranean Theater. Moreover, the facilities and techniques of a clandestine service were readily available. A communications net existed, equipment and personnel for undercover radio transmission could be provided, the secret transportation of personnel was a familiar and well-organized technique, and means could readily be devised to procure any special documents or equipment desired.

While the unconditional surrender formula postponed their successful conclusions until victory in the field was a certainty, OSS could gather valuable intelligence through secret negotiations and could, finally, make possible the cessation of hostilities at an early date.

Part VIII

THE LIBERATION OF EUROPE

OSS units were quick to follow the retreating Axis armies. City teams reached Athens, Sofia, Bucharest and Tirana ahead of Allied forces, and Belgrade on the same day. There they uncovered enemy agents, documents and equipment, reported political and economic developments pending the arrival of State Department representation and passed on battle order intelligence from local liaisons. Considerable opposition was encountered, however, in Communist-controlled countries, and, by September 1945, city teams in the Balkans had been de-activated. Meanwhile, in France and the Low Countries, OSS units provided similar coverage and, in addition, assisted the London base and the field detachments in the penetration of Germany.

Following the German surrender, additional city teams were established in Oslo, Copenhagen and northern Italy. Operational branches were withdrawn, but SI, X-2 and R&A moved into Germany to uncover Nazi officials and hidden assets and to provide basic intelligence for the U. S.

Group of the Control Council. Substantial OSS resources, including firsthand data supplied by an agent who had been for 38 days at Mauthausen, were devoted to supporting the U. S. prosecuting staff at the War Crimes Trials.

The issuance of the new and greatly reduced budget for the fiscal year beginning July 1945 resulted in the cancellation of most OSS projects in Scandinavia, Western Europe, the Mediterranean area, Africa and the Middle East. Agent chains which OSS had laboriously built up through the war years were dropped. While the pace of debriefing agents, de-activating operational and supply installations and closing off contacts reflected the efficiency of the liquidation program, it sacrificed extensive opportunities for laying the foundations of a peacetime intelligence procurement organization. The policy was followed throughout OSS of avoiding formal post-war commitments pending clarification of future American intelligence policies.

A. ATHENS

The German retreat from Greece moved slowly. It began in August, but did not clear Athens until 12 October, Salonika until the end of October, Crete and the Dodecanese several months later. Four members of the City Team for Athens arrived the day the Germans left, preceding British forces by three days. Another OSS group arrived in November and, by 10 December, there were 38 army and civilian personnel in Greece plus 6 men maintaining a supply base on the Island of Elba.

Control of Greek operations was transferred to OSS/Athens, and the advance bases at Izmir (Turkey), Edirne (Turkey) and Bari (Italy) were disbanded. SO, MO and OG personnel left * for operational activities elsewhere in Europe or in the Far East. Meanwhile, the total of ninety SI personnel still in Greece was cut sharply. Eight teams were maintained in territories held by the two main rival guerrilla groups, ELAS and EDES. A ninth team made a one-month photographic tour in November, covering war damage, German atrocities and general economic conditions. Finally, the base office in Athens acquired SI, X-2, R&A and Services personnel. Thirty-three OSS representatives were thus in Greece itself at the outbreak of Civil War on 3 December 1944.

The Civil War lasted about two months, with the British forces, supported to some extent by small Royalist and EDES groups, beating back the Communist-led army of the EAM.**

OSS maintained eight teams in the field, five in EAM-controlled territory, one in EDES territory, and one each in Salonika and Patras, cities whose control was disputed. OSS team PERICLES provided the only Allied liaison with EAM headquarters. Carrying messages to and from EAM leaders and reports of political and military developments, the leader of PERICLES crossed the lines in civilian clothes almost daily. The other field teams were cut off from pouch communication with Athens and depended on W/T alone. Although OSS agents tended to support whichever faction they accompanied, the resultant bias did not approach that of the reports by the participants. Since General Sir Ronald Scobie would not permit war correspondents to interview EAM leaders, even in the presence of British officers, OSS provided the only independent coverage of the Civil War.

An OSS team was further instrumental in the evacuation of 965 British prisoners in EAM hands. In late December this team located the group near Lamia without adequate food, clothing or medical care. The team obtained EAM permission for the parachutage of supplies by RAF planes to the prison camp. On 20 January, the OSS officers brought two representatives of EAM to Athens for conference with the British concerning an exchange of prisoners. At this conference, EAM refused the services of the International Red Cross (although this organization received public credit for the operation), and consented only to allow OSS officers to make arrangements for the delivery of the prisoners at an exchange point at Volos. On 23 January, the OSS party of three officers entered EAM territory with a British convoy of fifty trucks and nine

---

* Excepting the SO Medical Team. See "Greece", above.
** On EAM and EDES, and for other background, see "Greece", above.

ambulances, and by 24 January the evacuation had begun.

In Athens, meanwhile, the City Team operated under unusual difficulties. An R&A analyst reported:

During the first week the combination office-billet was situated a half block from the front lines. After the British managed to extend the area of their control, the front was pushed away from the office another block and a half. However, with a British-Greek police machine gun, which fired through the day and night, next door, and Greek militia barracks and a main military thoroughfare, which were targets for ELAS mortar shells, one-half block behind the office, there were few days when quiet prevailed enough to concentrate on a long report.*

Despite these difficulties, OSS continued to service the State Department, Foreign Economic Administration and U. S. General Sadler of ML (Greece). Selected reports were also forwarded to the British intelligence services.

Following the cessation of hostilities, OSS personnel was further decreased to 23 members. This allowed for a base staff at Athens, and for three two-man teams, complete with W/T sets, to cover the Greek-Yugoslav border. In June, one field operative was murdered by agents of the Okhrana (a movement for Macedonian autonomy). Trips by Athens personnel further augmented OSS coverage of Greece, Crete and the Dodecanese. An R&A representative maintained contacts with leaders of the Popular Party, Populists, Liberal Party and the Socialist ELD-SKE, and with various members of the cabinet.

A three-man X-2 unit had been working with the British and Royal Hellenic security services since October. At the time the Civil War broke out, these had formed an Anglo-American advance base in Salonika arresting German agents and collecting German sabotage and W/T equipment. To avoid involvement in the Civil War, these men returned to Athens in December, but

* History File 214a, p. 35.

continued their cooperation with British SIME and ISLD after hostilities ceased.

The main cells of the Abwehr sabotage section (IIH) had been left at Athens and Salonika to run some 120 agents in post-occupation sabotage and resistance. X-2 and the British identified the complete enemy group: seventy agents were apprehended; six more were killed; twenty-five left Greece and were traced to their hideouts elsewhere; four defected to the Allies; and ten served as controlled informers for the identification of like infiltrators. Several caches of wireless and sabotage equipment were uncovered. Two groups of parachutists, totalling 26 men, were rounded up and their equipment taken. Up to the termination of OSS in October 1945, no single enemy sabotage plan had been successfully effected.

X-2 also serviced other U. S. agencies, vetting Embassy employees, World War II pension applicants, Greeks in the American merchant marine, ML and ATC personnel, and applicants for visas to the United States. It cooperated with the State Department in studies of economic collaboration for the "Safe Haven" project.

OSS/Athens was also busied with the problem of agent release. Every step was taken to recompense the Greek agents. Death benefits were obtained for the next of kin of four Greeks killed in OSS service. Some 74 certificates were distributed. One hundred and seventy-six names were given to Hellenic Intelligence. OSS helped several of its former agents and sub-agents to find employment.

In the light of the new July budget, personnel was again decreased, this time to a total of thirteen, with one roving SI team (plus W/T), and two SI, one R&A, and three X-2 representatives in Athens. All communications were handled through the Embassy.

B. BUCHAREST

The anti-Nazi coup in Rumania on 23 August 1944 presented the two-fold opportunity of retrieving prisoners of war, and of gathering Rumanian intelligence on Germany. On 29 August, an OSS team of 21 men landed at Popesti airport in Fifteenth Air Force B-17's. In September the first reinforcement from Istanbul entered by Rumanian plane, flying over the Black Sea to avoid enemy Bulgar territory. Others followed by the same route.

OSS preceded the Russians and had a free hand for several days. Until the first week of October, the British had only one representative there, an SOE agent who had parachuted in late 1943.

The first task in Rumania was the evacuation of U. S. flyers. OSS/Bari had been informed by a representative of the prisoners (flown out in a Messerschmitt piloted by a Rumanian) that over 1,000 men were located near Popesti airport. Upon arrival of the team at Popesti, Rumanian officials obtained trucks at Bucharest to carry the released prisoners from their camp to the airfield. The evacuation began on 31 August, and, by the following day, over 1,100 men had been flown out in B-17's. Meanwhile fighting continued in the outskirts of Bucharest. OSS combed the Rumanian hospitals and with Russian help, once the Russians arrived, assembled and dispatched more U. S. flyers during the ensuing weeks, bringing the total of those evacuated to 1,350.

The second priority task was the examination of the Ploesti oil fields. Five R&A experts, entering with the first team, arrived at Ploesti on 3 September and commenced photographing damage and screening documents. The first of the sources to be tapped was Ruminoel, the official German oil mission in Bucharest. Although Ruminoel had been badly disordered after bombing, street-fighting and looting, documents were obtained detailing daily exports of oil products, monthly oil output since 1939, and the requirements and purchases of both the Wehrmacht and the Luftwaffe. From them it was learned that shipments of processed products to Germany had declined by sixty-two percent during the months when the Ploesti refineries were under air attack. Previously, thirty percent of all Germany's oil had come from Ploesti. Additional papers, obtained in the office of Schenker and Co. (German), revealed the destination of oil shipments to German territory, information which provided the Eighth and Fifteenth Air Forces with several new priority targets.

Further OSS investigations in and around Bucharest provided valuable documents. The general confusion occasioned by the German departure from, and Russian arrival in, Bucharest offered many opportunities for picking up manuals and equipment. Particularly remunerative were searches in Schenker and Co. (which proved also to be the center of German espionage in Rumania) and in the local Luftwaffe Hq. From these and other sources, OSS provided AFHQ, Italy, with ninety percent of its information on Rumania. This came from 24 personnel, including 11 SI, 6 X-2 and 2 R&A representatives.*

---

* The hiring of six Rumanians made for certain security weaknesses. In addition, the Rumanian liaison officers, attached to OSS and later to the Allied Control Commission, were reporting regularly to the Rumanian General Staff on OSS activities. It was not until August 1945 that all the liaison officers were dismissed.

A seven-man X-2 unit uncovered in September a large quantity of diplomatic documents of the former Rumanian Prime Minister, Mihai Antonescu, and transmitted them to the State Department. Some ten thousand dossiers were found in the office of the Nazi Party in Rumania and combed for information to be used in the War Crimes Trials. The German Gestapo files for Rumania were also acquired and transferred to SHAEF for disposition.

From these sources and from some sixty former Axis agents (some of them acting as doubles) X-2 identified over 4,000 Axis intelligence officials and agents, more than one hundred subversive organizations and some 200 commercial firms used as cover for espionage activity. Two hundred pages of such data were forwarded to General Deane of the American Military Mission in Moscow to be transmitted to Russian intelligence for action in Rumania.

Liaison with the Rumanian General Staff and with the 2nd Ukrainian Army produced a series of tactical targets, supply depots, airfields, enemy unit locations and communication centers, for OSS to cable back to the Fifteenth Air Force. Bombing and strafing lines were established, a liaison job which was subsequently taken over by a special MAAF unit, sent in for the purpose. After many setbacks, agreements were completed with the Russian NKVD and a sort of liaison effected. Counter-espionage information was exchanged, and OSS further obtained the right to interrogate German military and political prisoners.

Contacts with government and opposition leaders provided political and economic coverage of Russo-Rumanian relations. Trips to Slovakia, Transylvania and Debrecen (seat of the Provisional Hungarian Government) yielded reports on political developments, leading personalities and Russian occupation policies in those areas.

Examples of information obtained from the above-listed and other sources were:

(1) For ONI, reports on the Rumanian fleet in the Black Sea, navigation conditions, coastal defenses; an illustrated German analysis of naval and air operations at Salerno.

(2) For AFHQ, the first over-all coverage of Hungarian and German divisions in the area; unit identifications and composition.

(3) For the Air Forces, evidence that bombs used in raids on oil refineries should be fused no longer than 1/100th of a second; information on a German radar control apparatus effectively countering "window"; targets at Moosbierbaum in Austria (chemical works manufacturing aviation gasoline), and at Wismar (Dornier factory assembling FW-190's).

The OSS mission had originally entered under cover of an Air Crew Rescue Unit. The U. S. section of the Allied Control Commission arrived on 9 November (until which time OSS had been the sole American representation in the country), and the unit became a sub-section of US/ACC. Lacking local official approval, the station was closed in September 1945.

C. SOFIA

Like the other city teams, OSS/Sofia was the first U. S. representation in the country. The U. S. section of the Allied Control Commission (ACC) did not arrive in Bulgaria until November 1944, while British intelligence missions had been withheld until 21 September. On 23 August a two-man OSS team had been dropped on the Greek border and joined Greek guerrillas harassing the withdrawal of German troops. Advance through Bulgaria was hampered, however, first by the German troops and later by Bulgar celebrations; the team did not reach the capital until 17 September, where it found another one preceding it. This latter consisted of four men dispatched by car from OSS/Istanbul on 6 September 1944.

The first task was to arrange for the prompt evacuation of 335 airmen (mostly American). ˙ These were released from the camp at Shumen, Bulgaria, on 9 September and entrained for Sofia. Inasmuch as Sofia had not yet been occupied by the Russians, and was still subject to Allied bombing, OSS objected to this move. The chief of mission located the train some thirty miles beyond Gorna Orekovitsa, had it turned back and re-routed direct to Turkey. On the morning of 10 September, the Sofia railway station was severely bombed at about the time the aviators would have arrived. OSS cabled to Istanbul information of the trainload, and the aviators were met at the frontier by the U. S. Assistant Military Attache and a large Turkish reception committee.

The City Team provided the only independent U. S. intelligence during the critical and confused period of the Bulgarian transition from hostile to co-belligerent status. Besides political and economic coverage of Russo-Bulgar relations, OSS liaison with the intelligence section of the Bulgar operational staff provided daily reports on German battle order in Macedonia, plus several German and Hungarian military documents on training, weapons, etc.

The Russians, however, upon their arrival in mid-September, put a stop to further operations. On 24 September, the American and British intelligence missions were ordered to leave. Both parties demurred, stating that they would have to receive authorization from their respective headquarters. When the Russians repeated the order on 26 September, offering the alternative of imprisonment, the missions left.*

On 5 November, the OSS team obtained permission to re-enter, and resumed its military coverage (through the Bulgars and Russians), its political and economic reporting on developments in Bulgaria and its assistance in War Crimes investigation. An X-2 unit vetted State Department and other U. S. personnel and visa applicants. In December, Russian ACC pressure on the State Department representatives, who had arrived in November, again forced OSS withdrawal, this time permanently.

---

* Two explanations have been offered for this summary dismissal. The first (suggested by several members of the Bulgar Legation at Istanbul) was that the colonel commanding the British unit was suspected by the Russians of anti-Russian activity; in order to get him out of the country it was necessary to oust all missions. An alternative is that the Russians wished to establish their control of the area before any foreign missions were admitted.

D. TIRANA

Upon the withdrawal of German troops in October 1944, the two roving teams were recalled from northern Albania to join the base team in Tirana.* Coverage of political and economic developments continued. A medical officer made an inspection tour of the southern section of the country, reporting on hospital conditions and on the spreading typhus epidemic. On 27 November, the first Allied plane to arrive at Tirana airfield brought in an OSS officer. OWI films "Air Force" and "Here Comes the Navy" were loaned to the Provisional Government, and other OWI material was distributed.

Enver Hoxha, head of the Communist-controlled Provisional Government, delayed for some time the establishment of an OSS City Team, and the admittance of new OSS

---
* For background, see "Albania", above.

personnel. Finally, in February 1945, authorization was obtained, and the team was set up with eleven members, including five SI and one R&A. An interesting move by the Provisional Government was the refusal to accept any U. S. civilians. This order effectively prohibited the entry of the principal OSS expert on Albania (until he later joined the Consular staff).

The City Team continued its intelligence coverage, besides performing services for various visiting American representatives (State, Military Liaison, etc.). Until State Department representation arrived in mid-1945, OSS provided the only independent American evaluations of developments, and formed the only American link with Albania. Pressure from the Albanian Government necessitated the Team's departure in September.

E. BELGRADE

In September 1944, command of the fifteen OSS teams in the field was taken over from Brigadier Fitzroy MacLean (British SOE) by the Independent American Military Mission to Marshal Tito (IAMM).*

The joint U. S. Chiefs of Staff authorized IAMM to:

(1) Establish military liaison with the Partisans;

(2) report to AFHQ on military developments;

(3) handle all U. S. supplies to the Partisans; and

(4) command U. S. personnel in Yugoslavia.

An IAMM base at Partisan Headquarters had been established in August on Vis Island. Four of its members arrived at Valjevo on 9 October and, from there, advanced with the Partisan I Corps. They entered Belgrade on 20 October, with the last German units still surrendering in that city. The group sent in reports on economic conditions, war damage, military developments, a breakdown of the Partisan I Corps, and analyses of Partisan and Russian battle techniques.

The Mission established itself in Belgrade and became a city team. By January, this consisted of thirteen men, including four SI, three R&A and two X-2 representatives. The fifteen teams accompanying the Partisan Corps in the field were cut to eight by May. Liaison with the Partisans produced

* For background, see "Yugoslavia", above.

little on German battle order, Partisan cooperation having been notably poor since mid-1944. Political coverage was somewhat better. OSS maintained contacts both in the various government ministries and with the more or less silent opposition groups. Since the State Department did not arrive for several months, these OSS reports formed the only U. S. coverage of Yugoslav political developments.

An X-2 hope for the exchange of information with Yugoslav counter-espionage services came to nothing.

Economic and medical reports were also prepared. Members of various U. S. agencies (Typhus Commission, Red Cross, ATC, State Department, MAAF) were at one time or another attached to the mission. Until the arrival of an OWI representative, OSS itself distributed OWI publications. While the principal commitment for supplies to the Partisan army was British, OSS arranged for a contribution of some ten tons of drugs and medical equipment, and of eighty jeeps. About one hundred additional U. S. airmen, downed in Yugoslavia, were evacuated.

On 31 March 1945, the U. S. Ambassador arrived, and the Embassy took over many of the functions which the mission had been carrying out in the interim. Since the Yugoslavs refused clearance for a coexistent OSS unit, it was withdrawn in July. All field teams followed suit, excepting one in Trieste, which was transferred to SI/Italy jurisdiction.

F. LIBERATED FRANCE

Paris was cleared of enemy forces on 27 August 1944, and, in early September, an advance OSS base was established there to: (1) Direct intelligence activities against Germany; and (2) carry out various liquidation and post-liberation activities in France. In early September, due to the shortage of office space, SHAEF established a ceiling of 350 personnel for OSS/Paris, with the result that London was redesignated the main OSS base for operations against Germany. The field detachments were under Paris direction, but the long-range agent program for Germany and Austria was handled by London.*

Exchange of intelligence on Germany was continued with French DGER. DGER also entered into a joint project with SI to use ten two-man teams to be infiltrated behind German lines. Personnel was provided by DGER, equipping and processing handled by SI and expenses and intelligence shared equally by both agencies. The teams were dispatched to areas in front of French First Army and successfully wired back much battle order and other tactical intelligence. Additional recruits were obtained for SI/-London from the Communist Free Germany Committee. These agents were to be used for the infiltration of Germany and released immediately thereafter.

During the fall of 1944, important technical information was procured for Eighth Air Force through interrogations of a high Focke-Wulf engineer in Paris. Intelligence on the German Foreign Office was procured from interrogations of Blankenhorn of the Foreign Office's Protocol Division. Early in 1945, a representative of the Provisional Austrian National Committee (P. Oe. N.) was interviewed, and accurate information

was uncovered on the status of Austrian underground resistance.

On France itself, R&A economic specialists made studies on such subjects as "Present French Port Capacities" and "Damage to French Rail and Motor Transport". At the same time, political analysts produced a "Weekly French Intelligence Report" and drafted studies on such topics as "Communist Strength and Policy in France" and "Catholic Programs in France". They kept careful check on CALPO, the French Communist Free Germany Movement.

The rapid dissemination of secret intelligence to various continental customers was carried on during the fall by the SIRA Reports Board and later, after SIRA's dissolution,* by an informal joint SI/R&A Reports Board. Under this arrangement, OSS/-Paris developed into the central channel of OSS intelligence, not only for the armies in the field, but for all other OSS installations in ETO as well. The SIRA staff began operations at the end of September, with R&A political and economic specialists processing appropriate SI intelligence. The arrangement assured professional care in the evaluation of SI economic and political information.

SI/France handled the de-processing of London and Algiers agents in France, debriefing them, arranging for American medical care and paying insurance for agents killed in action. It was found difficult to obtain any quantity of American decorations. This was regretted, not only because the agents had performed missions of unusual danger in the service of the United States, but also inasmuch as it might in the future have proven worthwhile

---

* See those sections in Part VII, above.

* See section on Reports Board in "London Base", above.

to have maintained the support of those agents.

Elsewhere in France, SI analyzed types of currency in Alsace-Lorraine for SHAEF/-Civil Affairs. Franco-Italian tension in the Val d'Aosta was covered by the SI base at Nice for the Embassy. Two other of the more important OSS activities in France were those of the AQUITAINE mission and of the T-Forces.

AQUITAINE

The Germans, retreating from France, had left several pockets of German troops to prevent use by the Allies of ports on the west coast. Pockets at La Rochelle, Royan and Pointe de Grave, totalling 30,000, 15,000 and 1,500 men respectively, shut off the ports at Bordeaux and La Rochelle and the naval base at La Pallice. A French attack was planned for late December. The AQUITAINE mission in Toulouse, which had been established in October 1944 to liquidate the OSS/Spain chains into France, was requested by the French, through 6th Army Group, to assist in infiltrating the pockets.

In November, an infantry regiment arrived from General Le Clerc's division, and armored forces were to follow. The Ardennes counter-offensive, however, forced the withdrawal of the regiment, and the attack was temporarily postponed.

AQUITAINE continued its penetration of the area and was able to warn FFI forces, guarding the pockets, of several German foraging attacks. Within two weeks after the arrival of two operations personnel from OSS/Seventh Army, the first agent had been recruited, briefed, trained in short-range voice radio, and infiltrated into the Ile d'Oleron, and four additional agents were being trained. A total of eight local recruits, equipped with radio telephones (SCR-300 or SSTR-511), were infiltrated into Royan, Pointe de Grave, La Rochelle, Ile de Re and Ile d'Oleron. Due to the length of the sector to be covered, three

listening posts close to the German lines were established to receive agent messages. These were manned by former Spanish-French chain radio operators with SSTR-1's for contact with AQUITAINE headquarters near Cognac.

The methods of operation varied. For the Ile d'Oleron, a rubber boat operation was carried out from a 3-knot fishing barge which served as the mother craft. For the Ile de Re, it was impracticable to use the fishing barge, due to the distance involved and German control of the waters. Therefore, the agent was disguised as a fisherman and sent out on a fishing boat from a liberated village near the German lines north of La Rochelle. At the fishing grounds a rendezvous was arranged with a craft from the Ile de Re and the agent transferred. Arriving in Ile de Re shortly after dusk, he hid in the boat until darkness, whereupon he slipped ashore and proceeded to his safe house. The SCR-300 was concealed in the bottom of an oyster crate and subsequently delivered to him by friendly fishermen. The rendezvous of fishing boats also served as message center for transmission of long written messages and overlays.

Through-the-lines operations were run to Royan and the northern sector of La Rochelle, as well as Pointe de Grave. For one operation into the southern sector of La Rochelle, a point was found, on the coast near Fouras, which was only a few kilometers from a pinpoint on the German-held coast, and the infiltration was carried out at night by rowboat.

Practically all German movements were known. One agent penetrated Gestapo Hq. at La Rochelle.* The accurate information received by AQUITAINE, as compared with French reports, showed the effect of careful and experienced briefing and training. For example, on one occasion the French re-

---

* An Italian captain was awarded the Iron Cross by his German C. O. on the same day that he delivered to OSS a series of overlays of the enemy minefields around La Rochelle.

ceived a message, evaluated by them "possible" which merely said "Attaque prevue demain matin". The OSS agent sent a message at 5 p. m. which stated that an attack would be forthcoming the next morning at 6 a. m. in strength of about 3,000 in a specific sector, supported by artillery positions (with coordinates), and stating that he would follow up behind the attack with his radio, should OSS wish to station a receiving post on the French side of the lines to receive up-to-the-minute accounts.

In April, a French attack on Royan and Ile d'Oleron was carried out. AQUITAINE agents sent sixty to one hundred W/T messages daily and acted as artillery spotters behind the lines. The strongholds surrendered a few days after VE-Day.

Besides covering military developments in its area, the AQUITAINE mission reported on Spanish supply of the German pockets, on anti-Franco activities along the Spanish border and on the flight of Germans and German assets over the Pyrenees. The U. S. political advisor at SHAEF had requested information on these border conditions.

T-FORCES

During the capture of Cherbourg by Allied forces, OSS naval officers entered with advance army units to exploit documents, individuals and military equipment useful for later operations on the Continent. Acting on orders from the officer in charge of Naval Intelligence, ComNavEu, they joined a forward unit of the 39th Regiment on 17 June.

During the advance on Cherbourg, the officers found documents, including maps of fortifications, in overrun positions. Entering the city, they established the first U. S. Navy Headquarters there and canvassed all German naval establishments, including the Admiral's Hq. and the navy yard and arsenal. They examined the shore batteries and rocket sites from Cap de la Hague to Barfleur, finding a large quantity of secret papers and equipment, which were forwarded to the appropriate organizations for study. From harbor pilots, the OSS officers obtained urgently needed information on the location of minefields. On 12 July, they returned to London to report the first OSS quasi-T-Force mission completed.

Target-Forces were developed under G-2, SHAEF for the expeditious exploitation of enemy material and documents as soon as they were overrun. OSS first participated in the Rennes T-Force, but had no large representation until 12th Army Group T-Force, including both R&A and X-2 personnel, went into operation in Paris. There, R&A uncovered unexpectedly valuable material on the Far East, including numerous maps and plans of industrial installations in Japanese-occupied areas. Of more immediate interest was a set of French patents on parts for V-1 and V-2. X-2 shared with the documents sections of SHAEF and Communications Zone the inspection of former German Hqs. in and around the city, on leads supplied by T-Force and by local informants. This material, after processing, was forwarded to SCI units, to Comm. Z, the French Direction de la Securite Militaire and to X-2/London.

In March 1945, R&A turned out, for the T-Forces, a special study of the movement and secreting of German ministry archives. Representatives of R&A and X-2 moved forward with the T-Forces of the 12th and 21st Army Groups, microfilming and copying intelligence of interest for operations in Europe and the Far East in such towns as Brussels, Kiel, Berlin and Munich, in factories in the Ruhr and in areas eventually to be occupied by Russian forces.

G. BELGIUM AND HOLLAND

In accordance with a verbal understanding concluded by OSS and SIS in 1942, no SI activities were undertaken into Holland and Belgium before the entry of Allied troops. However, SI missions were planned before D-Day to enter Belgium and Holland immediately after liberation. They were to develop close working relationships with the Belgian and Dutch intelligence services for joint long- and short-range agent operations against the German forces. Both services approved OSS entry

Each mission went into the field early in September, attached to G-2, 21st Army Group, and reached destination later in the month— mission ESPINETTE (with five Americans and three members of the Belgian Surete) at Brussels, and mission MELANIE (with six Americans, three Dutch and one British officer) at Eindhoven.

ESPINETTE and MELANIE obtained, from the local intelligence services and resistance groups, recruits for the SI/London program to penetrate Germany, supplying cover stories, safe addresses and pinpoints. Final documentation, parachute training and actual dispatch of these agents was accomplished by London.* ESPINETTE furthermore supplied four W/T operators to Ninth Army Detachment and recruited other agents as requested. During the Battle of the Bulge, a stay-behind network of thirty "sleepers" was organized jointly with the British, but never used.**

Working with the Belgian and Dutch services, the two missions dispatched several short-range teams to work with resistance groups behind the lines for tactical intelligence.*** A close personal relationship with Prince Bernhardt, leader of the Dutch underground, facilitated operations and the exchange of reports. Considerable information came from the Dutch Intelligence Service's chains, previously established behind enemy lines, in exchange for cigarettes, candy, etc., and maritime equipment for river-crossings. Battle order material was generally wired to OSS/Paris, where it was edited and disseminated to the armies and army groups. Between September and April, a total of 3,200 pouch reports and 750 cables were dispatched to SHAEF in faster time than by the British service. Many of the items were included in the regular SHAEF and Army Group intelligence summaries; some were given the highest ratings on both importance and reliability. MELANIE, for example, was the sole source of information on the projected German invasion over the Maas, which was to complement Rundstedt's Ardennes offensive. Allied units were shifted on the basis of the MELANIE reports, and the German plan was called off. SHAEF estimated that MELANIE had provided the best coverage of all sections on the West Front.

The MELANIE performance was particularly significant in the general context of British opposition. The area of operations was a British-controlled area under 21st Army Group. For this reason, British opposition to independent American intelligence could be, and was, overt. The British attached an officer to the mission when it went into the field. At Eindhoven, the mission experienced initial and continuing difficulty in the establishment of any workable liaison with Dutch intelligence, because the chief was collaborating closely with the British. However, through the good offices of the Dutch officers attached to the mission, excellent relations were set up with Dutch resistance in the field. When it became

---

* See "Direct Penetration from London", above.
** See "West Front", above.
*** Ibid.

clear that OSS had every intention of carrying out its task in full, the British sent in high-ranking officials to dislodge it, on the grounds that it was unattached and operating in a British area. It was only by direct appeal to SHAEF, by this time well-pleased with the MELANIE performance, that the mission was permitted to stay.

British opposition appeared in the matter of penetration of Germany too. The obvious move was to use Dutch resistance, already behind the German lines, for the penetration of Germany proper. The chief of Dutch intelligence, at British instigation, declared this to be physically impossible; at the same time he pointed out that MELANIE's exclusive concern was Holland. It developed later that the British, with this man's help, had themselves made use of a Dutch resistance chain operating out of the Hamburg area. In any case, the mission never achieved penetration of Germany proper.

Belgium, on the other hand, was soon liberated, and ESPINETTE was little hampered in establishing excellent local contacts, for intelligence on Germany, with the Ministere de la Defense Nationale, the Belgian Surete de l'Etat and the various organizations of the Armee Secrete. In addition, it set up two independent intelligence sources: certain private individuals such as labor leaders, businessmen, editors and the like who could be expected to have extensive and reputable contacts; and a group of Belgian patriots who worked as a unit, calling themselves the MLF from the initials of the three key personalities involved.*

MLF was based at Liege, where it provided substantial aid to ESPINETTE in the accumulation of intelligence on Germany. This intelligence included information on safe houses, possible drop points and strategic operating areas for SI agents. MLF

---

* M stood for Marie, the prime mover of the unit. Said to be a prostitute, Marie refused the $10,000 offered her at the close of the operation, stating that she had worked as a patriot.

obtained the bulk of its data by interviewing workers, returning from Germany, on the areas in which they had been located.

In November 1944, the two SI missions had been reorganized to include other branches and to become regular OSS missions responsible directly to OSS/Paris. The original directive, authorizing only SI activities against the enemy forces, was broadened. R&A and SI worked together to cover political and economic developments in the two liberated countries. MO directed "black" propaganda toward the demoralized German soldiers. After VE-Day, MELANIE moved from Eindhoven to a suburb of The Hague, to liquidate its commitments, to help former agents to find employment, and to concentrate more effectively on political and economic reporting during the post-hostilities period.

One X-2 officer in Brussels worked with the British SCI unit there, which was chiefly concerned with the penetration of the remaining elements of the German intelligence services. A profitable independent liaison with the Belgian and Dutch services grew through the months of 1945. The X-2 officer worked also with FBI representatives on cases of captured agents with American backgrounds. With the assistance of X-2/-Paris, ten sabotage dumps were uncovered, and the chief of a sabotage organization working in northern France and Belgium was apprehended. X-2 files contained, by the end of September 1945, identifications of nearly four thousand enemy intelligence officials and agents.

SI and X-2 worked with the State Department in "Safe Haven" investigations, and SI/Belgium was responsible, in 1945, for uncovering one of the largest of the German fund transfer systems, the Fabelta combine. Sufficient proof was accumulated so that the case could be taken to the local courts, with resulting confiscation of assets and imprisonment of the more important persons involved.

H. OSLO AND COPENHAGEN

OSS City Teams for these two capitals were preceded by SO personnel, members of Special Force Detachments. These tripartite units were dispatched by SFHQ/-London, to represent SHAEF, as military liaison with resistance groups, and to aid generally in the restoration of order. Detachments for both countries arrived within 24 hours of VE-Day, set up their offices and established radio contact with the London base. Civil governments, however, took power without delay in both Norway and Denmark, British and American diplomatic representatives arrived, and the military liaison job was soon over. On 8 July the detachments were withdrawn.

Meanwhile the OSS City Teams had arrived in Copenhagen and Oslo on 11 and 12 May respectively. Each consisted of fifteen personnel, including representatives of SI,

X-2 and R&A. Political and economic developments were covered. War Crimes and "Safe Haven" studies were prepared, as were reports on Russian troops in northern Norway and on the Island of Bornholm. X-2's most time-consuming duty was the vetting of visa applicants for the State Department. The SCI teams, dispatched to Denmark and Norway by
were of considerable assistance in this work.

Upon the removal of SHAEF representation from both countries in July, the City Teams turned to the State Department for authorization. Although the Ambassador to Norway and the Minister to Denmark each cabled requests that the full OSS teams be included under diplomatic cover, the Department would approve X-2 representatives only. By October, all other personnel had been withdrawn.

I. ITALY

As organized enemy opposition decreased, German unit commanders sought to contact Allied authorities, but were reluctant to surrender to the partisans. Team MARGOT in Venice, after neutralizing the German garrison there, maintained telephone contact between the CLN in Venice and other CLN headquarters in the principal cities of northeast Italy. Numerous German and Italian Fascist units surrendered to Allied officers with resistance groups, or were so immobilized that resistance, even to the first wave of oncoming Allied troops, was no longer possible. One team, operating in the Udine area, arranged for the surrender to the British Eighth Army of 15,000 Yugoslav Chetniks who were still holding out in the Gorizia area.

On 26 April an OSS officer, dispatched from Switzerland, contacted Italian Fascist headquarters at Cernobbio and secured the surrender of the Fascist commander, Marshal Graziani, and several of his staff officers. In close collaboration with the CLN, he arranged for the neutralization of enemy troops in the area and then headed for CLN headquarters in Milan, escorting Graziani and the other prisoners. He entered Milan on the same day and arranged for a truce between the German commander of SS and police troops in Liguria, Lombardy and Piedmont and partisan headquarters. The two agreed to avoid demolitions and fighting within Milan until the arrival of Allied troops. Two days later, the first units of Allied IV Corps entered the city and took over Marshal Graziani, his staff officers and the German commander.*

* On the 2 May surrender of Axis forces in North Italy, handled through OSS/Bern, see "Secret Surrender Negotiations", above.

Throughout the winter, extensive preparations had been made by OSS for entry into North Italy immediately upon its liberation, to examine at first hand the effect of OSS and resistance activities throughout the country, to de-brief OSS agents, to report on conditions and developments incident to the liberation, to search for documentation and intelligence on Japan, and to uncover enemy resistance or stay-behind agents.

By March, teams were ready for Bologna, Genoa, Turin, Milan, Venice and Trieste. The first team entered Bologna on 21 April. On 26 April, the Venice team was in Verona and Padua, pending the clearing of Venice. It was accompanied by the Trieste team, which eventually moved to Udine, as it was not granted permission by the British to enter Trieste after the German surrender. The other teams had reached their destinations by the end of April. They worked rapidly, in close cooperation with Army G-2 personnel in units designated as S-Forces, and finally concentrated in Milan, where an advance OSS intelligence headquarters was established. With the German surrender, the teams expanded their intelligence objectives to include gathering of documentation on war crimes.

X-2 dispatched units to Bologna, Spezia, Verona and Genoa. Interrogations at all stations produced extensive data on enemy personnel, and long-range or stay-behind plans and organizations. In collaboration with the Monuments, Fine Arts and Archives Sub-Section of the Allied Control Commission, X-2 assisted in tracing individuals responsible for the looting of precious art objects.

When the final Allied drive was launched across the Apennines in April 1945, the elaborate registry and communications organization of SCI/Z Rome and of the Florence offices became the centers to which X-2 staffs with the City Teams reported. In May, X-2 field teams were located in Bologna, Genoa, Verona, Milan and Venice, and at 15th Army Group and IV Corps headquarters. In the following month, stations at Turin and San Remo were added.

Along with the counter-intelligence material gained, X-2 was able, from interrogations, to supply valuable information for later identification of Germans in Germany. Up to the end of the war, in collaboration with Allied services, X-2 work resulted in:

```
(1) Enemy agents identified...  3,575
(2) Apprehended ..............    675
    (a) Executed .........  30
    (b) Confined .........  635
    (c) Released .........   10
```

In February, a Coordinator of Far East Intelligence was appointed to control collection of information, principally on Japan, from sources in Italy. SI personnel on city team units were briefed on targets where data on Japan might be available. R&A prepared a list of specialized targets in northern Italian cities, in conjunction with ONI in Rome and the Intelligence Objectives Sub-Section of G-2, AFHQ, and material at S-Forces document collection centers was screened. A supplementary roster of Italians with possible recent or specialized knowledge of Japan was prepared, as well as a list of German prisoners of war who had been in activities relevant to the Japanese war effort.

The R&A economic staff completed and submitted to G-5 the final draft of a detailed study on "A Program of Imports for the Economic Rehabilitation of Italy", and made other reports and files available to the agricultural staff of the American Embassy. In addition, briefing material was prepared for the OSS North Italian city teams. R&A men were assigned to the city teams to interview partisan leaders, public officials and members of the CLNAI, principally in Bologna and Milan, and to report on economic and political conditions in major North Italian centers upon their liberation, as well as on the transition of resistance and political groups from the partisan and guerrilla stage to a peacetime political basis.

Research and Development Branch personnel made a 3,000 mile trip through North Italy, acquiring technical intelligence and data from Italian scientists, engineers and industrialists and searching for details on new Italian and German inventions, including jet-propelled engines and devices to stop airplane engines at long range.

OSS headquarters at Caserta completed preliminary plans for the reduction in force of OSS/MedTO immediately upon the cessation of hostilities. As early as February and March, specialized personnel, surplus to the immediate needs of headquarters, had been alerted for transfer to OSS in the Far East to relieve the critical personnel shortage in SEAC and China. Others were designated for return to the United States or for re-deployment within the Theater to other military units.

The de-briefing of agents and teams in the field was accomplished by de-briefing centers in Florence, Siena, Bologna, Milan and Cecina. At each center, representatives of the operating branch concerned, and of X-2, Security, Special Funds and Communications were present to participate in interrogation of the agent. In the month of May some seventy teams consisting of over 300 agents, both American and Italian, were de-briefed.

All agents had been instructed to report to the nearest city team immediately upon cessation of hostilities. The last clandestine radio went off the air on 12 May, the team having been instructed to move northward with the Germans in case of a last stand in the "Redoubt". Each agent, after interrogation, was given a certificate of service and approximately $100 for each month behind enemy lines.*

A regimental claims staff expanded its functions as rapidly as possible to liquidate outstanding claims by Italians against OSS. OSS and SOE jointly filed a claim on 1 May against the Bonomi Government for reimbursement of money advanced to the CLNAI in Milan, in accord with the SACMED-CLNAI agreement. The OSS share was 112,600,000 lira, the money received to be used to settle all claims against OSS in northern Italy.

SI was ordered to liquidate completely by 31 July. Originally the Branch had planned to establish a network of twenty intelligence centers in major Italian cities to serve as the basis of a post-war intelligence system. The lack of a directive on post-war work and the difficulties encountered by the SI staff during the campaign caused these plans to be rejected.

X-2 and R&A became the two predominant OSS post-hostilities activities in Italy. X-2 personnel functioned in Milan, Genoa, San Remo and Turin, interrogating leading figures of various branches of the German Intelligence Services in Italy and forming a detailed picture of the enemy organizations. In addition, the Branch conducted vetting operations for the State Department and other American agencies upon request.

* De-briefing officers reported that "many of the agents would have been completely content with the certificate alone." MedTO Monthly Report Summary, May 1945, History Files.

R&A completed reports on political and social conditions in the North Italian cities and prepared the only over-all Allied study of the situation in Trieste during the early days of Yugoslav occupation. Targets for the Far East, Latin American relations with Fascist Italy and late technical information on Japanese installations or materiel were also obtained. Other R&A officers continued political and economic reporting, on conditions and developments throughout Italy, for R&A/Washington and State Department. The Interdepartmental Committee (IDC) secured over 5,000 published or periodic items, hitherto unavailable in America, and dispatched them to Washington.

Until 30 September, OSS in the Mediterranean Theater continued programs of counter-intelligence, medical intelligence, the Intelligence Photographic Documentation Project,* and an R&A research program. OSS continued to report to the Commanding General of AFHQ and maintained a liaison officer at Caserta. In addition to the headquarters at Rome, R&A had an intelligence office in Milan, and X-2 personnel were active at various of the temporary stations in Italy. X-2 and R&A reports, and reports bearing on Italy from other OSS missions, continued to be disseminated to, among other customers, G-2, G-5, and the American Political Adviser of AFHQ, to the Ambassador, the Counter-Intelligence Corps and the Joint Intelligence Collection Agency, MedTO.

* See Washington section on Field Photographic.

J. CENTRAL EUROPE

On VE-Day OSS had intelligence bases covering Europe from Spain, Portugal, Cairo, Istanbul, various locations in Africa, Caserta, Rome and throughout North Italy, Stockholm, London, Paris, Brussels, Eindhoven, Bern, and the capitals of the Balkans (excepting Sofia *). New ones were about to move into Oslo and Copenhagen. On the German border, advance units were already established in Maastricht and Luxembourg.

In December 1944, after the Russian military progress in the Balkans, it had become apparent that the status of the city teams, most of which had been established by virtue of arrival prior to Russian occupation, must be formalized. Accordingly, OSS had sought and received a JCS directive to attach units to the U. S. delegations of the Allied Control Commissions in the countries of Southeast Europe. At Russian insistence, the Sofia team had already been withdrawn. As the end of the war approached and relations with the Russians grew more delicate and more important, General Marshall cabled General McNarney, in April, that no further efforts should be made to introduce U. S. personnel into Russian-controlled territory, except where essential to the U. S. war effort. On 1 May, the Budapest City Unit, which had been built up during early 1945 to a group of fifty intelligence and counter-intelligence experts, was formally refused permission by the Russians to enter that city. The Unit was disbanded. A Prague Unit of some fifteen personnel arrived in Prague on 7 May (two days before the Russians), and covered the formation of the Czechoslovak National Council. However, when the Russians arrived, the Unit not being excepted from Third Army orders that all U. S. military personnel be

---

* See "Sofia", above.

withdrawn, moved to Pilsen in the American-occupied zone.

No other OSS bases were active in Russian-occupied Europe, other than those already established in Bucharest, Tirana, and Belgrade. Between June and September 1945, these too were officially closed.

Large missions, which had been prepared during the months prior to VE-Day, moved in from ETO and MedTO to Germany and Austria, respectively. In each country, the principal OSS base was located in the U. S.-occupied zone (at Biebrich and Salzburg), while the chiefs of mission worked in the sub-bases at Berlin and Vienna.

Effective 12 July, a reorganization of OSS/ETO made the missions in England, France, and Germany independent of each other, reporting to OSS/Washington. Sub-missions in Norway and Denmark remained under London control; those in the Low Countries were directed by OSS/Paris; and that in Pilsen, Czechoslovakia was responsible to OSS/Germany. Communications and X-2 continued to be centralized under OSS/London. By 1 August, members of all operations branches had been withdrawn or transferred. X-2, R&A, and SI remained, with the various services.

In Germany, OSS was responsible to the U. S. Group of the Control Council; in Austria, to the U. S. Forces in Austria. Sub-sections were established in Bremen, Kassel, Heidelberg, Nuernberg, Hamburg, and Munich in Germany, and Salzburg, Innsbruck (later moved to Zell-am-See at French insistence), Klagenfurt (discontinued in June) and Linz in Austria.

From these various bases, SI developed chains of agents covering German and foreign activities in the various occupation zones of Germany and Austria. In this activity they were supplemented by chains into the British, French, and U. S. zones developed by the OSS mission in Maastricht, Holland.

In Czechoslovakia, SI had helped, just before VE-Day, to organize the National Council at Karlovy Vary, the first free parliamentary meeting in that country since the war. Continued contact with this group, and subsequently with the Government, provided good coverage of economic and political developments there.

An OSS team had received permission to enter Russian-occupied Vienna only in July, but had already built up excellent coverage of Austria and, to a degree, of Yugoslavia, particularly Yugoslav border developments. The unit provided ninety percent of G-2, USFA's dissemination of positive intelligence.

R&A in London, Washington, and Paris had been of particular assistance to G-5 (G-1, CAS, and CAD) in preparing handbooks, guides, and manuals for occupation forces and Civil Government units. The Branch also aided the U. S. Delegation to the Allied Reparations Conference in Moscow, and later the Big Three Conference at Potsdam, where reparations was one of the most important subjects on the agenda. For months prior to the actual departure of the Delegation, R&A engaged in preparing voluminous basic studies on Germany's capacity to pay, the amount of movable assets, probable effects of extensive reparations on European economy, comparative indices of European standards of living, the use of German labor as reparations, Soviet reparations intentions and numerous other subjects basic to the formulation of U. S. policy. The resources of R&A in Washington, London, Paris, and Germany were mobilized to make promptly available basic material or comprehensive spot studies needed in the course of the negotiations. Three R&A representatives were assigned to the U. S. Reparations Commissioner and took part in the negotiations at Moscow and Potsdam, two of them serving as the principal economists and one as the cartographer of the U. S. Delegation.

Similarly, X-2 was uniquely placed to assist the State Department in its "Safe Haven" project to trace the movement of German funds and physical wealth to hideouts in neutral European countries and to other continents. X-2 agents worked closely with State Department groups covering the various principal channels of flight, notably Bern, Madrid, Lisbon, Stockholm, and Istanbul. The X-2 Art Unit, in London, contributed a list of art objects bought and stolen in Europe by the Nazi leaders, and biographical data on their purchasing agents. X-2 also finished its job of identifying and interrogating members of German intelligence services,* vetted U. S. employees, visa applicants and local German and Austrian officials and protected U. S. agencies from penetration by foreign services.

Besides these general activities, OSS accomplished, both prior to and after VE-Day, various short-term services for the occupation forces.

SPECIAL ALLIED AIRBORNE RECONNAISSANCE FORCE

SAARF was activated by SHAEF on 29 March 1945 to send teams to various POW camps in enemy territory. The teams were to carry radios and a letter from General Eisenhower, were not to use arms, and were to approach directly the POW camp commanders in order to prevent forced marches, massacres, and other mistreatment of Allied troops. OSS, SOE, and DGER contributed personnel and the information which was used in preparing at SHAEF Forward a POW War Room, which listed the various camps in Germany and their estimated POW complements. If it proved easily

---

* See below.

available, the teams were also to gather intelligence.

Seventeen OSS personnel helped make up the sixty-odd SAARF teams. On 25 April, six of the latter (including four OSS agents, forming two teams) parachuted in uniform to the Altengrabow area. Here, one OSS team contacted POW laborers in the fields and picked up local military, industrial, and prison intelligence. The men worked jointly with a British major (using his W/T set, since their own had been broken in landing) and with a Russian captain, who had been operating in the area for some time. Together with their allies, they approached the Stalag commandant, established contact with the French base by W/T from inside the camp, persuaded the commandant to disobey orders to march the prisoners eastward, and eventually, on 3 May, were overrun by advancing U. S. forces.

No further teams were parachuted, but some thirty each were attached to 6th and 12th Army Groups to move forward with advance units. These ground teams were usually the first U. S. forces to arrive in POW camps, where they arranged for the organization of command and reported conditions to the Allied base. They were also instrumental in conducting many POW's out of areas subsequently controlled by the Russians.

UNCOVERING NAZI ORGANIZATIONS

All branches joined X-2 in the task of tracking down remnant Nazi organizations, including personnel and funds. It had been originally feared by the Allies (and planned by the Nazis) that underground groups would operate in Germany to hamper Allied occupation. SI had initiated the TWILIGHT plan to place agents trained in England to live in various German cities, where they would become assimilated with the population and be able to keep track of developing underground groups. Two SO projects, CROSS and AIRDALE, called for the employment of Communist CALPO * and of over one hundred previously trained Basque personnel as counter-sabotage operational units. The underground failed to materialize, and the SO and SI projects were therefore discontinued.

Special Counter-Intelligence (SCI) stations were located at Kassel, Erlangen, Stuttgart, Heidelberg, Munich, Bremen, and Berlin with the headquarters in Wiesbaden. With the exception of Berlin, these units, as in earlier operations in France, were attached to the American armies in each locality. The Berlin station was under the jurisdiction of the Allied Control Commission. In addition, SCI liaisons were maintained with the British at 21st Army Group and with the French through the Direction des Bureaux de Documentation, Allemagne, located at Bad Wildbad.

From the end of hostilities in Europe until 1 October 1945, activities of the X-2 field units were directed toward establishment of an underground network of German agents to penetrate any resistance movements which might arise, and, secondly, toward continued assistance to the Army Counter-Intelligence staffs in their respective areas.

Among the priority target individuals wanted for interrogation and/or detention was an SS Sturmbannfuehrer in Amt VI E, the Balkans section of the Reichssicherheitshauptamt. Third Army SCI located him in Alt Aussee, Austria, where he was in hiding with a number of SS officers. Subsequent to his apprehension he was, as were all leading German intelligence figures, evaluated and examined with a view to his use as a double-agent. Following the preliminary interrogation, a more thorough investigation was conducted in Germany and Austria, and the story told by the officer was confirmed.

About one year before the end of the war, he, along with several of his SS colleagues, had come to the conclusion that Germany

---

* Free Germany Committee in France.

had lost the war, and he foresaw what he felt was inevitable conflict between the western powers and Russia. Accordingly, he utilized his position in Amt VI to obtain technical radio equipment and to establish a network of agents in Rumania, Bulgaria, Hungary, and other countries in the Russian sphere. Sporadic contact was maintained with the agents of this network in the last year of the war, and, although the technical equipment was never used, a well-equipped base was found in a hunting lodge in the Austrian Alps about 150 kilometers from Salzburg. Complete technical data, including code sheets, transmission information and wave-lengths, were located in widely dispersed areas. When this network was offered to SCI for penetration of an alien intelligence service, it was necessary to investigate the case fully, since the possibility of its being used by other than the Americans could not be ignored. There was also the purpose of gaining any intelligence material inherent in the chain itself.

It was decided that SCI should take a small group of the SS officers to the mountain hide-out and see if actual W/T contact could be made with the alleged network. No positive intelligence was requested. The contacts were made merely to establish the existence of the chain, and the entire project was then abandoned as too insecure.

An equally interesting X-2 activity was the investigation of RSHA financial transactions. Among the more important divisions of the RSHA was Amt II which handled finance, administration, and legal work for the intelligence organization. In order to realize the importance of this group and to evaluate its potentialities, it must be remembered that Nazi Party functionaries in general, and intelligence officers in particular, were more than often inclined to use their positions for private financial gain. For example, huge counterfeiting projects were carried on, and the currencies of neutral and enemy countries were printed under governmental auspices through chan-

nels which defied detection even by banking officials. With such currency, numerous art treasures, gold, and other valuables were available to the Germans. In order to increase the enthusiasm on the part of persons engaged in converting this counterfeit currency to gold coin, the agents were allowed to retain about fifteen percent of the monies actually received for conversion. According to the head of Amt II, these operations ran well into millions of dollars, but his knowledge of the details of his office was too vague for exploitation.

Third Army SCI located a major who had been with this division, and, although his position was less impressive, his operational knowledge of Amt II was detailed and nearly complete. SCI took the man on several expeditions to Italy and Austria, and, as a result of these preliminary trips, over $500,000 in gold, as well as jewels, were recovered and turned over to the appropriate military authorities. At the same time SCI gave full details to the authorities in the American Zone setting forth the possibilities for further operations to locate and recover German intelligence currencies.

In Austria, X-2 handled nine-tenths of the interrogations of German intelligence personnel. SCI/Austria had been briefed to locate agents and, in particular, certain high-ranking German intelligence officials believed to have fled into the "Redoubt", south of Munich. As early as June 1945, SCI/A had interrogated several key figures, including the Befehlshaber der Sipo und Sicherheitsdienst, Salzburg, the Amt VI E chief for Italy, and Sandberger, a high-echelon member of the RSHA. Several caches of money and ammunition were also discovered. Working agreements with the Austrian and Swiss (through X-2/Bern) Criminal Police chiefs facilitated the location and handling of Nazi escapees. A postwar network of old-line Party members and Hitler-Jugend, forming a so-called "Werewolf" organization, was uncovered in southern Germany and Austria.

WAR CRIMES

OSS contributed its extensive resources to servicing the American prosecutors at the Nuernberg War Crimes Trials. General Donovan was appointed Associate Chief of Prosecution, and other OSS personnel assumed positions on Justice Jackson's staff. The Office of the General Counsel (OSS) was enlarged, its chief being appointed an assistant to Jackson, and in April 1945, the Office of the Theater Counsel (OSS) was formed in the European Theater, principally to contribute to the work. Aside from the extensive personality files which X-2, SI and R&A had developed during the combat period, all three branches continued to uncover material during the occupation period. The London Art Unit (X-2) investigated the looting of objects of art by the Nazi leaders, and assembled a list of agents who handled the expropriations. In MedTO, a War Investigation Section was organized in May, and all the SI personnel remaining in Italy joined in the task. A specially formed R&A Documentary Research Unit in London procured intelligence from British agency files and furnished experts to prepare memoranda for the prosecuting staff. Much background work was also done by R&A/Washington. The Field Photographic Branch collected photographic evidence of Nazi horrors, filmed important interrogations, uncovered incriminating German film and prepared a movie (shown at the trials) setting forth the basic indictments against the major criminals.

During the period immediately following VE-Day, OSS personnel had been re-deployed in large numbers to the Far East. Projects initiated to cover Germany over a longer period, should resistance continue (particularly in the mountain fortresses of West Austria and Norway), were closed. Agents were paid and de-briefed.

In Germany itself, between VE-Day and the termination of OSS on 30 September 1945, besides investigating developments in the U. S.-occupied zone, OSS gathered intelligence on the zones occupied by the British, French, and Russian Allies. R&A, for instance, prepared studies on Russian occupation policies, Communist activities in Germany, and related matters. SI and X-2 turned, with some indications of success, toward new secret intelligence and counterespionage objectives.

Section II

FAR EAST

A. INTRODUCTION

The defeat of Japan was assigned secondary priority in the strategy of the Combined Chiefs of Staff. The main Allied war effort was directed against Germany, and the bulk of Allied men and materiel was committed to winning the war in Europe. This factor had its effect on all agencies and units active in Far Eastern theaters. In most cases, it naturally resulted in reducing the potential of regular military organizations. This reduction served to raise to unprecedented proportions the reliance placed in certain areas upon irregular methods of warfare—upon heterodox techniques of operation depending less on the commitment of men and materiel than on the harnessing of latent forces or resources available in the areas of operation.

Furthermore, the basic techniques of penetration and preparation such as were used by OSS in Europe were not applicable to the Far East. The classic methods of intelligence penetration called first for the placing of key agents in strategic neutral countries from which to organize operations into the enemy's home territory. Thus, in Europe OSS initially established clandestine bases in Switzerland, Sweden and Turkey. In the Far East there were no accessible neutral countries about Japan. New techniques of operation were required, for the success of which tremendous additional barriers had to be overcome.

For example, the linguistic, racial and cultural affiliations binding the United States to Europe did not exist in the same manner between the United States and the Far East. Whereas language differences and differences in everyday habits of life could conceivably be surmounted, differences in race presented a formidable obstacle greatly limiting possibilities for penetration and cover. The opportunities open to white men for existence and circulation in Japan or Japanese-occupied territories were highly limited; the use of Americans of Japanese or Chinese descent in the Far Eastern theaters was, for reasons of military security, made virtually impossible.

As a result, new methods and techniques of operation were required, and OSS operations in the Far East from the start contrasted sharply in their application from those in the European theaters. In Europe, open guerrilla operations by uniformed or maquis bands were possible only subsequent to the initiation of Allied military operations in a particular region. Therefore, the emphasis was upon SO, clandestine acts of sabotage or harassment. In the Far East, much of the terrain of operations was either sparsely populated or actual jungle. This, together with the thinly spread occupation forces of the Japanese, made the situation ripe for open guerrilla warfare by American and native groups.

There was no experience in clandestine operations available to OSS in the Far East, such as had been to OSS in Europe. The liaison established with SIS and SOE in London and the lessons learned from the seasoned staffs of those organizations saved OSS in Europe many trials and errors. Operations such as OSS contemplated in the Far East, however, were unprecedented for the British as well as for the U. S.

In addition to its lower priority, the Japanese war was complicated by the tremendous distances involved, and by the initial military weakness, both of available American Navy and Army forces and of the forces of Britain and China. No bases of operations remained in Allied hands within the range of available types of military aircraft. The principal approaches to Japan itself were direct, across the Pacific—initially possible only for long-range submarines—or, alternately, across the Asiatic mainland—except that chaotic conditions within Chungking-controlled territory ruled out overland access to Manchuria and Korea.

The direct approaches to Japan were through the naval theaters of operation, or up from Australia through New Guinea and the Philippines. Lines of jurisdiction for gaining access to Japan from the Pacific were not clearly defined until shortly before the Allied landings in Normandy. This placed additional complications in the way of the establishment of OSS, an agency whose operations transcended theater lines, in the two principal Pacific theaters.

The OSS program called for the application of all possible techniques of intelligence, subversion and psychological warfare against Japan. In contrast, however, a theater commander's interest was predominantly on weapons and agencies which could be of direct service to his immediate objectives. On a smaller scale, OSS in Europe had faced a similar problem in initially establishing itself in early major European campaigns, such as Sicily and Salerno. In those campaigns, however, it had been possible to gain the recognition of the military commanders by expanding initial tactical responsibilities in the immediate zone of operations into indispensable strategic services, on the basis of which penetrations and operations into Germany itself could be built.

But the decision of the two Pacific theater commanders prevented even the assumption of initial tactical responsibilities by

OSS. In the naval theaters, OSS was admitted only to such strictly limited direct participation as an intelligence liaison office in Hawaii and some special teams for specific operations. General MacArthur did not accept OSS until after his designation as Commander of U. S. Army Forces in the Pacific, in the closing months of the war, and then his approval was limited to certain special weapons with their operators. This administrative situation forced OSS to make its major effort in the minor Far Eastern theaters on the Asiatic mainland.

The alternate approach to Japan was overland across the Asiatic Continent, and it was in the two continental theaters of operation—the China Theater and the Southeast Asia Command, or India-Burma Theater—that OSS operations were largely concentrated. The handicap this caused was as if, in the European theaters, OSS had been obliged to concentrate all its activities in the Balkans and in Norway, without making any contribution to the military campaigns in France or Italy.

This enforced strategy of concentrating in the lesser zones must be kept in mind in assessing the results achieved by OSS in the Far East as against those achieved in Europe. No OSS unit in Europe equalled the tactical combat record of Detachment 101 in northern Burma, just as no OSS group of any kind in the Far East could claim a direct contribution to successful major Allied amphibious invasions such as made by OSS prior to the landings in North Africa and, subsequently, in France. On the other hand, although numerous attempts at major subversion were made in Europe, none approached the thorough penetration of an entire nation such as was effected in Siam by OSS in Southeast Asia.

Intelligence penetration of Japan itself was accomplished, although no OSS agents reached the Japanese Islands. Indirect penetrations succeeded in procuring significant information, both original and confirmatory, on the situation in the enemy's home territory. Siamese representatives in Japan or Siamese students returning to their country from Japanese schools supplied first-hand and documentary reports which were passed to OSS through the Siamese underground. Thus, early in 1945 a mob attack on the home of a high-ranking Japanese staff officer in Tokyo shortly after a B-29 fire-bomb raid was described soon after it occurred, confirming with details similar reports received through other channels. For OSS, such other channels included information regularly forwarded through Swedish or Vatican channels,* through German pouch intercepts in Switzerland,** or data obtained in the interrogation of Japanese civilians overrun in the advance in Burma or in China. Although of varying reliability, reports from these sources were significant indications of trends and were important for individual items or the confirmation of data from other types of intelligence sources.

While, in general, the record of OSS activity in Europe emphasized the role of a clandestine organization in preparing for large-scale amphibious landing operations in major theaters of war, the achievements of OSS illustrated—among other things— how clandestine activity in a secondary theater could, to some degree, substitute for the direct commitment of front-line military forces, fulfilling the same strategic purpose at much smaller cost.

In China, the American military program called for keeping Chinese forces in action against Japanese forces with as small an expenditure of American personnel and equipment as possible. While Army units were assigned to advise and reorganize the Chinese military organization, the Navy,

through U. S. Naval Group, China, worked to develop and expand Chinese guerrilla activities behind enemy lines and along Japanese communications routes, and to aid China's intelligence and secret police service, the Bureau of Information and Statistics, headed by General Tai Li.

All American activity in China suffered from the soporific atmosphere pervading Chungking officialdom. Personal self-interest and corruption, as well as the partisan rather than national policy evidenced at all levels of the Chinese Nationalist Government, negated any efficient conduct of active warfare against Japan. The American program received Chinese cooperation wherever it entailed supplying or expanding existing Chinese agencies. Thus the activities of Naval Group, China, in building up China's internal security organization, evoked ample cooperation from the Chinese. On the other hand, the OSS plan for an independent American secret intelligence service in China, even though this would be aimed at Japan and Japanese activities, was blocked at every turn.

In the process of establishing bases of operation and, in general, gaining a foothold in the China Theater, OSS lost almost two years' valuable time. Only at the end of 1944, when China was made an independent theater of operations under an American Theater Commander, did OSS receive the support necessary for its operations. Until the last months of the war, however, it was impossible for OSS to break down Chinese resistance to American intelligence or operational penetration of northern China, Manchuria and Korea, or to get any closer to Japan than the Yellow River.

OSS, therefore, was obliged to concentrate almost exclusively on secondary targets: the Japanese armies of occupation, and the subversion of populations in Japanese-occupied areas in China and throughout southeastern Asia.

In Southeast Asia, OSS faced problems of liaison with the British in a sensitive area

* See Part VI, "Stockholm", in Europe-Africa Section.
** See Part VI, "Bern", in Europe-Africa Section.

of the British Empire. The British were re-luctant either to see the establishment of an independent intelligence service in In-dia, Burma, Siam, Indochina, and Malaya, or to permit the development of intimate contact between the Americans and the native populations. The predominantly British nature of the Theater, and the rela-tive lack of high-echelon American support, delayed the development of OSS activities until the last year of the war. An even greater factor, perhaps, was that of dis-tance. From airfields in India, patrol bombers could just barely reach the Gulf of Siam. The journey by sea across the Bay of Bengal required several days, into areas of changeable weather and sporadic enemy naval activity. New techniques were nec-essary in view of the terrain of the target areas; subversion applied toward jungle re-gions presented basically new problems.

In the Burmese campaign, OSS tech-niques became of immediate and valuable assistance to American forces. Burma was a zone of operations where available Ameri-can men and supplies were at a minimum. By organizing reliable and willing natives, skilled in survival and travel in the jungle, into intelligence teams and guerrilla bands, and finally into armed mobile battalions, OSS made it possible for the Air Forces to strike even the most heavily camouflaged Japanese targets, for the ground forces to out-flank and out-maneuver the main body of Japanese troops, and for the entire cam-paign in Burma to profit from the paralyz-ing effects on the Japanese of incessant cutting of their lines of supply.

As in Europe, OSS in the Far East was organized on a theater basis under Strategic Services Officers theoretically responsible to the respective theater commanders for all OSS activities in the given theater. Thus, in the broadest outline, OSS in the Far East consisted of OSS/Pacific Ocean Areas, lim-ited to the liaison office in Hawaii, OSS/-China, and OSS/Southeast Asia Command

(later, OSS/India-Burma). In the two Asiatic theaters, although a fairly high de-gree of integration had been achieved by the end of the war, the organizational pic-ture was complicated by both geographical and political factors, which had their effect from the first days of the organizational evolution of OSS in Asia.

Shortly after Pearl Harbor, the first of a series of individual COI representatives was dispatched to China to survey potentialities for operation there. Three of the officers reached China at various times between January and May 1942. Their principal in-terests were in operations such as were be-ing contemplated by SA/B and SA/G, the forerunners of SI and SO. The variety of their missions and the difficulties of com-munication caused overlap between them, but their reports, upon their return to Washington, helped condition subsequent OSS planning.

In addition, specially briefed teams were dispatched to initiate specific operations. One was an overland reconnaissance through Tibet; the other an SI project for China.

With the closing of the Burma Road by the Japanese, it was necessary to explore the possibility of an alternate overland route to China. A special OSS team of two officers was dispatched to reconnoiter the route leading from India across Tibet into China. The team bore letters and gifts from President Roosevelt to the Dalai Lama, and left from India for Lhasa, capital of Tibet, in September 1942. After 89 days of travel, it reached the Chinese city of Hwang-yuan, and from there proceeded to Sining, Lanchow and Chungking. The team was the first official American mission to make contact with the Tibetans, but, aside from its exotic aspects, the importance of its original mission was obviated by the Ameri-can decision to reopen the Burma Road by a drive through northern Burma.

Early in 1942 an American industrialist, with extensive connections throughout

China and the Far East, placed his resources and connections at General Donovan's disposal. A special cover corporation was established supposedly for the import and export of motor vehicles to China, and an undercover representative was dispatched in 1942.

The first operational unit to reach Asia— it was also the first complete operational unit to be dispatched overseas by COI/-OSS—arrived in India in the early summer of 1942. It was to serve under the Commanding General, China-Burma-India Theater, General Joseph W. Stilwell, and was intended primarily for use in China. The conditions under which it was to operate had not been completely settled with Stilwell before the party sailed, and, upon its arrival in the Theater, he diverted the group from its original mission by refusing authorization to operate in China and assigning it instead to a tactical mission in furtherance of his projected campaign into northern Burma. In accordance with Stilwell's order, the group was established near other American bases in the Indian province of Assam under the name: U. S. Experimental Station, Detachment 101, Office of Strategic Services.

Stilwell had two reasons for opposing the establishment of an OSS unit in China along the lines originally planned by Donovan. He felt that the unorthodox weapon placed in his hands by OSS could be used most effectively—if it could be used anywhere—in Burma. He also feared that OSS operations in China might lead to difficulties with the Chinese Government and to friction with the United States Navy, which had started clandestine and paramilitary activities of its own in China, only nominally under Stilwell's authority.

These naval activities were conducted by the U. S. Naval Group, China, under the command of Captain (later Rear Admiral) M. E. Miles, USN,* in close association with

General Tai Li, director of China's internal security and counter-intelligence service. The partnership between Miles and Tai Li in the fields of secret intelligence and sabotage eventually crystallized into a joint Sino-American clandestine agency, with Tai Li as Director and Miles as Deputy Director.

Strongly supported by the Chinese Government, this agency claimed a monopoly on Allied clandestine activities in the China Theater, based on the exclusive resources of Tai Li's service. This monopoly, however, actually existed only on paper for, although Tai Li's organization was the only Chinese intelligence service recognized by the Chungking Government, other Chinese services existed, maintained by various war lords in the areas under their control.

Although the creation of the agency was not formally approved by the JCS until April 1943, cooperation between Miles and Tai Li was already close when the Detachment 101 group reached India. The agency enjoyed virtual autonomy as far as any American military authority in Asia was concerned, both because of Tai Li's directorship and because the Navy Department in Washington fully supported Miles' position.

Stilwell himself was not an enthusiastic supporter of the Sino-Navy partnership, but he wished to avoid the jurisdictional—and inter-Allied—conflict certain to arise if OSS challenged Tai Li's intelligence position in China. Hence, he ordered Detachment 101 to remain south of the Hump.

The basic issue was that of independence of U. S. secret intelligence activities from foreign control. Donovan stressed throughout that this independence was an indispensable prerequisite to effective intelligence operations.*

Conditions in China gave additional impetus to the desire of the Chungking Government to prevent independent operations

---

* Miles also carried the title, Naval Observer, China.

* The issue had been joined in Europe, as in the initiation of OSS operations based on England.

by a U. S. agency. By keeping control, it would be possible to manipulate the sources, areas of procurement and the content of OSS intelligence and avoid independent reporting on China's war effort and internal situation. Furthermore, Tai Li wished to control paramilitary operations, and particularly wanted authority to determine which groups of guerrillas should and which should not receive aid. Then, also, keeping OSS constantly dependent upon the Chinese for intelligence and agents would facilitate exacting further supplies and facilities from the U. S.

Miles had discussed centralization of clandestine activities in China with one of the early COI/OSS representatives. He proposed that for the sake of efficiency he, Miles, be designated head of OSS in China, in addition to his naval responsibilities. At Miles' insistence, the Navy Department in Washington supported his proposal with a direct request to Donovan to make this designation.

Donovan acceded. There was no alternative open to him, and he entered into the partnership with Miles and Tai Li to broaden the Sino-Navy agency into a Sino-Navy-OSS organization, designated SACO (Sino-American Cooperative Organization). Donovan wished, first of all, to establish OSS in China, and, secondly, to meet the direct request of the Navy Department in Washington for help and assistance in developing clandestine operations.

The OSS contribution to SACO consisted initially of furnishing operational supplies and trained personnel. Administratively, Miles was designated Chief of OSS Activities, Asiatic Theater. This made him nominally the Strategic Services Officer for the whole CBI Theater, but, since Stilwell had already established Detachment 101 under his own direct command, Miles' authority over OSS personnel and operations was confined to China.

The next step in the complex process of OSS growth in Asia was concerned with

OSS-British relations and was likewise a problem involving the independence of intelligence operations. By the middle of 1943, Detachment 101 had established its usefulness to Stilwell and he approved plans for the expansion of the organization, both in personnel and in the geographical scope of its operations in Burma. The British, however, became alarmed at the expansion of an American clandestine agency completely free from their control, and, for a period, sought to check the growth of Detachment 101. In fact, at high theater echelons, the continued existence of the Detachment in any form was directly threatened.

Donovan found a solution to this difficulty when discussions at the Inter-Allied Quebec Conference led to the creation of the Southeast Asia Command (SEAC), an Allied Theater Command under Admiral Lord Louis Mountbatten which was superimposed upon the British forces on the southern Burma front and upon Stilwell's combat forces in northern Burma. With the approval of the JCS, Donovan negotiated an agreement with Mountbatten and Stilwell, whereby Detachment 101 would be confined to a tactical role in furtherance of the American campaign in northern Burma, while a new OSS unit would be established under the operational control of SEAC Headquarters for operations elsewhere in the Theater.

The new OSS/SEAC was activated after Donovan's visit to the Theater in November and December 1943, and soon began to grow rapidly. For administration, as well as questions of basic American policy, OSS/-SEAC was subject to the authority of the Commanding General, CBI. Detachment 101, under Stilwell's control, nominally had to clear its operations with the same section of Admiral Mountbatten's staff—designated "P" Division—which supervised the operations of OSS/SEAC and all other Allied clandestine activity in the Theater. The two OSS units in southeastern Asia—Detachment 101 and OSS/SEAC—naturally maintained close liaison, but there was no direct machinery within OSS for coordinating their activities and they functioned for all practical purposes as if they operated in two separate theaters.

In China, meanwhile, OSS-SACO relations had reached an impasse. OSS participation in SACO had not been satisfactory from the point of view of the contribution OSS hoped to make to the American war effort in the Far East. It soon became plain that, while SACO worked well as a lend-lease organization functioning on behalf of Tai Li's secret police, and unquestionably facilitated the important activities of U. S. Naval Group, China, it was producing very little useful intelligence. Furthermore, the OSS personnel assigned to it were unable to do much more than mark time and strive patiently to break down the intangible but consistent tacit opposition of the Chinese.

OSS could not withdraw entirely from SACO without virtually abandoning all activity in China. Miles, because of his close personal association with Tai Li, in effect afforded the Chinese complete control over OSS operations. Donovan modified the situation somewhat by relieving Miles as Strategic Services Officer, CBI, and giving Detachment 202, the name of the OSS unit in SACO, a status partially independent of that agency. This was done by designating the Commanding Officer of Detachment 202 the Strategic Services Officer, CBI, with vague supervisory authority over Detachment 101, over the OSS supply base which was being built up at Calcutta, and with direct control of a small Research and Analysis unit for China which was temporarily working in New Delhi, India. Thus, while the Commanding Officer of Detachment 202 was still subject to Miles for operations within the framework of SACO, he was independent of him administratively and was directly responsible to the Commanding General, CBI. It was a small but

significant step toward freedom of operation in China.

It was soon complemented by another and more tangible development. Without giving up participation in SACO, Donovan, as a counterpoise to this Chinese-dominated partnership, formed a new and purely American partnership, this time with General Chennault's Fourteenth Air Force, USAAF, with headquarters in Kunming. Under A-2, Fourteenth Air Force, there was created a joint Air Force-OSS group called the "Air and Ground Forces Resources and Technical Staff" (AGFRTS). Though administratively part of the Fourteenth Air Force, the OSS element of this group was responsible for operational coordination to Detachment 202. The standing in China of General Chennault was such that Tai Li was powerless to block AGFRTS' operational activities.

AGFRTS grew rapidly both in function and in effectiveness. Functionally, it undertook SI, SO, MO and R&A activities. Its agents and teams in the field quickly developed into an efficient tactical ground intelligence service, as well as rescuing fliers shot down over enemy territory and sabotaging enemy installations. After four months of operation, that is, by August 1944, AGFRTS was already supplying 50% of all intelligence used by the Fourteenth Air Force, and had begun obtaining significant items of strategic intelligence on conditions in Japan proper.

In June 1944 the OSS organization in Asia consisted of:

Detachment 101 — operating into northern Burma, with headquarters at Nazira, Assam Province, India.

Detachment 202 — Chungking, an administrative and coordinating headquarters for OSS activities in SACO and AGFRTS.

OSS/SACO — a unit participating in SACO at Happy Valley near Chungking.

363

OSS/AGFRTS	— OSS personnel in the joint OSS - Fourteenth Air Force group at Kunming.
Detachment 303	— New Delhi, a rear echelon base for OSS/SEAC.
Detachment 404	— Kandy, Ceylon, headquarters for OSS/SEAC.
Detachment 505*	— Calcutta, a supply base for Detachment 101.

This arrangement prevailed—except for steady growth of all these units—until the autumn of 1944, when the American CBI Theater was split into the India-Burma Theater, operationally subject to SEAC, and the new China Theater. Shortly thereafter, in February 1945, OSS in Asia was reorganized into its final form, following another visit by Donovan to the theaters.

At that time, OSS/SEAC was abolished and replaced by OSS/India-Burma Theater (OSS/IBT) with headquarters in Kandy at Detachment 404. This headquarters exercised full control over all OSS detachments and units south of the Hump and was responsible both to Admiral Mountbatten and to the Commanding General USAF India-Burma Theater for all OSS activities within the IBT and SEAC limits.

It was in China that the major reorganization took place. By order of the new Theater Commander, Lt. Gen. Albert C. Wedemeyer, OSS was made responsible for all clandestine activities (except Chinese) in China; AGFRTS was bodily transferred to OSS command; and OSS, as a whole, was given the status of an independent command responsible to the Theater Commander through the G-5.

OSS participation in SACO continued up to the end of the war, but effective OSS control over OSS personnel in SACO was eventually secured. From February 1945 on,

---

* This designation was not officially applied until the reorganization early in 1945.

the importance of SACO steadily diminished. In contrast, OSS in China expanded rapidly. It had finally achieved the two basic prerequisites to successful operation: integration of its forces, and independent American control.

The organizational development of OSS in China and Southeast Asia in effect followed the pattern evident also in European theaters: Initial establishment wherever establishment was possible; multiplication of specialized functions and administrative units in response to immediate requests or necessitated by theater conditions; uncoordinated and often inefficient expansion of all groups; finally, consolidation and integration in the performance of basic OSS functions.

OSS had to cope with Allied hostility and suspicion. More important, it had to win the support and confidence of the American theater commands. The degree of support it finally enjoyed in all theaters was the best measure of its contribution.

At the time of the liquidation of OSS, unsettled post-hostilities conditions resulted in the OSS units in China and the area of the Southeast Asia Command still bearing major responsibilities for the U. S. theater commanders and the State Department. While the strictly guerrilla and paramilitary personnel were returned to the U. S. for release, OSS intelligence, counter-intelligence and analysis staffs continued to operate at a high pitch of activity under the Strategic Services Unit, the agency of the Office of Assistant Secretary of War, War Department, established to liquidate OSS operations branches.*

---

* R&A field personnel in China Theater and SEAC (as well as in Germany and Austria) were included in the transfer to SSU, War Department, even though the R&A Branch was made part of State Department. Upon their return from the field, R&A personnel were assigned to State Department.

B. PACIFIC OCEAN THEATERS

1. OSS/Pacific Ocean Areas

An outpost office of COI was opened in Honolulu a month after the Pearl Harbor attack, and the small staff on duty there was continued after June 1942 under OSS. The principal functions of the office were liaison and research.

Liaison was established with the major Navy and Army commands and OSS materials, prepared by the intelligence branches in Washington, were made available to the intelligence sections of the various headquarters. Included in the materials were R&A studies, SI reports, and interview reports. By May 1944, new dissemination procedures went into effect in the Theater with the establishment of the Joint Intelligence Center, Pacific Ocean Areas (JICPOA). Thereafter, by the specific request of ONI in Washington, OSS materials from Washington were forwarded to the Pacific via ONI channels through JICPOA.

Research activities by the OSS office at first consisted mainly of collecting cartographic and other source material available in the Hawaiian Islands and of value to planning of future Pacific and Asiatic strategy. This material was made available both to agencies in POA and to OSS in Washington. Subsequent to 1944, the preparation of research studies by the Honolulu office was hindered by the unavailability of data disseminated by other intelligence agencies in the field. Despite repeated requests, OSS/POA, under direct orders from Admiral C. W. Nimitz, was denied access to documentation from JICPOA.* This was in line

with the Navy's program of concentrating intelligence research activities either to service intelligence agencies in the Theater or through Naval Intelligence headquarters in Washington.

The OSS concept of operations in the Pacific entailed both activities in direct support of theater programs, and close coordination with OSS projects on the Asiatic mainland to develop maximum access for OSS to the Japanese home islands. The development of OSS operations in the Pacific was outlined in a Basic Military Plan for Psychological Warfare in the Pacific Theater (JCS 403), presented for the consideration of the JCS in early summer 1943. The Plan stressed active reconnaissance and sabotage, as well as morale operations, against Japan and Japanese installations in the Pacific, and called for bases in Hawaii, sub-bases in the North and South Pacific Areas, and a staff of 50 officers and 266 enlisted men. The JSP forwarded the plan to CINCPOA, Admiral C. W. Nimitz, noting, however, that "the characteristics of this theater render impractical the employment of the specialized agencies which OSS proposes to place at the disposal of the theater commander." * Nimitz concurred, being "averse to establishing in Oahu, where housing is at a premium, an organization whose value at present and for some time to come is not apparent." **

In April 1944 Donovan conferred with Nimitz in Hawaii. Thereafter, a naval officer was appointed Chief, OSS/POA, and assigned to Nimitz' staff as Strategic Services Officer.*** In July, Nimitz informed him

---

* Letter from Nimitz to Chief, OSS Honolulu Office, 12 April 1944.

* Report by JSP on JCS 403, 7 July 1943.
** CINCPOA to COMINCH, Serial 00119.
*** Letter, Nimitz to Donovan, 27 April 1944.

that OSS should submit for CINCPOA approval detailed plans of operation as authorized by JCS for OSS. After a preliminary exchange of correspondence, OSS forwarded to JCS a detailed operational plan on 13 November, proposing SI operations in POA, specifically SI penetration of the Kurile Islands, as well as programs for R&A and Morale Operations. It was pointed out that this program did not constitute a complete application of OSS resources but would project operations which could and should be undertaken immediately. These plans, however, were not approved by CINCPOA, and consequently the approval of the JCS was never obtained. As a result, OSS/POA never developed the comprehensive functions represented in OSS units in other war theaters.

In the last year of the war, OSS reports from agent networks in China were relayed by OSS communications to the Honolulu office for rapid dissemination to Theater intelligence staffs there. In addition to this service, requests for specific items of intelligence on enemy installations or order of battle along the China coast, and reports of OSS coast-watching teams, were forwarded upon request.

Two additional specialized OSS activities were represented in POA. Field Photographic units were active in December 1941, photographing the damage to Pearl Harbor, and during the Japanese attack on Midway early in 1942. From the latter operation the film "Battle of Midway" was made.

The original OSS swimmer team, Maritime Unit Group A, trained in Catalina and the Bahamas, was requested by POA and served from August 1944 until April 1945 with U. S. Navy Underwater Demolitions Team #10 in pre-landing combat operations at Angaur, Ulithi, Leyte, Lingayen Gulf and Zambales. In addition, one group of five OSS men participated in a special submarine-borne reconnaissance of Yap and Palau.

2. OSS in the Southwest Pacific Theater

An OSS representative was dispatched to General MacArthur's headquarters in mid-1942. The representative had had long experience in Philippine affairs and was officially appointed Civil Advisor and consultant on Philippine affairs at General Headquarters, Southwest Pacific Area, in September 1943.

The office of Civil Advisor was first attached to the Philippine Regional Section of the Allied Intelligence Bureau, G-2, GHQ, SWPA, and later transferred to G-1 and G-5, GHQ, SWPA, and the Civil Affairs Section, Hqs. USAFFE, with the OSS representative as chief and his assistant, recruited and trained by R&A/Washington, as Executive Officer.

Starting with a basic library of documentation on the Philippines, assembled in Washington and shipped to Australia late in 1943, the Section became the center for information on social, economic and political conditions in the Philippines. After the reoccupation of the Islands, a basic library was established in Manila. Field trips were undertaken to all parts of the Philippines, and the processing of current information was continued. Major research studies were undertaken at the request of army agencies and of the Philippine Commonwealth Government, including a series of reports on the political situation in the various parts of the Commonwealth.

After April 1945, upon the priority request of General MacArthur, the OSS Special Projects Branch was ordered to transport the JAVAMAN weapon, together with the necessary number of technicians to operate it, to the Philippines for use against the remainder of the Japanese fleet.* The Japanese surrender came before the weapon could be put into operation.

---

* See "Special Projects" in Washington Section.

3. Other Activities

MO. In the late spring of 1945, using the OWI broadcasting station at Guam, the OSS Morale Operations Branch established a small staff of specialists on Guam. Until VJ-Day, daily "black" radio programs were broadcast to the Japanese homeland and occupied Asiatic territories.

Okinawa Campaign. In the preparation for Okinawa, a number of special OSS weapons were delivered to the Tenth Army Commander for use in the landing operations and the subsequent campaign. In addition, an OSS officer was assigned as OSS representative with Tenth Army headquarters in April 1945. Among his assignments were to investigate the possibilities of exfiltrating and infiltrating agent personnel onto the China coast from Pacific bases, so as to facilitate penetration of Formosa, northern China, Manchuria and Korea and the Japanese home islands by sea.* By means of special radio equipment, the latest intelligence on Japanese movements relevant to present or future Tenth Army operations was relayed from OSS/China and OSS/-SEAC to Tenth Army headquarters. The OSS representative was withdrawn with the close of the campaign on the Island.

Civil Affairs. R&A units were assigned to the Civil Affairs Staging Area (CASA)** in San Francisco to assist in planning and preparation for the occupation of Japan.

---

* The imminence of the Japanese surrender and the complications of inter-theater relationships, however, prevented use of Pacific bases to support operations on the Asiatic mainland.

** See "San Francisco" Office and also "R&A" in Washington Section.

C. BURMA — DETACHMENT 101

1. Assignment to Burma

The original objective of the group which became Detachment 101 was to conduct intelligence and paramilitary operations in China. It was intended to be of direct assistance to General Joseph W. Stilwell in the China-Burma-India (CBI) Theater and to prepare the way for the full development of OSS resources in the campaigns on the Asiatic mainland.

Recruiting and preparations had been carried on even before the formation of OSS, under the SA/G Branch of COI.* The group was trained in the SOE schools in Canada and an advance echelon of twenty officers and men, under the command of an officer who had served under Stilwell and was well known to the General, left for the field in May 1942.

When they arrived in the Theater, Stilwell informed them that he did not wish the mission assigned by OSS/Washington to be carried out. He was in desperate need of all possible help in the pending campaign to retake northern Burma, and the resources of manpower and supplies allotted to him were extremely limited. Moreover, he felt that the complicated political situation in China ** would only be aggravated by steps to introduce American clandestine operations there.

Therefore, Stilwell ordered the OSS group to operate in Burma instead. At that time, Stilwell was faced with the primary problem of reopening an overland supply route to China. U. S. policy called for the delivery of supplies to China, to support and maintain Chinese troops in the field against

the Japanese, provided that control of routes between India and China could be reestablished. The Japanese advance into northern Burma early in the war had cut the approaches to the Burma Road, and the Japanese were maintaining four divisions in the country to keep China isolated from the southwest.

Burma, a nation almost the size of the State of Texas, presented other obstacles in addition to its difficult climate and terrain. East-west transportation routes were virtually non-existent. A major engineering task would be required to carry the traffic entailed in the China supply program. Further, the majority of Burma's 15,000,000 inhabitants were natives of various races and tribes whom propaganda and latent anti-British sentiments had turned pro-Japanese.

The answer to the supply problem was the construction of a route to connect with the Burma Road. The Ledo (later Stilwell) Road was to begin at Ledo on the Assam-Burma border, follow through the Hukawng Valley and southward to Myitkyina, through Bhamo to join the Burma Road near the Burma-China border. The prerequisite to construction of the route, however, was the recapture of Myitkyina and the clearing of the Japanese from northern Burma.

Following the discussions with Stilwell, the OSS group was designated U. S. Experimental Station, Detachment 101, Office of Strategic Services. Authorization was given for the establishment of a base camp on a tea estate near Nazira, in Assam Province, and for the initiation of operations. The orders officially activating Detachment 101 were cut on 15 September 1942.

---

* See Washington section on COI.
** See "Background and Problems" in China, below.

Nominally the Detachment was placed under Miles,* who at that time was in charge of all OSS operations in Asia. It was recognized, however, that if the Nazira "Experimental Station" proved successful, it would function as an integral part of Stilwell's combat forces.

Stilwell's first operational directive to Detachment 101 was concise: to deny to the Japanese the use of Myitkyina airfield, some 150 miles inside Burma, through sabotage of Japanese lines of communication and by any other means that could be developed. Strategically it was imperative that the Myitkyina air strip be neutralized to prevent the Japanese from dispatching fighter aircraft either to attack American planes flying the Hump or to hamper progress in the construction of the Ledo Road.

No express limitation was placed on the scope of OSS activities. In Stilwell's mind, however, the basic purpose of Detachment 101 was to give direct tactical assistance to U. S. air and ground forces operating in northern Burma. While early OSS plans contemplated extensive clandestine activities throughout the Theater, the Detachment of necessity devoted its entire time to the assignment at hand. Stilwell's mandate to 101 was the initial step in the establishment of OSS in the field in Asia. The adequate fulfillment of that mandate would in itself show the potentialities of OSS in other Far Eastern campaigns and theaters.

Detachment 101 operations at first followed a pattern typical of clandestine activity. The initial 101 staff recruited Asiatic and Eurasian personnel in British territory, trained them hastily at the Nazira base and parachuted them in small groups near enemy targets. Wherever possible, these groups were to recruit natives and establish intelligence and resistance networks. As the Burma campaign progressed, and as 101 became more closely an integral part of

---
* Commanding Officer of U. S. Navy Group, China. See "Background and Problems" in "China" below.

Theater forces, this type of operation gave way to guerrilla activities which emphasized harassment of the enemy behind his lines and the procurement of tactical intelligence directly in support of the Allied advance. The first method of operating was never wholly abandoned, however, and throughout the campaign 101 successfully supported its jungle combat units with SI and SO techniques wherever possible.

Advance bases were established by American officers on the edge of enemy territory, in the jungle no-man's-land, deep behind enemy lines and close to his bases—always where the terrain afforded cover and protection. These bases were linked by radio with the Nazira base, with teams in the field, and, when necessary, with one another and with Allied forces in their areas. Usually they maintained small camouflaged air strips for the Detachment's light planes. Besides directing 101 operations in their respective territories, these bases performed a variety of supporting tasks. By diplomacy, by distribution of supplies and by giving medical aid they won the good-will of the tribesmen. They were thus able to tap the "jungle grapevine" for intelligence, in addition to recruiting agents and guerrillas from among the native peoples. Most native recruits were trained on the spot, but a number were sent to the Nazira base for special training. The advance bases also served as weather stations and air-raid warning networks, two services of vital importance to the heavy air traffic across the Hump to China. In addition, they organized a jungle network for rescuing crashed American airmen.

Within four months after the Detachment's activation, valuable intelligence reports were reaching Stilwell's headquarters and minor sabotage operations against the enemy were being attempted. It was not until the spring of 1943, however, that the strategic significance of 101 operations became clearly discernible. By that time, plans for pushing the Ledo Road across

North Burma to link with the old Burma Road to China were well advanced and Detachment 101 was assigned the mission of collecting the requisite intelligence, both military and topographic, required by the planners, of winning the collaboration of the tribes through whose territory the road would pass, and of acting as forward outposts for the Chinese troops protecting the engineer units working on the road. All these services helped to speed up the construction of the road itself, and time was vital from Stilwell's point of view. But Detachment 101 rendered him a still more valuable service, one without which the road might not have been possible at all.

To liberate northern Burma with his inadequate ground forces, nearly all Chinese, Stilwell had to rely heavily on his air arm and exploit it to the hilt. Aerial opposition was insignificant but the jungle terrain seemed to impose a severe limitation upon the effectiveness of air attack. Whether the problem was supporting ground troops, impeding movement along enemy lines of communication, or simple attrition, the bombs and bullets of Stilwell's Tenth Air Force had to have remunerative targets. In the heavy jungle which covered most of northern Burma such targets could not be located by any normal A-2 methods or recognized when found. Only agents on the ground could locate and identify the targets adequately, and the pinpointing of air targets came to be one of the great 101 specialties—so that at least sixty-five percent of the bombing and strafing missions flown by the Tenth Air Force were against targets designated by OSS.

Few of these targets were major ones, but the cumulative effect of this small-scale precision bombing made possible by OSS intelligence was a major factor in breaking the Japanese hold upon northern Burma.

In early August 1942, Stilwell instructed the Detachment command to return to India and build up his unit, and told him that he would be given a free hand but that he would be expected to maintain proper liaison. In New Delhi, the Theater G-3 informed the Detachment commander that 101 should give first priority to operations against Myitkyina airfield, the key to the Japanese effort against the American supply line to China.

The Detachment's first letter of instruction was received with the order for activation on 15 September 1942. It specified that the Detachment carry out the mission verbally assigned to it by Stilwell, subject only to the restriction that no important operations be executed without prior approval from New Delhi Headquarters. Tenth Air Force and SOS had been directed to cooperate with 101 but their existing facilities as to housing and transportation were inadequate and no requests were to be made to them for such assistance. In connection with denying Myitkyina airfield to the Japanese, the instructions further read: ". . . without any desire to restrict you, it is desired to indicate that destruction on the railroad, the firing of railroad cars, and the sinking of vessels carrying fuel will all contribute to the general success of your operations. Effective destructions of important bridges, . . . would reduce rail shipments of gasoline to a negligible amount. . . . Liaison with British authorities should be initiated to the end that no possible cause for mutual interference may arise."

Liaison with other U. S. Army units would be channelled through G-3. At the initial conference with G-3, the Detachment commander reported that he was in the process of preparing four groups of native agents for the following areas: (1) The "hunting preserve" northwest of Myitkyina; (2) the triangular region of which Myitkyina was the northern apex, the Irrawaddy River and the railroad the two sides, and the line Bhamo-Katha the base; (3) the vicinity of Lashio; and (4) down the Burmese coast to Rangoon. By late September, the nucleus of the first three groups had been recruited.

Initial emphasis was on the first two areas. It was planned that the groups would perform two types of operation: First, sporadic, widely separated small attacks to harass Japanese supply lines; and second, a carefully synchronized attack against a maximum number of objectives simultaneously on the railroad, the river, and in Myitkyina proper, with maximum emphasis on the airfield. The first would tend to alert Japanese occupation forces, which at that time were poorly organized, and would also stimulate Japanese reprisals on natives, possibly discouraging their desire to assist in further sabotage activities. On the other hand, if maintained continuously, these attacks would increasingly divert Japanese troops to security missions. The second, or synchronized, attack would take maximum advantage of the laxness of the Japanese occupation and would be particularly effective in coordination with other major Allied operations.

Close liaison was maintained at all times with the British through SOE. General Wavell approved the operations 101 had planned. There were two points of possible contention between 101 and SOE: shortage of qualified native personnel and duplication of effort. 101 conceded that SOE should have first claim on personnel; since, in this type of work duplication was advantageous, this factor presented no problem. Accordingly, 101 negotiated an agreement with SOE which contained the following provisions: (1) 101 would remain a separate entity, maintaining the fullest cooperation with SOE/India, collaborating in training, selection of personnel and use of supplies to the best mutual advantage, in addition to exchanging relevant information; (2) 101 operations would be submitted for approval to the Commander-in-Chief, India and the Chief of SOE/India; (3) 101 would act as liaison for SOE/India with American authorities, while SOE would perform similar functions for 101 with the British; (4) an officer of the Burma Army who would assist in liaison between 101 and SOE would be attached to 101's staff; and (5) there would be no objection to duplication of operations if care were taken to avoid competition between agents.

During the fall of 1942, emphasis was placed entirely on training. One of the Detachment's first tasks was to recruit someone with detailed knowledge of the projected area of operations. To fill this need, the Governor of Burma made available from his personal staff a colonel who had been for many years in charge of forestry work for the Government in northern Burma. When recruiting began, a number of this colonel's former assistants were secured from different units of the Burma Army.

By November, the Detachment had already begun to supply intelligence. Headquarters had been established at Nazira, and it was planned, subsequent to the initiation of operations in the north, to establish an advance base in southern Burma immediately to the north of the Japanese positions. The Tenth Air Force was being supplied with detailed information on Myitkyina, including a mosaic of the area.

2. · Establishment

The techniques used by Detachment 101 followed what might be called a model approach to paramilitary operations. After the establishment of a main operations headquarters, a supply base near the combat zone, and the installation of training and communications facilities small teams of trained intelligence agents were parachuted or infiltrated overland into the target area. Wherever possible, the agents were equipped with radio sets and maintained close communication with headquarters. Their function was not only to reconnoiter but also to make cautious contact with reliable natives and prepare the way for the arrival of combat nuclei.

When conditions were reported favorable, combat nuclei of eight or ten Americans each were parachuted to receptions arranged by the agents. The nuclei had the dual function of recruiting and training agents on the spot into guerrilla bands, and beginning operations to harass the enemy. Supplies, equipment and additional personnel were to be delivered regularly by air drop or, in some cases, by small planes landing on secret airfields cleared and maintained behind enemy lines.

When guerrilla groups were developed sufficiently and their activities had succeeded in driving the enemy from the immediate region, advance OSS operations headquarters were moved into the territory, and additional intelligence agents sent forward to the next target area.

Native personnel employed in northern Burma were the Kachins,* small, wiry, dark-skinned tribesmen who inhabited the area north of and around the town of Myitkyina and the upper Irrawaddy River. However, they lived in almost complete independence of the Rangoon Government. While the Kachins were not particularly devoted to the British, they remained loyal during the Japanese invasion of Burma when most of the other Burmese tribes and factions transferred their allegiance to the enemy.

Kachins were employed by numerous British and American units for a wide variety of tasks in the Burmese campaigns. The Kachins were by nature excellent soldier material. Native "forward companies," led by British officers, were effective in harassing actions against the Japanese, using a heterogeneous assortment of weapons—from ancient muzzle-loading flintlocks to Enfield rifles, captured Japanese arms and Bren guns.

Even more valuable than their military proclivities was the Kachins' thorough knowledge of the jungle and the terrain of northern Burma. They were perfect guides,

and were extensively used as such by both British* and American headquarters. Special raiding and reconnaissance groups, composed of Allied and Kachin personnel, were formed in Stilwell's Northern Combat Area Command. Some of these, designated "V-Forces," operated at some distance inside northern Burma ahead of American positions, as screening forces for engineer troops working on the roads and in such matters as recovery and return of downed Allied aviators.

Anglo-Indians and Anglo-Burmese were also used, extensively at first, either recruited locally in India or Burma or lent from British military units. Their relations with Kachins and other native Orientals were, however, frequently handicapped by the fact that they were apt to consider themselves as rating higher than natives who were not half-caste, and tended to emulate Occidentals in behavior, outlook and dress. A situation as in the Burmese campaign, calling for the close collaboration of men of many nationalities and ethnic groups, required great care at all times to avoid just such reactions as this behavior was likely to produce.

The first contacts between Detachment 101 and the Kachins in the field were made early in 1943. By that time, the Detachment's principal physical installations were taking shape. Most of the original group of twenty Americans and a small nucleus of Anglo-Burmese and Anglo-Indian trainees and interpreters were stationed at the Nazira headquarters. The trainees were being instructed in radio operation, cryptography, parachuting and guerrilla fighting, with the understanding that each would eventually pass on his knowledge and skills to Kachins recruited in the field. A rear area with radio station was maintained in Calcutta for contact with Washington and other Far East bases. A supply base and air dispatching area was opened at Dinjan,

* Also known as "Jingpaw," whence the name "Jingpaw Rangers," the unofficial designation of Detachment 101 Kachin battalions.

* The British maintained a force of 750 Kachin Levies based at Fort Hertz.

near Ledo, on the Assam side of the India-Burma border.

Clarification of the position of the Detachment was required, both in the Theater with regard to Stilwell's NCAC headquarters and within OSS in the light of general operations plans. It was necessary to convince many of the Americans in the Theater Command of the value of the heterodox type of warfare Detachment 101 was prepared to wage. From a strategic point of view, the Detachment's techniques were unconventional and unproven. Officers in individual units or sectors were concerned with immediate tactical problems, and tended to attach small significance to the long-range strategy on which 101's plans were based. However, an air of informality pervaded Stilwell's command, and problems of liaison could usually be worked out on a personal basis. When the Detachment exhausted its funds shortly after the first 101 groups entered enemy territory early in 1943, the officers of the Detachment pooled their personal funds and turned them over for the use of the Detachment as a whole. Stilwell himself heard of the Detachment's difficulty and advanced $50,000, pending the arrival of additional funds from Washington.

As reflected in correspondence, relations between 101 and OSS/Washington became strained, as a variety of recruiting, clearance and transportation difficulties delayed the arrival in the Theater of additional personnel badly needed by the Detachment for recruiting, finance, training and communications, medical and ordnance sections, research and analysis, and supply services. The situation was not relieved until the summer of 1943, but, for a while before that, the morale of 101 personnel was affected by a feeling that the Detachment was being neglected by Washington headquarters.

Particularly in its early days, the Detachment was obliged to rely more on "unofficial procurement" than on what it could obtain through official channels. This ranged from direct contact with commanders of supply and personnel depots to cash or barter purchases on local markets.

Procurement of specialist personnel was performed on a more legitimate basis. For example, "We needed Nisei who could interrogate prisoners," a sergeant with 101 reported. "Washington had trouble lining them up. There was a big security headache in clearing them for embarkation. Even if we could get Nisei in Washington, it took a lot of time and red tape to ship them to the Far East from West Coast embarkation ports. Feeling against Japanese-Americans was high in San Francisco and Los Angeles. So (we) looked around in New Delhi and found four Nisei enlisted men (whom we) borrowed . . . from U. S. Army Headquarters. Two were assigned to . . . the field and two to Base Headquarters. They were all good men, very reliable and hard-working, and they stayed right on with us . . ." *

The necessity for improvisation had its direct effect upon the utilization of Detachment personnel. OSS branch distinctions were sublimated to fulfilling the most immediate needs of the Detachment. While this was probably unavoidable in the circumstances prevailing during the early days of the Detachment, the pattern it set made the subsequent application of specific branch programs a matter of secondary importance to the Detachment throughout its existence.

3. Initial Operations

In late December 1942, an advance party of 15 flew to northern Burma to establish a forward base at Sumprabum. They arrived at Fort Hertz in two transport planes, with four fighter escorts, carrying a considerable quantity of supplies. They were in British uniform under the cover of members of the Kachin Levies; however, the British commander of the Levies had informed Fort Hertz that Americans were coming. Since

----
* Field Report, Sgt. Soo Lim.

this cover was blown, they stated that they were a Tenth Air Force radio unit. Shortly after arrival they proceeded by a convoy of 14 elephants to Sumprabum, northern headquarters of the Levies, 50 miles south over primitive jungle trails. This trip, which required six days, initiated the group into Burma field conditions, complete with the coolie elephant guides requiring daily payments and bribes to insure their continued assistance.

After a week of getting established at Sumprabum, a problem of command arose when the British commanding officer of the Levies demanded that OSS operate according to his directions, which not only conflicted with OSS policy but were apt to be changed drastically from day to day, apparently according to his personal whim. The Detachment commander had no other course but to withdraw his main unit, leaving behind only three men and a radio station. The British commander was thereafter instructed by 4th Corps command that OSS groups were to be assisted, not directed.

On 10 February, a new unit was sent in with instructions to move into the "Triangle" * and from there to work west from the hills to penetrate Myitkyina. Until March, the group sent daily weather reports to the Tenth Air Force in addition to indicating numerous bombing targets. They also forwarded British intelligence by radio to Nazira, whence it was relayed to Tenth Air Force, arriving there two or three days more quickly than through British channels.

Early in March, the Japanese started for Sumprabum in force, and the British fell back to Fort Hertz, taking the 101 group with them. The British then decided to evacuate to India, but the 101 group remained, reporting on Japanese situations until May when it returned southward to a point southeast of Sumprabum.

---

* Area between Sumprabum and Myitkyina, east of the former—see map.

The first 101 long-range penetration group was parachuted from Nazira on 7 February into the Kaukkwe (or Koukke) Valley area, 250 miles behind Japanese lines. Designated Group "A," it consisted of 12 agents led by a captain of the Burma Army. Its instructions were: (1) To determine whether the Japanese held the area and, if so, in what strength; (2) to cut the railroad between Mogaung and Katha after 1 March in support of a planned Theater push against the Japanese in this area; and (3) to recruit a guerrilla force from the Kachin hills southeast of Myitkyina, which would harass road and river traffic from Myitkyina to Bhamo. Parachutage of the agents, their radio and supplies was completely successful, despite the dense jungle and meager intelligence available concerning the strength of enemy forces in the area and the attitude of the natives.

Radio communication was established with Nazira, and one of the first messages reported 50 enemy troops patrolling the railroad to Myitkyina. The possibility of immediate discovery made the Group decide to start cutting the railroad ahead of schedule. They demolished three railroad bridges, but an attempt by part of the Group to derail a train was abortive. One of the men was killed in a premature explosion, and, in the resulting confusion, one man was lost and one captured, but two others escaped. The entire Group was imperiled and was forced to move to another location.

On 20 February, Nazira informed the Group that its operations were being coordinated with a different Theater offensive than originally planned. It was instructed to determine the attitude of the natives in their area and obtain information from them if possible. Group "A" reported that the natives in the towns "seem contented and definitely pro-Jap. Impossible to approach anyone." They also reported heavy Japanese train and road traffic at night. The Japanese were advancing northward, but the regular flow of intelligence from the

Group on enemy traffic and situations more than compensated for the hazards of their continuing operations. A series of supply drops reinforced the Group, although planes were scarce and the mission a difficult one, and drops had to be kept to a minimum. Intelligence contributed by Group "A" was commended by Stilwell's Deputy Chief of Staff in a wire to Detachment 101 on 2 March:

> AT FIRST OPPORTUNITY CONVEY MY CONGRATULATIONS FOR EXCELLENT PERFORMANCE OF A DIFFICULT AND DANGEROUS MISSION TO YOUR FIRST GROUP . . . KEEP SENDING US ALL INFORMATION AS EXTREMELY VALUABLE.

Information on Japanese locations became more and more important during March, as the Allies established definite air superiority and needed fuller information on possible targets.

Group "B" was infiltrated even deeper into Japanese territory near Lashio. The Group, composed of six Anglo-Burmese, had been recruited ·in October 1942 and underwent intensive training while awaiting Stilwell's approval. Since it was impossible to obtain air cover from India for this deep penetration, the Group had to be infiltrated from Kunming, China. Approval was delayed until February 1942, since Stilwell was primarily concerned with getting supplies over the Hump to the Chinese and weighed very carefully the value of every mission detracting from those commitments. Finally, in February, the Group was dropped from a C-47 with a six-plane fighter cover supplied by the Fourteenth Air Force. The parachutage appeared successful, but the Group was never heard from again. On 4 March Radio Tokyo reported that "six British spies" who parachuted into Burma in February had been attacked by "patriotic" Burmese, and that three of the six had been captured and three killed. The Japanese description was sufficiently accurate to indicate the fate of the Group. After this failure, it was decided that for fu-

ture drops reconnaissance flights would be made beforehand and a two-man reconnaissance team would first be dropped to determine the safety of the dropping zone.

Support to First Allied Offensive in Burma. The strategic situation in Burma began to change in the spring of 1943, when the Allies assumed the offensive with an experimental operation behind enemy lines. British Brigadier O. C. Wingate led long-range penetration units of the 77th Indian Infantry Brigade across the natural barrier between India and Burma into Japanese-held territory. From February to June 1943, his columns covered a distance of 1,000 miles. On 18 February, Stilwell directed Detachment 101 to give priority to: (1) Contact with British line units and SOE; (2) contact with V-Force (short-range penetration groups); (3) contact with loyal natives, with whom 101 was to establish friendly relations, reassuring them regarding Chinese treatment and obtaining from them information on Japanese activities. Meanwhile, 101 was to set up locations for overland supply lines and communications chains from Nazira into Burma in preparation for the coming attack on Myitkyina; (4) harassment of Japanese communications as far south as the halfway point between Mogaung and Katha and eastward, including the Myitkyina area. Stilwell specifically directed that the Japanese should be kept out of Sumprabum and confined to the area near Myitkyina, and a. Detachment 101 group should be put in the Taunggyi-Loilem-Lashio area (far south of Myitkyina) to work on the railroad and report enemy moves in the region.

Lt. Gen. R. A. Wheeler, SOS Chief in the India-Burma Theater and G-4 for NCAC, was contacted in regard to the proposed supply line as it would operate through NCAC territory in the upper Hukawng Valley. He quickly agreed to the advantages of having the 101 units move on foot into enemy territory ahead of his troops to supply information. The monsoon was about to start, but operations were to continue unabated.

By early March, Detachment 101 had a group working forward from Ledo, concerned primarily with protective information on road construction. The group consisted of five Anglo-Burmese, led by agent "Skittles." All of them spoke either Chinese or Burmese dialects; they operated in native attire and were familiar with junglecraft and the terrain. They carried two radios especially adapted for the operation by the 101 Communications section. From the point of view of 101, the group would serve five purposes: (1) Supply to Wheeler information on the enemy in the upper Hukawng Valley; (2) establish a supply route from northern Assam into Burma; (3) establish a base for placing future groups in Burma; (4) create friendly relations with the natives whom Chinese troops had mistreated in their retreat from Burma; and (5) serve as outposts in front of the Chinese to report any Japanese action designed to prevent the building of the Ledo Road.

The group divided into two sections, both operating about 50 miles ahead of army outposts. One, working east along the northern rim of the Hukawng Valley and commanded by "Skittles," was designated "L" Group. The other, in the Taro Valley and led by "Robby," was known as "M" Group. Both were subsequently augmented by additional personnel. Heavy rains began toward the end of March, and movement through the jungle trails became so difficult that it required Wheeler's forces ten days or more to advance 40 miles. The U. S. Army, Chinese troops and 101 groups in the field were supplied by regular air drops. All technical equipment had to be kept in waterproof containers, since the rainfall was extremely heavy and the driving rain penetrated anything that was not solidly encased in waterproofed containers.* Supply

---

* Annual rainfall in the area was 250 inches, all of which came during the few months of the monsoon season.

items were rotted quickly by fungi and mildew.

On 18 March, Wheeler requested that a third 101 group be sent into the Miao area to determine whether the enemy held the northeastern region of the Hukawng Valley, where two mountain passes were potential means of entrance into upper Assam. "J" Group was dispatched in late March. Heavy rains delayed its progress into the target area, since small streams were often transformed overnight into raging torrents, which, contrary to plan, were not fordable and could be crossed only by crude rafts constructed on the spot. The Group arrived at Miao on 31 March.

In April, when Wheeler was replaced, arrangements were made with his successor for Detachment 101 to be responsible for all activities behind enemy lines ahead of his position. All information would be immediately passed to him, and all 101 operations would be coordinated with his plans prior to execution.

Aid to British Offensive on the Burma Coast. In February, when the British under Wingate were attempting to invade Burma along the coast near Akyab, 101 was asked to participate. Lt. Gen. Irwin, commanding the Eastern Army, asked that 101 cut the Prome-Taungup road by which the strongly entrenched Japanese were being supplied from the south. RAF attacks on enemy motor and sampan convoys had failed to halt the heavy traffic, and it appeared that ground sabotage was necessary. 101 already had men in training for this area, having foreseen possibilities for operations along the Burma coast. Arrangements were made with the Royal Navy for a maritime landing on the night of 7-8 March. The commander of Detachment 101 accompanied the Group, which was designated "W." Despite bad weather, landing operations were carried out. British boats could not be made available at any other date and the landing could not be delayed much longer since the monsoon was about to start; the operation had to be performed at that time or not at all.

Group "W" departed from Chittagong on 6 March, arriving in the vicinity of the mainland at Sandoway the following midnight. The landing beach was uncharted and the many rocks created a heavy surf, but, after four attempts, the landing was finally accomplished successfully. The six Anglo-Burmese comprising Group "W" went ashore in small British rubber dinghies, moved by a guide line which the Detachment commander himself had secured between ship and shore. He had decided to swim ashore when, at the last minute, it appeared that the agents, who had had no training in night maritime operations, were too shaken by the bad landing conditions to continue on their own. By a human chain from the water's edge onto the rocks, they moved 1,000 pounds of supplies and equipment to the mainland. According to the Detachment commander's report, he then "shook hands with the lads, told them to get the stuff under cover before daylight which was almost in the sky, and if they were discovered, not to be taken alive. I said goodbye and pushed off."

Group "W" was never heard from. It had not been expected that radio contact could be made, since their radio equipment had been swamped during the landing. However, no trace of the Group was found even later in the Burma campaign when the territory surrounding the target area was liberated.

The Detachment commander stated in a report to Donovan that the fact that OSS did not have its own equipment was a basic reason for the failure of the mission. OSS was forced to utilize equipment and personnel of regular military organizations for transportation and thus was forced to rely upon orthodox military methods and timetables. He emphasized that successful OSS operations should use the methods of the smuggler, rather than the military. Whereas the Army, particularly the Air

Corps, gave first consideration to equipment, OSS should give first consideration to the trained agent—its most valuable equipment and a very expensive tool. For instance, Air Corps planes carrying 101's agents could fly only in the daytime and only with a fighter escort. Obviously, this did not give the agent every chance for the secret landing he should have for successful infiltration. Detachment 101 needed its own light planes for this work. For maritime operations, it required ordinary motor boats and also one larger operations boat of a type used for "rum-running during the days of prohibition . . . the fastest type boat on the West Coast."

Another important factor contributing to the failure of both Group "W" and Group "B" was extremely poor security, which, in turn, could be traced to the fact that 101 lacked its own operational equipment. In the U. S., security had been stressed, but in Burma, there was no way of maintaining anything approaching good security conditions. For example, at least twenty Indians, persons who could not under any circumstances be in an organization like OSS, had actually observed the landing of 101's agents on the coast of Burma. In addition, other Indians and British officers with no security training had taken part in the operations. Fifty or more Americans, none of them having security training beyond a look at the poster "Loose Talk May Lose Lives," had seen OSS drop agents behind the lines. Although the purpose of the organization had been kept a secret up to the time that operations began, the Detachment commander was compelled to state in April 1943 that "everybody in this theater knows who we are, what we are doing, and a lot of them actually know . . . what we are planning to do and when we will do it."

It was soon realized that the British offensive along the coast was a failure, due to the strength of superior Japanese forces, and 101 did not attempt to put another group in the area.

Pre-Monsoon Operations—1943. Before the start of the monsoon period in 1943, Group "A" had established a fairly reliable informant service. Its target area had been depleted of food and other commodities and extensive supplies were dropped by plane from Nazira in order to secure the good-will of the natives. Three of the four missing members of the Group had returned to Fort Hertz in early May with an abundance of intelligence. In June, the entire Group ceased operation. They had apparently succeeded in keeping the Burma railway out of action in their area, and supplied a great deal of information on economic, social and political matters in northern Burma upon their return. Included in the intelligence secured were lists of trustworthy villages and village headmen, as well as copies of newspapers, pamphlets and official credentials. Natives holding key positions under the Japanese were also listed, including former employees of the British Government who had transferred their allegiance.

Information supplied by Groups "A," "L," "M" and "J" on their methods of operations in the jungle greatly assisted the Army force engaged in constructing the Ledo Road, and also was used by OSS in preparing a manual on survival in the jungle.* The Groups provided information on foraging techniques, indicating edible fish, game, roots and fruit, the weapons most suitable for hunting, and meals which could be prepared.

During April, Groups "L," "M" and "J" were assembled for reorganization. Previously, they had been directly responsible to the commanding general of the Ledo force, but now were placed directly under the control of 101, closely supervised by Wheeler's

successor. The Groups were formed into new field groups under an advance base (KNOTHEAD), similar to the original advance base operating in northeastern Burma (FORWARD).*

In June and July the advance base in the Sumprabum area, FORWARD, moved farther into Burma, well ahead of the advancing British. This move was successfully effected, despite ravages of malaria, typhoid and black water fever, and an accidental strafing and bombing by Allied aircraft.

Monsoon Operations—June Through November 1943. Following Wingate's initial penetration, the seasonal rains again restricted ground activity. However, Allied bombers of the Tenth Air Force continued to attack Japanese supply lines in Burma (and Siam) with steadily increasing strength. 101 operations continued during the monsoon.

FORWARD was near Ngumla by September. It had recruited and trained 28 agents in the field in addition to 19 agents who had arrived from Nazira. Natives in the Kachin hills under its influence and control numbered into the hundreds. FORWARD was preparing to attack enemy lines of communication, and had been reporting information of such value that two additional units of Stilwell's command had asked to be included in distribution of 101 intelligence.

4. Reorganization — December 1943

By the end of 1943, Detachment 101 had established its two main advance bases, FORWARD and KNOTHEAD, and had intelligence and operations groups in the field, with eleven radios reporting regularly to headquarters from behind Japanese lines. Air delivery of supplies to these groups, in the month of December alone, totalled over forty tons, a peak figure up to that time. In the same period, twenty American com-

---

* This manual was prepared for the S&T Branch preparatory course on Catalina Island, where officers and men scheduled for duty in Southeast Asia received intensive physical training. See "Schools and Training" in Washington Section.

* The designations, FORWARD and KNOTHEAD, were not adopted until August.

missioned and enlisted personnel were parachuted into enemy-held areas. After October, when the enemy had begun activities against the Air Force, 101 had rescued 26 downed airmen by means of its jungle network.* It had also captured two Japanese soldiers, one of them a pilot, the first Japanese army officer to be taken alive by British or American forces in the area.

Headquarters in Nazira maintained close radio contact with FORWARD and KNOTHEAD. Fifty-seven students were in training at Nazira. Supplies and reinforcements arrived regularly from the U. S. at the rear echelon base in Calcutta.

The principal problem of the Detachment was shortage of personnel, partially caused by illness and casualties. Operations could not be expanded until additional personnel arrived. An administrative staff was needed to handle financial and other work pertaining to running the expanding native groups.**

Another paramount problem was security. The Detachment had 27 camps spread over an area of forty square miles, with a guard force of only 45 "semi-militarized" Gurkhas. A security officer was needed, plus more guards.

Communications with agents in the field presented still another problem. Agent sets had been constructed by 101 personnel, using limited facilities and equipment. Both SSTR-1's and communications personnel from Washington were urgently needed.

During December, Donovan arrived to inspect and reorganize the Detachment. The reorganization was designed to implement decisions reached at the Quebec Conference affecting the future of OSS in the Far East. It had been decided that an offensive should be undertaken in North Burma during the winter of 1943-44 and that the Ledo Road

should be extended to reopen the old Burma Road as rapidly as the progress of the offensive permitted.

Donovan made a thorough inspection of 101, including flying in one of the Detachment's liaison planes to an advanced group headquarters inside enemy territory. He observed at first hand 101's operating techniques and the multiple supply and combat problems which it faced in the field. Thereafter, he instituted changes to regularize the organization of the Detachment and clarify its status within the Theater. He also promised additional personnel.

Primarily, the Detachment was reorganized along more military lines. Donovan realized that tactical considerations were foremost in the operations of the Detachment and that it would have to work as an integral part of Theater combat forces. In order to permit the full application of OSS resources within this pattern, he ordered the tactical work of the Detachment broadened to include the entire scope of OSS activities. Other OSS branches were to be represented at 101, particularly R&A, MO and R&D. While it might not be possible for specific staffs to carry out the functions of these branches exclusively, the implementation of their respective activities was nevertheless to be undertaken wherever possible as a part of regular Detachment operations.

The status of the Detachment within the Theater and within OSS was thereby clarified. The Commanding Officer of the Detachment was to submit reports of current and pending operational plans through U. S. Army channels to "P" Division,* SEAC Headquarters, at Kandy, Ceylon. "P" Division had authority to coordinate the Detachment's operations with those of Allied military units in the Theater. In turn, the Commanding Officer, Detachment 101, served as the chief of "P" Division for Burma. Due to the predominantly tactical

---

* See section on 101 air activities below.
** The January payroll for non-American personnel included 225 instructors, agents and students, 50 cooks and bearers, 50 Gurkha guards and 30 miscellaneous employees.

* See "Problems of Theater Liaison" in OSS/-SEAC below.

nature of 101 activities, only nominal direction was given to 101 operations by "P" Division.

A new Commanding Officer of the Detachment was appointed, who was technically responsible to the Strategic Services Officer, CBI. New commanders were also appointed for KNOTHEAD and FORWARD. OSS appropriations for Detachment 101 were raised from the original monthly figure of $40,000 to $100,000.

5. Specialized and Auxiliary Activities

Although the organization of Detachment 101 did not specifically follow the branch lines of OSS/Washington, certain specialized and auxiliary activities became an integral part of the Detachment's scheme of operation. Close relationships with the air forces were essential for dispatching missions into the field by parachute and for delivering supplies by air to units and groups deep in enemy territory. OSS Communications personnel established and maintained base and field headquarters radio stations, prepared radio equipment for the field, improvising or adapting available equipment where necessary, and training native recruits in communications techniques. To combat the Burmese climate, highly developed medical facilities were essential. The medical staff gained immeasurable good-will for the Detachment as a whole by its services to the native populations encountered in the field.

At Detachment headquarters, specialized staffs were formed to check, evaluate and process intelligence reports from the field, to facilitate the rapid distribution of information to customer agencies, and to brief agents and issue intelligence directives to teams in the field. In addition, SI and R&A officers prepared intelligence analyses in greater detail to answer specific Theater requests.

Air Operations. Close relations were maintained with the Tenth Air Force from the start. Planes and equipment were made available to 101, and, on the long-range missions, fighter cover was provided. In return, as Detachment intelligence sources in the field developed and multiplied, the Air Force profited by receiving information used to select the majority of its bombing targets through 101. Ultimately, the Detachment organized an "air force" of its own, consisting principally of liaison planes and small transport craft.

Lessons learned from the operations of the original field groups, particularly "A" and "B," led to steady improvement and refinements in the technique of parachuting personnel and supplies. Pilots were briefed to approach their target sites with greater care and to drop containers more accurately. Since guerrilla troops in jungle and mountain terrain depended entirely on air drops for rations and ammunition, as well as for demolitions and radio equipment, it was of supreme importance that air operations be developed to a high degree and that each air mission be soundly organized, planned and executed. By the end of 1943, the Tenth Air Force had evolved a system of combining missions for 101 with strafing, bombing or reconnaissance flights. For example, in the course of one mission flown on 12 May, 7 containers and 34 packages were dropped to an advance group, from an altitude of between two and three hundred feet. Most of the supplies landed within the designated clearing, and the remainder was retrieved. On his return trip, the pilot made a wide sweep, flying low over the Irrawaddy River, to strafe targets of opportunity before returning to his base.

The Detachment's own air force was constantly used for observation purposes, courier flights or the evacuation of casualties. As field units effected deeper penetrations into enemy territory, new air strips were built. By the end of 1944, the Detachment operated eight C-47's, six of which were stationed at Dinjan for supply drop purposes and the remainder at Myitkyina. When escorts were needed, the Tenth Air Force provided requisite fighter craft or B-25's.

Nine-tenths of the entire weight of supplies delivered by air to teams in the field was flown out of Dinjan, the main air supply depot of the Detachment. In addition to the C-47's, the Detachment had eight L-5's, four L-1's, two PT-17's and two C-64's.*

Communications. The success of 101 operations depended upon the ability of agents to communicate their reports immediately to base headquarters, whence reports would be relayed to the appropriate Allied units on widely separated fronts. When 101 was first organized it was realized that this would be the case and expert Communications personnel were included in the original group. They established a radio shop in Assam in October 1942, began experiments for the construction of small field sets, and started a twenty-position school for communications training.

A rear echelon station was established at Calcutta in January 1943. Contact was made with the first field group in February. By November, daily schedules for urgent traffic were maintained with Army headquarters at Ledo and at Marguerita, as well as with British headquarters at Meerut. In January 1944, the field units themselves established direct contact with the U. S. or British stations in their areas.

Equipment for the construction of the radio station, which had been ordered from Washington before the departure of the original group, arrived only in part. Communications personnel were forced to improvise an emergency transmitter, using tin from cans for variable condensers, bamboo for coil forms, and any other available junk equipment and odd parts for the rest. Small field equipment was adapted from Army hand generators and scrap parts with great success. One type of radio invented

by 101 operated over a distance of 750 air miles.

By December 1944 traffic with field groups had reached such proportions that the small Communications staff was hard-pressed. With only ten personnel, and despite the continuing shortage of proper equipment, the base station handled 1,571 messages (140,471 groups) during December.

Research and Development. Stilwell requested 101's Research and Development staff to devise a counter-measure to Japanese anti-tank tactics.* R&D responded by developing an improvised flame-thrower which spread a snake-like incendiary fire over a wide area, to flush the enemy out of tall grass or other hiding places inaccessible to tanks. Among the other devices developed by the Branch were special booby traps and demolitions, mostly devised from "odds and ends" of materials and adapted for combat conditions in Burma.

Medical. The role of medicine and medical activities was significant, if not vital, from the earliest days of the Detachment. Due to the rigors of the Burmese climate, the American personnel required constant attention. In addition, from the time the Detachment began operations in the field, arrangements were made for medical care for the Kachins, both for the agent personnel directly on duty with the Detachment and for natives living in areas in the path of Detachment operations. Reports from intelligence agents repeatedly disclosed the failure of the Japanese—either by design or inability—to supply medicinal products to the natives in the territories occupied by them.

In late October 1942, at the request of Detachment 101, a U. S. Navy surgeon, several pharmacist mates and extensive medical supplies were turned over to 101 by Navy Group, China, and flown by plane to Fort

---

* The two C-64's ("Norsemen") were originally designed for service in Canada and the Arctic, and had difficulty in the jungles of Burma.

* Japanese infantry men used incendiary bombs which clung to the armor and forced tank crews to abandon their vehicles.

Hertz. Thereafter, supplies were moved southward overland, reaching FORWARD at Ngumla on 3 December 1943. A temporary field dispensary was constructed, and by the day before Christmas, when additional medical supplies were dropped by plane, a bamboo hospital and surgical clinic was completed, as well as a dispensary.

"The response of the (natives) to the advent of medical care was remarkable, even though their reactions were quite a surprise to the Western mind," the surgeon reported. "In the south Triangle there had never been a white doctor . . . the Kachins were at first cautious and then fascinated by medical procedures; . . . remained suspicious until the beneficial results were observed and then . . . came in such numbers that it was almost impossible to heal all of them."* It was noted that the Kachins accepted medical care in a very matter-of-fact manner, apparently feeling that it was no more than right that the Americans, who had come to live with them, should give them whatever they could in the way of help.

Successful medical treatment served to acquire staunch friends for the Detachment, with a minimum of effort and time expended. The Kachins' confidence was gained with such rapidity that when the original commander of FORWARD was recalled late in December, he was replaced by the Navy surgeon, who was named as his successor and directed both medical and combat activities. Shortly before the capture of Myitkyina, the surgeon's popularity reached unprecedented proportions as the result of a delicate and dangerous brain operation which he performed on a wounded Kachin, in a primitive hut, with meager surgical facilities, while a mortar section from FORWARD was operating with a unit of Kachin Levies ahead, attacking enemy road traffic.

* Lt. Comdr. Luce, MC (USN), final report, dated 1 Nov. 1943 to 1 April 1945.

After the capture of Myitkyina, the field hospital at Ngumla was moved to the Myitkyina region, and the original staff of Navy pharmacist mates was supplemented by Army medical corps personnel assigned to the Detachment. In addition, both Army and native surgeons and doctors were added to the Detachment for work in the hospital or at the aid stations. Medical aid was administered to all natives, civilians and troops contacted by the Group's personnel, to native Burmese troops under British command, to British officers and men and to Indian troops serving near FORWARD and in adjacent areas, as well as to Detachment 101 personnel.

In July the Navy surgeon was relieved of line command of FORWARD Group. In view of Stilwell's approval for still another expansion in Detachment 101's field forces, it was important to expand rear echelon medical facilities. A 50-bed hospital and three new field hospitals were completed under the surgeon's supervision in Assam. By November 1944, the rear echelon medical service also included a 70-bed hospital. The field operations of the Detachment at that time resulted in increased combat casualties, and necessitated added hospital tents and a rehabilitation camp. Both American and native casualties received treatment at the bases. The non-segregation of casualties by race created no problems; on the contrary, the nature of Detachment 101 personnel, structure and operations would have made any other policy an alien one, in view of the close spirit of collaboration in the field and in combat. Furthermore, non-segregation prevented breaches of security, which occurred in some cases where, due to the fact that Detachment facilities were unavailable, the wounded were treated in other establishments. The nursing staff of the hospitals included Burmese girls who had been trained by Dr. Gordon Seagrave, the noted American medical missionary.

Morale Operations. In December 1943, Donovan directed that morale operations be added to Detachment 101 activities. The following month, an MO officer arrived to survey the possibilities of morale subversion in Burma, particularly the techniques which could be employed and the media or channels through which the information could be circulated. However, difficulties and complications arising out of the local situation prevented the successful development of MO in Burma. Initial handicaps included lack of personnel and equipment, as well as a chain of command extending to Washington, thousands of miles away. There were still greater difficulties which were beyond the control of the MO Branch.

At the time MO initiated its program, Stilwell was preparing for the Myitkyina campaign. Chinese troops were being staged for the new offensive. In addition, seasoned volunteer U. S. infantry men were secretly en route from the southwest Pacific to Burma, where they were to be re-grouped as "Merrill's Marauders". Publicity regarding the imminent return of Chinese troops to northeastern Burma would only remind the natives of the looting and brutality perpetrated by some Chinese forces during Stilwell's 1942 retreat. Since the future deployment of the Marauders could not be revealed, MO was at a loss in attempting to prepare on short notice adequate themes for exploitation. Nevertheless, arrangements were made to have MO men advance with 101 teams deep into enemy territory. As they advanced, they found most Allied commanders indifferent to such innovations in jungle warfare as rumor-mongering and the distribution of subversive leaflets. Some of the MO personnel were diverted to interrogation or intelligence work.

In the late stages of the Burma campaign, MO initiated the "Gold Dust" mission for the purpose of directing natives behind enemy lines to propagate subversive and morale-destroying reports about the enemy, and to promote the Allied cause. The Mission included eight officers, four enlisted men, a native civilian and a photographic and reproduction unit with a five-ton press. Activities continued throughout the remaining days of the campaign, and much of the experience gained was useful for subsequent operations elsewhere in the Far East.

6.   The NCAC Campaign to Myitkyina

By November 1943, the beginning of the dry season during which a ground offensive was possible, Allied Air Forces had established definite superiority in Burma. At this time, there were indications that the Japanese offensive against India would be resumed. The Allies were also preparing for major offensive operations, from both India and China. The first Allied blow was to come from the north and was to be led by Stilwell, who had mounted an offensive to cross the Patkai Range, conquer northern Burma, and open a new land route to China. American-trained Chinese divisions constituted his main striking force. In immediate support of his advance, long-range penetration operations were to be carried out by combat teams of the 5307th Composite Unit (Provisional) under Brig. Gen. Frank D. Merrill. This unit came to be known as Merrill's Marauders.

By February 1944, when the Marauders reached the area of operations, Stilwell's offensive had made considerable progress. U. S. engineers had pushed a road over the Patkais 100 miles from the base at Ledo. However, the main enemy resistance was still to be met.

Merrill's Marauders had been organized pursuant to a decision made at the Quebec Conference. Five months later, on 1 February 1944, they were in India ready for employment.* They were the only American ground combat troops designated at this time for the CBI Theater.

Originally, Detachment 101 was to assist in the North Burma campaign by acting as an advance screen supplying intelligence to the main Allied forces, pinpointing bombing targets, rescuing downed airmen, and harassing the enemy from the rear. Since U. S. officers and enlisted men had had no experience in training and leading native forces behind enemy lines, the first attacks against the enemy were in reality a "trial run". These preliminary attempts, however, showed such promise that, by April 1944, Stilwell had ordered the Detachment to increase its combat troops to 10,000. Thereafter, guerrilla warfare played an increasingly important part in the Burma campaign.

In late February 1944, the Marauders started their drive; fighting began on 3 March. Early in the campaign 101 supplied the Marauders with at least two Kachin guides for patrols, and, in addition, established a pool of ten to fifteen Kachins at regimental command posts. Through its network of radio stations, patrols and native outposts, Detachment 101 kept Merrill fully informed of Japanese movements and concentrations along his route. Merrill maintained close liaison with 101 personnel in the course of planning his campaign.

The Kachins cleared trails, built bamboo bridges, located water-holes, and selected dropping grounds for air supplies. Particularly valuable was their selection of

<hr>

* Prepared in secret, they were transported on a "sealed" ship. An OSS/R&A man, en route from the U. S. to the Theater, was, by chance, loaded onto this ship at San Francisco with the Marauders. For security reasons, no one was permitted to be detached from the Marauders. The OSS man, therefore, although completely untrained for combat, remained with Merrill's forces through several arduous months of the Burmese campaign. Before his return to OSS, he had been awarded the Bronze Star Medal.

fields capable of receiving L-5 planes to evacuate the sick and wounded.

The Marauders were ordered to operate fifteen to twenty miles behind enemy lines, ahead of Stilwell's Chinese divisions in the Mogaung Valley corridor. The 1st Battalion of the Marauders on 15 March encountered heavy Japanese forces, and was almost surrounded. Although they were unaware of it at the time, the Battalion was receiving considerable assistance in its battle from a group of 200 Kachins led by a 101 lieutenant. This "Lightning Force", as it was called, actually a part of KNOTHEAD, was performing ambushing and harassing activities in the rear of Japanese forces in the area. Unfortunately, the colonel in command of the Battalion had no information on this unit's activities, and attempted to cut a trail around the Japanese force rather than meet its threat. Finally, on 18 March, contact between the Battalion and the "Lightning Force" was effected and the 101 unit supplied guides during the remainder of the Battalion's march.

On 20 March, the Kachin guides with the Battalion suddenly became talkative. Having no interpreter handy, the Marauders ascribed the natives' jabbering to a desire for food or cigarettes and provided them with both. Actually, the Kachins had announced that a Japanese machine gun position lay directly ahead, and they assumed that the food and cigarettes were rewards for this information. The machine gun soon went into action. Luckily, the Japanese had been impetuous in opening fire, and were able to inflict only three casualties. The Marauders had learned a lesson, however; thereafter, close attention was paid to the remarks of the natives.

Meanwhile, the 2nd and 3rd Marauder Battalions were active in the Mogaung Valley. On 15 March they were met by KNOTHEAD, which by that time consisted of 8 Americans and 331 natives. The two battalions were ordered to protect the south flank of the Chinese advance. With KNOTHEAD support, the Japanese were completely deceived as to the size of the attacking force. The Marauders later stated that, by creating in the minds of the Japanese an exaggerated idea of the size of the area held by the Marauders and of their strength, the 101 Kachins were probably of more assistance than anyone realized.

In late April, the Marauders were ordered to carry out a wide flanking move to the east of the main drive. This was to be their most difficult task, since they were to strike at Myitkyina itself, the chief objective of the campaign. This surprise thrust deep into enemy territory was designed to dispose of the principal air base, from which Japanese aircraft menaced American transport planes flying supplies to China, and to deprive the enemy of an important stronghold, the center of an extensive military framework.

By April, the original Marauder force, which had been fighting in exceedingly difficult terrain, was seriously weakened by casualties, and the remaining troops were depleted by illness and exhaustion. They had lost about 700 men, killed, wounded or sick, out of an original 3,000. There were no American replacements in the Theater to provide the strength necessary for the final attack on Myitkyina. Stilwell therefore decided to reinforce Merrill's forces with Kachin and Chinese troops. In accordance with this plan, a re-grouping of units was undertaken at this time and three new combat units, designated H, K and M Forces, were formed. For example, the former 2nd Marauder Battalion, reinforced with 300 Kachin guerrillas became M Force.

The plan of attack provided that the newly-constituted H, or Galahad, Force would make a surprise assault on the Myitkyina air strip, supported by K Force. They were led by PAT,* a 101 group commanded by American officers, on a devious course through paddy field and jungle in order to

---
* Originally part of KNOTHEAD.

reach Myitkyina without being observed by either Japanese or natives. On 15 May, just as the force reached a point about 15 miles from its objective, the chief guide was bitten by a poisonous snake. Despite his wound, he continued on horseback, leading the column until it reached its destination that night.

The attack came off exactly as scheduled. By noon on 17 May, the Myitkyina air strip was in Allied hands. The leader of the victorious Galahad Force cabled to the 101 Commander his recognition of the vital contribution of the Detachment: "THANKS TO YOUR PEOPLE FOR A SWELL JOB. COULD NOT HAVE SUCCEEDED WITHOUT THEM."

Other 101 groups had also helped support the capture of the Myitkyina air strip. 101 units, had, in fact, provided the only intelligence screen in advance of the Allied forces in North Burma. FORWARD, by that time composed of over 1,000 natives, performed diversionary operations northeast and east of Myitkyina. They harassed Japanese reinforcements to such an extent that an enemy battalion was halted and finally diverted from its objective.

The capture of Myitkyina itself was not effected until 3 August. During the siege of the town, NCAC relied on Detachment 101 to contain the enemy along the whole of the left flank from the Irrawaddy east to the China border. U. S.-officered 101 guerrilla units, totalling up to 1,500, served to divert a battalion of the enemy from Myitkyina.

In support of the main drive into North Burma, Wingate's columns had thrust deep into central Burma to cut enemy communications far to the south of Myitkyina. Detachment 101 furnished liaison and intelligence officers, as well as guerrilla scouts, to provide intelligence cover and combat patrols for both flanks during Wingate's march northward toward Mogaung. 101's agents also accompanied the British forces which cut the road south of Bhamo. The exchange of daily situation reports and summaries between the British forces and Stilwell's headquarters was effected through 101's liaison officers and its radio net.

In June Stilwell, in a message to the JCS, stated:

Services rendered by detachment 101 to Merrill's force in Myitkyina campaign were of great value. Information furnished on routes and enemy locations and strength assisted us greatly. We are further developing this organization because of its future potential value.*

By the end of the campaign, Detachment 101 had not only been ordered to expand but also was given responsibility for the coordination of Allied clandestine activities in the NCAC area.

7.   Aid to the Air Forces

Although the contribution of Detachment 101 in support of ground operations was perhaps its primary contribution to the U. S. forces in this area the Detachment also provided valuable services to U. S. air units.

Reports from the Tenth Air Force and ATC attest. to this contribution both with respect to intelligence on enemy air strength, bombing targets, escape routes or safe areas for downed aviators and the rescue of airmen.

A report from the A-2 of the Tenth Air Force in September 1944 stated that 101's services represented for Tenth Air Force the "most certain means of obtaining information concerning the enemy to the rear of the front lines." In Air Force "attacks on enemy personnel, stores and installations . . . the work of 101 was not only valuable, but actually indispensable." 101 information included both target data and damage assessment.

An example of the use of 101 intelligence was given as follows:

A C-3 report dated August 14 advised that 1000 Japs, with considerable stores, were located in Moda. . . . Photo cover confirmed the activity. Fighters, loaded with demolition and incendiary bombs, attacked the town

at once. Subsequent 101 reports indicated that enemy casualties actually totalled 200 Japs and forty armed Burmans; that many Japs were caught in houses and that a dump filled with ammunition and arms was completely destroyed. Previous to the original report Moda, an inconspicuous Burmese town had been disregarded and never photographed. Without the 101 report no enemy activity would have been suspected there.

Damage assessments by 101 were particularly important due to the difficulty of observing results from the air in view of the heavy jungle foliage.

Another important service to the Air Force was in the field of "escape, evasion and rescue" work. 101 reports revealed areas behind the lines where the natives were definitely pro-Allied or pro-Japanese in their sentiments; listed specific friendly or unfriendly towns; located secret light plane strips laid out by 101 forces behind enemy lines; and gave specific areas where 101 forces existed to give assistance. Special safe-area maps were provided. 101 was immediately notified whenever a pilot was forced down behind the lines. All 101 forces in the area then would at once conduct a search for the pilot and render all assistance possible, including medical care. By September 1944, some 180 ATC and Tenth Air Force personnel had been assisted by 101 forces in enemy territory. The morale of the pilots was considerably boosted by the knowledge assistance might be close at hand if they were forced down in enemy territory.

101 also served the ATC. Intelligence procured by the Detachment was useful in the briefing of ATC personnel before flights over the Hump and in indicating the numerical strength of enemy aircraft based on forward Burma fields.

8.   Reopening the Burma Road

With the successful liberation of Myitkyina, the first phase in the reopening of the Burma Road had been achieved. However, before the Theater Commander could fulfill his directive to reopen the supply route to China, two other key points,

---

* JCS Memorandum for Information No. 258.

Bhamo and Lashio, had to be cleared of enemy forces.

Detachment 101 was to play an important part in these actions. During the monsoon, FORWARD, KNOTHEAD and other groups were integrated into a system of operating bases directing the activities of agents and guerrilla battalions, Kachin personnel for which had been recruited and trained pursuant to Stilwell's orders to expand 101 activities. Up to ten battalions, each composed of about 1,000 Kachins led by Americans, were active in the field at various times.

In October, when NCAC plans for the march south to Bhamo were being formulated, 101 had established and was maintaining traffic tally stations on the important roads and rivers leading out of Bhamo.

Throughout the campaign to take Bhamo, 101 intelligence and combat groups operated ahead of the advancing Mars Task Force and Stilwell's Chinese divisions. Twenty miles east of Japanese-held Bhamo, a large field base was established, where air drops were made daily by Detachment 101 light planes with the full knowledge of the enemy. In addition, seven 101 battalions prevented the development of a Japanese flanking movement against the Allied drive, forcing the enemy to keep large forces in the areas east of this advance. 101 battalions also supported British and Chinese divisions during this period, operating forward in the area between the railroad corridor and the Irrawaddy River. Both flanks of the British 36th Division, which had been committed to the battle for Katha, were protected by 101, and the Commanding Officer of the 36th Division gave a substantial part of the credit for his success to 101.*

---

* In February 1945 agent "Ski" reported 500 Japanese advancing toward the Shweli River who appeared to be planning a surprise counterattack on the British 36th Division right flank. The British were able to deploy a brigade to meet the Japanese when they attacked, and the British commander stated "Ski" had "saved the Division."

From June until December 1944 Detachment 101 forces were the only Allied troops between Katha and the Chindwin River. They continually harassed elements of a Japanese division over a distance of 100 miles. This area was of special concern to the Allied command because of the possibility that the enemy might launch an offensive north against the Ledo Road. Activity of 101 troops not only guarded against such an attack but caused the Japanese to believe the Allies were planning an offensive in this sector.

As the campaign moved southward, the 101 forces which had been covering the right flank moved in advance of the British as they swept across the Chindwin River to the railway. 101 intelligence reporting during this period covered the advance of the Japanese units moving southwest to meet Allied forces from the north.

In the eastern sector, the occupation of Bhamo had set the stage for the advance on Lashio and the achievement of the NCAC goal of reopening the Burma Road. By that time, 101 had a small "army" of 9,000 guerrillas along the entire front.

The guerrilla tactics employed during the Lashio campaign were a very fluid type of warfare. The enemy's superiority in numbers and armament forced the Detachment's battalions to rely upon surprise, speed and freedom of movement. Ambushes, weapons blocks and hit-and-run attacks killed enemy personnel and destroyed communications and equipment without involving the guerrillas in pitched battles against overwhelming odds. The enemy acknowledged the effectiveness of these operations during the Lashio campaign by filling every open field with obstacles, and issuing a directive to the effect that all Japanese units in Burma had become front line troops due to the employing of "airborne battalions" by the Allied forces.

A Detachment 101 battalion was the first Allied unit to strike the Japanese on the Burma Road, in an action which took place between Wanting and Hsenwi. Another 101 battalion established the first contact of any Allied force with Chinese troops advancing down the road from China.*

To the west, guides were provided for the attack on Namhkan and combat patrols harassed the retreating enemy south of the city. By February Detachment units had penetrated to a point 40 miles south of the battle line and four miles southwest of Lashio. Other 101 units took up positions on the outskirts of the city and held them until Lashio was occupied on 7 March. These units then moved south to secure the Allied success.

The NCAC campaign to reopen the Burma Road was successfully concluded with the capture of Lashio. Detachment 101's main contribution to the campaign was the acquisition and dissemination of all types of intelligence. Eighty-five percent or more of all tactical intelligence received by G-2 during the campaign was supplied by 101; seventy-five percent of all Tenth Air Force targets behind Japanese lines were assigned on the basis of Detachment information; and nearly one hundred percent of the ground assessment of Air Corps action in enemy territory was made by 101 agents.

Casualties inflicted on the Japanese by 101 were conservatively estimated at 4,350 killed. Fifty-three Japanese were captured. OSS combat casualties consisted of 1 American killed, 75 Kachins killed and 125 Kachins wounded. 101 troops also guided 228 Air Corps personnel to safety. A total of 470 wounded American, British and native troops were evacuated by the 101 light plane squadron.

At the end of the NCAC campaign, the Detachment's strength was 566 Americans and 9,200 natives. Twelve combat headquarters and eighteen intelligence head-

---

* Friction developed due to looting and pillaging by Chinese troops inside Burma. After protests and direct police action by Detachment 101, the Chinese were ordered withdrawn across the border.

quarters had been established. The various headquarters were organized to plan field operations, supply field groups by air, and furnish field personnel with information concerning positions of Allied units, as well as positions and plans of other Detachment units.

Incoming intelligence was disseminated to G-2, P-I and A-2 of NCAC, by teletype. In addition, intelligence was distributed by Detachment liaison officers to the major units of the British, Chinese and American forces serving in Burma. A compilation of all intelligence obtained by 101 from its field units, by interrogation of prisoners, natives and returning field personnel, as well as from the photo interpretation section, was pouched weekly to rear echelon headquarters in China, India, Ceylon and the United States. The X-2 section of 101, working with CIC, sought out Japanese collaborators and espionage systems and reported on conditions which existed in territory under enemy control.

Throughout the NCAC campaign 101 relied heavily on its own light plane squadron to bring special equipment to units behind enemy lines and to evacuate wounded, prisoners, key native figures, downed Allied fliers and captured documents. The air strips utilized by these planes had been hastily constructed by natives and were often almost inaccessible, yet the flight record was nearly perfect. Forty-one strips were constructed behind enemy lines during the campaign. The squadron proved so valuable that after the NCAC campaign every effort was being made to augment its strength of seventeen planes and two officer and eight sergeant pilots.

A brief history of Detachment 101, prepared for NCAC records, by the Detachment Reports Officer in March 1944 concluded with the following statement:

There is reason to believe that Detachment 101, the first United States unit to form an intelligence screen and to organize and employ a large guerrilla army deep in enemy territory, has made a significant contribution to the success of the military operation in Burma. The G-2 of NCAC stated that the Detachment's efforts made it possible to fight the Japanese with more complete knowledge of enemy positions and movement than has been possible in most Theaters of this war. In the opinion of the Chief of Staff, the Detachment performed in an outstanding manner one of the most difficult and hazardous assignments that any military unit has ever been called upon to perform.*

9. Clearing the Shan States

Detachment 101 had demonstrated in the NCAC campaign the validity of Stilwell's belief that American-trained and led guerrillas could be of substantial support to Allied forces in actual combat. This success led to the assignment of a mission to be carried out without the support of other ground forces.

Lt. Gen. Sultan ordered 101 to clear the enemy from the Shan States down the Heho-Kengtung Road, thus securing the Burma Road against any possible counterattack and gaining control of the only escape route remaining to the Japanese in the central Shan States. The action would also assist the British in their drive east. The area defined was roughly 10,000 square

---

* During the North Burma campaign, American personnel at Detachment 101 decided that some appropriate recognition should be given the loyal Kachins, and requested that a medal be approved by Headquarters. The Rear Echelon immediately, but without authorization from Washington, prepared medals for the obviously deserving Kachins. In their well-meaning haste, however, they misinterpreted the cable as requesting the CMA medal, CMA actually being cable abbreviation for "comma." The medals, beautifully designed in the best tradition of fancy decorations, were delivered to 101 forward bases by the hundreds. 101 personnel immediately performed their usual task of making their improvisations better than the real thing, and conducted impressive ceremonies in Kachin villages where they gave village headmen and chief agents the rare American decoration, the "Civilian Military Award." Although the medals were ordered recalled by OSS/Washington, it was decided that such an action was impossible as it would cause ill-feeling among the natives and perhaps lead to loss of their further assistance.

miles, and it was specified that no enemy pockets of resistance were to be left.

Enemy forces were estimated to consist of 10,000 battle-hardened veterans, known to possess artillery, light tanks and motor transport, in addition to standard infantry armament.

Detachment 101 forces at this time numbered 3,200 American-led natives, but the bulk of the seasoned troops which had taken part in the Lashio campaign had been replaced. It was no longer practical to rely only on Kachins. The jungle tactics used in the Kachins' home territory were of little value under attack by large infantry forces supported by artillery and motorized columns. The area of operations had shifted to barren red-dirt hill country, which permitted the enemy to move artillery and supplies with greater ease and speed. Moreover, the Kachins were reluctant to leave their native regions. To counter Japanese artillery, 101 could rely on the 60th Fighter Squadron, one B-25 and several C-47's, combat cargo planes, left behind by NCAC to support 101 operations.

The nature of the 101 troops and their equipment prevented them from operating as regular infantry units. They relied upon hit-and-run tactics, or, if forced into pitched battles, inflicted the greatest possible number of casualties and then withdrew. On the basis of these operating principles, Detachment forces were divided into four principal battalions of 700 to 1,000 men each and a specific area assigned to each battalion.

After the fall of Lashio, the Detachment continued to press south in support of Chinese troops clearing the Lashio-Hsipaw road. By 10 April, guerrilla forces had advanced far south of the Chinese and were the only NCAC ground forces in contact with the enemy. The four battalions had been organized and were prepared to carry out their mission to clear the Shan States. The 1st Battalion engaged in several pitched battles wherein they sustained some losses, but such losses were only a fraction of those inflicted on the enemy. However, it was not the pitched battles but the cumulative effect of the small hit-and-run attacks which proved to be the decisive factor in the defeat of the enemy.

One ambush by the 1st Battalion on 17 May along the Lawksawk-Shwenyaung road deserves special mention. Hand grenades connected by primer cord were hidden every three yards along a hundred yard section of the road, while the ambush party took up positions at both ends. Two hundred Japanese came down the road with advance and rear guards of 25 men each. When the main body was inside the trap, the grenades were electrically detonated and the guerrillas opened fire. The Detachment suffered no casualties but the Japanese lost half their men.

Many smaller ambushes together with the destruction of bridges, motor transport and similar activity made all areas unsafe for the enemy and caused him to choose retreat rather than risk slow annihilation.

The 10th Battalion harassed the enemy in an area of 200 square miles for a period of two months during which hardly a day passed without action. On 25 April, an enemy force attempted to wipe out battalion headquarters. During a two-day battle the guerrillas drove off the attackers, killing 37 Japanese with a loss to themselves of two men. Harassing actions affected the enemy to such an extent that a force of 500 Japanese supported by artillery was sent north against the battalion headquarters. Although the guerrillas were forced back several miles, the Japanese losses in the offensive were so great that they gave it up after three days.

The 2nd Battalion distinguished itself in the siege on Loilem, which was fortified by a ring of enemy emplacements composed of pillboxes and bunkers some six feet in depth. An attack lasting over one week finally resulted in Japanese withdrawal.

The 3rd Battalion was responsible for an area containing a route of Japanese withdrawal and by 5 June was systematically patrolling the route.

During the entire Shan States campaign an exceptional degree of coordination was achieved between 101 and the 60th Fighter Squadron. 101 special agents operated far south of the combat line and continually supplied air targets which received extensive bombing action. Detachment 101 troops, as the only ground forces in contact with the enemy in the India-Burma Theater, had supplied all military intelligence in the area, with the exception of a small amount of data supplied by British Force 136 (SOE).

Detachment 101 had accomplished its mission by 15 June. The Heho-Kengtung withdrawal route could no longer be used by the enemy.* The area for which it was responsible had been cleared of the Japanese.

STATISTICAL SUMMARY OF ALL DETACHMENT 101 ACTIVITIES

Enemy killed (known)	5,447
Enemy killed or seriously wounded (estimated)	10,000
Enemy captured	64
Americans killed	15
Native personnel killed	184
Native personnel captured or missing	86
Bridges destroyed	51
Railroad trains destroyed	9
Military vehicles destroyed	277
Supplies destroyed (estimated) ..	2,000 tons
Supplies captured (estimated) ..	500 tons
Intelligence furnished NCAC	90 percent average
Targets designated for air action	65 percent average

* See attached summary below for operational statistics.

Enemy casualties resulting from air action instigated by the Detachment.................. 11,225 killed
885 wounded
Air Force personnel rescued..... 232
Greatest total number U. S. personnel, Det. 101.............. 131 officers
418 EM
American personnel not having had field service............ 5 officers
18 EM
Greatest number native personnel (Dec. 1944 - Feb. 1945).... 9,200
Agent groups with radio, parachuted or overland.......... 122
Total American personnel parachuted in.................... 87
Total native personnel parachuted in.................... 147
Total casualties from parachute jumps...................... 0

10. Deactivation of 101

Liquidation of Detachment 101 was begun in April and the Detachment was officially deactivated on 12 July 1945. It had been decided that after 1 July responsibility for the security of northern Burma would rest with British Civil Affairs Service. A British brigade remained for mopping-up purposes. All 101 personnel, both native and American, were evacuated by air within four days. Half of 101 military personnel were transferred to China, and the remainder reassigned to Detachment 404 or returned to the U. S.

D. SOUTHEAST ASIA

1. Establishment of OSS/SEAC

Had inter-Allied relationships been harmonious in the China-Burma-India Theater, it is probable that Detachment 404 would never have been created. Instead, OSS operations in the territory of the Southeast Asia Command would almost certainly have been conducted from an expanded Detachment 101 under the direct authority of the U. S. Theater Commander and as an integral part of the American military effort in the Theater.

The hostility toward OSS manifested by the Indian Government, the Headquarters of the Indian Army and the British clandestine organizations operating in the area—particularly British SOE—led Donovan to establish a new operational unit in the Theater, rather than to expand the basic one which already existed. This British hostility was, in part, a reflection of the bad relations that long prevailed between the American military forces in the Theater and all British civilian and military authorities. It was aggravated in the case of OSS, however, by the strong British misgivings about the political implications of American clandestine activities among the subject peoples of Southeast Asia.

By the summer of 1943 OSS-British relations were so bad that the status of Detachment 101 itself was being seriously impaired and its very existence was in danger. Hence, when it was decided at the Quebec Conference to superimpose an over-all Allied command with an integrated Anglo-American staff under the new Theater Commander, Admiral Lord Louis Mountbatten, upon all the American and British combat forces in the Theater, Donovan seized the opportunity to conclude a tentative agreement with Mountbatten permitting OSS to continue and even to expand operations in the new Southeast Asia Command. This agreement did not take final shape until Donovan reached New Delhi in November 1943.

Before it could be put into operation, a bitter five-way battle had to be resolved in New Delhi. The participants in this battle were OSS, striving for maximum operational freedom and maximum support from the American Theater Commander; British G. H. Q. India, which was reluctant to relinquish control of Allied clandestine activities to the new Southeast Asia Command (SEAC); the dominant British element in SEAC itself, which welcomed OSS participation in the Theater but hoped to effect a closer integration of OSS with British clandestine activities than OSS or the JCS were prepared to accept; Stilwell, the American Theater Commander, who felt that the risk of OSS coming under British political domination outweighed the advantages that would accrue from expanded operations; and Miles, head of U. S. Navy Group, China, who wished to conduct clandestine naval activities in Southeast Asia as well.

Miles and G. H. Q. India were eventually eliminated from the picture, and Donovan's visit to the Theater produced a compromise formula of which the following were the essential elements:

1. Detachment 101 remained under the close tactical control of the American military authorities in northern Burma. Nominally, 101 operations were to be cleared with "P" Division, SEAC, through U. S. Theater channels.

2. A new OSS unit was created for operations throughout the Theater, except in northern Burma. The officer who had been serving for several months on Stilwell's staff with the somewhat ambiguous title of Stra-

tegic Services Officer, CBI,* was appointed to organize and head this unit, which was designated Detachment 404.

3. The new OSS/SEAC establishment was, like all American forces in the Theater, subject to the administrative authority of the American Commanding General, CBI, and dependent upon him for shipping priorities, transport and other services. In addition, the U. S. Theater Commander retained the power to determine whether or not the operations and other activities of OSS/SEAC conformed to basic American policy and to his own Theater policies.

4. OSS/SEAC was to maintain headquarters at Headquarters SEAC, and all its operations were to be subject to the approval of a unit on Mountbatten's staff designated "P" Division, which was responsible for coordinating the work of all Allied clandestine operations agencies in the Theater.

5. Implicit in accepting the authority of "P" Division were two important principles: (a) The right of OSS to operate anywhere in the Theater, except when there was some direct or specific military objection to such operations; (b) the power of "P" Division to disapprove OSS operations programs when they did not serve the primary military interests of SEAC or when they might conflict with or endanger already established British (or other) clandestine operations.

Donovan, however, succeeded in securing from his discussions with Mountbatten the basic recognition on the part of the British of the OSS right to gather strategic intelligence independently, through its own agents, everywhere in the Theater that U. S. interests required, regardless of whether or not such intelligence was required or requested by SEAC. In other words, a distinction was made between OSS sabotage, guerrilla and intelligence operations of direct service to SEAC and wholly dependent upon the wishes of the Supreme Allied Commander, and intelligence-gathering activities primarily of service to the U. S. Theater Commander and the JCS.

This agreement as a whole, including its implicit and purely verbal provisions, meant that the British abandoned their opposition to the tactical mission of Detachment 101 in support of the American military campaign in northern Burma, and granted OSS wide latitude for what virtually constituted an independent American check on British intelligence reporting in the Theater. In exchange, it entailed accepting a close British supervision of OSS operational activities outside the 101 area, which could hardly have been refused in any event in a British-dominated Theater. It also meant supplying Mountbatten with a token force of specialized American troops for guerrilla and similar activities, valuable to him in view of the small representation of forces in the Theater. This token force included OSS saboteurs, guerrilla fighters, underwater swimmers and morale subversion experts. Their activities, in support of such SEAC military operations as took place were in line with American military policy of stimulating the maximum British effort in the parts of the Theater which were primarily a British responsibility, with only a moderate expenditure of American equipment and a minimal expenditure of American manpower.

OSS/SEAC played a significant role in implementing this policy. Its intelligence on the enemy situation, though never complete, was sufficient to supply some much-needed perspective on the claims of British intelligence which consistently tended to overestimate enemy capabilities. By its operational activity in Siam, in southern Burma and even in Malaya it spurred the British clandestine agencies to greatly intensified efforts. For example, the mere presence of an OSS unit on the Arakan coast * inspired British Force 136, the local

* See "Introduction" above.

* See "Arakan Field Unit," below.

394

SOE detachment, to accelerated and ultimately successful efforts in winning military recognition for the Burmese antifascist partisans lest OSS first establish effective contact with them.

This complex background of political conflict and compromise is essential to an understanding of OSS/SEAC. It had much to do with shaping what might be termed its operational personality and it had a determinant effect on relations with military authorities in the Theater.

2. Phases of Activity

The activity of OSS in the Southeast Asia Command falls into two distinct but organically related phases. In most of the first phase, extending from November 1943 to January 1945, OSS/SEAC consisted of Detachment 404—with headquarters and training camps in Ceylon—and Detachment 303 in New Delhi. The basic OSS mission was to begin clandestine operations against the enemy in furtherance of the military operations of the Southeast Asia Command; to render such direct services as the U. S. China-Burma-India Theater Command might direct, such as rescue of American flyers shot down over enemy territory; and to transmit to OSS/Washington intelligence or research material collected independently or through liaison with Allied agencies in India and Ceylon.

In the second phase, from January 1945 to the liquidation of OSS, all OSS units in India and Southeast Asia, including Detachment 101 and its rear supply base, Detachment 505 in Calcutta, were integrated in a new administrative entity called OSS/-India-Burma Theater. Detachment 101 maintained its administrative autonomy to a large degree in the reorganization, but Detachment 404 tended to lose its identity, its top staff officers becoming branch chiefs for all OSS activities in the Theater, while many of its operations personnel were transferred to Detachments 101, 505 and 303.

Although Detachment 404 was never abolished as an administrative unit, or even as an operational unit, it became more and more the headquarters organization for OSS in the Theater, and OSS/IBT became the executor of the mission originally assigned to OSS/SEAC. Nominally, OSS/-IBT also assumed final responsibility for the tactical mission of Detachment 101, in furtherance of American military operations in the Northern Combat Area Command between January 1945 and the liquidation of Detachment 101 in the summer of 1945. The really significant extension of the mission of OSS/SEAC after the formation of OSS/IBT lay, however, in assuming responsibility for the servicing functions of OSS/China through what became the OSS/-China supply base, Detachment 505 in Calcutta. In evaluating the contribution of OSS in the Theater, it must therefore be kept in mind that, through Detachment 505, OSS/IBT handled all personnel and supplies destined for OSS/China, in addition to the operational missions assigned to OSS/-SEAC and Detachment 101.

The main activity of Detachment 101 with the Northern Combat Area Command (NCAC), even after the inclusion of that Detachment in OSS/IBT, is treated elsewhere.* The activities of OSS/SEAC are here treated in their two phases: The activities of Detachments 404 (Ceylon) and 303 (New Delhi), as a whole, from their inception to 30 September 1945; and the activities of Headquarters, OSS/IBT, of Detachment 505 (Calcutta) and of certain phases of Detachment 101 (Burma) after January 1945. Thus operations on the Arakan coast of southern Burma and the contribution of Detachment 101 to OSS operations in Siam are here included as part of the general OSS effort on behalf of the Allied Southeast Asia Command.

This effort, though modest in terms of the larger Theaters, was on a considerable scale. During the 21 months of activity, operations were conducted in southern Burma, Siam, Malaya, the Andaman Is-

---

* See "Burma—Detachment 101" in "C" above.

lands, Sumatra and adjacent islands of the Netherlands East Indies, and, finally, in southern French Indochina. In addition, R&A and X-2 activities were conducted at numerous points in India and Ceylon.

At the beginning of January 1945, Detachment 404 alone numbered 595 officers, enlisted men and civilian personnel. At its peak strength, in the spring of 1945, OSS/-IBT, including Detachment 101, numbered approximately 1,500. A total of some 2,400 intelligence reports were transmitted to OSS/Washington, 215 native agents were trained and 125 different operations were launched.

The sparsely populated regions, long rough coast lines and mountainous or jungle-covered terrain of the Theater operating area made it fundamentally easy to penetrate into enemy-held territory. On the other hand, the primitive character of the natives in many areas and the absence among them of any deep hatred of the Japanese were as unusual and as formidable difficulties to .OSS as the profound American ignorance of Southeast Asia and the cultural and psychological obstacles to the recruiting, training and managing of competent and loyal native agents. The tremendous distances between bases and target areas and treacherous weather created peculiar hazards, and the very terrain which shielded agents and scouting parties from enemy observation often involved cruel physical hardships and serious health problems.

The tangled administrative structure of the Theater made it difficult—and for a time nearly impossible—to coordinate all OSS activities within it for maximum efficiency, and the jealous suspicion with which OSS was regarded by its Allied counterparts in a British-dominated zone was a constant impediment. Finally, the relatively slight strategic importance of the Theater, combined with the absence of any large-scale military operations during most of the period under consideration, inevi-

tably set a limit on the importance of the OSS contribution. Perhaps the greatest single service rendered to the armed forces, and the U. S. Government as a whole, by OSS in the Southeast Asia Command was that, in the face of innumerable difficulties, and despite formidable pressures, it maintained its status as a purely American agency and, by carrying out its assigned mission, supplied the JCS, the U. S. Theater Commander and the State Department with the only regular independent U. S. source of intelligence on the enemy that was available to them throughout much of the Theater. This was neither an easy nor an unimportant accomplishment.

3. Problems of Theater Liaison

The support and confidence of the Commanding General, CBI, were essential if OSS was to fulfill its mission. Uncertainties as to the proper channel and chain of command between him and OSS/SEAC, however, at first created complications. The CBI liaison officer at SEAC Headquarters, invariably a general officer, eventually became, through custom, the established channel except for routine matters. This greatly facilitated rapid decisions on OSS problems and enabled the Theater Commander to maintain the close supervision which OSS operations required. It did, however, tend somewhat to widen the gap between OSS and the Theater G-2. Relations between OSS and the U. S. Theater Command improved when the CBI Theater was split in two and all the OSS units south of the Hump were consolidated into OSS/-IBT.

Relations between OSS and the British, particularly between OSS and Force 136 (SOE), were conditioned by basic considerations of national policy. Only the integration of operational personnel in the two agencies or an agreement on exclusive spheres of operation in the Theater would have brought peace in their relations. U. S. policy ruled out integration; any effective agreement on spheres of activity was impeded by the clash of British imperial interests with the American desire for independent intelligence from all parts of the Theater. The various crises were ultimately resolved, and OSS maintained its status on the basis of the agreement arranged by Donovan in 1944, and the coordination afforded by "P" Division.

"P" Division was headed by a veteran British naval officer, with an OSS officer as his deputy. Its actual coordinating machinery was simple. Plans for operations were nearly always initiated by the clandestine services themselves and submitted to a weekly meeting, presided over by the head of "P" Division, and including representatives of OSS, SOE, SIS, the Supreme Commander's British Political Advisor, and staff specialists, such as the head of his Psychological Warfare Division, liaison officers from the Royal Navy and the Royal Air Force; and representatives of other military interests concerned with particular operations as required. If no objection was raised to a plan by one of the clandestine agencies or the Political Advisor, it was referred to the Royal Navy or the Royal Air Force, depending upon whether it involved air-drop or infiltration by submarine, to determine whether it was technically feasible or whether it conflicted with any other commitment.

The RAF maintained Special Duty squadrons for the use of the clandestine agencies, but the Eastern Fleet of the Royal Navy insisted upon combining clandestine operations with normal submarine patrols. The lack of adequate means of underwater transportation severely limited the operations of all the clandestine agencies. Except where submarine transportation was necessary and immediately obtainable, OSS generally sought to obtain air transportation from the American Theater Commander, especially when the nature of the operation made it possible to utilize the C-47's of the Combat Carrier squadrons based in eastern Bengal or in northern Burma.

Transportation approved, the staff specialists were then given an opportunity to express any comments they might have—for example, the Psychological Warfare Officer might request that a given operation be used secondarily to further some psychological warfare program. The plan was then formally approved by "P" Division and submitted to the Director of Intelligence and to the Chief of Staff for clearance. These obtained, the agency which had originated the plan was notified and from then on usually dealt directly with any military authorities concerned in its execution, with "P" Division intervening, when necessary, to eliminate administrative delays and expedite cooperation.

Apart from operations, "P" Division * acted as a general intermediary between the clandestine agencies and all the military or civilian authorities with whom they had to deal in regard to such matters as supply, housing and the recruitment of native agents or British military personnel. Although "P" Division itself was an organism of the Supreme Commander's staff, it managed to exercise some influence over the coordination of combat activities by clandestine agencies operating on the army, corps or task force level through persuading field commanders to set up their own miniature "P" divisions and by maintaining fairly close liaison with these field "P" officers. For example, by agreement with the American Theater Commander, the Commanding Officer of OSS Detachment 101 was designated as the "P" Division for the NCAC and was thus made responsible for coordinating his own and British clandestine activities in the area.

4. Problems of Command and Administration

Administrative problems loomed exceptionally large in the record of OSS/SEAC.

---

* Because of their special nature, neither the MO nor the X-2 activities of OSS came completely within the jurisdiction of "P" Division.

This was due basically to the combined effects of the geography, the military structure and the administrative history of the Theater as a whole.

The location of headquarters in Ceylon proved a serious handicap. When, in the spring of 1944, Admiral Mountbatten moved Theater Headquarters from New Delhi to Kandy, Ceylon, the Commanding Officer of OSS/SEAC was obliged to join in this military migration. Failure to do so would have violated the spirit of the Donovan-Mountbatten agreements. Since it was considered, probably correctly, that the Strategic Services Officer had to establish himself near SEAC headquarters, it was logical that OSS/SEAC should concentrate as much of its personnel and as many of its establishments as possible on the small island of Ceylon, the more so since it was originally expected that maritime means of transport would be utilized to a greater extent than air in operations and that the major military activity of the Theater would be directed toward Malaya and Sumatra.

These expectations proved unfounded, for reasons which OSS could not have foreseen. Ceylon proved logistically the worst spot that could have been chosen for headquarters in the whole Theater. Not only was the island excessively remote from both the fighting front and the main supply ports and military bases in India, but the air services linking it with other parts of the Theater were woefully inadequate. Even on Ceylon itself, poor communications seriously impeded contact between OSS headquarters in Kandy, the supply unit at Colombo and the training camps at Galle, Clodagh and Trincomalee.

This situation would have been serious even if all of OSS/SEAC could have been concentrated in Ceylon. Unfortunately, this was not the case. Because it operated under a divided chain of command, OSS/-SEAC had to maintain a liaison officer at CBI Theater Headquarters in New Delhi. This officer, whose main activity was obtaining transportation priorities for supplies and personnel, had to have a considerable clerical and communications staff. Thus, from the moment that the headquarters of OSS/SEAC moved from New Delhi to Kandy and the unit was divided into Detachments 303 and 404 (the move was completed in April 1944), vital functions of the Services Branch had to be coordinated between two points some 1,800 miles distant. With the foundation of OSS/IBT ten months later, the Services picture was further complicated by the addition of Detachment 505 in Calcutta, which became the most important Services base for OSS in the Far East. A Theater Services officer had functioned in Kandy prior to the creation of OSS/IBT, but afterwards the attempt to centralize the activities of the Services Branch at Headquarters was abandoned. In effect, the SSO/IBT was obliged to act as his own Services officer, devoting an excessive amount of time and energy to this phase of his command.

The work of other branches likewise could not be effectively coordinated from Headquarters. The MO Branch, for a number of technical reasons,* could not function properly from Ceylon and was obliged to establish its Branch headquarters for the Theater in Calcutta. This rendered supervision of its delicate activities more difficult and virtually cut it off from the other operational branches. Because the essence of X-2 operations was liaison with the British counter-espionage services in India, the Branch wished to establish its Theater headquarters at New Delhi with Detachment 303, and (though it was never formally allowed to do so) functioned for all practical purposes as if it had. The R&A unit, which dealt with Indian material, could only operate in India, so a semi-autonomous subdivision of the Branch was set up in Detachment 303.

There were also administrative difficulties in properly coordinating the activities of the various branches. The relative posi-

---

* See below.

tions of the individual branches ranged from the discarding of branch distinctions, as in Detachment 101, to the initial extreme branch consciousness at Detachment 404.

In terms of the immediate and specialized task it had to accomplish, Detachment 101 could see no advantage in the complex branch structure of OSS, and accordingly virtually abolished it in favor of a closer and more military integration of all personnel. Thus, while the whole of the Detachment served as an intelligence-gathering organization, it possessed no formal SI Branch, and was not by other means conducting true SI activities. Opportunities for collecting strategic intelligence in the jungle of northern Burma were rather rare, but they did sometimes occur without being adequately exploited. Above all, when such intelligence was collected it was not rapidly disseminated to all possible users. However, since 101's tactical contribution within NCAC was of such immense value, no strong attempt was made fully to integrate 101 intelligence activities into the general OSS framework.

On the other hand, Detachment 404 had begun operating as a highly branch-conscious unit. Upon the reorganization into OSS/IBT, the branches, instead of being abolished, were subordinated to the control of an Operational Planning Officer and a Theater Intelligence Officer, virtually a G-3 and a G-2, respectively. This formula was never wholly satisfactory: While it provided organizational order and formal allocation of functions, it tended to divorce the operations branches from control over their personnel who were sent into the field. SI, in particular, objected to the personnel whom it recruited and trained being arbitrarily diverted by the Operational Planning Officer to assignments of immediate priority instead of to SI missions long contemplated or awaiting approval.

On the other hand, it was felt that the scarcity of both agents and transportation ruled out, in most cases, operations conducted by or on behalf of a single branch; so far as possible each agent or party sent into enemy territory had to conduct activities on behalf of all the operational branches. Often this was not possible, but it was taken as the ideal at which to aim under the circumstances, and it implied joint planning, joint interpretation of results, and generally much closer interbranch collaboration between branches than Washington had envisaged.

A Planning Committee of branch heads (which was continually changing names, size, composition and functions) was also established. While, at its meetings the tensions generated by enforced branch coordination constantly erupted, it did, however, serve to focus the attention of branch heads upon problems to be faced, and the system of coordination gradually began to produce tangible results.

One vital result was the close participation of the R&A Branch in every phase of planning, from the determination of tactical objectives to the training techniques for native agents. Another was the acceptance of the principle that every operation against the enemy should produce some intelligence required by each of the intelligence branches. Also, the instruction programs of the Schools and Training Branch were kept abreast of the current operational requirements. This helped remedy one of the early deficiencies of inadequate or unrealistic training programs for operatives and agents. Finally, an efficient method was developed of distributing intelligence, obtained from operations, among the various intelligence branches. While the evaluation and dissemination of normal intelligence was the responsibility of the SI Reports Board, R&A and X-2 always had an opportunity to contribute to the interpretation of a given item before it was disseminated outside OSS.

Thus, a degree of functional coordination was attained in the planning and exploitation of operations by the operational branches at Detachment 404. Where the system was less successful was in coordinating the operational with the auxiliary branches. Special Funds and Communications worked smoothly with the operational branches, while Operational Supply, on the other hand, was never wholly satisfactory, due both to ignorance of supply problems on the part of planners and branch heads, and an insufficiently operational outlook on the part of the Services Branch which otherwise functioned efficiently. The same lack of operational indoctrination prevented the Medical Services Branch from making the maximum contribution to operations in a Theater which offered unique opportunities for medical intelligence and other related medical activities. The Visual Presentation Branch likewise was not used to the fullest extent in the training of native agents and in preparing for agents in the field visual aids on such matters as order of battle and the accurate identification of special enemy equipment. Certain individual branches presented more specific problems. Thus the R&D Branch, because of shortage of qualified personnel in Washington, was late in getting started and was always understaffed. These seem to have been the only reasons for its failure to make any useful contribution. The same applies to the CD Branch.

A small OG unit was set up at Detachment 404 with a special training camp at Galle on the west coast of Ceylon. It took part in a few scouting raids on the Arakan coast with the Arakan Field Unit in the winter of 1944-45 and was then sent to China, where there was a greater need for this activity.

It was expected that MU activities, because of the nature of the Theater, would play a considerable role, and a large unit, with a section of underwater swimmers and three 90-foot air-sea rescue craft (ARB's), was established at Detachment 404, with a marine base near Trincomalee. Most of the Unit went to the Arakan with the OG's and several maritime operations were launched with rather inconclusive results. It was found that the MU craft lacked sufficient range to operate effectively in the Theater. While additional fuel tanks on deck increased range, they decreased safety. Basically, however, the craft were too small for ocean conditions. This, combined with the fact that there were no suitable targets for the swimmers, caused the Branch to liquidate early. The boats were laid up, some MU personnel were sent to China. and others were given new assignments in the Theater. The remainder were used as escorting officers for submarine operations and as instructors for native agents.

An SO Branch was established early at Detachment 404 and plans for extensive SO activities were laid, but before they advanced very far, the head of the Branch and most of its personnel were called to China. Thereafter, OSS/IBT functioned without a proper SO Branch, but, despite this, projected large-scale SO activities in Siam. SI and SO personnel were used interchangeably in these activities. The experience of both OSS/IBT and Detachment 101 suggested that, for most wartime clandestine operations involving contact with native resistance groups, field personnel should be trained in both SO techniques and in intelligence procurement.

The MO Branch was first established at Kandy, then moved to Colombo, then to Calcutta due to greater access there to printing and paper facilities. Valuable services were performed by individual MO personnel at various times, but the contribution of the Branch as a whole was negligible. The equally meager results achieved by British "black" psychological warfare activities in the Theater would seem to indicate that the area was a poor one for MO.

Similarly, the X-2 Branch was never able to make a significant contribution in OSS/-IBT. Stations were maintained in all parts of India, particularly the cities of Bombay, Karachi, Calcutta and New Delhi. Although its officers were handicapped by lack of regional qualifications for the area, the principal reason for its failure was lack of cooperation from its British counterparts. This was directly in line with British reluctance to permit U. S. clandestine activities within India.

Except for Communications, no Branch rendered broader services than R&A. A peculiarity of the Branch in IBT was that it was almost excessively operations-minded, thus tending to neglect the preparation of strategic studies and reports for Washington in favor of assisting or supporting local operations. The terrain and other studies completed in connection with OSS operational plans were often so comprehensive and original that they were of great assistance to SEAC staff planners as well.

5. Recruiting and Training

The recruiting of native agents presented a crucial challenge to OSS/SEAC. Except for a small group of Siamese students and a still smaller group of Indonesians, no agents qualified for operations in the area could be found in the U. S. This situation was aggravated by an acute shortage of Americans with the regional experience and linguistic skills requisite for duty as instructors or conducting officers.

In India there were a few refugees from Burma and Malaya, and Indians themselves, or overseas Chinese who could be used as agents in certain regions. The Dutch colonial authorities, temporarily established in Ceylon, had a small personnel pool of Indonesians. Recruiting from either of these two sources was difficult for OSS, however, because of the intense competition, not only among the clandestine services but between all of them and various British military departments, chiefly Civil Affairs. OSS, being American, was at a disadvantage compared to the British and the Dutch in the scramble for native personnel. Under "P" Division, a system was finally evolved, whereby OSS shared equally with the British clandestine services in the meager native personnel resources of the Theater, and all the clandestine services as a group were given reasonable good priorities as against other military claimants. Rosters of all available native personnel were prepared at SEAC Headquarters from data supplied by the India Army, the Indian Government, the Government of Burma, the Dutch colonial government and other official sources. Recruiting outside this roster was banned, save in exceptional circumstances. To obtain the service of a native listed on the roster, OSS had to prove a greater operational need than any of the other claimants, and the native himself had to be willing.

Potential agents obtained in this way, plus a small number loaned or turned over to OSS/SEAC by Detachment 101, were too few in number, and usually of too low quality, to supply the organization's extensive operational needs. Consequently, OSS embarked on a large-scale program—seemingly fantastic, but actually quite successful—of recruitment in enemy territory. Whenever possible, it was made a secondary objective for all OSS operations to recruit and exfiltrate new native personnel. In Siam, where there was a large, well-organized underground and Allied planes could land safely on secret jungle airfields, this program presented no serious difficulties. It was not so easy on the closely patrolled, heavily policed Tenasserim coast of southern Burma, but it was done there nevertheless. One or two reliable, well-trained Karen * agents would be landed from submarines with instructions to set up a clandestine intelligence post communicating with Ceylon by W/T, contact their friends and select one or two reliable persons, willing to act as agents, who could be picked up by submarine at the next rendezvous and brought back to Trincomalee for training.

More forthright and even rather desperate methods were used along the Malayan and Indonesian coasts. The initial recruit-

* Southern Burmese natives.

ment was usually made at the point of a gun. The future agent would be taken prisoner by an OSS scouting party along some lonely shore or upon some isolated island, or an OSS escorting officer in the course of a submarine sortie would persuade the skipper of the submarine to board some small native craft and take the crew prisoners. The prisoners would be given glowing accounts of the life of a clandestine agent, promised big pay and confronted with the brutal alternatives of spending the rest of the war in an internment camp or returning to their homes in a few months as Allied agents. When such prisoners accepted employment as agents, they had to be listed on the SEAC roster and shared—if sufficiently numerous—with the British clandestine services, but by gentlemen's agreement, OSS always had first choice in the allocation of the human booty. Consequently, this modern wartime version of blackbirding was eagerly pursued and proved a valuable source of personnel.

A less high-handed and dramatic but no less dangerous form of recruitment was practiced along the Arakan coast of Burma, when the XV Indian Corps began its advance. Upon entering a newly liberated town or village, the OSS unit attached to XV Corps would offer employment to the most likely-looking natives encountered, and then, after two or three days' rudimentary training on the spot, would send them back into enemy territory to collect intelligence. The security hazard in these recruiting methods was obviously very great and the possibility of falling upon really good agent material slight. Curiously, although many of the native agents, particularly those recruited under duress, proved worthless for one reason or another, no case of treachery or attempted treachery was ever recorded.

Agent recruits were normally brought to Ceylon and sent for a few days to the "W" school at Clodagh in the center of the Island. The course here was primarily an assessment one. At first, the elaborate psychological techniques of assessment developed in the U. S. produced results of little value when applied to Asiatics, at least when applied by psychologists who were not familiar with Asiatic cultures and languages. However, the course as a whole furnished some useful indications as to the aptitudes of the potential agent. If the school staff judged him possible agent material, he was sent to "Y" camp near Trincomalee. Unless the student were earmarked for an early operation and specialized training of some kind was directed by Headquarters, he was put through a general training course in such subjects as use of weapons, unarmed combat, small boat work, jungle-craft, mapreading and mapmaking, demolitions, W/T, and intelligence gathering.

Students at "Y" lived in separate huts according to nationalities. Other huts, removed from the main camp area, were used to house agents training for specific operations. American conducting or escorting officers were assigned to such groups from the moment they went into training and sometimes lived in the same huts with the native students. In any case, they were obliged to accompany them through their different courses and they sometimes assisted in the teaching staff. The necessity of keeping in the same camp elementary students, some of whom would be weeded out as their deficiencies came to light, student-agents preparing for specific operations, and full-fledged agents returned from operations and awaiting reassignment, created a difficult problem for the camp security officer and staff.

But the greatest problem at "Y" was teaching agents, often illiterate in their own languages, to send code and read maps in English and to master the intricacies of Japanese order of battle. The instructors frequently had to operate through interpreters or even by sign language. Though several of the instructors and conducting officers spoke one or more of the Asiatic tongues, none was familiar with all the languages represented in the student body. Visual aids of various kinds were used, though not intensively enough. Many of the students turned out to be naturally keen observers and to have good memories. When visual aids were properly applied, the results were sometimes amazingly satisfactory. Thus, when accurate wooden scale models of various types of Japanese radar and communications equipment likely to be confused with radar were exhibited to Siamese students who had never heard of electronics, they quickly learned to distinguish between them, and, when sent into the field, reported accurate descriptions of the equipment at suspected Japanese radar posts.

The training system was far from perfect. It was notably weak on the intelligence side, and sometimes wasted hours teaching "jungle craft" to men born in the jungle. Yet, time after time, following two or three months of instruction, it succeeded in converting the most unlikely human material into agents capable of operating in enemy territory without being detected, and even on occasion of producing relatively high-level intelligence.

6. Operations

OSS/SEAC was confronted from the start with a series of strategic, logistic and policy problems which were to exercise a decisive influence in shaping the course of its operations. The first of these problems was the inaccessibility of the most important targets of clandestine warfare in the Theater. The other problems were political in nature—gaining support from American Theater authorities and recognition from the Allied Theater Command.

Distances were the basic problem. The main specific targets for OSS were Bangkok, Rangoon, Singapore and Palembang—in about that order of importance. These were the enemy centers where intelligence of some strategic value might be found,

where physical or psychological sabotage, if it were conducted, was likely to have the most significant effects. A secondary area of interest was the Kra Isthmus, the economically, rich, strategically vital, politically unsettled zone of the Malay Peninsula from Penang to Tavoy.

From the viewpoint of the American campaign in the Pacific, the most important area of all was the coast of French Indochina. This actually lay outside the Southeast Asia Command, as the boundaries were interpreted by the JCS, so OSS/SEAC was not authorized to conduct operations there except after involved inter-theater arrangements. However, the possibility of an extension of SEAC Theater lines—such as finally occurred—had to be kept in mind and the Siam-French Indochina border had to be considered a potentially significant area of SEAC operations.

All of these places or zones of interest were inaccessible to direct clandestine penetration when OSS/SEAC first began operation. Singapore and Palembang were beyond the range of land-based aircraft* and inaccessible to approach by submarine. Rangoon and Bangkok were within air range but set in the midst of vast rice plains which offered little or no initial concealment for agents. The French Indochina-Siam borderland and the Kra Isthmus were open to penetration if one knew where to penetrate, but were difficult to scout in advance.

It was therefore concluded by the OSS planners—either immediately or after fruitless attempts on these targets—that in order to operate in the areas of main interest it would be necessary, first of all, to establish bases in more accessible parts of the enemy's domain. The optimum requirements were: A base, accessible by sea, on the Arakan coast of Burma between Akyab and Bassein; a clandestine air base in the wild country on the Burma-Siam border;

* Carrier-based aircraft of the British East India Fleet were unavailable for OSS operations.

an island or coastal base, accessible by submarine, along the Kra Isthmus; a jungle air base in the highlands of Malaya, plus a sea base on an uninhabited island at the entrance of the Malacca straits; a base accessible, by submarine, on the southwest coast or southwestern tip of Sumatra; and a submarine or hydroplane base in the Gulf of Siam near the Siam-Indochina border.

Since submarine transportation available for clandestine operations was so critically short, the plan was formed at one time to complement this system of clandestine bases with a refueling station in the Andaman Islands so that craft of the MU Branch in quiet weather could cross the Bay of Bengal to the Kra Isthmus from a base on the Chittagong or Arakan coast. This plan was finally abandoned, partly because the MU air-sea rescue craft (ARB's) were too small for extensive long distance operations across the Bay of Bengal, and partly because the rapid expansion from the original OSS penetration in Siam made it unnecessary to maintain any longer the island base which had been established off the Kra Isthmus.

The problem of conducting operations to discover and establish suitable bases was paralleled by the need to conduct operations to recruit natives for further operations. The result, unless one were thoroughly familiar with the problems of clandestine activity in the Theater, was a series of seemingly uncoordinated and unimportant operations, but, bit by bit, a definite pattern emerged and the strategic concept upon which the operational program was based proved itself sound.

Since, however, many months had to elapse before any really valuable intelligence could be expected from such operations, OSS felt impelled to squeeze the last drop of intelligence out of every single operation in the course of justifying its activities to the Theater Command. Lacking the opportunity to collect tactical intelligence of a significant nature, the agents were also briefed to collect scraps of technical, medical, economic, political and other specialized bits of information they might come across. Where nothing else was available, they collected topographic and hydrographic data. Coast watchers sitting on lonely islands off the Malayan coast, scanning the seas for non-existent enemy cruisers, destroyers or even freighters, meticulously reported every native junk and canoe sighted. The reports on the movements of these small coastal craft—which were carrying the bulk of Japanese military supplies in that area—were correlated by the R&A Branch with the copious but unsystematic logs of British submarine commanders, resulting in the location of previously unknown ports and hideouts for coastal traffic.

Gradually, it was discovered that it was often possible to prepare studies of considerable interest for specialized branches of the Army and Navy by piecing together scraps of information picked up by low-grade agents operating in even the isolated parts of the Theater. Technical and specialized intelligence of various types was developed to an unanticipated degree by OSS/SEAC, and some of its most successful activities were in this field. Although this discovery was more or less accidental on the part of OSS, it revealed a striking gap in normal military intelligence procurement, as well as demonstrating how clandestine operations could help fill the gap.

The same need to justify operations caused OSS/SEAC to utilize its operational personnel for all sorts of ancillary services to the regular American forces in the Theater, particularly to the Air Forces, whose cooperation was essential to the success of its major missions. This led, in time, to the development of an extensive chain of weather-reporting stations in enemy territory, supplying daily weather data to the Tenth Air Force Headquarters in Calcutta, and to such close cooperation with air-force rescue and escape work that the security of OSS field posts was sometimes compromised. Whenever possible, specialized services of this sort were included as secondary objectives in operations planned as part of the main OSS program, but some operations were launched exclusively for such purposes.

Finally, the immediate needs and wishes of the Supreme Allied Commander conditioned the planning of OSS operations. The whole of OSS was more or less on sufferance in a British-dominated Theater: OSS/SEAC was to some degree cover for Detachment 101, while other activities of OSS/SEAC were cover for the more high-level intelligence activities in the Theater in which Washington was primarily interested. Thus, some operations were launched by OSS/SEAC primarily with the idea of winning British good-will.

The first operation by Detachment 404 in this category was an arduous, dangerous and ultimately valueless reconnaissance of Simalur Island, off the west coast of Sumatra, which would have been a mission for Mountbatten's Commandos except for administrative difficulties at that time which prevented their use. The same diplomatic considerations led to an overly-generous assignment of personnel—including OG's, underwater swimmers and most of the MU craft—to the XV Indian Corps for tactical operations on the Arakan coast,* though this was also part of the plan for establishing a base accessible to Rangoon.

As a comprehensive strategic program, the OSS operational plan did not attain its objectives. The largest single operation, however, the penetration of Siam, was highly successful. Not only Bangkok, but ultimately the whole of Siam, was covered by an SO and SI network whose extent compared favorably with the major European underground movements.

As for specific targets, Rangoon was not penetrated until a few hours before the Brit-

---

* See below.

ish forces entered. Singapore was never penetrated and Palembang was never reached, though both the Malayan and the Indonesian operations produced valuable intelligence after VJ-Day. The Kra-Tenasserim area was successfully penetrated, yielding valuable intelligence, but the permanent bases originally planned in that area were found to be both unnecessary and untenable.

The major operations, such as into Siam, and the various post-surrender teams, are treated in detail in separate sections below. The following individual operations are briefly summarized to indicate the wide range of missions undertaken by OSS and some of the difficulties which had to be overcome:

RIPLEY: One of the earliest operations launched by Detachment 404, this was also over the longest distance. The aim was to establish a high-caliber Indonesian SI agent with W/T transmitter in the Palembang area on Sumatra. As this crossed theater lines, special authorization from General MacArthur had to be secured. The agent was landed from a British submarine on the coast of Java early in June 1944, with the intent of proceeding to Sumatra by ferry or native craft. He lost his W/T set and was arrested almost immediately after his landing. He managed to talk himself out of a Japanese jail, however, and was waiting in Batavia with much valuable information about the Indonesian republican movement when the OSS post-surrender team arrived there.

Other attempts to penetrate Sumatra were equally unsuccessful. A party of native agents was established in the Batoe Islands off the western coast of Sumatra early in September 1944, but they were eventually betrayed by some natives they had approached and were seized by the Japanese.

BALMORAL: Beginning in September 1944, OSS launched a series of operations in the southern Mergui Archipelago aimed at discovering a suitable permanent base for subsequent operations along the coast and to the mainland. Finally, on 26 November 1944, a party consisting of three American officers, an American corporal and a Malay W/T operator was established on Chance Island in the Mergui group. The size of the group was expanded to fifteen; a weather station and a coast-watching station were established; explorations of nearby islands were carried out; and native fishermen were contacted and intelligence was obtained from them. Ten of the natives were forcibly "recruited" and sent back to Ceylon; one minor demolitions job was accomplished; escape-dumps for Allied aviators were established on neighboring islands; and contact was made with the Siamese underground on the mainland. Finally, after more than five months of operation, the party was withdrawn as this section of the coast was closely patrolled by the enemy and it was felt that the development of the clandestine network in peninsular Siam rendered it unnecessary.

NOAH: This operation was originally conceived as part of a daring plan to capture a Chinese junk, substitute an OSS-trained crew, and sail up and down the Malayan coast of the Malacca Straits collecting intelligence and organizing cells for the penetration of Singapore. The first stage, successfully carried out in December 1944, was to establish a coast-watching party of two Malays and two Chinese with W/T on a small island of the Sembilan group. This station was maintained for several months and some useful maritime intelligence was obtained, but enemy vigilance was so intense that the agents finally lost their nerve and were withdrawn.

CAIRNGORM: This was one of the most spectacular and daring clandestine operations attempted in the Theater. One American officer and three Chinese agents were parachuted into the highlands of Malaya at the end of November 1944. Their mission was to contact Chinese guerrillas believed to be operating in that general area. The drop-point selected was chosen because, from aerial photographs, there appeared to be a clearing in the jungle at that spot and because it was at the extreme range of B-24's based in India. No other information about the drop-point was available; nothing was known about enemy dispositions in the area, and no fixed plan existed for exfiltrating or even supplying the party in the future. If no feasible plan for eventual exfiltration could be worked out after they had scouted the countryside, they were simply to remain in the jungle until the end of the war. This is exactly what the party did. Their W/T was damaged and the operator badly injured in the drop. Three subsequent attempts to discover their camp from the air and drop a new W/T set failed, mainly because the planes could not carry enough gas to do a thorough reconnaissance of the area and return to base. Eventually, another OSS officer was dropped to a British clandestine party in northern Malaya and contact was made with the original CAIRNGORM group, which was found to have taken charge of a small guerrilla band that had been effectively harassing the enemy for months. All members of the party survived this extraordinary adventure.

BACON: Like several other minor operations, this one turned out to have unexpectedly good results. Three Americans and a Malay W/T operator were landed from a British submarine on North Andaman Island in January 1945. They discovered a site for an MU base and set up a weather station, thus achieving their main mission. They then began a thorough exploration on this enemy-occupied island and eventually discovered and photographed a Japanese radar station whose existence had, up to that time, been considered uncertain.

Arakan Field Unit: This was the name for the OSS unit attached to XV Indian Corps on the Arakan coast. It consisted of 175 officers and men, mostly OG and SI. A number of short-range operations were carried out by this group, both overland and maritime. Originally established by Detachment 404, the Unit was taken over and given improved leadership by Detachment 101 when the Theater was reorganized. Though not successful in its original aim of launching deep-penetration operations into the Rangoon area, the Unit was commended by the British for valuable tactical intelligence services.

After the liberation of Rangoon, the advance party of the Arakan Unit functioned like the city teams organized by OSS in Europe, collecting what intelligence material the enemy had not removed. Headquarters were then established in Rangoon and the Unit became a full-fledged Detachment, designated 505a. As such, it played a valuable role in supporting the Siamese operations.

A similar unit, of SI, R&A and X-2 personnel, was formed to accompany the projected British landing on the Malayan coast. When this landing was effected after the Japanese surrender, this Unit formed the nucleus for OSS city teams in Kuala Lumpur, Singapore and, later, the Dutch East Indies.

7. OSS Operations in Siam

The initial OSS penetration of Siam was made by Siamese students recruited in the U. S. and infiltrated across the border from bases in China.* The progress made by these agents was unsatisfactory. A later attempt to introduce more Free Siamese agents into peninsular Siam proved that such agents, if discovered by the Siamese police, were taken in custody to Bangkok. While they might be allowed to communicate by radio with OSS, they were only supplied with such intelligence as the Chief of Police was able or willing to give them. They were, however, kept concealed from the Japanese.

---
* See "China" below.

It was therefore decided at Detachment 404 to try to effect direct contact with the Regent of Siam, Luang Pradit, taking care to prevent the agent from being discovered by the Siamese police, at least until he had completed his mission. The need for secrecy was considered so great that it was considered inadvisable to clear this operation with the British, who themselves were in contact with the Chief of Police through British-dispatched agents in his custody.

Authorization was accordingly obtained from Stilwell to make a secret personnel drop in northern Siam from American aircraft at the end of the 1944 monsoon season. The two best Siamese agents were selected for this mission, one of them having close family ties with the Regent. Their instructions were to contact Luang Pradit secretly, inform him of the desire of OSS to organize clandestine operations in conjunction with the Siamese underground movement, and to press for permission to introduce an OSS liaison officer into Bangkok. The Regent was further to be informed—unofficially— of the sympathetic view of Siam's predicament taken by the U. S. State Department and offered the use of OSS channels for communicating with the American Government and the Free Siamese mission in Washington. The difficulty that both OSS and the British had been having with the Chief of Police was frankly explained to the agents, who were members of the Regent's political party, and they were instructed to attempt no intelligence activities until after they had seen the Regent.

The drop was faulty and the two agents became separated and had much difficulty in reaching the capital. They finally succeeded, however, and after some delay were authorized to send to Ceylon a message of greetings from the Regent and the expression of his willingness to receive an OSS liaison officer. It was final confirmation that Luang Pradit himself headed the underground. Since it proved impossible to find in one man all the qualities desired for this delicate mission, two officers were finally sent, representing SI and SO, respectively. One of them had been an American businessman in Siam before the war; the other was a young New York lawyer, at that time Chief of the SO Branch at Detachment 404. They reached Bangkok in January 1945, having been landed from a British-operated Catalina at Goh Kaidar Island in the Gulf of Siam, off the coast near the French Indochina border, and picked up by a launch of the Royal Siamese Navy, manned by members of the pro-Allied underground, which brought them to Bangkok.

The situation in Siam was different from any that had ever confronted OSS in an enemy-occupied country.* Instead of a resistance movement, such as was encountered in European countries, there existed in Siam what might best be described as a patriotic governmental conspiracy against the Japanese in which most of the key figures of the state were involved. The Regent himself, the Minister and Chief of Police, the Minister of the Interior, the Minister of Foreign Affairs, senior officers of the armed service, and many other ranking officials belonged to it.

At the same time, the movement was selective: In one government department, the chief might be an active member of the conspiracy while his deputy was not; in another department, the situation might be reversed. In one sense, the whole Siamese Army and Air Force constituted a guerrilla group potentially at the disposal of OSS, while the various intelligence services of the Siamese Government became, ipso facto, the OSS/SI network in that country.

It seemed a dazzling prospect, but, viewed critically, there was an enormous gap between the potential value of the Siamese

* Subsequent somewhat analogous OSS operations were mounted towards Hungary and the German armies in northern Italy. See "Secret Surrender Negotiations," Part VII, Europe - Africa Section.

underground and its immediate usefulness. The forces which OSS would have available to utilize for the prosecution of clandestine warfare were ill-equipped, poorly trained and uncoordinated. Except for a few scraps of rather low-grade intelligence, this national underground had so far contributed nothing to the Allied war effort, and the peculiar treatment accorded the earlier American and British agents sent into the country, who had been detected, suggested, at the very least, a dangerous lack of cooperation between the Regent and the Chief of Police.

In the first flush of enthusiasm at the unexpected success of their mission, and in the warmth of the welcome given them by the highest personalities of the Siamese state, the OSS officers underestimated what was really the most significant element in the situation: The fact that they were not dealing with the usual underground groups, but with the responsible and official heads of a sovereign state, naturally and properly concerned with obtaining for their country the greatest possible benefits at the least cost.

There was no reason to doubt the anti-Japanese and pro-Allied sentiment of the underground leaders, nor their conviction in the final victory of the Allies, but fundamentally they were motivated less by hatred of the Japanese, or sympathy with Allied war aims, than by the patriotic desire to serve the long-term interests of Siam. This motivation could have led the Regent and his followers to a policy of only verbalizing their sympathy with the Allies and taking action only at the last moment, if at all, thus sparing Siam from enemy reprisals. Very probably, the Siamese had originally hoped to safeguard their post-war position with the Allies by some such painless method.

As long as contact with the underground government in Bangkok was maintained only through Siamese agents and confined to the purely tactical level, it was possible for the Siamese to follow a wait-and-see

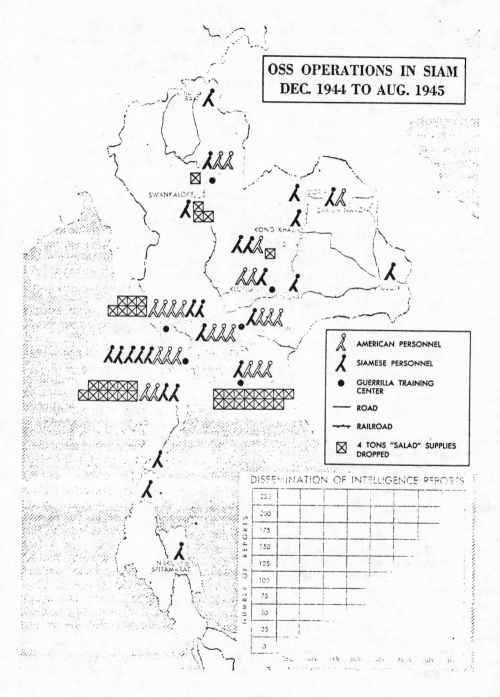

OSS OPERATIONS IN SIAM
DEC. 1944 TO AUG. 1945

AMERICAN PERSONNEL

SIAMESE PERSONNEL

GUERRILLA TRAINING CENTER

ROAD

RAILROAD

4 TONS "SALAD" SUPPLIES DROPPED

DISSEMINATION OF INTELLIGENCE REPORTS

225
200
175
150
125
100
75
50
25
0

DEC   JAN   FEB   MAR   APR   MAY   JUN   JUL

policy. By sending two American officers into Bangkok to discuss policy on the highest level with the Regent himself, OSS forced his hand and obliged him to commit himself to a course of action from which there was no withdrawing and only slight possibilities of major withholding. It was an achievement far more important than the discovery—or even the creation—of a normal resistance movement.

While the OSS officers probably did not realize the full implications of their success, they shrewdly diagnosed the peculiar character of the situation in Siam and developed an operational plan to meet it. To derive the fullest benefit from Siamese cooperation, they argued, it was necessary, first of all, to emphasize the political significance of the contact with the U. S. Government through OSS.* Yet the best political card OSS could play in Siam was to hold out hope of official American support to Siam in her struggle to maintain her independence and territorial integrity against suspected British designs.

This was a most delicate matter, for not only had care to be taken not to embarrass the U. S. Government, but it was also necessary to avoid stirring up the Siamese against the British. Military considerations required that Siam cooperate with the British clandestine services as well as OSS, and in the interests of the Siamese themselves it was essential to discourage any behavior that might be interpreted as obstructionism by the British.

Obviously, to carry out this policy, the fullest cooperation and the closest supervision of the U. S. State Department were essential. Both were obtained. All phases of OSS activity in Siam, including what to superficial examination might seem purely military activities, were carefully coordi-

* It should be noted that OSS was not authorized to make any commitments on behalf of the U. S. Government, and the State Department itself at that time had not formulated a definitive Siamese policy.

nated with American foreign policy, both in Washington by the Thai Committee (Thaicom), composed of representatives of OSS/-Washington SI and SO officers and State Department officials, and in the Theater by the political advisor to the U. S. Theater Commander. The success of the policy as a whole served as a striking illustration of the results obtainable wherever really close and confidential relations existed between OSS and the State Department.

Next, the OSS representatives in Bangkok emphasized strongly that, in operating in Siam, OSS should look upon the Regent as the head of a friendly state and the chief of all clandestine activities in his area. The Siamese were to be supplied, advised, prodded; but no attempt should be made to create a separate American organization in the country. Everything must be done through the Siamese underground movement. It was recognized that to obtain the fullest use of the Siamese underground it would be essential to have OSS liaison officers and instructors, not only in Bangkok but scattered at strategic points throughout the country. Because the Siamese Army was not everywhere considered completely trustworthy—and from political motives of his own—the Regent was eager to build up a separate guerrilla force, cooperating with the secret police and the patriotic elements in the Army, but under his personal control.

The Regent's attitude gave the OSS officers a chance, in effect, to make an independent American check on the extent of Siamese cooperation, and thereby to assure it. They proposed therefore—and Luang Pradit enthusiastically agreed—that OSS should send in SO instructors to be attached to the various guerrilla groups the Regent would organize throughout the country. The Regent further agreed that these guerrilla groups would be established as far as possible at points of greatest strategic interest to OSS, and that the American liaison officers would bring their own W/T operators and communicate directly with OSS headquarters.

In the Regent's mind the whole plan was geared to Allied invasion of Siam, preferably an American landing on the coast of the Gulf of Siam, and the entire Siamese Army, as well as the guerrilla units, would be used to strike a surprise blow at the Japanese on D-Day.

After working out in considerable detail a tentative plan of future operations with the Regent, one of the OSS officers returned to OSS headquarters by the way he had come, leaving the other officer to maintain the liaison with the Siamese underground and to edit the copious flow of intelligence which was now coming to the OSS "mission".*

Because of the exceptional importance of the matter, the OSS officer was flown to Washington, after reporting to the U. S. Theater Commander in New Delhi. In Washington he submitted the Regent's proposals to OSS headquarters and was closely questioned by officials of the War and State Departments. In general, the proposed OSS activities in Siam were approved, but the hope of any American military operations in Siam was scotched, and the implementation of the OSS program made subject to the approval of U. S. Theater Commander, who would have to provide transportation and supplies for it. The OSS officer returned to the Theater and was re-infiltrated to Bangkok.

Considerable difficulty was encountered in obtaining Theater approval. Theater Headquarters was interested in the intelligence coming from Siam but could see little value in the guerrilla training program. OSS fought desperately to convince the The-

ater Commander that the continued flow of intelligence from Siam depended upon furnishing the arms, supplies and instructors requested by the Siamese.* It was explained that not only did the program present a possibility of supervising native intelligence efforts by American officers at key points throughout the country, but that the program as a whole was necessary to convince the Siamese of America's keen interest. Unless the Siamese were convinced that America attached great importance to clandestine activities in Siam and that Siamese cooperation was really appreciated by the American Government, there was inadequate incentive for them to take the trouble and run the risks necessary to obtain high-grade intelligence.

Though these arguments failed to convince Theater Headquarters in New Delhi, they finally convinced the Joint Chiefs of Staff in Washington, and OSS was authorized to proceed with the program.** Several valuable months were lost in the process, however, so that by the middle of August 1945, OSS had only seven fully effective guerrilla bases, though several others were in the process of being developed. British SOE (Force 136), with the fullest support from British military forces in the Theater, had, in the meantime, forged ahead and established an extensive chain of Anglo-Siamese training camps throughout the country.

OSS efforts were re-directed towards intelligence procurement. Once it was clear that no American military operations would take place in Siam and that any British operations there would be of only slight interest to the United States, OSS shifted the emphasis in its Siamese plans from SO to SI activities, while continuing to press for the training and supply program which was considered necessary to strengthen intelligence activity.

---

* The "mission" was housed in a government palace close to the Regent's own palace, and for reasons of security the OSS officers were kept confined to one shuttered room during the daylight hours. The strain and the isolation caused temporary mental derangement of the remaining OSS officer, necessitating his relief. See below.

---

* The supply operations to Siam were designated "SALAD."
** JCS 1271, 16 June 1945.

411

To improve communications with Bangkok, which was just as vital for SI as for SO purposes, OSS secured from the Siamese underground the use of a remote airfield, hidden in the hilly jungle of north-central Siam. There American C-47's from bases in India or southern Burma could make dawn landings without much fear of enemy detection. Personnel or supplies for the Bangkok "mission" would then be transferred to a Siamese military plane which would land at dusk on the Siamese-held part of the Japanese air base of Don Muang, a few miles outside Bangkok. Immediately upon landing, the plane would be wheeled into a Siamese hangar and the freight or passengers would be placed in a curtained limousine and whisked into the city. To facilitate these movements, a safer and larger headquarters had been furnished OSS in an area of the capital studded with Siamese military and police barracks and not patrolled by the Japanese.

At the jungle airfield, which was near the little town of Pukeo, an American liaison officer was appointed, and for purposes of local protection he was authorized to distribute some arms and give some instruction to the guerrilla forces guarding the field. Similarly limited SO activities had been authorized by the Theater Commander at other spots, in connection with intelligence-gathering activities, pending decision on the main OSS guerrilla program. Thus, though more slowly than it wished, OSS was able to go ahead with the program of introducing American officers into Siam and to start at least token training programs on the strength of assuring local protection.

The first intelligence and training post set up was in the Kanchanburi area, near the strategically vital Bangkok-Moulmein railroad. Soon after, posts were established at the Siamese naval base of Sattahib and in the Lao tribal area along the French Indochina border. Depending on their targets, OSS parties were either landed at the

Pukeo field and transported from there to their final destinations by Siamese military plane, or else dropped by parachute.

Where it was not practical, at least immediately, to establish an American officer, OSS arranged with the Regent to establish an OSS-trained Siamese agent to transmit intelligence direct to OSS headquarters in Ceylon by W/T. Thanks to this system, OSS had direct coverage of every strategically important area in the country, in addition to the intelligence collected by the Siamese Government itself and made available to OSS at Bangkok.

Bangkok itself proved the most important source of intelligence in Siam. It seemed a bonanza at first, and indeed its volume remained tremendous. When the first flush of excitement had worn off, however, it was realized that much of this intelligence was of inferior quality. The subject matter was often extremely interesting. For example, there were Japanese analyses of Allied intentions; Japanese statements concerning their own intentions, communicated to the Intelligence Division of the Siamese Army; and reports on air-raid damage in Japan from the Siamese Legation there. The reporting of such information, however, was often lamentable. Significant details were omitted, facts were reported inaccurately, leads were not followed up and there was no careful evaluation of sources.

It soon became apparent that there was literally not one Siamese official or officer in the underground who understood the techniques of SI work—in fact, even the normal categories and criteria of military and political intelligence were not understood—except by the American-trained Siamese agents who, however, lacked solid official cover and had to be kept in the background. Order of battle intelligence, in particular, remained woefully defective. Not only did the Siamese not know how to report intelligence in a professional manner, but they did not know what was wanted or even where it was most likely to be found. For the OSS officers in Bangkok, SI work meant not only interrogating Siamese officials who were allowed access to them, and writing reports from what they learned, but simultaneously conducting an intelligence training course for the Siamese armed services, foreign office and police.

This informal schooling was supplemented by a still more informal correspondence course in SI work conducted by Kandy for the OSS officers in Bangkok, whose training was chiefly in the operational or procurement phases of SI, rather than in reports work. The problem was aggravated in February 1945, when the health of both OSS officers in Bangkok gave way. One officer was evacuated that month; the other shortly thereafter. Their replacement, a young officer with strong regional qualifications was quickly overburdened with his many duties. An effort to strengthen his intelligence output at Bangkok was made by dispatching a key officer of the SI/SEAC Reports staff to assist him. This attempt failed, however, when the plane carrying the Reports officer was shot down by an enemy fighter, so badly wounding the officer that he had to be evacuated. A few weeks later, OSS took the unusual and somewhat hazardous step of sending the Chief of the Reports Board on a temporary mission to Bangkok to aid in training the Siamese.

The program for strengthening SI work in Siam was further supported by bringing a large number of young Siamese out of the country for training at Camp "Y" in Ceylon and by indoctrinating the Siamese liaison officers who were periodically assigned to OSS headquarters.

The Japanese surrender terminated OSS operations in Siam. While the guerrilla program was never called into action highly significant intelligence had been procured. In addition, numerous downed American aviators had been saved from Japanese

hands. When hostilities ceased, the extensive OSS organization in Siam made it possible to evacuate all American prisoners of war in the country with maximum speed. At that time, it was learned that the Japanese had been aware of treachery on the part of the Siamese, and had redoubled their garrison in the country as a precaution, thus keeping several divisions from other fronts.

8. OSS Post-Surrender Intelligence Teams

Several weeks before the Japanese surrender OSS/SEAC prepared detailed plans for post-occupation teams to accompany British forces into liberated territory. The administrative structure and functioning of these teams had been carefully worked out on the basis of experience gained at the time of the liberation of Rangoon. The overt mission of assisting in war crimes investigation and prisoner rescue or evacuation work was to provide cover, if cover were required, for the collection of military, political and economic intelligence. Each plan contained a statement of intelligence objectives to be sought and the likely intelligence targets to be attacked. Such plans were prepared for Malaya, Sumatra, Siam and French Indochina. The possibility of Java becoming a post-surrender responsibility of SEAC had not been anticipated, but the plan for Sumatra was easily adaptable to Java, and the inclusion of southern Indochina had long been expected. Furthermore, an OSS unit comparable to the Arakan Field Unit, though smaller, had been organized and equipped to accompany the long-awaited British offensive in Malaya, with space in the convoys reserved. Only minor changes were necessary to convert this unit into post-occupational teams for Malaya and Java. Thus, OSS found itself better prepared for the surrender than either the regular British or American forces in the Theater.

The Bangkok team was the first dispatched, taking advantage of the OSS clandestine facilities to enter Siam unofficially before the surrender was formally signed. Thanks to this early start, all American POW's recovered in Siam were evacuated by OSS in the course of a few days. Thereafter, the team carried out its assigned intelligence functions.

The Malayan team, landing with the British forces and riding down to Singapore with them, collected much valuable political and economic intelligence, both from Malaya and from Sumatra. Permanent stations were established at Kuala Lumpur and Singapore and field teams were sent from time to time to Palembang or northern Sumatra.

The Saigon team and the Batavia team had the most adventurous histories. The leader of the Saigon team was accidentally killed, and another officer seriously wounded, by Annamese partisans in the guerrilla warfare against the French.* Faced with a return to wartime conditions, both the Saigon and the Batavia teams hastily established temporary networks of underground informants besides operating overtly as military observers attached to the Allied forces in these areas.

In addition to their intelligence functions, until the American consulates in all these

---

* The officers were mistaken for French military personnel due, in part, to the use of U. S. equipment and uniforms by the French, and British orders against prominent display of U. S. colors by American personnel in Indochina.

areas were reopened, the OSS teams looked after U. S. Government property, protected and evacuated U. S. civilians released from Japanese internment camps, and acted for the United States Theater Commander in various other ways.

The services rendered by the OSS post-occupational teams, particularly the intelligence collected by them and transmitted to Theater Headquarters and to Washington, were of great assistance, and for the first time in its long struggle for existence OSS/SEAC found itself enjoying the full support of the U. S. Theater Commander and full integration into his command. Also, the close relations which had prevailed between OSS and the State Department in regard to Siamese matters was extended to all phases of OSS activity in southeastern Asia.

Relations with the British naturally deteriorated, at least on the highest levels, as British activity in the newly occupied regions came to be one of the major OSS intelligence interests, but the firm insistence of the Theater Commander, backed by the State Department and the JCS, that the U. S. Government was entitled to first-hand information on what was happening in Southeast Asia blocked all British efforts to curtail OSS activities. Such official support and utilization of OSS resources, if it had existed two years earlier, would have eliminated many of the difficulties that hampered OSS in its beginnings in the Theater.

E. CHINA

1. Background and Problems

The Combined Chiefs of Staff viewed China as a secondary theater whose basic function was to contain the maximum number of Japanese troops at the minimum cost to the Allies in men and supplies. From the U. S. point of view, the strategic significance of China was twofold—a base for operations against Japan, and a potential replacement for Japan as the great power in the Far East.

The Chinese National Government of Generalissimo Chiang Kai-shek took a different view of China's role in World War II. Initially, it viewed itself as the principal front against Japan. It felt that Allied planning should accord it priority over the war against Germany. However, as the U. S. began to make substantial gains in the Pacific, China tended to relax its war effort and to permit the U. S. to take an increasingly heavy responsibility. This was accompanied by a growing concern on the part of the National Government with regard to the power and prestige of other political factions in China; some of Chiang Kai-shek's most effective armies were in the field to operate against their Communist compatriots rather than the Japanese.

Accordingly, OSS was faced with the problem of initiating operations against the enemy in a country whose prime concern was to use the striking power supplied by the Americans against dissident elements within the country. The OSS position was rendered doubly difficult by active Chinese opposition to the establishment of an independent American intelligence organization under the command of the American Theater Commander. This opposition was apparent in the Chinese determination to control the source and content of OSS intelligence, as well as all paramilitary operations.

OSS intelligence efforts were hindered by obstacles of a political and geographic nature. The political difficulties resulted from the activities of the Chinese Communists, particularly in the Communist-controlled area of North China with its capital at Yenan, and from the fact that the Japanese occupied substantial portions of the country.

The principal OSS intelligence objective in the Far East was the penetration of Japan and Japanese-occupied territory. But the use of China as a base for operations against Japan necessitated access to the northern parts of the country and through them to Manchuria and Korea. However, the northern area of China was under the control of Chinese Communist forces. The Communists also had a large net of guerrilla units operating in the Japanese-occupied areas of China. The constant struggle between Government and Communist forces rendered exceedingly difficult the task of a neutral organization, such as OSS, in trying to cooperate with both factions in a common struggle against the Japanese, since any agreement that OSS proposed or negotiated with the one immediately became suspect in the eyes of the other.

The Japanese occupied and controlled the coastal area of China, including the industrial centers, the major roads and rail lines and the major cities. They had established Chinese puppet armies, under Chinese quislings, who served the Japanese primarily as garrison and guard troops and sometimes even as combat forces. This had the effect of increasing the tremendous geographic problems which faced armies fighting in a country as vast as China.

The extent of the areas to be covered made general problems of services and supply extremely acute. China proper—without its outlying provinces—is comparable in dimension to Europe without Russia. This fact, taken in conjunction with Japanese occupation control of the main communications lines, both land and sea, produced a critical situation. Transportation inside China was inadequate at best, not only because of the great distances involved, which made it impossible to cover the entire area, but also because those transportation facilities which did exist were rudimentary. Land routes were scarce, except in Manchuria and southeast China, and the Japanese conquest of Burma in 1942 had cut the Burma Road, the only land connection to southern China at that time. By early 1942, the war had also cut off all of China's communications via the sea routes. It was not until 1945, when the Stilwell Road through liberated Burma was completed, that land communication between China and the Western Allies was re-established. For a substantial period, the only connecting link was the "Over the Hump" air route from India to China, over the Himalaya Mountains. Since r a d i c a l l y changing weather conditions accentuated the difficulties of air travel, planes flying over the Hump were forced to extreme heights with a consequent reduction in already small payloads.

It was against this general background of physical and geographical problems of distance, inadequate transport and a paucity of supplies, equipment, and all necessary materiel, as well as internal political difficulties and with China's opposition to an independent American intelligence organization, that OSS operated in the China Theater.

OSS played an important role in implementing U. S. strategy. Like all other U. S. forces in China, OSS had the mission of strengthening Chinese resistance so as to pin down as many Japanese divisions as pos-

sible. In addition, OSS had the mission of collecting full intelligence both on the Japanese, in support of U. S. military operations in the Pacific and in Asia, and on the general situation in Asia, important to the formulation of U. S. policy during the war and after victory.

Because the Chinese Army was incapable of taking the offensive against the enemy, it was important to develop as far as possible the only form of aggressive action China could take—guerrilla and clandestine operations. One of the primary assignments for OSS, therefore, was to stimulate, assist and guide Chinese paramilitary activity. More urgent and specific tasks in this line developed in the last year of the war. The first of these was during the 1944-1945 emergency in connection with halting the Japanese advance on Kunming and Chungking. The second was to assist in preparations for *CARBONADO,* the projected capture of Canton and other ports of debarkation for American forces on the Chinese coast.

The development of Chinese paramilitary warfare—and part of the intelligence mission—was accomplished, especially in the early period, by a combined U. S.-Chinese effort, involving OSS, U. S. Navy Group, China, and the Chinese intelligence service. All three participated in SACO, the Sino-American Cooperative Organization, directed by General Tai Li, the Chinese intelligence chief, and based on the resources of his agency.

Like most institutions in Nationalist China, the Chinese contribution to SACO was thoroughly inefficient and corrupt; the defeat of the Japanese was only one of the minor preoccupations of its high-echelon Chinese personnel. SACO was never completely reformed, and credit for such reform as took place belongs as much to Navy Group as to OSS, but it did finally fulfill some of the purposes for which it was intended. To assess its importance, it must be kept in mind that Tai Li really controlled a huge clandestine organization, in both free and occupied China, and that his agents often displayed remarkable ingenuity as well as daring and ruthlessness in accomplishing their missions.

the Tai Li organization had often demonstrated its effectiveness, but it was not geared either psychologically or technically to clandestine action against a foreign military enemy. Its top-echelon personnel lacked strong motivation for aiding the Allied war effort and its operatives were totally untrained in the requirements and techniques of sabotage or military intelligence. Furthermore, it had no concept of MO as a systematic attack upon enemy morale.

OSS faced a twofold problem in SACO: To induce Tai Li to use his organization against the Japanese, and to train his personnel to operate effectively. The first task had to be accomplished by a mixture of bribes and threats. If Tai Li did what OSS asked, he would continue to receive valuable military "wampum" in the form of supplies. If he did not cooperate, then OSS would act to withdraw from SACO and make Tai Li lose face by building up its own activities in China. This realistic approach finally proved much more effective than the earlier U. S. policy, followed by Navy Group, of unreserved confidence and unstinting generosity toward the man

It only proved effective when OSS, with the solid backing of the Theater Commander, was strong enough to defy Tai Li, and it could not have succeeded if OSS, by its independent operations, had not proved itself capable of operating without Tai Li's assistance.

The second task within SACO, that of training and directing the activity of the Chinese personnel, involved not only such standard subjects as radio work, how to report order of battle and other types of military intelligence, how to use special OSS equipment and how to perform effective demolitions, but it also involved selecting targets and the systematic planning of clandestine operations. The best results, it was found, were obtained when American OSS personnel accompanied Chinese field teams on specific operations or took over direction of part of the Tai Li organization in a given area. Little by little, through patient effort and continual struggle, the OSS unit in SACO worked itself into a position where it was able to launch and direct, from within Tai Li's organization, what were really OSS operations. By the late summer of 1944, SACO operations, inspired and to some extent controlled by OSS, covered most of the occupied areas in southern China. In 1945, when OSS obtained the right to launch independent operations, its activities within SACO simultaneously expanded in scope and increased in efficiency.

Though SACO was the first and main medium for OSS support to the Chinese military effort, it was not the only one. In April 1945, OSS, on orders from the Theater Commander, began training a special paratroop Commando force of 5,000 Chinese, selected from regular Chinese Army units, for long-range raids and penetrations. This force was organized into basic units of 178 men each—151 Chinese paratroopers, 19 Americans and 8 interpreters. Nominally these units were commanded by Chinese officers, with the OSS personnel serving as advisors and technicians. By late June, 2 of the units were ready for action in southeastern China and by 1 August, 20 of them were available for operations.

In addition to training and serving with this special Commando force, OSS frequently dispatched individual officers or small SO teams to work with guerrilla groups of the Chinese Army. Sometimes the OSS officers assigned to such duty managed to recruit additional forces and set themselves up as virtual guerrilla leaders. Whatever the relationship of the OSS personnel to the guerrilla group, and whether the relationship was arranged through the auspices of SACO, AGFRTS or by direct liaison with the Chinese Army, this guerrilla activity was an important phase of the

OSS program. In every case the twofold mission of OSS personnel attached to guerrilla bands was to stimulate their combativity and increase their military effectiveness by addition of OSS operational knowledge and SI techniques.

The scale of this guerrilla activity is indicated by an OSS estimate claiming 12,000 casualties inflicted on the enemy between 1 January and 11 August 1945. The significance of the figure is enhanced by the fact that, for the most part, the guerrilla attacks had specific and important strategic objectives beyond the general aim of keeping the enemy busy in China. They were intended to hamper enemy movements in the corridor between north and south China, first to slow down the Japanese drive on Kunming and later to facilitate Chinese counter-attacks. In execution of this strategy, OSS guerrilla and SO teams between 1 January and 26 June cut the Japanese railroad at 1,124 places between Chihsian and the Yellow River Bridge and from the middle of July to the middle of August they demolished two spans on the Yellow River Bridge of the Peiping-Hankow railroad, catching a Japan train as it was crossing the river.

During the great Japanese offensive in the last months of 1944 and the first few months of 1945 OSS guerrillas, and even OSS sabotage or demolitions teams working without Chinese assistance, played a valuable role. In addition to behind-the-lines attacks on enemy communications, OSS personnel were frequently called upon to destroy equipment which the Fourteenth Air Force had been forced to abandon in evacuating its forward bases—a hazardous mission sometimes performed only a few minutes before the arrival of advanced enemy elements.

Supporting the Fourteenth Air Force was a vital part of the OSS mission, for this organization was the main instrument of American military policy in China. Like OSS itself, but on a much larger scale, it had the dual role of enhancing the defensive or offensive power of the Chinese Army and of participating in the blockade of Japan by attacks on enemy shipping in Chinese waters. The main OSS contribution to the Air Force was through a joint OSS-Air Force unit, AGFRTS (Air and Ground Forces Resources and Technical Staff).

In AGFRTS, OSS carried on nearly every type of clandestine activity, including counter-espionage and MO in support of Fourteenth Air Force operations, but the collection of tactical intelligence was the most immediately valuable activity. As at Detachment 101 in Burma, teams of OSS-trained and OSS-led native agents pinpointed enemy targets, while a chain of coast and highway watching stations reported all enemy movements by land or water instantly to Fourteenth Air Force headquarters, thus enabling General Chennault to obtain maximum operational results from his over-taxed resources. Never less than one-third, and often two-thirds or more, of all the tactical intelligence received by Chennault's headquarters was supplied by AGFRTS.

The main strategic intelligence mission of OSS did not get under way to any extent until General Wedemeyer established OSS as an independent command with full authority over all its own personnel in China. This finally gave the SI Branch the freedom of action it needed. New forward bases were at once established and the development of an intelligence network in north-central China rivalling the SACO-AGFRTS-OSS chains in the south rapidly forged ahead. In the spring of 1945 all available OSS intelligence facilities were mobilized on orders from Wedemeyer to make an intensive survey of the South China coast in view of eventual American landings. OSS won high praise from the Theater Commander for the speed, accuracy and thoroughness with which it carried out this task.

As part of the mission to keep the Theater Commander and Washington informed of internal Chinese developments, OSS utilized the Army's DIXIE mission at Communist headquarters in Yenan as cover to establish trained observers there. As a result, OSS reaped a rich harvest of lucid, penetrating reports containing information of the highest value to American policy-makers. An R&A team established in Chungking collected intelligence directly from Chinese Government sources and used this, together with intelligence collected by OSS through SACO and other operations, in preparing comprehensive reports.

Most spectacularly successful of all high-level OSS intelligence activities was that of the X-2 Branch. Once the organization escaped from the yoke of SACO, the X-2 Branch, using various covers, proceeded to develop its own native agent networks in both free and occupied China. Besides collecting a mass of political and even military intelligence, the Branch was notably successful in exposing enemy espionage activities, one operation leading to the capture or breaking up of a ring of 175 Japanese agents. Unlike most X-2 operations, the one in China was neither limited nor strengthened by cooperation with other Allied counter-espionage agencies. Whereas in Europe the most important aspect of X-2 was the access obtained to British counter-espionage files, in China X-2 had to build its own files from scratch and develop its own undercover sources. From a long-term point of view, this had certain advantages. Since X-2 was not dependent on Chinese or British sources, it was able to continue exploiting these sources when the war ended and a greater degree of reserve characterized inter-Allied relationships in the field of clandestine activities. The outbreak of civil war in China, gravely disturbing to the U. S. Government, emphasized the continuing value of these sources.

In addition to its main intelligence effort in China itself, OSS/China developed SO-SI activities in French Indochina and launched the first American penetration of Siam, although the Siamese network was eventually taken over and raised to a much higher level of activity by OSS/SEAC.

Between 15 August and 30 September 1945 when OSS was officially dissolved, the organization rendered valuable services to the Theater Commander in war crimes and prisoner-of-war work, in the mopping up of enemy intelligence activities, and in covering the Nationalist-Communist clash in China.

2. SACO

The first COI/OSS group dispatched from Washington to the Far East to begin operations in China reached India in September 1942. However, Stilwell, Commander of U. S. forces in the China-Burma-India Theater, diverted the group, which was designated Detachment 101, from its original mission and assigned it to operations in Burma. Following this development, a special representative from OSS/Washington submitted plans to Stilwell at Chungking for OSS participation in the U. S. military effort in China through a unit to carry out strategic and tactical intelligence assignments, subversion and sabotage campaigns and such additional tasks as the Theater Commander might order. The general plan that emerged ultimately embraced the resources of the U. S. Navy, the National Government of China and OSS.

In the negotiations that ensued, OSS encountered for the first time a major obstacle which continued to hamper its operations in China throughout the war. It quickly became evident that the National Government of Generalissimo Chiang Kai-shek would not permit a foreign intelligence organization to operate independently in China.

The only U. S. intelligence organization at that time active in China was the U. S. Navy Group, China, commanded by Captain (later Rear Admiral) M. E. Miles, USN, American Naval Observer in Chungking. Miles had established close and cordial working relationships with Chiang Kai-shek and with General Tai Li, head of the Bureau of Investigation and Statistics, the Chinese National Government's internal security and counter-intelligence service.

Intent on gaining a foothold in China, Donovan acquiesced on 1 January 1943 in a tentative agreement which named Miles as Chief of OSS Activities in the Asiatic Theater (Burma and China). As it developed, Miles' authority in Burma was only nominal since Detachment 101 reported directly to Stilwell. But the agreement gave Miles control of OSS operations in China and stipulated that such operations could be carried out only with the full advance knowledge and authorization of the Chinese Government. A combined Sino-American agency would be formed, with a Chinese Director and an American Deputy Director. All decisions in matters of planning, policy and operations would be made jointly by these two officials. OSS activities would be planned and executed within the authority and under the control of this agency.

These terms were embodied in the Sino-American Special Technical Cooperative Agreement, approved by the Joint Chiefs of Staff in Washington 15 April 1943 in JCS 245. Under this Agreement, OSS was to initiate a training program for Chinese troops and Chinese agent personnel and participate in intelligence missions as an affiliate of Miles' Navy Group. The agency to carry out the Agreement was designated the Sino-American Cooperative Organization (SACO). Tai Li became its Director, and Miles the Deputy Director.

From the Navy Group point of view, the SACO Agreement, as it became known, was most satisfactory. Miles was assured of supplies totalling 150 tons monthly and the control of their distribution to OSS and Chinese elements, as well as to the Navy Group. He could also supervise the training and equipping of guerrilla forces, communications, and all operations. Being primarily interested in meteorological and coastal shipping intelligence, Miles could count on full Chinese cooperation. The Chinese did not object to such activities as he contemplated; their chief concern was the nature of the mission which OSS sought to perform. OSS was known to be an agency specializing in clandestine intelligence, and might obtain military, economic and political information which Tai Li believed the U. S. Government should not acquire.

Navy Group had no unit to perform a research and analysis function. Miles did not plan to engage in secret intelligence, large-scale guerrilla, counter-espionage and sabotage operations or morale subversion. His intelligence service began functioning in the field on an admittedly limited basis in July 1943. Field agents traveled in China and collected information primarily through Chinese officials. Throughout, the utmost importance was placed on maintaining cordial relations with the Chinese. This Miles succeeded in doing throughout the war.

In so doing, he was compelled to proceed slowly and patiently in building his organization, to give generously of his supplies and equipment to the Chinese—and to restrain OSS personnel in SACO from "alienating" the Chinese Government. Consequently, the establishment of training centers by OSS as a first step to operations was long delayed. The training program did not actually commence until September 1943, exactly one year after the first negotiations were opened with Stilwell.

Included in the training program were sabotage, photography * and intelligence research techniques. OSS would contribute instructors for the training, as well as specialized materiel for both training and operations. In addition, OSS would supply technicians and special personnel for the operations and, together with the Chinese,

---

* Photography was specially requested by the Chinese.

develop an extensive communications system for transmitting information back to Chungking.

Accordingly, SACO went into effect as a combined U. S.-Chinese arrangement under the control of Chiang Kai-shek; U. S. participation was divided between the Navy and OSS. Initially, three camps were established, and some 630 Chinese students took courses given chiefly by Navy Group instructors. Most of the administrators and service personnel also were members of the Navy Group. OSS technicians trained the Chinese in guerrilla tactics, demolitions, close combat and ambush.

The Navy followed a strictly legalistic interpretation of the unqualified Chinese control of SACO. Naval authorities did not recognize, or, in any case, did not choose to recognize, the fact that nominal acceptance of Chinese control was a necessary prerequisite for the development of U. S. clandestine paramilitary and intelligence activities in China. While paramilitary and guerrilla activities would profit by being staged cooperatively by U. S. and Chinese authorities, basic U. S. intelligence objectives could not be achieved without insistence on substantial independence from Chinese control over American clandestine intelligence procurement.

This placed OSS in China in a difficult position. Donovan insisted throughout that no intelligence agency could operate effectively without independence from the control of any other nation.* Nevertheless, SACO was the only means open to OSS to establish itself in China at all. Under the aegis of SACO, however, even a nominal independence was denied to OSS.

Tai Li consistently resisted the development of OSS. He claimed that his own networks comprised 400 intelligence stations and that these supplied sufficient coverage and information. His intelligence was reported to Miles, whose Navy Group staff

* See Survey, 27 October 1943 - 27 September 1944, in Washington Section II.

then spent considerable time examining and processing the reports before making them available to OSS. Apparently Miles held the information until he was sure it had been cabled to the Navy Department in Washington. To obviate this delay, OSS asked Tai Li for copies of the reports that were forwarded to Navy Group. His answer was a unique explanation for failure to comply—the Chinese did not use carbon paper, he explained, and lacked office supplies.

OSS in China offered to provide funds for missions, hoping that such offers would encourage Tai Li to react more favorably to OSS plans. One such mission was proposed in an area southwest of Shanghai. The cost, Tai Li estimated, would be $1,000,000 (Chinese), and only Chinese could participate in the operation. It would be necessary to exclude Americans lest they be killed in action. This tragedy would cause loss of face on his part, he said, because he would be responsible for the safety of the Americans. The project never materialized.

Such a   flavor characterized Tai Li's obstructionist tactics throughout 1943 and early 1944. In these efforts the Chinese received the support of the U. S. naval authorities.

Donovan had acceded to SACO in the expectation that, while the general spirit of the Agreement should serve as a guide both for the U. S. and the Chinese in the development of operations against the Japanese, it must not be allowed to sabotage basic U. S. intelligence objectives in China. This interpretation was, however, in direct opposition to that of the Navy, the co-partner in the arrangement, which took the view that an agreement with the Chinese had been undertaken and must be rigidly observed in every particular. In fact, the Navy went so far as to range itself on the Chinese side against OSS even in the original organizational discussions that were held, with the result that operational control of SACO passed entirely to the Chinese. In effect,

421

the Navy appeared to regard Chiang Kai-shek, rather than the JCS, as SACO's final authority.

Three separate courses of action developed, artificially allied within SACO but actually incompatible. The Chinese viewed SACO as the way to exact the maximum in arms and equipment from the U. S. for the minimum return—a return defined in the Agreement only as "intelligence available". Since Tai Li's main concern was to prevent the foreigner from knowing what was going on in China, the bulk of intelligence produced was meager and obsolete. As the U. S. was slated only to train and equip the Chinese agents, whereas the Chinese themselves directed all personnel and operations, it was not difficult for Tai Li to maintain a strict control.

The Navy viewed SACO primarily as a means to obtain information essential to the accomplishment of limited objectives in direct support of naval operations in the Pacific Ocean. Accordingly, operations to other ends than those which had immediate bearing on the accomplishment of these objectives were considered secondary. Matters, however, went further than this. The Navy also precluded OSS not only from phases of the intelligence field which it regarded as Navy Group's exclusive bailiwick, but, at the same time, undertook to exclude OSS from activities where the Navy itself, by its own choice, did not operate. For example, although the JCS enabling directive to OSS (JCS 155/11/D) made it clear that OSS was responsible for counter-intelligence in enemy or enemy-occupied territories, Navy Group undertook to organize a complete counter-intelligence service within SACO, that is, under Tai Li.

The Navy's attitude toward OSS became increasingly evident when it consistently refused or delayed transportation and supplies to OSS. During one particular month, for example, the Navy's total portion of SACO tonnage received was 130 tons. Of that total, OSS received nothing. Moreover, the Navy turned down an OSS request to attempt, within the framework of the original Agreement, a new formulation of objectives and mutual relationships with a view to permitting some measure of realization of OSS objectives in SACO. To insure a modicum of effectiveness, any such new formulation had, to some extent, to override Tai Li. This the Navy was not prepared to do: the result was that a veritable impasse developed. Actions of Navy Group, China, were supported throughout by the Navy Department in Washington, even in the face of protests from the American Theater Commander.

For the first eight months of SACO, OSS tried to perform its functions within the terms of the Agreement. However, during that time no significant intelligence was produced and no intelligence procurement operations were initiated.

Donovan attempted to improve the deteriorating OSS position in China by an amendment to JCS 245 which would give to OSS more freedom of action under the U. S. Theater Commander. Instead of a formal amendment, however, an "understanding" was reached in Chungking on 9 December 1943, following conferences between representatives of OSS, the U. S. Navy and China. The "understanding" undertook to define the spheres of activity between the Navy and OSS:

Navy	OSS
Weather Reports	Secret Intelligence (SI)
Aerial Reconnaissance	Counter Espionage (X-2)
Special Maritime Operations	Special Operations
Mining (of shipping routes)	(a) Physical (SO)
Radio interception	(b) Morale (MO)
Medical	Research & Analysis (R&A)
Supplies	Supplies
Communications	Communications
Training	Training
Repair Shops	Repair Shops

Following the conclusion of the "understanding", on 17 December, Donovan took a further step in asserting the identity of the OSS program within SACO. He ordered the activation of an OSS detachment, designated Detachment 202, in Chungking, and transferred several men from Detachment 101 to the new unit. This group was augmented later by the addition of officers and enlisted men en route to China from the United States at that time. The officer appointed commander of Detachment 202 was also designated Strategic Services Officer, OSS/CBI. OSS thus gained the status of a virtually autonomous unit under SACO.

Even though the "understanding" spelled out the relative functions of OSS and Navy Group, delegating to OSS even more clearly than before the implementation of a secret intelligence program, it did not relieve the main obstacle: ultimate control continued in the hands of Tai Li. As long as this situation obtained, OSS was effectually precluded from the field of secret intelligence in China.

Nevertheless, some progress became evident. In January 1944, the SI training base in Happy Valley, near Chungking, was in operation, with the Navy supplying most of the instructors. By April, training of the first group of Chinese agents was completed and a beginning was made toward the establishment of a secret agent net in occupied China to report military and general intelligence by radio. By that time, other OSS branches had made a start: SO had established two advance training and operational bases; R&A had begun to process intelligence; and MO had established one advance training and operational base and was planning to expand.

In spite of this, the barriers in the way of OSS remained unchanged. For example, there was consistent difficulty in obtaining translators for MO and R&A work, or in obtaining air and motor transport for supplies and personnel. Recruits selected by the Chinese as students for the SO and SI schools were, apparently deliberately, of inferior calibre, sometimes even entirely illiterate and uneducated.

While the intelligence aspects of SACO remained limited in output and value throughout the war, the guerrilla and sabotage activities, as well as the MO phase of enemy morale subversion, grew steadily. In regard to both the Japanese offensive and attacks on enemy communications SACO came to operate with telling effect.

Independent U. S. intelligence procurement, however, remained stalemated in SACO. OSS, in its own right, did not begin to achieve results in this field in China until January 1945, when it attained the status of an independent intelligence agency with sufficient personnel, authority, logistical and strategic support, in addition to Theater Command recognition. However, prior to that time, a means was found, through the development of close liaison with the Fourteenth Air Force, to initiate independent secret intelligence operations and develop the full scope of OSS intelligence, paramilitary and research facilities. The rapid success of the joint OSS-Fourteenth Air Force effort, through AGFRTS, provided a clear testimony to the importance of freedom from foreign control for the proper and effective establishment of strategic services.

THE JOINT CHIEFS OF STAFF
WASHINGTON

Captain Milton E. Miles, U. S. Navy,
Navy Department,
Washington, D. C.

You are advised that the Joint U. S. Chiefs of Staff take note of the proposed Sino-American Technical Cooperation Agreement for the conduct and support of special measures in the war effort against JAPAN, and, further, of the exchange of despatches between General Stilwell and the Chiefs of Staff in which General Stilwell expresses approval of the conduct of American participation in these measures by you directly under Chinese command. The Joint Chiefs of Staff approve this arrangement and desire that you cooperate with the responsible designated Chinese authorities in every way practicable for the prosecution of war measures against the Japanese.

The President has been informed and has given approval of the plan to place you in direct charge of the American participation, as set forth in the proposed agreement.

For the Joint Chiefs of Staff:—

WILLIAM D. LEAHY,
Admiral, U. S. Navy,
Chief of Staff to the
Commander in Chief of the Army and Navy.

SINO-AMERICAN SPECIAL TECHNICAL COOPERATION AGREEMENT

The National Government of the Republic of China, and the Government of the United States of America, animated by mutual desire to annihilate the common enemy and achieve military victory, have resolved to conclude an Agreement of Sino-American Special Technical Cooperation, and for that purpose have appointed their Plenipotentiaries:—

His Excellency the Generalissimo Chiang Kai Shek, Chairman of the National Commission of Military Affairs of the Government of the Republic of China:

The Honorable Dr. T. V. Soong, Foreign Minister of the Government of the Republic of China;

General Tai Li, Deputy-Director of the Bureau of Investigation and Statistics of the National Commission of Military Affairs of the Government of the Republic of China;

Lieutenant Colonel Sinju Pu Hsiao, Assistant Military Attache, Embassy of the Republic of China at Washington, D. C.:

His Excellency Mr. Franklin D. Roosevelt, the President of the United States of America:

The Honorable Frank Knox, Secretary of the Navy of the United States of America;

Brigadier General William J. Donovan, Director of the Office of Strategic Services of the United States of America;

Captain Milton E. Miles, United States Navy, Chief of the United States Strategic Services in the Far East:—

Who having communicated to each other their full powers which have been found to be in good and due form, have agreed upon the following provisions of the Cooperative Agreement:—

ARTICLE I

For the purpose of attacking our common enemy along the Chinese coast, in occupied territories in China, and in other areas held by the Japanese, the Sino-American Special Technical Cooperative Organization is organized in China. Its aim is, by common effort employing American equipment and technical training and utilizing the Chinese war zones as bases to attack effectively the Japanese Navy, the Japanese Merchant Marine, and the Japanese air forces in different territories of the Far East, and to attack the mines, factories, warehouses, depots, and other military establishments in areas under Japanese occupation.

ARTICLE II

The executive office organization of the said cooperation is named, "Sino-American Special Cooperative Organization". "SACO", will hereafter be used as the short title. Its organization and the distribution of its functions, are to be found in the attached diagram.

ARTICLE III

For facilitating the progress of the work, the United States Government is willing to cooperate with China, and to supply all materials gratis on the basis of friendship. Therefore, in the United States the name is "Friendship"; the English name in China is, "Sino-American Cooperative Organization", and the abbreviation in English is S A C O, which is pronounced similar to the American word, "SOCKO", with the significance of powerful or sudden attack.

424

ARTICLE IV

All members of this Organization are required to pledge their utmost effort to defeat Japan, and to keep absolute secrecy regarding the organization, and its activities as well as regarding the state of other allied units which have connection with said organization.

ARTICLE V

The present organization shall have a Director and a Deputy Director. The Director will be appointed by the Chinese side, and the Deputy Director by the American side.

ARTICLE VI

The functions of all the sections of this organization will be discussed and determined jointly by the Director and the Deputy Director.

ARTICLE VII

With a view to facilitating their movements and their identification in carrying out their functions in China, the responsible persons and the whole staff of this organization shall be appointed by the Generalissimo Chiang Kai Shek.

ARTICLE VIII

Personnel from Burma, Siam, Korea, Formosa, and Indo-China, who have completed suitable training in the United States, have proved their trustworthiness, and have sworn loyalty to the Allied Nations, upon being proposed by the American side and agreed to by the Chinese side, may be permitted to undertake various activities under the direction of the organization. However, in conformity with the principles of secret service, such persons shall be segregated and have no knowledge of the principal section of this organization. All matters regarding the arrangements at the places of their assignments and to the performance of their activities shall be so segregated.

ARTICLE IX

This organization shall establish a long-range aerial reconnaissance squad equipped with aircraft and flying materials and materials and personnel for reading, interpreting, and photographing. The aim and purpose of this unit shall be to take, study, and interpret photographs of all kinds of enemy activities in occupied territories in China, and other occupied territories in the Far East; thereby enabling the organization to maintain accurate knowledge of all perceptible activities of the enemy, in order to carry out all kinds of effective attacks. With the exception of the pilots, the photographers shall be in great part Chinese.

ARTICLE X

In order to facilitate the laying of mines in the ports, bays, and along the Chinese coast, to deal timely blows against Japanese vessels, the United States Government may dispatch airplanes to survey all the ports and bays, accompanied by participation of the Chinese personnel. In order to preserve military secrecy, all maps and photographs taken shall be exclusively for the use of this organization; shall be kept in archives and shall not be removed elsewhere.

ARTICLE XI

The organization shall establish a propaganda section for the purpose of carrying out psychological warfare against the enemy and the population in occupied territories in China, and other places occupied by the Japanese. All necessary equipment, such as wireless transmitters and receivers, special cameras, printing machines, etc., shall be provided by the United States Government which shall also be responsible for training Chinese personnel to use such equipment.

ARTICLE XII

This organization shall designate personnel at two places, Washington and Chungking, to take charge of the exchange of information between the United States and China.

All information from China for transmittal to the United States Government shall be released by the Director of SACO.

All information from the United States Government for transmittal to China shall be released by the Director of the Office of Strategic Services, or by the Commander-in-Chief, United States Fleet.

ARTICLE XIII

Any information collected by, or in the possession of this organization concerning sabotage, reconnaissance or mine laying, or any other information directly useful to activities of this organization, may be released for transmittal to the Military Authorities of the United States or China, by the Director and the Deputy Director, jointly, when they deem such transmittal to be necessary.

Wireless transmitting stations of this organization, specially authorized to do so, may communicate with wireless stations of the United States Navy, situated outside China; but use of all other wireless stations of this organization shall be restricted solely to activities of this organization.

ARTICLE XIV
[Omitted in original.]

ARTICLE XV

This organization shall establish its principal training center in the vicinity of Chungking. In case of necessity, subject to the approval of both High Contracting Parties, training classes may also be established wherever units are working.

ARTICLE XVI

Personnel of this organization for all kinds of training shall be appointed and selected by the Chinese Government, with the exception of those instructors responsible for technical training and of personnel for planning and directing the various types of technical training who are appointed by the American side.

The curriculum and the standards of training will be jointly decided by the Director and the Deputy Director. The distribution and assignment to duty of all trainees, after the completion of their courses, and after they pass satisfactory examinations and practical tests, shall be de-termined by the Director and the Deputy Director of the organization.

ARTICLE XVII

This organization shall keep a complete detailed record of all trainees, and of all Chinese members of its various sections, during the period of this training, and of their active duty. If any Chinese members acquit themselves with such distinction in their work as to merit a course of study in the United States, they may be selected by this organization, and upon approval being obtained from Generalissimo Chiang, they will be sent to the United States for study. The United States Government will pay lodging, tuition, and traveling expenses requisite to such instruction.

ARTICLE XVIII

In order to obtain enemy information, this organization will intercept and study transmissions of the Japanese Navy, Army, and Air Force. Personnel responsible for planning and directing such interceptions and study, shall be appointed by the American side. The Chinese side will appoint members to participate in this work.

Enemy codes intercepted and studies shall be dealt with in the premises of the section of the organization concerned, to preserve secrecy.

Should the necessity arise to transmit to the military authorities of both countries, the results of the interception and study of secret enemy codes, such results may be jointly released for transmittal by the Director and the Deputy Director.

ARTICLE XIX

The headquarters of this organization will be established in Chungking, the war time capital of China. Advanced stations and units will gradually be installed in various places, as required by actual situations, to conduct sabotage, reconnaissance, meteorological work, propaganda against the enemy, and for communication activities necessary to the functioning of this organization.

The following places are tentatively listed for establishment of advanced stations or units: 1: Kanchow, 2: Chenkei, 3: Wenchow, 4: Chuchow, 5: Foochow, 6: Chungchow, 7: Bias Bay, 8: Kaikong, 9: Peihai, 10: Kwangteh, 11: Lihwang, 12: Changteh, 13: Hengyang, 14: Loyang, 15: Area in the vicinity of Kaichow, 16: Area in the vicinity of Linchi, 17: Lanchow, 18: Wuyan, 19: Paoshan, 20: Chuli, 21: Anhsi, 22: Lahsa, 23: Tihua.

ARTICLE XX

Repair shops will be set up in the vicinity of Kanchow and Sian, to facilitate distribution and repair of materials for the various advanced units. These repair shops will be directed by American technicians.

ARTICLE XXI

All materials needed by this organization for sabotage, wireless, arms, ammunition, explosives, communication, photography, meteorology, chemicals, printing, medical equipment, and all other materials required for the diverse activities of this organization, shall be supplied by the American side, which shall be responsible for their delivery at Chungking, to the personnel designated by this organization. Transportation of the above materials from Chungking, to the various areas of activity, shall be taken care of by the Chinese side.

ARTICLE XXII

The Chinese side is to be responsible for salaries and working expenses of Chinese personnel.

ARTICLE XXIII

The American side is to be responsible for salaries and working expenses of the American personnel.

ARTICLE XXIV

The Chinese side is to be responsible for furnishing offices, laboratories, residences, and furniture of the various ranks and grades of American personnel of this organization in China.

ARTICLE XXV

All expenses of the activities of this organization in Burma, Thailand, Indo-China, Korea, Formosa, and so on, shall be paid by the American side.

ARTICLE XXVI

In case of necessity for altering the organization chart and functions, changes will be discussed by the Director and the Deputy Director, and submitted for decision to the Generalissimo and President Roosevelt.

ARTICLE XXVII

This agreement shall be effective upon being signed by the representatives of both sides duly authorized by the Chairman of the National Commission of Military Affairs of China, and the President of the United States of America. The period of validity will continue from the date of signing this agreement until the end of the war by the allied nations against Japan.

ARTICLE XXVIII

This agreement shall be drawn up in duplicate, both in Chinese and in English, both equally authentic; each party to hold one copy in each language.

T. V. SOONG,
Foreign Minister of the Government
of the Republic of China.

TAI LI,
Deputy-Director of the Bureau of Investigation and Statistics of the National Commission of Military Affairs of the Government of the Republic of China.

SINJU PU HSIAO,
Assistant Military Attache, Embassy of the Republic of China at Washington, D. C.

FRANK KNOX,
Secretary of the Navy of the United States of America.

WILLIAM J. DONOVAN,
Director of the Office of Strategic Services of the United States of America.

MILTON E. MILES,
Chief of the United States Strategic Services in the Far East.

Done at Washington, D. C., this Fifteenth Day of April in the Thirty-second Year of the Chinese Republic, equivalent to the Fifteenth Day of April, Nineteen Hundred and Forty-three.

3. AGFRTS

In December 1943 Donovan conferred in Chungking with General Claire L. Chennault, commander of the Fourteenth USAAF. The only U. S. combat command operating thoughout China, Fourteenth Air Force was badly in need of a widespread tactical ground-air intelligence service. Working with limited supplies over a vast area which presented few strategic targets, it was necessary to strike tactical points—enemy columns, concentrations, supply dumps—frequently discernible only by ground observation. Also, the Air Force needed a propaganda unit which would publicize U. S. airmen among the Chinese and encourage the natives to assist in the rescue and return of downed aviators.

The development of close OSS liaison with Chennault's forces promised to benefit the Air Force as well as permit the establishment of OSS intelligence procurement in China under exclusive U. S. control, albeit under the cover of Chennault's command. With Chennault's approval, OSS, as a preliminary move, attached two R&A officers to Headquarters, Fourteenth Air Force in February 1944 for duty with the A-2 Section.* The officers were assigned to assist in target analysis and operations, to assemble intelligence on air targets in Japan's Inner Zone for use in the field and in Washington, and to collect additional specialized intelligence. The results were highly satisfactory. The volume of additional documentation and the re-systematization of target selection, through access to OSS resources, proved of such great direct assistance to Chennault's operations that the establishment of a per-

* See the section on R&A in "Individual Branch Activities" below.

manent joint OSS-Fourteenth Air Force arrangement was proposed.

The arrangement was made official with Stilwell's order of 26 April 1944 which activated a new unit, the 5329th Air and Ground Forces Resources and Technical Staff (Provisional)—AGFRTS, popularly referred to as "Agfighters"—under the Commanding General, Fourteenth Air Force. Although the Air Force had built up a small and highly efficient ground intelligence organization, it had neither the trained personnel nor the specialized equipment and financial support to realize optimum results. The ground intelligence staff, composed of thirteen officers and two enlisted men, was transferred to duty with AGFRTS and its functions were absorbed by the new unit. Additional personnel representing the major OSS branches were attached, and operations began at once, with a total staff of twenty-four officers and thirteen enlisted men under the command of a specially assigned Fourteenth Air Force officer.

The prestige in China of Chennault and the Fourteenth Air Force was so great that Tai Li was unable to oppose it when it undertook independent intelligence operations. Tai Li, in fact, was not formally notified of the inception or composition of AGFRTS, although he was fully aware of its status.

AGFRTS succeeded where SACO had failed. It established independent operations which OSS had never been able to do under SACO. Fourteenth Air Force was effective cover and the addition of A-2 personnel to the OSS nucleus provided important specialized assistance on the problem of intelligence objectives. The Air Force personnel became an integral part of the organization, with the result that AGFRTS became a veritable OSS, operating effectively and with a minimum of organizational friction.

AGFRTS began to operate as an intelligence procurement and analysis agency for all U. S. forces in China, as well as for the

Fourteenth Air Force. It addressed itself immediately to the priority regions—the 1st, 3rd, 4th, 7th and 9th Chinese War Areas* in South China. The results, in the form of total intelligence available to the armed forces, were apparent almost immediately. All the intelligence branches of OSS went into action: SI and SO agents, attached to AGFRTS, were established behind enemy lines in a wide intelligence network which supplied a substantial amount of intelligence to headquarters at Kweilin; MO operated through the AGFRTS net; and R&A began to process numerous publications and other timely intelligence materials, rather than suffering the six to eight month lags characteristic of SACO activities. X-2 also found in AGFRTS a secure medium for its operations and, by the end of 1944, had made substantial gains.

In addition to collecting intelligence, AGFRTS undertook to digest and summarize data for dissemination in readily available form. A daily "Sitrep", or situation report, for Chennault and his staff was begun, as well as an "AGFRTS Weekly Summary", an "AGFRTS Monthly Report", a variety of spot reports for operational and strategic planning, and "hot" radio flashes for the Fourteenth Air Force on Tactical or spot targets, such as truck convoys, enemy concentrations, and the like. To increase the flow of current intelligence, AGFRTS dispatched mobile combat liaison teams to the War Areas to radio back front-line information and to relay requests for aerial tactical missions in conjunction with movements of ground forces.

AGFRTS provided other types of data in addition to its straight ground intelligence. For example, it supplied Air Force Headquarters with daily weather and meteorological reports from numerous points inside enemy-occupied China; these reports were also relayed directly to the Pacific Fleet. Regular coverage of Yangtze River traffic

and of coastal shipping, together with reports of train movements, were reported by radio to enable both the Fourteenth Air Force and the Pacific Fleet to hit Japanese supply lines with maximum efficiency. Ground and eyewitness reports of results of strategic bombing by the Fourteenth Air Force in China and Indochina proved invaluable in the assessment of bomb damage, particularly with reference to planning future attacks.

In addition, AGFRTS assisted the Fourteenth Air Force by air personnel rescue service, by sabotage of enemy air installations and supply lines, and by various means designed to mislead or deceive the Japanese, for example, leaving behind presumably authentic Air Force documents at air bases to be abandoned. In addition, rumors calculated to undermine enemy morale were circulated and selected Chinese soldiers recruited in War Areas were trained in combat intelligence and communications.

It is impossible to estimate with any accuracy the total contribution of AGFRTS operations. AGFRTS supplied valuable data, of both tactical and strategic importance, in increasing amounts. The significance of the intelligence itself was raised immeasurably by the speed of its reporting, since the acceleration of reporting, particularly on tactical objectives, meant that the Air Force could attack individual vulnerable points in the enemy's position while the opportunity was ripe. By August 1944, after some six months of operation, at least thirty-three percent of all intelligence credited to the various agencies in China in one five-day period was attributed to AGFRTS, and some fifty percent was credited to combined Fourteenth Air Force/AGFRTS sources.

AGFRTS continued to expand until early 1945, when OSS was reorganized in China. Up to that time, AGFRTS had maintained a steady geometric increase in intelligence as new sources were developed in the field and additional personnel was acquired. However, as AGFRTS results proved them-

* Comparable to U. S. Service Commands.

selves and the list of its customers continued to increase, the unit required additional personnel and supplies. OSS was not able to meet these requirements in China, in view of obligations to its units in Burma and India and its new unit to be organized in SEAC under Mountbatten. The problem was rendered more difficult because OSS was obligated to maintain its SACO connections, so that the Navy and Tai Li could not accuse it of reneging on its commitments. As a result, AGFRTS expansion plans suffered—something which could have been avoided if OSS/Washington allocations had permitted more effective support to China in the matter of personnel and supplies.

By early 1945, the question of the status of AGFRTS came to a head. The Theater reorganization established OSS in its own right under the Commanding General, China Theater. Both OSS and the Fourteenth Air Force wished full control over the joint unit. General Wedemeyer, Commanding General, China Theater, resolved the difference by assigning AGFRTS to OSS, in line with the new OSS responsibility for all American clandestine activities in the China Theater.

The timing for this assignment was exceptionally propitious for AGFRTS. By the end of 1944, there was a real need for a broader intelligence coverage than AGFRTS itself could provide. Inevitably, the priority interest of the unit had been intelligence in support of the air war in China. While this was not carried on to the exclusion of other activities, the need for greater emphasis on strategic intelligence to plan for future large-scale operations was increasingly evident. This constituted an assignment on a scale out of all proportion to AGFRTS capabilities. AGFRTS had performed excellently in the ways that were required at the time. Above all, it had permitted the initiation of independent U. S. intelligence operations otherwise politically and administratively impossible. With the

acceleration of the tempo of the war in China, however, an expanding program was required, one which would tax the full resources of OSS.

HEADQUARTERS
UNITED STATES ARMY FORCES
CHINA, BURMA, INDIA

A.P.O. 885
26 April 1944

GENERAL ORDERS NUMBER 36.

1. Subject to the provisions of Circular No. 59, this Headquarters, dated 8 September 1943; Circular No. 227, War Department, dated 22 September 1943, and Section II Circular No. 241, War Department, dated 5 October 1943, the 5329th Air Ground Force Resources and Technical Staff (Provisional) is organized this date with authorized strength of thirty-five (35) officers and sixty-five (65) enlisted men, and is assigned to the Commanding General, Fourteenth United States Army Air Force, with station at A.P.O. 430.

2. Personnel for this unit will be provided by the Commanding General, Fourteenth United States Army Air Force, from sources available to him within the Theater.

By command of Lieutenant General STILWELL:

VERNON EVANS
Brig. Gen., G.S.C.
Deputy Chief of Staff

JKD/flr
A.P.O. 879
March 24, 1944.

SUBJECT: Activation of Provisional Unit to be known as AGFTRS.

TO: Commanding General, Rear Echelon, Hq. USAFCBI, APO 885.

1. A request by the Fourteenth Air Force for activation of a provisional unit to be known as AGFTRS (Air Ground Forces Technical and Resources Staff) has been approved.

2. In accordance with paragraph 4, Circular 59, dated 8 September, 1943 the following information is submitted:

a. The purpose of this unit is primarily one of service and as a coordinator of all field intelligence functions of the Fourteenth Air Force.

b. The unit to be required for approximately one year.

c. The mission of this unit is:

(1) Liaison with Chinese Military Headquarters.

(2) Air-Ground Liaison when Military operations warrant.

(3) Secure all information possible on enemy Order of Battle, both air and ground, enemy shipping movement, industrial activities, documents, and publications.

(4) Arrange for Pilot Rescue.

(5) Submit daily weather reports.

(6) Train agents for working in the occupied zone and then place them there.

(7) Air Field Security and Counter Espionage to include trained Department of Justice agents and up to date methods of detection.

(8) General Ground intelligence.

(9) Prisoner of War interrogation.

(10) Morale operations.

(11) Technical Intelligence.

(12) Establishment of a complete radio net-work so that all reports of an urgent intelligence nature will be received in the quickest possible time, and so that the greatest security and efficiency can be attained.

(13) Instructional Branch for training of agent radio operators. This program will be conducted either at LINGLING or CHANGSHA according to decision to be made by the Commanding General, Fourteenth Air Force.

d. No table of organization to be submitted.

3. Due to the extreme secrecy of this unit, the minimum handling of this correspondence is required.

4. This unit is to be activated by order from Headquarters, Rear Echelon.

By command of Lieutenant General STILWELL:

EDWIN M. CAHILL
Lt. Colonel, A.G.D.
Asst. Adjutant General

AIR GROUND FORCES TECHNICAL AND RESOURCES STAFF

I. *PURPOSE OF AGFTRS.*

To have a self contained independent unit of selected men with a specific mission and with all of the means necessary to fulfill that mission in the most efficient manner.

II. *POLICY.*

AGFTRS to be operated as an intelligence-collecting agency for United States forces in China. Its position is primarily one of service and as a coordinator of all field intelligence functions.

Mindful of political embarrassments which may be imposed by the Chinese authorities to hamper the mission of AGFTRS it is imperative that a clear understanding of its role be impressed upon all personnel belonging to the unit. This calls for picked personnel who in their manner and actions demonstrate an intelligent and sympathetic understanding of the Chinese, their psychology, susceptibilities, and governmental problems. As AGFTRS will be aided materially by the good name enjoyed by the Fourteenth Air Force, it is incumbent upon all concerned to conduct themselves in the most circumspect manner at all times.

Cooperation with Chinese officials has been given to date largely because of the operational role of the Fourteenth Air Force and the long standing respect accorded the U. S. for its non-interference in Chinese national affairs. It will be the responsibility of AGFTRS to direct its attention to combat intelligence; and to avoid any semblance of prying into domestic problems either national or provincial. Personnel will be instructed to study the local picture and to understand its political implications thoroughly, but an attitude of prying is to be avoided scrupulously as rousing of Chinese suspicions would make further useful work impossible. Better combat intelligence is the goal of AGFTRS, and it must be stressed to the exclusion of all other objectives.

III. *PERSONNEL OF AGFTRS.*

It is proposed that the personnel for this unit be obtained as follows:

OSS to furnish certain personnel already in the Theater, and additional men as soon as they arrive.

The Fourteenth Air Force to furnish such officers and men as are already engaged in this work and are desired to continue.

The Theater Commander to be requested for such personnel as are especially well qualified and are doing like work.

All personnel with the unit will be attached to it as there will be no T/O for this unit.

If there should be any problem in promoting the personnel in this unit who are not assigned to OSS then it is suggested that such personnel be assigned to OSS and that their promotions be obtained in this manner. However, it is understood that this is only an administrative procedure dictated by circumstance and not designed to give OSS additional control or credit.

IV. *CONTROL OF AGFTRS.*

AGFTRS will be activated by an order issued by the Theater Commander and will be assigned to the Commanding General, Fourteenth Air Force, for direction and supervision. Copies of all orders affecting the policy of AGFTRS or the movement of its personnel will be forwarded to the Theater OSS Officer and the A-2, Fourteenth Air Force, for information.

V. *COMMANDING OFFICER AGFTRS.*

Major W. J. Smith, Assistant A-2, Fourteenth Air Force, will be designated the Commanding Officer, AGFTRS. Major Smith as Commanding Officer assumes full responsibility for direction of field functions and therefore will be given authority in all administrative matters pertaining to personnel in the field. Policies will be directed in conformity with the preceding paragraph. He will establish headquarters in Kweilin. Eventually a northern branch of this unit will be established with a site to be selected later.

VI. *POSITION OF OSS REGARDING AGFTRS.*

OSS will furnish personnel for AGFTRS under the Table of Organization approved for it by the Joint Chiefs of Staff.

OSS will furnish the special funds and equipment that are necessary in the performance of the assigned mission that are not available from any other source.

The Commanding Officer of AGFTRS will prepare and submit a monthly report outlining the physical set-up established, the work accomplished and the expenditures made. Copies of this report will then be forwarded to the Fourteenth Air Force and to Theater OSS Officer for information of the Theater Commander and the Commanding General, Fourteenth Air Force.

VII. *MISSION OF AGFTRS.*

Liaison with Chinese Military Headquarters.

Air-Ground Liaison when military operations warrant.

Secure all information possible on enemy order of battle, both air and ground, enemy shipping movement, industrial activities, documents, and publications.

Arrange for pilot rescue.

Submit daily weather reports.

Train agents for working in the occupied zone and then place them there.

Airfield security and counter-espionage to include trained Department of Justice agents and up-to-date methods of detection.

General ground intelligence.

Prisoner of war interrogation.

Morale operations. (See summary appended.)

Technical intelligence.

Establishment of a complete radio network so that all reports of an urgent intelligence nature will be received in the quickest possible time, and so that the greatest security and efficiency can be attained.

Instructional Branch for training of agent radio operators. This program will be conducted either at Lingling or Changsha according to decision to be made by the Commanding General, Fourteenth Air Force.

VIII. *PLANS*.

1. *Organization of III War Zone.*

a. Lt. Frillmann to command the base station at Shang Jao, Kiangsi Province. At present he has one radio operator and one code man and is using a V-100 set.

(1) Lt. Frillmann has two primary objectives at the present time, liaison with the War Area Commander, and establishing intelligence posts along the Yangtze River. Tentative points selected are Hukou, Anking, Wuhu, and Nanking.

(2) Agent sets and a more suitable base radio will be furnished to Lt. Frillman just as soon as they are available.

b. Capt. Leonard Clark with base station at Lishui to establish agents in Shanghai, Hankchow, Ningpo, and a minimum of two coast watching stations, one at Haimen and the other on an island to be selected in the Chushan archipelago. At the present time Capt. Clark is making reconnaissance in order to make the necessary contacts. Upon his return the necessary equipment and personnel will be available for his return to the area and establishing his base. It will also be Capt. Clark's responsibility for the placing of agents with radios on smuggler junks in the area. It is considered that major emphasis on coast watching stations should be concentrated in the Third War Area due to the present shipping lanes used by the Japanese and troop concentrations indicating a possible thrust southward.

c. A station to be established at Yungan will be at one of the main control points in the Fukien Provincial Warning Net. This station will be in touch with a coast watching post established near Kiangwo, immediately south of Amoy. It is anticipated that an agent will be placed on Que Moy Island, to report on Japanese airdrome activity and shipping movement. Another coast watching station to be established at Sungsia, immediately east of Futsing. It would be advisable to have another set located in Meihwa or on the Japanese held island of Wuhu. It is believed that arrangements could be made for the placing of an agent set on the Chinese Government launch which carries mail into Foochow at least once a week.

d. The Office of the Naval Attaché has already established a radio station at Foochow and has assigned an agent for duty on Pingtan Island. It is probable that the navy will expand present activities in the Foochow area, therefore it is proposed that the closest collaboration be established between AGFTRS and the Naval Attaché.

2. *Organization of the IX War Zone.*

a. The excellent work initially originated by Capt. Birch will be continued by Lt. Rosholt with a base station at Changsha. The agent set at Yochow will be retained as at present. It is expected that within the next two weeks the agent set which has been at Sienning will be pushed forward into the Wuhan area. This will be done as soon as another set can be obtained to cover Shihweiyao now being served by the Sienning team. For the time being the agent set near Nanchang will be retained. As soon as possible an agent will be recruited for the city of Hankow, trained and placed in that city with his own radio.

3. *Organization of the VII War Zone.*

a. Lt. Lynn, assisted by Lt. Gleysteen, will command the base station already established at Kukong. He will establish a radio set in Waiyeung for the rapid transmission of such information as is brought to that area; as soon as his assistant arrives and he is satisfied that he can carry on the work at the base satisfactorily, Lt. Lynn will proceed to Tsingyun taking with him two American enlisted radio operators and two agent sets. He will contact a nine-man Chinese guerrilla team that he knows of and leave the two American operators and one of the agent sets. When this arrangement has been completed Lt. Lynn will proceed to Shaping and contact the Government Guerrillas in that area and turn over the second set. It is intended that this second set be eventually worked into Fatsoong. It is assumed that these guerrillas will have personnel who will know how to work the set and also know English, and Lt. Lynn will teach them a safe code to be used in making radio contact with his base station at Kukong. In addition Lt. Lynn will contact Col. Au, Director Kwangtung Warning Net, and arrange for a coast watching station in the vicinity of Hui Lai. He will be charged with obtaining rapid reliable information from Swatow to the South of Macao and will recruit and train his own agents for this purpose.

4. *Organization of the V and VIII War Areas.*

a. In the V and VIII Areas a tentative base will be established at Sianfu. A radio station will be established by M. I. S. X. It will have liaison teams to be located in places to be determined at a future date. By having the base station at Sianfu established by M. I. S. X., it should later be possible for agents to be placed in the II and X War Areas, even though this territory is Communist. The cover of Air Rescue and the humanitarian work which this station will be doing should justify our making strong requests for the

contact regardless of the political implication which may be involved.

b. In the light of pending operations it is now necessary to furnish five liaison teams. These will maintain direct liaison with the Chinese Military and communicate by radio with Field Headquarters wherever it is established. Their function will be to effect Air-Ground liaison either in checking a Japanese drive or supporting a Chinese offensive. It is hoped that once the emergency is past the resulting "Good Will" will permit the establishing of a permanent base station and the procedure outlined for other areas will be followed.

5. It is hoped that once Capt. Birch and Lt. Drummond have established the liaison teams outlined in the preceding paragraph they will then be able to proceed to Fouyang and make arrangements for the establishing of a base station at that point. Once this base station has been established, it will be possible to tap and coordinate an extensive radio net already operating in guerrilla-held territory. This net now covers the Shantung Peninsula and extends as far north as Te Hsien on the Grand Canal. The officer in charge of the base station at Fouyang will be charged with the immediate mission of extending existing radio facilities to Tientsin, Peking, and the Kwantung Peninsula. The selection and recruiting of agents who will go to Korea via the Kwantung Peninsula will be possible once suitable contact has been established with the guerrillas in Shantung.

6. *Organization of the IV War Area.*

a. Intelligence data from F. I. C. are at present dependent upon the efforts of the Chinese military, Free French, and the Gordon-Bernard group. The usual shortcomings which characterize Chinese intelligence—namely, inaccuracy of reporting and excessive time lag—exist to a pronounced extent in this area. The Free French, who are only tolerated by the Chinese, maintain at best a precarious position. Their efforts are also weakened by lack of cohesion and internal administrative stresses. Experience to date has been that the Gordon-Bernard Group, sponsored by Admiral Yang Hsuan-Chen, Director of Intelligence, Military Operations Board, has demonstrated an effectiveness surpassing any intelligence group working in the area. This has been accomplished primarily because of the practical and aggressive policies of its co-directors, Mr. Larry Gordon (Canadian) and Mr. Harry Bernard (U. S. citizen), ex-Texaco employees in China, who now have an active and competent group of agents traveling to and from enemy held territory. Use of radios by agents and courier service has effectively proved that intelligence data can be accurately and promptly forwarded to operational headquarters.

b. It is proposed that Lt. Arthur Hopkins be stationed in Liuchow to act in the capacity of liaison officer with the B-G group and also to represent the Fourteenth Air Force at Fourth War Area Headquarters. His efforts should be directed toward training Chinese intelligence personnel in obtaining and reporting military intelligence accurately and promptly. It will be Lt. Hopkins' responsibility to supervise the transmission of all intelligence information via Fourteenth Air Force radio channels to Headquarters of the Air Force and all other interested agencies or units.

c. As one of the functions outlined for AGFTRS is pilot aid it would also be the responsibility of Lt. Hopkins to maintain close relationship with the Free French organization encouraging and assisting them to develop a practical program designed to return pilots to Free China. Major Wichtrich, Commanding Officer of the AGAS, will be advised of all aspects of the program as it develops.

d. At present the B-G organization maintains an outpost at Lungchow near the F.I.C. border. From this point agents are directed and incoming intelligence is transmitted by radio to Liuchow where it is now relayed by Army communications to Kunming and Kweilin. The radio now at Lungchow is at present inadequate to serve as a contact with Saigon where agents are now operating. It is the intention of the B-G group to establish a powerful station at Lungchow capable of working Saigon and points south. It will require the lapse of several months before the necessary equipment can be obtained and installed.

e. In the interim, it is proposed that the present routine of the Lungchow station be maintained. However, to profit by the contacts now existing in Saigon it is proposed that the recently improved Fourteenth Air Force radio station at Liuchow work a daily schedule with agents now in the Saigon area. Codes and schedules will be arranged by Messrs. Bernard and Gordon with cooperation of Lt. Hopkins.

f. Expansion of the agent training program should be undertaken by Gordon and Bernard. In order to facilitate their efforts AGFTRS stands ready to provide radios and other miscellaneous equipment as well as such funds as will be required to supplement the effective B-G program already in progress.

APPENDIX

Morale Operations

A. Objectives

1. To convince Chinese and other friendly residents of occupied areas of the necessity of bombing industrial, shipbuilding, and other targets, and the long term benefit to them therefrom.

2. To persuade Chinese labor in factories, mines, shipyards, godowns, etc., in occupied areas likely to be bombed and other areas to desert their jobs for their own safety and welfare.

3. To deceive, misdirect, and confuse Japanese military commanders concerning future Fourteenth Air Force bombing missions and targets.

4. To give false, misleading, and confusing directions to Japanese shipping for the purpose of entrapment or reconnaissance.

5. To discredit and otherwise neutralize or eliminate responsible Japanese (and collaborationist) officers and civilians engaged in coastal military or shipping operations.

6. To further arouse friendly Chinese and eventually the masses to passive resistance and as operations develop sufficiently, to sabotage and revolt.

7. To harass, confuse, and demoralize (where possible) Japanese troops and civilians, particularly at isolated garrisons or outposts.

B. Media

1. Agents, both professional and amateur—the latter, not agents in the ordinary sense of the term—can be organized to write hundreds of letters to relatives in occupied areas, urging them for reasons of safety to move out of crowded industrial areas. Students, merchants, refugees, and others can be organized, quite innocently, for reasons of self-interest, to carry on correspondence of this kind. The professional agents will be employed to go through the enemy lines into key points to carry out the objectives outlined above.

2. Rumors, both subversive and deceptive. These will be spread by word of mouth, by printed material, by black radio, and other methods. This technique was probably the most effective instrument employed by Germany in preparing the ground work for the downfall and defeat of France.

3. Subversive printed material, such as "black" leaflets, pamphlets, literary material from Japanese sources already banned by Japanese censors as "dangerous", false "Japanese" manifestos or documents, etc.

4. Black radio including "freedom stations, ghost-voicing of Japanese broadcasts, both at home and abroad, heckling, trans-mission of deceptive or subversive morse code (in Romanji) directions or news (such as news of Japanese losses) and following up regular Japanese broadcasts with news presumably from the same Japanese station.

5. Sonic and visual deception, by the use of special devices for sonic projection and dummy airplanes and paratroopers, etc., for visual deception.

6. Faked photographic and intelligence documents and orders, both American and enemy.

7. "Poison pen" letters regarding corrupt Japanese and collaboratist military, business, and political individual and interests.

C. Personnel

1. OSS will be able to provide, within the next six months, approximately twenty American personnel, both military and civilian, to organize and conduct the above operations. Agents can be recruited locally by men who have lived in the target areas. Certain other native personnel, with special talents as translators, writers, artists, monitors, and broadcasters are now being recruited in the United States.

2. As soon as desired by the Fourteenth Air Force, we will detach on temporary duty, an officer, fully experienced in MO media, to train other officers, enlisted men, and agents, and other training personnel en route.

3. Expert operating personnel, having special knowledge of particular media and techniques, are now en route or are soon to depart from the U. S. Approximately ten of these should be here in six weeks to two months, subject to unforeseen transportation delays.

D. Equipment

1. Special new printing and reproduction equipment, suitable for main base and field use, have been procured and are being shipped. Genuine Japanese documentary and special purpose paper (practically unobtainable and not produced outside of Japan, is also en route).

2. Both portable and stationary radio transmitters, particularly suitable for these purposes, have also been ordered, ranging in power from 300 watt to 50 kw. (The latter may be used in another Theater, if transportation over the hump is not obtainable, but its power and range would be especially useful in this Theater where distances are so great). All of these transmitters will be so converted by the manufacturer that they can be operated on both medium and short wave, adjusted to voice, telegraphic code, recordings, etc. Frequency changes can be made promptly.

3. Other equipment is also en route or on order, which will be useful in MO operations, including special deceptive devices and photographic equipment.

4. Penetration of Northern China

It was essential that OSS penetrate northern China in order to gain access to Manchuria, Korea, and eventually Japan itself. As a preliminary step, OSS proposed to establish an advance operational base in the Communist-held areas of northern China. Negotiations to this end were initiated with the Chungking Government and dragged on for a period of months. Finally, early in 1944, authorization was received for U. S. entry into Communist and guerrilla-controlled territory.*

A mission, designated DIXIE, was activated in July 1944 under the direction of G-2, CBI, and commanded by a G-2 officer. It was the first American attempt to secure intelligence from areas of China beyond the control of the Chungking Government. The purpose of DIXIE was to estimate the potentialities of the Communist areas to aid U. S. plans and possible offensives, both from the military and the intelligence viewpoints. The assignments of the mission specifically included the collection of Japa-

* Vice-President Wallace, then in China, assisted in obtaining Army approval of this plan, despite Ambassador Hurley's objections to it.

nese battle order data; intelligence from Japanese-language materials, prisoners of war and captured documents; data on weather; and information on the Communist military potential. Included in the first group of nine Americans who arrived at Yenan, the Communist capital, were four OSS men.* Additional personnel from OSS and other agencies joined DIXIE in August, bringing the total number of Americans to approximately twenty. Included were representatives of the China Theater G-2, State Department, 20th Bomber Command, Fourteenth Air Force, OWI and OSS.

During the first eight months, OSS men attached to DIXIE procured about eighty percent of the mission's intelligence data. Through DIXIE it was possible for the first time to obtain detailed, accurate Japanese order of battle information, train counts on the highly strategic North China rail lines, a steady flow of Japanese newspapers and magazines from North China, and data on the Japanese prisoner-of-war interrogation organization and Japanese intelligence and counter-intelligence units in China.

Immediately after the organization of the China Theater, OSS presented a series of plans for the expansion of DIXIE and the dispatch of other teams and missions into Communist-held territory. As long as operations from the Communist areas were interdicted to OSS, no access was possible to northern China, Manchuria and Korea. Therefore, OSS proposed a program for recruiting and training agents from among the Chinese Communists to develop SI, SO and MO operations in the regions dominated or occupied by the Communists. Discussions were held in Yenan, during which the Communists demanded nothing short of a complete OSS training and operations program. Chungking authorities, however,

* The OSS representatives were under the cover of G-2 or Fourteenth Air Force (AGFRTS), since Tai Li stubbornly and consistently refused to sanction the entry of OSS personnel into Communist areas.

objected hotly to any arrangements whereby the U. S. would give to the Communists any training or equipment which might be used against the Chiang Kai-shek regime after the war. The failure of the Chinese factions to reach an agreement prevented approval for any plan to penetrate or operate from Communist territory.

Another OSS project, designated EAGLE, was aimed at Korea. A unit of Koreans and Korean-American personnel was recruited in the U. S. and in China and trained intensively at bases in Anhwei Province and near Hsian. Although contact was made with the Korean underground, EAGLE never was cleared to go into action as planned.

U. S. representatives with DIXIE in Yenan were gradually withdrawn in June and July of 1945; all representation in Communist China was terminated in July, in view of the tense political situation developing incident to the impending capitulation of the Japanese.

The full support of the China Theater Commander was lacking in pressing for greater access to regions beyond the control of Chungking. Wedemeyer, himself, was preoccupied with southern China and Theater plans for a major offensive there. Operation CARBONADO * was to culminate in a drive to Canton and the South China Sea, coincident with an American landing on the China coast.

The failure to penetrate northern China was a crucial gap in U. S. intelligence coverage for the war against Japan. Operations into Manchuria would have definitively revealed the weakness of the vaunted Japanese Kwangtung Army—information which might have served to strengthen immeasurably the U. S. position at the Yalta Conference. The Japanese capitulation in August both obviated the OSS plans and caused Wedemeyer's offensive to be stillborn.

————
* See OG, in "Individual Branch Activities," below.

5. Operations into Siam and Indochina

The original authorization for OSS operations from China into Siam and Indochina was contained in JCS 245. Pursuant to the SACO Agreement, these operations were to be under SACO control. In this area, as in China itself, the obstructionism and lassitude of the Chinese, evident in all phases of SACO intelligence activities, handicapped OSS. OSS made little real progress until freed from foreign control. Certain minor penetrations into northern Siam were effected; in Indochina additional complications were present in the form of intra-French political differences, on the one hand, and, on the other, the activities of an existing spontaneous amateur intelligence organization.

(a) *Siam.* As early as August 1942 OSS recruited and began to train twenty-one Siamese, most of them students at American universities and schools. They were to be sent to China at some later date, following the approval of Stilwell and Tai Li. Their mission called for the establishment of an intelligence net in Siam and the implementation of all phases of psychological warfare against the Japanese forces occupying that country.

Early in 1944, following additional training in India, the group established a base at Szemao, in southern Yunnan Province near the Indochina border, and prepared to enter Siam clandestinely and begin operations. However, the Chinese succeeded in preventing such operations for a period of months. Finally, in September 1944, a small group was successfully infiltrated.* In October 1944 regular contact was established and maintained between the group in Siam and the advance base at Szemao. Since these operations were confined largely to northern Siam, only little significant intelligence was

————
* Using one excuse after another, the Chinese continually failed to provide the necessary guides, and OSS was forced to rely on its own initiative to recruit suitable personnel familiar with the area.

received. Not until early 1945, when OSS began operations based in the south and direct contact with Siamese officials was established, did intelligence results from Siam provide dividends proportionate to the effort expended. At that time, all OSS operations in Siam came under the command of OSS/SEAC Detachment 404.*

(b) *Indochina.* Two groups, entirely unrelated and separate, served to complicate the initiation of intelligence operations into French Indochina: (1) The Meynier Mission, and (2) the GBT group.

Meynier. China-based operations into Indochina were approved by Tai Li late in 1942, contingent upon compliance with his request that French, rather than American, personnel be used.** In the spring of 1943, OSS requested and obtained from the French military authorities in North Africa the assignment of several French officers for activities in Indochina. An officer on the staff of General Giraud, Commandant Meynier, was chosen to head the group. Meynier recruited several other French officers with experience in Indochina, in addition to some native soldiers from the French Army. Following training in an OSS area in North Africa, the group reached China via India early in the fall of 1943. They were held for further training and briefing at a SACO base in China. At this point a series of complications developed.

Meynier's wife, an Annamese princess and priestess who was related to several key administrative and ecclesiastical figures in Indochina, was in custody in occupied France. It was not possible for Meynier to proceed with plans for entering Indochina until his wife was liberated. Repeated efforts by OSS and British agents finally resulted in her escape from France in July 1943. She was brought to China to enter Indochina with her husband and his group.

---

* See Siam in "Southeast Asia", above.
** The Chungking Government recognized the Free French.

A thornier problem was that of political differences among the French themselves. Even though General de Gaulle had given his approval to Meynier and his group, relations between Meynier and the ardently de Gaullist French Military Mission in Chungking were strained from the start. Upon arrival in China, Meynier found that a new group, the Devereux mission, had been organized to begin operations into Indochina before the Meynier mission had embarked from North Africa. The Devereux group included French naval officers and was predominantly de Gaullist. The group was disbanded and its personnel reassigned. Despite the fact that de Gaulle had approved Meynier's activities, he was regarded as suspect by the other French groups in China.

By early 1944, the Meynier group had not yet made much progress toward penetrating Indochina. The intra-French political complexities appeared overwhelming, and OSS requested that the group be transferred to the full control and authority of the French Military Mission in China.

GBT. The other group with which OSS worked in Indochina was the Gordon-Bernard-Tan Group (GBT). It was organized in early 1942 by a group of employees of a U. S. oil firm in Indochina. The original purpose of the leader of the group, a Canadian, appeared to have been to bolster the morale of the employees' French friends in the country by maintaining contact with the outside world. However, what had originally been a casual arrangement began to assume the characteristics of an amateur intelligence agency. Subsequently, it developed into an actual intelligence network collaborating with Allied organizations.

GBT began operations with couriers. It acquired a limited number of radio sets from the British in India and established stations at Hanoi and Haiphong, as well as a headquarters station at Lungchou in China, across the Indochina border. The Chinese Government supplied operators for

439

the headquarters station on condition that all intelligence received would be sent to Chinese military intelligence in Chungking.

The first OSS contact with GBT was through AGFRTS, after the establishment of that unit in April 1944. Daily radio contacts between GBT and AGFRTS were arranged for the Fourteenth Air Force, which supplied money for expansion of the GBT headquarters and staff. AGAS (Air Ground Aid Service) used GBT for rescue work and donated radio and other equipment. Although OSS at first had no direct relations with GBT, in September 1944 it provided some financial support and assigned a liaison officer to aid the development of SO and MO operations and generally expand the GBT network. By November 1944, GBT radio contacts included: OSS, Kunming; AGAS, Kunming; AGFRTS, Kweiyang; Chinese 4th War Area Headquarters, Liuchow (Kwangsi); Chinese 4th War Area Sub-headquarters, Tunghing (Kwangsi); Chinese Director Military Intelligence and the British and American Military Attaches, Chungking; and Chinese Director Military Intelligence Sub-headquarters at Nanning. Some of these contacts were dropped as the Japanese advanced through southern China at the end of 1944, but GBT still maintained contact with the American, Chinese, British and French units.

OSS participation resulted in wide expansion of the GBT network. In the OSS reorganization at the beginning of 1945, the administrative and operational control of GBT was projected. However, by 10 March 1945, the Japanese completed total occupation of Indochina. The result was the inevitable disintegration of GBT. Its headquarters were transferred from Lungchou to Kunming in China. From there, infrequent radio contact was maintained with Hanoi, Haiphong and Saigon.

From early March to the end of May of that year, OSS attempted to bring GBT under its direct control. Aside from the fact that OSS was supplying the bulk of GBT

equipment and support, the problem transcended that of mere operational direction: matters of security of GBT operations were also at stake and, through them, the security of contiguous OSS operations. However, OSS overtures were declined, and, after 1 June 1945, connections with GBT were severed. GBT itself continued to serve AGAS and to operate under the direction of that agency.

In the spring of 1945, after OSS was given responsibility for coordination of all but Chinese clandestine activities in the China Theater, new OSS teams were dispatched into Indochina and a network of some twelve chains was active by May, which produced a rapidly increasing flow of intelligence.

6. OSS in the China Theater

On 31 October 1944, Lt. Gen. A. C. Wedemeyer assumed command of the newly constituted China Theater with headquarters in Chungking. The boundaries of the Theater included the Chinese mainland, Indochina and all islands adjacent thereto, with the exception of Formosa and Hainan. This split in what had originally been the China-Burma-India Theater was designed to increase efficiency by dividing U. S. command responsibilities between two theater commanders. From the OSS point of view, it was a development of the greatest importance: it at last permitted OSS to attain the independent status under the local Theater Commander that it had sought from the start.

The situation of the Chungking Government in China was extremely critical. The summer campaigns had been marked by a series of military and political disasters: The defeat of 700,000 Chinese troops by an enemy force of 100,000 in the Honan Province; the Chinese loss of Changsha in Hunan; the successful use by the enemy of well-armed fifth column forces; and the growth within Chungking-controlled territory of a separatist movement fostered both by quislings and by democratically-minded intellectuals and businessmen weary of gross incompetence, venality and government profiteering, as well as the acute inflation which threatened the country.

Wedemeyer's mission was to keep China in the war, to encourage the Chinese and to fulfill the agreements made at the Cairo Conference. The Japanese were advancing on Kweilin in a drive to establish an unbroken line of communications from Tokyo to Singapore. By 5 December 1944, embassies in Chungking were unofficially advising civilian women, children and unessential men to leave because of the enemy advance into Kweichow Province from Kwangsi Province. Wedemeyer's task was twofold:

(1) Support to the Chinese: The Chungking Government was attempting to maintain some 450 ill-equipped, underfed and poorly trained divisions. Chinese economy supporting this force was withering, and the transportation system did not include one effective railroad. Wedemeyer undertook a training program, providing veterinary, signal corps, transport and general staff schools to teach American techniques. At the same time, he attempted to simplify the Chinese command of field forces.

(2) Offensive action: Although the reopening of the Burma Road improved the supply situation, the secondary nature of China as a war theater had become patently evident in comparison with the Pacific theaters. Nonetheless, China remained a vital intelligence base and a front on which guerrilla warfare could be conducted with excellent results. In addition, there was the possibility of a major amphibious invasion on the China coast.

In Washington Donovan reported at length to President Roosevelt on the continuous difficulties encountered by OSS in developing intelligence operations in China. In a memorandum sent to the White House in November 1944, Donovan stated flatly that the Chinese throughout 1943 had opposed every effort of OSS to establish itself in China. He characterized the SACO Agreement as "the first breach in this resistance", but went on to say that it was only "a foot in the door, the first step". He cited the lack of Hump tonnages allotted to OSS in SACO and the "impossible" situation of that organization over a period of eight months in 1944, during which strenuous but futile efforts were made to mount the extensive operations required by the situation. Lacking equipment, resources and the cooperation of SACO, OSS was helpless. He added:

I discussed this situation with you before my trip last November (1943) to China. You agreed with me that we could not do our job unless we operated as an independent organization. You authorized me to tell the Generalissimo we must be permitted independence of operation. . . .

Donovan went on to review the record of AGFRTS. Under AGFRTS, with the cooperation of the Fourteenth Air Force, OSS had finally succeeded in initiating independent intelligence operations. The progress of OSS through AGFRTS was clear evidence of the need for operational independence. As a result of the shift in command in the Far East, OSS would now be able to perform its principal functions in China: To collect information necessary both for the defeat of the Japanese enemy and for making informed decisions on ultimate peace settlements in the Far East. "Now is the time to make OSS in China directly responsible to the U. S. Commanding General and to service him, his subordinates, General MacArthur and Admiral Nimitz", Donovan stated.

This wish was attained: OSS/China emerged as an independent agency operating under the command of the Commanding General, China Theater.

The Theater reorganization gave OSS the opportunity to re-assess its activities and functions in both of the new theaters, China and India-Burma. Conferences were held in Washington between Donovan and key

OSS officers from the field establishments. Following a general agreement on the future organization and plans for the Theater, Donovan himself went to the field in January 1945 to complete the reorientation of OSS installations. At that time OSS maintained three operating units in China: SACO, AGFRTS and an embryo Detachment 202 at Chungking. In December 1943 Donovan had activated 202 in a move to assert the identity of OSS and to emphasize its contribution to SACO. Detachment 202 operated as a headquarters detachment and spent a substantial portion of its time in a series of controversies with Tai Li over efforts to develop independent U. S. intelligence operations. The total OSS personnel in the Theater numbered 144 persons at the time of the Theater reorganization.

Wedemeyer worked to concentrate all U. S. personnel in China under his command and responsible to him. He insisted, and the JCS concurred, that in his capacity as Theater Commander he should exercise full command and operational control over all units and resources belonging to U. S. military, naval and quasi-military or clandestine operations agencies active in the China Theater. In line with this policy, OSS was not only accorded status as an independent agency operating under the Theater Commander but also was charged with coordination of all U. S. clandestine operations in the Theater. Wedemeyer conferred with the commander of Detachment 202 and studied the operations of AGFRTS. One of his first decisions was to relieve Miles of direct control of 202 and of its supplies. He also made recommendations with regard to operations in Indochina.* His decisions with regard to OSS were formalized in Operational Directive No. 4, issued on 6 February 1945.

Under this directive, the principal mission of OSS in the Theater was defined.

---

* Wedemeyer recommended that OSS operate independently in Indochina instead of depending on the GBT organization. See "Operations into Siam and Indochina" above.

OSS was to conduct operations, in line with JCS 155/11/D, as requested by and in accordance with the policies of the Theater Commander. Each proposed operation would be submitted for Theater Command approval through the appropriate general staff section and OSS was required to keep Theater Headquarters thoroughly informed on the current status of all operations undertaken, the implementation of Theater assignments and the coordination of such operations with the appropriate staff section.

In addition, to specific operations ordered by the Theater Commander, OSS operations included the following:

(1) The organization, supervision and direction of guerrilla activities or of special operations designed to effect the physical subversion of the enemy, including sabotage; the organization, direction, and conduct of guerrilla warfare; direct contact with, and support of, resistance groups, both underground and open; and the equipping and training of personnel required to carry out such activities;

(2) The delay and harassment of the enemy, and the denial to him of the use of lines of supply and communication and strategic facilities wherever located;

(3) The collection of secret intelligence by various means, including espionage and counter-espionage, in areas designated by the Theater Commander; the evaluation and dissemination of intelligence so collected;

(4) The subversion of the morale of enemy and puppet troops and enemy civilian personnel, wherever found, and the raising of the morale of friendly civilians in occupied territories;

(5) The accumulation, evaluation, and analysis of economic, political, psychological, topographic and military information concerning enemy and enemy-occupied territories, and the preparation of appropriate studies on those subjects;

(6) The expansion and improvement of the OSS communications network in China and contiguous areas in order to support and maintain adequately the operations of OSS;

(7) The performance of such special tasks, activities, or operations as might be required for the accomplishment of the OSS mission.

In addition, AGFRTS was placed under the command of the Strategic Services Officer * and the monthly allotment of supplies for OSS was increased from 25 to 150 tons, with Calcutta designated as OSS supply base. At the same time, OSS received informally a directive to begin the training of twenty Commando units of Chinese troops under OG leadership. Each Commando would comprise about 200 men to be used to spearhead future military operations.**

The SACO Agreement was continued, with the understanding that it would be amended to place all OSS personnel and supplies, as well as those of Navy Group, under Wedemeyer's direct command. On 6 April, JCS approved the transfer of Navy Group to the command and operational control of the Theater Commander and, by Operational Directive No. 15 of 15 May, Wedemeyer formally assumed command of Navy Group. This served to place the American contribution to SACO entirely under the Theater Commander—an arrangement that had been proposed by OSS as early as 1942.

The precise organization and functions of OSS/China crystallized in February 1945. General Order No. 5, issued by OSS/China on 1 March 1945, established an organizational pattern parallel to that of OSS/-Washington, yet drawing upon the experience of OSS in other war theaters. The position of Chief (Strategic Services Officer) and Deputy Chief were created, as well as that of Executive Officer. A Registry

was established and made responsible to the Secretariat. An Operational Planning Board was created to control the following:

(1) The Intelligence Officer, responsible for SI, X-2, R&A and CD;

(2) The Operations Officer, directing MO. SO, MU, Field Photographic and Special Projects;

(3) The Services Officer, controlling Finance, Procurement and Supplies, Reproduction, Transportation, military and civilian administrative and general office services;

(4) AGFRTS; and

(5) The OG Command, assigned to train the Chinese Commandos.

By this time the OSS roster had increased to more than 300. OSS headquarters for the China Theater were placed in Detachment 202, physically divided between Chungking and Kunming. The base headquarters was maintained at Chungking, primarily for liaison purposes. Kunming became the major operational and administrative headquarters and the Secretariat, as well as Hq. and Hq. Det., were established there. There was another OSS unit at Chungking, designated Detachment 203, which comprised small R&A, SI and MO staffs. In addition to the OSS personnel attached to SACO, several additional specialized detachments were established:

Detachment 204—the Schools and Training camp at Kaiyuan.

Detachment 205—at Dinjan, India; originally the Air Supply Base for Detachment 101 operations in Burma, it became a holding area for supplies and personnel south of the Hump and a supply base for OSS/-China generally.

Detachment 206—at Chengtu; primarily an X-2 base, also used for liaison with 20th Bomber Command units there.

In view of Theater priorities, the internal organization of OSS placed emphasis on three major branches: (1) The OG Branch which, in training Chinese Commando units, joined OSS directly to Theater tac-

---

* See "AGFRTS" above.
** See "Individual Branch Activities" above.

tical operations; (2) Secret Intelligence, responsibility for which made OSS the principal intelligence procurement agency in the Theater; and (3) Special Operations, to interdict enemy communication lines between northern and southern China in accordance with Theater plans and to organize guerrilla bands in support of the Chinese Armies.

To achieve staff coordination the Strategic Services Officer attended weekly meetings of the Theater Commander's Committee which formulated Theater policy, the membership of which included the commanding generals of Fourteenth Air Force, CCC, Theater G-2 and Army Service Forces. The OSS Executive Officer attended the meetings of the Committee of the Chiefs of Staff of those organizations.

OSS installations in forward areas were also reorganized. A system of Field Commands and Forward Bases was developed. From the Forward Bases, small teams, composed of four or five OSS men representing several branches, would be dispatched to operate behind the enemy lines. The Forward Bases served as supply centers for these teams and as relay points for the transmission of intelligence to OSS headquarters. Individual Field Commanders had the responsibility for implementing and coordinating OSS policies, projects and operations in their respective areas.

By 9 April, specific Field Commands had been established. OSS for its purposes divided the China Theater into three large zones:

Zone 1, Hsian Unit Field Command, north of the Yangtze River with base headquarters at Hsian.

Zone 2, Chihkiang Unit Field Command, south of the Yangtze River (primarily the 3rd, 7th and 9th Chinese War Areas) with base headquarters at Chihkiang.

Zone 3, Szemao Unit Field Command, comprising Indochina south to the 16° north latitude (the limit of the China Theater) with base headquarters at Szemao.

These areas remained substantially unaltered throughout the war, although their official designations were changed several times.

In addition to operations in these major geographical areas, OSS continued active participation in SACO, which by that time was operating in both north-central and southern China and which began to function with increasing efficiency in the final months of the war. A complete separation was maintained in the field between SACO operations and non-SACO activities; the latter soon far surpassed those conducted under SACO, both in scope and in number.

Throughout the first three months of 1945, AGFRTS continued much as before. After 7 February 1945, it operated fully under OSS command, continuing to supply valuable intelligence to the China Theater and especially to the Fourteenth Air Force. For example, during the period 8-19 February, AGFRTS supplied up to 57% of the total intelligence available to the Fourteenth Air Force, and from 19 to 22 February, 84% of the intelligence that the Fourteenth Air Force received was supplied by AGFRTS.* AGFRTS continued its operations until early April 1945. At that time, the Field Commands at Hsian and Chihkiang were activated. Since their areas of operation practically coincided with the AGFRTS areas, the latter organization was liquidated. AGFRTS personnel and activities were completely absorbed into OSS and the Field Commands.

AKRON. Outstanding among intelligence operations by OSS in the China Theater was the AKRON Project. It was activated in the beginning of 1945, at Wedemeyer's request, to conduct an intensive survey of the South China coast from Hongkong to Hainan Island. Personnel represented several OSS branches, particularly SI, R&A and Field Photographic.

---

* The percentages included ground and air reconnaissance intelligence.

444

The Project was started in February 1945; the deadline was 7 April, when all intelligence secured on the target area was due in Pearl Harbor. To meet the deadline, AKRON personnel were to be parachuted at the beginning of March and remain in the field for something over two weeks, whereupon they were to be recovered on or before 25 March together with the intelligence that they had collected during the period.

The drop operation on the east coast of China was successfully completed at the beginning of March, when eight men and their equipment were parachuted. Two weeks later, a supply drop to them was completed after two attempts had failed because of bad weather. AKRON then radioed that it had acquired the first intelligence installment in the allotted time and was ready for the pick-up.

The Theater, on request of OSS, approved the loan of a PBY-1, attached to the Air Sea Rescue Squadron in India, to effect the pick-up operation. The plane put in at Kunming on 19 March, and landed at the rendezvous point on the China coast on the same day as scheduled. The plane picked up 7 people, 2 of whom were OSS men bringing intelligence that they had compiled as the result of an extensive reconnaissance of the target area. Of the remaining 5 persons evacuated, 4 were Navy fliers who had been awaiting rescue for 3 months, and the fifth was a Catholic priest. The passage between the point off shore where the plane had landed and the coast was accomplished by means of two rubber dinghies.*

The first phase of AKRON was completed; the two members of the mission thus evacuated brought out with them a wealth of information, including 700 photographs. The remaining 6 AKRON men stayed in the area for an additional period to compile further requisite data and to organize coast watching units. In mid-April, one of the

remaining 6 men was evacuated and brought more photographic material. On 26 April, the chief of the Project was evacuated and assigned to take the completed AKRON report to Washington. The AKRON personnel remaining in the field were incorporated into AGFRTS on 1 May.

The survey of the coastal area from Hongkong to Hainan Strait—AKRON's mission—was completed within the time set. Wedemeyer commended OSS for this achievement, characterizing it as a "work containing clear and concise information of the terrain and facilities in that area" and constituting "an excellent study of the areas desired, thus making a timely contribution to the information on which theater plans must be based."

7. Individual Branch Activities

Details and examples of specific OSS activities in China are most readily provided by an examination of the work of the individual branches. In general, several branches collaborated on virtually all OSS/-China operations; OSS teams in the field were almost always composed of representatives of more than one branch.

The work of the branches was uniformly accelerated and brought to full significance by the organization of the China Theater and the establishment of OSS as an independent agency under the Theater Commander at the start of 1945. It took two full years for OSS to attain the necessary status and support that made possible the adequate development of its resources. Only in the penetration of northern China did OSS fail, and that due to factors far beyond its control.

SO. In OSS/China the Special Operations Branch was one of the first to be organized, its establishment dating back to the OSS/SACO period. SO activities at first consisted primarily of training and planning. A few OSS officers instructed Chinese agents in SACO training camps and several SO teams were dispatched un-

---

* The sea was so rough that it was not possible to use wooden boats which might damage the aircraft.

der SACO auspices and rigid Chinese surveillance. Since SO was denied both equipment for more extensive activities and Tai Li's authorization to engage in combat, demolition and sabotage missions, the Branch turned also to AGFRTS, upon establishment of that unit in April 1944. Under the aegis of AGFRTS, SO teams received explosives, radio equipment, arms and munitions. During the Japanese offensive in 1944, SO/-AGFRTS teams, employing guerrilla tactics, helped materially to delay the enemy advance.

A more significant phase in the history of SO/China began in February 1945, when OSS/China was reorganized and OSS was established as an independent command. Accordingly, SO initiated its own operational and training activities, in addition to continuing SACO and AGFRTS missions. In the field, the Branch developed extensive sabotage activities and amassed an impressive total; at the same time, it embarked on an expanded training program.

Although SO teams were authorized to operate everywhere in China, limitations of transportation, supply and trained personnel precluded an expansion commensurate with opportunity. Nevertheless, the teams operated in areas up to 500 miles behind enemy lines, with OSS men leading Chinese guerrilla forces ranging in strength up to 1,500. The American officers and enlisted men who served with such forces assumed both the battle dress and living conditions of Chinese guerrilla troops.

The main school and training base for SO units was established at Loyang in Honan Province. The SO forward base was situated in Kweilin in 1944, but was moved later to Liuchow in the face of an enemy offensive. During the subsequent Japanese drive on Liuchow, two SO teams directed the efforts of Chinese troops to defend their positions. Under their leadership, an estimated 3,000 Japanese were killed, 123 bridges of all types were destroyed and 19 river ferries were either burned or blown up.

At the same time, the SO units constructed 25 road blocks to help stem the enemy advance. Government buildings, abandoned by the Chinese, were booby-trapped; shipping installations and power lines in the enemy-held corridor between northern and southern China, along the Canton-Hankow railroad, and subsidiary and alternate routes, were destroyed. By 26 June 1945, SO teams nad cut the railroad at 1,124 places between Chihsian and the Yellow River bridge and between Sinsiang and Kaifeng on the only alternate river route. One team cut telephone and telegraph lines in 156 places, destroyed 7 bridges, removed 524 rails and 72 telegraph poles, and derailed 2 enemy troop trains, in which 145 Japanese troops perished. The next day another SO team cut the railroad between Hengyang and Leiyang, wrecking one train and stalling three others at points where assaults by air had been prearranged. In these operations the enemy reportedly suffered 1,300 casualties, including 10 staff officers killed. At Kinhwa, a special Japanese military train was wrecked by another SO team. Near Saichiapu, an enemy airfield was attacked on 29 June, as a result of which it was abandoned for two weeks. Japanese convoys were repeatedly ambushed along the roads and advance posts were frequently raided.

The basic OSS field unit consisted of a four-man team and 150 OSS-trained guerrillas. The teams operated in the 1st, 2nd, 3rd, 7th, 9th and 10th Chinese War Areas and at headquarters of the Chinese Combat Command. In areas threatened by Japanese offensives, OSS combat forces undertook to retard the enemy by scorched earth tactics, as well as demolitions and guerrilla attacks. In February, for example, the Hsinchang airfield was demolished by two OSS teams on orders from the Chinese commanding general six days after all Fourteenth Air Force personnel had been evacuated from the base.

OSS field teams, both SO and SI, were equipped with one of the latest Signal Corps developments, VHF (Very High Frequency) radio, to guide Fourteenth Air Force planes to tactical targets. The performance of this radio was excellent. Two teams operating in the Chinese 9th War Area were credited with the transmission of more than 211 important intelligence messages in two months; the information transmitted included order of battle of all enemy divisions between Changsha and Kweilin, the condition of the Hangchow-Kweilin railroad, the enemy's sampan traffic on the Siang Kiang River and the morale of individual Japanese garrisons.

SO activities were varied. They included assistance to the Chinese guerrillas, sabotage missions in support of the Chinese armies and general damaging action against the enemy wherever possible. SO operations in support of Chinese guerrillas were generally successful, when considered in the light of the inadequate training and equipment which characterized guerrilla operations. The SO units completed numerous sabotage assignments, perhaps the most spectacular single exploit being the destruction early in August 1945 of the famous Yellow River bridge on the Peiping-Hankow railroad, which also resulted in the destruction of an entire Japanese train. In the same month, a large bridge ten miles east of Loning was blown. Enemy attempts to repair the damage were frustrated by American airmen, who carried out strafing missions on virtually a daily basis.

Behind the Japanese lines, SO teams constituted the basis for the development of other OSS activities. By the summer of 1945, the teams were producing even more comprehensive results due, in some measure, to the addition of SI, MO and Field Photographic personnel to the original SO groups.

In addition to SO teams, the work of AGFRTS and SACO units led by or including SO personnel developed to telling effect, particularly in respect to aid given to the Fourteenth Air Force. During the Japanese advance on Changsha, for instance, two OSS Army privates at a SACO training school in Yolo Shan volunteered to lead teams of Chinese against the enemy. Sighting an enemy cavalry unit approaching the river near Yi-Yang, they immediately radioed a message, first in code and then in clear text, to the Fourteenth Air Force fighter base. Fighter-bombers responded at once, attacking the Japanese while they were in midstream. Chinese reports placed the number of enemy dead at 9,000, a figure to be regarded with skepticism; but, even by conservative estimate, the enemy suffered casualties in the thousands. Two days later, one of the same privates relayed an agent's report of Japanese troops crossing the Siang River in sampans for an attack on Yolo Shan. The message was received by Fourteenth Air Force planes already airborne. They proceeded to the target immediately. The "sampans" proved to be double-decked troop barges. The next day, Chinese sources informed the Fourteenth Air Force Wing Commander that at least 23 of the barges had been sunk and 1,000 Japanese killed.

SI. SI, as such, was not established as an independently functioning branch in China until January 1945. It had been active before this time, but not on a scale comparable to SO. The work of SI was complicated by the fact that the earliest SI agents dispatched into China operated towards objectives assigned by OSS/Washington, under covers arranged in the U. S., and reported direct to SI/Washington. As of 25 January 1945, the actual SI force at OSS/China Headquarters consisted of six officers and two enlisted men—a group which lacked organization and even such basic equipment as maps showing the disposition of enemy troops and the progress of the fighting, or complete data on other SI installations or agents in China. Very little collated intelligence was available, and SI/China exercised no control over secret intelligence operations by OSS personnel in SACO or AGFRTS.

On 31 January 1945, a reorganization of SI was begun, incident to the OSS reorientation in the Theater. The SI men who previously operated in unorganized fashion were collected and reassigned. Accurate information concerning all available personnel had been compiled by 1 March and the staff had been rearranged. At the same time, reinforcements arrived from Washington and the European theaters, many of them completely untrained for the Far East. Because of the pressing need for SI agents in the field, it was necessary to send relatively untrained men to target areas.

During the period between March and June, additional personnel arrived in China in sufficient numbers and with adequate SI training to undertake major assignments. In the same period, SI acquired new intelligence sources in the field and prepared reports on major political and strategic subjects. The new sources increased steadily, so that by July 1945 the reports on strategic and political subjects from the new sources exceeded all previous sources combined.

The over-all intelligence coverage of OSS in China expanded greatly. Teams penetrated the Shantung Peninsula, the Yellow River Bend area, the Canton-Hongkong area, Shanghai and vicinity, Peiping and Tientsin, the area extending from Canton to the French Indochina border, and Chekiang, Anwhei and Kiangsi Provinces. SI teams were established in these areas and assisted in the training of agents for missions elsewhere, such as Koreans for the EAGLE Project.*

Although OSS penetration of Indochina was proposed in the QUAIL Plan, the complications incident to collaboration with the French and with GBT delayed the development of independent OSS operations until the Theater reorganization.** The SI

Branch received Wedemeyer's authorization to dispatch teams to Indochina, both by land and water, but conflicting directives in April delayed the mission until firm support was received from the Theater Commander when he recognized OSS as the sole American intelligence agency authorized to enter the country. By May 1945, there were twelve SI teams in Indochina and the flow of intelligence from them was rapidly increasing.

SI achieved virtually complete coverage only in southern China, where it established stations in three war areas. In addition, longer-range agents, reporting to the Chihchiang base, operated in the Foochow, Hangchow, Amoy, Shanghai, Canton, Macao and Nanking areas. In coastal regions, SI agents reported data on ship movements, weather and enemy air traffic, which was relayed to the Commander-in-Chief, Pacific Fleet, who made formal acknowledgment of these services rendered by OSS. All SI teams in southern and southeastern China regularly relayed meteorological intelligence. In addition, a number of teams specializing in weather reporting were situated along the coast from Hongkong to Shanghai. Such reports were specially handled by communications personnel and were radioed directly to the headquarters of interested Navy and Air Forces operational units. In this phase of its intelligence work, SI cooperated with the 10th Weather Squadron, Fourteenth Air Force and Navy Group, China.

The increased coverage of SI was evident in the increase of its disseminations in the period between January and June 1945. In January, less than ten percent of SI's output was useful to G-2, China Theater. In June, G-2 was utilizing more than forty percent of the information contained in SI reports. SI scored several intelligence triumphs, such as the procurement of a list of Japanese Army Postal Code designations. This list contained the designations of new enemy military units then in the formative

---

* See "Penetration of Northern China" above.
** See "Operations into Siam and Indochina" above.

stage, as well as those already in action in China. More than 400 Japanese postcards and letters identifying numerous troop units were seized. Among additional intelligence items secured by SI/China were: A code used by the Japanese Navy operating in Shanghai waters; the identification and location of the enemy's 133rd Division; the identification, location and code name of the Japanese 129th Division; the location and confirmation of the existence of the 131st Division; and the movement of the 27th and 40th Divisions from central China to points east and south of Canton, and their subsequent shift into the Kanhsien sector.

At SI headquarters in Kunming, staff members processed, evaluated and edited disseminations sent regularly to the Theater G-2, the Air Forces, the American Embassy in Chungking, the Chinese Combat Command and other customers. In addition, SI produced spot reports on request. One such spot assignment was a survey for General Wedemeyer of the Chinese coast from Hongkong to Hainan. Conducted by SI, with the assistance of personnel from other branches, the survey won a commendation from the General for the entire OSS organization in the Theater.*

In China, SI teams cooperated closely with the Chinese Area Military Commands in the 3rd, 7th and 9th War Areas, where a wide variety of intelligence, chiefly tactical, was obtained. In addition, Chinese agents trained by OSS/SACO for SI missions began reporting significant data early in 1945. Following the closer integration of SACO into the Theater Command, progressively important results were obtained, and the problems of delay in relaying intelligence were largely overcome.

However, the key SI targets in the China Theater were not covered: Northern China, Manchuria, Korea and the Japanese home

islands were never directly penetrated. Certain indirect penetrations were effected,* but the Chinese political schism between Chungking and Yenan ruled out operations in the northern areas under Communist control, and consequently precluded the use of those areas as a base for operations into Japan itself.

MO. Like other branches which were repeatedly frustrated in early efforts to gain a foothold in the China Theater, MO was compelled to create a unit within the SACO structure in order to begin operations. A cooperative agreement was drawn up between the Branch Chief and the Chinese in April 1944, after four weeks of unproductive negotiations. On 21 April, the first MO unit in China was activated at Happy Valley under the nominal leadership of a Chinese official, with MO providing radio and printing facilities. The Chinese agreed to furnish morale intelligence and agents. At the same time, at the suggestion of the Commanding Officer of Detachment 202, MO turned to the newly formed AGFRTS, whose networks of native agents were free of SACO control and capable of planting deceptive rumors and subversive literature, in addition to executing regular intelligence and sabotage activities.

As in the case of other branches, MO operations within the AGFRTS framework were more successful than under SACO. The MO unit in AGFRTS directed two rumor-spreading groups in southern China in May 1944, during the Japanese advance on Kweilin. MO in the SACO establishment was notably successful in September, when a team led by a naval officer, operating from a headquarters in Nanking, built an extensive propaganda network in the coastal area of southeast China. By the end of 1944, this team had circulated some 35,000 pieces of literature, printed on native presses, behind enemy lines.

On the whole, literature prepared and reproduced by the MO staff in Washington

* See AKRON Project in "OSS in the China Theater" above.

* See "Introduction" above.

449

and sent to the Theater was unsuitable for use in China. Teams in the field, even behind enemy lines, could far more effectively produce propaganda and MO material on the basis of morale intelligence and the reactions to current political, military and economic conditions. MO personnel were assisted by men from other OSS branches serving on the same field teams. Although lack of equipment for publication and broadcasting purposes hampered operations, the teams improvised skillfully. During the last few months of the war they were successful in inducing large numbers of enemy and puppet troops to surrender, in direct implementation of Combined Chiefs of Staff directives on "Inducement to Surrender of the Japanese Forces." In Kunming, MO operated a 7,500-watt radio transmitter which could be heard in the enemy-held coastal cities.

MO's projects for radio, rumor-planting and subversive printed propaganda never fully materialized on a large scale for several reasons. In essence, the reasons were: (1) Lateness in gaining entry into China; (2) lack of equipment and adequately trained personnel for the completely unprecedented and exceedingly complex job of conducting clandestine propaganda activities in so vast a Theater as China; and (3) the traditional Chinese attitude of apathy toward, and distrust of, propaganda in general and alien-directed propaganda in particular.

X-2. The work of X-2 was complicated both by difficulty in establishing itself and by the problems involved in invoking positive or police action to support its findings. The efforts of OSS to perform X-2 functions in SACO failed,* but a start was made under AGFRTS. It was not until September 1944 that the Branch was officially established at Kunming. Prior to that time, counter-espionage for U. S. needs was to have been supplied through Tai Li's BIS. This was not an ideal arrangement. The

---
* See "SACO" above.

U. S. could not rely on counter-espionage on any scale, particularly for long-range use, if such information came exclusively from Chinese or Chinese-controlled sources provided by the Chungking Government. Further, the Chinese manifested little interest in counter-espionage. A study by X-2 showed that Chinese efforts were "expended much less in preventing Japanese espionage penetration than in their own jurisdictional disputes and in spying on the Communists, Americans and British." Even the elementary task of interrogating prisoners was neglected; a suspect in Chinese hands generally was held in custody indefinitely or was quickly executed.

China was the territory of an ally in the war; it was not possible to operate there as in other war theaters, where there was ready access to positive action in support of X-2 information. Independent positive action might prove embarrassing or harmful to Chinese or other agencies. Coordination with the Chinese was impossible and OSS was forced to operate by its own devices.

Thus the X-2 assignment in China was made more complex, but it still entailed identification and neutralization of enemy espionage and the protection of the operational security of OSS. Arrests of proven enemy agents could only be made by the Chinese, whose cooperation in this regard frequently was difficult and time-consuming to secure. In the China Theater, X-2 worked through the CIC, which maintained close liaison with the Chinese. A system of interchange of interrogation reports was devised and, in cases where action was necessary, X-2 sent information to CIC which, if it concurred, presented the facts to the Chinese.

After October 1944, additional X-2 personnel were trained, new field stations were activated, and a master card file, which eventually contained some 15,000 "black" names, was begun. By March 1945, the X-2 staff in China had increased to 27 from the September 1944 total of 12, and by April X-2 personnel totalled 31.

X-2 organized and established a system of native agents at its several field stations since it was practically impossible for an American to carry on X-2 work himself because of racial and linguistic barriers. The policy of using native agents under American direction proved very successful. One field office in North China alone had over 17 key agents in its network and many of these agents ran their own smaller networks. The agents were sent into occupied China where, in several cases, they succeeded in penetrating regional Japanese headquarters. X-2 identified numerous Japanese agents and turned the data for their apprehension over to the appropriate agencies.

X-2's investigations and reports were largely responsible for alerting U. S. agencies in China to the dangers of enemy plainclothesmen assigned to espionage and assassination missions. The most spectacular achievement of the Branch was the exposure of three large enemy espionage rings, one of which employed 175 known agents. The first lead to these groups came in May 1945 in connection with the interrogation of seven suspects seized in the Hsian area by a field team. Other investigations revealed the Japanese use of Chinese agents for the dual purpose of espionage and traffic in narcotics.

Towards the close of the war, X-2/China had compiled the largest file on enemy agents and suspects of any American organization in the China Theater. The files furnished information which led to the arrest of a number of enemy agents, and prevented penetration of OSS and other U. S. agencies in many instances. One important operation was the X-2 penetration of a Japanese network preparing to attack Wedemeyer and Chiang Kai-shek during their trip to Hsian in August 1945. The successful penetration led to the frustration of the Japanese attempt.

In addition to the uncovering of several enemy espionage nets, X-2 planned and activated two large-scale programs: (1) Penetration of South China, providing for penetration of the strategic coastal areas from Canton and Hongkong south to Haiphong in Indochina, and (2) penetration of East China, providing for penetration of the coastal areas from Shanghai south to Hongkong. Agents were dispatched and were producing intelligence in considerable volume at the time of the Japanese surrender.

X-2 plans and programs were fully realized only after VJ-Day. Following the Japanese surrender, X-2 stations were ordered to move into areas under Chungking control in an attempt to locate or cause the neutralization of suspects and known agents, conduct interrogations, enter Japanese espionage training schools and agent meeting places that X-2 had identified, capture documents, and in general fulfill the complete objectives of the X-2 mission. After the reorganization of OSS/China on 15 August, X-2 became the Counter-Espionage Section of the Intelligence Division.

The delay of the actual surrender of the Japanese in China permitted the enemy to eliminate many X-2 targets which might have been covered. In addition, the lack of transportation, difficulties encountered in clearing X-2 work in many of the newly liberated areas, efforts to curtail the size of the staff and permit high-point men to go home, and yet furnish the immediate coverage best suited for the national interests, all served to reduce the effectiveness of X-2 operations.

During September 1945, X-2 was able to send representatives into most of the major coastal cities in China. These men uncovered much valuable information on German and Japanese espionage in the area. The teams secured the names of key Japanese and puppet subversive intelligence officers throughout China, including leaders in the Kempeitai and various intelligence "kikans," informant and agent networks, location of headquarters and intelligence on Japanese post-war plans to continue operating undercover intelligence organizations. In Canton, X-2 uncovered a German transmitting station which had monitored Allied broadcasts between IBT and CT for the Japanese and also transmitted findings to Germany. One of the key German agents apprehended by X-2 was Fritz Wiedemann, former German consul-general in San Francisco. Wiedemann was later brought to the U. S. for further interrogation. Toward the end of September 1945, voluminous reports on Japanese and German intelligence activities were received from the field teams.

The difficulties of cover, the necessity of working alone and often blindly, problems involved in using native agents, limited personnel, language barriers, the lack of time, the absence of authority to take positive action against enemy espionage agents in the territory of an ally, and other factors frequently spelled individual or program failure. The X-2 mission, however, viewed as a whole, eliminated agents, broke up enemy intelligence rings, collected intelligence of both immediate and long-range strategic use, built from scratch to nearly 15,000 a master card file of suspects, collaborators, agents, meeting places, secret societies, etc., ferreted out and neutralized penetrations of U. S. installations, and prepared summaries of counter-intelligence data for the use of U. S. commands in China.

R&A. The first R&A staff in the Far East, a group of nine, arrived in India in December 1943. The staff had a dual assignment: To work in China under the SACO agreement and in India with the British on Burmese problems. Because New Delhi was the center of British intelligence operations in the Far East, and also offered better security and freedom from problems of Chinese liaison, it became headquarters for all R&A work in the CBI Theater.

One officer was dispatched immediately to China and arrived at SACO headquarters in Happy Valley, Chungking, in January 1944. The shortcomings of Chinese intelligence material and the apathy of Chinese officials toward the work of intelligence analysis were evident from the start. This was demonstrated in many ways, including the fact that neither original intelligence data nor essential publications were made available to R&A personnel. An official OSS protest resulted in improved working conditions and many promises for the improvement of the quality of the intelligence procured. A small flow of intelligence did result, but the Chinese never collaborated according to promise. The acute shortage of available research specialists made maintenance of R&A representatives an extravagance entirely out of line with the negligible results.

In February 1944, an arrangement was made with the Fourteenth Air Force to assign two officers of the R&A group to work with A-2 in Kunming in order to gain access to intelligence not available to SACO.* From the outset, this staff made a substantial contribution both to R&A and to the Air Force, whose intelligence staff was undermanned. Both strategic and semi-tactical intelligence reports, based largely on the flow of Fourteenth Air Force information from the field, were prepared and proved to be of such value to both agencies that the two-man staff was increased to nine in late summer 1944 and remained with the Fourteenth Air Force as an R&A detachment until the end of the war. Priority in reporting was given to China as the political center of incoming intelligence on strategic air targets in the Japanese Inner Zone for the use of the Air Force in the Theater and in Washington.

In May 1944, an officer from the original Far East group was sent to Chungking un-

---

* This was the precursor of the AGFRTS agreement of April 1944.

der AGFRTS cover to uncover and exploit a new source of intelligence to supplement those of SACO. Early in July, the Theater Command organized the U. S. Army Observer Mission to Yenan (DIXIE),* and this officer was chosen to be one of the four OSS men on the mission. The benefits that OSS derived from representation on DIXIE were somewhat lessened by the failure of G-2 to forward the reports, or, if they did forward them, the long delays in doing so. However, at the conclusion of the mission in October 1944, the team delivered to OSS microfilmed material which had been collected and prepared in Yenan, and reported in comprehensive detail on the Communist situation in the north.

The establishment of the China Theater in October 1944 enabled R&A to establish another section in Kunming, operating independently of SACO and the Fourteenth Air Force/AGFRTS unit. Three people were assigned in November to initiate this unit, which was designed to support the operational requirements of various Theater agencies and other OSS branches in China, as well as to prepare and transmit reports requested by Washington. These responsibilities were taken over from the Fourteenth Air Force detachment, which was thereafter enabled to concentrate on research and analysis activities in support of the air war. By March 1945, when OSS at last gained control over its own personnel, R&A participation in SACO was virtually abandoned.

R&A/China, following the Theater reorganization, carried out its assignment of obtaining military, political and economic information and documentation on Japan, Japanese-occupied territories and China. During the last ten months of the war, R&A completed numerous intelligence studies for the Theater Command, Chinese Combat Command, Army Service Forces, G-2, G-5 and the U. S. Consulate. Such studies included documentary material for future operations of the Theater Command, spot reports on specific topics and regional studies of areas in Southern China. In February and March 1945, the Branch participated in and prepared the final report on the AKRON Project.* In July, the first estimate of Japanese requirements in China was completed for the Theater Command.

R&A performed a variety of intelligence functions, one of the most significant being the preparation of target studies for the Fourteenth Air Force. On several occasions, Chennault expressed his appreciation of the importance of this work to the successful conclusion of the air war.

Special detachments were assigned to perform specific jobs. Upon arrival, in October 1944, a two-man team of geographers travelled widely in China, collecting intelligence, particularly maps, not previously obtained by the Army or any other U. S. agency. Additional R&A personnel were assigned to OSS Field Bases in Hsian to prepare strategic studies of North China and Korea. Another field team was dispatched to the 3rd War Area in occupied China to collect behind-the-front intelligence. R&A played an integral role in the briefing of personnel going into the field; in fact, the R&A Branch Chief in China was Chairman of the Briefing Committee.

Although greatly handicapped throughout by lack of personnel, R&A rendered substantial service to the Theater Commander, as well as to the other branches of OSS/China. Copies of all reports were sent to Washington, and numerous special economic studies were prepared for Washington, but shortage of political analysts in the field resulted in inadequate service for R&A/Washington headquarters, as compared with such services performed by R&A staffs in other theaters.

The Fourteenth Air Force Detachment completed more than 90 reports. Some

* See "Penetrations into Northern China" above.

* See "OSS in the China Theater" above.

were included in the Fourteenth Air Force Daily or Weekly Summary, a publication with 250 customers. Many special planning papers and maps were made available to specific Air Force groups. R&A/Kunming prepared reports, briefed outgoing teams, performed cartographic work for all branches and issued some 50,000 sheets of maps to numerous OSS branches and other agencies. The independent R&A unit in Chungking completed twenty reports on highly specialized Chinese economic, legal and political problems. R&A observers in Yenan, with DIXIE, prepared a series of comprehensive papers on conditions in Communist territory, and developed the flow of Japanese publications to IDC to a point where Yenan was the most important R&A source for this material. This continued until the termination of all OSS representation in Communist territory in July 1945.*

After VJ-Day, the R&A Branch staff was amalgamated with the SI Reporting Board into a new branch, Reports and Research. The emphasis on reporting was shifted from tactical and strategic subjects to surveys of political and economic conditions, with a view to keeping Theater Headquarters and Washington informed on the current situation. The Fourteenth Air Force detachment was disbanded and the Field Units were recalled. The Chungking unit remained in operation pending a move to Shanghai, and small units were sent to Shanghai, Peiping, Nanking and Canton in September.

OG. The mission assigned to the OG Command was the formation, training and equipping of twenty Chinese Commando units—each not to exceed 200 men of all ranks. The mission was decided upon at a conference between Wedemeyer, Donovan and Chiang Kai-shek during January 1945. It was based upon the belief that small units of Chinese, properly trained and equipped, together with assigned veteran American

---

* See "Penetration of Northern China" above.

officers and soldiers, would fight more effectively than regular Chinese divisions. OSS was to be responsible for the training program, for certain items of supply for the Chinese, and for assigning the American personnel. The Chinese Army was to furnish suitable personnel for Commando-type operations, and was responsible for Chinese pay, rations, uniforms, and the like. The Chinese promised some 4,000 men and OSS promised up to 470. The first OG detachment arrived in China in early March to begin training; 390 OG's were on duty with the program by VJ-Day.

The Chinese Army assigned the Chinese 1st Parachute Regiment, which had been undergoing intensive physical training for nine months, to serve as the nucleus of the Commandos, and the first five Commandos were formed from this Regiment. The Chinese had originally promised that OSS would be allowed to screen the Chinese Army to obtain the best possible personnel for the Commandos, but the Chinese failed to fulfill this promise. The personnel for the remaining 15 Commandos did not arrive on time, and when they did, proved to be of inferior caliber both physically and mentally—a performance reminiscent of the SACO experience with agent training. An increased ration allowance granted to the Commandos by the Chinese Ministry of War, coupled with a progressive program of physical hardening during the training period, improved the physical condition of the troops.

The program was delayed considerably by the discovery that the Chinese troops actually required basic training, even prior to the more specialized Commando exercises. However, orders from Theater Headquarters stated that all 20 Commandos had to be fully trained and ready for the field by 1 August 1945. A training schedule of eight weeks' duration was planned. Even this could not be followed because of the Chinese failure to provide personnel in time. However, training did begin on 16 April with an American staff of 16 officers and 30 enlisted men.

OSS organized a parachute training school at Kunming. Half of the 1st Commando unit began the four-week course on 4 July 1945. Parachute training progressed slowly because of Theater ceiling on American personnel, difficulty in obtaining aircraft, and poor weather conditions. By the end of the war, 6 Commandos had been fully paratrained, while 6 others were in various stages of training. For the first time in its history, China had Army paratroop units. The parachute school remained in operation until VJ-Day, when it was closed by Theater Headquarters.

The equipment authorized for use in Commando training was drawn through normal OSS and ASF channels. Hump tonnage was charged against OSS allocations. The Chungking Government and the Chinese Army again failed to live up to their commitments, with the result that the Chinese soldiers were not adequately supplied with such standard items of issue as uniforms, blankets, shoes, mess kits, and the like. In view of the Chinese defection, OSS was obliged to take on basic supply functions in order to insure the success of the project. For example, the 1st Commando unit approached parachute training practically barefoot and, since the Chinese Army still did not furnish shoes, OSS procured all available paratroop shoes in the India-Burma Theater and issued them to the Commandos. Another Commando unit ready for the field lacked sufficient blankets; OSS was obliged to make up the shortage before the unit departed.

During the training period, the Commandos were placed under the control of the Chinese Reserve Command. Upon completion of training, each Commando came under the operational control, for the Chinese personnel, of the Chinese military command, and, for the Americans, of Chinese Combat Command (CCC). This arrangement worked very smoothly. All operations

were agreed upon in conferences between CCC and OSS, whereupon proper orders were issued for OSS to implement the plans.

The first official news of Theater plans for the use of the Commandos did not come until March 1945, when General Wedemeyer returned from Washington to Chungking with JCS approval for Operation *CARBONADO*. The original Commando directive gave 1 August as the target date for the completion of training of all 20 Commando units. Preparations for *CARBONADO,* together with the increased urgency of the war situation in China, resulted in acceleration of the Commando training. However, although individual Commandos participated in the initial phases of *CARBONADO,* the war ended before the operational potential of the Commandos as a whole had been tested.

The original *CARBONADO* Plan entailed the launching of a limited offensive against the Nanning area, to continue, in its second phase, down the West River corridor to Canton. The schedule called for the opening of the port city during August; the preliminary period—from June to August— was envisaged as a preparation for the final attack. A Theater directive of 10 May allocated between OSS and the U. S. Navy Group responsibility in Indochina for demolition of communications, railroads and supply dumps, so that the flanks might be given effective protection in the drive on Canton. On 9 June, a further directive assigned to OSS areas of responsibility for the operation of guerrilla units under SO teams in support of Operation *CARBONADO.* There were nine such locations in the area. As of 1 July, 13 SO teams were in operation and an additional 4 were in the field training guerrillas and preparing for future operations.

The war situation in the Far East changed during the spring and summer of 1945. Operational emphasis shifted from China to the Pacific, and it became increasingly evident that *CARBONADO* would be merely a holding action designed to pin down as many Japanese troops as possible. In addition, since the Japanese withdrew from Nanning in the spring of 1945, the opening phase of the original plan was negated. On 19 June 1945, Wedemeyer issued Operational Directive 21, a modified *CARBONADO* Plan. Phase 1 of the original plan was eliminated, but the basic mission remained intact, namely, to seize and secure the Canton-Hongkong port area for future use as a base against the Japanese.

Except for the allocation of responsibility in Indochina between SO and the U. S. Navy Group with respect to demolition of communications, railroads and supplies, OSS, although included in the over-all strategy in China, had received no specific directions as to its role in support of *CARBONADO* until 4 July 1945.

On that day, OSS received instructions concerning the employment of SO teams working with the Chinese guerrillas and of the 20 Commando units that OSS has assembled. At the same time, half of the first Commando unit began parachute training. In accordance with the instructions, OSS was to undertake the support of these operational activities by the expansion of the regular intelligence service, in accordance with Theater directives. Such intelligence activities included such functions as MO and X-2. The mission of the Commando units and SO teams in support of *CARBONADO* was defined as follows: (1) To disrupt communications and to delay the movements of the enemy forces from the north, south and east; (2) to seize and hold for limited periods certain specific objectives, in accordance with orders of the Supreme Commander; and (3) to provide combat and tactical intelligence for ground and air forces. The instructions went on to state that, in order to control operations effectively, OSS would establish a forward headquarters with Tactical Headquarters, in order to maintain close liaison for operations and intelligence

with subordinate echelons, as required, and to direct all OSS operations in the zone of action of the ground forces.

When *CARBONADO* was launched, the Commandos were sent into action. On 12 July, the 1st Commando was parachuted successfully into the 7th Chinese War Area near Kai-ping, with the mission of interdicting road and river traffic along the West River. This operation, designated APPLE, was the first airborne movement in the history of the Chinese Army. The enemy attacked the Commandos, who fought well in their first engagement, but the mission as such did not accomplish much. On 18 July, the 8th, 9th and 10th Commandos, which had been formed into a provisional battalion, were flown to Liuchow, whence they went by sampan down-river to a point near the airfield at Tanchuk. The mission, BLACKBERRY, was to secure the Tanchuck airfield and then move east along the West River, ahead of the Chinese armies. The Commandos were scheduled to attack the airfield on 3 August, in conjunction with the 265th Regiment of the Chinese 89th Division. After it had occupied high ground overlooking the field, the Regiment was to attack and complete the capture of the airfield. The Commandos successfully completed their phase of the operation, but the Regiment failed to move in as planned. This resulted in heavy losses to the Commandos, who were forced to withdraw after holding their positions for six hours. The Japanese withdrew the next night, and the Chinese Regiment moved in and took the town and airfield the following morning. On the basis of this mission, CCC realized that the Commandos should not be used to replace frontal assault troops.

On 27 July, the 2nd Commando unit, in a mission called BLUEBERRY, was dropped successfully near the town of Chakiang, with the assignment of interdicting road and river traffic along the Paoching-Hengyang-Changsha lines of communication. The Commando, in conjunction with Chinese guerrillas in the area, attacked some Japanese positions on 5 August, but, due to faulty coordination between the participating units, the operation was unsuccessful. Two other Commando operations, CHERRY and CRABAPPLE, were carried out by the 3rd and 4th Commandos. They were selected to act as honor guard at the discussion of surrender terms between Allied and Japanese officials after VJ-Day. They were off-loaded at Chihkiang * on 21 August and proceeded to Nanking on 27 August, where they secured the airport.

8. Mercy Teams

When it became apparent that the Japanese capitulation was imminent, humanitarian liaison and rescue teams were formed by OSS in cooperation with other organizations in the Theater, particularly AGAS. There was extreme concern among Allied authorities over both the condition of Allied prisoners of war in Japanese hands and the treatment these prisoners might receive at the time of the surrender of Japanese forces.

Six-man teams, generally referred to as Mercy Teams, were formed to operate throughout the China Theater. They were prepared to parachute to prisoner-of-war centers, insure proper treatment for the prisoners at the time of their liberation and report on conditions, with specific reference to the possibility of war crimes evidence or evidence of violation of the Geneva Convention. In addition, they were to clear suitable airfields for evacuation purposes.

---

* The OSS base at Chihkiang was outside the area that had been delineated for the operation of guerrilla units and SO teams in direct support of *CARBONADO*. However, it was in a sufficiently strategic location to perform the following substantial services during the period of maximum operations: Chihkiang teams were credited with 4,833 enemy casualties; 31 sampans and trucks destroyed; 900 railroad cuts; and 4 bridge demolitions. In the same period, 41 combat missions were flown and 63 men and some 100 tons of supplies were parachuted into the field successfully.

Each Mercy Team included medical personnel and supplies to cope with the extremely poor conditions of health and nourishment anticipated among the prisoners of war.

A precedent for these teams existed in the European Theater where, in March 1945, the Special Allied Airborne Reconnaissance Force (SAARF) * was activated by SHAEF to send radio-equipped teams, each carrying a letter from Eisenhower, to contact specific prisoner-of-war camp commanders so as to prevent forced marches or other mistreatment of Allied troops.

For OSS, the Teams also provided opportunities to cover intelligence objectives otherwise possibly inaccessible, to collect appropriate data on enemy personalities, to prepare agent networks for information on post-surrender developments and Allied activity, and, if possible, to cover points of political unrest.

The OSS quota of Mercy Teams in the Far East was nine. All were to be mounted at the Hsian base, although they were ultimately destined for different areas, and the Fourteenth Air Force was to provide the necessary transportation facilities. The Teams comprised SI, SO, Medical Services and Communications personnel, as well as Chinese interpreters. On 15 August, the Theater Commander directed OSS and other organizations to give the highest priority to the Mercy Teams. Four missions were alerted at Hsian: MAGPIE, to operate in Peiping, DUCK in Weihsien, FLAMINGO in Harbin and CARDINAL in Mukden. Prior to departure, personnel were briefed thoroughly on various questions of Theater policy, such as supply, publicity, fraternization with the enemy, and the geographical limits of Team activity. FLAMINGO was cancelled on 18 August by a Theater order, since its target was under Russian control and no clearance with the Russians had been arranged. FLAMINGO personnel were assigned to EAGLE, destined for Keijo, Ko-

---

* See "Central Europe" under Part VIII, "The Liberation of Europe," in Europe-Africa Section.

457

rea. However, on 30 August, while still awaiting dispatch, EAGLE was cancelled in view of the imminence of the occupation of the Peninsula by American troops. MAGPIE, DUCK and CARDINAL were dispatched successfully by air. Three teams, in addition to the original four, were mounted in Hsian and subsequently also dispatched: SPARROW to Shanghai, QUAIL to Hanoi, and PIGEON to Sanya on Hainan Island. MAGPIE, DUCK, CARDINAL, QUAIL and PIGEON landed in their target areas and successfully carried out their assignments. SPARROW was parachuted safely, but was immediately interned by Japanese authorities in the Shanghai area and was unable to operate.

The conditions reported by the teams varied extensively. For example, DUCK found the prisoners at Weihsien in relatively good condition; on the other hand MAGPIE found among the internees in the Peiping area four of the Doolittle fliers who had been kept in solitary confinement almost continuously since the time of their capture and were in serious condition.

CARDINAL attracted the greatest attention. Following its landing at Mukden, the team was informed by the Japanese that all future landings and operations in the area must be cleared by the Russians who were occupying the region. By 21 August, Russian permission had been granted to the U. S. to unload one plane daily at Mukden and proceed with the evacuation of prisoners. However, a period of difficulty ensued, due to both undiplomatic conduct by American personnel and Russian reluctance toward U. S. operations in their zone of activity. At a camp 100 miles northeast of Mukden, the most notable prisoner of war in the Far East, General Wainwright, was liberated, as well as General Percival, the former British Commander at Malaya, Sir Benton Thomas, former Governor of Malaya, and other important British and Dutch officials. Following Russian pro-

tests, CARDINAL was withdrawn at the end of August.

Upon completion of the rescue missions in September, this activity was turned over to the Army and the Air Force. OSS either withdrew its representatives or redirected their efforts entirely to intelligence procurement. Wedemeyer officially acknowledged the OSS contribution to the success of the Mercy Teams. In a message to Donovan on 5 September he commended OSS for its work in creating:

. . . humanitarian teams which endured hardships and shared dangers in order to bring medical supplies and food to prisoners of war of various nationalities incarcerated in camps for the past several years. OSS was assisted by other organizations in the theater. However, your organization carried the brunt of the undertaking.

9. OSS After VJ-Day

Following the Japanese surrender, OSS/China was reorganized in line with its principal post-hostilities assignments: (1) Furnishing intelligence to Theater Headquarters and the Chinese Combat Command while American forces remained in China to assist the Chinese in their re-occupation; and (2) laying the foundations for a long-term intelligence program in the Far East.

It was evident that the OSS mission in China would be almost exclusively one of intelligence and counter-intelligence. Accordingly, intelligence activities of all branches were combined in a newly created Intelligence Division. In general, all field personnel were placed under the operational control of the Intelligence Division, while all services, other than local service facilities, were combined in the newly established Field Services Division, and all matters of administration and local services were placed under Headquarters and Headquarters Detachment.

The Intelligence Division became the core of all OSS operations in China; all field personnel (except the OG's, then in process of liquidation) came under the jurisdiction of the Operations Section of the Intelligence Division. The Operations Section was responsible for planning operations, for staging operations in cooperation with the various sections of the Field Services Division, and for directing operations following dispatch to the field. The MO Branch, redesignated the Morale Intelligence Section, was placed under the Intelligence Division; its assignment included the compilation of such morale and opinion studies as required by the Theater Command. The R&A Branch and the SI Reporting Board, combined in a Reports and Research Section of the Intelligence Division, processed all incoming intelligence except counter-espionage. The existing Central Intelligence Registry, an amalgamation of R&D/CID and the SI, MO and X-2 intelligence files, was placed in the Intelligence Division. The Map Division of R&A and the Geographical Intelligence Section of SI combined to become a Map Section in the Intelligence Division. X-2 was redesignated the Counter-Espionage Section of the Intelligence Division.

All branches and sections engaged in services and supply operations for the field, or for OSS/China in general, were consolidated into the Field Services Division. R&D joined what had been the Services Branch to form a Procurement and Supply Section. Its functions were limited to supply matters and major construction projects. The Schools and Training Branch was redesignated the Replacement and Training Section. Virtually all OSS training was suspended, except for some specialized intelligence training and civilian training for OSS personnel awaiting return to the U. S. The Communications Branch and Medical Services, substantial as they were, became sections of the Field Services Division. Since all parachute and air-drop training was abandoned, the Air Operations Branch was de-activated, although some personnel remained to arrange for intra-China air lifts performed by the Air Operations and Air Transport Section. The Reproduction and Field Photographic Branches were amalgamated into the Photography and Reproduction Section.

With the end of the war, all SO activities, as such, ceased. A large number of SO personnel, already engaged in the collection of tactical intelligence, was placed under the control of the Operations Section, Intelligence Division. A small SO Section was retained in the Field Services Division to liquidate SO operations and to furnish protection to any intelligence group entering areas where fighting or rebellion could endanger the lives of American personnel.

All military administration, discipline, and purely local services functions were placed under the Headquarters Detachment, together with the Personnel Security Offices.

The system of Field Commands was abandoned in the post-surrender period. Since the chief function of the OSS Field Commands had been to direct SO teams in the field, collect tactical intelligence on the spot and forward it to appropriate Army or Air Force Headquarters, the cessation of all SO operations and the greatly decreased importance of tactical intelligence made it unnecessary to maintain field commands. Operational control of field personnel was placed directly under the Intelligence Division at Central Headquarters and the Field Commands were redesignated "Field Base Commands". Their function became that of maintaining bases throughout China, to expedite and supply OSS missions and to implement Headquarters operational directives. The POW rescue teams in North China and Manchuria, for example, were staged from Hsian and the Hsian base performed very important functions in the supply and transportation of these teams. Since Headquarters was in constant touch with Theater Command, AGAS, and other interested agencies regarding the details of the POW rescue missions, the direction of the teams was a Headquarters function.

OSS Headquarters, together with Theater Headquarters, moved to Shanghai in September and October. The only staff left at Chungking consisted of intelligence personnel to report on political developments during and after the move of the Chinese National Government to Nanking. Kunming remained a large OSS base while property disposal and the liquidation of extensive properties and supply dumps were in progress. All personnel who could be returned to the U. S. via Kunming were dispatched from there. Shanghai became a headquarters unit large enough to implement the Theater order directing OSS to continue to supply intelligence to the Theater Command in the post-surrender period. By the end of September 1945, over one-third of all OSS personnel in China had been processed through Kunming en route to the U. S.* Such OSS records as were no

* After 1 October 1945, following the liquidation of OSS, the task of returning OSS personnel devolved upon SSU, which continued the general plan of processing U. S.-bound personnel through Kunming, although later some were procesesd through Shanghai.

longer required in the China Theater were assembled, catalogued and forwarded to Washington by officer couriers.

After the surrender, OSS worked out a publicity policy in conjunction with Theater Command, and an OSS/China Public Relations Officer was appointed. Subsequently, certain information was released for publication, including the names of OSS personnel and information on SO and OG activities. Such information did not at any time include data on branch designations, either of personnel or operations, nor any data on SI, X-2, MO or other intelligence operations in China.

As part of a plan for long-range intelligence operations in China, OSS/China laid the groundwork for a widespread network by setting up observation stations in Peiping, Nanking, Hongkong, Canton, Mukden, Tíentsin, Hankow and Tsingtao. Before any of these long-range plans could be further implemented and expanded, President Truman issued the Executive Order which terminated OSS as of 1 October 1945.